A TREE WITHOUT BRANCHES:
Anna's Journey

Helena E Kanak

First published in Far North Queensland, 2024 by Bowerbird Publishing

Copyright @ 2024 Helena E Kanak

All rights reserved. Apart from any fair dealing for private study, research, criticism or review, as permitted under the Copyright Act, no part of this book may be reproduced or transmitted in any form or by any means, electronic or mechanical, including photocopying, recording or by any information storage and retrieval system, without prior permission in writing from the publisher. The author's moral right to be identified and to have her text preserved is asserted. Enquiries should be made to the publisher. Images copyright, individual owners.

ISBN 978-0-6457433-4-0 (print)
ISBN 978-0-6457433-5-7 (ebook)

A Tree Without Branches: Anna's Journey
Helena E Kanak

First edition: 2024

Edited by: Crystal Leonardi, Bowerbird Publishing
Front & Rear Cover Concept & Design by: Helena E Kanak
Interior Design by: Crystal Leonardi, Bowerbird Publishing

Distributed by Bowerbird Publishing
Available in National Library of Australia

Crystal Leonardi, Bowerbird Publishing
Julatten, Queensland, Australia
www.crystalleonardi.com

In memory of Anna Kanak; my Mum and a friend to many.
For my family and all those who knew and loved her.

About the Author
Helena E Kanak

Helena Kanak was born in South Australia to immigrant parents, who, after WW2, arrived from Czechoslovakia. Her family eventually moved to North Queensland, where she and her two siblings, John and Diana grew up and began school.

Life started in Mareeba and then on a dairy farm in Euluma Creek before moving to Julatten and, later, remote areas around Laura. As the eldest child, Helena was the first to experience early separation from her family. During the school term, she was sent to board with friends in Julatten and later Cooktown, while her family remained in Laura due to work commitments.

After her father passed away suddenly, life became more Anglicized when her mother and siblings began integrating into the Julatten community.

Initially, the Kanak family only spoke Czech at home, but English was introduced once school started for the children. Words such as discrimination and prejudice were alien to Helena, so upon starting secondary education, lessons in social history enlightened her about the real world.

During her secondary education, Helena attended Blackheath College, a boarding school in Charters Towers, and then studied nursing at the Princess Alexander Hospital in Brisbane. Her nursing career took her abroad, living and working for several years in England, and Cairo Egypt. After returning and settling closer to home in North Queensland, Helena worked as a Paediatric Nurse at the Cairns Hospital until retirement.

Always a keen observer of life, Helena maintains journals, writing travel logs and keeps abreast with her art. Marrying later in life and upon retirement, Helena revisited her love for writing.

Although she has written and illustrated several unpublished fiction narratives for younger readers; 'When a Curlew Comes Calling,' 'Scallywags of Bushy Creek,' 'Trot Plod and Waddle Investigators,' 'A Spherical Puzzle 4 U' to name a few, her most challenging work has been her mother's biography, 'A Tree Without Branches.'

e: helenamaxd@gmail.com

Foreword

Harvey and I had the pleasure of meeting with Anna Kanak when we moved from Mareeba to Julatten in 1968. We share-farmed on James Lenahan's tobacco property near Hunters Creek. Becoming firm friends with Anna and her family, Anna and I also worked together at Mt. Kooyong Convalescent Home — I, in the office, and Anna as a nursing staff member.

Soon after we arrived in Julatten, Anna invited us for a meal at her home, and she was an excellent cook, making it a memorable evening. Anna treated us with one of her 'famous' apple strudels, which we often enjoyed.

When the tobacco season started, Anna worked with us for ten years on her days off from Mt. Kooyong. By this time, her children Helena, John, and Diana had finished boarding school and embarked on their own careers; John studied civil engineering while the girls studied nursing. Anna was rather proud of her children's achievements.

During this period, Anna decided she would learn to drive, so she and John bought a Mini-Moke, and John taught his mother to drive. Anna soon became confident, and from there on, we shared many shopping trips together into Mareeba, be it open-air driving in the Moke!

When Jim Lenahan decided to sell the tobacco farm to the Mossman Sugar Mill, we had to look for another job and bought the Millaa-Millaa Hotel. When Anna finally finished up at Mt. Kooyong, she would drive onto Millaa-Millaa and work with us thrice a week. Between us, we would organize kitchen duties, prepare menus and do the cooking.

When Anna finally retired, she continued to work at her home, passionate about gardening and caring for various farm animals, which had become her pastime.

We have many fond memories of Anna, spending time with her and attending various activities. Anna was a true friend to us.

Olive and Harvey Keys

Introduction

It was a cool Autumn Saturday during an evening storm on the 10th of August 1985 when my sister Diana and I sat around the kitchen table at Krhová in Moravia with Aunt Helena and Uncle Robert. The topic of conversation soon gravitated toward my mother's upcoming birthday. I had been living in Egypt when Diana and her then-husband Robert visited, and together we travelled to Czechoslovakia (as it was then known) to visit relatives.

The country was still languishing behind the 'Iron Curtain' (a term coined by Winston Churchill). Although I had visited previously with my brother John in the Autumn of 1983, for me, on that auspicious evening, there was to be yet another family revelation.

Our mother's birthday was less than two weeks away, and Aunt Helena reminded us that Anna, her sister, would be 69 on the 25th of August.

I thought nothing of it, except my sister immediately jumped in to correct her, "Mum is only 67, and her birthday isn't on the 25th! It's on the 28th!"

And so began a heated debate as to who was right. Uncle Robert soon became impatient with the family disquiet and laughed off the inconsequential matter but unintentionally adds fuel to the fire.

"Who cares when Anna was born? Besides, priests were often inebriated during this sort of weather in those days, and by the time they reached the house to baptize a child, most wouldn't know what day it was, let alone what year!"

Incensed by her husband's off-handed remark directed at the most pious institution, the Catholic church, Aunt Helena disappeared into their bedroom and soon returned with her sister's christening certificate. This created a certain amount of consternation as, by now, Aunt Helena was accusing her older sister of pretending to be younger than she really was. It nevertheless intrigued me that my mother's age seemed so significantly inconsistent with the evidence at hand; in as much, it began to dawn on me that there might be more to this oversight than simply just an error.

The mother I knew was practical and unpretentious and never showed a desire to make herself more youthful or glamorous, so pretending to be younger than she was, did not make sense. Aunt Helena was so incensed that she immediately wrote to her sister demanding a 'please explain!' This obviously reopened old wounds for my mother; memories she would have much preferred had remained buried, but fearing her relationship was being tested with her closest sister, Anna sat down and, in 1986, wrote in detail of her post-war epic; a journey that took her from Czechoslovakia to New Zealand. Much of what she wrote was being aired for the first time in decades, and very little had ever been revealed to any of us before, or her family, and so with it came unsettling facts of survival.

Years later, when I returned home from Egypt, my curiosity about my mother's past still remained on a list of things to discuss. Once home, I began a regular dialogue on the subject with my mother and started to understand why she, as a refugee, escaped Czechoslovakia rather than just immigrating on her own terms after WWII. From there onward, she bared her soul and spoke to me as if with a need to shed her past and put to rest some less pleasant memories from her journey. I would learn much later how much had been deliberately omitted from her 'explanation' letter so as not to further grieve her family. After the war, her country had fast become a satellite state of communist Russia, and for close to half a century there afterward, it would be reduced to an isolated nation, oppressed by a political regime that created a society of enforced and controlled ideals.

My mother told me, her prudence came early; grasping at the reality of what life would be like in post-war Czechoslovakia, leaving little or no opportunity for her or anyone else in her homeland. Sadly, she had to abandon her family and embark on a dangerous if not uncertain journey; leaving behind, her family, home, her dreams, and hopes of any future aspirations.

Unexpectedly, one day while visiting my mother a week or two before Easter of 1998, she casually mentioned that on 29th March, it would be her 50th anniversary since escaping from her homeland. Our conversation turned to her post-WWII journey, and I began to wonder if perhaps our local paper, 'The Cairns Post,' might be interested in doing a short feature on her. At first, she was reluctant but finally agreed to be interviewed and photographed. What followed was a pleasant surprise for my mother, as it rekindled a friendship of old, and opened a new chapter in Anna's life.

While sitting together, we searched through old photographs and discussed them at length and how each related to her past life, all the while recalling the faces staring back at her. It was during this time that she solemnly informed me, that she never had any intention or desire to ever return to Czechoslovakia, and nor upon her death did she wish any of her ashes to be returned there. About this, she was surprisingly very adamant. Although long freed from any fear of persecution or retribution, she felt safe and grateful in her new homeland and did not need to revisit and test the waters of her past.

Her life span in Czechoslovakia had been barely 32 years, as from there afterward for the next 60 years she had lived a completely separate life; an existence far removed from the parallel life she once shared with her siblings. Out of them all, my mother Anna was probably the real black sheep in the family; not only did she leave home, but she allegedly married beneath her family's expectations and religious parameters and instead chose a Protestant and a divorcee from a less intellectual background. However, she must have been long forgiven for this folly as she always maintained a loving and undisputed relationship with her family, albeit from the other side of the globe.

She had initially come from a family with property and money, but as with many families, fortunes gained were often just as easily lost, and the war did not discriminate. My mother recalled that on numerous occasions, whenever she and my father had crosswords about money, he would always remind her; "I wasn't born with the silver spoon in my mouth, and you accepted my marriage proposal!"

And later, when he thought she needed flattering, he would say, "You may not have been the most beautiful amongst your sisters, but I chose you because you were clever and the most practical one of them all!"

She once asked me quite unexpectedly, if I thought she had suffered. It was an open-ended question, one I had no immediate answer for, but then, I realized she wasn't seeking an answer but rather something to ponder. I wanted to comfort and reassure her with something positive;

save her from her past anguish, but no words seemed to suffice, so instead, my silence spoke. How could I empathize with all she had endured without walking alongside in her shoes?

Her life journey was one I could never have endured in face of such adversity. I do not possess the kind of stamina or courage to undergo what she had. It was as if she and my father had been uprooted from tumultuous Czech soil and transplanted like trees into a promising Australian landscape, briefly blooming, producing fruit, but failing to put out seed for future generations. And so, our family tree would too, cease to grow and put out new branches, leaving no life force for a future generation to sprout from its ancestral roots.

Surrounded by unmentioned but often palpable melancholy, through which she forfeited her own country for personal justification, it induced me to explore and try to understand the real woman who happened to be my mother. This, in many ways, became the launching pad for her memoir.

Throughout this endeavour, I turned to my Czech family for answers but soon came to the realization that many of my valuable sources (namely her relatives and friends in the Czech Republic) were fast drying up with the passing years. It would soon leave me with nothing to go on with, except my tattered notes that I frantically scribbled during conversations with my mother.

Anna rarely complained and graciously accepted any hardship in life as she went about doing something positive to improve her situation. From my perspective, her life had been a hard and unfair journey, and lonely at the best, from start to finish, especially when my father passed away, leaving her a widow at the age of 47 with three young children to bring up, find employment, and become two parents in one. Still, somehow, she overcame and endured all that was thrown in her path.

Anna continued to struggle stoically, both financially and emotionally, with our growing demands, while expectations within society often set her apart from other families. Anna always seemed the reluctant hero who preferred to remain anonymous, and always insisted her life was ordinary and of no interest to anyone, and reminded me that there was nothing special about her life and nothing that others in her circumstances would not have done as she, but on this; I waiver to differ.

She even suggested that if I was so keen on writing, why not write about the animal characters from my childhood?

She then began to tell me about her grandmother's bedtime stories which grew from fond animal characters on her family farm. At first, I took little heed of her advice. Still, upon my mother's death in 2008 and after defaulting on her memoir for far too many years due to emotional ineptitude and procrastination, I eventually did precisely as she suggested and began on 'Scallywags from Bushy Creek,' a tale somewhat reminiscent of Great Grandma Stolař's bedtime stories.

Realization soon stared me in the face, that if I continued to be distracted with other projects, I would soon forego the essence of these lengthy dialogues I had with her, and her memoir would never be written. So, with renewed vigor and a yearning to uncover more about our family, I embarked once again to revive these memories and search further afield for what else could support this narrative.

Although my mother may have only made a minuscule contribution to the colourful tapestry of Australian life, she, along with other immigrants and pioneering families of her time, helped to cement their lives into the foundations upon which our nation grew, creating the social fabric of unique Australianism. Even though by 1948, only some 160 years since colonization, Australia had already extended a humanitarian hand to so many desperate for a better life; displaced people ready to blend into the potpourri of cultures that we collectively today call Australia. It was during this era, still void of political sophistication and correctness but, already striving to become a mature nation, that my mother arrived and carved out her identity and new home.

Anna never dwelled on discrimination, letdowns, hate, regret, or holding grudges, but rather aspired to achieve something positive through hard work. She was courageous and sacrificed for survival. She helped others along the road and made lasting friendships. She may have loved and lost, but her sheer strength of character and the ability to laugh at herself pulled her through life's adversities. She strived to be accepted into society and become a worthy new Australian, overcoming the cliché of being a 'Wog' or foreigner from some unpronounceable alien country.

This memoir is only a brief glimpse into an ordinary woman's life, albeit in not-so-ordinary times, but who found her place in a new world, a place she called home; but yet at what cost?

Like with many ambitious projects, my aspirations were constantly daunted by the scope of this task, and I began to have self-doubts when I delved into the enormity of it all. I feared my account of her life would only be dwarfed by my efforts to discover the truth behind this remarkable woman. I also soon came to realize and appreciate that there would be conflicts of family opinions, differing interpretations of events, and memories levelled to which side of the truth best suited them. But, in the end, it was my mother's words that guided me.

No one can ever be an island unto oneself as life's trajectory crisscrossed the paths of so many; family, friends, acquaintances, work colleagues, or simply people briefly encountered only once in a lifetime. And it is also nature's creatures that bring so much joy, as no life could ever be fulfilled without them, and not leave us enriched for the better. And so was Anna's life by those who once knew and loved her and all the creatures that found a home in her heart.

Contents

About the Author	I
Foreword	III
Introduction	IV
Maps of Czechoslovakia	XII
Anna's Family Tree	XIV
Jan's Family Tree	XV
Footnote	XVI

BOOK ONE: Anna's Story

Chapter		
1	Moravia: Rural life in Lhotka nad Bečvou	2
2	Kurovec Ancestral History	12
3	Kurovec Family Life in Lhotka	21
4	A Prelude to War	56
5	Krhova and Lhotka: Anna's War under Nazi Occupation	68
6	End of WWII: VE Day 8th May, 1945	95
7	Anna's Escape Plans	109
8	Pulgary (Bulhary)	117
9	The Escape: Pulgary to Poysdorf	128
10	Vienna (Vídeň): Czechs on the Run	140
11	Steyr to Passau	153
12	West Germany: Regensburg - Burg 1948	161
13	Ludwigsburg: 1948-1949	181
14	Hošťálková: Jan Kaňák's Journey	213
14.1	Family Life	214
14.2	Jan's Brief Czech Military Career	220
14.3	France: A Short but Bitter Fight	227
14.4	1940-1945: Cholmondeley Cheshire & Formation of CIABG	237
14.5	1944-1945: Siege of Dunkirk and Finally Home	253
14.6	Jan's WWII Aftermath	258
15	New Zealand: Anna's Dream	266
16	Wellington New Zealand	275
17	Anna: Tokanui Psychiatric Hospital	281
18	A Close Call & New Friendships	289
19	Winter Engagement in Takapuna	302
20	Sunnyside Asylum Christchurch	313

Contents

BOOK TWO: Life in Australia

Chapter 21	Wanilla Forest SA: 1952 -1954	336
22	Wangary SA: 1955-1956	344
23	Road to Queensland: 1956	353
24	Mareeba: 1956-1957	358
25	Euluma Creek: 1957-1959	364
26	Julatten: 1960	379
27	Laura Station:1960-1961	389
28	Return to Julatten: 1962	408
29	A Year of Unbearable Sorrow: 1963	416
30	Julatten: A Tree Without Branches	421
31	Life without Jan: 1964-1968	425
32	Charters Towers: 1969-1972	448
33	Anna returns Home to Julatten	458
34	Anna's Life after Mt. Kooyong: 1976-1997	465
35	Anna's Life Full-Circle: 1998-2008	485

Epilogue	499
Acknowledgments	563
A Brief History of Czech Lands to the Birth of a Nation	566
References	579
From the Publisher	589

Maps

Nation of Czechoslovakia after WWI uniting Bohemia, Moravia and Slovakia.

Modern day Czech Republic comprising of Bohemia and Moravia.

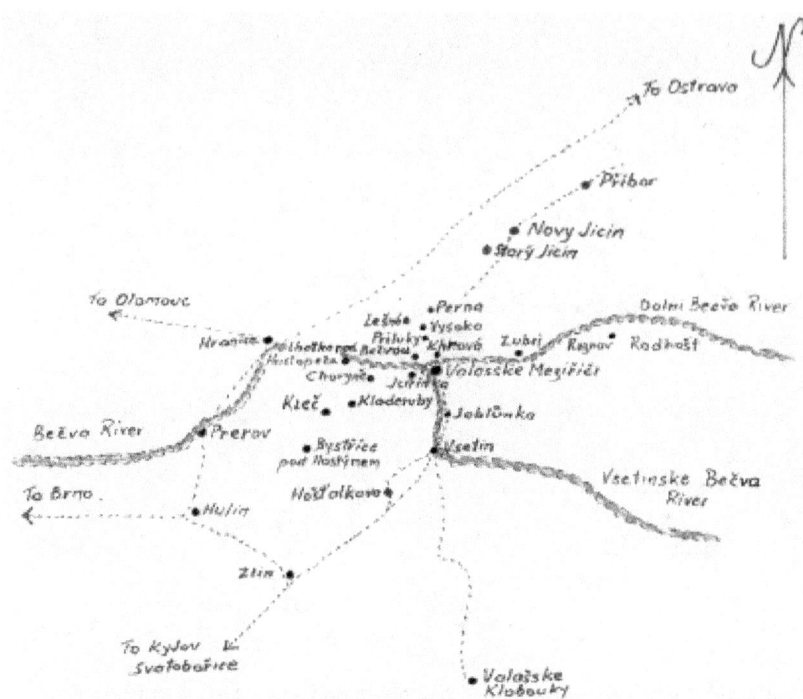

Neighbouring district around Valašské Mezirici in Moravia.

Family Tree

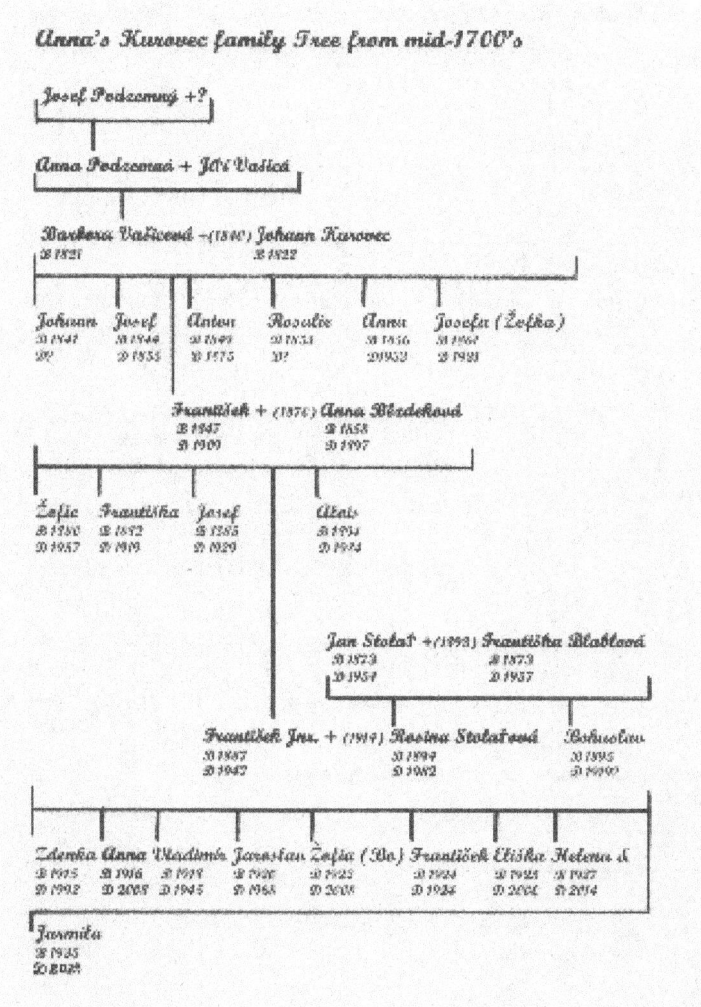

Anna Kanak's Kurovec Family Tree

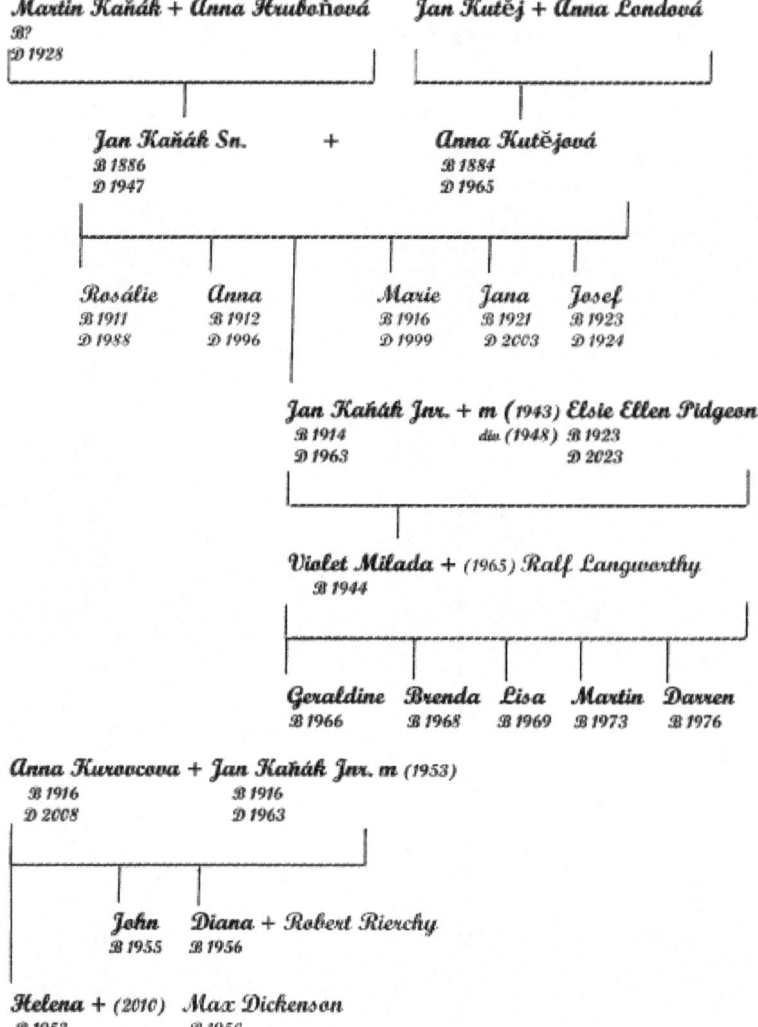

Jan Kanak's Family Tree

Footnote

I must stress that Anna's memoirs are her personal life experiences she shared with me as we discussed her past. These are not always in perfect harmony with information put forward by other family members. Many anecdotal stories and family memories may not always share the same enthusiasm or be recollected similarly, but the stories are as Anna remembered them. Fortunately, we had ancestral records to refer to, and together with my mother's knowledge, we brought many of these characters to life. Anna never wished for anything said to cause direct and deliberate harm to anyone; it was not in her nature to do so. On the contrary, I often experienced her reluctance to pursue the occasional avenue of research where someone's integrity came under the harsh light of scrutiny. Not to be too pedantic about the accuracy, but it is how Anna recalled her life and how it had to be written to give it authenticity.

Historical facts entwined into Anna's story were much easier to research and document than the lives of those who lived alongside her. On occasions, time frames may be slightly warped, or actual names of people differ or be misspelled, a task in itself difficult to rectify, as sometimes I only had an old photograph to reboot her memory or, more often, only the pronunciation of names in taped interviews to go by.

It bears to remind readers that names beginning with 'J,' as in Jan, Jaroslav, Jaroslava, Jarda, Jarek, Jiří, Jarmila, Jana, etc., are pronounced as if with a 'Y.' Additionally, the 'ova' suffix following a family name denotes the feminine form. I researched names and spelled them as closely as possible to what they resembled in Czech, and for any errors made on my behalf, I apologize.

Helena Kanak, 2024.

Book One: Anna's Story

CHAPTER 1

Moravia: Rural Life in Lhotka and Bečvou

The Provence of Moravia occupies most of the eastern part of what is now the Czech Republic. It is north of the Bohemian region comprising the northerly Bohemian-Moravian highlands and northwest of what is known as the Českomoravská Vrcovina. Eastward, the region reaches the Carpathian Mountains, where Moravia borders Slovakia to the east and Poland to the north. Here, the mountains are separated by the lower Moravian valley, comprised mostly of farming land. A portion of Moravia also borders Austria to the south, where farming and agricultural land again extends into the neighbouring country. Within the Provence of Moravia, its major centres are; the capital city of Brno to the southeast, Ostrava to the north, Olomouc located centrally to the west and Zlín in the central east. These all network with numerous other smaller but major municipal towns of Nový Jičín, Hodslavice, Valašské Meziříčí, Hranice in the Přerov district, Bystřice, Vsetín, and innumerable surrounding villages.

By the early 1800s, as public interest developed in the Czech National Movement under the writings of Moravian historian and politician František Palacký (born close by in Hodslavice), the Czechs began to demand equality and recognition of their Czech language in both schools and governments. Before this, German had been the recognized language taught throughout the Austro-Hungarian States.

The Austro-Hungarian Revolution of 1848 sparked renewed Nationalism, and with it came many changes as the Austro-Slavic movement began to define the future of Czech Politics. This Nationalistic revival gradually opened opportunities for the landless peasants to immigrate elsewhere and brought about a working-class political party in addition to the dominant Catholic Party.

The majority of wealthy landowners were for most Catholic nobility and middle-class families who inherited their ancestral land and dwelled in stately chateaus and castles, and standalone villas surrounded by their substantial parcels of land. At the centre of this existence small villages grew and created the social fabric and dwelling places for the workers who serviced these landed gentry.

Farming during the nineteenth and early twentieth centuries was relatively unsophisticated utilizing horse power and primitive means of automation. Many flour mills were located beside flowing streams and relied heavily on water to turn the giant wheels that powered the gavels to accomplish the task. Mechanization was in its infancy, with manual labour and horsepower still turning the wheels of agriculture. There was a plentiful supply of local labourers, many of whom were poor peasants who needed work to survive.

Rural life generally flowed in seasonal rhythm with planting, harvesting, and produce going to local markets, making profitable incomes for the landowners.

As summer days shortened under the weakening sun, harvest time would become the epicentre of farm activity. Men and women eager to earn money were engaged to reap barley, rye, wheat, and oats, dig potatoes, harvest sugar beet, and pick seasonal fruits and nuts from orchards. During the chaos of harvest time, an orderly routine under the supervision of overseers ensured tasks were accomplished before winter set in. Residential barn owls perched high in the rafters sheepishly oversaw the proceedings while hunting for any fat fury rodents concealed in the straw.

There was plentiful work to be done in the fields, sheds, barns housing animals, and domestic duties. Those with specialized skills tended to the horses, greased harness yokes and bridles, and sharpened the tools of trade in preparation for the next day.

Grain crops were mostly hand slashed with scythes, but some farms already used primitive horse-driven harvesters that had to be manually managed. As grain was cut, labourers followed to scoop and tie the straw into sheaths and bundled it into stacks to be manually thrashed of seed which was bagged for milling. After drying, some hay stacks would also be used for winter fodder, while the rest would be buried and turned into silage for additional winter and early spring feed for the housed animals. A successful harvest always made landowners happy, putting money in everyone's pockets at the end of a hard day's work.

Outside, youths, if not lazing and dreaming under shady trees or snoozing in hay stacks, herded sheep and goats while these animals grazed on stubble from freshly harvested crops. Flocks of geese honking in protest and with their wings spanned as if ready for flight, raced ahead of young children trying to corral the birds together. They could not afford to lose any bird, to a cunning and opportunistic fox often lurking in the brambles, waiting to snatch a meal. As the flocks joined other scurrying domestic birds darting about in the orchard in pursuit of last-minute insects, there was still time for the children to pick late season berries and flowers.

Throughout the year, nature harmonized with seasonal changes as every day breathed energy into the countryside. From fields of brilliant red poppies to pastel blue cornflowers of spring and onto golden waving fields of grain basking beneath hot and hazy summer days, time drifted along as lightly as clouds from one season onto the next. A late summer change in the breeze would herald autumn, and with it, each leaf would begin to change from green to earthy colours. As autumn deepened, so did the colour of the leaves, turning into shades of yellow, deep red, and gold.

Waves of harsh rustling breezes high in the tree tops would strip the leaves and shower them silently onto the earth below, leaving trees standing naked of foliage. Rustling amongst the fallen leaves and sniffing out edible morsels, squirrels scampered up and down trees carrying troves of nuts to stash into hollow tree trunks or secret in underground cavities for winter. In the end, only the fir trees remained green, ready to carry the burden of winter snows as a reinvigorated chill on the breeze signalled its approach.

As each day shortened and evenings closed in with the threat of inhospitable frost, the urgency of last-minute tasks stepped up for the workers as they raced to beat the inevitable weather. There were still horses to be shod, harnesses to be greased, and barns to be continually cleaned out. The remaining wheat not sold at the markets had to be milled, and the sugar processed earlier from the sugar beet had to be weighed and distributed into bags and stacked in the larder. The larder seemed an extravagant assortment of foodstuffs with jars of churned butter and homemade cheeses, vats of sour bubbling cabbage, jars of pickled onions and cucumbers, preserved apples, pears, peaches, plums, and cherries all stacked on shelves ready for the winter months.

As clear blue skies faded and became heavy with grey clouds hanging menacingly over stark bare trees and fallow fields, distant mountains too became shrouded in thick fog. From the first silent whisks of snow drifts, the falls increased in voluminous momentum, creating a landscape of white that enveloped every corner of the country in glistening snow.

Plumes of misty smoke rising from chimneys would blend into the grey sky and disappear, while indoor wood fires burned relentlessly, warding off winter chills that seeped through cracks beneath doors and windows. From there onward, low-lying dwellings, with everyone inside, would often become snowed in with minimal outside access until the thaw. Days could be arduous and bitterly cold, with families holding up for weeks without access to anything except what they had in their larders.

Although outdoor farm work ceased, the feeding and tending of animals increased. Apart from constant shovelling of snow to make inroads into farm sheds and roads accessible, there was also time for family fun, and in between schooling, the young would ice skate on frozen lakes and rivers and toboggan down slopes while the more agile older folk took to the local ski fields. It was time for friends and family get-togethers to enjoy a few celebratory drinks to ignite conversation.

Home-distilled Slivovitz, discreetly stowed away, was a traditional plum brandy of varying degrees of alcohol strength, depending on who and how it was prepared. During winter, over vigorous conversation, every household proudly presented it, tasted it, and compared it with other previous batches until everyone agreed on its quality, leaving no doubt that it was the best brew yet!

Slivovitz also had various other uses apart from being an alcoholic beverage. More often than not, it was a self-prescribed medicinal tonic taken regularly for whatever problematic health issue presented. It allegedly cured all sorts of ailments and diseases known to humankind! It could be used as a cleansing spirit for cuts and burns, but more significantly, it was a drink that could warm the body, heart, and soul in the coldest depths of a freezing and miserable winter. Each family had their special Slivovitz recipe, and each family guarded theirs fervently.

When winter finally retreated and the snow melted beneath the strengthening warmth of the still bleak sun, spring arrived, and the once empty fields that lay fallow beneath the snow once again breathed energy. A new cycle of life began, and with it, renewed hope of prosperity.

The small town of Valašské Meziříčí lies within the agricultural landscape between the confluence of two rivers, the Vsetínská Bečva and Rožnovská Bečva Rivers, which join to become the Bečva River. This area is located within the Vsetín district in the Zlín Region of Moravia, and geographically the town is in a picturesque location about 50 kilometres in a northerly direction from Zlín. Its urban region extends within the parameters of the Moravian-Silesian foothills to the northwest, easterly to the Rožnov Valley and southerly toward the Hostýn-Vsetín Mountains.

Eastward and overlooking the town of nearby Rožnov, Radhošť with its well-worn track winding up to its summit was frequented by pilgrims and visitors alike. At the commencement of the uphill track to Radhošť, visitors would pass a sentinel; a solitary statue of the mythical creature, Radegast[1]. This pagan god of war and victory, sun and abundance, had been erected near the forest edge in more recent times to welcome and oversee all who pass on their long hike to the summit of Radhošť. Here on a clear day, visitor's efforts would be rewarded with impressive views of the country side below, and perched precariously near the edge surrounded by steep pastures dotted with grazing sheep, the old historic wooden chapel of Saints Cyril and Methodius (Cyril and Metoděje) would be the pilgrim's ultimate goal.

Valašské Meziříčí historic beginnings date back to 1377, where its once original gothic church stood, but now in its place stands the historic Assumption of the Virgin Mary Parish Church. The nearby Renaissance Žerotín Castle and Kinski Chateau are all within the town precinct, and centrally the old town marketplace is skirted by well-preserved Germanic

Burgher houses. Neighbouring small villages of Krhová, Lhotka on the Bečva River, Lešná, Kladeruby, Choryně, Juřinka, Příluky, Vysoká, Perná, and Zubří are all within proximity and depended on Valašské Meziříčí as their focal point for marketing locally grown produce.

A short distance to the west from Valašské Meziříčí and close to the Bečva River, the little village of Lhotka is nestled in the undulating landscape that rises on both sides of the river extending out to where once temperate forests hugged hilltops, and wild animals took refuge from hunters who coveted their antlers and pelts.

This undulating and picturesque countryside around Lhotka was then dotted with tiled farm roofs punctuating the landscape through which a network of roads crisscrossed the country, dividing fields with tree-shaded lanes. These were shared with foot travellers alongside nimble horses and carriages while wagons trundled along ladened with produce destined for nearby village markets. Later early model cars would add to the traffic. A railway line with a regular passenger service from Valašské Meziříčí, passed through Lhotka linking it and other small provincial towns and villages.

Within the village of Lhotka, among the collection of dwellings, there was a local school and, further on, a small Catholic chapel with its spiral crucifix rising above the bell tower from where the chimes announced Sunday worship or any other religious and ceremonial occasion. From Lhotka, looking to the east on a clear day, the distant high mountain range of Radhošť would occasionally be visible but more often mired in a haze.

Family records dating back to the late 1700s show that the Podzemný and Kurovec families could be traced back to the Valašské Meziříčí district. The Kurovec Family were not of any notable or noble lineage, but they belonged to the intellectual and middle-class Catholic gentry who were wealthy enough to establish and maintain uninterrupted land ownership dating back to well before the eighteenth century.

For these well-heeled, educated and intellectual families with an ancestral farming inheritance passed down by successive generations, Valašské Meziříčí was their social hub for business and commerce; produce markets and shopping, ongoing higher education, and cultural entertainment.

Anna's father František Kurovec, (better known to all as Frantz), had inherited a large sized property in Lhotka, with money and a lifestyle to match. The Stolař family of matching wealth and land ownership would become conjoined through marriage and bless Frantz, Anna's father, with comfort, wealth, and community responsibilities, an inherited moral obligation to care for all those who worked for him as well as his own growing family.

And so began Anna's life in 1916, far removed from the threats of past empirical feudal systems but at a time when her country was growing into a Nation of self-determination and democracy. Anna was a child of modern Czechoslovakia rather than a product of the defunct Austro-Hungarian Empire.

Photograph 1: Valašské Meziříčí market centre, Postcard circa pre-early 1900s.

Photograph 2: Valašské Meziříčí town centre, Postcard circa the early 1900s.

Photograph 3: Village of Lhotka near Valašské Meziříčí. X marks Josef & Anna Kurovec' villa.

Photograph 4: Farming land around Lhotka.

Photograph 5: School at Lhotka.

Photograph 6: Winter in and around the neighbouring countryside.

Photograph 7 & 8: (L-R) Statue of mythical Pagan deity Radegast at the base of Radhošť. Wooden chapel Metoděje and Cyril at the summit of Radhošť.

CHAPTER 2

Kurovec Ancestral History

The farming village of Kladeruby on the southern reaches of the Bečva River is slightly southwest of Valašské Meziříčí and only a short distance over the river south west from Lhotka. Sometime during the early eighteenth century the Podzemný and Kurowetz families (Kurovec) settled and prospered in this region. Josef Podzemný was a landowner of substance with influence in the local community. His daughter Anna Podzemna married Jiří (George) Waschitze (Vasica) and they had a daughter Barbora.

Records in 1793 spelled the surname of Vasica, as Waschitze so it is often difficult to ascertain if these names simply indicate errors in spelling; or later took on a spelling that was better suited to the Czech identity. Either way, the pronunciation was much the same. Poland, Germany, and Austria all bordered the provinces of Bohemia and Moravia so it may be reasonable to assume that many people moved freely between these regions during the era of the Austro-Hungarian and Prussian Empires and their names would be spelled according to which language or dialect was prominent in their region at the time.

In 1840 Barbora Vasicová married Johann (Jan) Kurovec, the son of Johann Kurowetz (Kurovec) Snr., a landowner from Kladeruby and so these two influential farming families were brought together.

Johann (Jan) and his wife Barbora inherited farm No. 13 in the Lhotka area which in all probability had been passed onto them through Barbora's Vasica family. It was a sizable property measured by farming standards of the time, and here, the couple produced seven children; Johann (Jan) Jnr, Josef, František, Anton, Rosalie, Anna and Žofka (also referred to as Josefa).

Johann and Barbora's oldest son, Johann (Jan) Jnr. was born in 1841 and later as a young man met with an unfortunate accident, his leg being crushed by falling timber, which culminated to his limb being amputated. Little knowledge remains about him except that he married and had a son Tomáš.

Their second son Josef tragically died in 1855 aged only eleven years, and their youngest son Anton died in 1875 aged twenty-six.

Their three younger daughters left home once they married. Rosalie married and became a Gerlova and lived further north in the village of Perná. Anna also married and became a Polachová, while their youngest sister Žofka or Josefa, remained single.

František Kurovec their third son, was born on the 5th of June in 1847 and became the beneficiary of the family property, probably because his older brother Johann was too incapacitated to carry on farming.

By the time František Kurovec, grandfather of Anna Kanak, inherited the family property No. 13 near Lhotka, he had met and married Anna Bezděková. Anna Bezděková was born in 1858 in the nearby village of Příluky close to Lhotka. She was some eleven years younger than František and also came with a dowery, having inherited property from her family. At the time Anna and František Kurovec Snr., together owned and operated one of the largest farming properties in the Příluky-Lhotka area.

Life for František was typical of landed gentry with family life orientating around church worship, but also participating in grand picnics, organized hunts, and mingling with likeminded people at social and community levels. Although the Kurovec family had money to afford luxuries beyond the means of ordinary folk, they were neither wasteful nor extravagant. Wealth was mostly measured by ownership of farming land, but they were by no means as wealthy as some of the neighbouring nobles living in castles and chateaus who owned even larger swathes of land.

František was a benevolent and fair landlord to work for, and was never known to exploit his position, thus gaining respect from all who knew him. He possessed a passion for horses and was renowned for his fine breeds of working horses and those bred for traps and harness work.

But above all, František Kurovec was a lucky man who possessed a keen sense for agriculture, and had the ability to recognize opportunities he believed would benefit him and the farm in the long term. Upon these opportune moments, he acted without hesitation with rewarding results.

After the Austrian Empire Revolution of 1848, many changes took place. The huge exodus of Czech Protestant peasants who immigrated to elsewhere in the world, opened the way for those who previously struggled to find jobs and who now at last, had a chance to secure permanent employment.

František was able to recruit many such labourers for his farm during planting and harvest time and he also presented employment opportunities for permanent domestic assignments in the kitchen, caring for his young children, and attending to orchards, gardens and farm animals.

It was only the most trusted and proven employees who would ever be allowed near František's prized horses. František knew that his horses were the engines of farming and without their wellbeing, the farm could just as easily suffer the consequences of delayed or inefficient harvests.

With the National Czech Revival gaining momentum and influenced by fellow Moravian Frantz Palacký, Czech historian and politician, it was beginning to make way for a new political landscape with the ruling Hapsburgs now fast losing popularity. František Kurovec remained positive during this growing political movement and believed everyone would eventually benefit. In spite of this unrest, he took a gamble and forged ahead with his agricultural ideology and exchanged farm No.13 for the old ancestral farm No. 6 which had been once in the Podzemný family.

Josef Podzemný's family had originally owned farm No. 6 and built their home and fortune upon it in the early eighteenth century. Both properties were in close proximity and František's insight dictated it was a wise move which would benefit him, as the land was more conducive to agriculture and was only a short distance from Lhotka. Josef Podzemný, through Frantisek's ancestral maternal line, was his great-grand father, but this land acquisition was primarily a shrewd business transaction rather than a sentimental one.

The solidly structured home was rendered and painted in yellow ochre with a steel-blue tiled roof. It was accessible from the main road by way of an entrance enclosed by high wooden gates at the front which led into the courtyard. Here, horse-drawn carriages could easily assemble in the privacy of the enclosure and be shielded from the road. The house had sufficient attic space with room for storage and additional sleeping quarters. Down stairs the living and kitchen quarters opened into the large courtyard adjacent to the stables.

There was ample winter shelter at the distal end of the building for all vulnerable domestic animals. A barn to house pigs and an additional shelter for cows, sheep, goats and domestic fowl was situated further beyond this point. A water well within the courtyard was pivotal for both domestic purposes and for watering the garden and farm animals. However, the water from this well was not always suitable for drinking and an alternate water supply from the north was eventually gravity fed to the home from the nearby village of Vysoká.

Surrounding the house, a perennial flower garden flowed into the orchard where trees of apples, pears, cherries, and other various stone fruits and walnuts grew.

Beyond, the land opened into cultivated fields and grazing pastures that extended toward the distant densely wooded foothills. In the garden and standing a short distance from the house, a small solitary religious shrine marked the family's respect to their catholic faith. Such icons erected in fields and along lanes and roads were customary of the time as a measure of the country's obedience to the then ruling religious Catholic Empire.

The country side ahead appealed to František as he gazed over it filling him with pride and satisfaction. He was grateful to God for such privileged circumstance in life.

Farm No. 6 at Lhotka would remain in the Kurovec name for the next three generations, even though much later after reckless gambling debts incurred by František's son, the farm still survived and remained steadfastly in the family. It would not be until in the 1970s, that its ownership would eventually be transferred to the Hurtík family who themselves are descendants and great-grandchildren of František Kurovec.

By the late 1800s, František and his wife Anna Bezděková had five children; two girls and three boys. Their older daughters, Žofie or Žofka was born in October of 1880 followed in December of 1882 by Františka, who was also known as Funka. Josef their eldest son was born in 1885 and František Jnr, or Frantz, as he became known, was born in April 1888, followed by their youngest son Alois in March 1894.

Early in life, Františekʼs children were all taught respect and to be responsible and upstanding citizens. They were a close-knit family with moral and family values based on devout Catholicism. Every Sunday the older Kurovec family members attended early morning mass and would be later joined by the younger children for the family church service. As the children grew, they remained united and humbly accepted their status within the community.

In 1897 Františekʼs wife Anna, passed away unexpectedly from renal complications. At the time she was only thirty-nine and left her husband František a distraught widower with a young family to raise. Although much grieved by his loss, a few years afterward František suggested to his children that he would like to remarry. At the prospect of this happening, he was met with hostile resistance especially from his two daughters Žofka and Funka, who both strongly opposed any such union with his proposed bride to be. With a heavy heart František gave in to their wishes and in spite of this disappointment, he continued to farm, passing on most of the day-to-day responsibilities to his younger son Frantz.

This arrangement made way for František to pursue his passion in numerous philanthropic interests. As a prominent citizen of Lhotka, he remained involved within the community and local council of Valašské Meziříčí. He contributed much of his energy and money helping to build schools and improving local infrastructure.

Frantisek resolved to keep the family property as a whole and made it clear that there would be only one beneficiary inheriting the farm. He therefore made ample provisions for all his children giving each a share of his wealth without having to divide the farm.

Žofka his eldest daughter married Josef Flajšar. They had four children, František, Robert, Josef and Božena. Žofka put her inheritance toward her husbandʼs business venture but unbeknown to her father

František at the time, they were already grappling with financial problems.

Františka or better known as Funka, married Josef Šnajdar in 1909. They also had children; two daughters Marenka and Helena, and son Bohuslav. Both girls died early in life. The Šnajdars inherited a share in a local flourmill which some years earlier František had purchased from a company in Přerov. The mill was situated near Jurinka about four kilometres over the river from Lhotka and František appointed his son-in-law Josef as manager.

Josef Kurovec the eldest son went onto university to study agronomy. He married Anna Dobová a schoolteacher who was some ten years older, but did not bear any children. Anna Dobová had a brother, Roman, and two sisters, Funka and Julie. Both her sisters married; Funka became Zocková and had three children; Funka, Eda, (Edvard) and Helena, while the other sister Julie Kusáková moved north to Opava where they operated a grocery business.

After František Kurovec passed away in 1909 aged only sixty-seven, his son Frantz (František Jnr.) inherited the family property. In early 1914, young Frantz Kurovec married the daughter of Jan Stolař and Františka from Krhová. Jan Stolař was born in 1873 and was a well to do farmer. In 1893 he had married Františka Blablová, the daughter of a gardener from Jurinka. Františka was born in 1873, the same year as her husband, but had come from an entirely different background.

Františka's father had promised the young couple a dowry but at the time made numerous excuses why the money was not forthcoming. The sad truth being; he was a habitual alcoholic and would never be able to fulfill his promise and obligation to the young nuptials. Jan Stolař forgave his father-in-law for this indiscretion and never gave it any further thought. This fortunate union had remarkably elevated Františka's status in life. In 1894 the couple had a daughter Rosina, and in the following year in 1895 a son Bohuslav.

Marriage to Rosina brought Franz Kurovec a substantial dowry, which at the time was paid in gold by his father-in-law Jan Stolař. It was a handsome fortune setting them up comfortably on the farm in Lhotka.

Alois, Frantz's youngest brother enlisted in the army and went onto fight in Russia during WWI. Many young Czech men of the time including Rosina's brother Bohuslav Stolař, went off to war where in this instance he served his campaign in Italy.

Although the country remained relatively unaffected by the turmoil and upheaval occurring elsewhere in Europe during WWI, its earlier national revival led by Jan Masaryk and Frantz Palacký opened the way to independence, once the authoritarian Austro-Hungarian Empire was crushed at the end of the war. It was the finalé of one of the longest enduring empires in Europe, when on 28th October 1918, the Czech Lands were finally united as a nation of Czech people with Jan Masaryk as their elected leader.

When Alois Kurovec returned from war, he met and married Helena Zocková in 1923, a relative to his brother Josef's wife Anna Dobová. Helena was the youngest daughter of Funka Zocková; sister to Anna Dobová; so, Helena was not only her niece but became her sister-in-law as well. Helena Zocková was only 19 years and some 10 years younger than Alois when they married, but this did not deter the young nuptials from having a happy and fruitful marriage. They had three children; Milan, Marta and Pavla.

With his inheritance of land and livestock Alois Kurovec had a brief partnership with his brother Franz. However, Alois had limited interest in farming and was keen to be entrepreneurial and make money like his father had before him. Alois saw an opportunity in manufacturing and quarry mining rather than agriculture, so he began excavating rock on his share of the property processing it into sand and raw materials. He manufactured roofing-tiles, concrete pipes and provided neighbouring towns with sand and gravel for road construction.

Alois had a railway siding at his manufacturing plant and railed goods and raw materials to wherever business dictated.

Alois and Helena's son Milan Kurovec married and settled in Jakubovice with his family, but sadly passed away in 1981 aged only fifty-seven. Milan's sister Marta married Vladimír Berka and lived in Havlíčkův-Brod south east of Prague. They had a daughter Helena who went on to study medicine; became a cardiologist, married Jaromír Štrusa and had two sons; Jaromír and Vladimír. After her husband's death Marta passed away in November of 2020.

Alois and Helena's youngest daughter Pavla was beautiful and vibrant and married Ladislav Kristýnek. Together they had two children, but aged only thirty-five Pavla had an untimely death in 1975.

When Rosina's brother Bohuslav Stolař returned after having experienced the horrors of WWI; in 1922 aged only 27, he accidentally shot himself while cleaning his gun. However, this tragedy did not rest easy with everyone. It appeared that there had been underlying family friction which raised suspicion that it might not have been an accident. At least two more versions of this family incident circulated; one being that Bohuslav had suicided after being jilted by a young lass named Hedvika Mikundova and who chose over him, a publican for her husband, a man of lesser means, jilting the son of the wealthy farmer. The other scenario was that he hung himself in the family home attic because his parents deemed his choice of wife unsuitable and would not accept her. Whichever assumption was correct if any at all, some still suspected suicide as being the most probable cause of death that resulted from an unhappy love affair. Nevertheless, this sad and tragic event left his mother, Františka Stolařová inconsolable for the rest of her life.

She never recovered from this loss and steadfastly maintained it had been a tragic and accidental death so, no suggestion of suicide was ever mentioned in her presence. However, at the old Krásno nad Bečvou cemetery, it seemed to suggest anything but a normal burial as the original grave site did not appear to be within consecrated ground. His body was allegedly moved later and placed into the Stolař family crypt in Krhová. Much still remains unsubstantiated.

Photograph 9: Anna Bezděková & František Kurovec; paternal grandparents of Anna Kanak.

Photograph 10: František Kurovec. Anna Kanak's paternal grandfather František Kurovec Snr.

CHAPTER 3

Kurovec Family Life in Lhotka

During the first world war, on the 14th of January 1915, Rosina Stolařová (or Rosalie as she would later be known) and Frantz Kurovec had their first child. A daughter named Zdeňka. Soon afterward, in quick succession and midway through WWI, their second daughter, Anna Kurovcová, was born on the 25th of August 1916. Eighteen months later, toward the end of the war, their first son Vladimír Kurovec arrived on the 18th of January 1918. The other children were all post war arrivals; a second son Jaroslav Kurovec on the 20th of April of 1920, another daughter, Bohuslava Kurovcová (or Bo as she was better known) on the 20th of July 1922, and two years afterward, on the 3rd of April 1924 another son, who sadly died at birth. They christened him František.

Their fourth daughter Eliška Kurovcová was born on the 11th of November 1925, and three years later, on the 28th of November 1927, another daughter, Helena Kurovcová, was born. Finally, on 1st September 1932, they had their ninth and last child, a daughter named Jarmila. In a space of seventeen years, the Kurovec household was full and overbrimming with eight children!

Zużka Gerlova arrived to help Rosalie and became a nanny to the Kurovec children. Her husband was also employed and became an overseer on the Kurovec farm. They too came from a large family farm, but whether the Gerla family was related to Frantisek Kurovec, there was no mention of it, but nevertheless, Zużka was always referred to as 'Teta Gerlova,' meaning Auntie Gerlova.

Zużka was strict but very kind to the children, and Anna Kanak nee Kurovcová recalled on numerous occasions how her Auntie Gerlova would bring scraps of material and make dresses for her dolls.

When Anna's siblings were only babies, Auntie Gerlova used to feed them a paste, a concoction of butter, flour, milk, and a sprinkling of sugar. In those days there weren't such essentials as prepared baby formulas and tinned foods, so early infant nourishment often fell to the kitchen staff to create a palatable baby meal that was deemed best for the survival and growth of the infant. Today modern nutritionists would be appalled by these kitchen recipes! Zuźka was quite a bit older than Rosalie, and after retiring from service with the Kurovec family, she passed away before the onset of WWII.

With a large growing family to support, Frantz Kurovec believed he could still maintain them comfortably. However, he probably had little inkling that circumstances could change. His oversight of running short of money while maintaining an extravagant life style was most likely hinged on his lack of understanding concise financial management and which ultimately lead him down a path of false security.

Although Frantz was honest and trustworthy, he was easily swayed to waste money, especially if it gave him pleasure without reason to doubt his outlandish expenditure. Initially, during his youth, Frantz showed the potential of becoming a successful farmer under the stewardship of his father. However, after his father's death, complacency grew instead, and contentment seemed to overshadow any desire to work hard and build up wealth.

Sometime during this period, brothers Alois and Frantz had a falling out over family business matters. Some believed that their sister-in-law Anna Dobová, Josef's wife, was instrumental in the brother's partnership demise because soon afterward, Josef joined his brother Alois in an alliance, replacing Frantz.

The land shared by Alois and Frantz Kurovec was originally agricultural country, but after Alois quarried a large portion of it and finally exhausted the sand mining, the remainder of the reduced and untouched land holding had diminished agricultural profitability. Despite this family hiccup, Alois and Josef Kurovec continued to prosper and do well without their brother Frantz.

Having suffered from tuberculosis for several years, Josef Kurovec finally succumbed to it in 1929, and with it, the short-lived partnership with his brother Alois was absolved. Upon her husband's death, Anna had been well provided for financially by his estate, inheriting half of the value of Josef's share in the business and their family villa. Whilst they had no children and no encumbrances of outgoing financial obligations, Anna still felt she had been cheated out of her husband's total estate. Josef had bequeathed the other half of his partnership to his brother Alois, but Anna believed she was entitled to her husband's full share rather than only half of it. This caused considerable consternation and animosity between Anna and Alois' wife, Helena. Although both women were related, Anna could not bear the thought that her much younger niece Helena, should be far wealthier than she. Anna was so beside herself with anger and envy at the very prospect of such circumstances that she sought legal advice.

Failing to gain satisfaction and still distraught and resentful of the outcome, Anna called upon a séance to resolve the matter once and for all! Allegedly her dead husband Josef Kurovec relayed a message to the effect, "Leave me alone. I made my decision, and that is final. So, let things be as I had wished, and leave me to rest in peace!!"

In the end, Auntie Anna, as she became known to the family, eventually accepted her lot and lived out her life with whatever inheritance was accorded to her. But Auntie Anna was never one to live alone or be lonely for too long. She would remain at the forefront of all Kurovec family gatherings. She had the propensity to interfere or rather advise where she probably had no business. When she finally passed away in 1975, she bequeathed her villa to her niece Bo Kurovcová.

Since Auntie Anna's passing, her villa in Lhotka never seemed to bring happy outcomes to those, especially in the family who subsequently inherited it. It was almost as if the place had been cursed.

The only one not to benefit from Josef's estate was Frantz Kurovec himself, upon whose land, in the first place, this business venture had been developed. After all the family debacle, Frantz Kurovec was left with this portion of mostly useless agricultural land that had been intensely quarried, and with no further need for it, his brother Alois moved on.

As Alois prospered, Frantz's fortune and luck dwindled. By now, Alois had acquired another quarry near Jakubovice, and for some time, his business flourished. With the onset of Communism after WWII his prosperity would also make a decline.

Although Frantz and Alois managed to heal their differences, Alois was occasionally prone to snub some of Frantz's family. On one particular day, while Frantz's daughter Eliška Kurovcová was walking home from school with her girlfriend, Alois pulled over in his flash car and offered her friend a lift, totally ignoring his niece Eliška.

The young girl refused the offer, and both girls continued to walk home together. These petty incidents were seen as a slur on Frantz's family but were generally ignored by him, although his daughter Eliška felt hurt by her uncle's insensitive attitude.

Alois had a more cordial relationship with Frantz's two sons, Vladimír and Jaroslav, and their sister Anna. Although Alois enjoyed his niece Anna's company, their paths would cross again much later when their allegiance and support for one another would be tested under very different circumstances.

As the Kurovec children grew, so did their needs increase. It wasn't that they were demanding of their father Frantz, but instead, he desired to lavish them with gifts and treats, which were often extravagant and unnecessary. He had a soft spot for Anna, his second daughter, as she so reminded him of his own mother Anna Bezděková.

When Anna was about fifteen, Frantz took her on one of his business trips into town. Anna returned decked out in a fashionable and expensive outfit with numerous matching accessories. Rosalie, Anna's mother, was lost for words at such extravagance and harshly reprimanded her husband that he had five other daughters to provide equally for. Rosalie was so upset by her husband's reckless spending that she frequently reminded him they were living well beyond their means. Despite her mother's outburst, Anna felt chuffed with her new outfit and was relieved when it was not returned.

In appreciation, Anna shared her new wardrobe with her sisters, especially Zdeňka, whom she adored and was always eager to please. Zdeňka always presented immaculately dressed and was quite often the envy of her younger sisters. Anna hoped, in return, that Zdeňka would look favourably upon her and share a more affectionate sisterly bond.

Growing up in the pre-war years seemed abundant in happiness and social activity. These were the halcyonian days when the children were innocently unaware of financial stress or household disharmony. There were only wonderful memories for them with very little hardship to speak of and certainly never any idea of possible poverty in later years.

Favourable winter weather would bring the children out to play in the snow, skiing, ice skating upon frozen ponds, and tobogganing down icy slopes, which were once cow meadows and grain fields.

During spring and summer, families would dress up, and especially on Sundays after church, a whole range of outings would be enjoyed. From picnics by the river to hiking in the woods or excursions by train into cities to attend fairs, cinemas, and concerts. At local country fairs, amidst rollicking folk music and dancing, displays of traditional treats and foods were placed out for sale. Many families proudly participated, dressed in their traditional and regional costumes giving the fair a flare of flamboyance and colour.

There was always an occasion to celebrate, be it religious feasts, weddings, christenings, and name days, along with regular Sunday family worship. It was all a part of normal everyday family life.

As autumn approached, there were other traditional family and village gatherings. Domestic geese were carefully plucked of their fine down so as not to harm or stress the birds. These rather dishevelled birds would then be well fed and taken care of so their feathers regrew before winter set in. The plucked down would be steamed and cleaned on a muslin cloth secured over the rim of a copper which was filled with boiling water as it bubbled over a large fire. When the process was completed and the down dried of any moisture, it would be stowed away into dry attics until winter.

When winter arrived, the village women would gather at each other's homes, and everyone would strip off the fine down from the feather quills. It was a tedious job but a perfect time for chatter and catching up on village gossip, as most women were housebound with little to do outside. When one household was completed, everybody would progress to the next house until everyone had their new feathers bagged and ready to stuff into new pillows and duvets. Over the duration, each daughter would acquire a wedding dowry of feather-down bed covers and pillow sets packed into a glory box awaiting that special day.

In those days, village customs were steeped in tradition, with village women celebrating together once their tasks were accomplished.

The participating villagers would then join in creating a communal feast of smoked meats, pork sausages, goulash, and roasts of pork, chicken, goose, and turkey; all served with lashings of potatoes and sour cabbage. As the men drank their slivovic, the women passed around their sweet delicacies, each showcasing their favourite family recipe passed down over the generations.

With fields lying fallow and frozen over with snow, all domestic animals were housed in barns for the duration of winter. For the men, there was still plenty of housekeeping, cleaning the horse stables and barns, and feeding and watering the animals. A door-to-door saddler would come by, and strip and grease horse harnesses, repair and restore any that were faulty and prepare everything for the following season. There were all assortments of leather straps and boots to mend and brass buckles to polish before continuing onto the next farm. Knives and tools were also sharpened by a door-to-door serviceman specializing in this craft as he made his way around the farming villages.

Franz Kurovec kept sheep; fleece from which was hand clipped and sent to woollen mills in Valašské Klobuky to be woven into cloth for winter clothing, hats, and blankets. From his stock of sheep Frantz cherished one particular prized breeding ram that was exceptionally docile and with a gentle temperament. This ram was quite often left tethered onto a pole by the road on a grassy patch opposite the Kurovec home. Here the ram would graze peacefully along with whatever other small creatures wished to join him. However, whenever the Gypsies were in town, no sheep, nor any other animals, for that matter, were ever left grazing unattended.

As in most villages, there is always a village fool who shamelessly enjoyed the challenge of provoking peaceful animals to the end of their tether. Mr. Novosat, a local villager, had one such son, who, unbeknown to him at the time, had quite a reputation around the place for disruptive behaviour and who had been caught on numerous occasions causing disturbances in the village.

One particular day, this young lad decided to stir up Frantz Kurovec's ram that was tethered by the road. The lad set his dog onto the unfortunate ram, and the animal, not being used to such threats, took fright and, with a sudden jolt, reared and lurched forward and, with sheer strength, pulled the pole out of the ground taking it with him as he fled down the road. Still attached to a paraphernalia of things, including the bouncing pole, the terrified ram raced around the corner, colliding with an unfortunate cyclist headed toward him. A terrible crash followed, with loud screaming and cursing, much to the delight of the lad, who snickered with glee as he scurried home, followed closely by his equally guilty dog.

At home, still gloating and full of joy at his accomplishment, the lad boasted rather foolishly to his mother how he had witnessed Mr. Kurovec's wild ram being chased by a dog down the road and charging at a man on his bicycle. He simply couldn't wait to tell his father about Mr. Kurovec's ram.

With raised fists, bruised and bleeding from wounds and scratches, and covered in tattered clothes, the victim looked more like a homeless derelict rather than a gentleman as he picked himself up and dusted off the dirt and gravel. As he surveyed his badly buckled bicycle, he cursed and threatened Franz for letting loose such a wild ram. He swore and cursed loudly and vowed that Frantz Kurovec would pay for this and threatened him with the retribution of compensation through lawyers for damages incurred to him and what remained of his bicycle. "I will see you in court, Franz!" he shouted. Carrying his crumpled bicycle and limping with injured pride, the disgruntled victim staggered home but secretly relishing his day in court over this fiasco.

As Mr. Novosat walked in through his front door and came face to face with his eager son, the boy's exuberance paled, and his face changed to sheer panic as he silently looked upon his angry and injured father. The shaken lad knew all too well that this would not be the right time to indulge his father with Mr. Kurovec's ram, as in front of him stood an immensely angry man still gripping onto his mangled bicycle and mumbling seething threats of violence toward Franz and his dangerous animal! So obsessed was he with anger and revenge that Mr. Novosat didn't even notice his son sneak out of the room. Needless to say, no more was ever said about the incident.

The Gypsies, or the Roma people as they are known today, frequented country villages in their often-colourful wagons, but they were not necessarily the most welcoming sight as they filed through the rural countryside. They were a nomadic race whose origins are often debated. Some believe their roots originated from as far away as India and then migrated into Europe over the centuries. They did have a strong connection with Hungary and the Magyar tribes, but the Romany was an independent tribe of people that evolved without integrating into the society of the time.

These nomads would arrive unannounced and uninvited into villages, settle on nearby communal land, and set up camp with burning campfires. From their colourful horse-drawn wagons spilled out children and whatever else they had procured from previous villages. However, no sooner had they arrived when things would start to go missing.

They had the habit of taking anything that didn't belong to them and often would go to deceptive efforts to steal things they fancied, often with no need for them.

They found a use for most things, and anything surplus could always be traded later, even if it meant bartering with its original owner. When they saw the opportunity for a set of free clothes, they blatantly took the clothing hanging out on washing lines. These people were habitual thieves and partial to all sorts of livestock, especially sheep, goats, small piglets, dogs, and cats, and an extra horse was always a prized scoop, especially if it came at no cost to them. Many farm animals would sporadically disappear whenever Gypsies passed through villages.

They were particularly prone to stealing live poultry, such as chickens, ducks, and geese, and when capturing them, the women would secret the fresh meal under billowing layers of skirts while another diverted the attention of the poor victim.

It was difficult to outwit these people. While one would be busy apprehending the unfortunate farmer at the front door, others would be at the back helping themselves to anything edible, desirable, or moveable. They possessed blatant deceitfulness without being consciously aware of it and existed daily on opportunistic acquisitions. They were not workers but more of a nuisance in the villages rather than a threat, and quite often, some of the characters were as much likable as despised.

The Gypsy children always appeared in need of a wash, and this was more so evident in schools whenever they made the rare appearance. Most of them could not read or write as their schooling was always a brief affair, and the children only lasted there as long as the caravans were in town. However, one legacy that they generally left behind was head lice. It would not be long after their departure when the whole class would start scratching and continue to do so until the room was evacuated and disinfected and all the children's hair treated.

Most of the time, these visiting youngsters would be seated well apart from the local children, who were discreetly told not to play with the gypsies. But despite Gypsy folklore generated by the locals and how they supposedly stole children, this actually did not happen as they had more than enough children of their own. But having Gypsies in town was a good deterrent for naughty children in some cases, who were known to misbehave or disobey their parents or those who always appeared dishevelled and grubby; so, Gypsy kidnapping tales were often rewarded with improved behaviour.

Some of the Gypsies claimed to be fortune-tellers especially when there was easy money to be made. The ulterior motive was that the bigger the fortune, the more it cost, but just as many blatantly lied about hand palm readings, all the while ingratiating themselves to the poor victim at a price.

While Anna was still a young lass, a blind old Gypsy woman once held her hand and professed she foresaw a long journey ahead over the water to the other side of the world. Although Anna loved geography and had a childhood fascination with New Zealand, these sort of predictions were hard to imagine for a young girl living in a landlocked country. Anna took the old woman's forecast with a grain of salt and forgot about it. Besides, Anna's life at the time was a happy one, and she had no desire to stray beyond her family's comforts to seek new adventures elsewhere.

However, the Gypsy folk did bring misfortune to some, as quite often, their dogs were rabid, which was a threat to all village life. One day Anna's young brother Vladimír was playing at home with a stray and rather robust Gypsy dog. As Frantz watched the two playing, he thought the dog displayed odd behaviour symptomatic of rabies.

He also noticed that the dog had scratched his son while romping around with it in the garden. Fearing the worst, Frantz immediately took Vladimír to Dr. Malac, their local village doctor. Frantz's worst fears were soon confirmed when Dr. Malac made immediate plans for Vladimír to be taken to Prague for treatment with a course of anti-rabies serum injections.

In anxious haste, Frantz and his son left on the earliest train for Prague, and Vladimír was promptly delivered to the sanatorium attached to the Pasteur Institute for research. Vladimír would have to stay alone at the sanatorium for the duration of his treatment as it was far too busy on the farm at the time for any family members to remain with him. However, being an easy-going and placid child, he soon made himself at home as he wondered about the sanatorium corridors. Vladimír would spend a great deal of his time following the staff around and was especially happy to be in the kitchen with them.

When the young lad was almost ready for discharge from the sanatorium, one of the staff asked him, "What is your family name, and where do you live, little man?"

To this, he simply replied, "I live on the Bečva River, and my mother goes shopping in a big town!"

He was only preschool age and did not yet know his family name, let alone where he lived at the time, but he obviously felt this answer would suffice and get him home. Due to Vladimír's misadventure with the rabid dog, all the village cats and dogs exposed to the diseased animal at the time had to be destroyed.

Over the years, Jan Stolař, Franz's father-in-law, had his own fair share of dealings with the Gypsies and was often reminded by his wife how on one particular occasion, a Gypsy got the better of him.

A gypsy had approached Jan with a rather old and poor-looking horse. He asked Jan if he would care for his animal for just one day, as he had business to attend to in town, and that he would return later in the day and collect his horse and pay him. The gypsy, noticing freshly cut hay close by, pointed out that his horse would enjoy some of that, as well as some fresh water. Jan paid little heed to him, and when the Gypsy disappeared, Jan proceeded to feed the rather shabby old horse starved of nourishment and care. The day turned into tomorrow and the following day into the next, and so the days followed into weeks and months, and still no sign of the Gypsy.

For months the horse luxuriated on Jan Stolař's generosity, grew fat and content with the passing of time, and thrived in extravagance well beyond its means and worth, even without as much as a day's work in the fields, and still, nobody claimed him.

After several months had passed without any sign of the Gypsy, Jan finally concluded he had been well and truly foiled and was going to be stuck with the rather aged and useless animal, as well as its feeding costs. One morning, as usual, Jan went to feed the horses and, to his dismay, found that his star border had gone, and together with it, any prospect of reimbursement for its keep. Jan felt annoyed, but after all, this was the nature of these people, and he could only blame himself for being so gullible. No payment, not even an excuse or a thank you, the Gypsy silently returned, reclaimed his possession, and together they disappeared.

Jan Stolař was a keen horseman, and he kept thoroughbred stables for breeding carriage-drawn and riding horses. He also owned a small horse and chaise business, hiring out to anyone needing private transportation. Jan once received a message from his local doctor who was urgently required to attend to an ill patient outside the village. Dr. Malac always hired Jan's horses for his out-of-town calls and also for the village visits whenever he was called upon. He was Jan's family physician, as well as a good friend. Jan Stolař rode in quickly and collected Dr. Malac, and together made haste to the patient's house.

A frail, thin man met them at the door, wringing his hands nervously and looking most distraught. At first glance, it appeared that he was in need of medical attention, but instead, he ushered Jan and the doctor inside, pointing out that it was his wife who was ill, and anxiously explained to Dr. Malac that his wife was choking.

To their amazement and disbelief and somewhat relief, they found a very overweight woman sitting at the kitchen table, bent over a saucepan of fatty soup. She was so intent on her fatty meal, slurping, coughing, and spluttering over the contents that she was totally oblivious to her husband's panic over her coughing fits and near-choking episodes. The woman remained totally unaware of the visitors, head buried in her meal, and not even raising it to acknowledge them, let alone an apology for the medical emergency call-out she had caused. Dr. Malac was at odds with the pair but later confided in Jan that he suspected she would eat herself to death and leave her poor husband in grave need of a decent feed and urgent medical attention if he lasted that long!

Markets were totally reliant on community people who lived close by and contributed to its subsequent survival, be it selling farm produce or buying food for the table. Every Monday, someone would go to the markets at Valasske Meziříčí and sell seasonal farm produce, such as eggs, fruit, and vegetables, or any available farm livestock that had matured and was in demand at a good price.

During the pre-war years, chickens, ducks, geese, pigs, and goats were always in plentiful supply at the markets, and prices were often negotiated with some robust haggling before money was exchanged, and the animal sent off with its new owner. In return for the sale of farm produce, essential household goods would be purchased, including items of hardware, clothing, soap, coffee, tea, and anything else that could not be produced or processed at home.

With the onset of autumn, much of the fruit in the orchards would have ripened and been picked for the markets. Sacks of fruit would be loaded onto horse-drawn wagons and taken regularly to yet another market in Nový Jičín. This journey to Nový Jičín, some distance to the north of Krhová, required substantial planning as the loaded wagon with everyone aboard needed to start out by at least two o'clock in the afternoon to get to Nový Jičín by four o'clock the following morning. On arrival, all the stalls displaying individual produce would need to be set up by five o'clock before the morning markets opened.

This busy morning market, when opened, lasted only for a short duration, as milling crowds of farmers and town's people bartered and bought their goods. By eight o'clock, all would be over, and the town square, normally bustling with activity, would become deserted. By then, the only echoes heard would be clattering wagon wheels and horse hooves as they made their way homeward over the cobbled market-square toward the town's exit.

During these market excursions to Nový Jičín, Rosalie would often call in on her way home for a social chat and morning tea with her friend Maria Rýdlová. Both women as young girls had met at finishing school in Rožnov, and although now living some distance apart, Rosalie always visited Maria on these opportune occasions. Maria had also married, and for a while, during Rosalie's confinement with her children, their contact had been steadily maintained. During this time, Maria would come and stay at Lhotka with Rosalie and help with the birth of her children.

Most years, the Kurovec family would attend the annual Agricultural Fair in Olomouc. This city was quite some distance away and well to the west of Lhotka. Most towns were linked with a regular and efficient train service, and the family would once again set out early, catching the morning train to Olomouc. By the end of the day, after all the business had been transacted, everyone would eventually return home later that evening.

This Fair was often incorporated with school excursions so that all village children could have the opportunity to experience the thrill and adventure of a bustling city fair. In earlier years, when life had been more affluent and less restrictive, the Kurovec family would take the train to Prague and attend 'The Veletrhy Praha Expo.' This once-a-year Expo was a Spring extravaganza, a magnificent display of worldly goods and latest innovations presented for the Czech public to see. It was always a special treat for everyone, as it was one of its kind in the country and could not be compared to anything else offered unless you travelled further afield in Europe. Here would be displays of fascinating objects and innovations, many unusual creations from countries abroad or elsewhere from around the world. Samples would be sold, and further goods could be ordered as required from agents displaying these samples.

For the Kurovec family to prepare for such a journey to Prague, it took some meticulous planning to accommodate eight active children overflowing with excitement and anticipation.

They always stayed at Hotel U Holubů, in Václavské Náměsti, in Prague. At the time, Frantz was well acquainted with the hotel proprietor, who always welcomed his family and catered to all their needs during visits to Prague.

Anna had many memories of visiting Prague during these family excursions, where together, they would visit museums, churches, and shops and attend concerts and operas. It was a cultural revelation that did not exist in their village. As a family, they were fortunate and privileged to be able to afford such extravagant holidays so far from home.

In later years, preceding and after WWII, such opportunities never presented again, and holidays of this measure ceased to exist. Food and essential goods became a top priority with regular shortages, so most goods were bought sparingly with little money available. However, before the war, Franz Kurovec still frequented numerous Agricultural Fairs and, on one occasion, returned from Prague with a prized goat of a notable blood line, albeit with an expensive price tag! Unbeknown to him, this goat was already in-kid, and what should have been a double blessing for his money; turned into anything but!

The young troublesome kid was hard work from the day he was born. He learned early to escape and raid the neighbour's gardens. Mr. Hásha, one of the neighbours, soon became so incensed with the goat's continual invasion that he captured the animal and locked it in his barn. When no one came to claim the kid, he took it over to Frantz, demanding a bag of wheat as compensation for all the damage it had caused. As the little goat became more uncontrollable, Frantz took it to his father-in-law's place in Krhová, implying the goat would make good sausages. Jan Stolař accepted the goat in good faith but soon learned it was not a gift from the gods but from the devil himself.

As it clambered up into the barn rafters, the young animal had a nasty habit of urinating over bags of oats which all the other animals then refused to eat. One day Jan Stolař caught the animal in the very act of spraying his bags of grain, so he grabbed the rascal by its horns and hurled it downstairs. Regretting his angry outburst and thinking he had killed the poor creature; Jan quickly summonsed his yardman to bury it. However, by the time the yardman arrived, the goat had disappeared, and a frantic search began of the neighbourhood. The next thing Jan discovered the creature back in the loft.

The neighbour's children pleaded to buy the goat for 20 Koruna, but Jan Stolař refused the deal and instead said they could have it for nothing provided they promised never to allow it back onto his property again.

Františka, Jan's wife, often laughed about her husband's goat saga and created a tale about a little goat for their grandchildren.

With such a large family, the Kurovec children were often farmed out to other relatives. Still, it was their Stolař grandparents who were most glad of their companionship and help at Krhová. This co-sharing often lessened the burden for their daughter Rosalie and helped to fill the permanent void Františka felt after losing their only son, Bohuslav.

The Kurovec children had all been brought up on bedtime stories, and none more enjoyed than Jan Karafiát's 'Broučci.' These were the adventures of Brouček and Beruška and their friends. These little creatures were fireflies, and a new adventure would start each night, entertaining the children before going to sleep.

With a ready and eager audience, Grandmother Františka added her own version of bed time tales that grew from her husband's farming experiences with the animals. To the goat saga, Františka added a further circle of friends which entertained the children at bedtime. "Once upon a time, there was a naughty young goat who kept company with a lazy pig, a fast and quick-witted hare who always outsmarted the cunning fox, and a cranky goose who relentlessly pursued the goat while the bumbling old horse pulled all five of them in his horse cart."

When Anna was nearing six years of age, with four additional siblings already in the Kurovec family and another one on the way, she was sent to live with her Stolař Grandparents at Krhová. Anna would become the centre of attention and the apple of her grandfather's eye. Anna adored her Stolař grandparents as they spoiled her and once gave her a German Shepard pup named Ranní.

On the morning of her name day, Anna had been gifted a box of chocolate-coated cherries, a real delicacy at the time, which were placed by her bedside for when she awoke. Sadly, the box was torn apart and emptied of its contents when Anna awoke, and sleeping innocently by her bedside was the four-legged culprit who had indulged himself in the expensive treat.

As a young child, Anna idolized Grandfather Stolař and would be mesmerized by his long, flowing white beard. One day while she sat with him at the dining room table, staring at his beard, he asked her, "What are you staring at, little one?"

To which she replied, "Your beard, it looks like a goat's beard!"

This was probably the only time she recollected being so impudent and upfront with him as much later, Anna always addressed him politely and with great reverence.

Anna recalled many years later, "I very much revered my Grandfather Stolař's cleverness in business, and as much as I admired Uncle Alois for his ability to make money, above all, it was still my father I loved, whatever shortcomings or weaknesses he may have possessed."

Anna's growing up years were full of happiness while she shared her time between her family home at Lhotka and her grandparent's farm in Krhová. As with all village life and there were occasionally odd happenings which offered no explanation.

An old lady who lived alone in one of the village cottages was often seen sitting in her front garden, sunning herself. On many occasions whenever Anna walked past on her way to school, she would wave and greet her. One day the old lady failed to appear and remained absent for some days before her neighbours became concerned. Shortly after the old lady's protracted absence, Anna noticed the old lady at the front door of her cottage again and as always, they waved to each other. It was soon revealed that the old lady had actually passed away some days earlier.

From Krhová, Anna later attended gymnasium (a secondary tier of education) in preparation for university, where she hoped one day to study medicine. She would become her grandfather's biggest fan, and his influence helped to form the building blocks from which her character grew and developed.

Anna never feared hard work, and the fruits of her toil, together with her grandfather's guidance and encouragement, in the end, paid dividends, creating a positive and nurturing impact on the development of a confident young woman.

Anna's life with her grandparents was an idyllic and productive period for her, from which she gleaned life skills that would mould her from a young farm girl into a grown-up, mature woman. It was a halcyonian existence filled with happiness, and no doubt made easier because grandfather always had money, and all farm accounts were met and paid on time. There was always money to buy the necessities of life, and the farm remained progressive and productive, and well-managed.

By now, Anna's two other sisters, Bo and Zdeňka, were already teenagers and went on to live with Aunt Anna and Uncle Josef Kurovec and, on a rotational basis, spent time between there and their Lhotka family home.

Later during Anna's stay with her Stolař grandparents at Krhová, she would be joined by her younger siblings, Helena and Jarmila while at the same time, the other Kurovec children, Vladimír, Jaroslav, and Eliška, remained with their parents in Lhotka. When Anna was finally invited to stay on permanently with her Stolař grandparents she would do so until she was close to twenty-five years of age.

Grandfather Jan Stolař always had a good sense of humour, and with it came a touch of mischief that occasionally showed at the most inopportune moments. On one occasion, when Anna's little sister Helena, then aged about three years, was visiting them, she attended Sunday mass with her Stolař grandparents. After church and teasing his granddaughter, Jan Stolař asked Helena, "And what did you learn in church today, little one?" Much to his amusement, Helena straightened herself to her entire height and, with great seriousness and aplomb, sang a garbled recital of her Latin version of the service, "Keet-zee-ree-Meet-zee-ree!" Her devout grandmother flushed with embarrassment and indignation as she scolded her husband for encouraging sacrilegious nonsense from their granddaughter.

Jan Stolař's keen horsemanship and vast equine knowledge and experience made him a popular figure in his steed business amongst those of similar interest. He bred fine thoroughbred horses, and his stables had numerous colts available for sale at competitive prices. Jan quite often entertained important clients who shared his enthusiasm for horses.

One such customer was a well-educated young chap called Vladimír Pavlík, who lived close by and shared a passion for horses. Anna, Jan Stolař's granddaughter, met Vladimír Pavlík on rare occasions, but she did see him frequently with her grandfather discussing horses. However, she always felt embarrassed and intimidated in his presence, as she lacked qualities that he seemed to exude; poise, confidence, and self-assurance and having had a good education it enabled him to hold intelligent conversations with those much older than himself.

Vladimír would later join the diplomatic corps, which would take him throughout Europe and later onto America, where his untimely death would create family suspicion of a deliberate act by another party and which would never be satisfactorily resolved. However, it would be many years later, but well before settling in the USA, that Vladimir Pavlik's and Anna's paths would cross again, albeit briefly, under very different circumstances.

Vladimír Pavlík had a brother, Robert, who served in the army and would later join the Czechoslovak brigade (CIABG)[1] at Cholmondeley in England. Robert would remain abroad for the latter part of the war and serve as an officer in the Special Forces during WWII. In addition, he was an accomplished skier, an ability that would serve him well in the course of his specialized commission during the war.

He would rise through the ranks as Major, and some fifty-five years later, after communism was finally disbanded in Czechoslovakia, he would become latently recognized for his past achievements and decorated as General Robert Pavlík. He would also become Anna's future brother-in-law.

Anna's younger sister Helena would later live with their Stolař grandparents caring for them into their twilight years, but not before Frantiska and Jan Stolař celebrated together their Golden and Diamond Wedding Anniversaries surrounded by four generations of family.

After their passing, Jan Stolař in 1954 and his wife Františka in 1957, Helena and her family would make the Krhova farm their home. By then, with Soviet oppression, the farm would eventually be reduced to only a house, with the remaining farmland acquired by the government and utilized for collective farming.[2]

After Uncle Josef Kurovec passed away in 1929, Anna's oldest sister Zdeňka moved in with Auntie Anna and remained there until she married, and then afterward, sister Bo settled in with their aunt. While Zdeňka lived with Auntie Anna, she was already in the full bloom of youthful beauty, and with her long, thick, dark hair, Zdeňka drew the attention of many admirers.

During this time, Auntie Anna convinced her niece Zdeňka to have her hair cut and styled in the then-popular Japanese Mikado-like bop. A highly fashionable and desirable hairdo made famous during the flapper era of the 1920s through to the 1930s. Auntie Anna complimented Zdeňka on the new sophisticated look and, as always, fussed over her. This modern and glamorous image suited and delighted Zdeňka, so she went home to her mother to show off her alluring new look.

Rosalie was horrified, if not devastated when she saw her daughter's long hair had been cut so short. But what peeved her, even more was that Zdeňka sought advice from an old interfering aunt who suddenly had become her daughter's influential fashion guru! Rosalie did not hesitate to inform Zdeňka that she did not like her hair, especially now that she realized Auntie Anna was behind the latest fashion exposé. This only fuelled Zdeňka's determination for independence, especially when she saw how disapproving her mother had been.

Zdeňka was a beautiful lass, always flattering her good looks much to the admiration and approval of many young lads, keen to make their acquaintance. But, Zdeňka always maintained her countenance, only flirting with them occasionally but always keeping her cards close to her heart.

When Zdeňka was about sixteen, Rosalie sent her and her younger sister Anna to Svaté Hostýn on an outing. It was some distance away, so the journey had to be taken by train. Hostýn is a sacred mountain located east of Přerov and 735 metres above sea level. Here traces of civilization have been recorded as far back as the Stone Age. The small town of Bystřice pod Hostýnem rests at its base, and on top of the mountain stands a Basilica that is very popular with pilgrims and visitors, even to this day.

On this particular journey to Hostýn, Zdeňka had invited her close girlfriend, Funka Vahalová, to accompany them. The girls spent the night at Bystřice pod Hostýnem, staying in one of the cabins, and enjoyed the many tourist shops and stalls that lined the street heading up to Svaté Hostýn. The next day before they were all scheduled to return home, Zdeňka told her younger sister Anna to remain seated on the bench beneath the trees close to the railway station and look after all their cases while she and Funka went for a stroll. Zdeňka instructed emphatically that Anna was not to follow or disturb them and cause embarrassment. Obligingly, Anna remained seated with all three cases while the two girls, dressed in their finery, quickly flitted off, giggling, whispering, and flirting with some of the young lads present.

As time drew on, Anna heard the arrival of their train and promptly made her way toward it. Believing it to be their home-bound train as it was headed in the same direction from where they had come the day before, Anna soon realized that it remained entirely up to her to board with all three cases as there was no sight of the other two to help her. Anna assumed the girls, ashamed of her in front of their male admirers, had bordered one of the carriages further down, so she settled into the nearest vacant seat with all the baggage and proceeded on her homeward journey.

When the train neared Hranice, the conductor arrived to collect Anna's ticket, and she realized, much to her horror, that she didn't have her ticket as Zdeňka, the oldest and most responsible, had them all with her. Panic-stricken, Anna soon realized she had headed home alone, and the other two had missed their train. But what was even more worrying, Anna would now have to explain to her mother and Auntie Anna the absence of the other two!

Zdeňka and Funka finally arrived home, but it was many hours later. They had caught a train sometime after Anna but would soon discover it was the wrong one headed south to Hulín in the Zlín area instead of north toward Hranice. Fortunately, the conductor caught up with the two girls at Hulín, where they were offloaded, and then had to wait for the remainder of the day at the railway station until the next train arrived heading north onto Hranice. When the girls finally made it home, looking sheepish and lost for words, Auntie Anna smirked at them with folded arms and scolded sardonically, "Well! Well! Well! The stupid one finds her way home, but the two clever ones get lost!"

Zdeňka was twenty-three when she and Milos Hurtík wed in 1938. He was a high school teacher and regarded as a very acceptable suitor. Being the eldest daughter of Frantz and Rosalie Kurovec, Zdeňka had a wedding befitting her social status. She was dressed in a white gown and looked like the perfect bride. In return for helping and keeping Auntie

Anna company, Zdeňka received a dowry from her, which helped the young couple financially as they started life together.

Sadly, Zdeňka would be the only Kurovec daughter to dress in traditional white, as all the other girls, except for Bo, would choose to marry in more conservative suits at a time when money was fast becoming scarce for lavish occasions. Instead, weddings would be celebrated discreetly in times of austerity with minimal fuss and expense.

The older Kurovec sons by now, had left home to pursue their own lives. Vladimír, the elder of the boys, met Božena Čurdová and married in 1942. For whatever reason, the Kurovec families seemed to have distanced themselves from the young nuptials in as much that Vladimír never returned home to help and take over the family farm as would have been expected of the eldest son.

Jaroslav also left home, worked at the nearby Tobacco Factory, and had various other occupations before joining the army. He, too, showed no interest in farming the family property, so much remained with the Kurovec parents and Stolař grandparents to cope alone. In the end, it would be the older girls who came to their aid.

Bo, who had spent much of her time flitting between families, was a difficult child to please at the best of times. She never seemed to appreciate or be satisfied with what she had. She was attractive but fussy, and as with many romantically inclined young women of her day, she was always searching for impossible dreams. She, too, moved in and settled with Auntie Anna when her older sister, Zdeňka, left and married.

Auntie Anna, being yet again alone after Zdeňka's departure, welcomed Bo's permanent company. Perhaps both being similar in nature, they each helped to fill the void they had in their lives. Bo never married but inherited her Auntie Anna's villa when her aunt died in 1975. Bo lived in the villa for quite some time until she found living alone unbearable. She then opted to move in with her sister Eliška's family for companionship and, in exchange, forfeited her villa and gave it to her young niece, also named Eliška, being the daughter of Bo's sister Eliška. This would later become a bone of contention between herself, her family, and her niece. But even before Bo had formalized this deal, her own family warned her against such a rash decision. Bo disregarded their well-intentioned advice and proceeded to do as she saw fit. She refused to be swayed by the possible consequences of such an impulsive act and stubbornly refused to heed advice from those who wanted to safeguard her future. At the time, she had believed she was acting in good faith when she transferred her home to her niece.

However, soon afterward, realizing she had been hoodwinked and betrayed, it was too late. In hindsight, Bo came to regret her decision all too soon that being homeless and alone was entirely her own doing, and she could blame no one except herself. No matter what un-wrangling of this transaction she proposed, the deal was legally air-tight. This once again created a rift within the families, which only had begun to heal since Bo's passing in 2008. Once again, Auntie Anna's villa was at the epicentre of disenchantment!

Jarmila, the youngest Kurovec sibling, was delightful but spoilt, yet a constant source of endearment and entertainment to everyone she met. She was much younger than her oldest sister, Zdeňka, who was already 18 years old when Jarmila was born in 1932. Jarmila had very little recollection of the pre-war years but, like everyone else, would have to endure life in Czechoslovakia in the aftermath of WWII.

As a three-year-old, Jarmila would wander about with her favourite comic book under her arm, asking any stranger who came to the door if they could read. She would then thrust her book at them and promptly instruct that they read to her. Of course, by this time, she knew her storybook off by heart, and woe betide should anybody try and alter the wording of any passage or verse; she would immediately point out their error! On one occasion, the local headmaster visited and was promptly demanded to read. Being quite accustomed to her quirky ways, he created his own tale of events bearing no relevance to the book. Annoyed, Jarmila snatched back her comic book and dispatched him for not knowing how to read!

Jarmila was a busy child and had the propensity to be easily distracted. She was tasked to watch over a flock of turkeys at her parent's home at Lhotka. By late evening she turned up unannounced at her grandparent's farm some five kilometres away at Krhová. She was in tears because she had lost all the turkeys and feared her parent's repercussions.

The biggest concern was to inform and pacify the anxious family back in Lhotka that their daughter was safe and well, albeit minus the turkeys. So, it fell upon Anna, then living with her Stolař grandparents at Krhová, to walk the distance back to Lhotka with the good news.

Milos and Zdeňka who had married before the onset of WWII were now permanently settled at Vysoká. Before this, Milos Hurtík had taught at several other schools before transferring to Leshná upper school. At Leshna, Milos Hurtík had the added challenge of teaching his young sister-in-law Jarmila who lived close by. This schooling arrangement proved inconvenient for Jarmila as her brother-in-law constantly reminded her to do her homework, only all too aware of the consequences if she didn't.

By now, the Hurtík's had children of their own, and their oldest son, born in 1940, was only seven years younger than his Aunt Jarmila.

To further aggravate her annoyance, the biggest thorn in her side was her nephew Miloslav or Mila as he was also known, who attended the same school for a while. Although quite junior to Jarmila in class, Mila took a keen interest in his young Aunt's education. Young Mila would eves-drop in on conversations between his parents and then gleefully impart his own versions of Jarmila's progress reports to anyone who was prepared to listen. He would often embroider Jarmila's behaviour and relay this onto family and friends. Much to Jarmila's chagrin, she could hardly do anything but weather the storm of her nephew's constant broadcasts.

Afterward, the other younger Hurtík children, Zdeněk and Jaroslav, and much later, Pavla, didn't have the same schooling experiences as did Mila with Jarmila while attending tuition under their father's watch.

The threats of WWII were fast becoming a reality, and with it, the uncertainty and fear of losing any lasting peace loomed ominously on the horizon.

With increasing family demands, Anna was left with no doubt that her life was not destined to be what she had planned, but rather the constant pressure and expectation to help out with whichever farm demanded her. In the end, it would be her parents who needed her most to help salvage the family Lhotka farm from ruination when fate beyond Anna's control propelled her back into farming and hard work. Anna's hopes and aspirations of a medical career quickly faded, and instead of university life, Anna would remain at Lhotka for the duration of the war, by which time, at its conclusion, she would be twenty-nine years of age.

Photograph 11,12 & 13: (L-R) Rosalie Kurovcová nee Stolařová, Anna's mother. Frantisek (Franz) Kurovec Anna's Father. Zdeňka Hurtíková, Anna's sister.

Photograph 14, 15 & 16: (L-R) Anna Kurovcová, nee Kanak. Anna's brothers Vladimír Kurovec & Jaroslav Kurovec.

Photograph 17 18 & 19: (L-R) Anna's sisters Bohuslava or 'Bo' Kurovcová & Eliška Kurovcová (Vodová). Anna's younger sister Helena Pavlíková nee Kurovcová.

Photograph 21, 22 & 23: (L-R) Anna's younger sister Jarmila Švecová nee Kurovcová. Anna's cousins Milan Kurovec & Marta Berková nee Kurovcová.

Photograph 23 & 24: (L-R) Pavla Kristýneková nee Kurovcová, Anna's cousin. Wedding Helena Zocková & Alois Kurovec, brother of Frantz (Anna's father).

Photograph 25 & 26: (L-R) Alois & his wife Helena with son Milan. Alois Kurovec in old age father of Marta & grandfather to Helena Štrusová.

Photograph 27 & 28: (L-R) Helena Kurovcová nee Zocková.
Anna Kurovcová nee Dobova, wife of Josef Kurovec.

Photograph 29 & 30: (L-R) Josef Kurovec brother to Alois and Franz. Marta & Vladimír Berka's wedding with sister Pavla & cousin Jaroslav Kurovec.

Photograph 31 & 32: (L-R) Vladimír Berka husband of Marta.
Pavla & Ladislav Kristýnek at their wedding.

Photograph 33 & 34: (L-R) Helena & Alois Kurovec in old age. Their granddaughter Helena, daughter of Marta & Vladimír Berka with her husband Jaromír Štrusa.

Photograph 35 & 36: (L-R) Aunt Anna Kurovcová wife of Josef with niece Jarmila Kurovcová. Jarmila Kurovcová next to her Uncle Alois Kurovec's car.

Photograph 37: Zdeňka & Miloš Hurtík's family wedding photo 3rd September 1938 at Aunt Anna's villa.

Photograph 38: Anna & Josef Kurovec's family villa passed down to Bo Kurovcová and then onto Bo's niece Eliška Mullerová nee Vodová.

Photograph 39: Kurovec Family home on Farm No 6 Lhotka.

Photograph 40: Jan & Františka Stolař with granddaughter Helena Kurovcová, and great grandchildren Mila & Zdeněk Hurtík on their farm at Krhová.

Photograph 41: Jan Stolař handling horses assisted by granddaughter Anna Kanak nee Kurovcová and her sister Helena in background.

Photograph 42: Jarmila Kurovcová with working horses at Lhotka Farm during harvest.

Photograph 43 & 44: (L-R) Granddaughters Anna & Jarmila Kurocove with Jan Stolař at Krhová. Kurovec sisters; Anna, Helena & Bo.

Photograph 45: Bo Kurovcová with her mother Rosalie & grandfather Jan Stolař.

Photograph 46 & 47: (L-R) Golden Wedding Anniversary 1943; Back L-R; Eliška, Anna, Bo, Helena. Front L-R; Milos' mother, Jarmila, Rosalie, Jan & Františka Stolař, Milos & Zdeňka Hurtík with sons Mila & Zdeněk. The Stolařs grandparents 1943.

Photograph 48 & 49: (L-R) Rosalie Kurovcová & her mother.
L-R Anna, Bo & Eliška, Front (L-R) Rosalie Kurovcová, Jarmila, & Františka Stolařová.

Photograph 50 & 51: (L-R) Sisters Eliška with Anna sitting on toboggan. Frantiska Stolařová.

Photograph 52: Jarmila and Helena playing cards with farm-stay guest at Lhotka.

Photograph 53 & 54: (L-R) Jarmila entertains farm-stay guest. Bo second from Left, Helena, & Jarmila at end with farm-stay guests in Lhotka.

Photograph 55: Jarmila relaxing with guests on the Bečva River at Lhotka.

Photograph 56 & 57: (L-R) Jarmila Kurovcová playing with farm animals at home in Lhotka. Jarmila with family cat at Lhotka.

Photograph 58 & 59: (L-R) Jarmila with her mother's dog Brok on the Bečva River. Jarmila's nephews Mila, Zdeněk & Jarek Hurtik.

Photograph 60 & 61: (L-R) Jarmila on her birthday.
Jarmila with nephew Mila Hurtík.

Photograph 62 & 63: (L-R) Auntie Anna Kurovcová & her niece Zdeňka Hurtíková.
Brother & Sister Vladimír & Anna Kurovcová (Kanak).

Photograph 64 & 65: (L-R) Anna Kurovcová (Kanak) 1941.
Vladimír Kurovec & Božena Čurdová wedding 2nd May 1942.

Photograph 66: Farm 6 quarry remains owned by Alois & Josef Kurovec.

Photograph 67: Zdeňka & Miloš Hurtík's wedding 3rd September 1938; with Vladimír, Bo & Jarmila.

Photograph 68: Zdeněk Hurtík.

CHAPTER 4

A Prelude to War

By late 1937 home life in Lhotka had fast become a shadow of its former self. So much disarray and lack of upkeep stared back at Anna as the days of opulence, and rich harvests now seemed a distant memory.

Her father Frantz had continued to spend money impulsively and often needlessly, and certainly without any consideration for the future. He did so continually, even without prior consultation with his wife or family.

What added to the problem was that Frantz Kurovec became a habitual gambler, and much of the money that could have helped his family pay farming costs and debts was now squandered elsewhere, feeding a habit he showed no desire to control or end. He had become careless and reckless with money, and some even allege he had several indiscretions with other women. Either way, he still played card games, gambled, and, more often than not, lost.

In the past, he had suffered a personal falling out with his younger brother Alois, and now he suffered reproach from other family members as well. He knew he was a failure as a businessman because he lacked the luck and money acumen that his ancestors and brothers had. Although the Stolař grandparents were still running a successful farm in Krhová, for security reasons, some of their personal finances had been tied up with their daughter's family farm in Lhotka. Nevertheless, despite this, they had very little control over the undertaking of everyday financial farming management that Franz, their son-in-law, had on the Kurovec property.

Over time, the Stolař family had willingly covered debts he incurred on numerous occasions. During this gradual erosion of family fortunes, Anna's father Franz had twice gambled away the Lhotka farm, and each time, Grandfather Stolař came to the rescue and bought back the farm. By now, Anna had earned her grandparent's trust and appreciation, so on the third occasion, when the farm was lost to gambling yet again, Jan Stolař once more bought back the property but this time signed the farm over into Anna's name so her father could never use it as gambling collateral for any of his future losses. From there onward, the property remained in Anna's name until well after the war, and although still a beneficiary during the Soviet Russian period of influence, most of this farming land would become annexed for other Communist collective purposes without Anna's permission.

Anna loved her father but still could not bring herself to blame him completely for their downfall. She was aware he had many admirable traits, but it was his fractured and weakened esteem that she pitied the most.

Over the years, Anna had become aware of his propensity for gambling, but it was not in her place to rebuke him. Besides, there was a side to his character that others always saw, a man of integrity who often went out of his way to help many others less fortunate than himself. But all this came at great cost to his family as now he cut a tragic figure burdened with grief and regret that would continue to plague him for the remainder of his life.

With escalating threats of war and dwindling family fortunes, the Stolař grandparents, still having to maintain their own Krhová farm, could no longer rescue their daughter and her family from the spiralling demise of their once happier disposition. Before Anna's return to Lhotka, all the while, with the rumblings of war gaining momentum, Rosalie had taken it upon herself to earn extra income to supplement what little money remained for every day costs of living. She turned their Lhotka farmhouse into a country homestay for city folk on holiday. This homestay venture was successful for a while as it created a pleasant diversion for those who wanted to spend holiday time in the country. Most were well-heeled guests from different walks of life, such as artists and actors, and those who simply craved the tranquillity of country living.

One family who frequented for a while was Mr. and Mrs. Uretsky, a friendly young couple without children, who at the time enjoyed a break from city living. They would spend much of their time frolicking in the Bečva River or walking the fields amongst grazing sheep and generally enjoying the beauty and quietude of the place. They especially enjoyed Jarmila's company, who by now had moved back to her parent's home.

Brok, the Kurovec family dog, was a small shaggy dark coloured dog of an undetermined pedigree but very active and agile and a constant companion to Jarmila.

Even though Brok regarded Rosalie as his mistress, he seemed happy to exchange his loyalty for Jarmila's company; so, wherever Jarmila went, Brok went, especially if there was plenty of action and newcomers to entertain.

When war was about to break out in 1938, all of Rosalie's bookings for her farm stay dried up, and with it came an end to Rosalie's extra housekeeping money. Similarly, the Uretsky couple stopped coming, and even after the war ended, they never returned.

Various relatives were now chastising Rosalie for her over indulgent generosity toward her family, especially her children, and she was accused of giving them the cream of the crop, which she could ill afford. She was constantly hounded to sell more farm produce to make ends meet, instead providing extravagantly for her family at the dinner table.

Regardless of what others accused her of, Rosalie remained considerate and caring and would not deprive her family of anything that could be passed onto others, leaving her children to go without. She herself could do without many things, but never her children.

All the while, Rosalie continued to toil on the farm with little support from her husband, and it was beginning to take its toll on her. With surmounting hardship, and lack of money and support, Anna could see sadness and heartache etched into her mother's otherwise serene, blue eyes. Her mother's once beautiful and kindly face now bore a mask permanently displaying disappointment and pain that could never be erased. Anna knew her grandparents were acutely aware of their daughter's daily struggle both emotionally and financially and that life on the Lhotka farm was far from being a harmonious and carefree existence.

With Anna's help, the Stolař grandparents hoped that some of their daughter's burden would be eased with extra support. So, Anna returned home to help her mother.

No matter how scrupulous Anna was with money and cost-saving measures, the Lhotka farm was slipping deeper into debt. She tried to apply her grandfather's management principles, but it was not easy to achieve the same result as it had been with her grandfather's money. All seemed so methodical and easy when living at Krhová.

Anna blamed herself, in part, for the demise of her parent's fortune and wished, in hindsight, that she had been called upon much earlier to help out. She felt guilty that she could not save her family farm simply with hard work as it soon became evident that she was fighting a losing battle without capital. Had she remained with her parents right from the very beginning, perhaps these financial woes may not have occurred, but on the other hand, she would have been ill-prepared without the life skills her grandfather had instilled in her. It was futile to ponder irreversible outcomes.

Despite the circumstances, Anna felt morally obligated to lend a hand and alleviate some of the burden befallen on her mother, and with what little funds Anna had of her own, she would try to make the best of a bad situation. She decided that whatever produce was at hand, it would be sold to make ends meet. Anna approached other local farmers and bought goslings, which she raised and fattened, and resold when they matured. She acquired a clientele from Ostrava, who happily travelled to Lhotka and purchased these live fattened geese and paid her handsomely for them. With these funds, she managed to buy some everyday essentials.

Anna made it her practice to squirrel away some of her meagre profits and then, at her earliest opportunity, buy a young farm animal she could rear and eventually sell. She acquired a young heifer, which she raised for some months, and then sold it in-calf for over three times its original value, a profit which helped to sustain her family for a while. It was a tediously slow process but one with only a glimmer of hope.

These little business ventures, she had gleaned from Grandfather Stolař, who was always wheeling and dealing, albeit on a larger scale, and always making a clean-cut profit from his transactions. However, Anna always lacked the capital, so it never seemed as lucrative as her grandfather's business enterprises.

Grandfather Stolař had always stressed to her that whenever in business, no one should ever place themselves financially as a guarantor on behalf of another or equally never expect others to place themselves in a similar situation. He always advocated never borrowing money from strangers, friends, or family but rather going through reputable banks as unexpected demand for total loan repayment could cause further financial embarrassment; "But better still," he advised her, "Don't spend it all. Save some money for when you might really need it."

Her grandfather's principles may have been admirable, but when your life and that of others depend on your ability to provide during exceptional circumstances when no banks were lending money for farm debts, fine principles can often be muddied by desperation.

On occasions, despite pending doom, Anna would visit Valašské Mezirici, which often coincided with market days. It would become Anna's brief escape from the tedium of poverty, where she could attend a budget opera permitted only from her meagre personal savings. She recalled one enjoyable operatic comedy, 'Prodaná Nevěsta,' translated as 'The Bartered Bride' written by the famous composer Bedřich Smetana. A few months later, while window-shopping in Nový Jičín, Anna saw a blue and white porcelain dinner set for sale. It was decorated in character figurines from the opera she had attended in Valašské Mezirici. She instantly wanted to buy it for her mother. Anna's money was always put aside for emergency needs, but in this case, it was the thought of the pleasure it might bring her mother rather than the future prospect of needing the money to survive.

It may have been a reckless and impulsive gesture, but it did come with a genuine love for her mother, who met Anna's gift with some disapproval. Anna struggled to convince Rosalie to cast off her old set of battered metal cups and plates, which had come into use since falling onto hard times, and replace them with something new and more fitting. Rosalie had the habit of hiding away anything precious in hope of using these things when better days returned. She had a few family pieces of chinaware and crystal squirreled away, insisting they were reserved for special occasions.

Anna finally won her mother over to part with the old and bring in the new. Like her mother, over time, Anna too would inherit this trait and become reluctant to use precious things and instead hide them for those occasions which, in many instances, never eventuated.

During these latter years with her parents, Anna endeavoured to make home life comfortable for her mother while managing the day-to-day affairs of the farm. Her family no longer afforded domestic staff or labourers, so it was up to the family to do the labour-intensive work. There was no discrimination; men, women, and children all worked together. This was the case for many families, but at the time, there were still many who were far better off financially than the Kurovec family.

Anna's sister, Bo, seemed to be an exception to this rule. She always had an excuse whenever help was needed. On most occasions, she managed to shirk from her share of work and instead idle the day away out of sight, daydreaming or lazing about by the Bečva River. Bo was not used to working hard, and she was not about to apply herself to tasks that she disliked doing.

While the Kurovec family struggled, with it came the subsequent repercussions and uncertainty of approaching war. Yet, for many, they remained unconcerned and refused to believe that one day their lives could be at the epicentre of a conflict. This unpreparedness for the eventuality that Czechoslovakia might go to war or, worse still, be overtaken by a foreign power was not something that ordinary country folk envisaged.

By April of 1938, the Anglo-French alliance was to defy any invasion of Czechoslovakia by Germany. So, in the event of this happening, it would draw both Britain and France into the conflict, or so the Czechs hoped.

Shortly afterward, in May, Hitler and Mussolini pledged a lasting friendship. The Czech government responded and ordered that all men between the ages of sixteen and sixty years were to have defence training in preparation for a possible invasion, and the Prague government immediately ordered 400,000 troops toward the Austro-German border.

The Bren gun, so named after the two cities where it was being manufactured (Brno in Moravia and simultaneously in Enfield, UK), entered into service with production of these high-quality guns being fuelled by the probability of war, and so manufacturing escalated in readiness for any major ground-force combat.

By September of 1938, the Sudeten Germans held mass rallies calling for union with Germany. In response with growing Czech hostility toward the Germans, Czech Premier Milan Hodza appealed for calm.

Politician Konrad Heinlein[1], who once held pro-Czechoslovak views and was publicly anti-Nazi, still advocated autonomy for Sudetenland. Many of the Czechs protested against this happening until General Jan Syrový's sweeping mobilization of troops soon replaced Premier Hodza. As the crises escalated, it prompted France to send troops to the Maginot Line[2], a fortified defence set-up along the German border stretching from La Ferté to the Rhine River.

Hitler called for a 'four power' conference to discuss the Czech crises, and in September of 1938, 'The Munich Deal on Czechoslovakia' was made by Hitler, Mussolini, Chamberlain, and Daladier, without any Czech presence at the table.

The deal comprised the Sudeten Region with its German-speaking minority to be handed over to Germany, but it also stated that Germany could not enter these ceded territories through Czechoslovakia itself. Under the 30th September 1938 Munich Agreement[3], Germany was only allowed to annex Sudetenland, and the Agreement disallowed Hitler from invading Czechoslovakia.

The Czech people perceived this whole exercise to be a 'sell-out of their country' to Hitler when on October 5th, his army seized the once Czech-occupied Sudetenland.

Upon Hitler's occupation declaration, Konrad Heinlein was awarded Commissioner for the Sudeten Region and walked alongside The Führer during the procession. There afterward, Heinlein would organize the pogrom, a campaign to de-Jewify Sudetenland, and he would join the Reichstag and officially become a member of the Nazi Party.

While Germany was reclaiming Czech land, the Polish, in turn, claimed some 802sq kilometres of Zaolzie[4], Teschen-Silesia territory from Czechoslovakia. This further eroded Czech confidence, making them subservient to any future invasion.

Uncertainty in Czechoslovakia prevailed, with everyone eventually beginning to grasp the magnitude of the situation if Germany ever invaded. The Czechs were a nation of free thinkers and were steered by self-determination to achieve a stable economy driven by agriculture, industry, and infrastructure that had been inherited from the fall of the Austro-Hungarian Empire. So, by the end of WWI, they had become a new nation in the process of redefining their newly reinstated identity.

Edvard Beneš, who had been president of Czechoslovakia from 1935 to 1938, resigned on the 5th of October 1938 in protest against German aggression and was replaced by Emil Hácha. With the advent of WWII actually happening, and with growing uneasiness over further invasions in Europe by the Third Reich, it did not lessen Czech concerns of safety and security nor immune them from the clutches of Nazi occupation. President Emil Hácha, now President-elect, albeit for only a short duration until the 15th of March 1939, was faced with the unenviable task of securing his country from invasion.

In the unpredictable climate of negotiations, it may have temporarily halted Hitler's advance to war, but the Führer still had his sights on Bohemia and Moravia's vast industrial capacity to oil his war machine.

On the 14th of March 1939, after a short confrontation, overpowered and unprepared without military support, the Czech army was ordered to lay down arms and disband while Hitler's army invaded Czechoslovakia. The Czech's surrender was not of its choosing but instead based on obvious evidence that no allied nation was prepared to come to their aid. It was the dawning in history that no one could have predicted.

Hitler disbanded the Czech army, thus acquiring its military hardware to his advantage against the allies. He also maintained a small number of sympathetic Czech soldiers as a symbolic gesture. All remaining soldiers were discharged, many joining the Partisans to wage subversive agitations against the Nazis while many more fled the country and joined Allied forces; the Russians in the east and Europe in the west.

On the 15th of March 1939, when only six months earlier, Hitler having vowed he had no further interest in territorial claims in Europe, and only two days after his ultimatum that there would be complete independence for Slovakia and Ruthenia, Hitler entered Prague as a conqueror and raised his flag over Hradčany Castle[5]. In the past, this ancient palace had been the seat of Bohemian Kings, but more recently, the residence of the fast-vanishing Czech Presidents. Needless to say, Hitler's reception in Prague was anything but the tumultuous welcome he had received earlier in claiming the Sudetenland. Instead, many Czech demonstrators discarded their safety, sang their National Anthem, and opposed Hitler unashamedly. In response, Hitler imposed a curfew in Prague, closing cafes, restaurants, theatres, and cinemas, while thousands of Nazi opposers sought escape through crowded railway stations. It was the first time that Adolf Hitler occupied a land of non-German people.

By March of 1939, when Germany finally had control of Czechoslovakia and made the Czech lands of Bohemia and Moravia an established Protectorate of Nazi Germany, President Hácha became a powerless figurehead as the 'Reichprotektor' took control and became answerable only to Hitler. The newly formed Czech Government under Premier Rudolf Beran, took over from General Jan Syrový. Hitler then insisted that the Czech Government make all gold and foreign currency exchange payments to the Reich.

Czechoslovakia was desperate. Abandoned by her former allies, France and Britain, many Czechs blamed and held their allied friends responsible for this scourge.

During the earlier March invasion and subsequent occupation of Bohemia and Moravia, Slovakia was placed under the Presidency of Józef Tiso[6]. Ever since the declaration of Czechoslovakia after WWI, Józef Tiso always advocated for Slovakia to be recognized as a Republic in its own right and continued to agitate for its sovereignty. He had been a Catholic Priest who joined Slovakia's party politics and rose through the ranks and, after collaborating with Hitler, better placed himself to become President of the Slovak Republic by October of 1939. Regardless, his country would still remain a puppet state of the Third Reich.

In May, Mussolini joined Hitler, and together they signed a 'Pact of Steel', committing support for one another in the event of war. Germany's occupation measures were felt by every Czech as Germany prepared for an inevitable war. All produce grown was now earmarked for the Reich to control, and every aspect of industry and agriculture was scrutinized and controlled by them. Food supplies were primarily for the German troops, industrial workers, and administrators, and what remained would have to feed the remaining people. However, Czechs working for the Germans in essential services and factories often received more generous rations.

The structured monthly coupon system introduced by the Germans in 1938 maintained a steady supply of certain basic foods, but people could no longer be selective; however, neither did they starve. Ration stamps, smaller than the larger ration portions given to the Germans, were generally for meat, bread, potatoes, and milk and were more amply supplied to those living in cities, whereas those on farms still had access, albeit to much-reduced quantities of vegetables, fruit, poultry, eggs, and dairy produce which they grew.

Later, between 1944 to 1945, rations of animal products such as meats, fats, butter, and eggs would become scarce, so diets had to be supplemented with fish, and children much to their dislike were regularly dosed with fish oil.

Moreover, any perceived civilian disobedience within earshot of German authorities posed a constant threat to Czech citizens' safety and security, and if not complicit to Nazi demands, unexpected raids from the Gestapo with immeasurable repercussions were more often than not of fatal consequence.

By August, Hitler closed the borders with Poland in Upper Silesia, and as tensions increased, the Polish troops mobilized. By September, Hitler attacked Poland with his Blitzkrieg[7], destroying Polish railway systems and its Air Force, and then invaded the country.

The notion of an all-out European conflict had finally become a reality when war was declared on Germany on the 3rd of September 1939 by Britain and France. While WWII rapidly escalated, Winston Churchill was already in the process of replacing Chamberlain as Prime Minister of Great Britain.

Anna's once privileged life shared with her grandparents in Krhova was now a shadow in the past and replacing it was the unparallel and harsh reality of life that would soon engulf her family. Anna cared deeply for her parents and wanted to do her best to help, but it seemed an impossible task to deliver a farm from debt into solvency, especially during a war. From here on, Anna's life became a parody of everything she believed in, a life no longer in her control but rather at the mercy of Nazi Germany, who would dictate all future terms of conduct.

Photograph 69: Oil painting of Lhotka home circa 1970 commissioned by Bo Kurovcová.

Photograph 70 & 71: (L-R) A cup from Anna's dinner service purchased for Rosalie. Jaroslav's gift to his sisters.

CHAPTER 5

Krhová and Lhotka: Anna's War Under Nazi Occupation

In 1938 ex-President Edvard Beneš and his minister Jan Masaryk moved to Great Britain, and by October 1939, established a Czechoslovak Government-In-Exile with Beneš as President and Masaryk as Foreign Minister.

Beneš may have had the interests of Czechoslovakia at heart, but he also played politics, believing the Russians would be useful against Germany. He had a deep seeded hatred of the Germans and was believed to have had pro-Russian sentiments when the Allied nations ignored his earlier pleas for assistance. With information obtained from Czech Intelligence Agent František Moravec[1] and undisclosed Agent A-45, Beneš was able to use this gathered intelligence to bargain deals with the British. He also organized and directed numerous retaliations against the occupying Germans.

With war escalating and the Nazi grip on Czechoslovakia steadfastly increasing, the Czechs became isolated. Many, in response, joined the underground, a resistance movement to sabotage German occupation. These Partisans initially trained to use passive methods to penetrate Nazi strongholds with an emphasis on sabotage and collecting intelligence, intending to weaken and topple the regime. It was a brazen act by those bravely volunteering to resist the Nazis in face of their strength. And if the saboteurs were caught, severe repercussions followed, not only for them but their families.

Further still, many silent Nazi sympathizers shamelessly denounced their own people with differing views to the occupying Germans.

With a new government in place demanding allegiance to Hitler, disillusion spread amongst the Czechs who only desired peace and self-determination and instead became divided with growing resentment, anxiety, and fear.

Independent thinking became restrictive, and the Nazis did everything in their power to crush the Czech's National pride, even to erase association with their past leaders.

Czechoslovakia's future hung like an ominous cloud about to burst and deliver a harsh recourse to anyone seeking liberation from Nazi dominance.

Every aspect of life was controlled and scrutinized as war efforts were accelerated by the occupying force.

Surrounded by an enemy of faceless sympathizers, the Czech people grew not only suspicious, but fearful of being denounced by unscrupulous neighbours or even family and friends, on suspicion of unfounded allegations against the regime without any evidence except here-say.

Consequently, any subversive acts against the Nazis came at a huge cost to resistance fighters if caught, with on flowing consequences to innocent people.

In Krhová, a monument had been erected near the village chapel in honour of the nation's first President, Tomáš Garrigue Masaryk, who had passed away in 1937.

For many local Czechs, this monument was a shrine of hope in their darkest hour of Nazi occupation and was frequently visited and revered by all who believed one day their nation would rise again and become a true democracy.

Flowers were often placed at the foot of the statue, especially on the 14th of September, the anniversary of the President's death.

However, during Nazi occupation, as a determined gesture of reverence to their late leader, visits became more frequent and shadowy figures would pause, bow their heads, kneel by the monument, and place a posy of flowers at the site before slipping away undetected. For these believers, it was a case of never giving up hope, no matter how futile the road ahead.

This object of hero worship soon became a sore point with the local pro-Nazi police and opposed it vehemently, resolving to dispense with the monument once and for all.

One night the President's statue mysteriously disappeared, and despite a thorough search and much to their annoyance, the police failed to recover and dispose of it themselves.

It was alleged someone unknown in the local community had hidden it for safekeeping.

Anna recalled afterward; the site was still regularly visited as flowers would mysteriously appear overnight.

Very early one morning while still quite dark, Anna herself visited the monument site. On her way, she recognized Mrs. Pavlíková, mother of Vladimír and Robert, coming toward her. The women knew one another, but she ignored Anna and briskly swept past her. By the time Anna reached the place, fresh flowers had already been placed there.

At the end of the War, the statue of Tomáš Garrigue Masaryk mysteriously reappeared again. It is believed it had been concealed from the Nazis in the nearby school attic.

Today this monument stands on its original site and added to it are the names of local soldiers who fell during WWII and civilians who performed heroic acts in the name of freedom within the Lhotka-Krhová region.

It stands as a reminder that the fight for freedom came at the cost of many human lives, and it is still revered as a sign of ongoing hope, remembering all those who paved the way for democracy.

Anna's brother, Vladimír Kurovec, had been in the army all of three weeks when in March of 1939 the Germans took power and disbanded the Czech Army. Afterward, Vladimír gained employment at the nearby steel foundry but much to Anna's concern for him and her family she discovered he together with their father Franz had become active Partisans. Anna further learnt, her father kept a handgun at home

Book One: Anna's Story

and prayed her mother Rosalie knew nothing of his clandestine ventures. If Rosalie was aware, nothing was ever said and if she knew she was wise enough to keep any suspicions to herself. Besides, she had enough to contend with, hearing rumours that her husband was keeping company with strange women in discrete places!

Partisan activity became even more evident when sabotages of a subversive nature came to the attention of the Gestapo who followed up with interrogations of locals who either knew nothing of Partisan activities or became implicated by chance and were dealt punishment. Regardless, Partisan members continued to meet secretly at undisclosed places and monitor all Nazi movements.

Before the war, Franz had spent much of his time socializing and gambling at hotel tables, so during German occupation, he found no reason to change his habit of a lifetime, and instead, redirect his so-called habitual outings to cover up more intriguing agendas.

Over the years, his wife Rosalie had suffered silently with rumours of his so-called dalliances, but instead of growing resentful, she allowed him to continue his customary absences despite often accruing heavy gambling losses.

While continuing with these irregular hours, Frantz's untoward behaviour created no unwanted attention apart from being an annoying habitual absence from home when farm work needed attention. So, his so-called discrete indiscretions went unchallenged and Rosalie never once hinted she suspected his continual behaviour was now playing a more sinister role, if not a treacherous one.

Even less was known about Anna's younger brother Jaroslav, whose activities remained unspoken about and who for a while had a factory job before briefly joining the army. He generally did not visit home very often and even less so when he left the Czech army at the beginning of Nazi occupation.

Anna tried to remain impartial with family concerns and distanced herself from any subversive involvement with the full knowledge that the only way to protect herself and her family was to genuinely know nothing if ever questioned. It was far easier to remain innocent rather than lie if accusations were ever levelled against them. However, in most cases, the outcome was no different, especially if anyone was suspected of supporting the Partisans.

As Nazi supporters infiltrated society, disturbing news of arrests, purges, and executions instilled fear into everyone, with many victims often coming from close by communities.

In Prague in November of 1939, a demonstration against Nazi occupation was called on by Jan Opletal, a student leader from Charles University[2]. He was shot by German civilian police and died a few days later from wounds. Over three thousand students attended his funeral on the 15th of November as his body was prepared for transfer back to his home village of Náklo near Olomouc in central Moravia. Demonstration clashes with Nazi authorities followed, and by the 17th, all Czech Universities and colleges were closed after the arrest and execution of a further nine students and teachers. As a result, over 1,200 additional students would be deported to Sachsenhausen Concentration Camp.

The Gestapo regularly rounded up provocateurs demonstrating opposing views to the Reich and would readily execute them along with Jews, Romany people, and anybody else deemed an enemy or threat to Hitler.

Radios were listened to regularly to keep abreast of war progress but overall remained discreetly concealed and only used sparingly. But, by early 1940 a Nazi ban against anyone listening to foreign radio stations was introduced, and any unauthorised Czech person caught, the offense was punishable by death[3].

Unbeknown to Anna's family, at the beginning of 1940, her brother Jaroslav Kurovec together with several other patriots attempted to escape Czechoslovakia. They failed to cross into Hungry and at the border were captured, returned to Bratislava and imprisoned at Vacínu.

Again, sometime later, Jaroslav regrouped with Partisan comrades; Bohumil Menšík, Valentin Kubín, and Ludvík Pobořil, and this time escaped successfully, making their way onto Yugoslavia. Here they were assisted with crossing into Greece and the Middle East and from there afterward departed by boat onto France. They would eventually make their way into England on the Egyptian registered boat, the 'Rod El Farag.'

In June of 1941, the Nazis invaded Russia, and on 7th December of that year, the Japanese bombed Pearl Harbour, finally plunging America into the theatre of WWII.

Many welcomed America's entry into the war, except Hitler himself. He hoped the Americans would busy themselves with the Japanese, but his hopes were dashed when the Americans instead joined the Allied Forces to put an end to Hitler's proposed conquest of Europe.

Throughout the war, Hitler pursued his main objective to rid the country of Jews, and by his order, thousands were arrested and executed on prefabricated accusations, while hundreds of thousands were transported into labour and Concentration camps. It was a tempestuous time, not only for the Jews but for the many non-Jewish sympathizers working against the Führer and his Reich.

In May of 1942, after a botched attempt on Reinhardt Heydrich's life, a state of emergency was declared in Czechoslovakia[4]. Heydrich, the Nazi Governor of Bohemia, had been ambushed and fired upon while he drove in his open car to his Prague office. It was an orchestrated attack by Czech agents on behalf of 'Operation Anthropoid', and which had gone horribly wrong, leaving Heydrich only wounded but not critically enough to kill him at the time. However, a short time later, his injuries turned septic and gangrenous, and as a result, he died.

He had been known as the 'Hangman of Europe' and the architect of 'The Final Solution', and throughout, Reinhard Heydrich actually believed the Czech people admired him as their Reich Protector of Bohemia!

Reinhardt Heydrich's assassins were members of the Free Czech Forces who had been flown in earlier on the 28th of December 1941 from

England in a Royal Air Force Halifax plane piloted by legendary Group Captain Ronald C. Hockey. It had been a midwinter's night operation when they were parachuted into separate regions outside of Prague. Once on the ground, the seven Czech soldiers carefully regrouped before Jan Kubiš and Josef Gabčík carried out their mission, 'Operation Anthropoid,' which eventually succeeded in the death of their victim.

Upon the capture of Karel Čurda, one of the original Free Czech Force recruits, their safehouses, and their underground organizational networks were betrayed to the Gestapo. The six remaining undercover soldiers; Josef Gabčík, Jan Kubiš, Adolf Opálka, Josef Valcik, Jaroslav Svarc, and Jan Hruby eventually gained sanctuary in the crypt of St. Cyril and Methodius Church on Resslova Street in Prague. After a desperate battle, they failed to escape the Gestapo, and these Czech patriots were tragically killed.

It was hardly any wonder that this event fired off a Czech militia retaliation which cost many Sudeten Germans their lives; many of whom were not even sympathetic to Hitler.

Even though 'Operation Anthropoid' met its objective, its success failed to measure up against the cost of so many innocent lives just to rid the country of one human being, albeit an evil one!

The reprisal by the Nazis for this act was horrendous. Over three thousand Czechs were arrested, and of these, over two thousand died, either shot or tortured during SS police interrogations.

In June of 1942, the entire village of Lidice, a short distance from Prague, was completely erased[5]. One hundred and ninety-nine men and boys were slaughtered, while over one hundred and ninety-five women were sent to Ravensburg Concentration Camp, with the remaining older women going to Auschwitz, where they would be used, amongst other things, for medical experimentation. The children were sent to other concentration camps throughout the state, including the Chelmno extermination camp in Nazi-occupied Poland, where victims were gassed. Some children escaped the chambers, and being deemed suitable for Germanisation, were handed over to German families.

Added to these atrocities, people from the village of Ležáky suffered similar reprisal, where all men and women were murdered because a radio transmitter had been discovered there. It was a stark reminder that Nazi dominance ruled, and reprisals were severe for any retaliation against their authority.

Earlier in May of 1942, Anna's brother Vladimír Kurovec married Božena Čurdová and together moved to Kremlin near Ostrava. While his participation within the resistance intensified, waging a subversive campaign against the Nazis, Vladimír maintained regular contact with his father, Frantz.

Unexpectedly in September of 1942, the German Gestapo arrived at the Kurovec family home in Lhotka.

Frantz and Rosalie, with daughter Eliška, had been seated around the table in the kitchen when the Germans barged in on the pretext they were searching for Jaroslav Kurovec. Waving guns about, they demanded to speak with their son Jaroslav.

Jaroslav had already been absent for some time, and fortunately, his family had no idea where he was. The intrusion, although alarming, probably came as no surprise to Frantz, who half expected a visit from the authorities sooner or later looking for him or his son Vladimír. This time Frantz was briefly reprieved that their interests lay solely with Jaroslav.

Since joining the Partisans, Jaroslav had not been heard from for some time now, but the Gestapo were adamant he was hiding out somewhere close by, and so began searching the house. As was typical, all families of notifiable Czech escapees were frequently arrested for interrogation. Whether innocent or genuinely uninformed of Jaroslav's whereabouts and activity, it had been unfortunate they were at home on that day when the Gestapo came calling. But, nevertheless, the family was still taken in for further questioning.

When Anna learnt her parents and sister had been arrested, her heart sank, fearing the worst knowing her father possessed an illegal firearm.

It had been only by sheer chance that Anna and sisters, Helena, and Jarmila were on that day with their Grandparents at Krhová. The other two girls were living elsewhere, Zdeňka being already married, and Bo was with their Auntie Anna.

As a consequence of the Gestapo home invasion on the 17th of September 1942, Frantz, Rosalie, and their daughter Eliška were sentenced and jailed on suspicions of collaborating with Partisans and concealing their son Jaroslav's whereabouts. The mere fact that her family was being jailed meant they were still alive, which reassured Anna her father's fire arm had not been discovered. He had always kept it handy but well concealed from the family. Anna and her Grandparents suspected the family home would now be under surveillance and would continue to be on the Gestapo's radar in case further developments occurred.

Sudden unexplained desertion of any property always had tongues wagging, if not an open invitation for noisy intruders to snoop about, but first, Anna had to find the gun and get rid of it.

A few days later, when Gestapo activity eventually died down, Anna's prime motive was to return home as quickly as possible, find the weapon and dispose of it. Besides, if anyone stopped and questioned her, the farm still had to be looked after, so Anna had a valid reason to return.

One evening when all had gone to bed except Grandfather Stolař, and Anna, they quietly discussed a recovery plan.

During the night Anna had to sneak home alone, and hope her late arrival would not arouse further curiosity of neighbours.

At home she was greeted by her mother's hungry dog Brok as he excitedly jumped about her in the dark but luckily made no loud fuss while anticipating a much overdue feed. Anna calmed the excited animal and, together crept inside. The house felt cold, eerie, and deserted as Anna choked back tears and fumbled her way through the rooms. In the kitchen, everything was left on the table as it was on the day her family was taken away. She fumbled about searching with some aid from moonlight filtering in through the windows.

Wrapped in an old oiled cloth and hidden under some old papers in an alcove Anna found what she had been looking for. She retrieved the revolver and cartridges and outside in the garden, hurriedly found a mattock and dug a hole beneath an old pear tree. Here she buried the gun covering it with extra hay from the barn. Deed done; she hoped it would never need to surface again!

The incarceration of Anna's family at Svatobořice may have been unfounded and traumatic for everyone, but at least for the time being; there was no direct link or implication her father or brother Vladimir were under immediate suspicion, so what little knowledge Anna had, she kept to herself. However, future imprisonments were always concerning, if not problematic, should additional Gestapo information from ongoing investigations levy suspicion at her family, making them easier targets in the future to blame and implicate.

Sisters Anna and Helena knew they had a lucky escape but it did not ease their anxiety for their incarcerated family. Their brother Vladimír's whereabouts were always sketchy at the best of times, but having recently married, they hoped he was safely in Krmelin with his wife. As for Jaroslav, at the epicentre of the current debacle, his whereabouts remained a mystery.

News spread quickly and many in the village offered to help Anna and Helena. Although their grandfather was there to help, it was decided Jarmila would remain with their grandparents in Krhová while the two sisters returned home and did what best they could.

Anna and Helena made regular attempts to see their family in Svatobořice Prison, but it wasn't an easy place to visit. The prison was near Kyjov, some 100 km south west from their home and getting there was always a significant feat. The girls soon learnt prison life offered no comfort for the innocent. Family men and women were all housed separately, so Rosalie and Eliška did not have regular contact with Frantz.

However, Rosalie maintained a positive attitude, forever optimistic and tried to keep herself occupied.

Whenever she received letters from her daughters, Rosalie, in return, would only request some old scraps of cloth with sewing needles and thread to be sent. This way she could occupy her mind and keep her hands busy with needlecraft to while away the days. Rosalie was exceptionally talented at crocheting and tatting, and out of bits of cloth and frayed petticoats, she made beautiful handkerchiefs, collars, and inserts for coat pockets.

There were occasions when the female inmates tried to be light-hearted, and with some imagination and talent they would produce a puppet show for general entertainment. These puppet characters were made from odd bits of fabric found discarded in the laundry but always bore a vague resemblance to their wardens. The theme of the show was invariably satirical with black humour thrown in, and in many instances, portraying the brutal prison system at the expense of the puppets appearing like the obnoxious looking guards they were.

One evening, while showing one such puppet performance, Rosalie sat in the audience, preoccupied with her needlework.

As the others watched, entertained by the black humour, Rosalie was barely oblivious to the performance. Unexpectedly a few prison guards arrived and sat down. Everything suddenly went quiet, followed by a scatter of shuffling feet as all the women and the puppeteers disappeared from the scene. Rosalie remained seated, absorbed in her sewing when she suddenly realized she was alone. She attempted to leave but was apprehended from behind by two guards and marched off into solitary confinement. Her sentence for insubordination and lack of respect for the German Reich was to sleep in the morgue for an extended period of time.

Franz her husband, soon learnt of her ordeal and realized she would have little, if any warmth in the morgue. Rosalie had only been wearing an old and tattered, thread-bare dress, so with only one thread-bare blanket to keep her warm, Franz took it upon himself to smuggle an extra blanket to her through a small window, leaving himself with little or no warmth.

Rosalie took her punishment on the chin with courage. She told everyone later that those in the morgue did not bother her. She knew most of them during their imprisonment, so she had little fear from them; and even less now, as they lay peacefully around her. Perhaps they were much better off now than those still alive in prison.

Book One: Anna's Story

Anna was always worried about her parent's well-being and keen to deliver extra food whenever possible. For Christmas of 1942, she packed three large food parcels ahead of time and sent them onto the prison.

Her mother would later recall how excited she had been when she was called into the office to collect the food parcels, one for each of them.

Rosalie found herself amongst friends, so she could not help but share her food with them.

Anna had baked Vánočka, a lightweight bread biscuit made with citron, raisins, and almonds and after baking, it was rolled in sugar. Anna hoped it would provide extra sweetness for her family when it was dunked into their bitter coffee.

On the morning before Christmas, en route to Svatobořice, Anna and Helena went to church in Kyjov. While in church, each made a wish for something, but at the time, would not reveal to the other what each had wished for.

As always, the excursion from home to Svatobořice had to be well organized, with sufficient food prepared for not only their journey but for their imprisoned family. Anna together with grandmother Stolarova always included extra smoked meat and biscuits.

On such a lengthy trip Anna and Helena could never be certain if they would be allowed in to see their family, so they planned to leave the food parcels at their overnight loggings in Kyjov.

Walking toward Svatobořice, the sisters were passed by a truckload of turnips trundling toward the prison gates. Helena motioned toward the truck and, looking wistfully at Anna, whispered, "Wouldn't it be great if something happened to this load of turnips just before the prison gates?"

No sooner spoken, when the truck pulled to the side of the road, and the driver got out to inspect what appeared to be a flat tyre. To repair the tyre, all the turnips had to be offloaded, and soon, a stream of prisoners was summoned to pick bucket loads of vegetables from the off loaded truck and deliver them to the prison kitchen.

Anna and Helena stood by watching, not knowing where to go or how this holdup which they had hoped for, was going to benefit them.

An elderly man in prison clothes caught sight of them and cautiously approached and quietly enquired as to why they were standing about looking lost. Helena, at first was guarded, and reluctant to divulge too much information. She feared him and what might happen to her family as a result of this meeting. Holding onto his bucket full of turnips, he reassured her he was only one of the prisoners and asked Helena whom she knew inside. Apprehensively, she whispered back, it was their mother and father and sister whom they wished to visit. He went as far as to enquire the name of their sister, to which Helena returned, "Her name is Eliška." His face lit up, and he whispered back enthusiastically.

"I know her well. She works with me in the kitchen! When I return to the kitchen with my bucket of turnips, I will tell her she has visitors by the gate."

He was true to his word, and not only did Eliška, arrive but Franz and Rosalie as well. Grouped together, and bent over buckets of turnips on the ground, they spoke quietly, pretending to be busy, moving turnips in and out of the buckets while the other prisoners maintained a steady stream of turnips into the prison kitchen. Anna informed them they had a food parcel for them but hadn't brought it along, as they never imagined in their wildest dreams to be talking with one another outside the prison gates. Anna made hurried arrangements for the next day to meet her mother at a certain time by the prison garden boundary and hopefully deliver the food parcel.

The following day having borrowed a worker's outfit, Anna returned dressed like a peasant and attached herself to a group of workers hoeing and tilling the soil close to the prison fence. She enthusiastically tilled the soil making her way toward the prison boundary, all along maintaining a discrete distance from the others so not to appear overly conspicuous.

Near the fence, Anna crouched down and tugged at weeds with one hand while with the other, she extracted the food parcel hidden under her baggy clothes and forced the package beneath the boundary structure. Anna heard Rosalie on the other side and speaking quietly, thanked her daughter, and quickly slipped away.

To exchange a few precious words between mother and daughter was a risk worth taking as Anna remembered how thin and unwell her parents had become and likewise, her sister Eliška, who had appeared even worse, bloated and pale.

On her return to meet Helena for their train journey home to Lhotka, Anna came across a man by the roadside loading a dead horse onto his wagon. She noticed the dead beast in the field earlier on her way to the prison.

Curious, Anna paused and asked the peasant labourer where he was taking the dead beast rather than burying it in the field. "It's going to the prison down the road to feed the prisoners!" Horrified and saddened by the explanation, she hurried back and later exchanged their secret wishes made in church. The sisters both had wished to see their family for Christmas.

Frantz, Rosalie, and Eliška served close to five months in prison, during which time their health declined drastically due to poor nutrition and living conditions.

While Rosalie and her family were away in prison, Brok, her dog, used to wander every day down to the railway siding waiting and watching for the daily train to call in. It was only after the train pulled out without Rosalie alighting that he would wander home. During her incarceration, every letter Rosalie wrote and sent her family would be eagerly sniffed by Brok, wagging his tail profusely, anticipating her return. It seemed to give him great satisfaction that the scent of his mistress was so close by. Brok's daily jaunt to the rail siding continued for the duration of Rosalie's absence, without once failing to meet the train until one day, his persistence and patience paid off. Brok would be the first to greet his long-missed mistress when Rosalie, Frantz, and daughter Eliška were finally released from prison and returned home at the end of January 1943.

With his health rapidly declining, Brok held out long enough to welcome Rosalie home but died within the month of their release.

By February of 1943, Vladimír Kurovec and Božena had their only child, a daughter named Jaroslava, and a granddaughter for Franz and Rosalie. It was a brief moment of bliss only to be overshadowed by the ongoing scourge of war.

Since returning from prison, Frantz began to suffer bouts of tuberculosis he contracted during his incarceration. This illness would ultimately contribute to his early demise, but in the meantime, he remained an ardent supporter of the Partisans and their efforts would continue to frustrate the Germans throughout the remainder of the war.

Random Sabotage would cause obstruction and delays for the officious Nazi machine leaving them on constant alert for perpetrators as they followed up on leads for every subversive act. As much as the locals detested the Germans, they feared for their lives whenever a purposeful sabotage succeeded.

By December of 1943, the exiled Czech Leader, Edvard Beneš, placed blind trust with the Soviets and, in London, signed a twenty-year post-war co-operation permitting the Soviet Army to liberate Czechoslovakia.

By April 1944, Britain, France, and Poland signed a pact of support, and Hitler retaliated by destroying the 1934 Naval Treaty with Britain.

In October of that year, the Russians traversed over one hundred and seventy miles of Czech frontier and crossed into Warsaw and Budapest.

After numerous Soviet-trained Czech paratroopers were dropped into Slovakia, the Jan Žižka Partisan Brigade [6] was formed in August of 1944. It was named after 'Jan Žižka z Trocnova a Kalicha,' who, in the fourteenth to the fifteenth century, was a revered Czech General and a contemporary follower of Jan Hus.

This Czech Partisan group; the Jan Žižka Brigade, was a guerrilla-warfare organization, again mainly focused on sabotage and intelligence gathering. It attracted and recruited many local sympathizers, both men, and women who were trained to hinder and frustrate German occupation. It was a well-orchestrated organization, difficult to infiltrate and generally successful.

However, during August 1944 the Slovak National Uprising against the Nazi-backed Tiso Government, many of the partisans failed to achieve any measure of success with their activities, only to be retaliated against by the Gestapo; rounded up, charged, and murdered along with innocent Jews.

By January 1945 the Russians advanced upon Berlin and seized seven main German strongholds and some two hundred villages in the Silesian area. Allied troops liberated Bergan-Belsen, surrounded Leipzig, and advanced onto Hamburg.

In Czechoslovakia the Gestapo were becoming increasingly agitated and nervous, and through to March of 1945, directed their attention on Partisan activity in regional areas.

A branch of Jan Žižka Brigade began to concentrate operations in the Valašské Meziříčí area and with selected resistance leaders and various other partisan recruits including Anna's brother Vladimír and his father Frantz Kurovec, they met regularly at undisclosed venues, collecting intelligence and focusing on local German activity.

Frantz a known card player and gambler, maintained his undercover gambling persona arriving to attend meetings at irregular hours at hotels in Valašské Meziříčí and in local public houses. Much of Frantz's womanizing reputation may have been sealed during these clandestine gatherings where women were as much a part of the organization as the men were and each trained to play specific roles within the group.

During meetings with organization leaders, as described in 'Nešli Stejnou Cestou' by Jaroslav Pospíšil and Čestmír Šikola, and also later recalled in archival letters by Anna's sister Bo Kurovcová, most involved with the Partisans had a code name.

Frantz Kurovec's undercover identity was code-named (Dr.4-Táta 4). Whether it was a Pythagorean numerical code is anyone's guess.

Frantz's son Vladimír became VI Kurovec, and together they maintained regular contact with major players within the organization including other operative agents.

One notorious operative, Agent B-105, was as cunning as he was treacherous[7]. Agent B-105 (Velký Franta or Big Frank) worked on developing a trusted relationship within the Partisan organization and shortly after his introduction to the group, increased numbers of unexplained arrests by the Gestapo began to occur.

Through another Partisan activist, Frantisek Bednář or Malý Franta (Small Frank), B-105 managed to acquire high ranking names from him of those within the resistance group and then spruik their names with familiarity as if he knew them personally. B-105 then insisted on an introduction to Anton Bartoš, Commander of the Paratrooper Clay Group.

It soon transpired Agent B-105 had a checked past in subversive activity. After numerous imprisonments; another fact would emerge. Upon his latest imprisonment after which he was eventually released, he became a fully-fledged Gestapo agent. It was during this time in prison he had met Frantisek Bednář turned gestapo informer himself and gleaned valuable information from him. Agent B-105 would soon become a valuable tool for the Gestapo against the resistance movement, especially the Jan Žižka Brigade.

As results began to flow in his favour and to the Gestapo's list of arrests, Agent B-105 began to gravitate toward Valašské Meziříčí in the hope of infiltrating the Jan Žižka Organization.

Throughout, Big Frank met regularly with trusting Partisans at Hotel Snoza in Valašské Meziříčí while not far from their meeting place, unbeknown to them, B-105 maintained a secret liaison and collaborated with the Gestapo at Hotel Modrá Hvézda (Hotel Blue Star). Here the Gestapo regularly brought in their victims for interrogation and torture before dispensing with them.

However, Big Frank (Agent B-105) did not go entirely unnoticed, and began to gain attention from certain Partisan members. Gradually, information trickled in from within the organization that Agent B-105 was not to be trusted and he was placed under surveillance on suspicion of collaborating with the Gestapo.

Evidence soon pointed toward B-105 identifying him as the Gestapo double agent František Šmid, whose pseudonym was Velký Franta or 'Big Frank.' Initially, double agents caught infiltrating resistance groups were dispensed with very early, but Agent B-105 had eluded them long enough to cause irreversible collateral damage to the partisan's organization.

By January 1945, the Gestapo had infiltrated the Jan Žižka Brigade, regularly arresting prominent members.

Frantisek Šmid used many aliases to erode the organization but was soon well and truly on the Partisan's wanted list.

A group of four Partisans, including; Václav Březík, Emil Hanzlik, Čestmír Podzemný, and Vl. Kurovec (Vladimír) were ordered to apprehend Frantisek Šmid (Velký Franta) and if possible, deliver him alive to their resistance commander Major Murzin.

On the morning of 8th February 1945, Velký Franta was confronted by the group of Partisans and probably on a tip off was armed at the time.

In an admission of self-defence, Čestmír Podzemný shot him, but it seems the other two, Václav Březík and Emil Hanzlik, may have added to the certainty of his death. It was recounted later, that Vladimír Kurovec did not fire a shot when the traitor was finally liquidated.

Without alerting the Gestapo, Agent B-105 Šmid was quickly and quietly disposed of down a pit beneath a rabbit hatch. Agent Frantisek Šmid's presence was not missed until a few weeks later in February, when he failed to report in, and by then, the suspicious Gestapo came looking for him. His body was finally unearthed from his burial place and examined for forensic evidence to establish his killer.

On about the 16th of February 1945, and with new evidence emerging about Agent B-105's death, the Gestapo ruthlessly searched all probable places for the perpetrators. The resistance group had been tipped off, and many suspects were nowhere to be found when the Gestapo arrived.

František Kurovec and Drahomír Blažken, with the help of resistance fighter Jan Rychlik armed with a police gun and bayonet, were rushed to Zubří, where they were taken in by a local tailor and hidden down a well. Many others fled into various Partisan strongholds, while many more were rounded up and arrested for questioning by the Gestapo.

During Velký Franta's Nazi collaboration, the fallout from his resistance infiltration was nothing short of alarming, resulting in the Gestapo arresting over two thousand five hundred Partisans.

On 7th March 1945, Vladimír Kurovec was arrested by the Gestapo in Valašské Meziříčí, and along with some thirty-six resistance collaborators, they were imprisoned without trial.

On the 18th of April 1945, amid one family tragedy, another momentous event unfolded close to home, drawing Anna into the centre of local Partisan activity. That night at about 9 pm, a villa in Lhotka suddenly exploded, destroying the two-storied dwelling and scattering debris and bodies, mostly buried beneath piles of rubble.

Franz Kurovec immediately recognized the repercussions from this explosion and together with his brother Alois began to scramble volunteers to frantically search for bodies strewn beneath bricks and concrete slabs, hoping to reach survivors and remove them from the scene as quickly as possible before the police and the Gestapo arrived.

Shattered by the unfolding tragedy and still recovering from the shock of it all, Anna was commandeered by her Uncle Alois to stand by for assistance.

When all the bodies were finally accounted for, only two retrieved were still alive and within the short time of recovering the two badly burnt and injured men, the rescuers managed to administer first aid as best they could to keep them alive. They were quickly removed from the scene and prepared for evacuation elsewhere.

When the Gestapo and police finally arrived to inspect the scene and what remained of the villa; a once two-story dwelling, they soon made light of the situation and postulated scathing and derogatory remarks, insinuating that it was a terrible shame that only one house blew up and not the entire village of Lhotka with everyone in it.

The Nazis justified that everybody who died in the catastrophe was guilty and deserved what had come to them!

While the Gestapo authorities investigated and interrogated those present, Alois Kurovec had already put wheels into motion and secured safe refuge and urgent medical treatment for the injured men who had been moved away from the area.

One of the victims still alive was an employee of his, so Alois made arrangements to transport him to the old Chateau Monastery in Choryně. There the nuns from the order of Sisters of Mercy of the Holy Cross would care for him until he could be moved to an appropriate medical facility. Alois Kurovec summoned Anna with the task of delivering him there.

With all the mayhem at the explosion site, Anna was placed in charge of the horse and chaise as preparations were made for her passengers.

Feeling shattered and distraught by the tragedy, Anna did as she was told and did not question who her passengers were. She was only told her companions would be Vlastimil Menšik and another wrapped and dressed in woman's clothing, and together the three of them would make the urgent journey to Choryně. She was instructed not to panic and keep calm and proceed at leisurely pace on a hopefully inconspicuous late-evening journey.

The victim, dressed as a woman and his face discreetly covered with a head scarf, sat wedged between them. He was in considerable pain as blood oozed profusely from multiple injuries and severe burns. Blankets and bandages with extra wadding had been applied but had to be constantly reinforced. The sheer stamina and determination that he possessed, not to scream and bring attention to them all was heroic, at the very least.

Anna tried to concentrate on the task of steering the horse while Vlastimil kept the victim calm and seated upright between them.

Such pretence from a severely wounded man without giving away the absolute magnitude of pain was more than Anna could endure and struggled not to dissolve into an emotionally inept shamble.

Under tremendous duress to accomplish the journey to Choryně situated on the other side of the Bečva River, Anna mainly dreaded if someone should stop and question them.

Anna's only task was to deliver the wounded patriot to safety. She had been told not to panic and not gallop the horse but stay calm if they were stopped and leave the explaining to Vlastimil Menšík who no doubt had other contingency plans.

Although the victim struggled to remain alert, he was obviously in shock, but he cooperated every inch of the way without raising any suspicion for the length of the uncomfortable journey there.

Some hours later, just before dawn, Anna finally accomplished her mission, and the three arrived at the monastery and were met as arranged.

On her return home, Anna learnt the other surviving victim, Karel Haša, had died while being transported to hospital. His injuries had been so extensive that chances of survival faded rapidly, and he died soon after being moved. His family was devastated and they were soon to learn and grieve the loss of yet another killed in battle in Europe.

Anna's and Vlastimil's next arduous task was to help with Karel Haša's funeral arrangements. Karel had come from Kladeruby and was to be buried in Kelč, a short distance away. It had to be done in secrecy as the authorities were unaware that he, too, had been a victim of the Smolká blast. It remained with the Partisan's ardent supporters to arrange the burial without drawing attention as his coffin went to the cemetery in a horse-drawn manure cart.

The Smolká family at the centre of the disaster, were Partisan supporters, and the explosives stored in their down-stairs cellar were for various anti-Nazi subversive activities.

The villa had been occupied by the Smolká family living on the lower floor while the Home family dwelled on the upper floor. The youngest lad, Čestmír Smolká, was the only family member not in the house at the time of the explosion. The blast shook the neighbourhood with shattering force.[8]

The whole community was shaken and terrified by the blast, as most did not know what had caused it. Retribution by the Nazis was always first and foremost on everyone's mind, so, many chose to distance themselves from the blast so as not to be seen as overly inquisitive and become targets for questioning by the Gestapo.

It had been alleged that things went horribly wrong while the Smolká members were preparing gelignite explosives, accidentally detonating and causing the devastating blast. Afterward, some observers mentioned in statements that the boys were often casual with explosives, a cigarette generally hanging out of their mouths as they prepared the devices.

The Smolká and Home family funeral that followed was a sombre affair attended by community members in solidarity over the loss of their own, but some discretely distancing themselves from any association with the recent event. Many chose not to attend, while others constantly looked over their shoulders as they silently grieved.

The Partisans had gathered intelligence prior to the explosion that ten wagon loads of ammunition were to be railed north from Slovakia for Nazi war purpose. The locomotive with its cargo was to be travelling north from Hustopeče and on a specific date it would be passing through in the vicinity of Hranice. An approximate time had been calculated when the train later that night would cross the rail bridge between Hranice and Valašské Meziříčí, so the plan that evening prior to the house blast, was to sabotage the train as it neared Lhotka.

After the explosion, the Gestapo made no immediate arrests as the damage caused was self-inflicted, and all victims had been killed. However, it still raised the question over the nature of the explosion. The fundamental objective of all the stored incendiary material and devices was without a doubt directed toward the Nazis, so the authorities still had to investigate if further punishment was warranted.

The Gestapo knew that the Smolká family victims were only a tiny part of a larger group that needed to be rooted out and dealt with.

Numerous interrogations followed, and shortly afterward arrests were made, especially those close to the victims, including Josef Haša and Jaromír Pobořil's families.

Anna's Uncle Alois Kurovec was also apprehended on the 19th of April 1945, detained and interrogated in Valasske Meziříčí over the Smolká affair but was finally released a few days later on the 25th. Although increasingly nervous, the Gestapo continued with vigilant surveillance and patrolled main roads and railroads maintaining all transport routes remained opened and free of any proposed sabotage.

Although many condoned the actions of the Resistance, just as many preferred, these actions had not been carried out, ultimately dividing much of the village. Everyone feared being interrogated by the Gestapo and they equally knew every retaliation against the Nazis would be doubly returned with even greater vengeance.

Some alleged the train with its explosives at the epicentre of this disaster had eventually been derailed as planned, and if so, by whom nobody was admitting.

Vlastimil Menšik, owner of the local mill, regularly entertained Partisan meetings, but he was also frequented by the local German police officer Baumgarten, who was closely aligned with the Gestapo. During these inconvenient visits, Baumkarten expected complimentary drinks of slivovic.

Shortly after the Smolká family fiasco, and during one of his subsequent visits to the mill, Baumkarten was approached by members of the Partisans who demanded he write a letter to the local Gestapo authority requesting that all Partisans in his jurisdiction be allowed to voluntarily depart so that the rest of the people could be spared further persecution.

This demand was met with an abrupt refusal, so in return, Baumkarten was allegedly shot by Russian Partisan Jefrem Špochou, and the police officer's body disposed of some distance from the mill.

In early April of 1945, after Vladimír Kurovec's arrest, along with some thirty-six other detainees, all were taken to a high-security prison in Brno. At first, Anna's family believed he had been sent to Svatobořice, so Anna desperately tried to contact him there.

However, her hopes were dashed when she learned he had been moved onto Brno. Anna tried to garner support from Vladimír's wife, Božena, to join in achieving clemency for her husband, but Božena refused to be drawn into taking action as she feared for herself and her child.

Whenever Anna drew close to where her brother was being detained, she would again be told he had already been moved elsewhere. In the end, none of the family ever saw Vladimír again.

Although it was never established what Vladimir was accused of, the Gestapo still declared Vladimír an enemy of the Reich and would be punished in accordance with those undermining the Gestapo and refuting the authorities.

At the time, many more involved with the Jan Žižka Brigade were captured and incarcerated with other prisoners, and without any trial, many of those also ended up in Brno and from there railed on Transport KL3 onto KT Mauthausen in Austria[9].

At Mauthausen even before reaching the notorious gas chambers, thousands died as frail, emaciated skeletons from prolonged starvation and enforced labour, stumbling beneath heavy loads of crushed rock while slaving in the nearby quarry.

In a desperate effort to cover up, the Nazis tried to conceal the horrors of Mauthausen and surrounding camps by quickly executing as many inmates as possible.

As the Mauthausen gas chambers emptied, they would refill again with many more terminal cases from death camps elsewhere that were being emptied daily of thousands of wretched detainees who had already undergone insurmountable deprivation from beatings and torture, many psychologically broken.

All this evidence had to be hurriedly destroyed by erasing incriminating infrastructure before the allies would finally liberate all the concentration camps. If Vladimír witnessed any of this in his brief stay there, it will never be known, but the smell of death would certainly have filled the air.

The inmates who would eventually be rescued were scarred and traumatized for life and many later recalled horrifying stories of torture, starvation, slavery, and sufferance beyond comprehension.

One local village prisoner who survived Mauthausen; described the atrocities from firsthand experience. This witness, knew Vladimír and recalls seeing him when he arrived at Mauthausen. He described Vladimir as a tall and handsome young man who stood out in the crowd but as someone who probably already knew his fate was sealed, from which there was no escaping.

On that day, Vladimir and his group were marched from the train into holding quarters, not given any food or water, and then transferred into the gas chamber.

Vladimír had been a young married man, a father to a young daughter and husband to a woman who would never see him again. With a passionate desire to win against the Germans, Vladimír and others may have been denied life, but their endeavours would live on and keep their legacy alive. They would all remain in the hearts of their nation as patriotic human beings sacrificed by the hands of Nazis. Only after the war would Vladimír's family learn of his fate.

Vladimír died on 10th April 1945, only a matter of weeks before WWII ended in Europe.

Photograph 72 & 73: (L-R) Memorial to the erased Czech village of Lidice in 1942; a symbolic memorial to the children killed. Human statues to all those lost in Lidice.

Photograph 74, 75 & 76: (L-R) A statue symbolising the grief on that day. St. Cyril & Methodius Church on Resslova Street, Prague. The Cyril & Methodist church crypt where 6 Patriots died in 1942 after the assassination of Nazi Reinhard Heydrich.

Photograph 77, 78 & 79: (L-R) Vladimír Kurovec in uniform. Božena & Vladimír at their wedding. Božena Kurovcova with daughter Jaroslava.

Photograph 80 & 81: Vladimír & Božena Kurovec with family at home in Kremlin. Monument at Krhová to the local fallen Partisans 1945.

Photograph 82 & 83: (L-R) Anna's Uncle Alois Kurovec 1945. Monument to the Smolká and Home families who in 1945 died at the site of their house explosion in Lhotka.

Photograph 84 & 85: (L-R) Marta Kurovcová with cousin Helena Kurovcová at the Smolká family funeral 1945. Anna Kurovcová (Kanak) 1945.

CHAPTER 6
End of WWII: VE Day 8th May 1945

The old wireless that had been tuned into numerous unauthorized channels, especially the British BBC airwaves, had withstood the scourges of Nazi occupation. For much of the time, it had been hidden away, for fear that if it was discovered, the household would be implicated and punished. It had been illegal during the German occupation to listen to anything but Nazi propaganda. Anna's father had secretly listened to the wireless regularly, gleaning hints of news that might give some clue on the war's progress. As it sat on the bench close to the kitchen table, crackling away with the latest Czech news, the reception was no clearer than before, but in recent times, it seemed to crackle with added enthusiasm.

On the 1st of May 1945, Anna excitedly heard the announcement over the wireless that the US army had liberated the town of Cheb on the German border and a Token Force of Czech soldiers had arrived[1]. The Token Force was a symbolic gesture of 140 soldiers to raise the Czechoslovakian Flag over their homeland. The remaining Czechs stayed behind at Dunkirk to 'clean up' under Major General Alois Liška[2]. Ear glued to the wireless, hoping to hear an announcement that the war had finally ended, Anna felt a further surge of excitement and relief when later on the 6th of May, she heard that Plzeň had also been liberated from German occupation.

On the 7th May 1945 an unconditional surrender of the German Reich was signed at Reims in France which then on the 8th became known as Victory Day in Europe or VE Day. However, on the 8th of May, there were still skirmishes and fighting in the Streets of Prague, although the Czech war was declared officially over. It wasn't until the Russian Red Army captured Danzig (now the Polish city of Gdańsk) on the Baltic coast, and crossed from Hungry into Austria that, on the 10th of May 1945, Prague was officially the last European capital to be liberated from the Nazis.

By early May of 1945, many Czech soldiers, already gathered and waiting in Plzeň, were hoping for an early army discharge. For those who fought in Europe, the war was over for them, and after an absence of almost seven years, many were exhausted and yearning for home. However, it would only be after the Pacific war ended that the declaration on the 14th of August 1945 signalled WWII officially over.

During mid-May of 1945, the Czech Armoured Brigade that had landed earlier in Normandy in August of 1944 had returned, and many soldiers were waiting in Plzeň to advance onto Prague for their Victory March. Relaxing and basking in their victory over Germany, many were interviewed by Czech radio stations and urged to send messages to their anxious loved ones waiting at home. Many of the families had no idea where their boys were, or indeed, if still alive.

While desperately wanting to hear something encouraging, Anna was amazed by the sheer volume of messages sent, voices from loved ones that had not been heard in such a long time. Unexpectedly, a familiar voice crackled over the wireless, sending his love to his Kurovec family in Lhotka and reassuring them of a speedy return home.

It was Anna's brother Jaroslav, and she was beside herself with excitement, barely believing what she had just heard. Heart racing with joy, she bounded outside to find her parents. Breathlessly she informed them that Jaroslav was alive and well and would soon be home.

Anna believed she had been lucky to hear Jaroslav's voice amongst hundreds of other messages from soldiers waiting to be discharged and reunited with loved ones. At first, Rosalie was sceptical that such good news could be real. After so much pain and suffering, she feared it could be Nazi propaganda to incite further anguish, but Anna was adamant she had heard Jaroslav's voice.

Anna's immediate desire was to travel to Plzeň and meet her brother. Amidst protests, she was finally granted leave with her cousin Milan Kurovec, son of Uncle Alois, and together, they caught the train via Prague onto Plzeň. When they arrived, they were surrounded by throngs of soldiers and armoured tanks lining the streets and roads. Plzeň echoed with excitement and exhilaration as US soldiers distributed chocolates and canned food to children milling about them. Welcoming cheers were deafening as appreciative locals offered hospitality and temporary accommodation to the many returning young men.

Many soldiers eagerly awaited early discharge from the army or, at the very least, leave after the planned Victory march onto Prague had been accomplished. There was to be the official presentation by the USA, pledging all the amassed American Armory in Plzeň to the newly reformed Czech army. Additionally, there was the promise of aid from UNRRA (United Nations Relief and Rehabilitation Administration) [3] of food, clothing, and small goods to be distributed. Disappointingly, most of the American military hardware so generously donated to the Czech people to help rebuild their army would come to nothing and not necessarily remain in Czechoslovakia but instead end up in Russian possession to be relocated into Soviet territories at their discretion.

Anna found the crowds overwhelming as she followed her cousin through the throngs of cheering people. Whenever she asked for directions or names of people, everyone was more than eager to assist. Somehow, they had to find Jaroslav, but it seemed a near-impossible task with thousands of soldiers and civilians milling about. Finally, in desperation, Anna asked a passing Czech soldier if he, by chance, knew of a Jaroslav Kurovec. Much to her surprise, not only did he know him, but he took Anna and Milan to him.

When they finally reunited, Anna was so excited that she eagerly insisted Jaroslav return home with her. Much to her disappointment, Anna learned Jaroslav could be delayed in Plzeň for some days, if not weeks, before receiving further orders. His tank brigade was stationed close by, but even though the war was over for many, the troops were still beheld to the Czech Army until they received official discharge papers, which, for many, would only occur after the 30th of September 1945.

Jaroslav briefly introduced Anna and Milan to his fellow army colleagues, Jan Kaňák and Zoltán Farkáš, who served together in the same artillery regiment. While they made small talk, an announcement interrupted them, heralding a special thanks-giving commemoration at the nearby church. It was nondenominational and held on behalf of all returning Czech personnel, including a remembrance service for those fallen. Anna, Milan, Jaroslav, and Jan joined the service, where religious denominations did not matter for once, and the solemn occasion brought together civilians and soldiers to pay their tributes. Zoltán Farkáš was Jewish, so he chose not to join them in church but instead stood outside and listened to the service.

Once the service was over, Anna broached the subject of family and broke the news to Jaroslav about their parent's imprisonment and Vladimír's recent transportation to Mauthausen. She feared that he may already be dead, as no one had heard from him. Jaroslav was shocked at the tragic news, so he made it his mission to apply for urgent leave of absence on grounds of family bereavement so he could return home with Anna.

Added to Jaroslav's grief was the unenviable task of informing the Pobořil family that their son Ludvík had been recently killed in Belgium. Out of respect, he felt obliged to extend to them, the bereft families, an invitation to gather at the Kurovec home in Lhotka. With much assistance and good luck, Jaroslav finally secured an early pass, signed by non-other than the Foreign Minister, Jan Masaryk.

Their homeward train journey was interrupted several times by overzealous Russian military guards demanding Jaroslav's papers and why he had been allowed to leave his army post. Seeing his documents, they still demanded whose signature it was that authorized the leave. The name of Jan Masaryk meant nothing to them. Much to Anna's disbelief and horror, Jaroslav cursed them in Czech, insinuating they were stupid buffoons who had no idea who their Foreign Minister was. He further added insult, calling them ignorant and illiterate simpletons! This seemed to satisfy them, so they allowed Jaroslav to proceed.

Jaroslav, Milan, and Anna returned by mid-afternoon and were greeted by Rosalie, who ran to meet them when she heard the train arriving. Overcome with joy amidst tears and cries of welcome, yet emotionally frail and fearing something would spoil this long-awaited moment, Rosalie hugged her son and, with painful hearts, paid homage to his brother Vladimir. Jaroslav felt immense remorse and anger that his own escape from Czechoslovakia had caused his parents and sister Eliška so much grief.

Jaroslav spoke briefly about his years away but remained circumspect, disclosing only bare facts of those lost in battle around him. Out of the four of them who escaped Czechoslovakia together in December of 1939, only two of them returned; Jaroslav Kurovec[4] and Bohumil Menšik. The other two, Ludvík Pobořil and Valentin Kubín, did not return. Ludvík died in battle at Dunkirk in October of 1944, and Valentin, who joined the RAF and after three years of training, was discharged in 1943 due to illness. Valentin was never able to return home and died in Wales in March of 1945 at Sully Hospital and was buried in Barry.

Vladimír's tragic arrest and presumed death were beyond comparison to any heroic acts Jaroslav had seen or even beyond the courage he himself displayed toward the end of the war. Around the family table, Jaroslav recalled a particular incident while he was on sentry duty one night. He had stumbled accidentally into an enemy bunker occupied by some twenty or thirty German soldiers. The Germans were taken by surprise in the middle of their card game when suddenly apprehended by an allied soldier. Jaroslav was equally startled when he called their bluff to drop their guns and they did so. The Germans with hands up, rose spontaneously without any resistance, and unopposed, Jaroslav filed them all out of the bunker. He was completely stunned when they obeyed, all believing he had reinforcements outside and any attempt to escape would have been met by gunfire... or so they thought. In disbelief and shaken by his own brazen act, unaided Jaroslav marched them to his commanding officer. From this unexpected German surrender without shedding any blood that night, Jaroslav suffered immediate aftershock and attributed his hair turning grey as a result of it.

Jaroslav lamented the loss of many fellow soldiers, but none more than Alois Gabriel, or Gabish as everyone called him. On that fateful occasion, Jaroslav had been instructed to board and manoeuvre his tank to assist another tank crew in difficulty. When orders were issued, Jaroslav, who had not been in his complete combat outfit, was about to dress when Gabish, his ever-obliging friend, shouted out that he would do the job instead, as he still had all his combat gear on. Gabish quickly mounted the tank and climbed into the operational hole so that Jaroslav didn't even have time to respond to him. The tank had barely moved from its stationary position when it touched a mine, exploding into a ball of flames with shrapnel scattering everywhere, and within minutes, it was all over, and a dear comrade gone forever.

Jaroslav felt incensed by the futility of war, leaving so many killed and even more, maimed. So many innocent people were imprisoned, tortured and executed, for no fault of their own but only to become a statistic of war. Jaroslav resisted attending his medal presentation ceremony for mentions during combat. He was alive, and the medals should have gone to the poor soldiers who died and received nothing for their sacrifices. Jaroslav saw little value in medals, as the proper accolades belonged to those who were no longer with him. So many unsung heroes deserved better than the death mask that they had been dealt. For him, there was no glory in heroism. So instead, Jaroslav sent a friend to accept the citation on his behalf.

Unbeknown to all at the time, during 1942, Rosalie Kurovcová and Gabish's mother had become well acquainted while both were in prison at Svatobořice. At the time, neither had any inkling that their sons were best friends and together would be fighting in battle in Europe. It was a tragic fate that would bind the two families for the rest of their lives, and Rosalie would have to share this tragedy with her friend.

With Czechoslovakia now liberated and all fighting ceased, by June of 1945, the Russians ceded Carpathian-Ruthenia. In October of 1945, Jaroslav was employed as a driver for UNRRA (United Nations Relief and Rehabilitation Administration), a job that took him all over Europe delivering aid. He was given the use of a Tatra vehicle, PD 13230, allowing him to travel throughout the American-occupied territories. He distributed food and clothing, and during this period, his youngest sister Jarmila tasted peanut butter for the first time. Jaroslav remained with UNRRA until it folded in 1947. When the Soviets gained full control of Czechoslovakia, all foreign aid distributed throughout Europe was eventually refused by the Soviets on behalf of the Czech people.

When Jaroslav returned home, he presented Anna and each of his sisters with a small token. It was a meagre offering, but it symbolized his fondness for his sisters. There was little available to buy as most metals were scarce and authentic jewellery was rare and expensive. So, with this austerity, each received a trinket, an engraved aluminium bracelet, not unlike those sold at fairs or shows. The girls were delighted.

Jaroslav resumed his old job at the tobacco factory, where he remained until it closed. He was the last employee there and remained until the site was cleaned up.

By now, Jaroslav had grown sceptical of Czechoslovakia's future and planned to escape before communism completely controlled their lives. Unbeknown to her brother, Anna already had been having similar doubts and was planning to take similar measures, except that both had not shared their thoughts.

Czechoslovakia had become a desperate nation needing to unshackle itself from alien authority and was still haemorrhaging from these post-war inflictions. The country lacked any capacity or military might to ward off its circling prey, leaving her vulnerable and exposed to the very nation that liberated her in 1945 from the grip of Nazi control. Over the past ten years, all sacrifices made and aspirations fought for had come to nothing but still at the cost of so many lives that, in the end, it only resulted in loss of freedom and democracy, in exchange for Soviet ideology. The Soviets may have liberated the Czechs from one foe, but nobody seemed to have the foresight that the Czechs would remain beheld to the other. Liberation became a contradiction of terms.

During this brief period of leniency, Anna and Helena took a train trip to Lednice, a small town in the south near Břeclav. For many years, they had wanted to visit the Botanical Garden, which was particularly renowned for its scarce tropical flora grown in warmed glass houses. After visiting the gardens, they signed the guest book and made their way onto Mikulov, a nearby hilltop village. There they found a restaurant and proceeded to take tea. A young waiter serving them became smitten with Anna's sister and fussed incessantly about them, trying to please them both, especially Helena. Unfortunately, his overtures failed to impress Helena as she was either totally oblivious to his flattery or couldn't care less about the poor chap. Recalling this incident later, Anna teased Helena relentlessly about him as the sisters giggled about the young lad's constant fussing over them.

From the mountaintop, Anna gazed toward the Austrian border and beyond.

She remembered it all so vividly; a similar landscape belonging to another nation but then without any visible border dividing the countries. Undulating terrain with roads crisscrossing over it through forests, rolling green pastures, and vineyards spilling over from her homeland. Her eyes followed the horizon as if searching for a gap through which she could run and escape into this seemingly freer world. It was a fantasy that kept her hopes alive through which she was determined to somehow achieve freedom, even if the pastures only appeared a little greener on the other side. In the meantime, Anna consoled herself that it was an improbable dream as she felt physically inept in accomplishing such a feat alone. For her, it was still a distant crossing of one bridge too far.

Years after Anna left, Helena alone revisited Lednice Botanical Gardens to run her fingers over her sister's signature in the guest book to feel a tangible connection with her. The same guest book remained in use for many years afterward, but as tourist numbers grew, old guest books were replaced by new ones, and they eventually ended up buried somewhere deep within the archives.

By the 5th of March 1946, the 'Iron Curtain'[5], as Churchill christened it, was a Soviet border proposal to traverse from Stettin in the Baltic to Trieste in the Adriatic. The Czechoslovakian election on the

26th of May 1946 gave the Soviet-backed Communists increased political power, with more than a third of the Parliamentary seats allocated to them. The government agreed to restore Edvard Beneš as President and Jan Masaryk as Foreign Minister but in a marginally weakened capacity. In 1947, Foreign Minister Jan Masaryk indicated that Czechoslovakia was interested in participating in the USA-proposed Marshall Plan, a post-war European aid program. This did not appease the Soviets at all.

Anna saw her country in economic tatters, but to take away the pride of the Czech Nation and steal ownership of their land was not liberation; it was a deprivation of human rights and demoralization and destruction of a society. The land her family once owned was now about to be seized from them, and used for collective farming and industry, leaving behind, for some, only a house to live in.

Most buildings, in many cases, were already in disrepair from lack of maintenance during the war, so with little or no money for repairs and with no capital to kick-start farming; it was a near impossible task to rebuild foundations for a productive furfure. Standard of living was further hampered with the cost and availability of quality coal for heating, power for lighting and the freedom to choose career options which would fulfill personal ambitions.

Upon the formation of Czechoslovakia in 1918, the Košice Government Programme[6] had been the political tool for rural landowners. However, with new political land reforms which were in line with Soviet socialism, the Unified Agricultural Cooperative (UAC) would now be dictating the terms to property holders, and their rules would become progressively tough on the farmers. There would be limitations on the size of individual land ownership, and if rural landowners did not voluntarily join the UAC, there were also further consequences. Confiscation and division of agricultural land depended on whether it was held by Germans, Hungarian traitors, or enemies of the Czech and Slovak Nation. This left a broad interpretation depending on how the government viewed family loyalty.

Anna's mother, Rosalie, could have been in line to inherit her parent's property at Krhová, and it could have added to the established

Kurovec farm. Perhaps under different circumstances, it could have been divided between her children, and they could have continued as a family farming enterprise. However, to begin with, there had to be capital and a youthful willingness eager to farm as an enterprise without Socialist constraints.

Anna's name was on the title of her family property at Lhotka, but this neither protected nor helped her or anyone else in her family, as her aged parents had no means of engineering an income from their land. None of Anna's immediate family had able male descendants apart from her brother Jaroslav who was probably deemed an enemy of the State due to his British allegiance. This obviously created a dilemma for them all, so for the land to be confiscated and redistributed amongst strangers for collective farming seemed to be the only plausible outcome.

With nowhere else to turn, young people, educated or otherwise, would be required to work for the government at the discretion of bureaucrats, and those too old would receive a meagre pension and make do with what little they possessed. There was no compensation for the land seized. Everywhere, Anna saw the upheaval of people's lives as they struggled to achieve some level of existence. The pride and spirit of the nation had been broken, and now they had to cowl down to the injustices brought on by Soviet backed communism. It was an ideology that vehemently discouraged individual recognition and reward for achievement but rather a level of coexistence where everyone, regardless of profession and education, received the same benefits regardless of productivity.

Anna desperately wanted to hold onto the past and open her eyes to an awakening future full of promise. Instead, all that greeted her was the stifling reality of abandonment and regret.

Grandfather Stolař once consoled her, "When the war is over, my dear, life will be good again. One day you will have all the nice things you sacrificed while you kept everyone and everything together during the hard times. You will one day finish your education, follow your dreams, and be rewarded. This Anushka, I promise you."

Somehow, this promise felt so empty now, and it was to be the one promise Grandfather Stolař could never keep.

By now, Anna's greatest advocate Grandfather Stolař was already an old man, exhausted financially and emotionally and aware that his time of prosperity had run its course. Like everyone else, he was incapable of changing and rebuilding former lives.

What precious little money he had kept safely hidden for when it would be most needed had little value.

Despite looming hardships, they were still alive. They had food, shelter, and basic needs, even if coal for fires and heating was limited. Anna was beginning to feel nervous about her family's prospects, and there was little she could do to reassure herself otherwise. It would be only a matter of time before she would hear her own footsteps echoing down the dark corridors and following to the beat of another drum. One thing remained unfeigned; the good life was no longer.

On the 28th of November 1947, Anna's father, Frantz Kurovec, passed away. His untimely death was a heartbreaking time for the family, especially Anna, who loved him dearly. Frantz had been known as the 'Poor man's Advocate.' He had a heart of gold and was always willing to give a hand to those in desperate need of assistance. He had been the perfect gentleman, but his main downfall, apart from being a gambler, was his poor judgment in business.

Upon his passing, it was his burden of guilt and shame that transferred to Anna and weighed heavily on her shoulders seeing her family reduced to mere paupers. Life had been miserable enough under Nazi occupation, but now with her father gone and no one to shoulder family responsibility, Anna realized her choices would soon be not hers to make but rest with the collective powers of communism.

Anna confided in her mother and confessed she could no longer uphold family living standards as decisions were slowly being removed from her hands. She begged Rosalie to leave the country with her so they could start a new life elsewhere. Anna did not want her mother to remain alone now that Frantz had died. Although saddened by Anna's plight, Rosalie remained indifferent to her daughter's absurd suggestion, refusing to be drawn into conversations about leaving the country. Rosalie may have empathized with her daughter's dissolution and misery, but they had just survived a war, and although they did not achieve the outcome they had hoped for, it was regrettable that life did not offer brighter prospects; but at least they were still alive.

Rosalie was too old to relocate elsewhere in the world, and Lhotka and Krhová were where her home and family were. It was all she knew despite their lives being reduced to shambles. Besides, her mother and father were still alive, and they would soon need her even more.

She maintained faith that Anna's irrational and preposterous manifestation of fanciful dreams would fade in time, and she would settle down and return to some form of normality. She knew things were not quite as before, and there was an air of change that was creating uneasiness amongst the people, coupled with rumours of even more austere changes to come.

Rosalie was also aware that such matters of the heart, if made known, could put family lives in jeopardy. To mention escape with neighbours, friends, or other family members, even if only as a passing thought, was discouraged. Such conversations tended to leak beyond the walls of homes and could draw the attention of Communist sympathizers who were more than willing to gather such information to ingratiate themselves to the police to better position themselves with the authorities.

Anna adamantly focused on her so-called fanciful dreams, while her mother stubbornly refused to acknowledge her daughter's ideas and be drawn into undesirable conflict. Anna fleetingly considered taking her sister Jarmila with her, although, at the time, she was barely over fifteen years old. Helena, her other sister, shied away from any invitation of escape, excusing herself because she was recently engaged and it would be too risky to abandon her boyfriend and disappear without explanation.

She would later admit she had not even been in love with the young chap, but he was a good excuse at the time to cover up for her own fears and lack of courage to follow her sister.

Anna's failure to entice any of her family to join her only resolutely motivated her to do it and escape alone. She was determined to free herself from the demoralization of their culture and the erosion of freedom, which was destroying any chances of democracy. In hindsight, many probably regretted not joining Anna, but at the time, each had their reasons but probably lacked the foresight and fortitude to leave and follow her. With growing mistrust, jealousy and societal division and deepening fear of punishment for individual expression opposing government policy, descent ordinary people were regularly made an example of and disciplined with varying degrees of deprivation. Throughout, Rosalie maintained her silence, prayed for her daughter's tortured soul, and pretended nothing was amiss.

Much later, when others began reconsidering their options, it would already be too late to escape as security and borders became too impenetrable.

One small consolation for Czech Nationalists was that traitor and Nazi sympathizer Konrad Heinlein committed suicide in 1945 while held captive in Plzeň, and Slovakian Józef Tiso was executed in 1947 for treason.

Photograph 86 & 87: (L-R) Cpl Jaroslav Kurovec F2443. Jaroslav's War medals courtesy Kurovec family SA.

Photograph 88 & 89: (L-R) Jan Kaňák and Jaroslav Kurovec. Zoltan Farkáš included. (Alois Gabriel and Ludvik Pobořil died in battle). Anna's sister Zdeňka Hurtíková in National costume.

Photograph 90 & 91: (L-R) Jarmila Helena & Eliška Kurocove. Božena wife of Vladimír, holding their daughter Jaroslava with Vladimír's sister Jarmila Kurovcová.

CHAPTER 7

Anna's Escape Plans

As winter progressed, with it came snow and bitterly cold weather. Christmas of 1947 was going to be a bleak occasion for the Lhotka household, with Anna's father, Frantz Kurovec, not there for the first time. Anna also grasped that it may well be her last Christmas with her family.

The communist coup of February 1948 left President Edvard Beneš in a communist-dominated government with Jan Masaryk as the only non-communist member. On 10th March 1948, Jan Masaryk was found dead in the courtyard beneath his flat at the foreign office in Prague[1]. Speculations were aired over the radio that he had committed suicide after a nervous breakdown. Many followers believed otherwise. As news circulated about his demise, the mood of democratic politics began spearheading to the left, and so by April of the same year, the reorganized Czech government had a strong Communist contingent.

Communist Leader Klement Gottwald[2] and his supporters began nationalizing all major industries. He gained control of education, internal affairs, and communications portfolios and further ceded Sub-Carpathian Ruthenia to the Soviet Union; all Sudeten Germans were expelled from the country. Eventually, all pre-war conservative parties were banned, and any prominent anti-communists were either deposed of or exiled. Severe censorship of mail and telecommunication, literature, and free-thinking debates, were introduced and everything was closely monitored and stamped out if there was any inkling of opposition to the radicalization of Soviet ideology.

Professionals from all walks of life, other than government officials, educated or otherwise, were paid as much as unskilled labourers. So, any incentive to excel at work was fast fading when the prospect of no forthcoming recognition of effort failed to reward the employees. The regime would isolate the Czech people creating a secretive and suspicious society which often divided family loyalties, and even manifested jealousies among them. Fearful of reprisals for perceived disloyalty toward the political system, many simply bowed to the inevitable restructuring of government and went about collectively with their reassigned tasks.

Most Czechs would ultimately become foiled by the stealth of this indoctrination, and be convinced that Soviet-backed Communism should be embraced for its philosophy of delivering a professed truth that was best for everyone. The nation would eventually slump into social and economic stalemate, shielded from truths of western democracies by a constant barrage of anti-western propaganda from beyond the 'Iron Curtain' leaving the Czech people virtually invisible to western society for nearly fifty years.

Anna's brother Jaroslav Kurovec grew despondent when he saw Czechoslovakia remain under Soviet stewardship. In the short time since returning home from the war, Jaroslav and his comrade Jan Kaňák braced themselves against renewed political changes whilst remaining fearful of ominous threats directed toward them. The political powerhouse in Czechoslovakia had shifted so dramatically, that authoritarian pressure began to mount with persistent harassment plaguing them to sign their allegiance to the Soviet-backed regime.

They had fought as Czech soldiers, albeit with the CIABG in Great Britain, as opposed to the many Czechs who fought alongside the Russians. Regardless both endeavours had set out to achieve the same goal; the defeat of Hitler. Consequently, Jan, Jaroslav, and fellow compatriots were now deemed a threat to destabilizing Soviet authority. Both men had tried to readjust and make the best of re-establishing their lives, but their conscience would not let go of the ideological freedom they had fought for. All of this was now being eroded with threats of ending behind bars or in hard labour camps, with the very essence of freedom being tested.

Life was fast becoming difficult for everyone, and Anna imagined that this was merely the tip of the iceberg of what would follow. When Anna finally made it clear to her mother, Rosalie, and sister, Helena, that she was leaving and nothing would change her mind. Both cried and felt helpless, pleading for Anna to reconsider such foolhardiness. Her family was not prepared to let her go so easily.

It had already become increasingly dangerous to escape, and many who tried were invariably captured, made an example of, and in many cases, never heard from again. Many were also beginning to accept that Soviet Socialism would be their salvation and the only solution for moving forward after such a long war. Those who declared their allegiance to the new government were rewarded with more favourable jobs and promised egalitarian living conditions for their loyalty, so previously friendly neighbours were now prepared to spy on each other for the state.

With worsening threats of crises, it only fuelled Jan and Jaroslav's resolve to escape before it became near impossible to do so. They believed it would be only a matter of time before the nation's borders would be locked permanently, leaving Communism to rule and capitalize on all the nation's resources with unhindered interference from the rest of the world. For the time being, border crossings still partially accessible were now closely monitored, reducing flexibility of movement even for those who still owned land or worked outside the parameters of the Czech border. These people had to obtain special passes for daily entry and re-entry to attend their farms. However, security soon tightened as it had become apparent when many day-pass holders were not returning after a day's work but escaping as refugees into neighbouring Austria and Germany.

Much to Jaroslav's annoyance and displeasure, his sister informed him that she too was going to escape and wanted to team up with him, resolute he should take her with him. Jaroslav had enough problems of his own without worrying about his sister tagging along. However, Anna was adamant she was going, and that was that.

She informed her brother that there was a family obligation for both of them to carry out before leaving. It was an uneasiness that had long plagued her since her father's death; the proper disposal of their father's illegal weapon. Anna buried it in September of 1942 after her father, mother, and sister Eliška had been imprisoned. Since the question of its whereabouts had never been raised, Anna wanted to relocate it elsewhere with Jaroslav's help so it would never be found again. Together they reburied it deeper near the well at the opposite side of the house where it would be least likely dug up.

Decades later, in spite of numerous family attempts to locate this weapon, today, it still remains exactly where they both buried it.

When Rosalie heard that both intended to leave, trying to plead with them became a futile exercise. Rosalie reluctantly pledged her blessing and support so as to avoid any further distressing discourse.

Unbeknown to Anna, an escape contingency plan had already been well-advanced, considering different get-away routes. Due to numerous others involved in this exercise, not everyone could travel together. It would be easier to operate in smaller groups to avoid becoming conspicuous, and if any attempt was made to apprehend them, it would be easier to disperse and disappear.

Two courses were decided on, one group with Jan Kaňák leading them across the border from the south into Austria and Jaroslav with the other; west into Germany. Both routes were well distanced apart, and at different poles of the border, so neither group could be connected to the other. Both men knew the dangers of escaping over borders as Jan and Jaroslav both had been captured before during the war, and only on their second attempts, did they successfully escape from Czechoslovakia. Back then each soldier was responsible only for himself, and although now, under different circumstances with more people involved, similar challenges still remained, but with added responsibility for others. There could never be guarantees of success.

Secrecy was paramount between Jan and Jaroslav until all plans had been finalized, and the predetermined moment of the journey's start announced. Until such times, no escapees were privy to the exact route they would be taking. This would lessen chances of compromise for everyone should a leak occur.

Anna was relegated to Jan's group. During this time Jan lived in Pulgary, close to the Austrian border. It was a farming district and least populated, and he was familiar with the region's layout. The village of Pulgary would later become Bulhary during Soviet times.

Anna guessed there were others involved, but who and how many she had no idea at the time. All she knew Jaroslav would not be travelling with her but instead with another group of people through a region near Cheb and across the border into Germany. She was instructed to say nothing to anybody and told to make discrete family farewells as if she was going on a holiday before catching her train onto Břeclav on a predetermined date. Jan Kaňák would then meet her at the Břeclav railway station, and from there, they would continue onto Pulgary. In the event of any suspicion, her alibi would be that she was visiting Anna Kaňákova, the mother of her brother's friend Jan Kaňák. Anna had been instructed to pack lightly despite the cold weather and maintain a relaxed and casual countenance.

Most of her family believed Anna was embarking on a brief holiday to Pulgary, but beyond that, it was only her sister Helena and mother Rosalie who knew the real purpose. Anna felt guilty that her other sisters, Zdeňka, Bohuslava, Eliška, and Jarmila, as well as her grandparents, had to be excluded and not privy to a proper farewell. She knew it was all to safeguard herself and others, as well as her family members, from spilling the truth if plans were to go horribly wrong. Anna's youngest sister Jarmila would have been too young and innocent to understand the implications, but Bo, on the other hand who at the time was working at the local post office would soon have the village gossiping. Eliška, like Bo and Jarmila, would never know of Anna's plan and only learn about it after Easter when she failed to return home from Pulgary.

Leading up to Anna's departure, she casually visited her family to bestow Easter greetings, explaining she was off to Pulgary on a brief Easter break. On the day she greeted her Uncle Alois, Anna had been unusually reserved. They had their fair share of dangerous missions during the war, and since then, both remained close. Alois was as fond of his niece as Anna was of him. She was about to divulge her secret, as she knew he could be trusted, when his wife, Aunt Helena, walked into the room. At that moment, Anna had to double-check her motive for visiting and not go through with her prepared confession. So, in the end, so as not to embroil her aunt into the unnecessary foray of things, Anna paid her dues and left.

Her deceit and lack of courage haunted her for years afterward for not even hugging them goodbye. Alois Kurovec would recall many years later that he sensed Anna was up to something and had come to say goodbye but admitted knowing nothing of her plans.

Next, Anna visited Zdeňka, her oldest sister, to bid her final goodbye. Anna broke down and told her sister the truth without going into detail. Both were reduced into floods of tears as they hugged. Zdeňka's sons, Milos and Zdeněk were still only young lads and were playing close by. Seeing their mother in such emotional distress, they rushed over to her. Milos, trying to comfort his mother, scolded his Aunty Anna for upsetting his mother. Zdeněk, the younger lad, seemed to heed little attention to all the commotion and sat silently, concentrating on an old broken alarm clock that Anna had given him. Anna hugged them all and left. Many years later, Zdeněk would recollect that moment with his broken alarm clock as it remained his only real memory of his Aunt Anna.

Anna could not bring herself to confide in her Stolars Grandparents, who had been so kind to her throughout her life. They were elderly now, and she chose not to burden them with the worry that she was departing for good.

She nursed extreme guilt and shame for many years to come as they were her adoring family, and she was about to abandon her greatest allies. Never wishing for them to lie on her behalf if authorities arrived to question her whereabouts, Anna hugged them both instead, wishing them Easter homage, and with a heavy heart, choking back tears, she departed never to return.

Easter was fast approaching when Anna returned home to Lhotka, where her mother and sister Helena anxiously awaited her. Trying to be brave and conceal a deep sense of sadness and pending gloom, Anna spent her final days with her mother and sister all sharing their grief in silence. Helena took it upon herself to prepare a carry-bag for her sister. She was more prepared for a journey than Anna would have ever been. Helena packed tights, a light blue woollen jumper that Anna had knitted, a pair of new leather boots, long socks, underwear, warm clothing, and nick-knacks that her sister might need. Anna was deeply grateful, as she had very little of her own to take with her.

At the time most shops carried very few goods, and while Anna bought very little for herself in the past, most of her money earned went back into the family farm, paying off debts. She had scrupulously put aside 2,000 Koruna for emergency purposes. The current value of 2,000 Koruna would have been about US$200, and that was all she had to survive on after her departure.

While Anna readied herself, Helena helped secrete the paper money within the hair of Anna's two auburn plats which she wore entwined and pinned up around her head. This way, Anna hoped not to lose or mislay her money. Sadly, this meagre amount of money would later haunt and wound her family devotion when Bo accused her of taking the 'family fortune,' leaving the rest of them destitute in Czechoslovakia.

Her only memento of home was a gift from her grandparents; a small gold and enamel medallion of Madonna with child, hanging from a fine gold chain around her neck and concealed beneath her blouse.

At 5 am on a frosty March morning in 1948, just a week before Easter and while it was still unusually bitterly cold with plenty of snow, Anna picked up her full-length tweed coat and carry bag and silently stepped outside into the brisk air and closing the door behind her, she departed home for the very last time. Anna was now all alone as she purposefully walked to the nearby railway station.

Photograph 92 & 93: (L-R) Anna's sister Zdeňka Hurtíková. Helena Kurovcová.

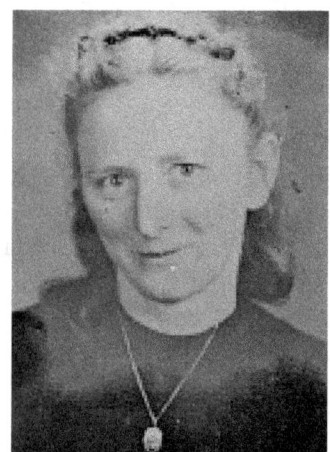
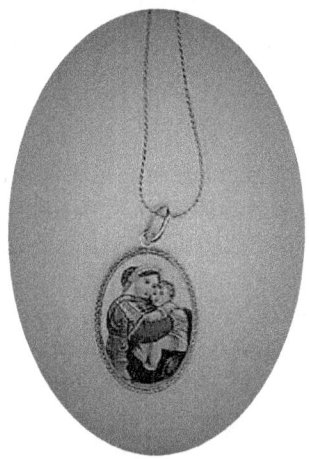

Photograph 94 & 95: (L-R) Anna Kurovcová 1948. Anna's gold and enamel pendant keepsake.

CHAPTER 8

Pulgary (Bulhary)

In the cold, awaiting the early morning train which would take Anna to south Moravia, she felt acutely self-conscious while mingling with others on the railway platform. Everybody was rugged up and anxious to board, destined for work or an early Easter holiday break. It was the week before Easter of March 1948, still crisp and cold with plenty of snow lying about when Anna bordered the train. She made herself comfortable in a seat well away from anyone in case she encountered someone she knew and became needlessly caught up in conversation, asking why and where she was travelling to.

The train rattled onto Břeclav through Přerov, Hulin, and Hodonín. It had been a lengthy trip as it was necessary to change trains to reach her final destination of Břeclav, a town in the winegrowing district of south Moravia, which was only a short distance from the village of Pulgary (Bulhary).

Anna remembered the countryside well from her summer excursion with Helena, but on this day, its lush green rolling hills covered in vineyards were still chilled by winter as the bare vines stood stark against the snow.

Her brother Jaroslav or Jarda as he was known to family and friends, had already left some days earlier, as his planned rendezvous was with another small group of people to the west near Cheb. There was always the risk of becoming a target when travelling in large numbers, making it so much easier to abort escape plans with smaller groups. Regardless, the risks and dangers were always there. If all went according to plan, a loose arrangement had been made between Anna and Jaroslav to meet somewhere in Germany.

As arranged, Anna arrived at Břeclav railway station and was met by Jan Kaňák with his horse and sulky to take her onto Pulgary. Apart from greeting her politely, Jan sat quietly, concentrating on his horse and the road ahead, his thoughts seemingly preoccupied with other matters. It was growing dark and cold, but Anna was well wrapped with an extra blanket over her knees, which Jan had provided. While there was still light, Anna occasionally glanced in his direction and thought he had a rather interesting face with a strong square jawline and distant eyes. She decided he was either very shy or terribly conceited and definitely not her type. They exchanged no further conversation until finally arriving in the village of Pulgary. Jan quietly pointed to the house numbered 57 with the high side gates and pulled up in front of the dwelling. It was snuggled next to similar houses which lined the main street.

Jan dismounted the sulky, opened one of the double gates, and through it, he led the horse and sulky with Anna still seated. This brought them into a small cobbled courtyard surrounded by numerous stone outhouses, sheds for tools and machinery, and a small stable housing domestic animals and chickens. Another barn stood further along, and behind it was a wine cellar. Beyond the dwelling and all these buildings, a narrow lane disappeared into the darkness dividing rows of vines still bare of foliage standing starkly against the slushy snow.

As Anna approached the back door beside a covered domestic well, she was met by a tall and upright elderly woman, not beautiful but perhaps once handsome in her youth, who was introduced as Jan's mother Anna Kaňákova. She greeted them warmly and beckoned them inside out of the cold. Anna was guided into a warm kitchen where, around the table, sat two young men who barely noticed her arrival. They were talking seriously between themselves, intent on tasting and discussing bottled wine on the table, when Jan joined in.

Anna Kaňákova, mother of Honza, a nickname for Jan, introduce Anna to the young men who looked up momentarily and acknowledged her.

One of the young men, probably out of politeness, looked up again, "Oh! Hello Sis! You must be Jarda's sister. I am Domin Červenec and this is Jara Kohut. Honza, you, of course, have already met!"

And with this brief interlude, they continued on with their wine tasting.

Anna was seated out of the way. Being already late evening and still sensing the chill, Anna remained rugged up, feeling self-conscious at being ignored as she watched on. She had met Jan once in Plzeň and was not even sure he remembered her. Their introduction through her brother had been brief as the jubilation and excitement at the time far exceeded any meaningful encounters. She wondered why she had been so gullible to entrust herself to a man she hardly knew, without knowing anything about him, his family, or his past. The only consolation was that he was a friend of her brother's, which surely had to carry some merit.

Jan got up, briefly catching Anna's eye, she smiled feebly, wringing her cold, gloved hands as he strode toward the fire and briefly stoked the coals and added another log. Anna felt a flush of embarrassment, and lost for words, she said nothing but realized against the glow of the fire that he had rather handsome features, if only in a rugged way. He had dark hair and blue eyes, was physically well-proportioned, perhaps a little too arrogant, and indeed a man of few words. Even if indifferent to her presence, she reminded herself that he definitely was not her type.

Jan returned to his place at the table with the others, and no more was directed at Anna as they continued on with their robust discussion. She only understood that they were tasting certain bottles from different batches of wine and deliberating prices. Soon afterward Anna Kaňáková returned from the kitchen larder laden with a tray of hot soup, some bread, and cheese and two plates, and placed the food on a stool beside Anna. Anna stood up to shed her overcoat, hat, and gloves as Jan's mother sat down beside her and motioned Anna to sit and join her for some supper. At the same time Jan's mother indicated that the boys were not ready for their supper as yet, and she would later prepare their evening meals when they were ready to eat together.

This somewhat eased Anna's self-consciousness as she sat down again and began to eat, politely chatting with the old lady. Nodding toward Domin, Jan's mother said both had served together during the war and were now inseparable. Domin more or less lived at their place as he rarely went home. She also explained why Domin called Anna 'Sis.' It was because she was Jarda's sister, but as this did not make sense, Anna did not press for further explanation.

During their conversation, Anna learned that Jan's major vine crops were planted outside the village. She was also told Jan had sold a consignment of wine to the Brněnsky Hotel for a large sum. The payment was to have been arranged upon delivery of the wine, but this had not happened. Although efforts were made to recoup the outstanding settlement, no money eventuated in the end.

The following day Anna was summoned to the Pulgary Post Office as there was an incoming call for her. Her sister Bo was anxious to know how everything was going in Pulgary. Bo was a gossip, so Anna could not trust her with any information whatsoever, and ringing her constantly in Pulgary could become a liability as there was always a chance it might draw unwanted attention to Anna's presence. Bo's intentions may have been genuine, but she was often reckless and foolish with her thoughts and did not pause to think who else was listening at either end as telephone calls were randomly tapped. This troubled Anna as it could potentially compromise her plans and embroil Bo in business which was none of her concern.

On the same afternoon, Anna's brother Jaroslav turned up unexpectedly to meet with Jan. Anna was over the moon to see him again so soon as she had already half expected he had left the country. Anna was beginning to feel emotional, as her life was hanging on the edge of a precipice, and she felt like she was about to go over it, not knowing how hard or where she would land.

That evening Jan invited Anna to join him and meet others he would be escorting over the border. Anna was surprised that there were so many. She counted at least sixteen of them but was relieved that women were also in the group.

The plan was to leave sometime during the week after Easter when there was no moon, and hopefully, by then, any recently fallen snow would have melted, leaving no obvious tracks to trace their course.

Jan's route remained closely guarded and would only be revealed when they were all on their way.

Afterward, during the evening, Jan, Jaroslav, Jara, and Domin adjourned to the cellar in the backyard for some more wine tasting, and Anna could hear them laughing as they debated its quality.

That night Anna Kaňákova had to cater for the remaining five of them although Jara Kohut, by then, had returned home. After a few too many wines, Jaroslav decided to give his sister a lecture on maintaining her silence and not be tempted to talk to any strangers about their plans. Anna had bought a small diary to keep track of the days, but without discussing it with her, Jaroslav assumed she was documenting her journey and scolded her, saying that if she ever lost it and outsiders recovered it, it could jeopardize innocent lives. Anna felt angry, embarrassed, and humiliated by her brother's outburst and his lack of tact, and for his insensitivity in matters which were based on no factual knowledge. All along, Anna acted discreetly, did not voice her opinion about the plans she preferred not to know about, and kept very much to herself. But as always Jaroslav wanted to lord over her and remind her, she had been included in this game plan only as a favour.

The following day, Jaroslav announced he was leaving and Anna felt almost relieved. Each politely wished one other a safe journey and a successful rendezvous in Germany in the not-so-distant future.

Realizing that Anna was becoming restless and trite, Jan lent her his book 'Zeměpis Člověka' (translated to mean Geography of Mankind) by Dr. Jiří Král. Anna appreciated this little gesture and soon absorbed herself into the literature.

By now, Anna had unpacked and repacked her bag numerous times over when she found Helena's 'Doxa' wristwatch packed amongst her clothes. This moved Anna to tears, as it had been her sister's prized possession.

Earlier, Jara Kohut confided in Anna, informing her he would not be leaving with them as initially planned. He explained he had Jan's horses and the vineyard to tend to but assured her that they would all meet again soon. Anna was disappointed that Jara chose to remain behind but agreed he had valid reasons and that someone had to look out for Jan's mother. During her short stay, Anna had many lengthy conversations with Jan's mother and learned that Jan had obtained the vineyard at Pulgary after returning from the war. With Jan's father now dead, she decided to join her son here as all her other daughters were married, and her second eldest, Anna Syptáková, was already living in the family home at 125 Hošťálková.

After Anna's brother departed, Jan observed her repacking her case and commented that she was carrying far too much. He suggested being sensible with what she brought along, as they would be hurriedly covering vast distances on foot with little time to rest. She alone would be carrying her case, which would become heavier as she tired. Anna felt incensed that he thought she was incapable of shouldering her own load, so to annoy him further, she also packed his book into her bag. 'I have suffered extreme pain from toothaches in the past without ever complaining, so I can survive this.' She thought to herself.

Jaroslav's departing advice to Anna was to listen and heed instructions and not speak her mind until she thoroughly thought everything through. He added that whatever Jan asked her to do, she was to do it without question as her life may well depend on his advice. Anna was a headstrong woman who had learned quickly to become independent and was used to making her own decisions. She had also learned to be frugal, organized and capable of confronting issues that stood in her way, but she had the propensity to become outspoken whenever she felt cornered, denigrated, or threatened. On the other hand, Jan was a person of few words but direct and to the point when he needed to say something. By nature, he was nonconfrontational and had no desire to have an argument with a woman he hardly knew, albeit someone he had to lead safely across the border.

Jan was a facts and figures man and had been meticulous with his planning, and his faith rested in those joining him, hoping for nothing more than they possessed common sense and a strong drive to prevail against all adversity. Anna had almost reached the point of no return, and so far, she had no reason to turn back. She had left her heart behind in Lhotka. What she now possessed was a strong determination to forge ahead and not become a victim of emotional upheaval, uncertainty, and, above all, failure.

Leading up to Easter was traditionally a busy time of the year. It was not only about worshiping and going to church but also participating in festivities to celebrate Easter as a family holiday. March weather in Pulgary was still brisk, with frozen snow lying on roads and in the fields. Fir trees were still weighed down with hanging frozen icicles, and the silent countryside was waiting for Spring to warm and revive the dormant life beneath its crust.

On Easter Monday evening (29th March 1948), a dance was being organized at Pulgary, to which Jan invited Anna to join him. He reminded her she had to be seen to act normally and not be viewed as fostering suspicious antisocial behaviour. Being stubborn and independent and determined not to curtail to Jan's wishes, Anna refused the invitation that evening and instead chose to spend the evening with his mother. Besides, she wished to keep a low profile and not be seen unnecessarily around the village.

During this brief but unconventional stay in Pulgary, Jan's mother and Anna developed a mutual understanding and deep respect for each other. Their friendship, as brief as it was, made Anna realize that Jan's mother had suffered considerable hardship in the past, but she was forgiving and possessed compassion and consideration for others. Despite their differing backgrounds, their paths may not have crossed otherwise were it not for the challenging times surrounding them. Anna always remained grateful for the opportunity and privilege to have met Anna Kaňákova.

The anticipation of escaping no longer held any great appeal or adventure for Anna but rather a fear thwarted by daunting possibilities of the immeasurable magnitude of blunders that could lead to the ruination of her life. So, before she changed her mind, she cast all doubt out of the window, and by 9 pm, both women were fast asleep.

Shortly after nine that evening, Jan rushed home from the dance and awoke Anna. She was about to complain about having to get up but thought better of it. Besides, she had already resolved not to let Jan down and be prepared to take on her share of responsibilities regardless of what befell them.

As Anna stood half-dazed in the doorway, she realized Jan was serious about her getting up, as he was anxious and agitated by something that had happened that evening. As he dashed about stuffing things into his knapsack, he demanded Anna to hastily get ready as all plans had been changed, and they had to leave immediately.

By then, Jan's mother had woken as well, and while she was keeping her emotions in check, she fussed about her son, regretting that this moment had finally arrived. Jan made one last-minute attempt to convince Anna to reduce her baggage weight, reminding her that the bag was far too big and heavy. He even tried to grab it and empty out its contents to repack it, but try as he might, Anna was not about to budge and give in to his demands. Anna protested loudly when he even attempted to snatch back the book, he had lent her, declaring she had not yet finished reading it. She let Jan know, under protest, that she, alone, would carry her own bag, no matter how heavy it was or how tired she might become, and she did not need any help or advice from him. Anna's feisty defiance was sufficient to make Jan back off and leave her to it.

Domin rushed in shortly afterward carrying his packed knapsack and appeared equally anxious and eager to get going. He looked at Anna's bag and frowned but said nothing. As they assembled together by the back door with their meagre life's possessions, Jan's mother stood by in tears, overwhelmed by their pending departure.

Jan sensed her grief as he, too, had tears when he hugged his mother and reminded her if anyone should ask their whereabouts; he had gone to Mikulov, and Anna had returned to northern Moravia.

Amidst tears, his mother bid them farewell and told Jan to be nice and care for Anna. Before emotion overwhelmed him, he turned away and led Domin and Anna through the back door into the darkness. In the shadows of the courtyard, Jan paused by the old well and hurriedly grappled with its cover for a few minutes while the music and laughter from the dance filtered through the cold and still air.

A short while later, Jan reappeared and thrust a revolver into Anna's hand. She was mortified. He quietly but firmly told her it was loaded and hers to use if necessary. She was only to shoot at the enemy if there was no other option; a case of her or the enemy's life. The other revolver he handed to Domin, while Jan kept the Stengun 32-round automatic[1] for himself.

Jan had concealed the guns in the well, away from his mother's realization, protecting her from any knowledge of illegal arms being hidden in or near their home. Nor was there time for fire-arms lessons, as unexpectedly, on that evening, certain events had drastically changed Jan's carefully laid out plans.

Upon departure, they agreed on one simple strategy. In the event of becoming apprehended by Czech authorities, firstly, they would try and bargain with them and plead to be let go, on the pretext that there were others following at a short distance who were armed and which would ultimately only lead to a shoot-out. If this failed, they would have no choice but to shoot to save themselves.

Jan's escape plans had been so meticulously revised over the weeks preceding this night that he had the whole route indelibly imprinted into his memory. The only shortcoming was that the execution of these plans was for the week after Easter and not for tonight. It had been predicted that most of the snow would have melted by the week after Easter, and the night would have been totally dark without a moon. Jan had even timed the walk to the proposed rail crossing to coincide with the midnight Express from Prague to Bratislava.

It had been fortuitous that Jan, Domin, and Jara had attended the evening dance that night, as otherwise, the outcome could have been vastly different. Jan did not drink socially but was there only to observe and mingle with the crowd. There had been numerous police officers and discreet personnel circulating about in the crowd, all looking for anti-social behaviour. It soon became apparent that many of whom were to go with Jan were having a jolly time, and drink was beginning to loosen their tongues! The circumstances leading to their hurried departure came about by chance when Jan overheard a particular conversation from one of his group members. The rather drunk young chap was slurring and drooling over his female companion and boasting to his audience how Jan Kaňák would soon take him and others over the border into Austria. Jan immediately suspected it would only be a matter of time that evening before the authorities would piece together information, be it gossip, pipe dreams, or otherwise, and round up the silly fools, arrest them and charge them with inciting escape, and then come looking for him. What would follow the next day when all facts were squeezed out of the unfortunate drunks could range from imprisonment to execution.

Remorsefully, the fate of the remaining innocent people did not rest well with Jan, but he had no time to contact them and instead had to leave everyone behind, and he himself quickly disappear. In the end, each had to be responsible for their own life. There was no time for heroics, and from then on, Jan's plans immediately changed.

Anna reluctantly followed into the cold darkness for their final pep talk with her revolver tucked deep into her overcoat. Holding her carry bag in the other hand, she was reminded she must keep up as the walk would take some hours in partial darkness over rough and frozen terrain, mainly through the woodlands.

She clung on to her treasured dream, a dream as a young girl, travelling to New Zealand after having read a book about the Māori people dwelling on the Waikiki River. Her brother Jaroslav joked at the time, saying it was only a dream she would never be able to fulfill, and besides, why would New Zealand even want her?

Perhaps, what the old Gypsy predicted all that time ago, was destined to happen.

Anna thought of the remaining party of thirteen left behind as a result of someone else's resolve to blabber recklessly after several drinks too many, endangering everone's life. The thought of what might be happening would only accelerate their pace to reach their rendezvous point before midnight without being followed and captured. Anna was already having a niggling regret of ignoring Jan's earlier advice, but there was no time for regrets now, as the burden of her bag was beginning to numb her hands as she stood in the cold waiting to proceed. She dared not utter a word of complaint, and nor could she simply throw away her bag without leaving behind evidence of her presence and besides there was no time remaining now to reorganize her luggage.

Anna's journey was almost at the point of no return, carrying the burden of her own convictions, but at what cost?

Photograph 96 & 97: (L-R) Jan Kaňák far right with a friend at Pulgary 1947.
Anna Kaňákova (Jan's Mother) at Pulgary in 1948.

Photograph 98 & 99: (L-R) Vineyards close to where Jan Kaňák grew his grape vines, Circa 2005. Rear of Jan Kaňák's house No. 57 at Bulhary (previously known as Pulgary) with old well in foreground. Circa 2005.

Photograph 100 & 101: (L-R) Backyard of house No. 57 Bulhary where Jan grew some of his vines, Circa 2005. Remaining backyard sheds at rear of Jan's house in Bulhary. Circa 2005.

CHAPTER 9

The Escape: Pulgary to Poysdorf

On Monday, the 29th of March 1948, just after 9 pm, three silent figures slipped hurriedly into the shadowy lane beyond the house and away from the village of Pulgary. The reedy-like organ music from the Easter dance still reverberated through the air but faded quickly the further they travelled. The short-lived bright light of the moon was slipping beyond the horizon, and with it came an eerie uneasiness. Soon it would be totally dark shrouding Jan, Domin, and Anna beneath a cloak of blackness. Jan and Domin seemed to know their way, but Anna stumbled and faltered with her heavy case as she struggled to keep up. She silently cursed herself for being so stubborn and not listening to Jan, but it was too late now, so she carried on without complaint.

Jan seemed to have had extraordinary night vision as he never faulted and led them first through what must have been lanes between dormant vines. Here Anna grappled with the dry vine tendrils as she scraped past, almost falling in a heap amongst them. The snow was slushy and crunchy beneath her feet, so hopefully, all boot tracks would dissolve before morning. It felt like she had been walking for ages, well past the three hours it was supposed to take them; up hill and dale, through woods, along invisible tracks, and past sleeping farm cottages. Every so often, a barking dog would startle them, and shortly afterward, the nearby farmhouse would light up as someone ventured out to investigate in response to the dog's agitated growling. Everyone would stop briefly until everything settled and then doubled their pace to catch up on lost time.

Jan deliberately stayed away from any main roads as border guards were already widening their patrol with guard dogs, and any unfortunate encounter with these animals would be hazardous. Most of the guards carried torches or lanterns, so their presence was always visible at a distance and could be easily avoided, but the dogs, with their keen sense of smell, were the real enemy.

With the absence of moonlight, it was reassuring as it hid their presence, but it also shrouded the landscape and tracks they were passing through. It was easy to become disorientated and lost were it not for the sound of trudging boots ahead of Anna that reassured her she was still on track. There was no talking, just the urge to follow without lagging behind. Anna's ears were alerted to every sound, even the crackling of a twig or the hooting of an owl made her jump and jogged her heart into adrenalin overload. She had no time to think how cold she felt but only prayed silently that nothing impeded their urgent getaway.

Up ahead and slightly to the west of them, the township of Mikulov twinkled high on a hill, its lights creating an aura on the black horizon. It was like a beacon showing them the way.

They were now trudging over the very landscape when only a year or so earlier, Anna with her sister Helena had crossed while heading for Mikulov. Anna remembered then how her mind navigated the roads and contours of hills and fields, subconsciously tempted by the coercion of freedom, which was why she was here tonight. Anna tried to recollect this invisible and sparsely populated countryside covered like a patchwork quilt of vineyards, encircled by forested hills under late summer skies. However, all landmarks were invisible right now, and the dark silent hills only seemed to mock her as she stumbled and slipped on the partially frozen snow. Tonight, it was real and not just some fanciful pretence of escape.

Anna knew the border was well beyond Mikulov, so they still had some distance to cover. She followed as if in a trance, holding off the notion of weariness under the burden of her heavy case, desperately striving toward that invisible divide. Gradually the terrain changed beneath their feet, and now they were treading over wet and marshy ground, which formed a system of waterways and lakes. Numerous streams of insignificant size flowed from far off hills into this area, creating an inhospitable habitat to walk through. This wetland was fed by the Včelínek Stream, which flowed north from Austria and entered beneath a railway bridge on the Czech side into a lake and wetland complex. Throughout this region, access on foot to the border would have been nearly impossible, especially after the winter thaw or recent rain when the area becomes a floodplain of swampy marshes. Inhaling deeply, the air was brisk and smelt dank from sodden vegetation, as each inward breath stung Anna's nostrils. Beneath her the earth was spongy and slippery. No sympathy was ever forthcoming from her two companions, whenever she blindly misjudged her footing and stumbled with both her boots sinking ankle-deep into the sloppy quagmire.

One major consolation in this inhabitable swamp was that the Austrian border ran closely parallel with the railway which traversed the only elevated dry land over the swampy marches. Somewhere in the darkness numerous small rail bridges spanned the chilly water below gushing into the nearby lake system. However, the biggest obstacle and challenge was that these rail tracks also functioned as a temporary section of the border between Austria and Czechoslovakia and which was always heavily patrolled. Needless to say, crossing into neighbouring Austria was perilous as chance encounters with enemy guard patrols were ever-present.

Due to the recent glut of escapees, surveillance along the Czech border had escalated. It was becoming increasingly difficult to cross undetected into West Germany or Austria as security guards with dogs constantly patrolled the borders.

As they hurried along, Jan, Domin, and Anna had no way of knowing if security police had already been alerted and were in pursuit of them. Jan was familiar with the outlay of the land. From his numerous reconnaissance surveys, he calculated time and distance to coincide with the express train passing over one of the larger bridges in the area. He had walked this escape route alone on numerous occasions but, for security reasons, kept all this knowledge to himself. It had been fortuitous after this evening's fiasco that they still had sufficient time to leave and follow his carefully orchestrated plan; otherwise, under different circumstances, it could have turned into a calamitous situation.

In a direct line or if travelled by conventional methods, it was not of great distance from Pulgary to the border but hiking hurriedly overland in the dark without any light or a road to follow and maintaining cover, made for a strenuous effort. Anna could only measure this distance in time, and after almost three hours in the dark, going at a pace just short of running, it was nothing short of exhausting, if not the very least, terrifying. Her feet were numbed, and those bits that still had some sensation ached from endless tripping and slipping over tree roots and stumps as bare bramble branches grasped, whipped, and scratched her face. Her body ached from the cold and the strain of humping such a heavy bag. It was far too late to dump any of her luggage as it would only leave a trail for enemy guard dogs to follow.

The journey seemed to have no end, and slushing through uneven marshes in the dark made it all the more foreboding. She was sure she would not have dared to enter this murkiness in broad daylight. Jan's instructions reverberated: "Shoot first if it means your life!" Anna knew how to handle a gun, but she had never used it to kill anyone before, and she prayed it would never come to that. Her laboured breathing became heavier by the minute, and at times it was the only sound she heard, pushing all other audible senses out of reach. She was alone with her dread, as the other two seemed to show no fear and strode effortlessly ahead.

It was a painful ordeal, but only the fear of being caught, humiliated and punished kept Anna going.

Suddenly, Jan stopped in his tracks. He motioned silence as ahead of him, some distance away, were guards with dogs walking abreast along the rail tracks. They had torches and were heading in their direction. Their voices had disturbed the stillness and filled Anna with dread as they waved their torches from side to side along the rail track. The torchlight, although strong, could not pick them up at this distance, but a dog's keen sense of smell was more of a threat. Anna heard a dog wince and whimper, and fearing the worst, she froze, but when nothing followed, she thought that perhaps the poor animal was just cold or hungry.

Luckily, Jan, Domin, and Anna were downwind but remained crouched low and very still, so the dogs could not pick up any movement or sound from their presence. At a short distance ahead of them, the patrol passed and then shortly afterward turned and returned the way they had come, proceeding toward the rail bridge. The guards with their dogs were soon on the bridge signalling to someone ahead, perhaps a sign that all was clear, before proceeding forward and finally disappearing from sight.

Jan signalled everyone to quickly move ahead with him until they were close to the rail bridge that crossed a flowing waterway. He then quickly clambered beneath the bridge and motioned everyone to follow and sit by the stream's edge and wait. Jan whispered urgently that the train would soon be passing overhead, and at that moment, they all had to jump into the water on his command and wade against the current beneath the bridge to the opposite bank further upstream.

They sat huddled together on the stream's edge for what seemed like an eternity, shivering from the cold while the dark swirling water gurgled past them. Jan mumbled something about the train being late, but his biggest fear was that the guards might return to do another patrol before it arrived.

It must have been shortly after midnight when the silence was broken by faint chugging. As it grew louder, the clattering along the lines echoed from above and reverberated through the woods, sending a shiver of apprehension down Anna's spine.

Bracing themselves, Jan suddenly yelled, "Jump!" and all three landed in the water together.

Anna had no time to think as the icy water pushed up against her, almost making her lose her balance before regaining her footing. Finally, her boots gripped the rocky bottom as she struggled waist-deep in the water against the current. Her bag was almost soaked as she wrestled with it, trying to keep it above water level while she struggled on the uneven and slippery bottom against the flow of the stream.

Despite the urgency to ford the torrent, Jan noticed Anna struggling with her heavy bag, barely holding it at chest level as the current slowly dragged her back toward the bridge. In good faith, he suddenly grabbed her bag and threw it toward the opposite bank, but unfortunately, he misjudged the distance, and it landed in the water with all its contents now completely drenched. Domin quickly retrieved it before all of Anna's possessions floated away.

Over the past weeks, Jan had meticulously calculated and timed the arrival of the Bratislava Express, so their approach at midnight at the bridge had been crucial to coincide with the train crossing it. The roaring of the train overhead would have muffled any sounds they made while crossing beneath the bridge. Before the guards with their dogs had time to return and resume their patrol, Jan, Domin and Anna would hopefully be further upstream on the other side of the rail track.

It was hardly a time for protests as Anna scrambled over the rocks and made for the bank. She silently cursed as she picked up her carry bag, now twice as heavy. Soaking wet and shivering with cold, there was no time to sit down and cry as the sound of the train was fast disappearing, and only the lingering smell of coal remained.

No sooner had the train passed when they spotted the re-emergence of guards with their dogs as flickering lights bopped along the rail tracks. Jan only hoped that no scent of their presence remained by the water's edge on the other side of the bridge to attract the dogs and induce a full-scale search. Maybe there was still sufficient steam and smoke about to confuse the animals if they detected something. The voices of guards soon became audible, and with no more time to spare, the three quickly crept into the thicket and hid. It was always best to crouch down and keep still instead of running while patrols moved past.

The true border or fence, or 'Iron Curtain' as it would become known, had yet to be constructed, but efforts were already underway to erect it. Numerous labour camps were being set up in remote areas along the Czech border to carry out the framework for these new partitions, eventually forming a preposterous barricade between east and western Europe. For the time being, many railway lines were being used as temporary boundaries, which made attempting to cross rail lines in the open foolish, if not a hazardous risk.

Jan calculated they were still on Czech soil and in danger of being captured. The true border was still a short distance away, and they would have to run for their lives to make it safely there. With Anna's waterlogged contents now weighing her down, the task was twice as arduous as she heaved up her soaked bag and hurriedly trudged after the other two.

It was well into the early hours of Tuesday the 30th of March when they probably crossed the invisible line separating Czechoslovakia from Austria. It had only been some 12 km to the border from Pulgary, but there was no way of telling how far they had gone or exactly where the border was.

The cold was incapacitating Anna's weary body as her joints pained and felt fused, but she knew the only way to resist becoming frozen altogether was to keep moving. Both men had been through the war and, like Anna's brother Jaroslav, experienced far worse than they had just been through. But for Anna, it was a first, and the realization of what real desperation, fear, cold, hunger, and homelessness were really like, was an experience she would never forget. It would become a journey under the heavy burden of her own doing.

Anna dared not think about what she had left behind but focused on what was ahead. Either way, there seemed little comfort as uncertainty was all she had. With everyone trudging on in silence and with the eastern sky hinting at the dawn of a new day, visible road signs finally indicated that they were, in fact, in Austria.

Before sunrise, while it was still relatively dark, Jan spotted a grove of vines with remnants of mulch from the previous season. Here he paused and asked for all the guns to be handed over. Rather reluctantly, Anna retrieved her handgun from her damp coat and gave it to him. As she watched him unload the pistol and bury it beneath the straw with the other two, for a moment, Anna felt naked and vulnerable to all invisible dangers, leaving her nothing with which to protect herself.

Seeing her questioning expression, Jan reminded her that it was illegal to carry arms. If caught, it would ruin any chance of repatriation elsewhere, and instead, it would land them all in prison, and if returned to Czechoslovakia, they would most certainly be shot.

As the eastern sky lightened with a chilly breeze whipping their frozen faces, they still pushed on through fields and dormant vineyards. At the crossroads, signposts heralding the Austrian word 'dorf' instead of 'vesníce,' meaning village, was almost music to them as they trudged on like weary travellers with a glimmer of a song in their hearts. They circumvented the sleeping little hamlets still shrouded in the bleak and frosty dawn fog as they slipped past Drasenhofen, Fünfkirchen, and numerous other villages.

Dogs began to bark more frequently as they passed quietly by farmhouses, still fearing someone might come out and ask who and what they were doing. The countryside was very similar to that of southern Moravia, with fields of dormant vines waiting for spring, but nevertheless, it already had an alien feel to it. Although not particularly hostile, it was definitely not welcoming.

They arrived at Poysdorf in Austria just before midday, some 30 km south of Bulhary. By now, they were sufficiently distanced from where they had buried the guns and well beyond the border. They had been on the road for almost fifteen hours, damp, cold, and hungry; they yearned for a hot coffee and something to eat. A bath and a change of clothing would have been high on Anna's wish list, but just sitting out of the cold was a luxury.

At a tavern on the outskirts of Poysdorf, they decided to risk their chances with the locals. This small, isolated Inn seemed safe and inconspicuous, so Domin, who spoke a smattering of German, volunteered to check out the premises. The Publican seemed friendly enough and paid little attention to them. They ordered cups of coffee and paid in Czech Krona as obviously the steady trickle of Czech immigrants was nothing new to him. It just seemed business as usual.

They could sit down and relax for the first time in hours, each with their black coffee and taking in their surroundings. Yet, it was only the beginning of a very long journey with no turning back.

During their break, Anna discussed the possibility of having a bath and changing her clothing and considered seeking out a catholic church where she was sure the priest would be charitable and help her. Jan replied that it was not a sensible idea to involve outside people as it only highlighted their presence in the village and could complicate matters. Besides, before reaching Vienna, they still had a long way to go and had to remain constantly vigilant, traversing the Soviet Zone of Austria.

They were about to leave when suddenly; two Czech police officers entered the Inn. They all exchanged cursory glances as escalating fear took hold and froze the trio to their seats.

Anna's immediate response was, "What should we do now? Make a run for it, or bluff our way out somehow?"

Neither one of them had valid papers or passes for Austria. Anna only possessed a half-soaked birth certificate and Czech Identity card hidden in her damp carry bag. Their presence, as it was, only confirmed their illegal status in the country, but it might be their only saving grace from the Czechs.

They must have stood out like terrified and wretchedly defenceless people on the run. While they sat, huddled together with droplets of sweat building up on their foreheads despite the cold, their hearts pounded loudly in their ears. The two unarmed Czech police officers briefly spoke with the Publican, who replied courteously and gestured toward the back of the Inn. Satisfied, the officers bid him goodbye, and as they passed, they nodded at the three terrified customers huddled together by the window and, in Czech, wished them a safe journey.

Stunned and almost paralysed by such a close encounter, and for a moment forgetting they were free from Czech persecution, they soon realized that Czech police were powerless to arrest and enforce their return home. However, the same did not apply to the Russian occupying forces in Austria, who had every power to arrest them and do as they please.

Domin spoke up first after the police disappeared and whispered that he recognized one of them as a policeman from Mikulov. The Publican, who briefly chatted with Domin earlier, said a tractor at the back of the inn had been used as an escape vehicle a few days ago. Domin guessed the police were here only to retrieve it and return the machine back to Czechoslovakia.

Austria was in a tumultuous situation at the time, suffering economic decline and food shortages due to exploitation by the Soviets. The country was also under threat of annexation into the Soviet bloc. Austria had been liberated from the Nazis by the Soviets in 1945. After the 'Vienna offensive' [1] (siege of Vienna by Soviets), joint allied occupational forces consisting of American, British, and French military established themselves alongside the Soviets in Austria, dividing the country into Occupational Zones[2].

Vorarlberg and North Tyrol were assigned to the French, Salzburg and Upper Austria (Oberösterreich) south of the Danube River to America, East Tyrol, Carinthia (Kärnten) and Styria (Steiermark) to the British, while lower Austria (Burgenland) and Mühlviertel region of Upper Austria (Niederösterreich) north of the Danube River went to the

Soviets. The Capital, Vienna, was similarly divided into four Zones, with its central district administered on a monthly Rota by all four occupying nations.

The American and French Zones conveniently bordered West Germany, while the Soviet Zone bordered the future Warsaw Pact states, including Czechoslovakia. However, the border between Czechoslovakia and West Germany was in the American Zone, no doubt much to the vexation of the Soviets, but nonetheless, this border would receive extra security, making it almost impenetrable. The initial purpose of joint foreign occupation was to rebuild and revive war-torn Europe, unite rather than divide, and establish a free independent democratic rule. It also became a valuable tool for gathering Intelligence. The allied occupation would remain in Austria until it ended in 1955 with the Austrian State Treaty. Ahead of Jan, Domin, and Anna was a minefield of trepidation as they prepared to head for Vienna and the safety of friendly allied-occupied Zones. But first they had to traverse the Russian-occupied Zone of Austria.

Photograph 102 & 103: (L-R) The marshy wetlands near the Czech Austrian border. Circa 2016. Rail Bridge in distance over the waterways near the border. Circa 2016.

Photograph 104 Terrain around escape route near Bulhary. Circa 2016.

Photograph 105: Vine growing region near Bulhary and Austrian border. Circa 2016.

Book One: Anna's Story

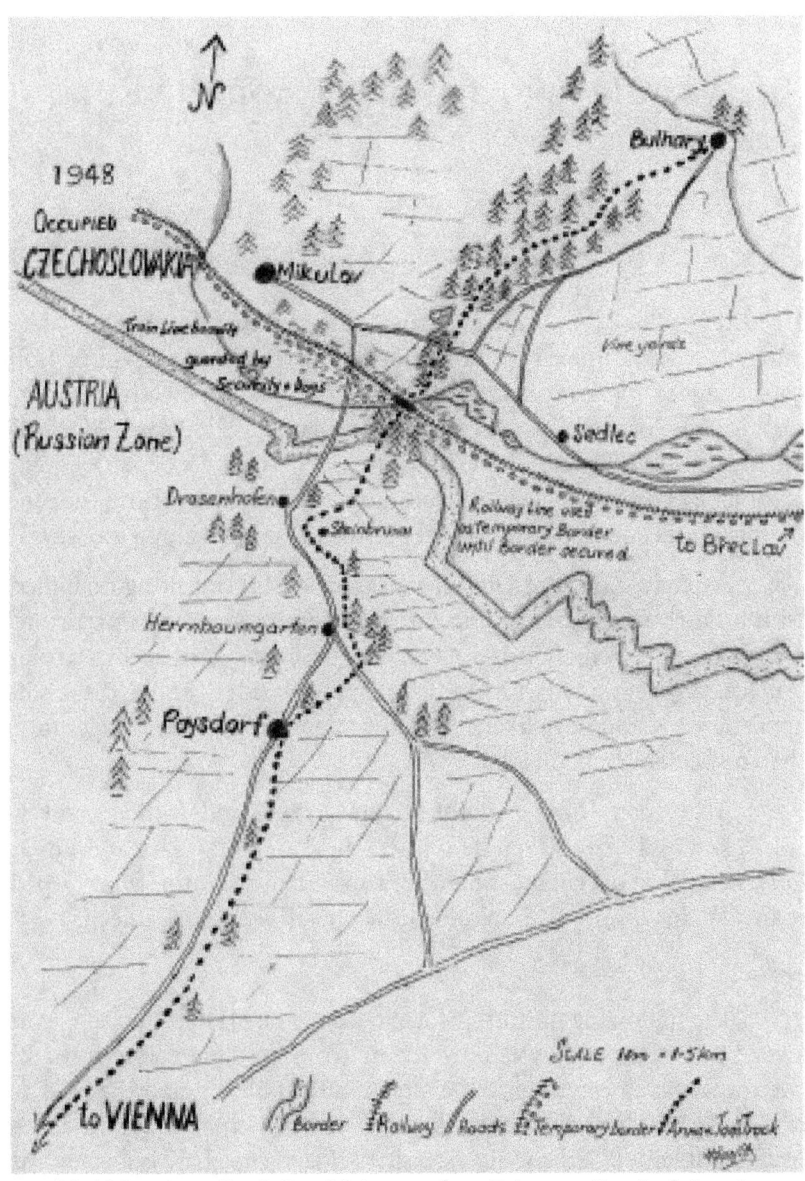

Mud Map: Anna, Jan & Domin's journey from Pulgary to Poysdorf, Austria, 29-30th of March 1948.

CHAPTER 10

Vienna (Vídeň): Czechs on the Run

Just after midday, Anna and her group departed Poysdorf and proceeded on foot down a quiet country road. It only had sporadic farm traffic consisting of local farmers and travellers who were going back and forth from Poysdorf. Ahead of them remained a long and uncertain journey onto Vídeň (the Czech name for Vienna), some 68 km away, and embracing a fate that held no guarantees of success for them, they took their chances and hoped no Soviet patrols intervened along the way.

As Jan, Anna, and Domin carried no valid transiting documents with legal reason to be passing through Austria, they were particularly conscious of remaining inconspicuous and cautiously avoided unnecessary contact with local people. Besides, their dishevelled appearance would have likened them more to wandering gypsies rather than respectable folk on a hike.

After many hours, nightfall approached, and with it came the cold again and like starved field mice, they were all weary and hungry. They needed to overnight somewhere and finally, spotting a pit near the roadside, they promptly bunkered down together and fell asleep.

The following morning, Wednesday the 31st of March, Anna awoke early. Her body was now aching from the damp clothes she had been wearing since crossing the stream after Pulgary, and the cold and cramped night in the hollow only worsened her situation, but she never once complained. No sooner had she stood up to thaw out, they were back on the road again.

After some hours, a man in a vehicle headed their way paused and asked where they were going, and reluctantly Domin admitted that they were heading for Vienna. At first, they were all wary of the traveller, but after speaking with him, they were offered a lift into Vienna. When asked if he could drop them off near the British or American Lager (camp), he assured them he could do so, as coincidently, he was headed close by and was happy to by-pass Russian authorities and deliver them to the British Camp. Everyone felt relieved when he further added that the English Forces were currently administering central Vienna. After negotiating a fee, the three of them with their meagre possessions, crowded into the back of the farmer's truck and crouched down out of sight beneath a tarpaulin covering the cargo of produce. It was a long and bumpy ride, but it rested their feet and minds as they fast-tracked to their destination.

To be taken directly to Vienna and to an English DP Lager, or Displaced Person's Camp, was more than they could have wished for, so they were eternally grateful for the lift. Each occupying force, America, Great Britain, France, and Soviet Russia had a shared responsibility for managing the massive exodus of displaced people from war-torn Europe. After the Potsdam Conference in 1945[1], involving America, Great Britain, and Soviet Russia, any refugee transfers had to be conducted in a humane manner. However, many reports indicated otherwise, with disturbing intelligence claiming brutal Soviet maltreatment of these captives and forced repatriation back into the countries of their origin, resulting in heinous injustices.

For many, arrival time at these Lagers had to coincide precisely with advanced knowledge of which allied country occupied which Zone so that the most vulnerable did not end up in Russian caretakership[2]. The worst thing Jan, Domin, and Anna feared for the duration of their flight through Austria, was to be caught in the Russian Zone and repatriated against their will back to where they had fled from.

Finally late on that Wednesday afternoon they arrived in Vienna and were dropped off by the gates of the Lager within the English Zone. Before the driver departed, he suggested which bank to go to in Vienna where they could exchange their Czech currency and assured them, he was happy to wait for his payment until later the next day. It was reassuring that some compassion still existed and not all displaced people were treated with disdain and contempt for imposing themselves unintendedly onto another struggling society.

Vienna should have been an enjoyable destination graced with opulent architecture, alive with artistic culture of operatic musicals and ballets, and its famous Dancing Horses. But all these were subdued by recent post war events and the influx of newly arrived refugees all wrestling to find refuge and a means of survival, only placed a heavier burden on the local polulace who were already themselves in desperate need of simple basics such as food and security.

The renowned grey Lipizzan stallions from the Vienna Dancing School, were select horses acclaimed for their strength, agility, intelligence, and graceful equestrian performances. This school had also undergone its struggle during the war resulting in a grave threat to its equine future. In 1942 during Nazi occupation these fabulous world-renowned creatures were poached from Piber in Austria and moved to Hostouň in Czechoslovakia. In early 1945 fearing the advancing Russian army would eat these threatened species, Colonel Alois Podhajsky and General George S. Patton devised 'Operation Cowboy'[3] and temporally relocated the horses to Wimsbach in Austria until such time in 1955, when all the breeding Lipizzan stock including the brood mares, would be finally returned to Piber. However, in 1948 the school was unfortunately still closed. It would not be until 1955 when the Lipizzan stallions would be returned to Vienna, and with it, the dancing school once again reopening,

Although the Lipizzan breed originated from Slovenia, in recent history, they have been bred in Austria.

As much as Anna loved history and culture, during her time in Vienna, opera and entertainment were not recreations afforded to her. Austria was in the midst of its own food crises and economic struggle and was forced to cater for the milling chaos of needy refugees. Anna could not believe the sheer volume of crowds as they joined the long queue of desperate, displaced human beings patiently waiting to be processed. Every day, thousands of people like themselves were pouring into these makeshift camps to access food and shelter and a bit of humility. But above all, simply seeking protection from persecution from those they were escaping.

After what seemed like eons, Anna and her crew were finally let through the gates, with their names added to the growing list of displaced people and war victims.

It was a humiliating experience for Anna, but at least she was not alone in this exodus of desperate masses, and surely here, at least, there would be some salvation with positive guidance to a new future. Each one was issued standard housekeeping items consisting of a blanket, one spoon, one tin cup, and one plate and a reminder that they could only stay for one month from the date of arrival. All their menial items must be returned and accounted for upon departure. While she still had the presence of mind, Anna quickly calculated that they would need to be organized to leave by the end of April.

Passing through the gates into the Lager, Anna entered a time zone that stole a part of her life that could never be recovered and, in most instances, not even accounted for.

From here on, time and memory began to blur into one momentous rollercoaster of often inhospitable refuge, unprecedented challenges, unavoidable circumstances, and the inevitable migration to destinations of uncertainty along with thousands of other strange faces, desperate to survive. Days and dates would melt into months, creating a motion of meaningless and often disoriented measures of time. There seemed no precise date or time to match many of the following events that unfolded, and with no measure of time, the calendar would become a blank page of nameless months, dates, and days as their journey unfolded. There would appear to be no real purpose for a past or a future but only the motivation of survival from day to day. Along with others, Anna's existence would become a series of events suspended in a surreal nightmare from which no one could wake. Only much later fragments from this existence would return and many times haunt them with the passing of time.

The Lager accommodation was a very basic dormitory-style building with wooden floors and thin walls offering a perceived safe haven, and although it kept out the dampness and wind, it did nothing to stop the evening chills. Each had a spot to sleep and basic washing and bathing facilities. Above all, there was some scant, if not bland food available, even if primarily unpalatable, it did help to stifle hunger for a brief period. Anything nourishing had to be bought with what little money could be scraped together. Outside of their designated quarters, a large copper was available for boiling water, cooking, and washing. This appealed to Anna as she could at least cook their own meals with whatever foodstuffs they could scrounge.

The following day Jan and Domin went to explore the city of Vienna and find the relevant bank they had been advised to go to and exchange their money for Austrian Shillings. Central Vienna was safe as it was being administered on rotation by one of the four Allied nations. While they were in Vienna, it was temporarily under British administration.

As there were three of them, they made a pact that one would always remain to guard their possessions while the other two did the chores and shopping. The men found the bank and exchanged their currency but were told the bank preferred to exchange larger sums of money rather than small amounts at a time, so Jan transacted all his money.

When Jan returned, Domin took Anna to the bank so she could exchange her 2,000 Koruna into shillings. On returning, she sewed together two small handkerchiefs and made a pouch for her money which she wore on a string around her neck. They paid the driver who delivered them to the camp and added a little extra for his kindness.

The next time Jan and Domin went into town, they bought an oversized wrought iron casserole dish and a large spoon to go with it for Anna to cook their meals in. The rule of the abode was that each had to do their own washing and contribute to keeping their place clean and tidy, but Anna was happy to do all their cooking. Soup became their staple diet and it became even more palatable when titbits of meat could be added. The leftovers could then be stored in the casserole for days during cold weather, providing tastier supplements to the less desirable rations.

While once alone with Anna, Domin confessed somewhat apologetically that he had left his money back in Pulgary.

She reassured him it was no fault of his own as they did rush off in rather an unexpected hurry but added, rather philosophically, "Life is more precious than money; once a life is lost, it is gone, but money can always be earned again."

When in Pulgary, Anna had learned from Jan's mother that Domin's mother had died very young. She had been unmarried and employed as a domestic to some man when Domin was born, so he never knew his father. Domin, whose actual name was Vavřín Červenec, was a decent chap who spoke a smattering of German, French, and English, which he picked up during his war years in Great Brittain with Jan. To Domin, Anna was always 'Sis,' and all three became requited friends, always guarding each other's backs.

In the camp, they encountered many other Czechs, all in similar circumstances and each with a dream to fulfill in a new world. Their allowed time in Vienna was nearing to an end, so future planning had to be considered. Between the three of them, they decided to stick together and devise a way onto the next leg of their journey. Toward the end of their stay at the Lager, Jan and Domin unexpectedly bumped into Jara Kohut. It was a surprising encounter, albeit a joyous reunion for the three friends, as they eagerly embraced and summonsed Jara to their abode. Anna was delighted to see Jara again, although hardly knowing him; having only met him briefly in Pulgary, she nevertheless greeted him enthusiastically as any old friend would.

By choice, Jara had remained in Pulgary when the others fled the country. During that time, he had assured Anna that they would meet again one day, somewhere in the world; but this soon was an unexpected delight, if not a miracle! Jara looked somewhat dishevelled as he stood before them in his worn-out shoes, being the sum of his possessions. His shirt might have been in shreds, tattered trousers split and barely covering his legs, and yet, his face lit up like a child elated in a candy store when he joined his equally motley crew. Everyone fussed over him as if he had been absent for years rather than weeks and welcomed him back into their fold like their long-lost prodigal son. Jara Kohut began to outline the aftermath of Easter Monday when, at such short notice, Jan, Anna, and Domin fled Pulgary late that evening. The harrowing ordeal due to their departure caused so much consternation within the community that Jara began to regret not having left with them. It did not take long for the security police to round up and arrest the other thirteen people from the group, and by Tuesday morning, authorities were knocking on Jan's door.

At first, Jan's mother imagined the worst, that her son and the other two had been arrested on the border, but it soon became evident that their visit was a reprisal for Jan evading them. Anna Kaňákova dutifully informed the police that she believed her son had gone to Mikulov. They also inquired about Anna Kurovcová, and once again, Jan's mother revealed nothing more except to her knowledge the young woman in question had returned to northern Moravia. The following course of interrogation surprised her when they began to question her about Jan's suspected illegal weapons.

She admitted honestly that she knew nothing about guns while they searched her house. Making no headway with the old lady, the police finally warned that when Jan returned, he was to immediately report to them.

The fallout from the botched escape had horrendous repercussions for those arrested at the dance and others suspected of involvement. Most placed the blame on Jan as the instigator and most significant player in the whole idea, and that they had been coerced into believing his plan promised them all a safe getaway. With limited information and knowledge, none could demonstrate which route Jan had supposedly arranged for their run away, nor could they add when exactly this was supposed to happen, except soon. They blamed and implicated one another, and neither was prepared to shoulder any responsibility. Many were beaten, some imprisoned, while others disappeared, presumed to have been executed. The small village of Pulgary was shaken to the core.

Jara Kohut realized it would be only a matter of time before he, too, was sought out and arrested for collusion. So far, his name had not been on the list of suspects, so he quickly dispatched Jan's mother to the nearest railway station and saw her off to Hošťálková. He then discreetly went into hiding until he hatched some kind of a plan to leave the country.

The following Wednesday morning, Jara picked up his rake and, disguised as a peasant labourer, walked toward the border where all other workers had congregated to proceed through the partition onto their respective farms in Austria. When stopped and questioned about the lack of a day pass, he simply indicated he was but a poor peasant who had been employed to do some raking in the nearby field. The guards seemed unbothered in following up an identification check on a desperate-looking hobo carrying a rake over his shoulder, so they left him to proceed over the border. Jara could not believe how easy it had been to rake his way over the tightly guarded border, whistle happily down the road, and make a miraculous escape in broad daylight.

Jara Kohut was a lad of about eighteen, good-natured but with plenty of 'front.' Although this impulsive act could have been fraught with consequences, instead, it simply worked like a charm without any planning. Once over the border in Austria, Jara did not look back but kept walking and raking until he eventually reached Vienna.

Once with his friends, Jara was sent to bathe and wash what little clothes he was wearing. Jan gave him trousers, a shirt and boots and also some money, while Domin added a sweater and socks and an old suitcase he had obtained from someone in the camp. Jara was so appreciative of all the help received that he was content to sit at their campsite and look after everyone's possessions while the others went off to shop and search out means of moving onward from the camp.

Every morning Anna prepared food for the casserole and left Jara to watch over the meal while it cooked. By now, Anna was sufficiently confident in finding her own way around Vienna and happily walked about alone. Jara quickly settled into their camp routine and enthusiastically assisted with ideas to formulate a plan for the next stage of their journey into Germany. They were all determined, as it was imperative, that they all remain in the American Zone and not be apprehended by the Russians.

Their final days at the camp passed quickly, as Jan, Domin, and Anna prepared to depart. They had lived at the camp for almost a month, but Jara Kohut still had several weeks' grace and could have remained longer, but he chose not to stay and instead travel with them on the next stage of their journey. The Vienna Lager had been a temporary reprieve and although it may have lacked privacy and comfort, it offered a safe haven with shelter and meagre food rations but it also provided the footing for enduring comradery. In the short time they had been there, they made many acquaintances and exchanged personal stories, always promising to keep in touch with one another.

While at the Vienna Lager, Domin was always keen to look ahead and proved to be industrious with efforts to seek out new avenues of how to move on. He made contact with a man who promised them for fifty Shillings per person, a safe passage onto the Steyer Lager within the American Zone. The huge cost incurred was for guides to chaperone fleeing refugees from Vienna through Austria within the Russian occupied Zone to near the Enns River which flowed from the west into the Danube. Still within Austria, the Enns River formed a divide between the Russian and American Zones. The proposed escorted passage onto Steyr required upfront payment before further negotiations were entered into. Upon payment, any further follow-up communication regarding this transfer onto Steyr, would be made through contacts at a designated place and time at the Vienna Railway Station. It was indicated that at least ten others would be joining Jan, Domin, Anna, and Jara if they decided to proceed. With so much money outlaid without any guarantees of a valid escape mission or authenticity of those involved, there was little choice but to take the risk and proceed with the offer. There would always be the chance of losing all their money to unscrupulous charlatans or worse still not even making it safely to Steyr. Such were the risks; whichever options came their way.

Finally, early in May, they were packed and almost ready to leave when Anna had a sudden dilemma. How would she manage to carry the cumbersome casserole dish? Her small carry bag was bursting at the seams, yet she was determined to take the dish with them. Before the other two became embroiled in Anna's predicament, Jara Kohut quietly offered to pack it into his practically empty case and carry it for her.

Later that evening, at the Vienna railway station, they were met and accompanied by a female guide and directed to board the train for Linz. It was imperative that the group stick together, and when signalled to disembark the train, everyone did so and not continue onto Linz.

The train trip was a nightmare, covering a distance of some 155km at slow pace. Inside the carriages were no functioning lights, and all the seats were broken. The shattered windows were barricaded with timber slats, and the passengers felt like prisoners huddled together on makeshift seating. In the dim light, they soon made out several Russian soldiers with guns seated alongside one another further down the carriage. With no means of defence or proper identification, Anna dreaded that, at any moment, they would be sighted, interrogated, and rounded up. She wondered if it all had been a trap to catch them. She had never in all her life felt so terrified. Only the darkness hid her true fear and apprehension. The train journey seemed endless, but not one of them dared to sleep, and at the rate they were travelling, it would be a nervous all-night trip.

The journey into Steyr could only be accomplished by traversing through the heart of Russian-occupied territory before accessing the

Book One: Anna's Story

township in the American-held Zone. It would be an anxious trip, albeit thwarted by danger and possible apprehension by Soviet guards. The Russians were already controlling the Austrian Czech border and adjoining borders with Germany preventing anyone from leaving their controlled Zone into American-controlled territory. At the time, five people had been recently caught and marched back under military escort into the Soviet Zone. It was imperative for them all that they did not end up the same.

Their anxiety grew as time progressed, as nothing outside was visible from their partially barricaded carriage windows. Concern grew as nobody really knew where and when they were to get off the train. Possibly sometime after midnight, a woman with her face heavily concealed passed them and signalled to get off at the next stop. Anna did not like nor trust the woman, but what else could she do?

Finally, the train wheels screeched to a halt at some obscure and poorly lit railway platform, where Anna and her companions finally prepared to disembark. Anna's heart was racing and sweat precipitating on her forehead, as the file of shuffling passengers passed down the corridor in an urgent but orderly manner. Although the Russian soldiers remained undisturbed and slept throughout the whole ordeal, the nervous refugees once alighting the train, only then breathed a sigh of relief when the train finally moved off with the Russian soldiers still onboard. The guide then urgently motioned everyone to quickly follow and gather around her into the shadows,

Their disembarkation spot was somewhere near Sankt Johann (not to be confused with Sankt Johann in Tirol, between Salzburg and Innsbruck), a couple of village station stops before the Enns River crossing. At this point, the railroad was nearest to the town of Steyr, although separated by hilly and densely forested terrain.

Ordinarily, this train journey would have continued veering north toward the Enns River crossing, before continuing onto Linz in the American Zone. The demarcation line with its checkpoint between the Soviet occupied zone to the south and the American Zone to the north was somewhere near the Enns River crossing, where it would probably be busy with strict transiting formalities, and anyone without proper papers would no doubt be apprehended by the Soviets and returned to their country of origin. At least by now, they were off the train, and no undesirable followers seemed to be shadowing them.

After a short briefing, their guide pointed the group down an obscure track and then promptly disappeared. Another heavily cloaked figure appeared from the darkness and beckoned everyone to follow and walked briskly for some distance until they reached an open field. In the shadowy moonlight, they realized they were not alone but amongst even more nervous strangers who, upon seeing the newly arrived, scattered in all directions dashing for cover.

After they regrouped, they were all handed over to yet another female guide, who again was heavily concealed behind a dark scarf. Once more, everyone was instructed to start walking for the remainder of the night and only come to rest at daybreak, where they would need to remain discreetly concealed for the duration of the day. It seemed a very organized, if not a costly scheme, to traffic desperate refugees into safer territories. As they proceeded down the road, disorientated by the shadowy darkness and following on blindly one after the other, no one knew precisely where they were or which way they were headed. One could only hope they were being led out of Russian territory and directed safely toward Steyr.

Anna counted well over sixty people in the whole group, many in far worse condition than themselves. Whenever unexpected lights appeared along the road, such as those of vehicles or somebody on a bicycle, everyone had to quickly run for cover and crouch silently on the ground until the traffic passed. This happened numerous times, especially later during the early morning hours when local travellers began using the road again.

When the skies lightened just on dawn, everyone was instructed to stop walking and hide, resting inconspicuously amongst the forest trees, but not gather in large groups drawing unnecessary attention to themselves, should somebody spot them. Some were in small family groups, some as couples, or as singles, all fatigued, hungry and apprehensive as they scattered about hidden in the grass under trees. Those fortunate enough to have food and drink, snacked on their meagre rations to build up stamina and a positive mindset for the coming evening when their trek would resume.

As a group, Jan, Domin, Anna, and Jara kept close resting together amongst the trees but well away from the road or any farmhouses. They positioned themselves centrally within the crowd as this offered a better chance to scatter and flee should they need to, rather than trying to escape from either tail end. They shared amongst themselves what little water and food rations they still had and made the best of resting while one of them always maintained vigil.

Anna had wanted to walk up front, near the guide, but Jan pulled her back and reminded her to be patient and remain well back of the line, as it would be easier to run away should they ever be apprehended.

A young Hungarian man hobbling along on his wooden leg, aided by a stick and carrying a large bundle of possessions, was trying to keep up with his pregnant wife and child. The uneven rhythm of his wooden peg clipped the cobbles on the road and resonated through the silence. Anna wished the road had been softer and kinder to him so the noise of his efforts were not so audible and a constant reminder of his impediment. It was heart rendering for Anna to listen to him clomping in the darkness, which made her want to help him. She mentioned it to Jan, who pointed out that walking on a firm surface was probably much easier for him than on grass or sand. He added he was only too familiar with this sound and how tiring it must be walking with a wooden leg, as his father had also been an amputee.

Watching his pregnant wife struggling with her bags and trying to carry their infant child, Anna could not bear to watch any longer and offered to take and carry the child so the pregnant woman could at least help her incapacitated husband. Without a word Jan automatically took Anna's carry bag from her and carried it. He had never offered to carry anything for her since that unpleasant incident in Pulgary when she fought to keep and carry all her possessions. But now it was a case of helping another fellow human being in far worse circumstances.

During the day, the countryside reminded Anna of home, a place near Raichovu Hutŭ where one would travel by train through the dark forests. She felt a brief pang of homesickness, but reality soon kicked in.

Their journey had taken much longer than it should have. At some stage, their guide had lost her way and discreetly had to ask for directions the next day. All this took extra time and additional effort, especially for the old and incapacitated, when everyone had to retrace their footsteps and walk further to the missed road intersection before proceeding on track. They later learnt that their guide had not travelled this road in many years, and her recollection of this particular route had been somewhat clouded.

However, much later, while still in Europe, Anna heard the tragic news of how the last contingent of refugees to ever cross this route was captured by Soviet authorities and retained within their Zone and, against their wishes, returned to their respective countries. The guide responsible for that folly was apprehended and imprisoned for aiding in the illegal escort of refugees. Such were the risks for everyone. Even though the cost of freedom was high, there was never any guarantee of successful outcomes for either party.

After about two and a half nights of walking and just on the sunrise of their final stretch, the party finally stopped on the crest of a hill. At the end of the road, as it continued down the slope, everyone saw a white barricade across the road, and beyond near the township was the Steyr Displaced People's Camp[4].

The Austrian town of Steyr was mostly industrial, and in the distance, its established manufacturing plant was involved in ball-bearing logistics. The distance to Steyr in a straight line was only about nine miles from where they disembarked near the small rail siding of Sankt Johann, but the journey had to be negotiated along a winding and often challenging track through steep and hilly terrain which had been deliberately used to avoid unnecessary contact with mainstream traffic.

While everyone stood in the middle of the road, pondering the view; others began to ask; "Where to now?"

At this point of contemplation, without any warning or further instructions their guide disappeared. Her work was done.

CHAPTER 11

Steyr to Passau

Access into Steyr was barricaded by a sturdy white gate and guarded by American military personnel. Much to everyone's relief, there was no evidence of Russian presence prior to the entry gate. Down the road in front of this barricade, a large contingent of earlier refugees was already lined up and milling about, waiting to pass through the partition. Crowd control and entry into Steyer seemed to progress methodically, albeit slowly.

The crowd of over sixty dishevelled refugees led by Domin, cautiously approached and gradually blended into the throng of people waiting outside the blockade. After some hours, everybody eventually passed the barrier and was transported into a controlled area of makeshift offices. Here the American officials counted and documented everyone; many without identification papers but only here-say names and places from where they originated.

Thousands of refugees were inside the camp, and the latest incoming group barely made a dent in the swelling congestion of displaced people. The multitudes comprised all ages, families with young children, young men and women, and the elderly. In this exodus of human beings, some stood alone while others, like Jan, Domin, Anna, and Jara, stayed firmly together like a family nucleus so as not to become separated as they proceeded through the formalities of assimilating into the camp.

Although now free from any Soviet intervention, their disappointments at Steyr arrived early. There were at least five thousand people ahead of them, all jostling for food and shelter, and they also learnt that accommodation could only be secured for a concise period. However, at least for now, they were safe in American custody.

A Tree Without Branches: Anna's Journey

Since departing Vienna, Steyr Camp had reasonable freedom of movement for the refugees. Many from Anna's group, with whom she had become acquainted over the past few days of trekking, were already absorbed into the Camp and invisible. Train trips from Steyr to elsewhere in Austria within the American Zone were cheap. Earlier during their stay, they all travelled individually as far as they could afford to search out better camp options. As always, one from their group would remain behind to care for their belongings. Numerous Czechs began to argue and complain loudly about unreasonable and poor living conditions and anything else they could gripe about. Looting and unruly behaviour were rampant, and more often than not, Jara Kohut volunteered to do their house-sitting. With Jara offering to look after Anna's belongings on numerous occasions, she was free to go off and explore. Anna even ventured to Innsbruck, where she found a large intern camp. The camp closer to the town of Salzburg really appealed to her. She considered moving there as this camp was less crowded, and unlike elsewhere, one could remain there as long as need be. Anna would have remained there had not her bags been back at Steyr.

Domin reminded everyone that many people had already departed from Germany to migrate overseas. What purpose would Salzburg serve Anna if she had already made plans to meet her brother somewhere in Germany? In the end, Anna remained in Steyr but refrained from further train trips as she had to hold on to what remaining money she had. Anna prayed she would soon be united with Jaroslav and hoped he would bring their sisters. However, for the duration of their stay at Steyr, the four remained discreet and maintained a social distance from certain rowdy and disruptive fellow countrymen.

Finally, they could bear it no more, and Domin expressed a desire to find another camp within the American Zone, which would be less unruly. Out of necessity, they packed up and prepared to leave the Steyr Lager and head toward Linz on the Danube River, which was within American control. To catch a train from Steyr to Linz at the time would probably mean re-entering back into the Russian Zone, so the only viable and least expensive route of some 32 km was to do it on foot. Thousands of people were still flowing into the camp, and nobody seemed to be doing a head count of those present. It was perpetual chaos, and everyone was too busy coping with the continuous influx of new arrivals that a few departed inmates would barely be missed. Unnoticed, they left Steyr one evening and, with all their possessions, headed off on foot toward Linz.

This journey was a much longer walk but not as challenging as before, and at least secure in the knowledge of not being pursued by Soviet guards. Being displaced people without proper identities, and so to avoid complicating their plans, they had to avoid the attention of Austrian authorities. With their recently acquired knowledge of how to be cautious and discreet along roads, they applied these strategies and walked by night and rested during the day, hoping their frugal food rations would sustain them long enough. They had minimal rations from Steyr when they started out, each carrying only a small chunk of stale and hard black rye bread and a slice of salami, barely enough to garnish a meal. The lack of food would plague them constantly. Even roadside trees were bare of fruit, so the walk into Linz became a hungry one.

In Linz, aided by an American Refugee Relief Group, Domin finally found them accommodation. They were put up on a large transport barge that had been moored along the bank on the Danube River. All were too tired and hungry and in need of a bath to concern themselves that a short distance across the river was the Soviet Zone.

Each was allocated a basic cabin with bunks made up of clean linen. Anna thought she was in heaven as she had not slept in such indulgence since leaving home, and once settled on board, everybody was served a meal. This was another unexpected treat with each plate topped with a pork schnitzel and crumbed cauliflower additional to a cup of black coffee. A far cry from the meal scraps of recent times, and for Anna, it had been a true blessing from God. It once again reassured her faith in humanity and that there were still good people in a world so deprived of food and security.

The Russians had their own 'refugee' zone on the opposite bank of the Danube. This realization sent a shiver down Anna's spine when she realized how close her enemy was. To be so close and see them was unnerving, as many reports were already circulating about their inhumane treatment of refugees. It was inconceivable to believe that Soviet guards had the power to please themselves, resulting in the mass rape of women, murder, and the pillage and looting of fellow humans.

The Danube was a swirling current of murky grey floodwater, a formidable river descending from its source in the Black Forest near Donaueschingen and flowing toward Vienna and beyond. Anna wondered if the strength of the river's undertow as it pushed water up against the sides of their barge could break the mooring and set them all adrift toward the other side. It was a constant worry for some days, as this dreaded thought preoccupied much of Anna's time and made for many sleepless and uneasy nights. After everything Anna had been through, she would rather dive into the icy depths than give herself up to the Soviets.

At the time, one can only ponder if Anna ever realized that only some 13 miles beyond the Danube River toward the Czech border, the concentration camp of Mauthausen was quietly rotting in its abhorrent history. Here, barely three years ago, her brother Vladimír was exterminated. Somewhere in its desecrated surroundings, his remains or ashes were disposed of in unknown mass graves with thousands of other wretched souls.

Mr. Škrášek, an elderly Czech man also residing on the barge, was practically beside himself when Domin pointed out that the enemy was only across the river.

"Should our mooring break, we could all end up with them!"

The poor old chap was so shaken that Anna had to reprimand Domin and appease the poor man before he had a nervous breakdown. The visible Soviet presence was a harsh reminder of why everyone was on the barge in Linz; destitute, homeless, and on the run. Mr. Škrášek was more relieved than anyone else when the day finally arrived, and all had to leave the barge and once more continue their journey on dry land. However, in the meantime, some thought had to be given to crossing the border at Passau, some 89 km upriver from Linz.

While in Linz, Jan, Jara, and Domin met some Czechs from Prague, with whom they became acquainted and who supposedly had connections with manufacturers in South America. These South Americans allegedly manufactured religious icons and were in the business of exporting them. Such potential work with lucrative business ventures was all very enticing to Jan and Domin at a time when their futures depended on a lucky break. Anna overheard Jan and Domin planning to immigrate to Argentina or even Brazil. This was all planned without including the other two: herself and Jara Kohut. It disappointed Anna that they lacked loyalty toward the rest of their group without including or considering Jara and herself in their conversations. As always, it seemed to be only about them. Anna learnt very early on that each had to fend for themselves, and in many ways, she had to feel grateful that she had been accompanied thus far. However, she also felt vindicated when Jan's and Domin's plans came to nothing.

Their scheming never rested, as Jan and Domin soon met another Czech family from Prague who was set on immigrating to Argentina. They had a printing business in Prague and, before the war, had purchased equipment and things they hoped to take with them to Argentina. They invited Domin and Jan to join them and offered them lucrative opportunities. Included in their promise was Jan's and Domin's paid passage to Argentina. Again, it sounded all too good to be true, and there was no welcome for Anna and Jara to join in except that everyone was invited on several occasions to dine with the highflyers; all expenses paid.

Anna surmised these people must have had plenty of money and good connections in high places as they seemed extravagant during such austere times. Meals were costly in Austria and could only be paid for with coupons. A privileged acquisition that Anna and her group did not have. Anna recalled, "Here, you still paid handsomely with these vouchers, but if you didn't have them, then you paid double the price!" In other words, it costs their hosts a small fortune just to entertain them. Their extravagance so enticed Jan and Domin that it was like the blind being led without any notion that there may be an ulterior motive for such generosity. At the time, Anna believed Jan and Domin were so blind-sided by promises of prosperity that she and Jara would eventually be forgotten and left behind in Germany while the other two chased their paper dreams. Ultimately, both 'romantic visionaries' decided to join Jara and Anna instead and continue with them onto Passau, where Jan and Domin still wishfully believed that good would eventuate from their newly found benefactors. Anna was relieved they had come to their senses thus far, but whatever happened afterward would be of their own choosing. It only reaffirmed that she had to finally take charge of her own destiny and not be swayed by the pipe dreams of others without any reality checks.

With about ten additional people attached to their party, they prepared for yet another long walk from Linz onto Passau, a journey of some distance that was anticipated to take them several days. With difficulty, Anna had to tear herself away from the comfort and safety of their barge where for a limited period their tumultuous world was at peace but only long enough until their billeted accommodation expired.

The road to Passau was again walked mainly at night to avoid unnecessary confrontations with those who resented refugees in their country. Although their journey kept them on the west side of the Danube River within the American Zone, many newcomers were not so easily convinced and constantly feared they would be captured and passed on to the Soviets across the river. As a result, everyone kept a low profile during the day, resting as couples in the fields and making themselves as inconspicuous as possible as the days passed. However, their constant companion, as always, was hunger.

Some days later, they arrived at the Austrian-German border town of Passau. Here at Passau border control, migration into Germany was a serious business, and authentic identification papers were a strict requirement of West German protocol. Otherwise, entry could be refused. Anna, like many others, possessed nothing more than her Czech ID card and her birth certificate as ownness of proof.

Once processed, everyone had to be photographed, and their bona fide identification had to be checked by the officials for authentication in exchange for newly prepared documents. Unfortunately, in her fervour, Anna handed over her birth certificate and Czech ID card, which the controller gleefully accepted. It would be the last time she would see her birth certificate.

Despite the queue, Jan, Domin, and Jara were processed in no time, but Anna remained standing and waiting for what she perceived would be her birth certificate and a new pass into Germany. As hours passed and the line shortened, Anna stood firm without any identity. When told to move on out of the way, as the officials were about to close their booths for the day, she refused to budge or let the devious officer out of her sight. She stood her ground and accused him of theft, dishonesty, and unscrupulous behaviour, and under no circumstances was she going to move. She added that she would tag along with him wherever he went if he did not return her original documents. He used the excuse that he no longer had them and that all her papers had been lost. He even argued that she should return tomorrow for a new pass when the next consignment of documents arrived from Belgium.

There was obviously a lack of compunction by many border officials to check that all applicant's papers were honoured and processed in accordance with the displaced person's status unless there was reason to suspect criminal activity. Anna was no different from any other refugee but felt she was being treated like a fool with total disregard for her rights. She was desperate and needed to cross the border on the same day as her companions. She feared the prospect of being detained alone as an anonymous refugee to fight another day for her true identity. Besides, she had little to bargain with now that her only identifications had been seized.

Jan, Domin, and Jara were becoming impatient and concerned by her prolonged absence. It was Domin who returned to see what had delayed Anna. In Domin's presence, Anna once again begged the official to return her original documents. Eager to rid himself of the annoying woman who by now was in tears, and with Domin now abetting Anna's defence in his smattering of angry German, the irritated official hastily issued Anna with a document, albeit on flimsy paper with her photo, which they miraculously found and stamped just to appease her. For this help, she was most grateful to Domin, although unforgiving of herself that her birth certificate was never returned.

They were already late, and the train scheduled for Regensburg was about to leave. Once bordered and seated on the train, a head count was done, and everyone was left in relative comfort for the duration of the journey. It was a civil train trip for once, and at leisure, Anna finally inspected her new document. It had been date stamped appropriately and carried her correct photograph and name, but to her indignation, her date of birth was recorded as 28th August 1918 rather than 25th August 1916. It had been a battle just to acquire an improvised ID, let alone a bona fide document, so from that point on, Anna could do nothing about the discrepancy without arousing suspicion. On that day, by crossing the border into West Germany, Anna was returned two years of her life.

With a differing date of birth now recorded on her new Identity papers, this may have raised questions had Anna ever returned to Czechoslovakia. But as her original birth certificate and ID card had disappeared (probably illegally acquired for want of proof), Anna always maintained that these documents had been stolen from her and probably paved the way on the black market for another woman desperately needing to conceal her true self and past, and who was prepared to pay an unscrupulous black marketeer handsomely to resume her life under a similar identity to Anna's. During such chaotic times, there was no time for forensic investigations!

CHAPTER 12

West Germany: Regensburg – Burg 1948

Under normal circumstances, any such error in Anna's identity would have been a joke or even seen as a deliberate faux pas to suddenly become younger, but not so with her. It confused her self-identity and sense of security as she did not know if and when actual facts would come into question and cause further complications when applying for future documents. Besides, she was not in the habit of concealing or creating untruths about herself.

It was no longer a case of languishing in the vanity of one's former youth but taking on the persona of someone much more experienced and wiser who had to shoulder the responsibility and burden of being whom she had become. Since leaving home, Anna's life had undergone a catharsis of sorts, but her numerous initiations into the real world now left her as a displaced human being, a persona non grata with no real home.

Upon reflection, she was walking a tightrope over a warped space of time into obscurity where nothing seemed predictable anymore. It was now like a journey of distressing proportions, where once it was a dream for a better future. "In the end, I suppose no one really cares how old I am anyway? Nobody is really interested enough to question me. There are too many of us to question, so I must go it alone to wherever I am going! To borrow my dead brother's birth year; I am sure he won't mind!" she sadly reflected.

The distance from Passau to Regensburg was about 120 km, and the train journey was probably one of the most civil trips that they had experienced in a long time. Even though the train to Regensburg was slow, constantly interrupted, and delayed, Anna saw it as a positive journey. It was taking them further away from everything they had fled so far, and into a country once deemed a hostile nation, it was now subservient to the allied forces[1].

When they finally set foot at their destination and lined up with all other new arrivals waiting for formal registration into the refugee camp, the Regensburg Goetheschule (Götteschule)[2], an old school building, the ever-increasing numbers of destitute people continued to swell about them. Anna's new identity papers served her well, and here, nobody questioned their authenticity as she proceeded unhindered. They were informed that they would remain in Regensburg for only three weeks and then be transferred to Burg.

The Goetheschule, originally a school, had wooden floored open classrooms creating a dormitory-style accommodation space. Sleeping arrangements were communal with no segregation of sexes. The mattresses were packed side by side in rows on the floor, and everyone found a spot to sleep next to their meagre possessions. The inside toilet and bathroom facilities were few and often with long queues of impatient inmates needing to use them. Food rations were even more scarce.

Everywhere Anna and her group had been, food shortage was a constant plight confronting them. In the Goetheschule, their rations consisted of a mug of black bitter coffee with a slice of hard black rye bread for breakfast and, twice a day, a serving of soup made of raisins in sweetened water and thickened with a little bit of flour. Anna found the concoction unpalatable and could barely eat it, but she had to be grateful for whatever food came her way. She would have preferred a handful of raisins with a little flour and sugar served separately so they could cook something more digestible with it.

The casserole dish, which Anna so ardently guarded and was carried along with them by Jara Kohut, had hardly served its purpose since Vienna as there had been so little food available to cook with. On rare occasions, after using a few of her fast-dwindling Austrian shillings, Anna bought some mushrooms and a few bones from a butcher and, for her group, enthusiastically made bone-flavoured mushroom soup in the casserole dish. On a good day, if lucky, she even managed to buy Bloodwurst (blood sausage) from the butcher. The downtown baker only sold bread for Austrian shillings. It was the same with everybody who traded with the locals, as they only accepted more desirable currencies other than the local Reichsmark (RM). The overinflated German currency may have been abundant, but it was valueless.

Crowds were huge and forever growing, but there was constant movement in Regensburg. It felt like being caught up in a wave of perpetual human motion driven by energy drawing everyone, as if instinctually, toward some obscure homing beacon. It was constantly buzzing with activity, new arrivals, and those leaving.

Anna made many friends at Regensburg, and each served to reassure the other, a shoulder to lean on and help survive through the hard times. During her stay, Anna helped many to cope with their hardships and bereavements and was always a willing advocate for anyone in distress. She also managed to find ingenious ways to acquire extra food to supplement their meagre food rations. She developed a positive attitude, and nothing was beyond her. Every problem had to have some kind of solution, no matter how inadequate or short-lived the outcome may have been.

In Regensburg, Anna met and befriended Veřa Duchková from a family of doctors in Hodonín (now in Slovakia). She married a Slovak named Dvořáček, who earlier had studied in Switzerland. Veřa Dvořáčeková, as she became known, already had family in San Paolo in Brazil, to where she and her husband were hoping to immigrate.

Veřa told Anna, at that time, that they had amassed a considerable sum of American Dollars but which were confiscated from them upon arriving in West Germany. The authorities assured them that this money would be returned again upon their departure from Germany once their visas for Brazil had been formalized.

Anna's friendship with Veřa continued for some time, but they would eventually lose contact and drift apart once Anna left Germany. Anna never did find out if their money had been restored to them on departure.

One day while still at Regensburg, Veřa informed Anna she had found a cheap butcher shop just down the street, and convinced her to try it out, so Anna went ahead and bought a large salami for Two RM (Reich mark). As she was hungry and craving meat, she immediately sliced off a large portion and began eating it. Glancing up at the Butcher's sign above his shop, she noticed a horse's head on it. Her hunger overruled any desire to throw up, although her stomach squirmed as she remembered the dead horse on her way after visiting Svatobořice Prison, where her parents and sister had once been incarcerated. Nevertheless, the salami tasted good enough to be eaten; besides, she had felt hungry enough to eat a horse! She decided to give the remaining salami to Jan to divide between himself, Domin, and Jara without telling them what it was made from. It had a sweet taste, but at the time, it didn't bother her, nor did it seem to bother the men. They were too starved, and besides, she reasoned, what they didn't know, wouldn't hurt them. On another occasion, Anna made arrangements with a fellow émigré to do his washing in exchange for food. Despite everyone's impoverished state, there was always someone else worse off.

Věra was forever on the lookout for newcomers arriving at the Goetheschule in case someone was known to her and brought news from their home country. Whenever she heard of new arrivals, she immediately summoned Anna, and together, they would rush over to the assembly area and hang about, looking for familiar faces.

Time was fast approaching for Anna and her contingent to prepare for transfer onto Burg in the district of Hessen when Věra announced excitedly that she heard a group of Czechs had just arrived from the western border of Czechoslovakia. Any news of arrivals always raised Anna's hopes that her brother Jaroslav would miraculously appear. So many times, in the past, there had been disappointment after disappointment as arrivals filed past her without any sign of him or anyone else bringing word about her family. Time was now running out, and they were soon due to leave Regensburg. She had not heard from Jaroslav since Pulgary, and it was several months since last seeing him. Given the grievous stories circulating about captured escapees that came with every newcomer, Anna still held hope that Jaroslav would be alive somewhere.

As usual, on such days, Věra and Anna gathered in the assembly area, hoping to catch sight of somebody who might look familiar. On this occasion, Anna spotted a small case in the corner of the room with a familiar tweed coat thrown over it. Her heart leaped, "Could this be

Jaroslav's?" Anna had a similar coat made of the same fabric her family purchased from Valašské Klobuky. Maybe it was just a coincidence, but she could not help but feel hopeful that the case and coat must belong to him.

Anna hung onto her belief, watching the case and coat steadfastly should it suddenly disappear. She pressed Veřa to wait just a little longer in case her brother appeared from inside the office. Both waited patiently until every last person had been registered. It seemed a futile wait, and both were about to return to their quarters when Jaroslav appeared and collected his belongings. He was still recognizable even if his much thinner frame and drawn pale features overshadowed his former self. Anna was so relieved he was alive and unharmed. She had waited so long for this moment as she eagerly called out and rushed toward him. He turned in surprise, and his face suddenly lit up like a child's as he waved back and greeted her.

Without thinking, Anna pleaded, "Which of our sisters did you bring?"

Taken aback as if hurt, he replied, "Aren't you satisfied that I alone made it here alive?"

Anna immediately felt ashamed for being so brash and insensitive at a moment when it was meant to be a joyous reunion. However, it still hurt and haunted her that the rest of her family had remained behind. She knew there would be much to talk about when Jarda (Jaroslav) caught up with Jan, Domin, and Jara.

When they finally assembled together and huddled outside away from everyone, Anna could see her brother was emaciated and starving after his protracted journey, so without further delay, they shared with Jaroslav what little food there was to go around. Their reunion was a momentous moment as they related their tales of abandonment, survival and lucky escapes. More so, everyone was eager to hear about Jaroslav's narrow escape from the communists as he fled Czechoslovakia into Germany. Jaroslav's initial plan to abscond was near the town of Cheb. This came undone when he and his group of about twenty were set upon by Soviet-Czech guards. Jaroslav's group fled in all directions; many were shot, wounded, and captured, while Jaroslav and a few others managed to escape deep into the forest. His planned escape route turned out not as straightforward as he had anticipated, and in hindsight, it was not the most practical or safest way out of the country either, as Jaroslav soon found out.

Although traversing this region should have offered quicker access into Germany due to the border's proximity to the American Zone, the Soviet-Czech guard patrols were concentrated in greater numbers in this area, making it nearly impossible to penetrate the border. Much to the Soviet's frustration, this border with Germany lapped the American Zone, and once escapees were over it, there was very little they could do except shoot them down on sight if caught fleeing.

Dangers remained even once crossing the border, as many escapees could still be fired upon by Czech patrols in the American Zone, which was not always patrolled by allied forces. With only a handful of remaining escapees, most of whom lost everything they had been carrying, Jaroslav fled further south, steering clear of occupied villages and farms and making it into the higher rugged mountains. This densely forested region of Šumava National Park[3], renowned for hiking, was some 65 miles south of Cheb and over 110 km (68 miles) in a direct line east from Regensburg and offered only inhospitable refuge for the escapees. Traversing on foot over precipitous and steep terrain while avoiding detection by enemy patrols and trying to maintain a westerly momentum without a compass proved harrowing without food.

Numerous Soviet-Czech patrols with dogs had occupied areas near the border but kept to the more favourable and popular routes out of Šumava National Park. It became a case of crossing into Germany, where it was least guarded in the less accessible regions. Jaroslav and his diminished party may have survived their ordeal, but it was their determination and fortitude on very spartan energy reserves that eventually brought them to Regensburg.

Outside in the courtyard during numerous late evenings, they would often sit together, discussing and plotting future stages of migration and from there on, Jaroslav became a fixture in their group. The four men were always full of ideas, some outlandish, but each would lead with suggestions and opinions which seemed acceptable amongst them, even if little heed was ever paid to Anna's contribution. Her opinion did not seem to matter. Anna recalled, "Amongst them, there was never a shortage of leaders and ideas!"

One agreement received unanimous approval: they all wanted to immigrate somewhere, but where to was always hotly debated. Jan initially preferred Africa or Australia or even back to the United Kingdom. Jaroslav said he wanted to go to Italy, where he could choose where else to go overseas. Domin was undecided between France or South America, while Jara hoped for Belgium or perhaps even the Belgium Congo in Africa. Whenever Anna mentioned New Zealand as her preferred destination, her brother immediately jumped into the conversation, imploring that she should stop talking nonsense in front of them and choose a country that would have her.

"What would they want with you over there?" He would always sharply rebuke her.

It annoyed and hurt Anna that her brother could be so mean in front of the others and constantly thwart her say in choosing a place to live. After all, New Zealand had been her dream; it kept her hopes alive when there was no other pleasure within her grasp.

They had all been through a lot, but still, Jaroslav could not show brotherly compassion toward his sister and continued to be intolerant of her fanciful ideas. It was always a case he knew better, and she should follow his example. Anna may have forgiven her brother for his faults of intolerance, but nevertheless, she resolved to follow her own intuitions even if it meant in quietude from the others. Only Jara Kohut supported Anna and quietly said she would go where her heart took her. His encouraging words often helped reinforce her belief in herself and take charge of her destiny, and go down a path of her own choosing, making her more determined to prove others wrong, especially her brother.

Their stay in Regensburg was ending, and a few days later, they were all scheduled to leave separately for Burg, a town in northwest Germany near Dillenburg and Herborn in the district of Hessen. Men and women were now segregated, and this time everyone was dispatched onto trains according to family status. First, families with children were bordered and sent, followed by married couples, then single women, and finally single men. Many of Anna's friends had already gone by the time she departed the camp.

The men, including Jan, Jara, Domin, and Jaroslav, followed sometime later onto Burg, leaving on the last transport train out of Regensburg. Jaroslav had caught up with them just in time and, given his unfortunate circumstances, still had managed to rendezvous with everyone as had been loosely planned in Pulgary. This seemed so long ago when they contrived this unpredictable exercise to escape Czechoslovakia.

The train transfer to Burg was long; it took days of being delayed for whatever reasons by lengthy stops and always giving way to daily commuter trains. Most of the train journey was done at night when most rail tracks were freed from regular day traffic. However, sitting on the train for long periods was as bad as standing, and again with these prolonged stops, there was little room to move about to allow adequate blood circulation and avoid swollen feet and back stiffness. Food was scarce as usual, and only second daily rations of Bloodwurst, black rye bread, and water were provided.

Anna's next place of abode was the DP Camp at Burg, known as 'Flüchtlings Lager Burgerhütte'. The site was once an abandoned airfield with standing infrastructure, but after the war and from 1947 until about 1949, it became a refugee camp[4]. From her group, Anna was the first to arrive at Burg, but she soon met up with friends she had recently become acquainted with in Regensburg.

In the milling crowds, differing nationalities and people from all walks of life were crammed into the camp. There were Jewish and political refugees: doctors, lawyers, professors, dentists, milliners, labourers, domestics, teachers, actors, artists, housewives, cooks, administrators, and even titled people. Dr. Hřebík, once chief of the Czechoslovakian National gymnastics team, Mr. Pobucký and his wife, administrator from Prague, Professor Středa and his family, and somewhere in their midst Count Kinsky of Czech nobility. They were all in the same boat and desperate for a positive renewal in life after escaping political persecution. They were all on this journey together and on equal standing as refugees seeking a new future. Despite any previous social status and education, most were people with humanity and humility and availed themselves to help each other, especially those less fortunate.

The Lager, where Anna was to be housed, consisted of two large double-storied iron and steel structures that had once been a part of an iron and steel works. One building was set aside for the Slovaks and the other for the Czechs; every compound had a German camp leader. Each floor of the Lager was split into smaller rooms like pokey storage chambers. This space sometimes accommodated up to nine people and was divvied between families with children, married couples, single men, and single women.

The establishment was ill-equipped for accommodation; the wind would whistle through the gaps in the walls. Even though it covered a vast area, it was once again extremely overcrowded, with each being allocated a small mattress stacked on the floor without any privacy and everyone slept side by side, cramped in with all their possessions.

Earlier in Regensburg, Anna had befriended Mrs. Tušlová and her three daughters, who had been amongst the first to leave Regensburg and arrive at Burg. Anna's strengths and attributes made her visible, appreciated, and endearing to people.

Due to her caring and considerate nature toward people less fortunate, and without exception, Anna always shared and rarely overlooked their needs above her own. She was neither gregarious nor attention-seeking but rather reserved and discreet and always availed herself to be helpful in times of need.

In Burg, it had been initially organized for Anna to be placed with the single women, but while pending her arrival, arrangements by the Tušle family overrode these plans when they offered to accommodate Anna with them, her readymade family. Mrs. Tušlová considered Anna as much a daughter as her own three daughters, Irena, Dagmar, and Milena. Irena, the eldest, was five years younger than Anna, while Dagmar was seven years younger. Their youngest, Milena, had become ill during camp transfers and had to be repatriated to Switzerland for treatment. Mr. Tušle had already made plans for his family to immigrate to Canada and alone had arranged to travel there first before sending for the rest of his family to follow.

The accommodation in the Flüchtlings Lager was very basic, food scarce, and conditions overcrowded, to say the least. However, Anna found security and family companionship with the Tušles, whom she could trust. From there on, the Tušles became Anna's adopted Czech family.

Mr. Mazanec an elderly Czech, had a job as a yardman at the camp and was invited to share the Tušle family abode. As a yardman, he had handy access to timber for the wood-fired 'donkey', a hot water apparatus shaped from a drum that provided bathing and cooking water and warmth for their room. His sleeping arrangements were next to this fired heater so he could keep a close watch and maintain it throughout the blustery cold weather. Like everybody else living in this poky little room, he was rostered weekly to scrub the floors in these shared quarters as a contribution to his keep.

Anna was always amazed by the vast number of children gathered outside in groups, either being taught by women or their mothers or other educated people such as Professor Středa and his wife. It was sad that these children were missing out on proper schooling and instead holed up in camps without childhood socialization or any definite education plans for the future.

Everyone regularly walked to Herborn or Dillenburg looking for work opportunities or searching to buy cheapest food available. Anna met many people in Burg, all struggling to find adequate food. In this camp, Anna experienced some of her hungriest days in living memory.

Some weeks later, when Jan, Domin, Jara, and Jaroslav finally arrived, Anna was already settled into her domestic routine. Although the men were billeted in another section some distance away from Anna's shared accommodation, they still had their meals together, and Anna felt obliged to help them as much as she could.

Jara Kohut, having finally arrived with the casserole dish, it was again deemed almost superfluous to requirement as there was very little to go into the dish for their communal meals. Food here was even more scarce than in Regensburg. The refugees were uninvited guests in Germany at a time when there was so little food available, much less enough to feed the German nation. Nobody seemed to want the local Reich Mark, and on numerous occasions, Domin complained to everyone that it would have been far better if they had remained in Austria. On the other hand, Jan reminded them he experienced far worse in late 1939 when captured in Hungry and imprisoned in Toloncz Haź Budapest[5]. "At least here in Burg," he prompted them; "We are still free people, albeit a little starved."

To make ends meet, everyone tried to contribute something from their efforts, be it work or selling some personal items (often precious or sentimental), so proceeds could put food on the table. Anna found employment for a while as a house cleaner for a Polish Jewess; however, after a few days of hard work, Anna only received black coffee and some bread and little else for her efforts. The woman was pleasant but not particularly keen to pay Anna in money.

They were always hungry, and finding food for everyone was the most challenging task. Women seemed to use more initiative and imagination and were prepared to sell almost anything to put food on the table, whereas the men, if they were not working and earning money, relied more on the women to find a way to be resourceful during this ongoing crisis. However, with little prospect of any food forthcoming for the table, Anna and newly arrived Veřa Morovková, whom Anna befriended, decided to walk into Herborn to sell Veřa's engagement ring. It was a desperate, if not drastic, measure for Veřa as she only received 60 Reich Mark.

Nevertheless, she reminded Anna. "You need money to eat, and you cannot eat diamonds!"

On the spur of the moment, Anna decided to match Veřa and sold her only good boots that she was wearing and which her sister Helena had given her. For this transaction, she received a small bag of potatoes and flour, a loaf of bread, some eggs, and a small portion of sugar and margarine. Anna felt elated, as now she had food for the table. Any long-term consequences of this snap and the foolhardy decision to sell her best foot ware never once crossed her mind. These boots had been her best ware, and good shoes or boots were like gold, especially when it was cold and long distances had to be walked.

However, when hunger sets in, it dictates terms of survival, and there is very little else to do other than find a means to an end to stop the pains of starvation.

Anna had another pair of tattered boots back at the camp, but they were beyond repair, with soles worn through, and the parted sides held together with string. They may have been worthless, but soon would become even more precious. However, for now, Anna had no choice but to walk barefoot back to Burg.

That evening there was plenty of cause for celebration when Anna finally prepared a tasty soup in the well-travelled casserole dish. Jan and Domin immediately wanted to know where she got the money to buy such food. Anna held her silence for a while as they hoed into their meal. Finally, Jara got up and thanked Anna, and left the room. After further questioning from the others, Anna relented and told them she had sold her good boots.

As Anna recalled, "Jan almost had a stroke! Demanding angrily, 'How on earth will you get about barefooted?'"

Jan realized she had done it for everyone but could not accept her selling something as important as her only good boots. Fortunately, that evening her brother Jaroslav was away in Butzbach looking for alternate accommodation, as otherwise, Anna was sure he would have added his sarcastic veneration. Anna soon accepted it had been stupid to sell her boots, but what could she do now? The deed was done, so she had to move on, boots or no boots.

Jan eventually informed Jaroslav about Anna's boots saga, and as expected, Jaroslav chastised Anna for her stupidity. He suggested Anna find two hessian bags and wrap her feet in them to walk about, as otherwise, she would have to sit at home and forsake her walks into Dillenburg and Herborn. Later when asked by others why Anna had not been seen walking about as often, Jara came to her rescue and explained diplomatically she had terrible blisters on her feet, but Domin was more forthcoming with the truth and announced she had sold her boots for food.

Over time, Jan's anger subsided, and on occasions, he too remained at home with her, but whenever they had heated words over something, like the proverbial elephant, he never forgot her boots and was quick to remind her how foolish she had been.

During these complex and often despondent times at Burg, romances flourished, and celebratory occasions filled the otherwise wretched void in people's lives. A young couple, Eliška and Simon, who had met in Czechoslovakia some years before, were Jaroslav's acquaintances and, by chance, were brought together in Burk.

Amidst all the chaos in the Burk refugee camp, they had a whirlwind romance and decided to get married. The wedding was to have no trappings of family fusion but rather an open invitation to all, promising music and some joviality. Their only request was, "bring your own food."

Earlier, Domin had given Anna a small glass bowl he found during one of his walks. As Anna had no use for it, she thought it would make an acceptable gift for the nuptials, but when she searched for it, she discovered it had been hidden because it was broken. Disappointed, she nevertheless went along with the others and enjoyed an evening of traditional music and singing.

Soon afterward, the couple immigrated to France and kept in touch for a while. With so many upheavals in Europe at the time and each trying to create a new life, eventually most people lost contact.

Anna's book 'Zeměpis Člověka' by Jiří Král, which she had borrowed from Jan back in Pulgary, finally became useful. With so much time on their hands and with little to do, many people constantly badgered her to lend it out. A young law student Zdeněk Dobrovský borrowed it, but when Jan found out, he immediately demanded it back. Anna sided with Zdeněk and told him to read it before passing it on to someone else, but Jan would have none of it and accused them of being in cahoots against him.

Regardless, the book proved popular until it finally fell apart as people shared the pages amongst themselves, reading it all simultaneously.

Many people passed through Anna's life while at Burg and were kind and considerate to her. A young man named Ben Wilhardy had a dental clinic in London. His English wife was already in London, but he and his brothers Sam and Frank were caught up in Burg. They were all keen for Anna to immigrate to the UK, suggesting that she would easily gain employment as a domestic, and once she learned English, Ben would employ her as a nurse in his clinic. It all sounded very fanciful and interesting, if not promising, but Anna had her heart set on New Zealand.

One day Ben asked if he could borrow Anna's carry bag as he had some shopping to do in Frankfurt. Upon returning her bag, and as a thank you, he left her several tins of fruit conserve in the bag.

Anna also became friendly with three Jewish sisters; Edit, Margaret, and Judi Löwe (pronounced Levy). The girls had two brothers, Frank and Will. Frank, the eldest, was about 32 years old at the time but quite bald, and during the war, like Jan, had served in the United Kingdom in the Czech army. After the war, Frank returned back to Czechoslovakia to aid the escape of his remaining family members. Their parents had died in Terezin Concentration Camp, but the four younger siblings escaped.

The girls were quite chatty and always keen to give Anna financial advice. They told her, "You must always buy land and property, and if you need to move on, then cash it in for diamonds and gold!"

Anna paid heed to them but decided such advice during overwhelming austerity would hardly benefit her, as any riches were well out of her reach.

Frank Löwe also borrowed Anna's bag numerous times whenever he went shopping and rewarded her with tins of preservatives. Anna was most grateful for this additional food as it was well out of her affordability, but all her hungry friends always appreciated it. Jara Kohut would go out regularly and pick mushrooms from the fields where around Burg they grew in abundance. Anna would fry them with margarine in her casserole dish, thicken the contents with flour and water, and whip up everyone's favourite dish of mushroom soup, just like her mother used to make.

One day Jara Kohut arrived excited and revealed to Anna that he had been granted refugee status in Belgium. He had always wanted to go there and perhaps even venture further abroad onto Belgium Congo (modern-day Zaire) in Africa. Everyone was overjoyed for him and saw the young chap off at the railway station, promising to remain in touch with him. Nobody heard from him after that, but Domin Červenec was soon granted a permit to immigrate to France. He also promised to write, but as with all promises in those days, letters rarely eventuated.

It would be the last time Jan and Jaroslav would see Domin. Anna's group was slowly shrinking; by now, it was down to three of them. Anna always felt a tinge of sadness with departures, but it always heartened her to see friends go onto new, safe havens to restart their lives. While Anna contemplated her future, she heard Jan telling Jaroslav that the Czechs he had met while in Linz were still waiting to be granted visas into Argentina.

Anna felt a pang of satisfaction and wanted to shout, "See, I told you they weren't genuine!" But, instead, she kept silent.

During this time, Jan had written to the British War Office for assistance in immigrating to the UK and directed his application to Col. Alois Liška[6] who was now residing in London. He had been Jan's commanding officer during the war and always supported his troops. Jan received a prompt reply from Liška informing him he had personally delivered Jan's letter to the Home Office. Jan received his visa approval in no time and, by the 27th of July of that year, was issued a temporary pass in Wiesbaden to depart Germany.

Anna's brother Jaroslav was still away trying to organize his own immigration papers when Jan received the good news. He decided to wait for Jaroslav to return, as Jan wanted to personally farewell him before departing. Finally, Jan was ready to leave Burg for Frankfurt and journey west to England.

At this time, Ben and Frank Wilhardy were also travelling to Frankfurt on business, but as their brother Sam decided to remain in Burg, they offered Anna the spare return train pass. She accepted it gratefully and headed off to Frankfurt with Jan and Jaroslav. On farewelling Jan, Anna thanked him for his help and for looking out for her over the past months. He seemed genuinely taken by her gesture and replied that they would no doubt catch up again somewhere. This gesture Anna took with a grain of salt as she did by now with most farewells. She had realized there was so much tumultuous unpredictability during this stage of their lives that many paths would never cross again. Jan and Jaroslav shook hands, acknowledging their good luck in as much that everything they had contrived so far had gone in accordance with most of their plans.

When Anna returned to Burg from Frankfurt, she was met by Mrs. Tušlova, who presented her with a pair of large boots. Jan had left them behind for her, but it was on the proviso that she exchanged them for food again. Jan had confided in Mrs. Tušlova, saying he was not game to give them personally to Anna as she would have hurled them at him. In no time, Anna proceeded onto Dillenburg and did as was agreed by the terms of his bequest and bought food and soap. Besides, the boots had been far too large for her, and to exchange them for smaller boots of similar quality was near impossible, so with plenty of soap, Anna joined Veřka Morovková down on the river and, for the first time in months, gave all their clothes a proper scrubbing.

With plenty of soap, Anna even offered to wash her brother's clothes when he next visited from Butzbach. After Jan's departure, Jaroslav often called by for a meal, and being the only two remaining from their group, they even managed to maintain a civil countenance toward one another.

Throughout their stay in Germany, Jaroslav had kept in touch with Pepik (Josef) Chmelař, who earlier had immigrated to Kenya and was now working for Baťa Shoes in Nairobi[7]. Pepik agreed to help Jaroslav with his immigration, but firstly Jaroslav would need to immigrate to England, and from there, he could apply to continue onto Kenya.

Over time, Pepik became helpful in keeping many in touch. He was a great correspondent and maintained contact with many people he met throughout his stay in Germany, and if anyone needed to find someone's whereabouts, he was the man to go to.

Some weeks after Jan's departure, Jaroslav arrived from Butzbach on a visit and informed Anna he finally had transport arranged for Italy and that she should also come along. Jaroslav always managed to infuriate Anna with plans to suit his needs. He wanted her to return with him to Butzbach, some forty-five kilometres away, but Anna stood her ground and refused, as she was not about to jump to his tune each time he whistled.

After talking it through with her, in the end, Anna decided to appease him and agreed that if nothing else eventuated for her after he applied to immigrate to England or Kenya, she might reconsider it.

Jaroslav returned to Butzbach without his sister and began planning his departure.

Shortly afterward, Ben, Frank, and Sam Wilhardy left for London and passed onto Anna anything they could not take along with them. They were convinced Anna would follow on not long afterward. Many who left for new destinations, like Anna's friend Růženka, wrote disheartening letters afterward, dispelling any myth of how great life had become. If anything, it was never positive news, but rather how difficult life was and how hard it was to earn money to make a living. Although survival for many had become easier, everything cost so much more, and so little could be afforded.

Earlier on the 20th of June, within the western occupied Zone of Germany, the Reich Mark was finally replaced by the new Deutsch Mark (DM) to overcome the black marketing of goods. Not until the new German Mark (DM), was introduced did German currency finally gain value[8]. Everyone was eventually given 40 DM in exchange for the now-useless Reich Mark, and another 20 DM was later allocated. This was good news for Anna and everyone else who remained in Germany. They had real money with value, but still, it was so little to survive on for any length of time.

In Burg at the time, Anna and her inmates were not recognized as Displaced Persons (DP). This initially only applied to the Lithuanians, Estonians, and Latvians, so the following good news was that Anna and everyone else in all refugee camps were to be taken over by IRO (International Refugee Organization)[9] and moved on out of Burg. As usual, there was much speculation about where they would end up while families were being organized for onward transportation. Again, those with children went first, followed by married couples, single women, and, lastly, single men. By now, Anna was the only one remaining from her original group, and, for that matter, not only in Burg but the whole of Germany. Her companions had all left and set out on their own journeys into the world.

About to be separated from the last of her friends and with no further need for her large cooking pot, which had accompanied Anna since Vienna, she finally parted with it and presented the heavy and cumbersome casserole dish to Mrs. Tušlova and her family when they departed Burg by train.

Ten days later, in early September, Anna was summoned into the Flüchtlings Lager Burgerhütte office, and Mr. Pobucký informed her that she too would be finally departing; destination Ludwigsburg.

Photograph 106 & 107: (L-R) Anna & brother Jaroslav in Burg 1948.
Veřa Morovková in Burg 1948.

Photograph 108: Anna and her brother Jaroslav Kurovec in Burg, Germany, 1948.

Photograph 109: Anna, Jaroslav Kurovec & Veřka Morovková in Burg Germany 1948.

Photograph 110: Flüchtlingslager Burgerhütte Burg 1948: Anna's friends Karel, Veřka & Bravoš.

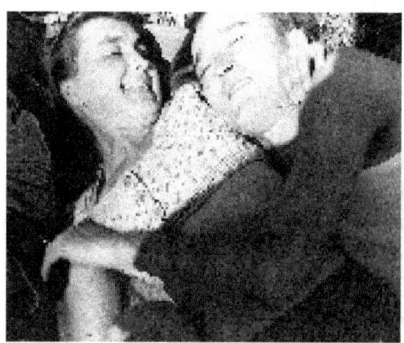 

Photograph 111 & 112: (L-R) Young Love: Veřka Morovková and husband Vlada in Burg, Germany 1948. With a friend, Veřka Morovková and husband Vlada on left, a day in the sun, Burg, Germany 1948.

CHAPTER 13

Ludwigsburg: 1948-1949

It was common practice to remove all seating on refugee transportation trains to fill the wagons to capacity. Everyone had to stand side by side, cramped together like sardines. The journey of nearly 300 km was a slow and painful process, almost an unbearable quest of human fortitude. The train would again stop, allowing faster commuter trains to pass, and it was more often held up for seemingly no apparent reason. Regular trains always had priority over all the refugee transportation being dispatched to and from various Camps. Being caught up in congested rail traffic during the day could keep everyone standing for hours, waiting for these scheduled trains to pass through. The refugee trains often remained stationary at railway stations for hours while others came and went.

Due to this lengthy transportation process, people crouching or standing in such confined spaces would suffer painfully swollen feet and legs as nobody was allowed off the train while being transported except for designated toilet stops. Long hours turned into days of insufferable endurance as, again, most of the travelling was done by night when rail lines were freed up from regular goods and passenger services.

Food was scarce as usual, and unless it had been brought along on departure, there was very little available on board, and to beg or barter for it with little or no money left many starving.

When finally arriving at their destination nearly a week later, everyone disembarked at Ludwigsburg railway station and late that evening filed down the road staggering toward 'Jägerhofkaserne,' or Jägerhof refugee barracks[1]. Three camps in the area probably accommodated close to two thousand people. Anna was hungry, weary, and personally conscious of her stale sweaty, and foul odour as she proceeded with her belongings on aching and swollen feet. Anna recalled that her feet looked like two fluid-filled buckets and felt rubbery as she plodded along.

At the barracks, Anna was overwhelmed to see so many familiar faces from Burg eagerly awaiting her. Mrs. Tušlova even pre-arranged Anna's rationed blanket, mattress, and stretcher; everything was ready and laid out for her in their clean and tidy room. Again, Anna felt immensely grateful but was divided when she realized the Pobucký family had also arranged for her to stay with them. Although Anna was immensely fond of everyone, Mrs. Tušlova and her girls suited her best.

Exhausted after such a long journey, she bathed and promptly fell into a deep sleep for the first time in over a week. She slept all night, the following day, and again the following night. When Anna finally awoke, she did not recognize herself! Her face was beyond recognition. She was covered in a spotted red and angry rash from tip to toe! Mrs. Tušlová immediately called for the camp doctor, who diagnosed Anna with a severe case of bedbug bites. Many who had arrived at Jägerhof Barracks before them had also suffered the same. It was a constant curse for everyone when new arrivals from overcrowded sources due to poor hygiene brought along these infestations. The doctor prescribed Anna DDT powder (an organochlorine $C_{14}H_9Cl_5$) which was widely used as an insecticide after the war. It is now a banned substance due to its severe long-term side effects. Anna was instructed to sprinkle the powder all over her bed and was further prescribed an oral substance which she ingested dissolved in water.

Mrs. Tušlová had a very practical approach to such matters and ordered everyone to air their bedding while the floors were thoroughly disinfected and scrubbed. From then on, every week, their sleeping quarters were cleared out, and floors scrubbed until the bedbug plague was eventually exterminated without further reoccurrence for the duration of their stay. Anna's unfortunate bedbug incident captured the attention of an aspiring young artist Mr. Teichmann, a camp lodger who sketched a comic caricature of Anna sleeping while being bombarded by parachuting bugs. He gave Anna the drawing, but over time it was unfortunately lost.

Living conditions from then onward improved significantly with better access to food. Whatever rations came their way, these were always appreciated and accepted gratefully with outstretched hands. As always, Anna was keen to find paid employment, but most approved positions within IRO were retained indefinitely unless people moved on or were sacked for obvious reasons. Nepotism seemed endemic as positions were often passed on to those known to the employee, so it was often a lengthy waiting game for the rare opportunity of paid work within the organization.

Living with the Tušle family, Anna was always keen to help and often remained to room-sit their possessions whenever the family went out. At first, Anna did not venture far, but on selective occasions, she would accompany the Tušle family into town. By now, Mr. Tušle had departed alone for Canada to pave the way for his wife and family to follow on as soon as possible.

One day Mr. Pobucký visited Anna and asked if she could assist his wife. He explained he would not be able to pay her but would give her extra food rations instead. Anna gladly jumped at the opportunity; at long last, she could contribute extra toward the household meals.

A short time afterward, Professor Středa called in on Anna and asked if she could cook. Anna never admitted to being a cook but implied she would be happy to try anything to secure employment. He told her he found a position as an assistant cook in the children's kitchen, where she would be responsible for around 150 children. She would be in charge of two younger female assistants, but above all, she would receive from the IRO, suitable clothes, cigarettes, and money for her work. She allowed herself no time to think or become overwhelmed by the number of mouths her cooking would feed, as it was too good an opportunity to forfeit. Anna accepted the position without hesitation as by then, she was down to her last few remaining pfennigs.

Mr. Pobucký and Professor Středa, amongst others, acted as refugee advocates and on behalf of them liaised with the IRO administrators and assisted many people with job applications and the processing of immigration requests. Hence, it was fortunate for Anna that they considered her sufficiently capable for the kitchen job.

The following day, her camp leader took Anna to the children's kitchen and introduced her to a well-rounded and formidable Polish cook and her two young Polish assistants. The Polish cook took an instant dislike to Anna, but the camp leader sensing the woman's disdain, immediately warned her that if she as so much laid a hand on Anna, she would be instantly dismissed and taken to the police. The Polish cook had been instructed to teach Anna the ropes, and in return, Anna was to record a list of all her duties and how to go about them. Anna felt somewhat relieved that she had backup, but it did not clear the air after the camp leader departed. Instead, the old woman became verbally abusive and cursed Anna in Polish, which she, fortunately, did not completely understand. Obviously, the stubborn old woman was not about to share with Anna any kitchen knowledge which would grant her the job so readily. Besides, Anna was terrified of the cook and preferred to follow the routine and make notes from a distance rather than have the woman hovering about her.

The next day, two new assistants, Marie and Božena, arrived with the camp leader, and Anna was informed that the two previous girls were being replaced. She was also advised that the Polish cook would soon be leaving, and if Anna could cook for the children, she would step up to the job of chief cook. Anna was delighted, if not daunted, by the prospect of all the responsibility. She later learned from Mrs. Pobucká why the Polish cook had been dismissed so quickly. Evidently, the Polish woman strongly opposed all Czechs and took a knife to one of the Czech girls, making the terrified assistant flee from her workplace.

Anna's two new assistants Božena and Marie were Czech and efficient workers. Božena had been a schoolteacher and was now placed in charge of peeling potatoes and preparing all the vegetables. Once a hotel owner, Marie was experienced and understood the running of a large kitchen but happily worked as Anna's subordinate and assisted with whatever tasks were at hand. All women needed employment and money, so they were glad for the jobs offered.

On many occasions, Anna felt inadequate by her lack of training, as those around her seemed better qualified for the job, and many times, when things went awfully wrong in the kitchen, everyone rallied behind her. Even Mr. Pobucký, with his administrative background, would come to the rescue and lend a hand.

There were three kitchens at Jägerhof, each with its own cook and staff. The head kitchen was for adults, the next for children, and the third for infants, where in the latter, preferred knowledge and experience in milk and food preparations for infants was needed.

Anna's job consisted of long hours beginning at 4:30 am, by which time the night watchman would have the water boiler on and all the stoves lit, ready for Anna to commence cooking. On arrival, Anna would collect their daily allocation of milk and bread delivered overnight, and before any kitchen staff arrived, she would prepare the porridge and coffee. After a short break, lunch had to be prepared, and after that, for the next two hours, Anna would take her break before resuming with the children's evening meal. She was consistently on the go, but the money was more than adequate for a woman in her circumstances, and she could now contribute to her host family's budget.

It was during this time that Anna seriously took up smoking. Before that, she would only have an occasional puff on someone else's cigarette, but now that she received a steady supply of her own cigarettes, she had plenty to share with others. Initially, the stress of work would be alleviated by an occasional cigarette. Still, in the end, like with all smokers, the habit grew, and she became a habitual smoker throughout her time as head cook in the children's kitchen.

Many people crossed paths with Anna throughout her journey, all destined for somewhere in the world but it did not stop friendships forming for however briefly.

Once while sitting in the courtyard during her two-hour break, a youth strolled by and started talking to her. Anna had noticed him looking her way a few times before but thought little of it. On the day he ultimately gained enough courage to approach Anna and ask her politely, "Were you ever in Mikulov in early Autumn of 1947?"

Taken by surprise, Anna thought momentarily, before replying that she may have been there but was puzzled where this conversation was leading. The youth then smiled broadly and elaborated, "But there were two of you on that day in the restaurant. What happened to the other girl?"

It suddenly dawned on Anna, that it was on the occasion when she and her sister Helena had visited Lidice and later had gone onto Mikulov to take tea. He spoke for a while and told Anna he was waiting to go to Canada, where he had relatives. "Such a small world, isn't it? And so many of us hoping and waiting to go somewhere!"

At Jägerhof, a large hall had been reserved for entertainment. Here concerts, plays, and various recitals by local artists were held, amongst which were some well-known Czech performers. One Czech stand-up comic of the time from Prague was Jara Kohut (not to be confused with Jan's friend from Pulgary), who presented regular comedy skits.

Dr. Jiří Král, who wrote 'Zeměpis Clověka,' also gave recitals. Anna would have loved him to autograph Jan's book, which she had coveted some months before, but sadly, it was now in tatters with loose pages and some missing due to popular demand. Besides, Anna felt too embarrassed even to approach him, let alone ask him to sign what remained of the book in such appalling condition. She also desperately wanted to ask him if he had ever been to New Zealand. When she later spoke with Professor Středa and told him she had listened to this author speaking and wished she had been introduced, Professor Středa told her she should have come to him at the time. He would have gladly introduced her. Unfortunately, Dr. Jiří Král left soon afterward for America.

For Anna and many fellow Czechs, the most moving performance of the evening was when two instrumentalists, one with a guitar and another with a saxophone, played one of their national tunes, 'Čechy Krásné Čechy' (Czech Beautiful Czech). It brought tears as homesickness griped and overwhelmed everyone with emotion; they sang together, remembering their homeland. For Anna, it was reminiscent of the 1940s Czech film 'To byl Český Musikant' (There was once a Czech Musician), a war drama directed by Vladimír Slavínský. Anna paused and thought about her parents and family and wondered how they were all coping under Soviet-backed Communism. Bits of information about Czechoslovakia would occasionally filter through from someone recently arrived. It never seemed good news, but nonetheless, it was news.

In June of 1948, President Beneš resigned after citing that a totalitarian regime would never work in Czechoslovakia. Pity he had not realized earlier that he had been used and hoodwinked by the Soviets. After failing to address the Nation publicly, Beneš disappeared amidst fuelled speculation that he was being restrained somewhere against his will. Klement Gottwald, previously General Secretary and Chairman of the Czech Communist Party, became President on the 8th of June 1948 with the total backing and approval from the Soviet Communists. Groomed and following Soviet Ideology, Gottwald believed the country's political system and Military forces had to be purged of western thinkers and re-educated, and if resisting, then removed from office and rehabilitated in Labour Camps.

It wasn't only those in power; all Czechs had to embrace Communism. Despite his harsh approach, Gottwald was a moderate compared to his Soviet Communist counterparts and advisers that Starlin had vested into the Czechoslovak government. It was fast becoming evident that even the communists themselves were not entirely above scrutiny. Many deemed too ambitious or unpopular with Starlin, and a consequential threat to the Polit Bureau were dispensed with from their government jobs and many of them not heard from again.

Anna also heard churches were being attacked, with worship and attendance restricted. Education was now to be taught along Marxist lines, with cultural and intellectual life re-organized to suit their doctrine. Industry, commerce, and transport were nationalized, with the Communists purging the system of any anti-Communist subversives, who were either sent to prison or labour camps. How fortuitous that Jan and her brother had foreseen this coming, as by now, both could be in labour camps doing their penance. Anna felt despondent and helpless, but she had chosen to leave. While she, her brother, Jan, and many others succeeded in escaping, just as many failed, creating new dilemmas for the Czech government to overcome. Her arch-enemy, the Soviet-backed Czech Communists, for the time being, remained at arm's length from her.

The Jägerhofkaserne inmates had access to a chapel, and Anna often went there to pray. While there, one day, Anna met Mrs. Krapačová, an elder lady from her camp who had a string of children of varying ages fed simultaneously by the three Jägerhof kitchens. This woman so much reminded Anna of Josef Gerla's wife, Aunt Tynka, who sometimes looked after them when they were children. Tynka had been the daughter of Granny Zuzaňakova, but Anna's mother, Rosalie, always referred to Tynka as Zużka; and so, Anna began referring to her new acquaintance as Granny Krapačová. At the chapel, for no apparent reason, Granny Krapačová began telling Anna how difficult life was with children at Jägerhofkaserne. From there onward, Anna would sit and listen to her woes whenever they met at the chapel.

One day she asked Anna if there was any possibility of getting a job for her in the kitchen. Anna was hardly in a position to give anyone a job but feeling sorry for her, she promised to keep a lookout in case a vacancy occurred at work, and if so, Granny Krapačová would be the first to hear of it. Anna told Mr. Pobucký about the woman and her plight. Instead of receiving a sympathetic hearing, he became vexed with her for discussing such matters and promising future employment to strangers. He reminded her he was not in the position to employ so-called acquaintances regardless of their situation. Anna felt annoyed with his apparent lack of compassion, but there was little she could do.

Jägerhofkaserne employed a chimneysweep who regularly cleaned the kitchens' chimneys, stoves, and boilers. He was also an escapee from beyond the border and lamented how everything they once owned was left behind and he and his wife would have to start all over again. His woes rested on Anna's sympathetic ears as almost everyone else she knew at the Kaserne would empathize with him as they, too, had lost their livelihood and home, a symptom of the times. The Chimneysweep and his wife were not housed at Jägerhof but lived elsewhere beyond the city parameters. For his work at the Kaserne, he was not being paid at the time but instead received coffee and food from the kitchen, which he appreciated as it was costly to buy food in Germany.

On his following visit to the camp, his demeanour had improved, and after work, he invited Anna to meet up with him and his wife whenever time was suitable. The following Sunday afternoon, it was agreed that Anna, with Mrs. Tušlová, would meet with the couple in the local park. They were a decent couple, and although not Czech, they spoke the language fluently, and all enjoyed one another's company.

Like a good Samaritan, Anna would have brought them to Jägerhofkaserne if she had her way, but this was disallowed. Instead, they all met regularly in the park, and while exchanging family accounts, Anna learned they had lost both sons during the war.

In the end, their plight got the better of Anna, and once again, she approached Mr. Pobucký and told him where and with whom she and Mrs. Tušlova had been spending their free Sunday afternoons. Once again, Anna was met with hostility and given a lengthy reprimand.

"What do you think you are doing? Sticking your nose in amongst the Germans and running some sort of a refugee ring! You would be better to keep out of it all, as you may well jeopardize your own chances of immigration if this ever gets out!"

Anna felt disheartened, but even Mrs. Pobucká warned that any adverse behaviour, no matter how well-intentioned, could go against her application for refugee asylum, so it was best to get over it, and all would soon be forgotten.

During this time, a lot of foreign aid and food were being pumped into Europe, and countries like Australia contributed their share toward the needy cause. The IRO distributed this food into its various camps, and on one occasion, Anna's children's kitchen received 50 kg of Australian honey. It was beautifully presented in colourfully decorated tins with bees and an idyllic Australian scene depicting gum trees and grazing sheep. The tins were stamped 'Foreign Aid not for sale.' The empty tins were equally desirable even compared to the honey which was like liquid gold. Božena, the kitchen hand had the tins, once empty, earmarked for herself, and Anna encouraged her to take the empty tins home as they took up too much needless space in the kitchen pantry. However, Božena refused as she feared someone would steal the decorative tins from her abode, so the empty containers remained stacked away in a corner.

With so much honey at their disposal, many administrators believed it should all be dispensed to the children immediately, while others believed differently. For Anna, it did not matter which opinion proved right, either way, this portion of honey designated to her children's kitchen would be somehow distributed equally amongst them, and it was up to Anna and her kitchen staff to devise how to do it. Anna only needed a suitable means of giving every child its share of honey. Given out all at once would only give the children a short, if not intense, sugar hit, and once it was all gone, there would not be anything left afterward for treats.

It was well into Autumn and already becoming cooler when the chimneysweep returned on his bicycle to carry out his regular cleaning.

Unbeknownst to Anna, on his way to work he left her a large bag of apples in Mrs. Tušlova's kitchen. When Anna returned home that evening, Mrs. Tušlová was flustered, fearing they would all be accused of stealing apples. At the very best, she could only cook a few of them without raising too much suspicion, but to cook them all would create alarm, and soon questions would be asked. After some deliberation, it was decided to immediately peel and slice the fruit and take it into the children's kitchen so that at the earliest opportunity the fruit would be ready to be made into an apple compote. However, the children's kitchen had insufficient sugar for such a large quantity of apples to make the fruit palatable, but they did have honey.

In the end, Anna pleaded with the head kitchen to supply her with additional flour and yeast as she told them she was about to cook something special for the children. Whether Mr. Pobucký knew about the apples is debatable. Still, when he heard dumplings were on the menu for the children, utilizing some of the recently acquired honey, he helped by sourcing an old sheet on which the dumplings would be placed and steamed over a large pot of boiling water. Anna washed the old sheet several times before starting her epic mission. The aim was to steam 400 dumplings, each filled with apple compote. It was no mean task, so with her voluntary kitchen helpers; Božena and Marie, Anna was up at 3 am to start on their dumpling project. The steamed apple dumplings were further smeared in butter and honey and delighted the children as they hoed into them. The children so appreciated them that by popular demand, Anna had to promise to make them again. Even Mr. Pobucký was taken in by Anna's cooking prowess when he tasted her dumplings. Although Anna humbly admitted to using her mother's old yeast recipe, she pointed out that the dumplings were nowhere near as good as her mother's.

News arrived that Edvard Beneš, Czech Ex-President, died on the 3rd of September 1948. After hearing earlier reports that he had disappeared from politics, it was reassuring that his death announcement had finally been made. It was a sad reflection on a man who tried his best to save Czechoslovakia but made poor choices by dealing with the devil incarnate. He may have disliked the Germans with a passion, but it would be the Soviets who would be his final undoing. For Anna, it was no longer a case of who was at the helm of her country as she was aware that whoever it was, they would only be a puppet of Soviet intervention, as Czechoslovakia was rapidly turning into a Soviet satellite state.

Sometime during the latter part of October 1948, Jägerhof Kaserne received an unexpected visitor, a United Nations Commission on Human Rights representative. At the time, Anna was still working in the children's kitchen when she was presented to Mrs. Eleanor Roosevelt. Eleanor Roosevelt was once the longest-serving First Lady of America until her husband, President Franklin D Roosevelt, died in 1945. From then onward, Mrs. Roosevelt devoted her life to Human Rights issues and was an ardent campaigner for Women's Rights.

Anna remembered her introduction vividly when this rather tall and statuesque woman, perhaps once handsome rather than attractive, extended her petite white-gloved hand to Anna. Anna was asked through an interpreter if there was anything she needed.

Never one to be lost for words, Anna replied, "I need nothing, but many here are very cold, and some extra blankets would be good."

A few weeks later, bundles of new blankets arrived.

Professor Středa arrived one day to hand Anna her pay and paused to discuss something. He told her he had a problem in the baby kitchen as their head cook had become ill and had to be hospitalized. Professor Středa offered Anna the position. Anna drove her end of the bargain and told him only on the condition that she maintained her afternoons off and that he gets someone to replace her in the children's kitchen. She could not possibly do both jobs with so much preparation required before meals. She had over 150 children, and there were as many infants again, under the age of two years, to be catered for in the baby kitchen. Before he had too much time to think about it, Anna quickly offered him a solution. She knew of a suitable candidate who would fit the cooking job in the children's kitchen. Finally, Granny Krapačová got her job.

Granny's kitchen was always immaculately kept, and whenever she finished her work, she would voluntarily go to the baby kitchen and help Anna to complete with cleaning up after the meals.

All kitchens were out of bounds to others at Jägerhof, except to the IRO staff, such as those employed in the kitchen or recruited to do certain maintenance. The IRO health inspectors were exceptionally particular about hygiene and stock accountability, and once a week, they would carry out a full audit and inspection. Although everyone in the camp envied the kitchen employees, nobody paused to think about the amount of work involved and all the early morning starts that were a part of their daily routine. The pay may have been enviable, with certain personal perks included, but those in kitchens worked hard for small rewards.

The International Refugee Organization (IRO) provided many clothing items for the refugees through Red Cross. Shoes, dresses, socks, long-sleeved thermal singlets, trousers, skirts and blouses, shirts, sweaters, and raincoats. Many may have been second-hand goods from America, but all were in immaculate order and exceptionally well made. Anna and Mrs. Tušlová would send any excess clothing that was allocated to them, to the chimneysweep's wife which was always gratefully accepted.

Boots that needed mending, Mrs. Tušlová soon sourced another bootmaker downtown upon the advice of the chimneysweep, as the poor Jägerhof man was so inundated with shoe repairs. There was never any guarantee within the camp that boots delivered for repairs would ever be recovered again, as repair kits and replacement leather was regularly unavailable. Eventually, most of these boots and shoes were lost.

Over the weeks, Anna's face became a familiar and much-loved fixture in the baby kitchen as parents with infants were always met by her at the window as she delved out baby rations. She always tried to give the littlest and most vulnerable a little extra sugar where ever possible. While working in the kitchen, many remembered Anna by name. She hardly knew these people as they were numbered in thousands, and all she could ever recall was their faces as they presented with babes in arms at the kitchen window.

One day, quite unexpectedly, Veřka Morovková turned up on a visit, and on that afternoon, she and Anna decided to go to Stuttgart, some 15 km away. They had been friends in Regensburg and Burg when in desperation, Veřka had sold her engagement ring for food. It always played on Anna's conscience that she could do such an admirable thing, so she let Veřka choose a gold band to replace her ring, and Anna paid for the gift. Veřka was delighted with Anna's gesture but added that her husband could always buy her another diamond ring when they arrived to Brazil.

Mrs. Tušlova and Veřka always got on well and were interested in fortune-tellers. Anna never believed in such predictions, nor did she ever want to know what would happen in the future.

She always said, "Let it be, and meet your future when it comes to you."

On this occasion, Mrs. Tušlova knew of a woman who was quite reputable with card reading, so she invited her over. Anna shied away from the visiting clairvoyant, but when their session was over, they convinced Anna to partake. At first, Anna resisted, but soon the woman was looking at her and dealing out the cards on the table.

"You will soon travel over the ocean, but before you depart, you will receive very sad news, and there will also be death. Someone close to you and you will shed a lot of tears. After you leave here and travel overseas, you will become gravely ill and nearly die..."

Anna couldn't bear to hear anymore, so she got up and left the room. She never believed in such hocus-pocus or believed that for one minute, this woman had any idea about her life.

Shortly afterward, Mr. Pobucký called Anna aside because he had something important to share.

He had a concerned look on his face, and Anna's heart sank as she thought, "Oh no! Is it about Jaroslav? Is he dead?"

She was near tears with worry as she had not heard from him in months. When Mr. Pobucký asked if she knew anything about honey going missing from the children's kitchen, she felt instantly relieved but similarly confused about his line of questioning. He added solemnly that somebody in town had illegally sold 20kg of Australian honey. When the culprit had been apprehended and questioned, to absolve himself from blame, he said he had been given the honey from someone in the Jägerhofkaserne kitchen. Mr. Pobucký further informed Anna that it had now become a police matter, but he was only ordered to collect any evidence before everyone was formally questioned. Anna suddenly realized she was under suspicion and informed him she knew nothing of it. At the time, she and only the girls, Božena and Marie, held the keys to the kitchen, and when off duty, these keys were always kept in Anna's room. Anna was not in the habit of keeping tabs on every skerrick of food used but had to go with Mr. Pobucký to inspect the kitchen and exclude any possibility of her being involved. Her kitchen had been allocated only 50kg of honey, and she had to prove beyond reasonable doubt that every kilo was accounted for. As they counted the tins and tallied up the score, Anna was exonerated from any crime and felt forever indebted to Bozena for keeping all the empty tins safely hidden in the kitchen rather than taking them home as she had suggested.

One day quite by chance in Ludwigsburg, just shortly before December, Anna crossed paths with Vladimír Pavlik from Krhová. She was shocked to see him but equally relieved if not excited that she had finally found someone from her neighbourhood in Moravia. Vladimír and his brother Robert had been well acquainted with Anna's grandfather Jan Stolař, and although she never formally spoke to either of the Pavlik men, she recognized them by sight. Robert had become a professional soldier, and Vladimír chose a career in the Diplomatic Corps.

On this occasion, Vladimír approached Anna first and initiated the conversation. Like everyone else who escaped Czechoslovakia upon the onset of Communism, he was in no man's land, unsure of his future. He did not have any news from home but, for a price, managed to make contact with his wife, Leila, who was still there. Although he had been posted to Belgium in the past, Leila had been separated from him on this occasion and, for some reason, had been caught up at home in Czechoslovakia. Vladimír was in a brief financial bind, and Anna offered to help, giving him 700 Deutsch Mark from her savings.

"What use is money otherwise, if a life now depends on it?" Anna added. Vladimir thanked her and promised to repay her when Leila was delivered safely over the border.

War did many strange things to people, but in so many cases, it became an equalizer in society; those who started with something ended up the same as those who started out with nothing.

At Jägerhofkaserne, Anna promised something special for the children during the Christmas festive season. The cooks put their heads together for suggestions to create a special occasion for Christmas Eve. Once again, the chimneysweep arrived to do his task in the kitchen and arrived again with yet another bag of apples. Much to her relief, he told Anna that this would be the last of the fruit as winter was approaching. Grateful for fresh fruit but once again conscious of possible implications, Anna paid him this time with her own money. He was pleased and promised to deliver some poppy seeds to garnish her baking. Anna was quite excited at the prospect of fresh poppy seeds but soon discovered that instead, he meant a flat and hard poppy seed cake and not loose seeds like those she was used to at home. However, moistening the flat poppy cake in milk with additional sugar made it palatable enough but hardly usable for sprinkling onto baked food, as Anna had hoped.

Anna's Christmas Eve cooking endeavour again became a major exercise, but this time she was offered the head kitchen as their production base. It was decided to make 'Vánočka,' a yeast-based dough flavoured with whatever fruit was available, in this case, apples, and baked into small rolls. It was planned that every child would receive one for Christmas.

Once again, with all hands-on deck, the primary baking task started in the early hours at about 3 am. After the dough was prepared and allowed to rise, the production line began. Božena scooped out a portion of the dough. Marie cut it into six thin lengths, and Anna inserted a scoop of fruit between the dough and platted the six pieces into a roll while Granny Krapačová basted the rolls with egg and sugar. After a short rest so the dough could rise again, each loaded flat tray was placed into the hot oven to be baked. This process went on for hours until, once again, some four hundred Vánočka rolls were baked. That morning, a pleasing aroma filtered from the kitchen throughout Jägerhofkaserne. For the enthusiastic cooks, there was no time to rest as breakfast had to be prepared, followed by lunch before the children's Christmas Eve party.

That evening the hall was decorated with a Christmas tree adorned with hundreds of red crosses, one for each child, together with a small gift, some dry sugared fruit, and a Vánočka roll. The look on the children's faces profoundly affected Anna and the kitchen staff as each child stared in wonderment at the tree and food. Anna was moved when so many children wanted to give her their gifts. She received various fun toys from them, but Peter, a little boy with his grubby but cute face and congenital leg deformity, pulled at Anna's heartstrings the most. He gave her his wooden soldier without legs and as it had just been washed, he told her he had wrapped it up especially for her. Another child gave Anna her doll, minus an arm. Anna was overwhelmed with such thoughtfulness from the children as these spartan toys, for most were all they had to play with.

While the children busied themselves with their treats, Anna returned the toys to their respective mothers, knowing they would fully appreciate them. Monika, a young girl of about four years, presented Anna with her small dog on a lead. Monika was often seen walking her fond pet around the camp, so it was heartfelt to be given such a gift. For a while, Anna was speechless as she had no idea where she would keep this poor flea-ridden pup. When Mrs. Tušlova came to inspect him, she rolled her eyes disapprovingly as it could not possibly live with them. In the past, they had their own fair share of vermin and certainly did not need fleas. Sensing an awkward situation, Mrs. Pobucká came up with an immediate solution. She found a red neck tie for the pup and attached a note for Monika, "I miss you so much. I want to come home." Someone informed them that Monika lived next to the Post Office and offered to deliver the pup back to her home. No one seemed more happier than Monika and her puppy to be reunited again!

Through the children's simple but heart-warming and sharing gestures, all the hard work in the kitchen had paid off. Preparation for the party was Anna's and her staff's gift to the children, and it was made all the more worthwhile and memorable when the children's faces showed genuine pleasure for so little.

It had been a long day when Anna walked into Ludwigsburg on Christmas Eve to attend midnight mass. She attended the Catholic Church of the Most Holy Trinity and sitting inside on her pew, she felt insignificant in its huge vestibule. With profound sadness and loneliness, she thought about her mother, grandparents, and sisters. It was Anna's first Christmas away from her family and without any news of them, she felt exceptionally sad and isolated. She was afraid to write telling them where she was, as there was always the fear of repercussions should her letters be intercepted and connected to her escape. She at least had hoped for news from her brother, but at the time nothing was forth coming.

After midnight the Czechs in town began to play music and sing melancholic national songs. It again brought tears to Anna as she pushed aside any joyous thoughts and joined in their sorrows, remembering her home, her loved ones, and those who were no longer here.

After church, a few friends, including Veřka, her husband Vlada, and Anna, were invited to Mr. and Mrs. Pobucký's place for coffee. Here, they all exchanged small gifts, and somebody with a camera took a photo of them. From the Pobucký family, Anna received a dressing gown, pyjamas, slippers, and a hairbrush. She was most grateful for these thoughtful gestures, but it was news of her family that she wished for the most. Even a small note from her brother Jaroslav would have sufficed.

During her Christmas melancholia, Anna was beginning to have grave regrets for not having gone with her brother to Italy, and then England, or even Kenya. As she reflected on her past year, it was already Christmas morning, and too late to go to bed.

Anna went straight to the kitchen to clean up after last night and begin preparations for the children's breakfast and all the meals for the coming day. She was totally exhausted by the time she arrived for her afternoon break.

The Tušle family was waiting for Anna, and although well past their lunch, they were eager to share the Christmas meal with her, regardless of how meagre it was. Anna had not eaten all day and could barely keep her eyes open, but nevertheless, she stayed up and joined them for a while. They gave her two letters; one from her friend Eliška in France and the other from Jan Kaňák in England. From France, Eliška, her Czech friend wrote of disturbing news of unrest in Valašské Mezirici, where many people were arrested and imprisoned for antigovernment petitions. Still, there was no mention of anyone Anna knew. Jan, on the other hand, wished her season greetings and, in his letter, gave some news of himself. He had already been in England for close on five months and, much to Anna's surprise, told her he was quite versed with her life in Ludwigsburg. He frequented a Czech Club in London, and many who had arrived from Ludwigsburg knew of her, and although she probably knew none of them, he, regardless, had plenty of news about her.

New Year's Eve of 1948 arrived, but with it very little snowfall. It had not been as cold as expected. Anna spent another sad and lonely evening in church praying for her family and contemplating her future. She still had no news about her application to immigrate to New Zealand, nor had she any news of home or her brother Jaroslav. All she had was her work and friends here, who still, nevertheless made her life worthwhile; otherwise, her own world remained in limbo.

Professor Středa was aware that Anna had set her heart on New Zealand and, on many occasions, reminded her that, according to his sources, New Zealand was not as yet taking in refugees. He told her not to despair but also not to set her heart only on the one country as there were other places in the world where she could immigrate to.

However, in February of 1949, Professor Středa came to see Anna again with promising news; New Zealand was finally accepting refugees but had already made a large recruitment from Austria and was only taking a few from each camp in Germany. He discouraged Anna from raising her hopes too high as there were so many people for them to choose from. In Jägerhofkaserne alone, there were close to two thousand people waiting for visa approvals. In the end, Professor Středa concluded that he would apply on her behalf and wait and see what happens.

Finally, only fifteen names from Jägerhofkaserne were forwarded to the New Zealand Consulate in Frankfurt, and only ten would eventually be selected; three women and seven men. Anna was over the moon when she learned her name was on the pending list of fifteen, but even more ecstatic when she finally learned she was one of the ten approved. She felt that, at long last, the sun was shining on her with God's blessing. She also heard she would be leaving within the next two months. Finally, her life was beginning to show promise of moving forward in a direction that could only have happened in her wildest dreams. Everyone was happy for her and congratulated her on her near-to-impossible dream.

From there on, there was so much preparatory work ahead of her departure that Anna decided to resign within the month and teach someone else the task of cooking in the children's kitchen. All those who had potential ability were not prepared to take over from her, and each expressed an excuse. They had seen Anna work, and she left big shoes to fill. Her kitchen hands Maria and Božena both shied away from the responsibility and did not want to get up early in the morning even if their pay would have been much better. All of a sudden, nobody wanted to work and earn money!

Some even said, "Why work when everything is freely provided at Jägerhof?"

Mrs. Tušlová's daughter Irena even turned the job down. Eventually, Mrs. Tušlová came to the rescue and took over Anna's post.

During Anna's last week at work, a melancholy overcame her as she realized how much she really enjoyed working in the kitchen. Everyone began telling her how much she would be missed. People started leaving notes of appreciation, and even the chimneysweep and his family wrote and thanked her for everything she had done for them.

Now that she was free from work, Mr. Pobucký encouraged Anna to travel and enjoy a little of Germany's countryside. She often travelled with Irena, Dagmar, or Mrs. Tušlová and visited places like Wiesbaden, Darmstadt, and Karlsruhe. One particular trip that remained imprinted in Anna's memory was when she and Dagmar went to Stuttgart to do some shopping. On their return to Ludwigsburg, Irena, Dagmar's sister, awaited them excitedly at the railway station and informed Anna she had a visitor waiting for her at home. Anna was expecting it to be Jaroslav, her brother, but to her surprise, it was Domin Červenec from France.

He greeted her with his usual "Hello, Sis!" and explained that Jan had written and informed him that she was still in Ludwigsburg.

Anna was delighted with his visit, and Mrs. Tušlová immediately invited him to stay with them, which he gratefully accepted. Anna was very fond of Domin, even perhaps 'in love' with him, but he always seemed to maintain a brotherly affection toward her and whether or not he sensed her interest, he never let on. They had many long talks, and he was delighted she was finally going to New Zealand. He hoped they would always keep in touch and reassured Anna he never doubted she would achieve her dream in the end.

As for himself, he told Anna he felt drawn toward Australia or America as France did not prove particularly desirable in the end. Mrs. Tušlová advised him that Canada would be the best place for him, but he was his own man and not easily swayed by well-intentioned suggestions. Domin stayed for a few days, and each afternoon he and Anna would walk together into the town square to sit and talk about their aspirations in life. One afternoon he confided in Anna, telling her he had something to do before he immigrated abroad. He recalled the incident in Pulgary when they were not paid for a consignment of wine. He told Anna he had been in touch by letter with the hotel proprietor, who promised to meet him close to the border town of Cheb, some 350km east of Ludwigsburg, and deliver the money. Anna felt uneasy about the plan and shared her ominous feeling about it all, and pleaded with Domin to forget about this money and move on. Domin could not be swayed.

As Anna was no longer committed to work, she could freely travel. However, when Domin suggested she join him on his trip to Cheb, Anna feared the prospect of being so close to the Czech border. She declined because she had a prearranged trip to Baden-Baden with the Pobucký family and Irena Tušlová, which was true. Anna begged him again not to go and to forget the so-called-owed money as he could do well without it. Instead, she invited him to join her on the planned excursion to Baden-Baden. She even offered Domin her Deutsch Marks, but he was always too proud and reminded her that in the past she had always paid for everything, like when she sold her boots in Burg and added that he could no longer remain dependent on others to continually help him. No amount of coercing from Anna could draw him away from his objective. It was as if fate was dragging him back to his home border.

A week later, Anna received the tragic news that Domin had been shot close to the border near Cheb.

Anna was heartbroken and wept for him, "Why take a man's life when you already have taken his money?"

She had loved him, but time did not allow this love to flourish. It was a fate preordained, and there was no escaping or turning back from it. Was it an orchestrated payback for escaping from Pulgary? Anna alone had to move on from this tragedy.

Many German towns held Spring Festivals during March and April.

Anna and her friends attended such Spring Festivals or Frühlingsfest in Stuttgart and again in Ludwigsburg. It was time for some light-hearted entertainment, to taste traditional foods and indulge in ice cream.

Sometime after Domin's death, while Anna was attending these festivities in downtown Ludwigsburg, someone came to her and said people beyond the gates wanted her. Anna felt afraid and cautious, being so soon after Domin's death, but was pleasantly surprised when she recognized Vladimír Pavlik and with him an unknown woman. Anna had not really expected to see him again, as life in Germany was one continuous revolving door of people; one day here, and the next thing gone forever. However, Vladimír wanted to settle his debt with Anna, return the loan she had so graciously given him, and introduce his wife, Leila.

Anna had never met Leila before but was more eager to hear news from home. Vladimír detailed recent events about his brother Robert and added he had been imprisoned for ten years with hard labour. It was a bitter outcome for a man who served his country during the war with the British Army and was now deemed an enemy of the state because he did not comply with or uphold communist principles. But worse still Leila informed Anna, Helena too (Anna's sister), was in prison. Anna paled in shock as the unfortunate account unfolded.

In late September of 1948, Helena had been caught with four other young women possessing anti-communist propaganda leaflets, and each was charged in Olomouc and sentenced to prison. Helena received five years, while the older girls received even lengthier sentences. Leila also elaborated that she heard Helena was being tortured while in prison. Anna was devastated.

"Why didn't she come away with me when I asked her to?"

Anna was inconsolable. Anna's friend Eliška from France had earlier relayed that there had been unrest in Valašské Meziříčí. Still, for one minute, Anna never suspected that it involved any of her family or friends. Even though Anna had to carry this troubled news for many years, only afterward would she learn from her sister Helena that she was never tortured by anyone while in prison. Regardless, imprisonment was still a deprivation her sister had to endure.

Life in Czechoslovakia under President Clement Gottwald's

Communist Party was anything but democratic. While Starlin let the Czech Communists know that it was, he who was now in charge of their country, it was still his chosen Soviet advisors who oversaw the running of Czechoslovakia. In time Gottwald's moderate communism would keep abreast with Starlin's methodology of purging the country of anti-communists. Eventually, they would begin to purge their own Communist party.

For many who were devoted to Starlin and the Party, suspicion, jealousy, and revengeful hatred with prefabricated lies would see many senior Czech Communists removed. In most cases, within party politics, fear, paranoia, accusations of collaborating with western spies and future threats to leadership resulted in revengeful dismissal and even execution. This fear and paranoia not only rested with the Communist Party but also with people at large as their democratic freedoms became eroded, followed by indiscriminate executions on allegations that were often baseless. Starlin held no sympathy for them, although he knew many innocent people would be implicated and executed in order to purge the system of nonconformists[2].

Anna was caught between a rock and the deep blue yonder. She could not return back home, only to end like Domin. Nor could she write, as it would only add complications and possible harm to her family. So close yet so far, Anna could do nothing from this side of the border except pray for them. So, with a heavy heart, Anna prepared for her departure from Germany.

Anna travelled to Wiesbaden, and on the 29th of April 1949, she received her official transit document from Germany to New Zealand. By departure time, Anna had spent over seven months employed by the IRO at Ludwigsburg. During her stay, she had become sufficiently proficient in German to understand the basic language and to get by with shopping in town.

On the day Anna departed, she received a rousing farewell at Ludwigsburg railway station. She could not hold back tears as she was leaving behind genuine friends. Friendships established under such austere times were precious and irreplaceable, needless to say, the goodbyes were heart-wrenching. Everybody promising to write and keep in touch as they wished her a safe journey and a happy new start in New Zealand.

From Ludwigsburg, Anna's train journey would be long but in relative comfort compared to all her earlier transportations from camp to camp. She travelled south through Stuttgart, back into Austria, and onto Innsbruck within the friendly occupational Allied Zones. She passed through the Alpine region via the Brenner Pass and into Italy, passing Trento and Verona. (Today, the Brenner Pass between Austria and Italy is an impressive tunnel carrying trains and a dual highway for cars.) [3]

During the day, the Alpine scenery was devastatingly beautiful, with snow-capped peaks and deep valleys. She had almost forgotten how beautiful the world really was outside of the refugee camps.

From Verona, the train continued south eastward onto Bologna, Rimini, and Senigallia, where during a lengthy pause, everyone had to remain on board and not allowed to alight from the train. They were informed there had been delays at the New Zealand camp in Ancona, so all new arrivals were being stalled from entering.

While in Senigallia, Anna peered from her rail carriage window and was enthralled with the view of the ocean. It was her very first glimpse of such a vast body of water. It may have only been the Adriatic Sea, but the sight was beyond imagination compared to anything she had encountered before. The ocean's vastness and blue hue was mesmerizing as her homeland was a country landlocked, with only rivers and lakes making up the waterways.

The next day they arrived at the coastal town of Ancona, their temporary destination for the time being. Having travelled over 700 km, Anna was already feeling weary, but it was a new and exciting start for her, and she was beginning to savour her newly found lease of life.

With her new acquaintances, Lida and daughter Miluška, they walked toward their New Zealand camp when they met a woman who remembered Anna from Burg. The woman told them that after she and her husband had left Burg, they were moved onto a camp in Fulda, a city in Hessen northwest of Frankfurt, where they were to wait for their passage onto Venezuela. In the end, nothing came of it, so now they were waiting to go to Australia. Anna did not remember this woman or husband while stationed in Burg, but on meeting them, like with all refugees, they immediately struck up a friendship and were invited to their new acquaintance's place for a meal.

The woman told them that while waiting for their passage onto Australia, her husband worked in a downtown hotel frequented by Americans. As he always paid them special attention, he was rewarded with generous gratuities and often certain goods unavailable to others. Anna, Lida, and Miluška were treated to the best fried bacon sandwich Anna had ever tasted.

During her brief stay in Ancona, Anna began inquiring about her brother amongst the arrivals from Butzbach, who since last year had been waiting at the camp. Nobody seemed to know Jaroslav Kurovec, but Anna persevered with her search and gave strangers her and her brother's name if, by chance, somebody should come across him. Anna just wanted to know that he was well and pass on that she was finally on her way to New Zealand.

Nobody in the camp had much idea about what was going on or when the next stage of their journey would begin. Some even suggested a further month could be spent waiting before setting sail. However, on the following day, it was announced that preparations were being made for all those travelling to New Zealand, and Anna was called up for her medical check, X-ray, and inoculations. It would be yet another lengthy train journey as Anna's group headed away from the coast, westward and inland, onto Turin, where they were to be housed in a transit camp. Nobody for the duration of their stay was allowed outside of the IRO Turin Transit Camp.

Before departing Turin, Anna received a congratulatory telegram from her brother Jaroslav. He was alive, and she was over the moon! It read he was at DP (Displaced Person) camp at Bagnoli near Roma but left no other information or forwarding contact address. Nevertheless, Anna was relieved her brother was alive even though she had no idea what plans he had made or where in the world he was going. She hung onto his telegram for many years, but it was lost somewhere in her later travels.

Anna's final leg of their train journey from Turin toward the Port of Trieste was travelled throughout the night. Again, it was another long and tiring trip of some 480 km, which eventually transited through the coastal town of Monfalcone, where on the 20th of May 1949, Anna received her visa and proceeded onto the Port of Trieste.

It was the beginning of a beautiful European Spring that Anna would fondly recall. "The Italian weather was already beginning to warm with so many plants in full bloom."

After a brief introductory message from a New Zealand Consulate representative, none of which Anna understood, she was now truly alone. Ready to leave Europe with hundreds of strangers and embark on a journey of her life time, after which Anna would have to take full responsibility for all her decisions.

It was a surreal moment for Anna on that Friday, the 20th of May 1949, when she finally began her walk up the gangplank toward the 'Dundalk Bay.' Her eyes remained focused only on the grand ship ahead, not daring for one moment to look back in case her mirage evaporated and disappeared in front of her.

The 'Dundalk Bay,' majestically marking time in the Harbour, was finally ready to begin her long sea voyage onto New Zealand [4].

Photograph 113 & 114: (L-R) Emi Tomasova Ludwigsburg. Mr. & Mrs. Tušle Ludwigsburg 1948.

Photograph 115 & 116: (L-R) Irena Tušlová with Murmir 1948. Irena, Mrs. Tušlová & Dagmar 1948.

Photograph 117 & 118: (L-R) Murmir in Ludwigsburg 1948. Dagmar with Murmir & her sister Irena 1948.

Photograph 119: Christmas get-together 1948; Back row; Tušlové girls; Irena & Dagmar, Vladimír & Veřka, Mr. Pobucký & Anna.

A Tree Without Branches: Anna's Journey

Photograph 120: The Krapačov Family; Mrs. Krapačová even tried to matchmake Joe Vejt with Anna after the family immigrated to America sometime in the early 1950s.

Photograph 121 & 122: (L-R) Olomouc paper announcing Helena's prison sentence circa Sept 1948. Postcard of Butzbach circa 1948.

Photograph 123 & 124: (L-R) Circa 1949 New Year postcard from the International Refugee Organization. Tušle Family; Irena, family friend Murmir, Dagmar and Mrs. Tušlová in Ludwigsburg 1949.

Photograph 125 & 126: (L-R) Ludwigsburg Spring Festival 1949, left Mrs. Tušle, Murmir, Dagmar, Irena, Anna & Veřka Morovková. Veřka Morovková and Anna eating ice cream at Ludwigsburg Spring Festival 1949.

Photograph 127: Near Krabbenloch Kaserne Ludwigsburg in 1949; from left Mr.& Mrs. Tušle, Anna, Irena, Dagmar and Murmir.

Photograph 128: Irena & Dagmar Tušlové at Krabbenloch Kaserne Ludwigsburg 1949.

Photograph 129: Anna second on left with Tušle Family near Krabbenloch Kaserne Ludwigsburg 1949.

Photograph 130: Anna second on left with the Tušle Family and Murmir in Ludwigsburg 1949.

Photograph 131 & 132: (L-R) Postcard of Senigallia beach promenade circa 1949. Postcard of 15th century Duke's Fortress in Senigallia circa 1949.

Photograph 133: Anna on left with friends at IRO Transit Camp in Turin, Italy, in late May 1949.

Photograph 134: The 'Dundalk Bay,' which transported 932 passengers to New Zealand in May 1949.

Anna Kurovcova's alien registration application for New Zealand granted in the American Zone of Germany 1949.

CHAPTER 14
Hošťálková: Jan Kaňák's Journey

*"According to the grace of God which is given unto me,
as a wise master builder, I have laid the foundation,
and another buildeth thereon.
But let every man take heed how he buildeth thereupon."*

Corinthians, Chapter 3, Verse 10

CHAPTER 14.1

Family Life

Hošťálková is a small Wallachian village[1] within the Hostýn Hills about 10km west of Vsetin in eastern Moravia. Overlooking this picturesque landscape stands its highest peak, Maruška, of some 664m.

Since the mid-13th century, this countryside had passed through differing nobility families. Still, it was not until the 16th century that arable land was developed for Wallachian colonization's expanding and growing population. As these people were mainly of peasant stock migrating from the eastern neighbouring countries, notably Romania, they brought arable grazing of sheep, goats, and cows.

The region became an independent estate by 1678, with Julius Karel Podstatský of Prusoinovice as the new landlord. By 1707 a manor house was constructed with additional developments; a pub, brewery, distillery, and timber mills, followed by a school in 1769 and a Catholic Church in 1798.

As a result of the Revolutionary Wallachian movement and the Patent of Tolerance issued in 1781 by Emperor Joseph II of the Hapsburg Monarchy, a Church of Protestant faith was finally allowed in 1831. This edict led to the additional recognition and practices of Lutheran, Calvinism, and Serbian Orthodox worship rather than only Catholicism. Control was maintained by printing the Edict pamphlets only in German. However, most of the population it targeted did not understand German. By 1918 the Lutheran and Calvinist churches would unite as the Evangelical Church of Czech Brethren (ECCB).

During 1834, much of the country except in the valley around Hošťálková was less desirable for intensive agriculture, so timber became the chief industry. Timber was transported by wagons to Jablůnka and then onto the Bečva River, from where it was distributed throughout Moravia.

By 1842 a chateau was erected by Count Frydrych Chorynský of Ledská, managing his estate with its prime source of agriculture being subsistence farming, grazing, and timber. Today, the village has evolved with a population of about 2,200 people. The town has progressed with modern development in industries of carbon steel, alloy, stainless-steel production, and leather works. It is also a popular skiing destination for local tourists during winter.

Jan Kaňák's ancestral history is sketchy, but his family tree can be traced to the mid-1800s when his grandfather Martin Kaňák married Anna Hrubřova. Jan's father, also named Jan, was born on the 10th of October 1886, and in 1910 on the 27th of July, he married Anna Kutějová, born on the 12th of February 1884. Their first child Rosálie was born on the 1st of January 1911, followed by Anna on the 14th of October 1912, Jan on the 14th of December 1914, Marie on the 26th of July 1916, Jana on the 7th of August 1921, and finally Josef on the 16th of January 1924. By the 12th of February 1924, young Josef contracted pneumonia and passed away. At the time, Jan was only ten years old, but little is known about how this ordeal affected him, except that he now remained an only son with foreseeable pressure of becoming the breadwinner to help with his two younger sisters.

His father, Jan Kaňák Snr., sustained his family by working in the lumber industry, cutting timber for the local mill. Sometimes during this period, Jan's father had an accident, and judging by his stance in old photographs, his right leg had been amputated. This brought additional hardship to an already struggling family, but with it came despondency and a penchant for alcohol. Jan often reflected on his father's drunkenness and lack of money left to feed the family, but somehow, they managed with what they grew at home and produce from the domestic animals they raised.

Later photographs show Jan's father as an elderly willowy man with a moustache and always smoking a pipe but standing tall despite his disability. His appearance always seemed dishevelled but he remained a strong presence within the family.

Not much was spoken of Jan's formative years except that he left school at about fifteen. Although his end-of-year school report card described him as satisfactory in lessons, his strength lay in drawing, calligraphy, singing, and manual arts. At the time, there seemed no prospect of further education.

All the while, life had not been easy for his mother, so as soon as he finished school, Jan took on labour work and, for the next six years, worked around the village and helped build his family home, replacing the rather old dilapidated wooden dwelling he had been brought up in.

After leaving school without any possibility of further education, Jan's two older sisters found work and eventually married. His eldest sister Rosálie moved away from home and in this case Jan's elder sister Anna, began married life sharing the family home living on the upper floors of the newly built two-storied house.

By 1935 his two younger sisters, Marie and Jana, were fourteen and eleven years old, respectively. They had all been a close-knit family, but Jan was affected by his father's habitual drinking and associated behaviour, so much that he resolved to move on and find his own road to separate himself from this anguish.

One thing that would always remain instilled from his upbringing; was never to drink alcohol in excess, nor smoke and gamble with money that was the only means to place food on the family table.

If Jan had any sweethearts during this time, little has been disclosed, although there had been a lass named Milada who may have been deemed a potential suitor. For whatever reason, Jan showed no interest in her, so after the war, when her name was raised again, he chose to ignore the lure and move on.

In 1935 aged twenty-one, Jan left his home village of Hošťálková and joined the Czech army in Vsetin.

Photograph 135: Jan's old Hošťálková family farm painting circa the 1970s commissioned by Bo Kurovcová for the Kaňák family by artist unknown.

Photograph 136: Village of Hošťálková postcard circa 1943.

Photograph 137 & 138: (L-R) Hošťálková No. 125 Jan's family home with his mother Anna Kaňákova at the front. The family home in later years.

Photograph 139 & 140: (L-R) Jan's mother, Anna Kaňákova, Aunt Adámková, & Aunt Kutějová 1940s. Jan's sister Maria Palová in later years.

Photograph 141: Jan & Anna Sypták, (Jan Kaňák's sister & brother-in-law) with their daughters Draha & Lenka in Hošťálková.

Jan's school leaving certificate 1929.

CHAPTER 14.2

Jan's Brief Czech Military Career

Jan Kaňák (F-3502)[1] began his career in the Czechoslovak army. As with most enlisted men of the time, it ended abruptly on the 14th of March 1939, when Adolf Hitler invaded Czechoslovakia and disbanded the Czech Army. Upon German invasion a few military skirmishes occurred near the border due to delayed communication with their Czech Military headquarters; one in particular at Čajánek's barracks in Frýdek-Místek [2] and another possibly at Moravská Třebová; but these seemed to be the only known resistance encounters by the Czech Army against German forces during WWII.

Jan's exact whereabouts at the time of disbandment are not fully known. Still, during this time, it is suspected he may have joined the earlier Partisans, who at the time were small groups of resistance fighters disrupting and boycotting public transport and creating skirmishes with German police forces. Their Nationalistic bearing would become more relevant as WWII progressed[3].

Whether Jan was disarmed at the time of the Czech Army being disbanded, or if he escaped with firearms is uncertain. However, after being demobbed, Jan did return to Hošťálková briefly to visit his family and his old dog Lumpa before he disappeared into obscurity amidst the looming uncertainty of Nazi occupation.

As Germany's stronghold over Czechoslovakia gathered, any opportunity to weaken this pernicious Nazi grip was a partisan's ethos to uphold. Jan was determined to fight for his country but to do so in Czechoslovakia could only be achieved by belonging to the Partisan movement, which, if caught, exposed him as nothing more than a terrorist, and ultimately the penalty would be execution. Jan, at the time

Book One: Anna's Story

kept well distanced from his family during Partisan subversive activities to safeguard them from any untoward blame.

Over the months, German presence increased daily with soldiers marching through the countryside. In their wake, terrified villagers hid to avoid confrontation whenever their homes were entered and burnt in search of Partisans or suspected collaborators. Jan's family was never far from the numerous skirmishes in the hills around Hošťálková as exchanged gunfire between the Partisans and German soldiers echoed down the valley. Once the family was holed up in the cellar and watched in silent terror as German feet marched past them on the outside footpath visible through the small outside gap from the cellar beneath the home.

Jan's only solution was to escape Czechoslovakia, reach Europe, enlist in France or England, and join Allied Forces to fight Hitler's Germany. Jan was not alone in this struggle, and many like him wanted to reach Europe and join in the fight.

The next twelve months were uncertain and dangerous times for Jan and his cohorts as they planned to flee through guarded borders of German-held territories before negotiating an escape route through the Balkans. During this period, there was already a huge outpour of Jewish families together with disenfranchised Czech, Slovakian, and Polish soldiers escaping eastward through Hungry and Jugoslavia in order to gain access to the west. The well-oiled machine of resistance fighters and sympathizers was already in motion, collaborating with embassies and assisting many persecuted people in mobilizing and reaching their objectives. But like any illegal underground organization, with it came severe recrimination if suspected and, worse yet, if caught.

The Resistance network was only as effective and operational as it was secure until infiltrated by enemy spies, double agents, betraying those of trust. However, despite numerous organizational cells willing to assist, too many innocent people beyond the network's capability were still being rounded up (especially if they were Jewish, Romany, or political traitors) and transported to concentration camps for involuntary labour or execution..

Many fleeing Czechoslovaks captured by the Hungarians were often assisted by these underground volunteers and eventually able to make their escape through the Balkan Route onto the Hungarian-Yugoslav border[4]. Upon reaching the Drava River border, further assistance would be arranged with crossing the swollen and heavily patrolled river enabling escapees to reach Barca and other towns. Here many would not necessarily be held prisoners by the Yugoslav government, which at the time had little sympathy for the Nazi war machine but instead allowed to be furnished with identity papers and travel permits to continue on their journey toward the Middle East.

With the aid of these brave humanitarian souls, Jan's aim was to cross the border into Hungry and head toward the Drava River separating Hungry from Yugoslavia, in hope these Resistance supporters would facilitate him with onward passage through the Balkans.

Jan's first escape from Czechoslovakia aimed to reach Budapest in Hungry failed, and he was captured by Hungarians still sympathetic to Hitler. He and others were imprisoned at 'Toloncz Haź,' a harsh state security penitentiary on Mosonyi Street in Budapest[5]. Here, Jan was interrogated and held captive with other partisans and would-be warriors. Toloncz Haź was a notorious, filthy, overcrowded prison of criminals, petty thieves, and prostitutes who were tortured and beaten into submission. Unspeakable punishments were carried out, like inflicting nasty bites to the soles of inmates' feet and other body parts that were not always visible but left prisoners with excruciating pain from infected wounds. Jan later recalled the blood-curdling screams of women as the guards dealt with them.

Prisoners were photographed, fingerprinted, and details undoubtedly forwarded to Gestapo headquarters. Jan and fellow Partisans were not dealt punishment in prison, but instead these captured inmates would be returned to the Slovakian border and handed over to the Gestapo to be dealt with.

It would have been about mid-April of 1940 when Jan's imminent transportation from Toloncz Haź back to the Czechoslovakian border had been scheduled. Shortly before this appointed date, Jan was met by a Catholic priest at the prison. The priest did not disclose any other purpose for being there except to avail himself to the prisoners as any Priest would. Not being of the Catholic faith, Jan tried to excuse himself because he was a Protestant, but nevertheless, the Priest persisted and initiated the conversation about Jan's plight. The priest quietly informed Jan that an escape was being prepared to coincide with the next transportation out of prison.

"Before you arrive at the Slovakian border, your transport truck will briefly stop. You must all get out quickly, run and disappear. From there on, you are on your own, and if you are caught again, I or anyone else here cannot help you anymore. So, go, my son, may you have a safe journey."

The Partisan's spy network was well entrenched inside the Hungarian bureaucracy, infiltrating the prison system and other higher echelons of organizational modus operandi. Organized escape plans and routes were constantly arranged by these groups, who saw it their duty to set free and help as many as possible from persecution by the Nazis.

The transport driver was most probably a member of the Resistance network. While employed as a Hungarian prison warden, he was supposed to deliver the captured defectors to the border and hand them over to the Germans. It was a plan with a short-lived time span, but while it lasted, it spared the lives of many young men. After doing his final delivery of prisoners to the border, the driver, before coming under suspicion would too eventually disappear and abandon the truck somewhere in the forest.

Jan's eventual escape from Toloncz Haź Prison took an unexpected turn. Unbeknown to Jan, the Catholic Priest himself was departing just prior to the next transportation of prisoners to the Slovakian border. The priest, at his own request, was allowed two inmates to accompany him as assistants. The Priest chose Jan Kaňák, a non-Catholic, and one other, and together, they left Toloncz Haź and travelled out of Budapest. Jan's journey to freedom would ultimately take him toward the heavily guarded Yugoslav border along the Drava River.

German and Hungarian security forces were already well entrenched along the border and any escapees they failed to detain, would occasionally be observed being apprehended by Yugoslav police with the hope that the fugitives would not be granted entry but rather returned back over the border. The Yugoslavs were fully aware of how Germany treated captured fugitives, so people on the run were often removed from view of the Germans and released. In the end, the Germans had little idea who was being held captive and who wasn't.

Until 1940, most of these fugitives were generally free to transit Yugoslavia onto Greece, Syria, Persia, and Lebanon, where they would join the ranks of the French Legion [6] and be dispatched to fight in France, North Africa, or where ever else these able-bodied volunteers were needed. For the time being, the Balkan route was the most reliable and safest means of escape that was within the control of the freedom fighters, but it could suddenly fold if infiltrated by enemy agents.

At the time, most people in Yugoslavia were more than ready to assist as their country had not yet entered the war. The Serbs were helpful, whereas the Croatians, on the other hand, were generally known to return many of these runaways back to Hungry. All that would change after the April War of 1941, when Yugoslavia would be conquered by the Axis forces of Germany, Italy, Hungary, and Bulgaria and dragged into capitulation [7].

Jan's Balkan escape route eventually led him much the same way, to the Yugoslav border and then over the swollen and swift Drava River onto Zagreb and Beograd (Belgrade), where travel documents were organized before catching the train onto the Middle East.

This train journey would have taken some eight or nine days as it traversed Greece through Salonika into Türkiye and across the Bosporus at Istanbul and via Ankara onto Aleppo in Syria, and finally Beirut in Lebanon, where French garrisons were stationed. With the advent of the French Mandate for Syria and Lebanon 1923-1946 (a type of League of Nations Mandate founded after WWI), it was possible to pass into these countries relatively unhindered [8].

In October of 1939, France and Czechoslovakia signed a Treaty of Cooperation. The 1st Czechoslovak Infantry Division was already formed by January 1940, so French Military garrisons in Beirut were well prepared to sign on the influx of soldiers offering themselves to fight along with the French.

In Hungary, due to numerous interruptions with prearranged prisoner deportations back into Slovakia, the Germans soon began to suspect that many prisoners were escaping. Their primary concern was that these trained Czech soldiers would find their way to Great Britain and Russia and fight against them in Europe. In retaliation, Hitler's henchmen began to scour Czechoslovakia with a vengeance, searching for these truants and failing there, then redirecting their revenge onto their families.

During Jan's brief stay in Beirut, while awaiting transportation, he enjoyed some favourable military hospitality and, like any visitor, even had time to sightsee.

In early May 1940, the soldiers finally bordered the Mariette Pacha*, a luxury steam liner. They were dispatched for Europe over the Mediterranean via Haifa and Alexandria and onto the French port of Marseilles.

*During her final days by 1942, the 'Marietta Pasha' was moored in Sète, France, and eventually moved onto Port Le Bouc and then Marseilles, where, for a while, her crew refused to abandon her. Finally, in 1944, the Germans scuttled her in Marseilles.

Photograph 142 & 143: (L-R) Jan Kaňák in Czech Army 1935-1939. Jan during his Partisan Days 1939.

Photograph 144: Jan as a tourist camel riding in Beirut Lebanon, in early May 1940.

CHAPTER 14.3

France: A Short but Bitter Fight

Along with the contingent of recruits from Beirut, Jan arrived in Marseilles on Monday, the 13th of May 1940. At the time, Marseilles was the biggest functioning port in any German unoccupied Zone. The city was steadily swelling with an exodus of refugees, many of whom were escaping from other German-occupied Zones into southern France. All were seeking assistance, safe houses, and means of escape either for personal safety or to seek active fighting outside of France. It was like a city within a city; one element carried on as usual, with its shipping business, and the other, a city full of activity, processing, and dispersing into the world, its overwhelming influx of new arrivals.

Marseilles would later become known as 'the first Capital of the Resistance' by Victor Serge, a Russian Revolutionary, Marxist, novelist, poet, and historian, whom himself would eventually escape from Marseilles to live out his life in Mexico[1].

Paris, some 775km to the north, had been in denial that the war would affect her. The Parisians had already once before prepared for war in September of 1939 when France and the United Kingdom declared war on Germany. In the beginning, during the eight-month Phoney period of little actual warfare involving France, it became known as the Phoney War [2]. Afterward, with the war raging on elsewhere, it was clearly a notion shared by many of its inhabitants that Paris would remain safe and free for all its citizens. But, by the 10th of May 1940, just days before Jan's arrival in France, people's attitudes were beginning to shift when refugees appeared in large numbers and had to be quickly absorbed into the Parisian landscape.

During this surmounting chaos, Jan's brief reprieve in Marseilles as a newly arrived soldier left him mostly unaware of what was happening in the city and elsewhere in France, except that he was hungry and needed a substantial meal. Neither understanding French, Jan and his fellow compatriot ordered the most expensive item on the menu, hoping for a hearty spread to satisfy their appetite. The café waiter arrived with condiments and a large covered charger, set the platter between them, and, removing the lid, bid them, "Bon appétit!" Both startled diners sat back, as in horror, their eyes followed numerous slithery creatures trailing over a bed of lettuce. For such slow and slimy individuals, it was surprising how quickly these snails moved toward the parameter of the plate and over the edge before trying to escape. All Jan and his fellow diner could do was herd the snails back together toward the centre of the platter.

Before the declaration of war in Europe, any Czechs wishing to fight in France for the freedom of their own country could only do so by joining the French Foreign Legion. However, after the declaration of WWII in September 1939, France had been pledged aid from the Czechoslovak Army abroad to support the Allied Forces.

On the 15th of May 1940, when Jan re-enlisted through the Central Recruitment Bureau of the Tchécoslovaque (Czechoslovak) Army on 52 Bourdonnais Avenue Paris, he was now eligible to join the 1st Czechoslovak Infantry Division in France.

All newly arrived recruits were then transported to nearby training camps. Jan was based at Agde, a short distance west of Marseilles, where with a combined strength of about 5,000 soldiers, the Czechoslovak Division was established into two infantry regiments [3]. Jan was attached to the 2nd Regiment 12th Company.

Camp conditions at Agde were primitive, with very limited resources for combat training. By the end of May 1940, the Division had grown in strength to over 11,400 men, including voluntarily enlisted soldiers and conscripts already domiciled in France.

Between the 12th to 15th of May 1940, after making an unexpected offense through the mountainous and forested Dardennes in northern

France, the German Wehrmacht (1st Panzer Division)[4] won the Battle of Sedan along the Meuse River [5], capturing bridges and creating a base from which to advance toward the English Channel. (This battle outcome was reminiscent of the Battle of Sedan during the Franco-Prussian War of 1870 when Emperor Napoleon and his troops were captured). With this advantage, the Germans pushed westward, eventually encircling the British and allied forces around Dunkerque. Although the added support of Hitler's 1st Panzer Division contributed to the battle and forced the British out of France, the division remained just 25km short of Dunkerque at the time.

Between the 26th of May, to the 4th of June, 'Operation Dynamo'[6] was in earnest with its massive evacuation of British and allied troops from Dunkerque. With so many soldiers being evacuated from the north after retreating from the Germans, what remained of the French fighters was fast becoming a fractured army in disarray.

On the 3rd of June 1940, Germany bombed Paris. As enemy soldiers swept in, an exodus of Jews and escaping fugitives desperately fleeing the Germans, flooded streets and roads leading south out of the city[7].

After brief 'Unarmed' military combat training at Camp Agde, all activity was suddenly suspended for the 1st Czechoslovak Infantry Division. Soldiers in the 1st and 2nd Regiments were armed with antiquated guns and limited live ammunition, some mortars, and two anti-air guns and prepared for redeployment.

On the 9th of June, orders came for the two regiments to be transferred by train to Chatillon-sur-Seine, some 600km north, for further combat training. Having arrived at Chatillon-sur-Seine and barely with time to assemble and test their equipment, orders arrived to pack up and move further north. With troops packed into remodelled and militarized old Parisian buses, and only under the guidance of dimmed vehicle lights the cavalcade trundled north throughout the night for the next 180km, giving way only to prioritized army personnel.

The column of buses finally arrived on the front in Coulommiers in the early morning hours. Intelligence flowed in, reporting that the Germans had already crossed the Marne River at several locations. Although Jan had over three years of military training in the Czechoslovak

Army, many with him had no formal training in armed combat and were ill-prepared for the battle ahead.

By the 13th of June, the 2nd Regiment, to which Jan was attached, was already in action at La Ferté-sous-Jouarre near the confluence of the L'Ourcq and Marne River when the 1st Regiment took up main defence positions on the south side of the Grand Morin River, east of Coulommiers. Unbeknown to most soldiers in the 2nd Regiment their battleground was a WWI historic site where in September 1914, the Battle of the Marne had been fought. It was then a significant battle that the French and British Expeditionary Forces (BEF), won when Germany's sweeping invasion was reduced to fighting in the trenches.

Mobility around Coulommiers had been made easier because most of the population in nearby regions had already evacuated. Still, road congestion with retreating and advancing units was more of a hindrance.

Jan had very little preparation for what awaited him and even less armament at hand, as some only had hand grenades, a hand rifle with limited ammunition. However, the support and additional artillery from the 240th French Division and 7th French Army helped cover the section between La Ferté-sous-Jouarre and L'Ourcq River.

With French Pioneers blowing up bridges to retard the advance of German forces, it was only a temporary measure as the enemy used other means to cross rivers. The German fighting infantry was backed up with air raid bombings, and with large numbers of their soldiers parachuted in behind defence lines. With both Czechoslovak Regiments defending together with French armies, the fighting was unabating and intense. The horror and carnage after each battle would remain imprinted in the minds of all who fought and those who survived the blitzkrieg by the Germans.

Earlier in May, by way of Belgium, during the Evacuation of Dunkerque, the Germans bypassed the Maginot Line[8], and by the 14th of June 1940, Germany occupied Paris. On the 15th of June, the 1st Panzer Division this time breached the Maginot Line, entered France through the Ardennes, and invaded unhindered from the east, spreading north and south while advancing westward at momentum. After a brief standoff by the French, the Germans soon captured the Citadel of Verdun, and before long, the Germans were only about 35km out of Laon, close behind the retreating French armies.

For the French and Czech units defending territories from the southern side, and with battles fought along major Rivers of the Marne, Grand Morin, Seine, and Loir, they were always stationed along the lower banks and so had to defend at a maximum distance from the river. The Germans stationed on the opposite higher banks always had advantageous views of the French and Czechs on the lower ground across the rivers. Having retreated southward toward the Seine River and with the Germans not far behind, the battle of Montereau began on the 15th of June.

With the French Pioneers already destroying bridges ahead of retreating Czech and French units, many were stuck on the northern side of the river. To cross, the Czech Division had to jettison much of their heavy armaments and ammunition while bombarded overhead by heavy enemy aircraft fire. Bridge destruction designed to hinder the gaining Germans may have delayed their advance, but it did not stop them. Instead, the enemy quickly built pontoons over the rivers, allowing them to cross and continue their rapid advance.

By daybreak, German reconnaissance Fieseler Fl 156 Storch aircraft[9] would whiz overhead, photographing and pin-pointing Allied bearings. A few hours later, the relentless screaming of dive-bombers, Junkers Ju 87 or Stukas[10], would strike these positions. Having no antiaircraft weapons, retaliation was powerless, with only small artillery guns aimed against the invading Luftwaffe[11].

Machine guns stationed and positioned overnight on a dam wall near the Seine River were used instead but were too exposed without time for camouflage. By daylight, these were soon attacked by German planes.

Shortly afterward, during this battle, the Germans retreated, obviously looking for another route to penetrate the defence barriers. While overnight, the French 3rd Armoured Division was deployed to defend this position, the two Czech Regiments marched 40km south to Dordives. From Dordives, the troops caught the last freight train for Gien on the Loire River.

Failing to garner support from the USA, Paul Reynaud resigned as French President on the 16th of June, and by the 18th of June, the French armament centre at Le Creusot to the south was occupied by German forces. On the same day, a radio call from Charles de Gaulle exiled in the United Kingdom urged all French people and their military to unite against the Nazis. In response, the French Resistance fired up, and its clandestine activity would soon hit the core of German occupation.

By the 17th of June, both battle-weary Czech Regiments were now stationed near the Loire River, with the German 1st Panzer Division not far behind. While the 2nd Regiment was ordered to defend from near St. Gondon across the Loire River just west of Gien, the 1st Regiment was to defend the flank near the tributary River Ocre and Loire River. Other Battalions took up positions on the southern side amidst French engineers still trying to demolish bridges, including Gien's notable historic stone bridge over the Loire River. Remnants of this main bridge were left open for as long as possible to enable refugees to pass and continue toward Argent-sur-Sauldre some 20km to the south.

The main objective of the defending armies was to hold the southern side of the Loire River and its crossing points. With the northern side of the river being agricultural with orchards and no buildings, the region was exposed should German soldiers attempt to advance.

While bridges were being blasted and made impassable, homes and buildings with civilian lives in Gien and neighbouring villages were being destroyed by enemy artillery fire as rounds bombarded the towns and allied strongholds. The French and Czech forces held out for about two days against the superior armed Germans, but once again, with the aid of pontoons, the enemy crossed the wide Loire River and continued its rapid advancement.

For the first time, Jan confronted the full carnage of war as it played out before him. Death and destruction were everywhere as villages burned and lay flattened and smouldering, with corpses of soldiers, civilians, and animals strewn in their path.

In a nearby village, with its Church still intact, Jan and a small troop of foot-weary soldiers headed toward it to take temporary shelter. It was late at night, and the church was deserted, but the relentless boom of artillery still echoed and flashed in the night sky, pouring out shells that sporadically pounded in their direction. Jan had a sense of foreboding about the place, and had he been alone, he would have preferred to push

Book One: Anna's Story

on toward a sheltered trench from where to resume fighting at dawn. However, on this occasion, he was vetoed by the others, as all were desperately tired.

Once bedded down on their rucksacks inside the once peaceful sanctuary, sleep came quickly to the foot-weary and hungry men. Jan was suddenly woken from his sleep. He had felt a hand on his shoulder, signalling him to get up and get going. Startled, he sat up, but there wasn't anyone around except sleeping bodies scattered about him. He immediately stood up and shouted for everyone to quickly get up and run. From about twenty men, most of them responded and staggered on behind as Jan raced out of the church. A few remaining soldiers refused to budge, too tired to move. Running at speed but still only a short distance from the church, Jan and his followers suddenly heard the ominous sound of an approaching mortar shell when it slammed into the church with a deafening blast turning the site into a burning inferno.

It was all too apparent that the German 1st Panzer Division was unstoppable against French defences, pushing the Czech soldiers to continually retreat, and forcing them to march south throughout the night.

The German incursion had a faster method of transportation, either on motorcycles or in vehicles, and was determined to outflank the retreating Czech and French armies. This had to be avoided at all costs, so forced marches by commanding officers continued all night while the Germans mobilized during the day. As skirmishes raged and shelling continued, the Czech Division was again forced to march, this time some 40km further south toward Presly. From Presly, they marched onto Vouzeron, to Vatan, and then onto Chateauroux, covering over 90km on foot and pursued all the way by Nazi soldiers. During the day, they would dig in and return with gunfire whenever attacked. Still, during the night, without food or rest, they footslogged onward as shelling by enemy artillery reverberated behind them.

For ten days, they marched day and night in a stupor of fatigue with little or no food and sleep. During these night retreats, many of the troops staggered under fatigue and hunger and some even straggled behind their regiments. Once, out of sheer exhaustion, Jan briefly sat on a bench next to a resting soldier whose face was covered by his helmet. On closer probing, Jan realized his companion was dead, with his face completely obliterated beneath the helmet. Jan's fatigue quickly dissipated, and with renewed vitality, he resumed marching, outstripping his earlier lassitude.

Jan and his group of four or five paused briefly beneath a large tree to rest. Some dozed while others, out of sheer exhaustion, fell asleep. Jan woke suddenly from what he believed was a dream, during which time he thought he heard someone warning him to get moving as otherwise great harm would descend upon them. Again, he immediately urged everyone to get going, telling them he sensed bad vibes about the place. All followed, but one refused to budge as he was too tired, so they had no choice but to leave him behind. What became of him, nobody knew, as he was neither seen nor heard from again. Once again, Jan's premonition saved them from unforeseen catastrophe.

France was collapsing, and with no aerial backup from allied forces, the Germans quickly occupied much of France's territory. The biggest challenge for the Allied commanding officers was yet to come, should any threat of capture by the Germans eventuated. That issue was how to save the Czech soldiers from German retribution at the end of this retreat,

Skirmishes continued until arriving at Chateauroux, where the French High Military Command announced that everyone would march for another 190km onto Nontron. Here, the Czechs would surrender all arms and hand them over to the French. From Nontron railway station, those who did not wish to continue would be sent back to Agde camp and demobbed, while those wishing to continue the war against Nazi Germany were to be transported by trucks onto the Port of Sète. By now, time was becoming critical as the advancing Germans rapidly eroded their chances of shipment out of France.

Some historians theorize that Germany's WWI Schlieffen Plan (a strategy devised by Count von Schlieffen to allow Germany to wage war successfully on two fronts)[12] may have had similarities implemented by Hitler when he invaded France by first attacking Belgium, followed by the Netherlands. This tactic seemed effective to a point, as Hitler's invasion was swift, and for the time being, Germany was in control of all the European Atlantic coast to the Spanish frontier. Only the southern part of France, along the Mediterranean coast, remained open to allied shipping.

After retreating on foot from all battles fort, and leaving behind war-ravaged countryside over the past 330km, Jan's final truck journey over the next 550km from Nontron to Sète must have felt almost like a holiday trip.

Amongst various other ships, the 'S.S. Rod El Farag' and 'S.S. Apapa,' both Egyptian, were regularly departing from Marseilles. Sailing for Gibraltar, troops and civilians were then transferred onto other ships, either the 'S.S. Neuralia' or 'Viceroy of India,' and then shipped to Liverpool and Plymouth, respectively[13].

Over the past few months, transport carriers were becoming less frequent despite the sheer volumes of people expecting evacuation from France. This time, from her normal port of departure, Marseilles, the 'S.S. Rod El Farag' was instead berthed in Sète and loading a final evacuation of Czech troops from France destined for Liverpool. The never-ending line of battle-weary men, numbering over 800, hurriedly boarded, leaving behind their major failure, to defeat the German invasion, the very objective that brought them all to France in the first place. After barely one month of intense combat in the battle for France, it was an undeniable defeat for the French and Czechs alike, and it was a failure that was even more painful than the drudgery and horror of war.

For now, fighting in France had ended for Jan and his cohorts, who were leaving one battle behind in anticipation of others to come. During the battle of France, they were fortunate not to have been taken prisoners by the Germans and returned to their home country to suffer humiliation and retribution; this was at least one sobering reminder they managed to escape. For Jan and his Czech compatriots, the Battle of France was one of retreat, a bitter failure and a humiliating experience, constantly fleeing from the advancing and superior, and unstoppable German military might.

•

The failed destruction of Hitler and his Nazi army weighed heavily on their conscience when on Saturday, 22nd June 1940, Jan and close to

800 fellow Czech soldiers sailed out of Sète for the UK. Regardless of De Gaulle's earlier patriotic plea, Marshall Phillippe Pétain's representatives signed the armistice agreement on the 24th of June. From thereon, the French Government moved on to Vichy[14] and became a puppet to Hitler's regime. With Charles De Gaulle in exile, he was tried for treason in absentia and sentenced to death.

A rather expensive, if not surprising live banquet in France in 1940.

CHAPTER 14.4

1940-1944: Cholmondeley Cheshire and Formation of CIABG

Jan arrived at the port of Liverpool in late June 1940, and it was surprising how welcoming the British were; a stark contrast to the French he had just left behind, where no one was keen to communicate with the Czechs. Here the local crowds welcomed the troops while they boarded conventional passenger carriages rather than being transported in cattle wagons before heading for their destination.

The newly arrived troops railed from Liverpool onto Cheshire were disembarked near Cholmondeley Castle Estate. They joined some 300 other Czech troops who had arrived earlier and were already stationed on the estate's grounds.

Cholmondeley Castle [1] in Cheshire has a Norman history dating back to 1200. By 1940, the 6th Marquess and his Marchioness, Lady Lavinia Cholmondeley, inherited the title. During the war, the grounds were reserved as the first campsite for the Free Czech Forces in Exile, mostly arriving from France.

Toward the end of July, signs of disharmony within the ranks of the Czechoslovak soldiers gave warning of the potential mutiny[2]. Soldier dissensions rested with the fact that proportionally officer numbers far outweighed the non-commissioned soldiers, and to counter this disproportionate balance many officers had to be reduced in rank. However, the biggest dissatisfaction arose from Communist supporters within the brigade who refused to recognize the Czechoslovakian Government in Exile. Czechoslovakian President in Exile, Edvard Beneš, tried to quell the situation. Still, failing to do so, the military command signalled a roll-call on the 23rd of July, and those not wishing to abide by the set down military code were disarmed and separated from the others. Finally, on the 26th of July, the matter was resolved after some 539 mutineers, refusing to comply, were expelled[3].

Many expelled and judged undesirable had the choice of joining the Pioneer Corps, Churchill's 'Foreign Legion.' This proved unsatisfactory, with discipline being challenging, and the Corps befell a somewhat checked history[4]. By the 1st of August, there were 3,324 soldiers remaining in the Czech Brigade, which would soon become known as the Czechoslovak Independent Brigade Group (CIBG)[5].

From August through to October, Jan and the others made do with the temporary accommodation on the grounds of Cholmondeley Castle. The grounds were dotted with sleeping tents, and all communal laundry and bathing facilities were outside. Apart from regimental parades, no serious training had actually commenced. Most of it was housekeeping and assigning soldiers to duties. For now, Jan was assigned to the kitchen as one of the cooks in the mess, and most meals were taken outside, sitting about casually with their chosen groups. This was acceptable while the weather remained warm, but in early October preparations were already underway to move to Leamington Spa southeast of Cholmondeley.

When the troops were not working on assignments digging trenches and setting up make-shift infrastructure, in between times, most sat about sharing their cigarettes, smoking, and playing cards. Those in the camp with musical talent managed to acquire a piano accordion, and sing-a-longs in the evenings were common as national songs resounded throughout the camp. The Czech version of the WWI Irish lyric 'It's a long way to Tipperary' was compiled in their language and became a favourite marching song;

"Jaká dálka do Tipperary
Jaká dálka je tam
Jaká dálka do Tipperary
Kde své sladké děvče mám
Sbohem Piccadilly
Zdráv bude světe můj
Í být dál, dál bylo Tipperary
Zůstanu vždy jen tvůj."

While at Cholmondeley, Jan met Jaroslav Kurovec, who experienced similar drawbacks when escaping Czechoslovakia before succeeding to cross borders into the Middle East and onto France. Although, like Jan, Jaroslav fought in France but did so with minimal experience.

Jan met his cousin Karel Kutěj from Hošťálková, who also fled home, however, under different circumstances. Karel initially had worked in a Baťa Shoe factory in the Moravian town of Zlín. The Baťa Shoe Company had a history dating back to 1894 when it was started by an entrepreneurial Czech named Tomáš Baťa. By the onset of WWII, the company had grown and spread far and wide. While working at the Zlín factory in 1939, when his country was already under German occupation, Karel was given the opportunity to transfer to the Yugoslav Baťa factory branch. He failed to stay on at his new post for any length of time, and like many young men of the time, he grabbed his opportunity and, without any army experience, eventually made his way to Great Britain.

By mid-October, Cholmondeley camp moved to its winter quarters in Leamington Spa[6], where training and manual labour was interspersed by visiting dignitaries and Military Generals carrying out inspections and pep talks. Jan, by then, was attached to the Field Artillery unit under Col. Alois Liška[7].

In April of 1941, Mrs. Beneš, wife of Prime minister in Exile Edvard Beneš, opened a canteen for the Czechs in Leamington Spa, which was met with great approval from the men starved of social interaction. Prime Minister Winston Churchill, accompanied by Mr. Beneš and other dignitaries, including US President Roosevelt's representative, also visited the camp and inspected the CIBG.

During this time, Special Operations Executive (SOE), with their Special Group D, began recruiting suitable volunteers from within the CIBG for classified missions into Occupied Czechoslovakia[8]. These recruits until 1943, were trained in secret locations in remote parts of England and Scotland.

In Leamington Spa, there was no end of visiting dignitaries, ceremonial functions, conferences, and dinners for distinguished officials and officers. However, the lack of English understanding among the troops remained a constant handicap in communication. Although some already had limited comprehension of English, others learned as they went along. It was then decided to introduce English instructors and eventually make it mandatory for all officers to attend lessons. Jan and his fellow cohorts with limited spoken English found it especially difficult when on leave, and like many young men, the notion of chatting up young women came with its downfalls.

During one evening while downtown, Jan met a young lass keen to meet him again. He made the necessary arrangements as he was again on leave the following weekend.

"Not today. Not today. Not today. Not today. Not today. But today, yes!"

Needless to say, the date came to nothing. However, it wasn't always the young men who missed out; young women also had their share of lost chances. Whenever an accompanying lady's gaze fell upon some young dashing Czech officer outside of Jan's circle of friends, the boys were always more than willing to offer introductory lines whenever asked. Armed with their precise Czech, the ladies would approach their officers of desire and politely repeat the Czech phrases. Jan and his crew would snicker in delight as the poor officer, astounded and red-faced, was left to handle the embarrassing situation in front of equally shocked, if not bemused, colleagues. Then, leading up to Christmas in 1941, an unexpected announcement brought everyone to their heels.

On the 7th of December 1941, the theatre of war was about to change when Japan bombed the American naval base of Pearl Harbour. This became a significant moment, and its consequence brought the USA into the WWII arena. The earlier Tripartite Pact of September the 27th, 1940, established a defence alliance between Germany, Italy, and Japan to deter the USA from entering the war[9]. The bombing of Pearl Harbour was planned to impede any immediate American retaliation in the Pacific. At the same time, Japan hoped to capture and occupy as many South East Asian European colonies as possible while the Americans were recovering from the unexpected attack, or so the Japanese thought. Instead, America retaliated all too readily, which did not help Japan nor Hitler's campaign to conquer Europe as the might of the US was quickly brought into the fold of war in Europe.

In April of 1942, exiled HM King Peter of Yugoslavia inspected the CBIG. Still, from there onward, little time was afforded to entertain visiting dignitaries, as the Brigade became heavily involved in exercises and Field Artillery firing programs. From May 1942 until August of the same year, the CIBG was transferred and regrouped in and around Ilminster[10] in South Somerset. Battalions stationed there for a predetermined duration trained at specified army drill locations, and during August of that year, the Field Artillery to which Jan was attached under Col. Liška, Anti-Tank, and Reconnaissance Companies from the Brigade were deployed on exercise to the Merivale Ranges, near the edge of Dartmoor Moorlands in Devon.

Here intensive lectures and training in camouflage were also added to the itinerary. When the remainder of the Brigade finally moved onto Lowestoft[11] in East Suffolk for coastal defence drills and army assignments along the southern North Sea coast, the Artillery and Brigade Ordnance workshop remained in Devon to hand over to the 9th Battalion of the Devonshire Regiment which, at the time, was providing extra training to the brigade[12]. *(Public records office WO 166/7898 War Diary August 1942).

During Jan's service in Somerset, and whenever he and fellow soldiers were granted leave, they often socialized in local community villages where they met with young ladies for an evening out. However, transport back to the base was always problematic, and they often had to hitch a lift with whatever means were headed their way.

On one rather inclement afternoon, two of them hitched a ride back to base in a lorry loaded with goods of various descriptions, all stacked up around them and exposed to the rainy weather. They squeezed in amongst the boxes and perched themselves on barrels while resting their feet on a coffin. For the time being, the weather was overcast and holding out, but if it began to rain again, it would be a race who would first score shelter inside the coffin.... provided it was empty!

A short while into the journey, with the rain still abating, the coffin lid creaked beneath their feet and suddenly shifted. Startled, both hurriedly lifted their feet and paled in horror when a hand squeezed out and began to wave about near their feet. The two stunned soldiers, still very much fixed to their seats, could only stare in dread as the lid slowly opened and a vagabond crawled out, smiled at them, hinted for a cigarette, and without a word, sat on top of the coffin and joined them in the ambiance of the late afternoon.

During this period, while still stationed in Sommerset, Jan met and fell in love with a young lass, some ten years younger, who lived in neighbouring Devon. Elsie Pidgeon came from Dalwood in Devon, and their relationship became a whirlwind romance. Soon afterward, Jan returned to his brigade quarters at Lowestoft, and any romance carried on between him and Elsie had to be long-distance. It was only during Jan's leave that they were able to meet. Elsie had a strict upbringing, and her parents, Alice and Fred, never allowed her to go out alone with Jan, but nevertheless, their relationship flourished.

Regimental exercises at Lowestoft kept Jan occupied, and for the time being, he remained attached to the Field Regiment. Between regular inspections by visiting Major Generals, their Prime Minister in Exile Edvard Beneš and his wife, and numerous other dignitaries, the camp had its usual schedule of drills and special training courses, all in preparation for their eventual call to battle.

By September 1942, Jan received his promotion to Lance Corporal, and by the 25th of February 1943, he and Elsie lodged an application to marry but had to do so within three months of its lodgement.

During February 1943, the CIBG moved to Harwich[13] on the coast in county Essex just south of Lowestoft, and during his leave, Jan and Elsie had a small but traditional marriage on the 11th of March at St. Peters Parish Church in Dalwood. It was a small wedding party, and Jan's cousin Karel Kutěj and Elsie's father, Fredrick Pidgeon, were present as chief witnesses. While Elsie continued to live at Danes Hill Cottage, Jan divided his time between there and his posting.

Jan and his new father-in-law Fred Pidgeon had a good relationship, but Alice, his mother-in-law, did not seem to rest easy with the intercontinental marriage. Elsie recalled, many years later, attending a London underground basement with Jan, where Czech civilians were tailor-making clothes for the London rich. Jan knew many of these Czechs, but by then, Elsie was already beginning to feel uncomfortable and alienated among people whose language she did not understand.

During March 1943, while stationed at Harwich, Jan's commander of the Field Regiment, Colonel Alois Liška, was promoted to Commander of the CIBG, replacing Colonel Jan Kratochvil[14], who would later be deployed to the Soviet to command Czech units. Lieutenant Colonel Marek now headed Jan's Field Regiment.

Following the Western Desert and Middle Eastern Campaigns between 1940-1943 [15], many Czech troops began arriving to the UK, and numbers within the CIBG swelled to over 5,000 when these newly arrived joined the brigade and resumed rigorous training exercises. Numerous inspections with guards of honour and march passes followed, honouring the fighting men who received mentions from recent campaigns. Later that month, advance parties left for Arthingworth[16] Northamptonshire, as the North Netherlands Brigade moved in to take over the Harwich Garrison.

By September 1943, the Brigade was stationed at Arthingworth. It was reorganized into the Czechoslovak Independent Armoured Brigade Group (CIABG)[17] and Col. Alois Liška was promoted to General, while recently arrived Lt. Col. Karel Klapálek [18] became his 2IC. No sooner had Jan arrived at Bulwick Camp at Arthingworth headquarters when he was transferred and attached to the 2nd Armoured Regiment under Lieutenant Colonel F. Šeda. Jan would remain with this unit for the duration of his army service.

On the 5th of March 1944, Jan and Elsie celebrated the arrival of their firstborn, whom they named Milada Violet. Jan had very little leave remaining for any lengthy home and family visits, as by now, the Czech Brigade was in full preparatory training for their inevitable landing in Europe.

Between May and August of 1944, Jan was based at Langton Camp Duns near Galashiels[19] close to the southern border of Scotland. Army drills, work-outs, and preparations were in full swing, overseen by a constant flow of Military and Government dignitaries, including a visit from the Foreign Minister of the Czechoslovak Republic Government in Exile, Jan Masaryk.

In August, the CIABG was finally transferred to the coastal town of Bridlington[20] in west Yorkshire. Jan's 2nd Armoured Regiment was based along Vernon Road, where final exercises, battle plans, and equipment checks were made for their imminent transfer onto the continent. During this period, Lt. Col. Karel Klapálek left the CIABG and was deployed to the Soviet Union to command the 3rd Czechoslovak Independent Brigade, and replacing him was Lt. Col. A. Barovsky who became 2IC to General Alois Liška.

It had been a frustrating four-year absence from battle for the Czech soldiers who eagerly prepared and waited to be called on to fight the Germans. With so few of them, these men could not be readily replaced. Instead, their contribution to the war effort was hampered by political intervention, which prevented this small brigade of Czech soldiers to be called on earlier.

Finally, at the end of August 1944, all the troops of the 1st Czechoslovak Independent Armoured Brigade (CIABG), under the command of Major-General Alois Liška, were finally called on and prepared to depart for France.[21]

Photograph 145: Visit from Mrs. Beneš in Cholmondeley, 1940.

Photograph 146: Mrs. Beneš with Czech troops in Cholmondeley, 1940.

Photograph 147 & 148: (L-R) Both photos of Cholmondeley Castle 1940.

Photograph 149, 150 & 151: (L-R) Jan's Army photo album. Jan in the Army fatigues 1941. A Czech musician at Cholmondeley Camp.

Photograph 152: A musical evening with Jan standing second on left.

Photograph 153 & 154: (L-R) Jan far right at Cholmondeley 1940. Jan in Army uniform.

Photograph 155: Card game, Jan standing second on left.

Photograph 156: Cholmondeley barber.

Photograph 157 & 158: (L-R) An athlete at Cholmondeley camp 1941. Jan third from left 1941.

Photograph 159: Christmas dinner at the castle 1940.

Photograph 160: Celebrating Christmas with Jan left of Musician in 1940.

Photograph 161 & 162: (L-R) Troops at work 1940.

Photograph 163 & 164: (L-R) Jan operating the cement mixer on right. Troops at work.

Photograph 165 & 166: (L-R) Jan in foreground on right. Construction site at Cholmondeley.

Photograph 167 & 168: (L-R) Lunch break with Jan holding the concrete mixer on right. Keeping warm during training.

Photograph 169 & 170: (L-R) Training at the camp. Tank manoeuvres during training.

Photograph 171: Boating exercises in the fog.

Photograph 172 & 173: (L-R) Moving the boat on exercise. A spot of bother on the road.

Photograph 174 & 175: (L-R) Truck bogged in the snowed-in ditch. On exercise.

Photograph 176: Ready for France 1944 with Jan top left.

Photograph 177: Winter at their camp in UK with Jan fifth from left back row.

Photograph 178 & 179: (L-R) Jan with Elsie Pidgeon 1944. Jan Kaňák in uniform.

Photograph 180: Jan and Elsie on their wedding day.

CHAPTER 14.5

1944-1945: Siege of Dunkirk and Finally Home

At the end of August 1944, waiting ships in the port of Bridlington were loaded with CIABG troops, artillery hardware, tanks, and transport trucks ready to sail across the English Channel. For any ships at the time, crossing the channel toward the Normandy coast of France was hazardous as they posed easy targets for German bombers or risking being torpedoed by enemy U-boats. Rough weather conditions, seasickness, and the possibility of hitting mines and losing a shipload of troops were always at the forefront of any crossing. Even with mine-sweepers, the risk of hitting an explosive device always remained.

The presence of accompanying mascots on board ships, either by chance or as the consequential result of someone's pet, momentarily may have alleviated apprehension and redirected attention from what lay ahead, as in one case, when a cat joined the troops crossing the channel. It would either bring luck or be unlucky while it, too, made the perilous journey. The cat was black with a white strip from its face tip down onto its breast. A curious young feline with sturdy sea legs but, in this instance, not destined for the battlefields of France but still on an equally perilous mission aboard the ship, even if only relegated to catching vermin.

For Jan and those who retreated from France in June of 1940 after being defeated by Hitler's army, it was a poignant moment to be returning so close to where they had fought; but this time, it came with a renewed commitment to finish the job that they had so long ago set out to accomplish; and that was to destroy Hitler and the Third Reich once and for all.

Nearing the Normandy coast in choppy seas, the Czechs were offloaded with their heavy armaments onto smaller US carrier barges within reach of Oistreham near the mouth of the Orne River. As the soldiers disembarked and clambered down ropes onto the swaying barges docked alongside the ships, it would soon be the dawning of reality for all to see the aftermath that the war over the past 4 years had left behind. The sandy beaches and reefs on the coast of the inlet made it unsuitable for large ships to enter. With all their artillery, the troops had to be ferried upstream inland toward Caen before disembarking and moving onto Épaney, where the Brigade was to be initially based for re-equipping, further training, and familiarization with tasks ahead.

At Falaise, the CIABG then joined the 1st Canadian Army (later becoming the 21st Army Group), where they continued to exercise until October. Only a few months earlier, on the 4th of June, after the Normandy D-Day landings by allied troops, this area around Caen[1], Épaney, and Falaise[2] had seen intense fighting and carnage against the German forces. The 1st Canadian Army had already participated in numerous strategic battles, during which time the Germans were finally forced to retreat. What remained after the liberation was a bleak and charred landscape in ruination with devastating civilian losses after bombing raids and intense armoured and artillery exchange flattened most villages. People now trudged through the rubble remains, some with their horses and carts, seeking what remained of their livelihood and trying to survive by piecing their lives together.

By the 6th of October, the CIABG was ordered north to Dunkirk with their headquarters now stationed at Wormhoudt[3], an area notoriously mentioned during the earlier Battle of France in May of 1940, where German Waffen-SS massacred British and French POWs[4]. The CIABG may have been subordinate to the 1st Canadian Army, but the Czech unit became an integral part of the 'Dunkirk Force' with Major General Alois Liška as its Commander.

Their first major engagement during inclement weather surprised German garrisons defending Dunkirk. The attack occurred on 28th October (Czechoslovak National Day), and the 2nd Armoured Regiment carried it out. It proved to be a successful mission resulting in over 200 German troops killed and a further six officers and 343 enemy soldiers captured. Compared in this instance to the Czech casualties which were low with five killed, 50 injured, and three missing. *(Public Record Office WO 171/3467 War Diary of 22 Liaison HQ October 1944).

The next major attack was in November but not as successful, as by then, the Germans were ready, and any element of surprise by the 2nd Armoured Regiment was markedly reduced. However, heavy opening attacks by British Hawker Typhoon bomber fighters (Tiffies)[5] soon retaliated against heavy enemy fire from German-occupied French bunkers at Chyvelde near the Belgium border. The British Spitfires attacked Leffrinckoucke, a Nazi stronghold of impenetrable cement bunkers secreted amongst sand dunes, forming part of the Atlantic Ocean defence fortification.

At the time, the Allies also targeted a close-by factory of specific interest. German night aircraft began dropping in supplies for their soldiers, but from greater heights, and as a result, many of these drops were often jeopardized and landed in the sea. For the Czechs, every inconvenience to the Germans carried merit even if enemy mine explosions became notably heavier than before, causing substantial damage to allied tanks and rendering many unrecoverable. At the end of the attack, allied casualties were recorded as 8 killed, 76 wounded, and 17 regular soldiers missing, with at least 2 German prisoners of war taken and identified.

It became extremely advantageous when captured enemy soldiers carried detailed mine-field maps indicating where mines had been placed and even stacked 3 to 4 on top of the other when laid out. *(Public Record Office WO 171/3468).

Throughout December and into early 1945, mortar attacks by the Czechs continued to bombard the parameter of Dunkirk. Still, orders remained to keep the Germans under siege rather than an outright attack to try and complete the mission. During the 30-week siege of Dunkirk, the CIABG suffered 668 casualties; 167 dead, 461 wounded, and 40 missing[6].

By April 1945, a Token Force[7] was being discussed and proposed as an advanced group of Czech soldiers to be sent onto Prague in preparation for the Czechoslovakian liberation from the Germans. Jan was not included in this selection but remained with the CIABG maintaining the siege at Dunkirk.

On the 23rd of April, this symbolic 140-men-strong unit led by Major Sítek detached from the CIABG and joined the 3rd US Army. A week later, on the 1st of May 1945, they raised the Czechoslovak flag at the border town of Cheb.

Many German soldiers in allied-held territory were already trying to surrender along with their wounded and all the equipment they held.

Under General Eisenhower's directive, these surrenders had to be stalled by roadblocks or whatever means to prevent German infiltration behind allied lines and subsequent movement to the west [8]. It was also instructed that any German or displaced Russian civilians who tried to bypass blockades would need be handed back to the Russians.

On the 7th of May 1945, but coming into effective on the 8th, Germany capitulated with an unconditional surrender signed in Reims, France, virtually ending WWII in Europe and the fall of the 3rd Reich.

Between the 5th to the 9th May, during the Prague Uprising, German Field Marshal Ferdinand Schörner was redeployed to the Czech city. He was a dedicated Nazi known for his brutality, and after Germany's capitulation on the 7th, he had ordered continual fighting against the Red Army and Czech insurgents in Prague [9]. A later alert from the Allied Command Post cautioned that if Field Marshal General Schörner [10] surrendered he was to be handed over to the Soviet High Commander for appropriate action to ascertain if any acts committed against Soviet Forces contravened the violation of the Military Capitulation Act [11].

On the 9th of May, General Alois Liška finally accepted the surrender from Admiral Frisius of the German garrison at Dunkirk with over 10,000 German soldiers and three captured U-Boats. It was a notable accomplishment for such a small brigade to ward off so many enemy troops that numbered twice as many as the Czechs surrounding them.

By 11th May, orders arrived from the Czechoslovak Government for the Token Force to proceed from Cheb onto Prague, leaving behind at Dunkirk the bulk of the CIABG. *(Supreme Headquarters Allied Expeditionary Force (SHAEF) 11th May 1945).

With the Czech siege of Dunkirk over, on the 12th and 13th of May two columns of soldiers (some 5,800 men) followed by Military armament left Dunkirk and headed back to Czechoslovakia [12]. On the 14th of May, the US Army Radio in Luxembourg reported that a 200-kilometre-long column comprising of the Czechoslovak Brigade had passed through the city. The CIABG file passed over seventy locations as the Czech soldiers made their way home[13].

The main force of Czech soldiers began reaching Plzeň by the 18th of May and then continued onto designated areas on the demarcation line between the American and Soviet Forces. On the 30th of May, as many troops as possible were called upon to attend the Victory Parade in Prague, after which they returned to their positions on the demarcation line [14] to await further orders.

CHAPTER 14.6

Jan's WWII Aftermath

The Victory Parade was met with jubilant cheering, but soon afterward, the Soviets began to accuse the Czech National Council of collaborating with the Germans during the Prague Uprising. "After the parade, the commander of a light repair workshop was sent ahead to check if the highway to Plzeň was free of obstacles. On his way, he was stopped by a Red Army soldier brandishing a submachine gun who attempted to steal his motorcycle…." *(Extract from Gustav Svoboda's 'Unconditional Surrender and Aftermath' - from 'On All Fronts- Czechoslovaks in WWII edited by Lewis M. White).

Not all who had fought for their country's freedom had a warm welcome, as they soon discovered. Much to their grief, many families no longer existed. Their dwellings had either been requisitioned under German force and its dwellers dispossessed of their homes or, worse still, banished to concentration camps such as Mauthausen[1].

Many high-ranking officers, such as Jan's commander of the 2nd Armoured Regiment, Lieutenant Colonel F. Šeda, and General Alois Liška, commander of the CIABG, soon found that their Western military alliances served against any career prospects in the newly liberated but now communist homeland. Many were relegated to the 'War College,' indicating they were no longer trusted within the newly reformed military chain of command and its higher levels of intelligence and responsibility.

In June, when General Liška was appointed Commander of the 'War College in Prague,' General J Koutňák, now a Communist, was appointed Commander of the Brigade. As pointed out in Gustav Svoboda's 'Patria Ingrata' [2], he comments that the Communist Party was having a decisive influence in re-organizing the 'New Army,' and also on the fate of all high-ranking officers such as General Alois Liška and the likes of Lieutenant Colonel Alois Šeda who fought with the British in the west. The ruling communists refused them any promotion, and instead, these officers were gradually demobbed; many military commissions illegally terminated or reduced in rank and deprived of any retirement benefits. For many, it was time to escape and return back to the west.

For the very few remaining, they would finally receive their notification of termination.

The general reason being "They failed to have a positive attitude toward the People's democratic system…. or were too pro-Western in orientation."

This termination decree, however, stipulated that the demobbed officers must always maintain silence on any Army matters.

After Jan was formally discharged from the Army on the 1st of September 1945, he returned home to his family in Hošťálková. He was overwhelmingly greeted at the front door albeit silently, by Lumpa, his faithful old dog. Lumpa had remembered him after an absence of almost six years.

Jan's mother was shocked when he unexpectedly walked into the kitchen, escorted by the overjoyed old canine. Jan soon learned how difficult life had been for his family after he disappeared into Yugoslavia. They had to endure the uncertainty and wroth of the occupying Nazis. For many, it was less confrontational in country villages than in larger cities such as in Prague, where there was always an abundance of Nazi security officers searching out suspects and making arrests. However, retaliatory actions against the Nazis by Partisans and their supporters were always followed through regardless of location and with no less severe repercussions from the German security forces.

Hošťálková had its fair share of action during the German occupation when a regiment of 300 to 400 marching German soldiers had been suddenly fired upon by Partisans hidden in the hills. It would never be a battle, as the Partisans were so few in numbers and disorganized, unlike the well-armed and disciplined German Army. Sporadic skirmishes continued to occur between the Partisans and the Germans until Czechoslovakia's liberation [3].

Throughout Nazi occupation Jan's family concealed themselves for most part in the underground cellar of their old home and silently watched through the cracks in the wall as the boots of marching enemy soldiers passed by. During such times, some local women in total ignorance of consequences, stood by the roadside to observe files of German foot soldiers marching until the foolish onlookers were dragged inside by family members and reminded that these soldiers were the enemy and everyone was at war.

Jan learnt from his family that when he and many others, especially ex-Czech soldiers, disappeared at the onset of German occupation, many families were arrested and interrogated over this regular and defiant truancy. In 1939 after Jan's disappearance, both his mother and sister, Anna Syptáková, had been interrogated by the Germans over his whereabouts and then incarcerated in prison at Svatobořice. In all honesty, neither knew anything, so Anna Kaňáková was released in December, and her daughter Anna Syptáková, finally, two months later in February of the following year.

While in prison, the women keenly informed Jan that they had met Olga Klapálekova, wife of Lt. Col. Karel Klapálek. Karel Klapálek had been a member of the 'Obrana Národa' organization before leaving to fight abroad. This organization had the same motive as Jan's partisan group, but many such groups often carried a strong communist philosophy. Jan remembered him well in Great Britain but was unsure if he agreed with his politics.

Karel Klapálek had also escaped Czechoslovakia. While in the Middle East, he became commander of the Czech 11th Infantry Battalion after the French Vichy Government capitulated to the Germans in 1941; his battalion had fought with the Allies invading Syria and Lebanon and bringing an end to its French occupation. Afterward Klapálek fought in Tobruk, northern Africa, and in 1943 arrived to Great Britain after his Middle Eastern campaigns. Jan remembered him in CIAB (the Czechoslovak Independent Armoured Brigade), when he was General Alois Liška's 2IC for a while, after which Klapálek was deployed to the Soviet Union to command the 3rd Czechoslovak Independent Brigade under General Ludvík Svoboda[4]. The Soviets would groom Ludvík Svoboda and upon returning to Czechoslovakia after the war, he and Klapálek would join the Communist Party and, for a while, both advanced their careers within the Military-Political field. After 1945 with favourable approval from Soviet motivators within the newly established Czech Communist Government, Ludvík Svoboda would make a political career for himself and eventually become Czech President from 1968 to 1975.

At this point, Jan and his family had differing political views, and no matter how decorated or esteemed these national heroes seemed, they were Communists and Jan steered clear of associating with their ideologies. Jan's war may have been over, but ahead of him remained another battle. He had a wife and daughter back in England whom he had not seen for over a year. After marrying Jan, Elsie automatically became a Czech citizen. While it was still possible to migrate into Czechoslovakia, Jan wrote to Elsie asking her and their daughter, to accompany Karel Kutěj to Hošťálková. For whatever reason, apart from witnessing Jan's and Elsie's marriage, Karel was back in England and maintained steady contact with her.

Although Elsie had promised to join Jan after the liberation of Czechoslovakia, much had happened in the past year, and Czechoslovakia was not going to be the democracy that Jan had fought for. It probably came as no surprise when Elsie replied that she and Violet were happily ensconced at home with her family in Devon and well distanced from communism. It became apparent to Jan that any future reunion with his family would be met with stiff opposition, especially from his mother-in-law Alice, who refused at point blank to allow her daughter and granddaughter even to consider joining him in Czechoslovakia. Had Elsie been alone in this equation, their matrimonial outcome may have progressed differently, but the strong-minded and controlling Alice made any marital reconciliation or negotiation near impossible.

The main reason the union failed in the first place was that Jan was determined to remain in Czechoslovakia. After all, he had fought for his country, and although Elsie made him a promise that she would follow once the war was over, she had many plausible excuses. Elsie mainly felt she would be lost and isolated in a foreign land. She was also worried about Jan's political stance, as he was already being tested regarding his noncompliant allegiance to the newly rising Czechoslovak Communist Government.

Karel Kutěj, who was the go-between, maintained contact with Elsie. Elsie wrote to Karel and Jan, "Divorce would be preferable to a marriage in which each lived in a separate place."

Realization that their marital situation was irreconcilable, Jan finally filed for divorce in 1946. By this time, Jan was already residing at No. 78 Pulgary. He had secured a job as a National Administrator on a landed estate and stated later in his divorce proceedings that he had badly needed a housekeeper. Not exactly the genteel homecoming persuasion for a bride. By the 17th of November 1947, their divorce had entered its final effect, and on the 17th of September 1948, divorce was granted.

Their daughter Violet recalled many years later, receiving numerous visits from Karel Jan's cousin. However, while Jan was in the UK after he had fled Czechoslovakia, a somewhat clouded memory led Violet to recall that in around 1948, when she was about five years old, her father did visit her once. At the time, Jan had taken up temporary residence in a bed and breakfast not far from where Elsie and Violet lived. Once during this time, Elsie and her brother had cycled to visit Jan (as recalled by Elsie's brother), but apart from that, little contact had ever been encouraged or maintained as, by then, they were already divorced.

Relocated and settled in Pulgary at No.75, Jan remained there from 1946 until early 1948. He put aside his failed marriage, hurt, and regrets and pursued a life in wine growing, searching out local markets for the red wine he produced. On 25th December 1947, Jan's father, Jan Kaňák Snr., died, but despite an often-difficult relationship with his father, it was still a sad Christmas for Jan, his mother, and his family.

The political climate was rapidly changing, and Jan was beginning to sense a mood that was not favourable but one opposing his personal beliefs. Although having been discharged from the army for some months, he began to gain regular and unwanted attention from the Communist authorities. He received numerous visits for 're-education,' coercing him to sign his allegiance to the Communists.

He constantly heard criminal charges being fabricated against various ex-military personnel who had served with him in Europe. For whatever crimes they were allegedly charged guilty of, these officers and regular soldiers alike were imprisoned with arbitrary hard labour as punishment or never heard from again. It seemed the Communists intended to cleanse the Czechs of any western persuasion that would threaten their ideology. It was becoming a menacing possibility that Jan too would end up in prison one day. He had come too far to be bullied against his will, and to remain in Czechoslovakia was fast becoming unpredictable and dangerous. All their Communist doctrines went against his grain; the right to democratic freedom was something he fought for and held close to his beliefs. Frequent and threatening visits continued to mount, until in early 1948, after the unexpected death by suicide of Foreign Minister Jan Masaryk was announced [5], Jan concluded that the harassments he was subjected to was only the beginning of what was to come.

Jan visited Prague to pay his respects and to attend Jan Masaryk's funeral. As the late Foreign Minister lay in state, Jan's own suspicion had been confirmed, as would be by any experienced soldier, that Jan Masaryk had probably been shot rather than killed by the tumble out of the window that had been reported to the public. His partially concealed temple wound spelled the markings of a suspiciously different case scenario to the head injury of a suicidal tumble. Some weeks later, the doctor who certified Jan Masaryk's death, also committed suicide.

Edvard Beneš, with whom so much hope and faith rested, was now powerless and unsupported to implement the voice of his nation and was overpowered by a new ideology far removed from the democracy they had all strived for.

It would be only a matter of time before Jan, just a regular soldier, would meet a similar fate as Jan Masaryk, but instead, he would go scarcely noticed and soon forgotten.

Unashamedly, Jan's family could not be convinced that their homeland was succumbing to an unyielding threat about to mould society against their wills and control their lives. They were all too easily hoodwinked into believing everything would eventually get better. But no one thought much about how long it would take to get better. For Jan, escape was either now or repent later!

Photograph 181 & 182: (L-R) Jan with his parents in Hošťálková 1945. Jan with parents and family in Hošťálková 1945.

Photograph 183 & 184: (L-R) Jan with family Hostalkova 1945. Jan with all his nieces and nephews in Hostalkova 1945.

Photograph 185, 186 & 187: (L-R) Jan on his horse in Bulhary 1946. Jan with his dog Lumpa on horseback with family member Bulhary 1946. Jan's sisters at Bulhary 1946.

Photograph 188 & 189: (L-R) Jans nieces; sisters Draha and Lenka Syptáková. Jan's nieces Liba and Jana Hříbková.

Photograph 190 & 191: (L-R) Karel Kutěj with wife and daughter Anna in Budapest after the war. Elsie with Violet in Devon, UK after the war.

Photograph 192: Violet Kanak (Langworthy) as a young lass with her dogs in Devon UK.

CHAPTER 15

New Zealand: Anna's Dream

Anna's philosophy had always been throughout her life. 'If you dream and believe you can achieve your dreams, somewhere a door will open, do not hesitate but take your chances and never look back with regret; just keep walking ahead, believing in your own judgment.'

Once on board the 'Dundalk Bay,' a group of musicians below on the wharf began playing a Czech Farewell song. Anna was moved to tears as it was a melody, she and her brother Jaroslav knew well.... 'I say goodbye to you, my faithful friends, for now, I am leaving the road where so many young people no longer go....'

The 'Dundalk Bay' glided out of Trieste on the 20th of May 1949 and slowly descended the Adriatic Coast. The port soon became a distant dot on the horizon as they continued between Italy and Greece and finally away from land into the Mediterranean Sea. Anna had never seen before such a vast body of perpetually rolling water, and this small portion of the ocean was only the beginning.

Her first night on board seemed a lap of luxury after all her past sleeping arrangements. Anna was shown her sleeping bunk neatly covered with clean linen and blankets and next to it was one of the ship's portholes with an outside view of the ocean. Anna shared her immediate space with three others, across from her a young woman of similar age and above them in the upper bunks, another woman and her child.

Breakfast was yet another culinary delight for Anna. They were served bacon and eggs on toast, and Anna drank coffee with milk for the first time! They were left not wanting for anything and everybody received an allowance from the New Zealand Government equivalent to about US$5 each to spend in the ship's canteen, which provided incidentals such as chocolates, cigarettes, and toiletries. Anna bought herself a comb, soap, socks, and cigarettes, saving the remainder of her money credits, hopefully for when she arrived to New Zealand. However, at the time, nobody had explained that this money allowance could only be spent on board for the duration of their sea voyage.

It was to be a six-week journey, and already some passengers were feeling queasy and confined to lower decks, meant claustrophobia only added to their woes. After finding her sea legs, Anna was determined not to fall victim to seasickness and discovered that sitting outside in the fresh air on the deck kept her balanced while she focused on the horizon as the ship swayed in the swell. Here on deck, Anna found camaraderie with others as each shared their cigarettes and exchanged future aspirations. They were a mixed bunch of young single men and women, some elderly, some with families and children, but each looked forward to a bright future in New Zealand.

The 'Dundalk Bay' carried 932 passengers of varying nationalities during the voyage. There were Estonians, Latvians, Lithuanians, Russians, Ukrainians, Yugoslavs, Poles, Hungarians, Czechoslovaks, and even some stateless souls.

Their first port of call was Alexandria in Egypt. Here the crew collected boxes of supplies and mail, but by the time they arrived in Port Said, some 45 passengers had to be disembarked because of severe illness. The captain could not afford so many being ill on board as sick-bay facilities were limited, and least of all, he did not want anyone dying on his ship.

Port Said was rife with hawkers who shouted up at the fascinated passengers leaning over the decks. All the while, these hapless salesmen drifted alongside the moored ship, haphazardly clinging onto it while trying to sell their chattels and wares from overloaded punts. At no point on the journey were the refugees allowed to disembark, but every now and then some absconded and during the voyage, for whatever reason, at least ten passengers defected.

The Suez Canal crossing highlighted a fascinating feat of engineering for Anna as she marvelled how this 100-mile waterway could shorten the distance and time travelled to New Zealand. Numerous ships lined up and moored ahead of them, all destined in the same direction, while equally numbered ships arrived from the Red Sea and passed them, heading back into the Mediterranean. It seemed that all ships heading west, sailed during the day, and later in the evening, those heading east would be escorted through during the night. Finally, by about midnight, the 'Dundalk Bay' began to move toward the canal, and from on top of the deck, Anna could see the canal lit up on both sides as two tugs, one at either end of the ship, guided it through the Suez Canal.

By morning, Anna saw that both sides of the canal were a vast nothingness of parched sand. On the Sinai side, it was an inhospitable stretch of flat sandy desert as far as the eye could see, occasionally broken by a camel train that blurred into the dusty horizon like a mirage. On the opposite side, it was much the same, except the monotony was punctuated with primitive mud brick huts occasionally shaded by date palms while loaded donkey carts hurried alongside the shore, whipped along by impatient Arabs.

When they arrived in Port Suez, it was stinking hot with a blistering wind carrying swarms of flies that soon roosted on the decks annoying passengers and crawling into every crevice of the ship. The stench was overpowering, consisting of every foul odour imaginable. Once again, the hawkers paddled out and nosily juggled for position showing off their goods and hoping for a quick sale. Fortunately, the ship remained only briefly in port before continuing into the Red Sea. The voyage over the Red Sea was exceedingly calm and balmy, and on many occasions, Anna found it difficult to sleep down in her bunk. She spent most nights on deck watching the starry sky overhead as the ship glided through the still and stifling heat of the Mediterranean.

Their next stop was at the port of Aden[1] in the gulf country by the same name that extended northward into the Arabian Sea. Aden was then a British Crown Colony, but the port today is in the renamed People's Republic of South Yemen. Despite its earlier history with Jewish unrest in 1947, followed by the first Arab-Israeli War of 1948, and although British relationships with the Arab world were already strained, during Anna's journey, Aden was a busy shipping destination and a viable port for any passing vessels through the Suez Canal. Anna's first impression of Aden in early June of 1949 was of barren cliffs and hills covered in goats and sheep. Not a very hospitable place, and Anna recalls many elderly people on board were still suffering from ongoing illnesses, but did their best to hide their ailments so not to be disembarked there by the ship's captain.

The journey onto India across the Arabian Sea was more pleasant with constant sea breezes, but with increased rocking of the ship as giant waves rolled and splashed against the lower deck portholes. The next port of call was Bombay (Mumbai), which once again was a noisy and busy seaport. Here on the wharf, goods were offloaded and additional supplies loaded amongst the argy-bargy of hawkers shouting enthusiastically at the passengers. From the ship's deck, Anna remembered seeing the distant view of Bombay city prettily nestled amongst tropical trees and palms. Once more, their stay in port was brief before the 'Dundalk Bay' sailed and headed south along the coast toward Ceylon.

Upon arrival in Ceylon; now known as Sri Lanka, the ship remained in the port of Colombo for a few days. Here, the non-refugee and paying passengers were allowed to disembark and enjoy their stay, visiting bazaars and tourist spots and over-night in exotic hotels. However, as per immigration directive, the refugee contingent had to remain on board, but it did not stop them from interacting with the locals. Multitudes of pestering Ceylonese hawkers on boats loaded with goods of all manner of things were determined to make a sale as they closed in on the ship berthed in port. The Ceylonese were only interested in American Dollars, but as the refugee passengers did not have any, many were still keen to trade their souvenirs regardless. The vendors improvised ingenious means of trade with a basket attached to a rope and throwing it up over the railings, the passengers could then lower the basket back and forth exchanging money or whatever means were used to barter for the goods being sold. There seemed to be an element of trust amongst them while the bartering continued. Anna had no money, but in exchange for the dressing gown she had received as a Christmas gift from Mrs. Pobucká in Ludwigsburg, she souvenired a wooden elephant with ivory tusks, some bananas and a pineapple. She was delighted with the fruit but most pleased with the wooden elephant statue, a souvenir that still remains in her home.

During the journey, the passengers were continually updated on their travels through an extensive global map pinpointing their ship's daily movement and locality. After some days out of Colombo, they were now nearing the Equator. Whispers were beginning to circulate that there was to be a party on board. On the day of crossing the Equator, everyone was instructed not to wear their best clothes. Not that many of the refugees possessed anything too flash. The 'Dundalk Bay' had a swimming pool on the top deck for its first-class passengers, and for the first time, all passengers regardless of being steerage class and who had not crossed the Equator before, were invited onto the top deck to be initiated by King Neptune. King Neptune dressed in full green aquatic regalia, who just happened to be the ship's captain, sat regally in his chair, waiting to meet his uninitiated subjects. It was a frivolous occasion with plenty of gaiety and shrieks of laughter as all the partaking passenger's faces and bodies were smeared with green slime by King Neptune and then thrown into the swimming pool by his attendants. Anna took her initiation with excellent humour as intended and, being a hot day, enjoyed the refreshing dip in the pool.

With so many refugees allowed to venture onto the top deck to be initiated, not all residing in their upper cabins saw the humorous side of this charade; for them, it was a class invasion. Anna cared nothing for their snobbery as she knew many people on board in the lower decks, and many more in Germany's refugee camps; were well educated, many even titled who mingled freely with the lowest of refugees without demanding preferential treatment.

During her time in Germany, Anna remembered seeing Count Friedrich Kinsky of noble Czech lineage [2]; not only was he a man of social status but a learned one who spoke several languages. While the Count had been a political refugee in Regensburg and later in Ludwigsburg, Anna was amazed that he appeared and acted like all other displaced Czechs and never demanded priority in both camps. She had seen and experienced it all there; the hunger, the poverty, and grief from family loss and separation; but now on the ship, she and others had a moment of reprieve and were appreciative of the pleasures bestowed upon them, even if short-lived.

Anna decided during this voyage that one day she would earn and save enough money to travel the world in style. For the time being, life on the ship had its own hurdles to overcome. Anna's sleeping quarters were situated on the bottom level. There were some 200 other women and children in double bunks side by side on this level, and whatever bunk allocation you were given at the beginning of the voyage remained so for the duration of the journey.

Anna had befriended Lida Dudova (Ludmila) and her 13-year-old daughter Miluška (Miloslava). Lida was a widow, and Anna met them in Trieste, so with newcomer Alena Lišková, they became a team and did everything together. By sheer luck, Anna had drawn a lower bunk right next to a porthole, and opposite her on the lower bunk was Alena's berth, with above them Lida and her daughter Miluška. However, those who slept at the ship's lower level were responsible for keeping their respective areas clean and tidy. Alena was a great companion, but she was a reluctant early-morning riser and lagged in sharing these domestic responsibilities.

Anna was delighted with her sleeping possie as the circular window was occasionally opened, bringing in a fresh air flow to ventilate the otherwise musky sleeping quarters. Everyone seemed keen to sit on Anna's bunk and gaze out to sea through the porthole, so much so that many friends would be waylaid staring out in contemplation and often arriving late for their meals.

After much begging and persuading from Lida, Anna finally gave in to her and Miluška, so mother and daughter moved to the lower bunks, while Anna and Alena relegated themselves to the upper quarters. One day while Lida slept by the opened porthole, an unexpected wave gushed in through the opening, leaving Lida in a bedful of seawater. All her bedding had been thoroughly soaked; the sheets, blankets, mattress, and even Anna's bag stowed beneath Lida's bunk. Anna had nothing to laugh about as this bunk had been allocated to her, so it was now her responsibility to clean up the mess. From there on, Lida was obliged to spend most of her time in this bunk and remain on watch in case someone opened the port hole. Below deck had been ventilated, so any fresh air coming through this opened porthole hardly made much difference to the ambient temperature.

There were only five showers on Anna's level, so the morning line-up to the bathroom could take hours. Anna soon discovered that if she awoke at least a quarter of an hour before rising time, she would be first in line with enough time for a shower and wash her smalls before anyone else was up and about. She would then go up on deck and dry her washing, at which time there would already be others to watch her washing should it look like flapping overboard in the breeze. During these early morning jaunts, there was time to share a cigarette while waiting for sunrise. On numerous occasions, dolphins often appeared, racing playfully ahead of the ship's bow wave. Dolphins were present notably whenever the ship neared island reefs, and for many hours these delightful creatures entertained the passengers with their aquatic antics as the ship glided along. Sea birds would also appear and land on deck whenever the ship sailed past islands and land.

One morning while on deck, Anna met Jarmila Drozdova. Anna initially believed her to be Polish as, for some reason, she had been relegated with the Poles but soon discovered Jarmila spoke fluent Czech and had come from Frenštat, not far from Anna's home. Jarmila had been studying medicine at Brno when she, too, had escaped and ended up in a refugee camp in Salzburg, from where she applied to immigrate to New Zealand. After meeting on that morning, they both had breakfast together, and Anna never dreamt that from there on they were destined to become lifelong friends.

Many years later, Jarmila would visit Anna in North Queensland, and they would reminisce about this boat trip to New Zealand and how they both started their new lives after arriving to Wellington. She was referred to as Aunty Jarmila by Anna's children, but Jarmila always reminded Anna that Julatten, where Anna finally settled, was far hotter than the Red Sea!

As the 'Dundalk Bay' sailed southerly toward Australia's western coast, outside temperatures began to cool, although the weather remained sunny. It was already June when they arrived at the Port of Freemantle. Anna was reminded that it was winter in Australia but not as cold as she had experienced back home in Europe. In Fremantle, they remained for a whole day, but again none of the refugees were allowed to disembark.

A week or so later, while berthed in Melbourne, Anna remembered all too well the cold wind that froze her to the bones. She once read that Australia was close to the Equator, where it was always hot. Still, Australia was a large continent straddling two Zones; one tropical and the other temperate, so she soon learned it was an island continent of very cold to freezing winters balanced with very hot summers.

While in Melbourne, further ill passengers disembarked before the 'Dundalk Bay' continued her journey through Bass Strait and into the Tasman Sea toward New Zealand. They were now sailing in the Southern Pacific Ocean, and Anna was beginning to sense excitement as their next port of call would be Wellington, her final destination.

One afternoon, only a few days into the Tasman Sea crossing, an unexpected loud-speaker announcement ordered everyone to get their life jackets and have them stowed and readily accessible during the night. Anna had entirely forgotten about life jackets and lifeboats since their emergency drill at the beginning of the voyage. Without further explanation from the captain's crew member, many passengers became anxious and began to pray. Further orders instructed all windows and port holes to be immediately closed, locked, and not opened under any circumstances. Furthermore, at least for the time being, nobody was allowed on deck.

By late afternoon, the 'Dundalk Bay' suddenly began to sway from side to side.

Nobody below deck could see the horizon, only seawater foam lashing up against the port holes. No one was game to stand up for fear of toppling onto someone else, and soon, anxious passengers were seasick. Once again, Anna managed to hold off any illness, but Lida and Miluška succumbed to seasickness along with most others. The ship was nearing the west coast of New Zealand, and sailing conditions in these parts of the Tasman Sea were often rough and unpredictable.

By morning no one was keen to have breakfast as the ship began approaching the passage between North and South Islands. The channel known as Cook Strait was also notorious for rough sailing, and the seas showed no sign of abating. Later during the day, it was announced that on the following morning, breakfast would be served an hour earlier, but to expect continued rough weather while the ship steamed through the passage.

Photograph 193: Anna Kurovcová 1949.

Photograph 194 & 195: (L-R) Lida & Miluška Dudova & Anna Kurovcová with an unknown child, June 1949. Czech lads on the 'Dundalk Bay' June 1949.

Photograph 196 & 197: (L-R) Czech lads headed for NZ in June 1949. Czech lads on the deck of the 'Dundalk Bay' June 1949.

CHAPTER 16

Wellington, New Zealand

After a turbulent journey across the Tasman Sea, the ship was rolling her way toward the end of Cook Strait that divided New Zealand into North and South Islands. Toward late afternoon the 'Dundalk Bay' finally steadied her speed as she approached the harbour. With the Winter sun already set, the 'Dundalk Bay' glided into Wellington Harbor on the evening of the 26th of June 1949. Her cargo of post-WWII immigrants who, some six weeks earlier, embarked from the Port of Trieste in Italy on a much anticipated, albeit uncertain, journey, had finally arrived.

Beyond the harbour, a deepening hue of rose rested on the horizon. Amongst the misty line of hills, lights twinkled like tiny jewels at the foot of the winter sky. The 'Dundalk Bay' sat almost motionless, anchored in the wintry waters of the harbor while white caped waves slapped about her anchor chains. The ship was lit up like a Christmas tree as she settled for the night only a short distance from her final disembarkation point, where she would finally offload her passengers in the morning.

The twinkling sprawl of Wellington became brighter in the gathering dusk, and despite the cold wind, it still delivered a serene and warm welcome to those finally allowed to gather and huddle in groups on the deck. There was an air of anticipation and excitement amongst the passengers as they embraced each other and, leaning against the railings, stared into the twilight horizon hugging the Harbor of Wellington. Even though Wellington was renowned for its windy disposition regardless of season, this had gone largely unnoticed as the passengers breathed in the crisp air whipping about their faces.

For Anna, it was difficult to imagine the scenery ahead in daylight as tomorrow morning could not arrive fast enough for her. Having to leave the 'Dundalk Bay,' Anna was beginning to have some sad misgivings as the ship had been home to them for over six weeks now and, for most, the only safe haven they had in recent years. Anna had made many friends during the voyage, and she hoped they would remain in touch and be there for one another in times of need and loneliness.

In hindsight if Anna had only known that everything would end safely in a harbour in New Zealand, she wished for one moment she could turn back the hands of time and convince her family when she fled home it would end in a safe journey. How happy this would have made her, vowing she would never have asked for anything else if only her family had come with her. Regrettably, they were destined to remain distant in a world that was now out of Anna's reach. She felt a deep pang of regret and sadness as she thought of them at home, knowing they had no idea where she was. Her emotions had become a mixture of sadness and nostalgia blended with jubilation at what tomorrow might bring. She reminded herself that tonight was supposed to be a very special moment, and she must savour every precious drop of it. It was her reward for enduring so much in recent years and not giving in to adversity but striving to achieve her goal against many odds. "New Zealand will now be my home." She reassured herself while grappling with the reality that she had actually achieved her goal, a goal that, until recently, had only been a childhood dream. There was no war here, only peace and tranquillity, even if a cold wind whipped her sad face and stung her already weeping eyes. Wiping away tears, her blurred vision steadily focused ahead on the twinkling lights dancing like stars that was the city of Wellington. Her thoughts returned to the present, and she wondered what this chilly cloak of darkness masquerading in sparkles would reveal tomorrow morning.

That evening Anna missed her final dinner sitting aboard the 'Dundalk Bay,' as excitement blended with anxiety, began to unsettle her stomach making the prospect of eating almost unpalatable. Tonight, the soul was hungry, not the stomach; somewhat ironical as not so long ago, Anna gave her all and sold her only pair of boots to abate the chronic hollow pangs of hunger... How quickly one forgets such deprivation!

To her unpreparedness, reality struck fast and hard. Suddenly, Anna felt embarrassed and very vulnerable. She was no longer in a refugee camp where equality remained unchallenged. She was now about to set foot into a sophisticated country and somehow assimilate with its equally sophisticated society. She had nothing to offer in return.

Book One: Anna's Story

No education, no wealth, only herself; a dishevelled stranger, shabbily dressed without money, profession, or even the comprehension of written or spoken English. It was a daunting prospect. It may have been an epic journey to Anna's fortunate dream's end, but the real obstacles were now formulating an equation without any counterbalance. For the first time, Anna realized she had not thought about how she would tackle her new life.

The following morning nearly everybody sat down to an early and hearty breakfast, but Anna was still without appetite. After breakfast, the passengers gathered with their meagre possessions and assembled on deck in preparation to disembark the 'Dundalk Bay,' which by now had been berthed alongside the wharf. Each step brought them closer to their destiny, onto foreign soil of a country that showed no animosity but welcomed them not as refugees but as people. On the wharf, the Māori people sang their song of greeting, which none of the passengers understood, but the swinging poi-pois in rhythm to their fluid swaying and singing exuded a genuine sense of welcome. Apart from this orchestrated welcome, the remainder of the wharf was busy, unusually brisk with milling throngs of people meeting the ship.

When Anna was about to embark onto the train bound for Pahiatua; a township set aside for newly arrived immigrants and which was situated some distance to the north, two kindly ladies approached her and presented Anna with a luxurious fawn-coloured coat, some biscuits, a food parcel and wished her well. Anna was overwhelmed with such unexpected but genuine kindness from total strangers.

At Pahiatua, the new arrivals lined up outside, while inside the hall, rows of make-shift customs and immigration desks manned with officials awaited them. Everything was orderly and efficiently processed as the refugees were ushered in amidst anticipated apprehension and confusion. Finally, all concerns were quelled, while patient staff assisted everyone with customs and immigration formalities; aiding with completion of documents to be presented to the officers at the desk.

All newcomers were issued a New Settlers Identity Card with the individual's personal details, including date of arrival, Employment Registration Number, Social Security Registration, and place of

Resettlement and Employment. These were all methodically stamped and dated as everyone passed through the centre.

Anna's ID card number was 2/495, processed from Pahiatua block No. 14, and showed she had arrived in New Zealand on the 27th of June 1949 from aboard the 'Dundalk Bay.' She was described as Roman Catholic, born on the 28th of August 1918, with auburn hair and hazel-coloured eyes. She stood 5 ft. 7½ inches tall and had a vaccination scar on her right arm. She passed through customs on the 30th of June 1949 and was registered as No. 81849. On the 5th of July, she received her Social Security clearance [1].

Being frugal with money, Anna had chosen not to use much of her allowance during the voyage from Trieste to Wellington and instead saved these credits for her arrival to New Zealand. When Anna enquired about her unused canteen credits, she was informed that this allowance had only been made available for the sole purpose of the journey and that now she had no further claim. She felt somewhat cheated and cross with herself for being so stupid. Many times, during the voyage, Anna hungered for a piece of chocolate, a soft drink, or chewing gum, or often hankered for a pretty handkerchief, a scarf, or even a pair of nylons; but sacrificed all, instead watching friends luxuriating in their purchases.

Pahiatua was a small rural service town, some 130 km or 81 miles, in a direct line north of Wellington. Its Māori name-sake meant either 'God's resting place or the place of a God,' and close by, a WWII internment camp for foreigners had been established in 1944, which became a refugee camp for Polish children. Anna's first and most memorable sight of Pahiatua camp was the colourful flowering geraniums growing protected against the walls of the disused barracks. It was winter, yet these plants flowered in red, pink, and white clusters. The flowers appeared so welcoming that Anna believed it had to be a sure sign of good things to come.

While they lived at Pahiatua, temporarily housed in the disused army barracks, each received a weekly allowance of 10 shillings until they gained permanent employment. During this stay, everyone had to attend English-Speaking Classes for the next two weeks. Their teacher was a pleasant woman whom herself had once visited Prague as a child and consequently developed an amicable relationship with Anna and her Czech friends. They also had table etiquette lessons, mainly on using a fork correctly. It was not to be used for shovelling food into your mouth but rather for picking up food and placing it delicately into the mouth. Many valuable tips that were commonplace to New Zealanders but not necessarily to Continental Europeans, were taken into account and taught.

Anna's immediate friends were a mixed bunch of characters. Dagmar Cihlová, who preferred to be called Dasha, was 20 years old and single. Jarmila Drozdova was 30 and single, but she had some nursing experience while studying medicine in her home country. Ludmilla Dudova, also known as Lida, was 35 and a widow. She was accompanied by her 13-year-old daughter Miluška. Alena Lišková was 27 and also single. Vlasta (possibly Pavlikova) was 25 years old, married, and the only occupation she ever knew was being a housewife. Although each had come from vastly different backgrounds with differing personalities, they shared a voyage with little expectation of what their futures might bring. Still, over the past six weeks at sea, each had supported and cheered up one another during their lows and uncertainties.

While some in the group were introspective and cautious, others were gregarious and humorous, and even adventurous and daring, throwing all caution to the wind. Still, together they were young Czech women who wanted a better future after escaping the hardships they had endured over the past years. This mixture of personalities gave Anna an opportunity to develop her own character, which until now had been thwarted by her own lack of self-esteem. She was a country girl who never had the opportunity to grow up and socialize under normal circumstances.

During that time, her brother Jaroslav and his friend Jan did not help matters inferring she was too timid and needed to wise up about world affairs if she was to survive on her own. Although all that Anna knew was farm work and still often craved life in the country, she was prepared to be educated for the better.

Her Czech friends often greeted her, "Hello, Country Bumkin!"

However, throughout, Anna never lost sight of her dreams and believed that one day she too could become 'an educated woman' and aspire to a fulfilling life regardless of fallen fortunes and shattered post-war hopes. In her youth, she had wanted to study medicine and become a doctor, but as it was not to be, at least here in New Zealand, she might carve out a career in a similar field. So, together with her circle of Czech girlfriends, Anna accepted her education graciously, and adjusted to new surroundings, embracing the new way of life and its culture.

A short time later, the two women who had showered Anna with gifts arrived at Pahiatua to visit her. They had made pleas to Anna to work for them in their shop in Hamilton. In accordance with government terms of Anna's immigration conditions, private employment was disallowed. All female migrants had to choose a vocation within the government system, factory, or health work. Anna, Dasha, Vlasta, and Jarmila chose careers in nursing, while Alena and Lida chose otherwise. Lida, opted for factory work and begged Anna to join her, but Anna was determined to study nursing.

Finally, on the 1st of September 1949, Anna and her friends were discharged from Pahiatua Training Centre. Those opting to study nursing were sent to Tokanui about 130 km south of Auckland. Tokanui Psychiatric Hospital was 14 km from Te Awamutu and about 29 km south of Hamilton.

Photograph 198: A small section of the Tokanui Hospital complex.

CHAPTER 17

Anna: Tokanui Psychiatric Hospital

On arrival to Tokanui the women were welcomed with tea and biscuits and then measured for uniforms. Anna's initial uniform was pale pink with a white collar, and all dresses were individually numbered along with their names for laundry purposes. Each was also given a laundry bag, and it too was numbered accordingly.

On Anna's first day, she started in Ward 15 under the charge of Sister Palmer. Anna was relegated to work alongside another experienced nurse but found herself often helping domestic staff with sweeping floors and cleaning windows.

Sister Palmer was a formidable character and not a force to meddle with. Initially she appeared unapproachable, unfriendly and mean, but she was officious and thorough. She spoke so fast that Anna understood very little if anything at all that was said with no inkling of what she was supposed to do. On numerous occasions, after receiving orders from Sister Palmer, Anna would wander off into oblivion hoping that someone would come along and rescue her and point her in the right direction before being chastised. One of Anna's saving graces was an inmate, a friendly and caring old lady named Mrs. Java, who would listen out for orders and then discreetly approach Anna, explain patiently what was expected, and point Anna in the right direction.

For some time, Anna remained under the watchful eye of her mentors, rotating shifts with nursing staff who were generally helpful and patient, explaining nursing procedures while working together. From the start, Anna tried to keep busy with whatever mundane tasks she was delegated and even assisted domestic staff so as to appear busy without drawing unneeded attention from Sister Palmer.

It was a difficult and frustrating beginning for Anna, with embarrassing moments, but as her rudimentary understanding of English improved, so did Anna's confidence. With newly gained nursing proficiency, she soon became hands-on with the inmates. Over the following month, Anna and Sister Palmer grew to tolerate one another and after becoming better acquainted, eventually became steady friends.

Anna's first pay was the princely sum of £3/10 shillings*, which Anna was most pleased with. (*Interestingly, the Gisborne Herald, December 10th, 1949, advertised for Psychiatric nursing training at Tokanui and amongst other hospitals in North Island, it stated; 'after-tax with board, lodging, and uniforms provided, the starting pay was £4/ 8 shillings per week.')[1] This amount of money had enormous potential for Anna, and although determined to save, she first wanted some niceties that her New Zealand counterparts had. So, she went on a shopping spree at the very first opportunity and bought a pair of shoes, as the only pair she had were the standard ones issued for work. Her other footwear, the boots that had seen her through Europe, were well and truly worn through, threadbare, and barely held together with string. She also bought stockings, underwear, a new dress with a handbag, a hat, and gloves to match, and afterward still had money left over. It was a great feeling to have money of her own and the independence to spend it as she wished, albeit on herself for a change.

Anna was finally beginning to feel like a worthy young woman and someone who could subtly fit in with her newly found friends without feeling too embarrassed about her impoverished predisposition. She earned money only once before, while in Germany working in the Children's kitchen at Ludwigsburg. It was menial pay then but because of necessity it compelled Anna to share it with her equally impoverished friends.

During her time in Tokanui, some of Anna's refugee friends still in Germany had managed to track her down through the IRO which forwarded letters from them onto her. Anna felt somewhat guilty about her fortunate circumstances while her refugee friends in Germany were still waiting for visas onto the USA and elsewhere. They frequently placed pressure on Anna to join them in America when they finally located there. Anna became torn between her pledge to remain in New Zealand and their persistence to join them.

Before leaving Germany, Anna had promised her friends that she would always remain in touch and perhaps one day she would join them. She heard that the Tušle family was finally happily settled in Canada, but the Krapačov family was still in Germany awaiting resettlement. Both urged Anna to join them. She replied to everyone, explaining her contractual circumstances binding her to New Zealand for the next three years, but it all seemed to fall upon deaf ears. Anna was happy in New Zealand and if it was not for her Ludwigsburg friends trying to influence her life, she would have had no particular desire to go elsewhere. Slowly they whittled her down, and Anna's guilt began to prick her conscience as she gave in to their pressure. Anna's written English was not at any acceptable standard. So as not to appear totally illiterate, she persuaded her friend Sister Collier to assist with a letter to the New Zealand Immigration Office. Sister Collier advised Anna that applying to leave New Zealand was not a good idea. Although she disagreed with Anna's idea, she dutifully wrote a letter stating that although Anna was happy in New Zealand, she wanted to immigrate to America.

Adding to Anna's quandary, she had a preconceived idea that all who lived on the South Island were Quakers and whose women folk abided by principles of simple and honest living in peaceful coexistence with others. Anna believed she would never measure up to such ideals of simplicity as she still desired to dress elegantly, enjoy dances and parties, and generally have a good time. She did not ever want to wear shabby or dull clothes again and deprive herself of feminine niceties. In the end, Sister Collier had to explain and assure Anna that Quakers were only a minority of people who did not forcibly impose their ideals onto others and they were not the only people whose lifestyle influenced New Zealand society.

Here in New Zealand, Anna was informed, she at least could choose her own philosophy in life and live accordingly. Still, more to the point, Anna was reminded that she had a binding contract with the New Zealand Government for at least three years which she had signed in Germany. However, without considering any consequences, Anna's so-called girlfriends Jarmila and Dagmar egged her on and told her not to be a pushover and just do it and go to America, both promising to follow her. In the end, Anna decided to go to the Wellington Immigration and Information Centre and ask for herself what her terms and conditions meant. She was given the name of Mrs. Růzickova, a Czech woman, and posted her a letter outlining all the dilemmas. When Mrs. Růzickova replied later in September, she invited Anna to come to Wellington and discuss the matter. She also added that it would coincide with Count Kinsky's visit as he too had issues to sort out. Anna was surprised to hear that he had also ended up in New Zealand, but she only knew of his family by sight.

Count Friedrich Kinsky was a Czech aristocrat. Anna remembered him briefly passing through Regensburg and Ludwigsburg but perhaps recognized him for no other reason than that he belonged to Czech Nobility. Fred Kinsky as he became known in New Zealand, was like many other refugee immigrants and, for the time being, without his wife and two daughters.

Count Kinsky sat down with Anna, advising her to be true to herself and not only allow her heart to be manipulated but also use her head to dictate her own course of action and not be drawn into futile promises just to appease others. After all, why did she want to go to America? Was she not grateful to be in New Zealand? He reminded her of the binding contract with the New Zealand Government, which many refugees would have given their all to be in her position. Afterall it was only of short duration, after which time she would be free to leave and go anywhere in the world she desired.

Anna settled into her nursing role at Tokanui Hospital and pushed aside all fanciful notions of immigrating elsewhere when actually, she was more than happy to be where she was.

Tokanui Psychiatric Hospital[2] may not have been the happiest environment in the world as a mental institution. Many of its inmates never left, or if they did, they only too readily returned. As with many such Institutions, allegories were always attached to these places, which kept many superstitious staff on edge. At Tokanui, for instance, nobody was ever allowed to place red and white flowers together in a vase as that invited death which came in the form of a visit from the 'Lady in

Grey,' who allegedly would sit on the bed or be seen hovering over her next victim. Anna once hinted that she thought she saw an apparition before the death of a patient but never really knew if it was the case or her vulnerability to be convinced that such matters occurred.

Cats were another source of superstition. If the residential cat was ever found sleeping beneath a patient's bed or paying unusual attention to them, this was also deemed an omen of pending death.

Apart from certain disturbing mental health work ethics that came with the territory of psychiatric nursing at the time, and which Anna had to accept in her role, New Zealand had become Anna's living dream. It was a stunningly beautiful country with snow-capped peaks and lush green hilly pastures dotted with grazing sheep. At the time, there were about one million people in New Zealand compared to its six million sheep. This always amused Anna.

Christmas of 1949 arrived with the full bloom of flowers, rather than cold wintery snow, as Anna remembered at home. Despite the glorious weather, Anna could not remember a sadder and more miserable Christmas while she quietly carried a heavy heart and grieved for her family.

She had not heard from her brother Jaroslav since the telegram in Italy prior to her departure. She knew nothing of his whereabouts, nor had he written as she was sure he could have tracked her down, knowing she was already somewhere in New Zealand. Anna felt desperately isolated and depressed about it, but she dared not spoil the festive season by drawing her friends into her own melancholia.

Christmas dinner was a memorable occasion for the Tokanui Hospital staff, and Anna made the most of the delicious spread of traditional English food. It was a tradition Anna was not accustomed to, and for the occasion, she put aside her sadness and enjoyed the friendly camaraderie and excellent food.

After Christmas, a New Year's ball had been arranged at the nurse's quarters, and all the young nurses were excited and eager to attend. Unfortunately, Anna had to work until late on that evening, but like all the other nursing staff, she was keen to attend at least some of the dances.

Anna finally arrived without an escort, dressed in a stunning black silk blouse tucked into a long white velvet skirt. It was well onto midnight when she entered the ballroom, and a gentleman promptly asked her to dance.

Soon afterward, she was reproached by Sister Champion, one of Anna's less affectionate work colleagues, demanding to know what she thought she was doing last night, dancing with her boyfriend. Needless to say, their relationship at work did not improve, and Anna was often banished to cleaning toilets when they next worked together.

While at Tokanui Hospital, her fellow Czech colleague Dagmar fell madly in love with a Czech lad called Mirek. Dagmar was not as conscientious about work as Anna, and thought nothing of being late, even missing the occasional shift at work. After failing to turn up at work on two consecutive days, and realizing much would need to be explained to plead for clemency, Dagmar begged Anna to accompany her to the Supervisor's office. Dagmar had already decided to bypass their Charge Sister and Matron and instead go directly to the top, taking Anna with her. Unannounced, they presented at the Superintendent's office to present Dagmar's case. Dr. Hunter, the hospital Superintendent was known to be approachable and compassionate toward his staff. As Dagmar believed he was especially fond of Anna in his protective way, surely, he would not reproach her in Anna's presence.

When the two women arrived, it is uncertain whether Dr. Hunter knew what they were on about as Anna explained Dagmar's situation, "Dagmar not come to work. Too much love!"

Somewhat bemused with the opening address, he took it to be an apology of some kind and turned to Anna and said, "You mean she is in love?"

They nodded in agreement, and without waiting for further redress, they scurried back to work. When they returned to the ward, they were both met with hostile glares from the Acting Matron, Sister Puk, who demanded an explanation for their unauthorized visit without her prior approval and an appropriate appointment with Dr. Hunter.

Photograph 199 & 200: (L-R) Anna early 1950 still in old boots. Anna posing at Tokanui Hospital in 1950.

Photograph 201 & 202: (L-R) Anna posing at Tokanui Hospital in 1950. Anna far right standing in uniform with nurses at Tokanui Hospital 1950.

Photograph 203: Anna far left sitting with nurses at Tokanui Hospital 1950.

Photograph 204: Staff fancy dress tennis match Tokanui Hospital 1950.

Photograph 205 & 206: (L-R)Anna at Tokanui Hospital in 1950.
Anna's friend; a young Māori nurse at Tokanui Hospital.

CHAPTER 18

A Close Call & New Friendships

During the weeks leading up to winter, there had been an outbreak of flu. The weather had suddenly turned dismally cold and windy, and many of the staff and inpatients succumbed to respiratory illnesses. Even Anna ended up with a croupy voice and began to cough incessantly. As staff shortages needed filling, Anna continued to work, thinking she would get over the worst of it before too long. Many inmates were already afflicted; some elderly and weaker ones even died. Despite feeling ill, Anna tried her hardest to carry on. She almost paid with her life for her efforts, however.

As Anna said in her own words, "We make these plans, and then God changes everything!"

With her cough unabating, she became exhausted and developed high fevers. With it came delirium, and she was finally transferred to Waikato Hospital in Hamilton, where the staff tried treating her with Penicillin. Anna reacted with a severe rash from tip to toe. Her Tokanui colleagues, Vlasta, and Dagmar came to visit, but only once, as Anna did not recognize them, so they did not return while she remained ill in the hospital. Only Jarmila persevered and visited as often as possible, even if Anna did not recognize her and for most remained unresponsive to her presence. It turned out that within her group of Czech friends, it was Jarmila who proved to be her genuine and caring friend.

During Anna's critical stage, somebody wrote to friends in Germany, informing them that Anna was gravely ill and dying. Another wrote to Mr. Pobucký at Ludwigsburg IRO Jägerhof (camp), informing him Anna had died and her ashes had already been scattered into the sea!

When Anna's distant acquaintances heard the distressing news, many grieved for her and passed on the upsetting news to others. How many in the end believed her to be dead at the time, Anna never really knew, but during her real-life crises, doctors did all they could for her while her life hung in limbo. There was even talk of surgery to find the source of her sepsis. But by a fortunate stroke of luck, a senior doctor from Auckland had arrived to consult on another case when Anna was referred to him. He concluded that her teeth were the source of her sepsis, so all her teeth were extracted. Shortly afterward, Anna's condition slowly improved, with fevers gradually subsiding.

One morning she awoke and turned her head toward a ringing telephone down the corridor to hear a conversation. The person who answered the phone expressed how well her patient had been progressing and that she would soon be ready for discharge. Anna had no idea the conversation was about her.

When Jarmila arrived to visit, Anna was full of smiles, albeit toothless, while they chatted about what had been happening in her absence.

With Anna's health and strength returning, the doctors began talking about sending her to a sanatorium for a month to convalesce. Anna did not want to go. She only wanted to go home, where ever that may be. Her belongings had been packed into her bags and placed in storage, and another nurse now occupied her room at Tokanui Nurse's Quarters.

When Anna finally returned to Tokanui, she was allocated a new room and given five weeks of sick leave. She had an appointment with a dentist at Te Awamutu and was soon fitted with new dentures. Slowly her health improved, and throughout her convalescence, she was never without friends fussing over her. Vlasta and Dagmar wanted to restore their friendship with her, and although Anna was receptive to them, she never trusted or became a part of their social circle again. Instead, much of her time was spent with Jarmila.

Although Jarmila and Anna were like chalk and cheese, their friendship remained firm. Both were proud individuals, whereas Jarmila was flamboyant and always on the go, Anna was quite the opposite.

As Anna put it, "We were like a pair of peacocks! Both proud, but one being the ostentatious and colourful one while the other was less visible and dowdy!"

Whenever any of the nurses went on home leave for a few days, they would invariably invite Anna along so she could see the countryside and enjoy life outside of the Tokanui hospital grounds. Katy Black was a sister (Registered Nurse) who often socialized with Anna's circle of friends. Katy's family were dairy farmers, so one day, Katy invited Anna to join her with her family.

Anna was surprised at how large Katy's family farm was and became fascinated with cows being milked by machines. She was eager to help and learn about their farming methods as it was nothing like how things were done back at her home in Czechoslovakia.

They also visited the neighbouring farm, which the Plummer family owned. Elizabeth, their daughter, was a great friend of Katy's, and while there, Anna was introduced to George, Elizabeth's older brother. Elizabeth was about to start work at a radio station in Auckland, and George seemed destined to remain on the farm. Anna obviously made an impression as Mrs. Plummer invited her back. Katy smiled at the invitation but said nothing to Anna at the time.

Shortly afterward, George visited Tokanui and confided in Katy that he fancied Anna and so began a relationship. Although he was shorter than Anna when she was in heels, he was the perfect gentleman, and his family always welcomed her.

At the end of her convalescence, Anna returned to nursing and once more settled into her work routine. Once again, her thoughts began to dwell on her family at home, and after her own recent calamity, she realized that if the worst had happened, they might have never heard of her again, so she finally decided it was time she made contact with them. She remembered the fortune teller's prediction in Ludwigsburg some twelve months previously, a reading she reluctantly participated in and one which she was even less inclined to believe. To say the least, it was uncanny and yet very disturbing that this woman's predictions so far, had accordingly manifested in her life. Anna's journey over the sea could have been a general prediction for anyone in a refugee camp in those days, but the other eventualities; great sadness; her sister Helena's imprisonment, tragic death; Domin's execution; and now her own grave illness which she would survive; were a sharp reminder to tread cautiously, or in the very least maintain some distance from so-called fortune-tellers. It sent a shiver down her back, but at least for now, these ominous predictions had come to pass, and Anna could put them all behind her and move on.

It was May of 1950, and her mother's birthday was nearing. She knew that she had to write to her family one day and let them know she was still alive and well. Anna was still fearful of writing home but there was no other sensible option rather than write and hope their lives would not be compromised. Her family had probably last heard of her when she was still in Ludwigsburg, but that was over twelve months ago. In the end, Anna decided to send her mother a birthday telegram. Still, as it could not be dispatched in Czech at the post office, she sent a brief English message, during which time she also posted one kilogram of chocolates and attached a lengthy letter inside.

Anna learned afterward that her telegram caused them more concern than not hearing from her. It had arrived at the Lešná Post Office during the early morning hours, and immediately, the postmistress dispatched it to Lhotka, where Anna's mother, Rosalie Kurovcová, was living. Everyone feared the worst as it was in English, so it immediately went onto Krhová, some eight kilometres further on, for Robert Pavlik to translate when he was next visited in prison. Robert spoke and understood English from his military service days in Great Brittan. After the war, when he returned to Czechoslovakia and was arrested and charged with trumped-up allegations, he was sentenced to prison for ten years. After six years, his sentence was eventually commuted to paroled labour for government regulators for the next ten years.

Reading the telegram, Robert soon reassured them that Anna was well and was only sending Birthday greetings to her mother. When Anna finally re-established frequent contact with her family at home, she always posted them items that could no longer be easily bought, so when she heard her sister Zdenka finally had a baby girl following her three boys; Milos, Zdeněk and Jarek, Anna immediately dispatched a belated gift, a pink woollen jacket and bonnet for newly arrived Pavla who had been born earlier in March of 1950.

In late 1950 Anna received a rather belated letter from Jan Kaňák, who was living near London. Jan had written earlier to Anna while she was still in Ludwigsburg, Germany. Due to her hectic travel developments, circumstances were such she could not reply immediately and, in the end, she forgot all about him.

When they parted in Burk in 1948, they made a pact to keep in touch and nominated Pepik Chmelař as their mutual contact as he always managed to keep tabs on everybody no matter what the circumstances. He enjoyed writing letters, and for the time being, he maintained regular correspondence with many he had met in Germany. However, as the envelope indicated, this was a well-travelled letter covered in many stamped date marks. Anna later discovered that while at the London Czech Club, Jan had met a young Czech journalist at a dance, and both realized they had mutual acquaintances. During the conversation, while they discussed their past lives, Jan made mention of Anna. The young woman immediately insinuated she knew Anna well but warned Jan not to waste time pining for this 'chimney smoking woman' who, by now, no doubt, was having the time of her life with her many suitors!

Her unprovoked attack on Anna disappointed him, but the sight of Anna smoking while in Germany always appalled him. Despite this scathing appraisal, he was determined to prove the Czech journalist wrong, so he again wrote to Anna. Not knowing what had become of her, Jan forwarded the letter via Pepik, who by then was living in Nairobi, Kenya. Pepik had been employed by Baťa Shoes and was believed to be managing a rubber plantation somewhere near Nairobi. Upon receiving the letter, Pepik forwarded the letter to Anna in Ludwigsburg as, at the time, he believed she was still living there. By the time the letter arrived, Anna had already departed and was on her way to Trieste in Italy.

When Anna finally received the letter in Tokanui, it had already travelled half around the world, stamped with a trail of places that read like a tourist map. From London to Nairobi and onto Ludwigsburg, Turin, Ancona, Senigallia and Trieste, Port Said, Aden, and Colombo, following her via Fremantle, Melbourne, Wellington, and finally Te Awamutu. It had been posted sometime in 1949 before finally reaching her at the hospital sometime in the middle of 1950.

The envelope had been admired by Sister Collier, one of Anna's colleagues at work, so Anna happily gave her this well-journeyed envelope. A stamp collector's dream!

In his letter, Jan described a woefully dismal existence in London and how it was impossible to make ends meet and get ahead. He told Anna that he was now a British Subject and carried a British Passport and would very much like to visit the other side of the world where Anna now lived. However, the cost of living was so high in London, he could never save enough money for such a trip. His only hope was to borrow enough money for his passage to Australia. In between his troubles and hoping Anna would understand his plight, he hinted at a hopeful reconciliation between them and perhaps even a life together.

By now Anna had established contact with her brother Jaroslav, probably at their mother's insistence, who would have prompted Jaroslav to write to his sister at her newly forwarded address in New Zealand. Anna learned from Jaroslav's letter that he had departed Italy after being processed by the IRO as a displaced person at Bagnoli Camp. He sailed on board the 'Svalbard' from Naples on the 9th of September 1949, just three months after Anna had departed from Italy. Jaroslav arrived to Melbourne on the 8th of October of the same year and from there, he moved to South Australia and found work around Port Lincoln. Feeling uncomfortable and guilty for not replying to Jan earlier, Anna promptly wrote to her brother in Australia, hoping he could help his friend.

She always knew her brother had never been keen to encourage a relationship between her and Jan as Jaroslav always maintained Anna was far too fickle and unreliable for any of his friends and that they deserved better. So, with some satisfaction, she forwarded to her brother, Jan's 'love letter to her' and waited to see what would transpire.

During mid 1950 it was nearing to over a year since starting work at Tokanui, and Anna was due for four weeks of fully paid holiday. The notion of being paid and not working was totally alien to the Czech girls, so instead of taking a holiday somewhere away from the hospital, they pleaded permission to stay at the Nurse's quarters for the duration. After all, it was a nice place, and a home holiday would be fine for them.

Dr. Hunter, the Superintendent of Tokanui Hospital at the time, reluctantly agreed to this arrangement but nevertheless allowed the young women to settle into domestic bliss at the nurse's quarters. Anna was good at sewing and soon was making dresses for herself. Her first effort was a handmade frock created from a fabric of a sheer green voile delicately embossed with raised cotton dots. It was a simple but stylish frock worn with a thick black belt and matching black accessories. As stylish as it was, Anna never got to wear it, and sixty years later, it was still hanging in her wardrobe.

Anna also earned extra money sewing for the other girls or whenever there was the opportunity to work extra shifts for staff if they had something else planned. Anna was always happy to oblige, but while on holiday she had to settle with only sewing.

Toward the end of 1950 when Anna had a further two weeks of paid leave approved, she thought she would again stay with her friends at the nurse's quarters. After all, they had everything provided for them, and they could go to the movies and do their reading and sewing at leisure. Dr. Hunter was not so amenable this time, and firmly suggested that for a change, they all take a holiday somewhere by the sea.

Sister Katy Black, or Blacky as she was affectionately known, decided to take Anna, Jarmila, Vlasta, and Dagmar on a seaside vacation. This created plenty of excitement for the girls who immediately went shopping for new bathing suits. Anna bought a fashionable and flattering yellow swimsuit but, at Jarmila's insistence, had to swap it with her as Jarmila could not fit into her new navy-blue two-piece as it was far too small. Anna felt disappointed but obliged her friend.

Blacky booked them all into self-contained cabins by the sea at Mount Maunganui, a seaside resort in the Bay of Plenty of North Island. This was a first-time life experience for Anna and her friends when Blacky introduced them to their first swim in the open sea and the taste of fresh seafood. Feeling the salty waves wash over her and tumble her into the sand was magic. Anna had never entirely experienced such a sensation, as before, she had only swum in the local freshwater rivers at home and, more recently, in a saltwater pool on 'Dundalk Bay.'

"This most certainly must be the watery kingdom and true realm of King Neptune," she smiled.

Anna also discovered and enjoyed the delicious flavour of seafood. Fleshy muscles and pipis, which, when shown how to collect these small molluscs from beneath the sand and then cook them in garlic and butter, were even tastier than the larger muscles.

They remained at Mount Maunganui for the duration of their stay, soaking up the sun, swimming, relaxing, and photographing one another before returning to work.

Throughout much of 1950, Anna was introduced to the somewhat shaky landscape of New Zealand but learned to endure a phenomenon that was very much a part of everyday life. At first, Anna felt sheer terror when the land rumbled, vibrated with such intensity, and swayed with her. But later, it almost became the norm, and even the small tremors would rarely rate a mention. Despite regular earth tremors, Anna travelled unperturbed throughout the North Island and ventured amongst the bubbling volcanic thermals of Rotorua, the often rumbling and steaming peaks of Mt. Tongariro and Mt. Ruapehu. She also explored the majestic but dormant Mt. Egmont or Mt. Taranaki, as it is now known, which erupted for the last time over 300 years ago. Another popular destination was Lake Taupo which sits in the caldera of a not so dormant super volcano.

From February through to June of 1951, there were no less than four significant earthquakes in North Island shaking the ground beneath her feet, as the tremors registered between 6.1 to 6.3 on the Richter Scale,

Anna always said, "If people only knew how unstable New Zealand was, no one would ever live there!" Otherwise, New Zealand remained Anna's perfect place to call home.

Eventually late in 1950, Anna received a reply from her brother informing her that through Thomas Cook Travel in Adelaide, he had paid a berth for Jan on board the 'Strathmore.' Jaroslav added that he remembered him fondly as Jan always helped him with money while they both served in the army at Cholmondeley.

During his army years, Jaroslav always existed from pay to pay and only managed to hold onto his money for a short time.

Jaroslav added in his letter to Anna, "I was unable to secure an economy berth for him on the 'Strathmore,' but could only pay for a first-class passage when a cabin became available!"

Anna later learned from Jan how delighted he was with Jaroslav's kind offer, but unaware it was a first-class ticket until he boarded the 'Strathmore' in London. At the time, he proudly showed the letter to their once-commanding officer General Alois Liška with whom Jan kept in touch. The General raised his eyebrows in surprise, telling Jan he remembered Jaroslav Kurovec very well…

"This soldier never had any money! Whenever he was paid, he immediately lost it all!" So, on the 5th of March 1951, Jan departed on board the P&O liner 'Strathmore' from the Port of London for Adelaide.

A Tree Without Branches: Anna's Journey

Photograph 207 & 208: (L-R) Rotorua 1950 Māori house. Rotorua thermal mud springs.

Photograph 209 & 210: (L-R) Anna facinated by the size of the tree. Anna and friend in Rotorua 1950.

Photograph 211: Anna far left at back in Rotorua with friends in 1950.

Photograph 212, 213 & 214: (L-R) Next two photos; Anna at Tokanui Hospital 1950. Anna posing with friend Katy at Mt. Manganui.

Photograph 215 & 216: (L-R) Mt. Manganui Anna's first swim in the sea in 1950. Mt. Manganui holiday Anna & friends 1950.

Photograph 217 & 218: (L-R) Mt. Manganui 1950: Jarmila, Anna & Katy.

Photograph 219 & 220: (L & R) Anna at Mt. Manganui 1950.

Photograph 221 & 222: (L-R) Mt. Manganui at sunrise 1950. Mt. Manganui Beach with donkey rides 1950.

Photograph 223 & 224: (L-R) Mt. Manganui Anna & Jarmila superimposed photo 1950. Jarmila & Katy with friend at Mt. Manganui 1950.

Photograph 225 & 226: (L-R) Anna, Katy & Jarmila at Mt. Manganui 1950. Jarmila, Anna & Katy on top of rocky outcrop at Mt. Manganui 1950.

Photograph 226 & 228: (L-R) Anna with friends 1950. Anna and George 1950.

Photograph 229: Anna and Katy 1950.

CHAPTER 19

Winter Engagement in Takapuna

Initially, Anna had no serious male relationships, although she was never short of potential suitors. George Plummer became a fixture in her life, and one day, Anna was invited to meet with his family in Wellington. George had booked himself and Anna into separate rooms at a hotel in Wellington with plans to take her to the races with his family, as they were keen racegoers. Anna remembered George's father as being a very tall gentleman, whereas his wife standing next to him was ever so petite.

While Anna occupied herself wandering about the living room admiring the residence, she spotted an impressive wall mural of a large bridge.

With interest, she peered at it and quickly tried to read the small print beneath when George stepped forward and said, "I bet you don't know where that is!"

Anna had never seen this bridge before but recalled the word 'Sydney' written at the bottom of the frame, so she quickly replied, "Sydney Bridge!"

George stood back, somewhat surprised by her apparent knowledge, and exclaimed, "Oh! So, you do know the Sydney Harbor Bridge, then?"

Anna felt chuffed with herself for being so clever, but in reality, she had never been to Sydney, let alone had any notion that such a bridge even existed. As they sat down to dinner, Anna's confidence soon faded when the main course arrived; roast mutton with a selection of vegetables including a cob of steaming yellow corn. It all looked very appetising but for the corn. At home, corn was fed to the animals.

"Why should people eat corn here when they are rich and have so many other vegetables?" She thought to herself.

As everyone proceeded with the course, Anna followed suit and wondered what she was supposed to do with the corn. She watched closely to avoid appearing ignorant and patiently waited to see how the corn would be eaten. As others picked up their cobs with two tiny skewers, Anna managed to do the same with some difficulty, but decided it was definitely an acquired taste.

The family dinner and racing event went smoothly, but Anna found George too intense. Although he treated her with tremendous respect and was attentive to her every need, she was deterred by his earnest nature and lack of spirited adventure and fun.

Some months later, in early June of 1951, Anna received a letter from Jan telling her that he was in South Australia working near Port Lincoln. After working for two months, he had managed to repay Jaroslav the debt owed for his passage to Australia and still managing to save money. As he had been too busy to go into Port Lincoln to spend it, he hinted he was keen to visit her in New Zealand when she next had some leave from work.

Jan's proposed visit to New Zealand came as a complete shock to Anna. While she feverously discussed his imminent arrival with Jarmila and Katy, Jarmila quickly concluded that Anna must not invite him to Te Awamutu, as he might accidentally run into George and instead, suggested they plan a trip to Auckland. After all, they had another two weeks leave scheduled for the end of June, and it would be far too cold to holiday in Te Awamutu. Auckland would be much better as it had a warmer climate by the sea where at least they could swim. Jarmila even ventured to add that it would not look good for Anna if she went alone to meet a male stranger and suggested that she accompany her.

Anna was in a quandary; she had exams before the end of June, after which, in July, their holidays were due to start, and now Jan was about to descend upon her, and Jarmila was inviting herself along as well. Anna's seemingly orderly life quickly became a complicated mockery of its former existence.

Rather than writing to Jan, she wrote again to her brother Jaroslav explaining her situation with pending exams, hoping he would be sympathetic and persuade Jan not to come to New Zealand. His reply was prompt and, as always, straight to the point. Anna had to be honest with everyone and think it through clearly before inviting Jan. She had to be upfront with her intentions and not toy with him and treat him like some love-struck fool for whom she did not care, only to make a mockery of him. After all, he was Jaroslav's friend, and while in England, Jan had endured enough of his own anguish with a failed marriage, a daughter, and divorce without adding Anna's love charades into the mix. Such was her dear brother's sympathetic advice.

In reality, Anna did not want to hear any of this, but she knew better than to reply to him, so instead, this time she wrote to Jan.

Anna booked and paid for two week's lodgings at Takapuna, a seaside suburb in Auckland. Initially, she booked the accommodation for only two people but added a third, a friend expected to arrive and join them from Australia. She had posted Jan all the details for their proposed vacation in Takapuna and hoped it would be satisfactorily received.

Before departing, Anna had yet to receive any letter of confirmation from Jan regarding his arrival plans, so, with no other option, Anna and Jarmila proceeded with their holiday plans for Takapuna. However, just before leaving on holiday, Anna and Jarmila went to Wellington. There they met with some of Anna's friends, Alena, Lida, and Mrs. Růzickova, for impartial advice about their proposed vacation. After two days there, Anna achieved nothing positive to quell her dilemma. Instead, she received aggravation from Jarmila and Alena, who never did like one another and who only argued since their arrival. By that time, Anna had had enough of them all.

When Anna and Jarmila finally arrived at Takapuna, they were met by the caretaker, who handed over the keys to their cabin and promptly asked, "How was your trip over the Tasman?"

As Jan had not arrived, Anna made some weak excuse that perhaps their Australian friend was sick and had missed his plane. Between them, they decided that if Jan did not turn up within the next few days, they would enjoy a short stay, dine out and go to the movies before hoping for a refund and returning home. In the meantime, they busied themselves with cleaning the three bed-roomed cabin and washed crockery and utensils until the only thing left to do was to rewash everything again. They planned to cook breakfast and lunch and then go out in the evenings for dinner. In the mornings, they went swimming for the next two days, and later in the afternoons, they would catch the trolly bus into the city. On the third day, although a few days late, Jan finally managed to track Anna down. He had just arrived from Sydney to Auckland by TEAL[1] on the short S.45 Solent Flying boat, the 'Ararangi' ZK-AMM, which serviced the Trans-Tasman run at the time. TEAL, which stood for Trans Empire Airways Limited, would later, in 1965, become Air New Zealand.

When Jan announced his arrival, it was a surprise to be met by another young woman he had never met or heard of before, and he asked her if Anna was staying there.

Jarmila immediately called out to Anna, 'Hanko!' (As Anna was often fondly referred to by her Czech friends), "There is someone here who wants to see you."

Jan was quite taken by Anna's appearance when she came out to see who the visitor was. Smiling at her, he complimented Anna on how lovely she looked after remembering the somewhat bedraggled young woman in Germany some years before. Jarmila was quite smitten by this young Czech when she was introduced to him and made it her endeavour to keep the two apart as much as possible. After all, Anna had a boyfriend, and this stranger was not about to derail her friend's relationship with George.

After some light conversation about their recent holiday travels, Jan suddenly changed the discussion and directed the following question at Anna. Much to her surprise and embarrassment, Jan unexpectedly proposed marriage to her in front of Jarmila. Anna was so taken aback by the sudden proposal that she had no time to think if he was serious or joking, and totally lost for words, could only blush instead. However, during this awkward predicament, stunned and awkward by his sudden proposition, Anna meekly accepted the proposal in a moment of weakness.

Jan sensed he had put Anna on the spot, so he quietly added that she had time to think about it.

Afterward, he asked Anna and Jarmila about their work and life generally before confronting Anna with another personal question; "By the way, do you have a boyfriend?"

For Anna, the question came something like putting the cart before the horse, but before she could respond, Jarmila was quick off the mark and said, "Yes, she has a boyfriend. He is a farmer, and he is very rich!"

Anna felt a defensive pang of pity for Jan, but unperturbed, he quietly directed his reply at Jarmila, "I don't have much to offer at the moment, but I believe I, too, can achieve something in my own right."

Jarmila would later remind Anna, "What were you thinking, Hanko? You actually said 'YES' to his proposal!"

Jan made no further mention of his proposal but instead left it to Anna to resolve in her own time. However, he did add that no matter how beautiful New Zealand appeared, he did not think he could ever live here permanently. He explained that it was far too cold for him and he much preferred the drier climate of Australia. He also knew Australia could offer him numerous work opportunities, whereas in New Zealand, work options would still need to be explored. Fortunately, during Jan's brief stay in New Zealand he did not experience any earth tremors which without doubt would have really unnerved him.

Over the next few days, much to Anna's relief, their conversation took on a lighter note, and the mood became friendly and relaxed as they reflected on their lives. If Anna ever desired intimate moments with Jan, it was never to be, as an opportunity for any private conversations with him was always overshadowed by Jarmila's persistent presence, and who always managed to either wedge herself between them or accompany them on every walk along the beach. Anna felt like they were the 'Three Musketeers'; everywhere they went, it was never without the third one!

However, they briefly had time to talk during one early morning stroll along the seafront. It was then, Jan confessed to Anna his failed marriage to Elsie and their child Violet and how he had to abandon the marriage and child, leaving him broken. Whether Anna had already gleaned this knowledge from Domin while still in Germany, apart from Jaroslav briefly mentioning it in his letter, Anna never admitted it. It became a subject she guarded vehemently and kept Jan's past marriage very much to herself. Jan admitted to her that when they had briefly met with Jaroslav and Zoltán Farkaš at the end of the war in Plzeň in 1945, he was still married but would soon realize afterward that his marriage was over. In hindsight, he admitted making some unwise decisions that affected him and hurt others close to him. It was a lesson that taught him not to dwell on the fall-out of these poor choices but rather take heed and not repeat them again and move on in life.

When again the three of them sat around in light-hearted conversation, Jan began to tell them about his journey from England to Australia.

"Here I was with only £40 to my name, and I was sailing on the 'Strathmore' [2] like a gentleman in a first-class birth with even my own cabin steward!"

Jan explained how he received an unexpected message from Thomas Cook Office informing him there had been an unexpected berth cancellation and to come immediately, collect his prepaid ticket, and proceed to board the 'Strathmore.' With such short notice of embarkation, he was rushed to pack whatever he owned.

"The weather was always miserable and cold in England," he continued.

"And with travel arrangements at such short notice, it barely left me time to collect my ticket from Thomas Cook; but nevertheless, it felt like the sun had come out at last and shone despite the bleak English weather. I had just done my washing, and all my soaking wet clothes were hanging on the line with no chance of drying! Everyone had to be on board by 4 pm and settled into their cabins as the 'Strathmore' was due to sail early the next morning. I quickly packed a shabby little case with what little I had in dry clothes; two dry shirts, a few extra things, plus some wet clothing as well, and this was the sum of my entire wardrobe barely filling my case; I grabbed my British Passport, and my total savings of £40 and dashed for the port. When I arrived, I was ushered into my cabin, and only then did I realize I was travelling first class!"

And so began Jan's Sea voyage.

Jan's account of his journey entertained the young women as he described the astonished look on his personal steward when he relieved Jan of his small shabby case and unpacked it for him. Embarrassed, Jan explained that he had left in a hurry and suggested he could buy a few things on board. The steward quickly advised him to save his money as things were far too expensive on the ship and that he would do far better when in a few days' time, they berthed at Alexandria in Egypt.

In Alexandria, the steward was most helpful and accompanied Jan into the bazaars and showed him where to shop. For £1, Jan acquired three new shirts, some tailor-made trousers, and as well some new shirts for Jaroslav. Jan upgraded his travel case to one of crocodile skin and purchased a pair of leather shoes for a few extra pounds, which still left him with £30.

As all meals were provided on board, Jan had little need to spend any more money except on postcards in Bombay and Ceylon. Jan received a transit pass in Freemantle for the 26th of April 1951, valid also for Adelaide and Melbourne until the 3rd of April, so when he arrived to Australia, he was still flush with cash.

He finally disembarked in Adelaide after a pleasant voyage, where Jaroslav met him, and from there, they continued onto Port Lincoln.

Jan found work, and before long, as he had written before to Anna, he repaid her brother in full. While Jarmila listened intently to how good life was in Australia, she quickly suggested to Anna, "Hanko, we will both go to Australia!"

By the time they were ready to return to Te Awamutu, Jarmila had already forgotten about Australia.

One morning Jan insisted on going downtown Auckland to enquire about land prices, so the two women remained alone. Anna confessed to Jarmila that she was in a quandary and did not know what to do about Jan.

"I don't even know if I like him!"

Jarmila quickly came to the rescue and concluded, "Don't get rid of him just yet, Hanko! I might take him off your hands for myself!"

That suggestion quickly resolved Anna's matters of the heart, and she decided there and then that if anyone would have Jan, it would be her and definitely not Jarmila!

When Jan returned, Anna quickly accepted his proposal and suggested that they have a celebratory party at a local restaurant to mark their engagement. For £50, Anna chose a simple gold band with a cameo instead of a diamond for her engagement ring. She was conscious Jan was not flush with money. Jarmila was miffed with Anna's choice and pointed out that this ring was far too ordinary; it should have been a diamond and nothing less. In the end, they had dinner at home. Jarmila bought the wine to celebrate the occasion while they listened to a well-known Czech Opera, 'Prodaná Nevésta,' 'The Bartered Bride,' composed by Bedřich Smetana.

The girls sang certain verses while Jan joined in with others, all becoming carried away with the operatic story. Anna remembered this impromptu engagement to Jan in July of 1951 as one of the most joyful moments in her life. Jan assured Anna that he would announce their engagement to family and friends and take care of Jaroslav's indifference should it arise.

Before parting, Jan made one request of Anna; "Promise me you will be true to yourself and truthful with your own truths."

Anna farewelled Jan in Auckland harbour as he departed on the flying boat for Brisbane, where in Queensland he planned to look for further work prospects.

Photograph 230: P&O Strathmore; Jan's passage from London to Adelaide post card circa 1951.

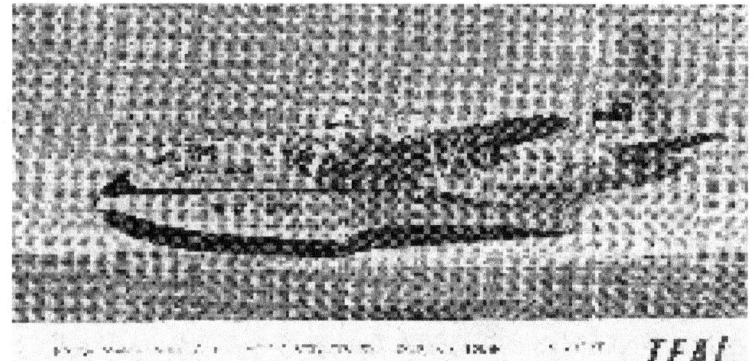

Photograph 231: Flying boat similar to that Jan caught from Sydney to Auckland circa 1951.

Jan Kaňák's transit pass for Freemantle 26 March 1951.

Photograph 233: Auckland view of both coast lines Postcard circa 1951.

Photograph 234 & 235: (L-R) Auckland: Takapuna fashionable caravans of the time in 1951. Jan & Anna in Takapuna July 1951.

Photograph 236 & 237: (L-R) Jan & Anna on their engagement July 1951. Anna & Jan July 1951.

Photograph 232: Auckland view of beaches Postcard circa 1951.

Photograph 238 & 239: (L-R) Anna & Jarmila in Takapuna. Anna at Tokanui 1951.

Photograph 240: Anna & Jarmila farewelled by nurses at Tokanui Hospital August 1951.

CHAPTER 20

Sunnyside Asylum Christchurch

After Jan returned to Australia, Anna was left to resolve her dilemma with George. She was now officially engaged to Jan, but only she and Jarmila knew about it when they returned to Te Awamutu. To make things worse, George was there to meet her on their return. He often told Anna that he liked her very much but, on that day, she had to break the news to George, that now she was engaged to someone else whom she planned to marry.

No one could believe how forthright Anna could be when she delivered the tidings. It was probably devastating for him, but George took it on the chin like a true gentleman. It upset Anna to make such a sudden and unexpected announcement as she was fond of George but knew that she could never reciprocate his feelings, besides, there had never been any official arrangement between George and herself. When Anna wrote to his parents, Mr. and Mrs. Plummer, of her recent engagement to Jan, she hoped it would all be settled amicably and without any resentment.

In no time, Jarmila began spreading the news amongst their nursing colleagues of Anna's engagement to Jan. Everyone wanted to know who this stranger was and where Anna had found him. But above all, when was she going to Australia to get married?

Before they left Takapuna, Jarmila had arranged for their examination results to be forwarded onto them from Tokanui. Jarmila was keen to know how she scored in her exams, whereas Anna was happy to find out when she returned to work. Jarmila was always on the go, racing ahead with new plans and keen to transfer to other hospitals. In contrast, Anna was content to stay and continue her studies at Tokanui, flanked by her many friends and George to escort her to places. But all that was before Jan Kaňák reemerged on the scene.

For Anna, the whole exposé of her personal life had become untenable. Vlasta, from whom Anna had distanced herself, was particularly harsh by accusing Anna of being; good for nothing; 'Slezské Kopyto,' which translates to no less than a Silesian hoof! So, Anna agreed to transfer with Jarmila to Sunnyside Psychiatric Hospital in Christchurch on South Island. Besides, at Tokanui, both spent all their money on clothes, and as Jarmila was always fashionably attired, Anna followed suit. Jarmila sewed well and could copy any of the latest fashions to a tee without buying them and had over three times the number of dresses as Anna.

When their transfer had been approved, Jarmila immediately took charge and booked their trip to Christchurch. Anna had been at Tokanui Hospital for over eighteen months, so she accepted it was time for a change without disrupting her studies. For once, she might make a serious effort and save money.

After their farewell, Katy came to see them off in Wellington, but it was Vlasta's friend, Dagmar, both of whom Anna did not have the closest friendships with since her illness; who was going to have the parting last word.

"Anousko! (Also, another pet name for Anna) We are sending all our wishes to you!"

It may or may not have been intended as sarcastic, but Anna cared not to know what these parting wishes were either way.

Anna and Jarmila travelled overnight by boat from Wellington to Lyttelton Harbour and arrived in Christchurch early in the morning. Christchurch was a beautiful city built on the meandering Avon River as the stream flowed through numerous leafy suburbs and parklands. This waterway was popular with local sightseers and punters rowing up and down the stream. It was just as popular with ducks constantly being fed by onlookers who stopped and watched them, mesmerized by their quirky bird antics. It was a city of beautiful Georgian and Gothic Revival structures. The city was very English provincial dotted with dark basalt stone buildings and churches with towering steeples; the main one being Christchurch Cathedral in Cathedral Square. Whereas Wellington was a windy city by the sea, Christchurch calmly sprawled on the flat landscape, mostly protected from the sea winds by a small range of hills to the east.

Beyond these eastern hills was the coastal suburb of Lyttelton and the Port for Christchurch. To the north was Brighton, and here during the summer months, the beaches would be swamped with relaxed locals enjoying family picnics and swimming. Further south of Christchurch along the coast was Akaroa, a quaint fishing village cradled in an inlet virtually surrounded by a mountainous range except for the narrow opening into the sea.

Sunnyside Psychiatric Hospital[1], known previously as a 'Lunatic Asylum' but at the time referred to as a mental asylum, was a vast multi-storeyed gothic complex. Tokanui could be described as a pretty place compared to this Victorian architecture of grey austerity, almost resembling something out of medieval times.

Behind its foreboding façade, deep dark secrets could quite easily manifest without ever being discovered. It sent a chill down Anna's back as she braced herself for what lay ahead. There was no turning back now as the two young women each received a set of new uniforms and were allocated accommodation in the nurse's quarters.

Sunnyside was an acute psychiatric facility with many of its patients, after treatment, either moving on with their lives or becoming habitual readmissions, the latter being the more significant.

Condemnations of psychiatric institutions were already being voiced as early as the 1900's when 'The Auckland Star'[2] wrote; "However mild the illness they arrived with, to a lifetime of insanity."

'The New Zealand Herald'[3] added, "They were treated as incurable, and so are made incurable."

And as Sir Henry Maudsley allegedly said with illuminated frankness, 'asylum-made lunatics.' Extract from 'Kingseat a Vision in Gray.'[4]

It was then not the most endearing compliment for any such institution.

Those who could afford at their expense to convalesce away from the acute arena of psychiatric care went onto Hornby Lodge[5], a ten bedded establishment for women overseen by Sunnyside staff. Originally, Hornby Lodge was known as 'Stoneycroft' and was built by George Ross[6] in the late nineteenth century. It was eventually sold to the Crown in 1919, becoming Hornby and then Hornby Lodge to provide accommodation for women as a part of the Sunnyside institutional complex.

Even though Sunnyside stood and looked like a dismal fortress from the outside, within its grounds were lawns and flower gardens full of butterflies, humming bees, and birds, and numerous paths skirted by overhanging trees that led to various outbuildings. Within its grounds was a chapel and a serene lily pond spanned by a small wooden bridge that connected various paths traversing the grounds. A central feature in the pond was a tiered fountain peacefully trickling water to create tranquillity in stark contrast to the often-tumultuous chaos within its walls.

Sunnyside may have been a gruesome institution, but behind those solid walls were everyday people struggling with an illness that an unfair hand had dealt them.

Anna recollects that all female patients that she came in contact with were always cared for reverently and she always respected them regardless of their illness. Psychiatric management in New Zealand was as on-trend as elsewhere in the modern world of psychiatry. Although, what may be unconventional and outdated today, was very much acceptable mainstream practices in psychiatric care. Anna remembered patients with mental illnesses such as schizophrenia who were managed with insulin coma therapy and placed daily into induced comas over a prescribed period of time. Although this therapy was controversial and least understood, it was still carried out until later replaced with modern neuroleptic or antipsychotic drugs.

Anna once cared for a young woman who was scheduled for ECT treatment and was terrified of what would happen. Electroconvulsive Treatment, or Electroconvulsive Therapy as it is known, had and still has its place in the Psychiatric arena. Although this procedure may be daunting and unconventional to the healthy mind, it remained, for most, an effective treatment in conjunction with psychotherapeutic drugs of the time. Both methods were used to manage certain mental illnesses, such as chronic endogenous depression and bipolar conditions.

Being familiar with this chilling methodology, Anna assisted as was expected, comforting and reassuring her patients that she would remain alongside them for this rather traumatizing session. However well-premedicated these patients were, and regardless of whether it was their first time or subsequent treatments, they were always haunted by the procedure. In many cases, Anna found mental illness challenging to comprehend, in as much that this inner turmoil could disrupt the lives of so many. Many of Anna's female patients seemed to have everything to live for except seemingly, peace of mind.

On one occasion, a frail and vulnerable young woman had been battling demons for some time and had undergone ECT treatment on numerous instances before arriving in Anna's care. She was young and attractive and had a beautiful home and family but was unhappy with this seemingly wonderful life as Anna perceived it to be. How could she make her understand that what she had in life far exceeded the expectations of so many people Anna had crossed paths with after the war, herself included? It was not as simple as that, as Anna would come to understand, but rather a battle for these poor souls trying to find a neurophysical balance that neither swung them into depression nor sent them into overdrive in the opposite direction.

Over the weeks, Anna accepted the revolving door of convoluted mentality and realized that all these people deserved the same respect and reverence as any other human being. Whenever opinions differed, she avoided conflict with them and offered reassurance and understanding. She became their confidant and listened patiently while many women poured out their troubled minds.

Many of Anna's patients made good progress. Eventually, those who could afford it were transferred to Hornby Lodge, the halfway house and stepping stone toward being discharged from in-house psychiatric care.

At the time, nursing staff shared working shifts between Sunnyside and Hornby Lodge, so Anna had her share of work rotations there. Although rostered to work at Hornby Lodge, the Sunnyside nurses still maintained their accommodation at Sunnyside nurses' quarters.

One night when Anna was on duty, a young woman became agitated about being discharged. Anna was exceptionally busy that night, so she avoided becoming too drawn into renewed self-doubt and troubling excuses until she found the woman threatening to jump out through an opened window from the top level. Anna was so shaken and upset with this sudden turnabout of slow but positive healing over the past weeks that she suddenly grabbed and pulled the young woman back inside. Still shaking with trepidation as to what might have just unfolded, Anna's forthright reaction was instantaneous and out of her own control; as she scolded the woman for such unprovoked foolishness. Anna reprimanded her for not considering her loved ones at home and being preoccupied with selfish obsessions. Anna reminded her that not only could she have harmed herself, but this threat to self-harm undid all the positive efforts she had achieved over the past months. Anna's uncompromising tone surprised the young woman, as it must have shocked Anna when she finally cooled down. Still, it seemingly jolted her inmate into realizing what an ugly situation she had got herself into.

The acknowledgment of the inevitable return to Sunnyside for repeat treatment was more than the young woman could endure. Anna calmed her down and made her promise never to contemplate such an act again, and with this solemn oath, Anna promised never to speak of the incident. Anna had placed blind faith in someone who had just contemplated an impulsive self-harming act, and now she was trusting her to honour a binding pact. In hindsight, considering the woman's past history, it was a deal she was more than capable of forfeiting. Anna could not reverse the compromise she had just negotiated without losing the young woman's confidence and trust. If either failed, it would not only spell demise for both; a young woman's life and Anna's career for not reporting a potentially life-threatening incident. Both would have to live with this on their conscience; one for putting a trusted confidant into a compromising situation and the other for not carrying out her duty of care.

Sadly, many patients once admitted to Sunnyside never returned to the normal world as we know it. Others struggled with their demons, briefly overcoming them, but only to return again time after time and recommence treatment. However, if successfully treated and discharged, some of these never returned.

When nursing tutorials began, Anna found the lessons challenging. Everything was in English, so she obtained an expensive five-volume set of a Nurse's Encyclopedia, 'The New People's Physician' to aid the process. She was determined to finish and become a sister; a Registered Psychiatric Nurse.

Anna was committed to her career as so far she had done well in her exams, and despite the language barrier, her knowledge of Latin helped her enormously. Anna discovered the Māori language was far easier to learn and speak than English, so she more often made friends with the Māori nurses. However, people always seemed to gravitate toward Anna, befriending her, so she soon became comfortable in her new surroundings.

One day while at work, Anna received an unexpected visit from her old friend Lida and daughter Miluška. Lida had called to see Anna, but unfortunately, at the time, Anna could not be excused from duty, but catching sight of them, she begged Lida to remain a while until she finished her shift. The last time they met was briefly in Wellington just before Anna's holiday to Takapuna in late June of 1951, when Lida coincidentally had time off from her factory job. However, this meeting had been disrupted by Jarmila, who had little tolerance for most of Anna's outside-of-work friends. Anna had desperately wanted to catch up with her friend and even invite her to stay over, but sadly Lida did not remain. Why the unexpected visit? Anna never found out as Lida and her daughter Miluška were not heard from again.

On another Saturday, while Anna and Jarmila were free from duty, they received some unexpected visitors. Jarmila quickly excused herself to make herself more presentable, while Anna received the guests. Anna recognized two of the three Czech lads as those who had travelled with them on the 'Dundalk Bay' to New Zealand. Mirek and Steve had been to Wellington recently, where they learned that two women with whom they had travelled from Trieste were now stationed and working in Christchurch.

Rudy, Mirek, and Steve were invited to have tea with them, and unexpectedly, the invitation was extended to lunch at Matron's insistence. Rudy excused himself as he had to go downtown while the other two lads gratefully accepted the lunch invitation.

Rudy was their camp cook, while Mirek and Steve were employed cutting timber at Hokitika on the west coast. As Rudy did not immediately return, Mirek and Steve remained for some hours with Anna and Jarmila, catching up on all the news since last seeing one another. Anna remembered it was Steve who had the camera when they all travelled on board the ship, and he took numerous photos of everyone as they made their journey to New Zealand. He promised Anna he would bring some photos the next time he visited.

They made plans to catch up again, but the lads apologized that the following weekend would be unsuitable for them. Rudy had gone downtown to source ingredients for a particular recipe for a special celebratory dinner that was to be held at their camp that weekend. Anna soon discovered; the honoured and distinguished guest was Count Fred Kinsky, who would be escorting and introducing the new Parish Priest to their camp. It was the same Count Kinsky Anna had met in Wellington only a few years before.

Jarmila and Anna found the boys entertaining, so they agreed to meet the lads whenever they were in Christchurch again. Anna knew Steve quite well but needed to learn more about Mirek.

Mirek was a handsome chap, quiet and definitely taken in by Jarmila.

As Anna put it, "He had eyes only for Jarmila!"

During the next meeting, Steve happily elaborated on Count Kinsky's visit and the successful dinner, but Mirek remained reserved. Steve explained that Rudy had made an excellent spread of traditional Czech food, including dumplings. Anna smiled at the thought and wondered if Count Kinsky remembered when her dumplings were the talk of the camp in Ludwigsburg.

Steve laughed as he jokingly described Rudy's culinary efforts. "He had his batch of dumplings ready but soon discovered he did not have any muslin cloth upon which to steam his dumplings, so he borrowed Mirek's shirt."

Some weeks later, Steve turned up again, this time in a car but without Mirek. Steve invited the girls to the movies so for the occasion, Jarmila promptly changed into fashionable attire and high-heeled boots.

It was a small car with enough seating for only two people in the front, but they managed to squash in together and set out like three mega-stars on a Sunday drive. Barely a mile into the journey, the car came to a grinding halt. Jarmila became indignant and angry as a hornet when they all had to push the vehicle off the road. As it rolled downhill, the axle snapped, probably from all the extra weight, and eventually had to be towed into a garage. Anna felt deeply sorry for Steve as his outing to impress the girls had come to such an embarrassing end, but instead, they all ended up sitting by the roadside eating fish and chips bought from the local cafe.

After having worked at Sunnyside Hospital for some time, Anna was surprised one day to meet Dr. Hunter[7] on her ward. He had been Superintendent at Tokanui Hospital while Anna worked there. He told her he had taken up the position of Superintendent at Sunnyside Hospital and had arrived shortly after Anna's transfer from Tokanui. She always liked and respected him as he remained helpful and supportive to all his staff. Having acknowledged Anna on the ward, it did not go unnoticed and immediately created a stir amongst her senior staff, who demanded to know from where she knew him.

Anna's student days at Sunnyside were never dull, sometimes less conventional, and certainly not always for the faint-hearted. Nevertheless, she had many happy memories there and felt quite at home amongst her nursing colleagues and inpatients, were it not for the fact that Sunnyside was a mental asylum.

Christmas arrived, and Anna diligently forwarded Christmas greetings to Jan and her brother Jaroslav, and on New Year's Eve, as it was about to ring in 1952, Anna was rostered on night duty.

By now, she had graduated into a senior nurse's role and was generally in charge of her shift and responsible for the running of the ward.

As with every New Year, there was bound to be plenty of festivities for the off-duty staff and occasionally for those on duty, as merriment blended in with the tinkling of glasses overflowing with celebratory drinks. Anna felt disappointed having missed the staff party, but someone always had to work. Midway through Anna's shift, one of her aged female patients passed away. After medical formalities had been completed and the death certificate signed and produced, Anna and her assistant proceeded to prepare the patient for her last office. As customary then, every shroud for a deceased patient was numbered and had to be signed for by the nurse in attendance.

When the wardsman finally arrived with his trolley to collect the neatly wrapped body, Anna suspected he may have had a celebratory tipple or two too many, as there was a definite smell of alcohol wafting about. It was not Anna's duty to reprimand the wardsman as he stumbled about lifting the deceased onto the trolly. All she could hope for was that he delivered the body into the morgue safely and with dignity.

The journey from the ward onto the mortuary building on the other side of the complex went over a dimly lit garden path that crossed the bridge over the pond. Shortly afterward, Anna heard an eerie howling followed by a cry for help muffled by splashing water as it echoed from somewhere outside in the darkness. Anna grabbed her torch and raced outside, flashing her light about, fearing the worst that one of her inmates had managed to escape and had thrown themselves into the pond.

Somewhat relieved, she saw it was probably only an inebriated party reveller struggling out of the pond covered in slime and water plants. Thinking she would help the hapless stranger, her heart sank when she realized it was the wardsman cursing loudly as he clambered out, but worse still, the trolley with the body was half submerged in the pond next to him. Anna was mortified and felt like shoving him back into the pond to sober up, as now she had to explain the crises and write a lengthy incident report and redress the corpse and document the missing shroud.

Anna's life in Christchurch with her many friends also had lighter moments. She became especially friendly with three young women who were sisters. Rhoda, the eldest of the sisters, was Anna's favourite. Together with the other two, Peggy and Mavis, they spent many memorable occasions travelling and exploring the city in their free time. However, one of Anna's most enduring friendships while she lived in South Island, New Zealand, was with their half-sister Margaret, a married woman of about Anna's age who lived in Christchurch and at the time had three young children; Roger, Julie, and Christine.

Margaret became one of Anna's dearest friends, and although she did not belong to the nursing fraternity circle, she blended in well with Anna's friends and joined in on many outings.

When Anna met Margaret, it was as if she had found a soulmate, a sister she could really confide in with her own mixture of scattered emotions that she had been struggling with. Margaret was the perfect sounding board and would patiently listen and offer solace but, in the end, Anna would always follow the path of her own choosing. She cherished this long and lasting friendship that spanned many decades. Theirs evolved into a friendship free from personal judgment, and each very much became a part of the other's family life. They were always honest with one another and shared many secrets as only close friends do. Although each had a different philosophy on life, they always agreed to disagree respectfully whenever ideals were at odds.

Margaret's gentle manner and genuine concern for other people, especially those less fortunate than herself, were one of her many attributes. Margaret would spend as much time as she could afford with Anna and her friends and remained an integral part of Anna's life while in New Zealand. Although distance would separate them in later years, they never failed to keep their friendship firmly cemented into their families for the duration of their lives.

Anna had the occasional faux pas, and one such incident occurred one morning after night duty at Sunnyside in early February of 1952. Anna was about to give her morning report, and, in those days, patients were always referred to by their surnames, followed by their overnight progress report. When the day staff arrived that morning, there seemed to be a lot of unusual chatter and excitement.

As Anna prepared to present her hand-over, one of the nurses leaned over and whispered, "Did you hear our King is dead?"

Anna looked horrified at the unexpected announcement and returned in astonishment, assuring the nurse.

"No! He is not dead! I saw our King walking down the corridor in his dressing gown!"

Mr. King may had been alive and well, but King George Vl certainly wasn't.

Anna and some of her colleagues were scheduled to take some leave, so they booked a holiday package to Eastbourne near Wellington. Since arriving in Christchurch, Anna kept quiet about her engagement to Jan, so her newly acquired friends were none the wiser. Although Margaret was privy to Anna's many secrets, her life generally was not open to others except the few who shared in their humble beginnings when first arriving to New Zealand. Anna's friend Katy Black from Tokanui was about to join Anna on holiday, and while they were downtown Wellington doing some shopping, they unexpectedly ran into Steve. By now, Mirek and Steve had completed their timber contract at Hokitika and both were in Wellington looking for work.

While Jarmila and Mirek developed a more serious relationship, Anna always remained good mates with Steve. Anna introduced Katy, who found Steve charming and suggested he might like to join them for tea at their holiday cottage in Eastbourne.

Soon afterward, their hostess, Mrs. Nelson, enquired if their guest would be staying for dinner. Anna hoped Steve would decline and leave for Wellington, but in the end, Mrs. Nelson offered him a room, so he remained for the ten days of their holiday.

Katy laughed at the outcome and asked Anna, "Do you think we have started a fashionable trend? Every time we invite someone over for tea, they end up staying on with us!"

Anna enjoyed their summer break with compatible camaraderie, while playing tennis, swimming, and dining out over jovial conversation. Relaxing in Eastbourne on holiday with friends was lots of fun for Anna until personal relationships again became problematic for her. Anna clarified that she hoped to go to Australia one day but had not mentioned the reason. Having heard these plans, Steve pleaded that she remain in New Zealand with him. Anna had not written to Jan since her Christmas greeting card, and neither had he made contact since his departure some months earlier; She was beginning to have second doubts and wondered if Jan had gone cold on their engagement and had already forgotten about her.

Before Anna left Eastbourne for Christchurch, Steve had already secured employment, working in a garage in Wellington and Anna was beginning to think that perhaps New Zealand was to be her true homeland after all. She decided her long-distance relationship with Jan was not really working, so she resolved to write and call off the engagement when she returned from her holiday. But even all carefully thought-out plans can often fail.

When Anna returned to Sunnyside, she found a letter waiting for her from Jan. Reading it, Anna's heart softened, and out of the window flew her much deliberated 'Dear John' letter, calling off their engagement. Jan wrote that after leaving New Zealand and arriving in Queensland, he went to Toowoomba and then continued onto Dalby, where he found employment on Erland Erlandson's property.

Erland and his wife Marjory took Jan in and treated him with great affection while he managed their farm during Erland's illness. Jan was given a cottage on the property and begged Anna to consider joining him there.

Anna always felt a sense of compassion for Jan as whenever he was on verge of making a difference in his life, something always seemed to counter this opportunity; such whenever he poised himself in self-employment; certain people he contracted for, either did not pay him or failed to honour prearranged contracts. Anna imagined he needed more business acumen. But then, in many ways, Anna and Jan were similar. Both struggled to achieve, and both made wrong choices at different times.

Although Anna never got to meet the Erlandsons until many decades later, she would soon begin a yearly Christmas correspondence with Marjory that would ultimately bring them closer, joining them in a pen-pal friendship that would last for the remainder of their lives. However, for the time being, Anna believed she could stave off the pressing indecision to commit herself to Australia but remain engaged to Jan while still continuing her nursing at Sunnyside.

Shortly after receiving Jan's belated letter, he followed it with an urgent telegram. The telegram had arrived via the main office at Sunnyside, so its news also came to Matron's attention. It read something like: 'Travelling to Port Lincoln. Jarda had an accident. Will write and explain. Honza.'

Jarda was a nickname for Jaroslav like Honza was for Jan. Suddenly, Anna's life was in turmoil, and Anna was beside herself with worry. She immediately wanted to leave for Australia. The hospital Matron was very supportive and tried to console Anna, offering whatever help she could.

Soon afterward, a second letter arrived from Jan and had an additional letter written in English by D. Vaughan, Commonwealth Employment officer. It read; 'Jaroslav Kurovec was seriously injured in an accident and lost his right lower leg. He requests that you do not tell your mother or sisters but hopes that you might be able to come as soon as possible and help him.'

This finally tipped Anna into emotional overdrive as she pleaded with her employer to allow her to travel immediately to Australia. To hasten matters, Anna tendered her resignation, but it was refused, and instead, she was granted five months compassionate leave. Anna was praised for being a good nurse, and the Nursing Fraternity did not want her to resign but instead return and complete her studies. She had been asked to reconsider all travel plans until at least after her brother's leg had healed and he was allowed home. She was reminded that she could do little for him while hospitalized.

When next free, Anna promptly travelled to Wellington to apply for an Australian visa as it could be a considerable wait before being granted. While there, she prebooked through Thomas Cook a return passage to Australia on the 'Wanganella'[8], a regular shipping service across the Tasman Sea between Wellington and Sydney. As she needed to be closer to the Australian Embassy in Wellington, Anna was granted a transfer to work at Porirua Psychiatric Hospital.

Porirua Hospital[9] had a progressive and different model of care compared to its contemporary mental institutions. It led the way in physiotherapeutic treatment challenging inmates to physical drills, massage, and electric treatment but also committing them to hospital farm work. The patients were housed in villas instead of institutionalized accommodations, which probably prepared them better for ongoing community-based care in the future. Anna remained working at Porirua for about six months before she was finally granted leave from nursing and prepared to travel to Australia.

While Anna was rushing about preparing for her voyage to South Australia and putting her nursing career on hold, unbeknown to her, other plans were already progressing along and gaining momentum. Jaroslav had met and fallen in love with a young Australian nurse. Anna received a photograph of a young woman shortly afterward from her mother. This photograph had been sent by Jaroslav to their mother, informing everyone in the family that he was about to get married.

On the back of the photo the greetings read, 'Mummy, this is my bride!'

Nothing was said if this news had any bearing on Anna's ongoing plans, which had already been put into motion. Regardless, Anna continued with her leave of absence from work and planned her journey to Australia.

On the day of Anna's departure, her old friends and nursing colleagues arrived to see her off and presented her with a crystal dressing table set and an inscribed Ronson cigarette lighter as a parting gift. She had been at pains to conceal the fact from Jan that she still smoked Players Cigarettes, and now with a cigarette lighter with her name on it, evidence would mount up when they next met.

Once again, Steve pleaded with her not to go but at least to return when he heard the reason for her hasty retreat. There was no mention of being engaged to Jan, only that her brother had had an awful accident and needed her support.

On her birthday, the 28th of August 1952, Anna boarded the 'Wanganella' in Wellington harbour, and amongst the fan-fare of friends who came to see her off, the mournful strains of Māori singing 'Po Atarau' [10] (Now is the Hour); set the scene for a tearful send-off. This somewhat melancholy melody, initially composed by Clement Scott but with Māori lyrics inserted later in 1915 by Maewa Kaihau and Dorothy Stewart, had become New Zealand's national farewell song. It always filled departing passengers with nostalgia and sadness as they left New Zealand on their voyage.

It was an emotional moment for Anna. Only four years earlier, she had been greeted by these melomaniac people who had welcomed the 'Dundalk Bay' into this harbour. As grass skirts swayed and poi-poi circled rhythmically about them, the Māori sang;

"Po Atarau -E moea iho nei
(And now is the hour when we must say goodbye)
E haere ana – Koi Ki pamamao
(Soon you'll be sailing, far across the sea)
Haere ra- Ka hoki mai ano
(While you're away, o, then remember me)
Ki I te tau – E tangi atu nei.
(When you return, you'll find me waiting here.)"

So, on that day, as the 'Wanganella' glided out of Wellington Harbour, Anna parted with Steve and her many New Zealand friends.

Footnote;
In the end, Steve married Anna's friend Alena Lišková, with whom Anna admitted to doing a bit of matchmaking. They remained living in Wellington while Steve made a success of his life. He died in the 1990s aged 74.

Photograph 241, 242 & 243: (L-R) Sunnyside Hospital - Anna, Sister Laura Wessler and nursing friend. Anna, Sister Laura Wessler and Matron. Sister Laura Wessler, 1952.

Photograph 244 & 245: (L-R) Anna with hospital matron. Anna at Sunnyside in 1952.

Photograph 246 & 247: (L-R) Anna at Hornby Lodge Christchurch, 1952.

Photograph 248: Anna at Hornby Lodge Christchurch, 1952.

Photograph 249 & 250: (L-R) Anna with the cook at Hornby Lodge. Anna with grounds manager Hornby Lodge 1952.

Photograph 251, 252 & 253: (L-R) Margaret Lewis in Christchurch. Anna in Christchurch. Margaret Lewis in Christchurch, 1952.

Photograph 254, 255 & 256: (L-R) Anna in Christchurch. Rhoda in Christchurch. Margaret Lewis with daughter Julie, 1952.

Photograph 257, 258 & 259: (L-R) Anna with Katy Black. Alena, Anna & Katy. Alena, Steve & Anna, early 1952.

Photograph 260, 261 & 262: (L-R) Alena with Steve. Anna, Steve & Katy. Margaret Turner & Laura Wessler, Christchurch early 1952.

Photograph 263: Lois Rischmueller, Jaroslav Kurovec's bride. Anna's sister-in-law circa 1952.

Written note by Jaroslav to his mother Rosalie on back of photograph.

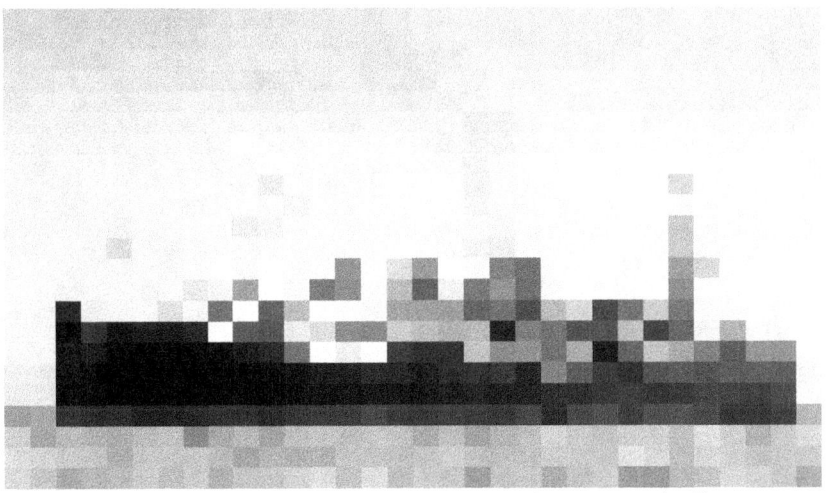

Photograph 264: The Wanganella. Curtsey Mr. Reuben Goossens' collection S.S. Maritime.

Photograph 265: Hornby Lodge drawing by author. Structurally it would have been similar in 1952.

A Tree Without Branches: Anna's Journey

BOOK TWO: Life in Australia

CHAPTER 21

Wanilla Forest SA: 1952-1954

Anna suffered from seasickness crossing the Tasman Sea and could barely stand as enormous swells swayed the ship. It had been a horrible journey and a far cry from the conditions when she first crossed the Tasman some years earlier. Calm only prevailed once they entered the waters around The Heads into Sydney Harbour, Australia. Anna finally came face to face with the Sydney Harbour Bridge as it spanned Port Jackson. She nostalgically recalled how she had outwitted George some years earlier by recognizing the name of Sydney on the wall mural in Wellington.

When Anna departed Christchurch, she had taken all her possessions as her future was uncertain, and she had mixed emotions. She travelled first class in style with four massive trunks; two green and two black, and eight other suitcases. Her luggage had already been forwarded onto Port Lincoln when she caught the overnight train from Sydney to Melbourne and another connection to Adelaide. She travelled overnight until she finally arrived at the Adelaide railway station, where Jan awaited her.

At Jan's suggestion, they remained in Adelaide, taking in the sights and catching up since the last meeting in New Zealand and discussing future plans. Jaroslav was in Victor Harbour, a small coastal town south of Adelaide, where he was having his new prosthesis fitted. Afterward, Anna and Jan flew onto Port Lincoln. Jaroslav finally arrived on the MV Minnipa [1], a twice-weekly goods and passenger boat service between Adelaide and Port Lincoln. This service lasted until 1960.

Finally meeting with her brother and his wife Lois, now her sister-in-law, for Anna it was probably not quite the reunion she anticipated. Anna now had to share his attention with a stranger who seemed indifferent to Anna's presence. Lois Rischmueller had been a nurse, was some ten years younger than Anna, and she and Jaroslav were already expecting their first child. Anna felt like an outsider coming into this already united circle of friends that her brother and Jan had created, with Lois very much a part of it. Worst of all, Anna resented the scrutiny from someone she did not know, especially when that person was her sister-in-law. Anna complained to Jan, but he remained impartial and reminded her that it was her brother's choice and that they were happy together. In this case, it was not what Anna wanted but what Jaroslav wanted. He further added that Anna should be happy for them and stop imagining she was being constantly scrutinized. But Anna remained sensitive to every remark her sister-in-law made, and probably read more into the comments then was intended. Even though her relationship with Jan wasn't a mutual catholic alliance, as was with Lois and Jaroslav, this also pricked Anna's conscience, sensing it was frowned upon by Lois. It seemed Anna would have to earn her stripes before becoming accepted by all parties.

Jan had joined the Wanilla RSL sub-branch sometime earlier, so he already had numerous acquaintances well before Anna's arrival. Apart from several fellow countrymen including a Czech couple Gizela and Jaroslav Dufek, Australian couples; Bob and Joyce Deer and Bob and Jean Blann and the Bradfords were amongst Jan's friends.

Bob Blann was the forestry foreman living in Wanilla Forest, a short distance northwest of Port Lincoln, so Jan rented a cottage near Bob and Jean's place, and from there, Jan carried on with timber contracting. And so, it followed that Anna and Jan's first home would be at Wanilla Forest, which neighboured onto 'The Fountain' where Jaroslav and Lois lived.

Although located in relative isolation from city life, they were not alone in this bush community. During this time, Anna pleaded with Jan to reconsider and return with her to New Zealand, but he was determined to remain in Australia. After some soul-searching, Anna decided to stay on and began befriending some of the local families.

Although Anna and Jan's childhood backgrounds and upbringing were poles-apart, here in Australia they stood on equal ground. The war saw to it that it left no winners, only survivors. Anna still secretly indulged in her cigarettes. It was a curse she had to kick if she and Jan were ever to live under the same roof.

After Christmas, Anna and Jan arranged to get married. Between them, they decided on a civil marriage in the Registry Office with a discrete celebration afterward. With money allocated for a more substantial wedding, Anna instead wanted to spend it on a new four-piece bedroom suite, a new kitchen table, chairs, crockery, and cabinet for their new home. Anna's only pièce de resistance for the occasion was to be a new frock. She had it ordered and made to fit from Adelaide through a boutique in Port Lincoln. It was a fashionable classic design of deep mauve crepe, with three-quarter sleeves and a mandarin collar. The bodice was sequined with rows of navy-blue beads to the waist and completed with a peplum and pleated train at the back matching the length of the frock. It cost Anna 22 Guineas, which was £23, and 1 shilling in pre-decimal currency, which today would equate approximately to $580. She did not come cheap!

So, on the 30th of January 1953, Jan and Anna married in Port Lincoln with Bob Blann and Jaroslav Kurovec as their witnesses. From that day on, Kaňák and Kaňákova became Angelized, and Anna became simply Mrs. Kanak, dropping the Czech suffix 'ova.'

Their honeymoon was in Adelaide at the same hotel they had stayed in when Anna first arrived. The establishment was run by a Jewish woman and her South African husband, a doctor. The accommodation was affordable, comfortable, clean, and well-appointed. During their stay, they attended the cinema and saw the film 'With a Song in My Heart,' starring Susan Hayward, Rory Calhoun, and David Wayne. It had been released earlier in 1952, a biographical film about Jane Froman, an American songstress crippled after a plane crash, who went on to entertain the WWII troops in Europe.

When they returned to Wanilla Forest, Anna busied herself with domestic chores while Jan pursued in timber contracting. During this time, it was not unusual for Jan to bring along a few mates after work; one of whom would occasionally bring along a fresh chook, and Anna would be expected to cook it for them. Anna was a competent and willing cook, but the unexpected arrival of people often placed her at odds with her evening routine.

Although Anna was happy to be close to her brother, it did not improve her relationship with his wife Lois, which was often far from cordial. Anna felt Lois' expectations of her housekeeping skills fell well beyond par, and what bothered Anna even more was her religious conscience in the presence of other practicing Catholics. The fact that Jan refused to be drawn into trivial matters of housekeeping and religious concerns did not help her. In the end, the two women maintained mutual tolerance of one another in respect for their husbands.

By now, Lois was busy with their baby son, Vladimir, and Anna was also expecting her first child. Anna's and Jan's firstborn was a daughter, arriving on the 20th of July in Port Lincoln Hospital. Dr. Kneebone attended the birth, but he did scare Anna at one stage when he said he could not hear a foetal heartbeat. Anna was relieved when she heard her baby's loud screams upon delivery. Sister O'Hara, the assisting midwife, was most helpful to Anna, which led to a new friendship.

Anna's life took on a new meaning; for most, she enjoyed motherhood with all its challenges. Jan left the children's upbringing to Anna, especially those dealing with religion. Being of the Evangelic Faith and an advocate of Jan Hus' philosophy, he did not enter into religious debates with Anna and left her free to choose how she wanted their children brought up. Coming from the Catholic faith, she would inevitably raise them as Catholics. However, one real obstacle was the naming of their daughter. Anna wanted Zena, but Jan would have none of it. He only asked for one request; a name that was not Russian sounding, so in the end, they agreed on Helena.

Their little girl was very much the apple of Jan's eye and his 'Little Lamb' as he called her. So, six weeks after their baby's birth, Jan and Anna's daughter was baptized Helena Elizabeth in the Catholic Church with Anna's midwife, Mary O'Hara, standing in as Godmother.

By now, Jan was building up his business. His mobile mill with bench saws, a Hargan-saw, a blue Fordson Major tractor, and a red international truck made his business versatile. As he now had a family, he bought a bottle-green Zephyr sedan car, which allowed for family outings to the beach and regular shopping trips to Port Lincoln.

In late January of 1954, Anna's friend Margaret Lewis arrived from New Zealand, so Jan took the opportunity to see a bit of Australia. He wanted to visit North Queensland, so he decided on a three-month trip by car. Jan travelled north from South Australia onto Cobar in central west New South Wales, and by the 3rd of February, he finally arrived in Charleville, Queensland. He wrote to Anna that torrential rain had flooded the roads and he had to spend considerable time by the roadside. It was so hot that he tried sleeping outside the car, but the mosquitoes attacked him. With so much water lying about, he at least could bathe himself and wash some of his clothes. At one stage, he stopped beside an Artesian bore and had a hot bath before settling in the car for the night.

From Charleville, Jan headed for Roma along the newly constructed road toward the east coast. Jan's following letter came from Brisbane on the 9th of March and that his arrival there had coincided with that of the Queen and Prince Philip, so this time traffic held him up. He made the most of his time visiting the Botanical Gardens and attending an outdoor concert. After resuming his trip north and passing through Gympie and Gladstone, he crossed the Tropic of Capricorn and arrived at Rockhampton. So as not to get caught up again in Her Majesty's visit, scheduled there for the 15th, Jan headed west inland toward Emerald. While driving some 200 miles over terrain that reminded him of the Marble Ranges north of Wanilla, he once more saw the devastation caused by recent floods. During this visit, Emerald and Clermont were nestled in green countryside. In his letter from Clermont dated 12th of March Jan commented on how pretty the townships appeared but streets seemed deserted, with no children running about. However, he soon discovered most of them had travelled to Rockhampton to see the Queen! In his lengthy letter he wrote about his Queensland adventure thus far and made constant mention of floods and rain. He was amazed by the amount of water that would remain on the roads for lengthy periods even after the rain had abated. A fact he had overlooked when leaving South Australia was that he would be travelling through Queensland during the monsoonal season.

Jan visited the coal mining town of Blair Athol before traversing the dirt track onto Charters Towers. It was rough going in the Zephyr, but roads were graded in places, and it was only when nearing Townsville that roads became sealed. Jan had laid out his plan for Anna, and although ambitious, he calculated it would take him three months to complete the trip.

He wrote again on the 17th of March from Cairns, describing how impressed he was with the countryside, its vegetation, and the lush sugarcane paddocks. He told Anna he had driven about on the Atherton Tablelands and had written to the Lands Department in Brisbane to enquire about purchasing land in North Queensland. He reassured Anna that the car was still in good order and travelling well.

He posted Anna cards of the Barron Falls at Kuranda and the lush countryside of Cairns, no doubt trying to convince her that it was the place to move to.

Jan's car journey would eventually take him south past Mt. Garnet and further away from civilization, southward along the gravel Hann Highway built to skirt most major wet-season rivers before joining a major road connecting the east with western outback towns and those of the north west gulf region. This unsealed road from Hughenden onto Julia Creek traversed flat and featureless black soil downs country, with roads impassable during the wet. From Cloncurry onto Mt. Isa the terrain was barren and inhospitable interspersed with rough rocky hills covered in spinifex. Further westward it became more isolated covering mostly flat and shrubby countryside peppered with dry spinifex as the road headed onto Camooweal on the Georgina River (passable when dry) near the Northern Territory border. Reaching the black soil downs of the Barkley Tablelands, here on the road, were more cattle and drovers than vehicles until eventually reaching the intersection of the dusty red and straight Stuart Highway tracking north to Darwin. Later, heading south to Alice Springs, Jan decided to load his car on the train and travel by Ghan to Port Augusta before finally returning home.

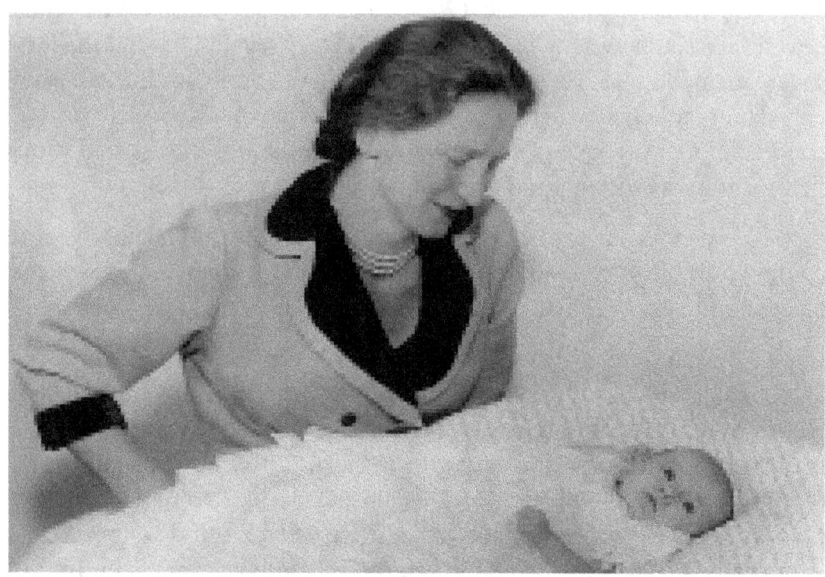
Photograph 266: Anna with Helena on her baptism 1953.

Photograph 268: Jan and Anna with Helena late 1953.

Photograph 267: Anna with children Helena and John, late 1955.

CHAPTER 22

Wangary, SA: 1955-1956

Some of Jan's timber contracting work took him north to Edillilie and Cummins near the region of Yallunda Flat[1]. Earlier during the nineteenth century the Mortlock family who once owned Martindale Hall, an 11,000-acre sheep property near Clare, were South Australia's wealthy pastoralists. They expanded their pastoral interests into Eyre Peninsula and acquired numerous properties around Coffin Bay and Port Lincoln and also country near Tumby Bay calling it Yalluna Station. The Puckeridge family also settled in the area owning large wheat and sheep grazing properties and near Wangary, northwest of Wanilla Forest and to the north of Coffin Bay, they owned country with a plentiful source of timber. After securing accommodation on Reg and Adeline Shepperd's property; wheat, and sheep farmers next door to the Puckeridges at Wangary, Jan and Anna moved into the Shepperd's old farmhouse. Here once more Jan continued cutting timber railway sleepers which he loaded and delivered to rail sidings at either Wanilla, Cummins or Edillilie.

Anna missed Bob and Jean Blann and their young girls Christine and Patricia (Yvonne their youngest not yet born at the time), at Wanilla Forest, while next door her brother, Jaroslav and his wife Lois already had their second child, Jaroslav or Jaryn, as he became known. Although Anna was delighted for them, she was now sufficiently distanced from her sister-in-law and any criticism over domestic shortcomings.

Reg and Adelie Shepperd had children of their own; Adrian, Gerald, Peter and Helen. Their youngest, Helen was similar in age to Helena, so they became playmates. Reg and Adeline would become lifelong friends, their family connection and friendship enduring for decades and eventually passing onto the younger generations to maintain ongoing contact. Many memorable family get-togethers were held at Shepperd's place, and the outdoor, open farm life suited Anna. She was once again in a rural setting with the familiarity of wheat and sheep surrounding her, like at home but in Australia on a much larger scale. Anna had the use of a quiet brindled dairy cow called Cherry, who would just stand in the paddock chewing her cud while Anna perched herself on a three-legged stool and hand-milked her into a bucket. Fresh milk was as abundant as was the country camaraderie forwarded by the Shepperd family.

Anna was now pregnant with her second child and kept busy with their eldest, almost two years old. Although Anna was slowly becoming a lapsed catholic due to the difficulty of attending Church with a non-Catholic husband, she was still determined to bring up her children with some faith instilled in them.

She began a private ritual with her daughter at bedtime and shared in a child's prayer.

Helena would kneel on the table facing her mother and together recite a Czech children's prayer, which, when translated, sounded like, "Little Angel my keeper, Look after my soul, Guard it every nightfall, from harm and all evil. Amen."

At first, Jan and Anna's life revolved around their daughter, and they probably overindulged in her as most parents do with their firstborn. However, there were many instances when this shy but stubborn little girl, with or without her guardian angel, cost them dearly. Their doctor had informed Anna that their daughter was pigeon-toed and would require corrective Posturepedic boots. After a costly trip to Port Lincoln to have their daughter fitted with these expensive orthopaedic boots, they discovered that Helena was wearing only one of them on their return home. It was soon established she threw the other boot out of the window somewhere along the road. From there on, her pigeon-toe treatment was relegated to mainstream children's foot ware.

Whenever travelling, and if their daughter ever became overly quiet in the back seat, it was often with good reason to become suspicious. On one occasion, when returning by car from Port Lincoln after shopping at George Mareolas' greengrocer's shop, Helena sat in the back seat in one of those exceptionally quiet moods. Old George Mareolas was a tight-fisted character, and many customers fell victim to his 'accidental' overcharging discrepancies. Anna was generally irked by his attitude toward her as whenever she shopped alone in his store and prepared to pay with Jan's signed cheque, the old grocer would refuse her and not accept payment until Jan himself presented the cheque. On this occasion when Anna turned around to look at her daughter in the back seat, she was horrified and demanded that her husband immediately stop the car. Looking back at Anna was a clown-like face with a sheepish smile splotched in a mask of technicolour. Not only her face but her new blue coat was smeared in colour! Soon numerous small bottles of food tincture were discovered and extracted from their daughter's coat pocket, soaking everything in a blended mass of dye. Cleaning up their child as best they could, still stained in a plethora of streaky colour extending from her face to her hands, and all over her clothing, Jan could only laugh and muse how his clever little 'Lamb' had managed to put one over the old scoundrel.

Christmas at Port Lincoln was always a special treat for Children as they would all line up by the Pier and wait for Santa's arrival in his speed boat. Helena was as excited as the next child to receive a present, but when she came face to face with the snowy-haired and bearded gentleman in red, no amount of persuasion would convince her that he was someone nice and friendly giving out gifts. She screamed the place down and began backing away, pushing the other children behind her into a pile of equally screaming and terrified youngsters.

While Anna was in Port Lincoln Hospital having their second child John, Jan took Helena to visit, but they first had to negotiate an elephant in the park on the waterfront. The elephant was there to entertain the children. As Helena stood mesmerized by the huge creature, and holding tightly onto her still, unopened packet of peanuts, the elephant casually dropped his trunk into her hands and snatched the treat. No consolation would appease the child, not even the promise of a new brother.

During mid-1955, some six weeks after the birth of their son, the baby was baptized Jan Martin, with Jaroslav Kurovec and Gizela Dufek as God-Parents. Baby Jan would change his name many years later by deed pole to John, but in the interim, he grew into a chubby and happy baby, a great favourite with Gizela, who at the time had not started their own family. Many subsequent jaunts to the beach showed the little chap wallowing in someone's lap until finally, he could sit up unaided and pose in front of the family Zephyr 'SA 369-816'... Jan's pride and joy.

Between work, Jan managed to make time for his family, which included many weekend jaunts to the beach. Beach attire to Anna was just as important as every day ware, and whenever she was at the seaside, she would wear her stylish swimsuit and matching beach outfit. Helena would also be dressed in her frilly white and yellow polka dotted costume and sport one of Anna's creations; a large well-shaded green triangular cotton bonnet trimmed with white zigzags. Although Jan loved the seaside, he rarely ventured in for a swim. He much preferred to remain on the sand playing with his children. Friends would often congregate for picnics at nearby Coffin Bay and Farmer's Beach, at Port Lincoln on the Pier, or further afield at Tumby Bay along the northeast coast. These functions always drove Anna's societal life as she drifted effortlessly into these gatherings.

Fishing in Port Lincoln or at Tumby Bay was a big attraction for both professional and recreational fishermen. Tuna was plentiful and readily available from the many fishing boats tied up in the harbour. At the time, a well-recognized fixture of the fishing fraternity was Pompa. Everyone knew him, and he was always Pompa to everyone, with his Christian name never used although it was surmised by some to be Wilf. He always had his dog Harris with him. During this time, it was believed Pompa was a bachelor, but he was likable and friendly and lived simply in a shack with his dog. Jan would often tease Anna that Pompa fancied her. But apart from owning fishing boats, Pompa also had a car and remained popular with Jan and his friends.

On weekends when Jan had free time, he would go rabbit shooting with his mates in the Todd River. But as always, he would return with them, and Anna would have to cook up whatever they hunted. When one of them, on another occasion, presented her with a rooster, she tried to do her best with it, but the old bird was far too tough to eat even when stewed; the dogs even turned away from it. At times Anna and the children would join her husband and his band of hunters on these weekend excursions, and together with their families, they would make it a bush picnic.

After work late in the evenings, Jan would invariably travel home on his tractor, arriving well into the night. He had excellent night vision, and driving along the quiet and deserted tracks; he never drove with his tractor or truck lights on. Anna would only hear the approaching sound of a vehicle in the dark, knowing he would soon be home. There was no traffic on those logging tracks, so after a day of hard work, it must have been a relaxing reprieve for Jan to follow along a familiar track surrounded by darkness with only the purring of his tractor breaking the silence. Perhaps this same nocturnal visual stealth served him well during the war and alerted him to nocturnal enemy activity. Many often spoke of his extraordinary night vision when they themselves floundered in the dark.

Jan worked hard and, together with Anna, still maintained a tight budget to accomodate their growing family. They retained specific traditional values at home but adapted to their new country, which involved changes to their lifestyle but also brought them into the fold of society rather than isolating them. Anna soon realized that certain social niceties she had grown used to in New Zealand had to give way to the harsh reality of starting out as a poor immigrant family. All money had to be put to sound economic use and not fritted away.

Whenever they went out with friends, and despite their relative poverty compared to other established European families, both were always well groomed. Jan readily swapped his working-day navy 'Jackie Howard' singlets for the opportunity to dress up in casual slacks and a jacket (even wearing a tie, on occasions) and always sporting a cap or hat depending on where they were going.

Anna presented stylishly dressed and posed a striking figure whenever they were in the company of others. After all, she had arrived with trunks of fashionable clothes from New Zealand which had to be worn. The children were also well groomed, and Helena would often wear new outfits which Anna hand-sewed complimented with a large bow almost overshadowing her daughter's short hair. By now, amongst their English-speaking friends, Jan's name was Anglicized to John or Jack, and baby Jan was called little Johnny.

Even though in the earlier days, Anna possessed an abundance of photographs of her growing family in South Australia, the novelty of regular photo shoots dwindled as the children grew, and more emphasis was placed on more immediate and pressing issues rather than filling shoe boxes with photographs. Their lives were changing, and by mid-1956, pregnant with her third child, Anna and Jan decided to leave South Australia, and with their household goods and machinery packed to follow on later, they were ready to migrate north to Queensland.

Photograph 269 & 270: (L-R) Anna, Helena & cow Cherry 1954. Anna, baby John & Helena at Wangary late 1955.

Photograph 271 & 272: (L-R) Anna & children at Farmers Beach. Jan & children at Farmers Beach 1955.

Photograph 273 & 274: (L-R) Jan on his tractor SA. Christmas at Shepherd's Wangary.

Photograph 275: Pompa & his dog circa 1952.

Photograph 276 & 277: (L-R) Jan on the Pier Port Lincoln 1954.
Jan in front Pier Hotel Port Lincoln.

Photograph 278 & 279: (L-R) Jan with Helena & Helen Sheppard and a family acquaintance. Pub scene Jaroslav Kurovec & friends Port Lincoln SA during early 1950s.

Photograph 280 & 281: (L-R) Jaroslav with friends at the Pier Hotel.
Jaroslav Kurovec and friends.

Photograph 282 & 283: (L-R) Jan, Helena & Reg Sheppard 1954.
Jan & Anna with baby Johnny with their vehicles.

Photograph 284, 285, 286 & 287: (Above) Jan & offsiders milling timber sleepers, Wanilla Forest SA 1952.

Photograph 288 & 289: (L-R) Jan & Anna & children at the seaside SA.

CHAPTER 23

Road to Queensland: 1956

When Jan made his first trip north to Queensland between early January to March of 1954, he suffered numerous road delays due to the northern monsoonal season. It was only the prelude to exceptional adverse weather conditions that would begin by the end of 1955.

In October 1955 and again in March 1956, flood water levels in the Murray-Darling catchment were among the highest recorded. The countryside was saturated and flooded with these two weather events so close together.

In early March of 1956, Cyclone Agnes (the first Tropical Cyclone to be tracked on radar) hit Townsville, Ingham, and Cairns before going inland and causing insurmountable damage and flooding. With unprecedented rainfall throughout Queensland and fuelling the rivers draining into the Murray-Darling River catchment, this only added chaos to the already saturated landscape stretching from Queensland down through western NSW and into South Australia. By early May, it was reported that the Darling River was experiencing high levels of flow, and with that, the Murray River was slowly rising. By the end of May 1956, many areas of the low-lying country were becoming flooded[1].

Jan did not seem to have much luck picking ideal weather conditions for overland travel. He may have reasoned that by leaving a few months later, in June-July, he would avoid any major flooding, but he did not realize; in Australia, you need not necessarily have rain falling onto you to have significant floods!

During mid-winter of 1956 it had also been a wet season on Ayre Peninsular in South Australia, with creeks running and swamps overflowing and, in many instances, blocking local roads to traffic. So, in spite of a heavy wet season, Jan and Anna had their farewell. All those determined to attend Jan and Anna's farewell party came from far and wide in trucks and any means of transport suitable to cross the waterlogged and boggy roads.

Recollections from Gerald and Peter Sheppard, and Peter Bradford; Jan and Anna had some send-off on Sheppard's farm. Two pigs were roasted on a spit over a big fire; one for lunch and the other for tea. The first pig was started at 5 am, while the second one was put on the spit at 11 am.

The red International truck was loaded to the hilt. Jan had removed the wheels from his Fordson Major Tractor and sat the body in cut-out trays on the back of the truck.

Amongst all the household furniture and saw benches, Peter Sheppard said, "It was one hell of a load!" Maybe, Main Roads Inspectors were not as diligent then as they are today with overloaded trucks.

Reflecting upon this migration to North Queensland in those days and now in the absence of Jan and Anna, those who vaguely recollected the family departure from Wangary debated how it was achieved. Some believed it to be a single journey with both vehicles departing at the same time, however the family's initial arrival to Mareeba was certainly by car. As Anna did not drive then, Jan had to drive both vehicles at different times from Wangary onto Mareeba in Queensland.

The little green Zephyr fully loaded with the four of them additional to clothes and bedding packed in the back seat and the boot, together with extra tinned food, water, fuel, and spare tyres; was a load in itself. The family's odyssey north in their Zephyr read something like 'I've Been Everywhere' by Australian country singer and writer Geoff Mack,

Anna recalled the trip vividly when they left Wangary and headed north to Cummins and out to the coastal town of Tumby Bay before proceeding up the coast onto Whyalla and Port Augusta. After that, as the experience became more confronting, the names of outback towns blurred into the landscape while their journey became influenced by unpredictable weather and road conditions. From the beginning, the weather was hot during the day and cold at night. Their only reprieve, the ocean breeze that they had earlier, soon became a memory as they drove from familiar coastal landmarks and headed north into the arid countryside. Anna was already five months pregnant, so it was a challenging and tiring trip with two children who were by now aged three and thirteen months. For most of the journey, the children slept in the back seat, but it was not always comfortable when Johnny had to be bottle-fed and would only settle to sleep in his mother's lap.

They headed east along the Port Pirie-Broken Hill Highway parallel with the railway line, keeping well northwest of the flooded catchment systems still fed from earlier torrential rains in the north. To the south, the Murray River had significant flooding, and crossing this river anywhere was always challenging.

The road northwest to Broken Hill was reasonable; although unsealed, it was rough with numerous wash-outs as it traversed the normally featureless countryside. Sandy creek beds had no culverts over them but rather stony crossings and even fewer bridges. The ordinarily barren landscape, covered in Blue Bush and Salt Bush, which after good seasons was fodder for sheep grazing, was exceptionally green as it stretched toward the horizon over flat and often water-logged panorama.

Nearing the mining town of Broken Hill, the Barrier Range finally broke the monotony.

Eastward to Wilcannia, the landscape was much the same, and what would have been usually a landscape of dry watercourses was now covered in sheets of water crisscrossing the flat plains.

After crossing the swollen Darling River at Wilcannia, Jan continued east toward Cobar and onto Dubbo. However, due to numerous diversions caused by the flooded river systems of the Macquarie and Castlereagh Rivers and coupled with infinite patience they could only make slow progress north toward Walgett. From there they made their way north east to Moree and eventually arrived at Goondiwindi on the Queensland border.

By the time they arrived in Queensland, days had already turned into weeks, and the weather was becoming steadfastly hot, with swarms of flies settling on them whenever they stopped to feed the children. In the evenings, when they finally pulled up to settle for the night, the mosquitoes arrived in droves, having breed profusely in all the water lying about from recent flooding and rain.

After Miles, they travelled westward to Roma and then continued inland in a northerly direction through the centre of Queensland, toward Rolleston and Springsure. Despite winter, the days grew hotter as further north they drove, and with it, a swag of flies always accompanied them. Anna began to wonder what she had let herself in for. It was a long journey over remote, gravel, and dusty roads. Numerous signposted cattle properties pointed down likely tracks from the main road, but no sign of life appeared close enough to make contact with these remote dwellers. It seemed lonely in the bush, and Anna wondered how they coped with being so far from civilization. It was only the sparse and dusty, ram-shackle settlements that popped up along the way that hinted any presence of life. But each township was like a remnant of bygone days, once filled with hopeful dreams but failing to deliver a sustainable future.

Anna desperately needed fresh meat, milk, eggs, fruit, and vegetables. Everything so far had been from tinned cans to sustain them. Food supplies were dwindling, and more was needed, but these remote towns relied heavily on fresh produce from elsewhere to feed their own communities, and here supplies were short. Boiled drinking water for the children was Anna's biggest concern. They only carried a small amount of water and coped with a small primus to boil the water and cook all their meals. But, despite it all, nobody became ill.

And the journey continued; onto Emerald, Capella, Clermont, Blair Athol, and Charters Towers. Most roads were rough, dusty, and washed out, but in places, still covered in churned-up boggy soil; a reminder of recent rains.

At last, Charters Towers felt civilized, and the road onto Townsville a dream compared to what they had endured over the past weeks. The further north they drove, the lusher the countryside grew as sways of green cane fields dominated the landscape. Encouragingly, Jan pointed out the beautiful rainforest mountains to the west and reminded Anna that it only improved the further north they went.

Around Ingham, out of desperation, Anna begged Jan to stop by a farmhouse so she could ask for some boiled water for Johnny's milk formula. The Italian lady spoke no English and not only gave Anna boiled water but fresh eggs, salami, bread, and milk. Anna was overwhelmed by the kindness from this stranger, as it hardly compared with what little they had received along the road since leaving Wangary.

Their journey introduced Anna to how vast and isolated Australia was at the time. It was an experience she would often reflect upon; that distance and isolation were of no meaningful measure for human endeavour to achieve something in the most challenging of places. In Queensland, the annual tropical monsoons bucket down, cutting off roads for days, sometimes lengthening into weeks, and leaving many thoroughfares damaged and impassable for months; all this would become a way of life for Anna. It was not only the climate and its Tropical Cyclones to contend with, but the environment with its own share of hazardous native predators to be reconciled with.

CHAPTER 24

Mareeba: 1956-1957

When Jan and Anna finally reached Mareeba, they were offered a hut as temporary accommodation on the banks of Atherton Creek on Stevenson's farm.

Some ten years earlier, the whole area had been a WWII airstrip. Although much of the land was slowly reverting back to tobacco farming, some of the countryside still had the tell-tale scars of crisscross runways and shelters used during the war.

The hut was a basic army barrack with three rooms and open-shutter windows without glass. Inside, the walls were unsealed and there was no electricity or running water. Water had to be carried up from the clear running stream only a few yards away and light at night was with kerosene hurricane lamps. But there was a wood stove for cooking and boiling water. For Anna it was a pleasing diversion from the cramped conditions all cooped together in the car for over six weeks on the road.

With Anna and the children settled in the hut, Jan returned to South Australia to collect the truck load of timber milling equipment, his tractor and all the household furniture including Anna's numerous travel trunks. Prior to leaving Wangary in the car with his family, Jan drove the pre-loaded truck in tandem with another driver following in a vehicle, as far as Port Pirie. The truck was then left safely at a conveniently prearranged place close to the rail link so once Jan returned by train from Queensland, he was able to collect his loaded truck and continue driving north.

When Jan finally returned with the loaded truck, including the much-awaited furniture, Anna was dismayed that the mirror on her bedroom dresser had cracked. However, as everything else was in order, she soon overcame her disappointment and made the shack comfortable while Jan searched for work.

Jan soon discovered work was plentiful, and Mareeba was a thriving community sustained by hard-working immigrant families. Many of them were predominantly Italian, Yugoslav, and Albanian, who grew tobacco, but like themselves, there were other nationalities within the community, including Czechs so Jan and Anna were always conscious of integrating into society rather than becoming a click with people of their own identity.

However, in Mareeba at the time, English-speaking people were less visible downtown. On busy days groups of farmers with their women folk would gather on street corners and have loud discussions in their native language. The foreign dialogue was so common that one could easily think Mareeba was a town in distant Italy or some other European country rather than Australia.

Early upon their arrival to Mareeba, Jan and Anna met Ivan and Anna Filcoff; tobacco share farmers. Ivan was Bulgarian, and Anna was Czech, and they had two daughters, Maria and Ann. It was probably through this casual acquaintance that Jan became interested in tobacco growing. Although Jan hated the idea of smoking, he realized there was big money to be made in the industry.

Australia's tobacco industry, on a worldwide scale, could not compare with the Americas and Asia, but it was still a lucrative industry at the time. Jan had become so immersed in growing tobacco that he and Anna often discussed the possibility of migrating to New Guinea or even Rhodesia (now Zimbabwe), countries still within the Commonwealth, and offering encouraging prospects to those prepared to take the gamble, but Anna could not be persuaded.

Anna's husband began cutting timber for the Forestry Department and from the forestry office at the old Assay Office in Walsh Street, Jan obtained permits to log timber at nearby Davies Creek Forestry Reserve. By then, Jan moved his equipment into the forest, and began logging and hauling specified trees before trucking them onto the Mareeba sawmill. He yearned to make money so he could eventually buy his own land as tobacco share farming did not appeal to him.

By the end of November 1956, their third child Pavla Anna Diana was born in Mareeba hospital and delivered by Dr. Patrick Flecker. Again, Anna readily made friends with women in the maternity ward and became friendly with the Goodhew family whose daughter was born at the same time as Diana. On the day Anna and her baby were discharged, their eldest three-year-old met the new arrival with some resistance and scorn and suggested they leave the baby in the hospital, and all return home quickly. But Johnny, almost eighteen months old, was delighted with the new addition and pointed out otherwise.

"Look! She has a nose and eyes like me, so we better take her home." The baby became known as Diana.

Anna's hands were full as she cared for three children under four years. She kept house and cooked, and even found time to bake traditional buns for the family. The baby was easy to care for, but the other two children were wanderers, and although warned never to go down to the creek, this often fell upon deaf ears as flowing water drew them like a magnet.

Swimming in the creek was always a family get-together, and on occasions when Anna washed their clothes, the children were allowed to splash about while she happily sang Czech songs to amuse them. The children had already been warned about 'Hastrman,'[1] a mythical Czech waterman who was evil and lurked hidden in the water. This creature was not unsimilar to the bunyip, so with this warning, the children were generally cautious not to paddle too far.

Jan once caught a penny-sized tortoise and gave it to Helena. She was delighted with it as she had never owned a pet before. The tortoise was meant to be a temporary visitor and was soon released. When it disappeared, Helena was dismayed and in tears, but she was told it had left because she was too untidy. She tidied everything in her room briefly, but soon the tortoise was forgotten, and so was the tidying up.

Although Helena was a wilful child, Johnny always caused the most concern for his parents.

On one occasion, when the children wandered, they came close to the creek. While leaning and peering over the bank's edge, a small sapling that Johnny was hanging onto gave away and he tumbled several feet into Atherton Creek. Fortunately, he did not plunge into the water, but instead landed unscathed amongst rocks.

By now, Johnny was sleeping in the large wicker cot beside the window while Helena was moved onto a makeshift bed on a mattress covering two of Anna's large travel trunks, which were pushed up against the wall. During summer, the window shutters had to remain open at night to cool the house and allow a breeze to pass through.

Johnny was a habitual night owl. No matter how often he was put to bed asleep, he would invariably wake up in the middle of the night and crawl over the cot sides and out through the window. Jan and Anna would only be alerted when they heard him crying outside. Cold and naked and holding onto Jan's axe, Johnny would be standing at the door, howling to be let in. The following morning, they would find his pyjamas by the wood heap. It was not a one-off episode, and it did not matter how much they child-proofed the cot, the young 'Houdini' would be found time after time, in the middle of the night whimpering on the doorstep.

Apart from a few domestic hiccups and less-than-ideal accommodation, Mareeba offered Jan and Anna a start in an assorted multicultural environment. The town's people were friendly, and where Jan and Anna lived out of town, it was still close enough to all the necessary amenities, such as the hospital and chemist, Post Office, and the NSW Bank. Although Penney's and Jack and Newell Department stores were larger and handy with various commodities, Jan and Anna did most of their household shopping at Bill Hastie's Grocery Store at the southern end of town.

During their time in Mareeba, Jan bought Anna a new Singer treadle sewing machine for £76. It was the best gift Anna received and she greatly appreciated it as, in the past, she had done all her sewing by hand. With renewed sewing enthusiasm, she made herself known to the elderly Mr. and Mrs. Jebreen, who owned Jebreen's Drapery. The shop was a family affair, with their children already learning the trade: so, the elderly Mrs. Selina Jebreen often made time for Anna to chat about family and life. She once told Anna how she and her husband met when she was young.

"One day, a man came to see my father, and when he left, the man gave me a present; a little box with a ring in it. I thanked him and ran off to play Hop-Scotch with my girlfriends," She laughed.

"He returned some years later. You know it was the happiest marriage imaginable!" Mrs. Jebreen concluded.

The area around where Jan and Anna lived on Stevenson's Farm, was flourishing with tobacco farms belonging to established farmers like the Murat family, the Celledoni family, and the Myrteza family, just to name a few. Amongst them, on a farm, lived an elderly and somewhat eccentric woman known to most as Aunty Flora. Aunty Flora would cycle into town wearing her billowing dress and a large hat and, from beneath it, peered a face with heavily applied red lipstick, which often exaggerated her lips. People paused to look at her as she rode by, but most children, unsure of her, instead hid behind their mother's skirts to watch on. She was never known to upset anyone but was a memorable character from that era.

Apart from timber contracting, Jan occasionally did work for various farmers whenever opportunities arose. Once, Jack Murat asked him to do a job, but after some time, Anna noticed that Jan still had not been paid. Jan was not too bothered as he believed it was probably an oversight, and if he did not get paid, he simply would not work for him again. It was not in Jan's nature to hound people for outstanding debts. But Anna was different, so she took it upon herself to deal with the matter personally. Mr. Murat must have been surprised when a woman unknown to him arrived and demanded payment for her husband's unpaid work. Whatever the reasons behind the circumstances, Jack quickly paid up. He probably realized it was best not to argue with a scorned woman.

Author's interpretation of young Johnny Kanak in 1956.

CHAPTER 25

Euluma Creek: 1957-1959

By mid-1957, after twelve months of living on Stevenson's Farm, Jan and Anna were ready to move from Mareeba. They began looking for a place that would be more comfortable for their growing family and one that would give them an added income. Jan had been told that there were timber contracting opportunities in Mossman, supplying sleepers for the network of rail lines used to carry cut sugarcane to the Mossman Sugar Mill.

Anna came from a farming background, whereas Jan only knew timber and the army, so when he secured a lease at Euluma Creek on what was then known as Mick Evans' Dairy Farm, Anna was delighted with the prospect. Mick Evans, having recently married, had moved into Mossman, so the farm presented an ideal opportunity for them.

The Euluma Creek community was far more isolated from amenities than in Mareeba. Again, there was no electricity, but there was running water. Although telephones were scarce, Mrs. Margaretha English, on a neighbouring dairy farm, ran the local telephone exchange where messages, be they telegrams, could be received and dispatched.

The closest Post Office and rail service was at Julatten, several miles away. The Euluma Creek Primary School had closed a few years before Jan and Anna's arrival, so all community schooling was now at Bushy Creek State School in Julatten.

Euluma Creek was on the upper reaches of the Great Dividing Range, some eighteen miles inland from the coastal town of Mossman. This farming community was mainly accessed from Mossman by way of the Rex Range, winding up over a steep and rough gravel road which, after the summit, the road either went ahead onto Julatten and beyond, or branched off onto Black Mountain Road toward Euluma Creek, from where it continued around onto Julatten forming the loop road. The remaining Black Mountain Road headed south as a logging track, skirting the coastal range onto Kuranda. It was seldom used for any other purpose than logging, although earlier, people within the community advocated upgrading it into a usable road.

As it is still known, the old Cobb and Co. track, or Bump Road[1], passed close through Euluma Creek and over the range toward Port Douglas. But it was already overgrown and only used by those adventurous enough to search out its native fauna and flora or dare to either hike or drive their 4x4 vehicles down the steep decline onto the coast near Port Douglas.

Most Euluma Creek dairy farms were at the canopy's edge of the thick rainforest. In the 1950s, Forestry Department permits still allowed timber logging in forestry reserves.

Mick Evans' Farm literally sat on the watershed, dividing the coastal water courses from those which flowed east into the Pacific Ocean and those west, eventually emptying into the Gulf of Carpentaria.

The farmhouse was a low set rambling Queenslander-style dwelling about three feet above the ground, painted white with bottle green trim. It was spacious, with a large kitchen-dining area and a living area at the centre from which a small back landing opened into the orchard. It had a large open veranda facing east, accessed through French windows from two side bedrooms. This veranda overlooked the undulating valley below through which flowed the stream, Euluma Creek.

Beyond, on the opposite side of the creek, two neighbouring farmers, the Pashen Family and the Larsen Family, were Jan and Anna's closest neighbours. Alongside the house were numerous out-sheds, barns, a chicken run, and an outdoor closed-in shower beneath a high tank stand. All toilets in those days were outside. Further south of the house by the fence gate where a disused old horse wagon was partially concealed in weeds, the track continued toward the dairy sheds and cow yards. Some cows and an old horse came with the property, while additional dairy herds for milking had to be eventually sourced. The dairy bales were basic, and hand milking with two people over twenty cows twice daily was a task. Once the milking herd was started, there were no holiday breaks afterward.

The cow's established routine was a perpetual cycle that could not be broken if milk and cream productivity was to be achieved. Jan could not always be there to help as he had to supplement their income with outside work. It was a new era for Anna as she braced herself for the job ahead.

Anna's hands were always full with the children, and while she milked the cows, Diana would be close by strapped in her pram while Helena often strayed into the bales to share molasses with the cows from the feed trough as they were being milked. Johnny had to be harnessed close by, as whenever he escaped, he would invariably climb the railings.

He once tumbled from the railings down into the yard below where a cow with her newborn calf were penned. Not too happy with her unexpected visitor, the cow charged and pinned him into the muddy ground. He had to be quickly rescued before the anxious and cranky beast caused him real damage.

Jan eventually found work cutting railway sleepers for the Mossman Sugar Mill. During this work, Jan met Max Davidson, a cane farmer from Miallo who brought him in contact with numerous other cane farmers from whom Jan would source discarded sugarcane stalks as additional fodder for his farm animals.

Through these contacts, Jan met Ned Cobb from Daintree. His family were long standing dairy farmers and went from dairying into grazing beef cattle. A more profitable enterprise. Their farm had been one of Daintree's last dairies to operate, if not one of the oldest in the area, and all the milking machines and equipment were up for sale. Jan made an offer, and so their Euluma Creek dairy farm became mechanized!

For Anna, the task of milking cows twice a day may have become easier, but with all the milking apparatus came the additional work of fastidious washing of every stainless-steel gadget and purging all milking hoses and suction caps after each milking session. The cream was now automatically separated into a stainless steel vat rather than being left to settle for a few hours in the milk before rising to the surface and then skimmed off and scooped into the cream cans. Although it took time to fill each cream can, Robin Clacherty another district farmer had the weekly cream run and collected the farmer's cream so that it could be forwarded onto the Malanda Butter Factory on the Atherton Tablelands. Anna took great pride in her quality cream production, where at the Malanda Butter Factory it was tested, graded, and certificated. These certificates brought greater pride and satisfaction to Anna than the measly income generated by the cream. Later when Robin retired and moved from the district, Bill Jorgenson took over the cream run for a while until the local cream delivery onto Malanda became unviable. Although the local Julatten Butter Factory had long ceased to operate many decades before, milk deliveries onto Malanda remained in place until dairy farming finally declined in the Julatten district.

The separated milk from the dairy, was generally left for the older poddy calves, but later it helped to supplement feed for rearing pigs. With a readily available source of molasses from the Mossman Sugar Mill and home-grown corn, Jan established a piggery that once housed over eighty pigs. With the additional fodder produced, the milking herd also increased in number as well as the workload, but not necessarily the income.

Jan bought shares in the Mareeba Bacon Factory Co-operative and regularly travelled to Mareeba to sell his pigs. Pigs generally made good money, but they probably ate double what they were worth.

Dairy farming at the time was gruelling, and the financial rewards were never lucrative for a small producer, but Anna persevered, taking it all in her stead. The small compensation for the work effort and time spent achieving it, was hardly worth it, as Anna needed more time to spare with her small children as well as maintaining the family house hold.

Evenings were Anna's only time of relaxation if churning cream into butter for home use and sewing and mending for the family could be regarded as a relaxing vocation! But, as with most European families, salted pig lard on bread was always preferable to butter!

With occasional visits from neighbouring Pashen and Larsen families, Anna needed more time for social interaction, apart from just attending rare community functions. Although there were several other farming families in the vicinity, namely the English family, Tommy, and Janet Twart, two elderly brothers George and Jack Diehm, and the Rebetzke family (of whom Cyril Rebetzke drove the school bus to Julatten), these were mostly people who Jan conferred with. However, Mrs. Twart, who farmed further along Black Mountain Road, would regularly walk over for a chat with Anna.

Jan's timber cutting was constantly in demand, and he often needed hired help. For a short while, he employed Les Webb from Julatten, who while working for Jan, found the work too dangerous after being chased by a wild boar in the forest. Several other men also lasted for only a short time, so for most, Jan did all the sleeper cutting alone. He was strong and not afraid to do the yards, but on many occasions, he would arrive home late, by which time the children would already be in bed.

Louie Nohl, a fellow countryman, arrived from South Australia on a short holiday but remained for a few months to work for Jan. Louie was a sociable and entreating chap and was quite handy with the piano accordion, which entertained the whole family if not the community. Louie enjoyed going to dances and chatting up the local young ladies, and on occasions, even babysat the children while Jan and Anna went to Tom Brown's picture theatre at Mt. Molloy. He was known as Uncle Louie to the children and would often saddle up the old horse and treat them to a ride.

The annual Mossman show was the yearly highlight, and the children would be taken down for the day between dairy milking sessions. Louie would return laden with prizes from the shooting gallery, while Helena returned with a gaping hole in her new tartan skirt ripped out by a monkey that reached and grabbed at her.

By now, Diana was beginning to walk and talk, and at dusk, she would lead Louie outside by the hand to the mango tree swarming with flying foxes.

With one hand pointing at the tree and the other with her finger to her lips, she would whisper a cautious warning, "Shoosh! Puncosh!"

Her expression for "Quiet! Flying foxes!"

Diana was a fair-haired child and was always by her mother's side as a willing helper. The old farm rooster saw her otherwise, and every time she entered the hen house with her basket to collect eggs, the old bird invariably attacked her. He would fly at her, landing on her shoulders and pecking at her head, ending their encounter in a flurry of screams with eggs and feathers flying everywhere.

Their next-door neighbour, Mrs. Pashen, used to visit regularly, and as she sat and chatted with Anna, she would invariably place Diana on her knees and search through the child's hair as she spoke. This happened numerous times until it got the better of Anna, and she spoke about it to her husband. He simply replied, "Then ask her if it bothers you that much!"

Anna soon discovered that Mrs. Pashen was searching Diana's head for paralysis ticks that could be fatal to the very young or elderly.

Johnny remained a constant cause of worry. Following his father every inch of the way, he soon discovered how to start the tractor. Unable to reach the peddles while he sat in the seat, he still managed to switch on the ignition and being in crawl gear, the machine began moving toward a large pile of timber off-cuts. By the time Jan heard the labouring noise of his tractor, and rushed to the scene, he arrived just in time to see his son seated at the wheel as the tractor began mounting the high wood heap.

Johnny had many scrapes, once falling off a log and ending up with several sutures to his eyebrow. Sister Lill Gadd in charge of the Mt. Molloy Clinic, was available then, so she stitched Johnny's brow, and the family ended up going to Tom Brown's movie theatre afterward. Johnny also had a stint in Mossman Hospital after a petrol-siphoning episode. Before being discharged, he disappeared beneath the low-set hospital and refused to be coaxed out. The scared lad understood no English, so everyone had to wait until Jan arrived. He was eventually beckoned out, holding onto a collection of cigarette buts!

Whenever Jan had the opportunity, he spent as much time as possible with the children, relieving Anna from her childminding role so other chores could be attended. Much to Anna's horror, he taught Helena how to use the new sewing machine. After the two of them cut out two pieces of fabric of equal shape, Helena proudly sewed them together, making her first rather rudimentary blouse. Jan was handy with the sewing machine as well, and made each of his girls' bikini bottoms to run about in outside.

Mostly the children ran naked around the yard whenever playing with the water hose. With the farm situated on an elevated ridge, plenty of downhill races with the children curled inside old tyres were carried out as they rolled speedily down the gully. It was one of their favourite past times with their father as they wheeled their tyres back uphill, huffing and puffing, only to be eagerly ready to set off again. In those days, the dangers associated with these games did not occur to anyone as the raw exuberance of being fearless made it all the more fun. However, the game was only allowed when their father supervised them.

During this time, Jan acquired two blue cattle dog pups; Kiki and Puntja. He trained them to herd cattle, but, in the end, it was only Kiki that showed promise of obedience to command, whereas Puntja would scatter the herd rather than round them up. Kiki remained with the family while the other pup was found a home elsewhere.

For the first time, the children had a pet, and over time, whenever Kiki was not with Jan, she began to accompany the children wherever they went.

When Kiki grew into adulthood, she used to get unrequited attention from the Pashen Family's farm dog. This annoyed Jan, and he once asked Mrs. Pashen if she would mind keeping her dog tied up at home. As she did not have a collar, Mrs. Pashen obliged and used her husband's necktie around the dog's neck and tethered him to a rope. He no sooner loosened the rope knot and escaped, once more visiting Kiki. Jan could only laugh this time when Kiki's suitor arrived with his necktie.

"Well, at least he now dresses up for the occasion!"

Due to the location of Euluma Creek being at the foothill of Black Mountain within the coastal ranges, rainfall was abundant during the monsoonal season, with spectacular displays of lightning that would craze the sky during thunderstorms. Nearby streams and gullies would flood during the wet season, especially Devil-Devil Creek. This branch of the creek was a short distance down the road toward Julatten, and on many occasions, the stream would break its bank, rise above the old wooden bridge, and spread across the low-lying swampy land blocking traffic onto Julatten and beyond. The alternate route would be to go around the loop road back toward the Rex Range and turn left over a higher but equally rickety Devil-Devil Creek bridge. On one such journey, the school bus, on its homebound route, lost two of its back wheels as the axle broke, sending the loaded vehicle of school kids to a shuddering halt in the middle of the road. The children were finally rescued and taken home by other means. Had it not been so close to the start of the Christmas Holidays, putting the school bus out of temporary commission, this would have delighted the children even more.

After some heavy rain, Jan borrowed Anna's expensive all-weather coat and left it hanging on a post by the dairy. By the time Anna retrieved it, it only had one sleeve. Dolly, one of Anna's dairy cows, had a peculiar habit, albeit an expensive one; a penchant for rubber, cloth, or anything chewable. On another occasion, Dolly let herself into the dairy, and by morning numerous machinery belts had been chewed through. Her days would have been long numbered, if she had not been such a good milking cow.

During one of Jan's regular trips to Mareeba with a load of pigs, Anna remained home with the children and busied herself with domestic chores. The two older children were left to play quietly on the veranda while Diana, the youngest, was having her afternoon nap in the cot. After some time, Helena and Johnny wandered off to play in the garden, and before long, the two of them, along with Kiki, made their way down the gully toward the creek. Anna had not noticed their absence until much later when after school the Larsen children unexpectedly arrived.

Although Anna's children had been drilled never to go to the creek alone, their sense of adventure always drew them to new, if not forbidden, places. What became evident, was when the two reached the stream and after testing the water with their feet, soon waded in waist-deep with all their clothes on. Smart enough to realize the consequences of being wet upon returning home, they both stripped off and hung their clothes on a small tree branch to dry while resuming to paddle in the stream.

A short time later, when the Larsen children returned from school and saw the pair alone in the creek, they instructed them to remain put while the neighbouring children dashed up the hill toward Jan and Anna's farmhouse. Sensing they were about to be dobbed on, Helena and Johnny raced to retrieve their clothes and get home as quickly as possible.

Standing beneath the tree, and enjoying the last of a very satisfying cud, Dolly the cow would have posed a sight of absolute contentment as she glazed her dreamy eyes over the naked and horrified children. Needless to say, when the naked pair returned home, Anna was more than ready for them, but she left the real punishment to be delved out when their father returned from town.

Jan worked tirelessly, as did Anna, but they soon realized this life would not make them financially rich in any great hurry. Jan craved the independence of owning his land, and Anna wanted a place that was theirs to call home and not be a slave to something that neither brought them money nor security.

Despite the tedious work load, Anna always managed quality time with her children, and at bedtime, she would recite Czech fairy stories. A great favourite was 'Broučci' by Czech author Jan Karafiát, a tale about a family of fireflies who set out each evening on an adventure. Upon returning in the morning, and before their bed time mother fire-fly would treat her children to a bowl of delicious soup.

All stories ended with the Czech version: "On top of the hill there was a bell, and so once it rings the story must end!"

However, the children's growing up years on the farm remained challenging for Anna as their increasing need to explore seemed to know no boundaries. So, by juggling farming with housework and continually watching out for them, Anna wished for a life less constraining that would allow more time for her family. Family life on the farm was simple and without any extravagance and festive occasions were celebrated without the commercial fanfare that was fast becoming popular with Christmas and Easter. Attending Worship during these festive occasions was out of the question as no churches were close by. The children had not been introduced to chocolate, so Easter eggs were the hard-boiled variety which Anna decorated with artistic flare. This simple gesture gave the children immense pleasure. Christmas was also kept low-key with a small she-oak tree decorated for the occasion, and only small gifts of purposeful use were ever exchanged.

As the children grew older, Anna introduced books for Christmas and Birthday gifts as the preferred choice and from there on, it became the accepted norm. However, Anna had one dilemma to overcome as her children grew older: how best to introduce them to vaccination injections. She was very fortunate at the time to have had a wonderful family doctor in Mossman. Dr. Blackburn used the 'Ice-cream' trick, bribing the children to cooperate. He only rewarded them with ice cream if they behaved and accepted their immunization shots without howling or objecting. Anna's brood soon became more than happy to go to Mossman for their vaccinations!

Anna and Jan made many acquaintances in their early days at Euluma Creek, people who would remain in Anna's life for many years to come. Although an isolated community, people always found one another and offered friendship and support. People like Ben and Elsie Kerr, whom Anna and Jan met when they attended Les Jenkins' funeral in November of 1958. It had been a sad occasion for all family and friends in the Julatten and Mt. Molloy district when Les being so young, tragically passed away and left behind Addy, a grieving young widow with their two small boys.

Elsie Kerr and Addy Jenkins were sisters with brother Ike Roberts. Together with their mother, Alice Roberts, who lived in the Mossman district at the time, they were all born on Curraghmore Station and raised by the Roberts family. Addy Jenkins and Anna would find common ground and become firm friends. At the time of the funeral, Anna and Jan had asked Edna and Bill Head of Julatten, if the children could remain with them for a few hours while they attended the funeral in Mount Molloy. It almost ended in disaster, being an equally sad occasion for Edna's cat's kittens when Johnny decided to give them a bath.

Johnny created more mayhem when he discovered Edna's gum boots and shoes. With his own shoes on, he placed his feet into another pair of sandshoes and finally inserted his feet with all shoes on into the gum boots. In the end, extracting him from the gumboots took some time!

One evening in early December 1958, after the children had gone to bed, and while Jan and Anna were talking quietly at the kitchen table, suddenly, all-night noises ceased, and everything went exceptionally quiet. A distant rumbling was heard not long afterward, becoming more audible by the minute. At first, it sounded like stampeding horses coming toward them, becoming louder as the thunderous noise approached and vibrated the house. Soon it was rumbling beneath them, and everything inside rattled and shook. Anna sat unperturbed while in front of her, Jan paled with beads of sweat rolling from his forehead. He looked terrified as he sat amidst the rumbling and swaying. After a few minutes, the thunderous commotion faded into the distant darkness, followed by the unusual deathly silence that lasted for only a short while.

Anna would recall later that it was not the first time she had experienced such an event, as earthquakes were common in New Zealand. Still, she added, it was the first and only time in her life that she felt stronger than her husband and had to reassure him it had only been a passing earthquake. The next morning, they heard on the wireless that a magnitude 5 tremor had hit the area, and the Mossman hospital apart from the startled patients had suffered only very minor damage [2].

One of the family's favourite past-times, would be the occasional weekend trip to the beach; an outing which had to be slotted between milking the cows. Port Douglas was always their beach of choice. Arriving there, over a sandy road that turned off from the main highway was the only way by road into this quiet seaside hamlet. Macrossan Street for most, was an unsealed sandy road lined by mango trees under which old Queenslander dwellings stood taking in constant sea breezes. A couple of old pubs lined the street, and one or two amenity shops selling ice cream and soft drinks, fish and chips, and various household and hardware goods, was about the sum total of the shopping precinct.

Between this main street, at one end was the beach, and at the other amongst mangroves was the fishing jetty with its old shed jutting out into the inlet surrounded by numerous moored fishing boats. Port Douglas had seen its heyday before the turn of the century as a port originally servicing the hinterland mining towns and later the wharf was used for shipping bagged sugar from the Mossman mill. Gradually over its declining years the township slumped into a sleepy seaside nook purposeful for its small residential population and visiting locals. With its expansive, coconut-shaded sandy stretch of Four Mile Beach littered with shells and coral pieces, it was then only sparsely frequented by beachgoers and seasonal tourists. However, it was still an idyllic paradise for local fishermen and beachcombers.

In late 1959, Jan and Anna visited Ivan and Anna Filcoff, who were holidaying in Port Douglas. They had met the family some years earlier when the Filcoffs were still tobacco share farmers in Mareeba. By the time Jan and Anna departed Mareeba, the Filcoff family had supposedly departed for Mary Kathleen, a uranium mining settlement between Cloncurry and Mt. Isa in western Queensland. At the time, when Jan and Anna visited them, they were living in one of the mango-shaded old Queenslanders along Macrossan Street. It was a happy reunion, but it would be the last time they would all meet as soon afterward, the Filcoffs moved south.

Toward the end of 1959, Louie Nohl visited again, but this time he brought along his fiancé Rita. They did not remain for long as they were on a 'honeymoon,' and Louie was not looking for work.

Anna and Jan's two older children were free-spirited and whenever there was an opportunity to escape parental attention and explore beyond parameters of their farm, they occasionally did so without detection. However, many of their misadventures did not always remain without consequence.

Euluma school, a short distance from the farm, had closed some years earlier on Friday, the 29th of June 1951, and on that day, Mrs. Florence Sides, the school teacher, had only seven pupils turn up. These children would finish their education in Herberton, bypassing the Julatten school. (Oral history from past student attending school at the time; Betty Lawford nee English, daughter of Margaretha English late of Euluma Creek.)

Although the nearby school had been closed for seven years, it virtually stood there, unlocked upstairs with books and papers scattered on the disused class room floor. When the intrepid adventurers returned home, Bill McGrath, the local Mt. Molloy policeman, was at their place. Dressed in his official khaki uniform, he made a formidable impression on the two guilty youngsters. Terrified that he had come for them, they confessed to their mother that they had only taken two pencils from the school. Anna was somewhat bewildered but eventually learned the two had trespassed upstairs into the deserted classroom. Although the class room door had been closed it had not been locked. Bill had only come on a friendly courtesy visit to see Jan, but the children did not know this and instead unwittingly gave themselves up to their mother after this misdemeanour.

In those days, the country policeman had additional administrative jobs in the community; it was not only about catching unregistered motorists speeding or drunk driving but also dealing with issues of vehicle registration and insurance, forestry permits, driving tests and licenses, and numerous other government formalities.

Truancy, following up on children who failed to attend school was yet another task. The local policeman was regarded as a pillar of society and a keeper of law and order. Families generally liked and respected their local Constable, but most children remained very weary of his presence.

During their time at Euluma Creek, Jan and Anna became well acquainted with the McGraths. Shortly before the end of 1959, when the McGrath family was transferred, Jan and Anna received boxes of children's toys and books that the older McGrath children had outgrown. Amongst the toys were a child's writing desk and stool, a small wooden seated tricycle, a rubber monkey, and a brown-faced Bakelite rag doll. For the first time, the children had many books and toys to play with.

Before the end of the 1959 school year, Charlie Todd, the soon-to-be transferred school headmaster of Bushy Creek State School, was being replaced by Wally Crear, who had been appointed as the new school headmaster at Julatten.

Prior to the school year ending, Jan and Anna decided to send Helena along to school for a few weeks to familiarize herself with speaking English in preparation for class enrolment in the new year. At home, the children and family only spoke Czech, so she needed to be prepared for the sudden language change. Most of their children understood a smattering of English, although no encouragement had been made to speak it at home. Whenever English-speaking visitors arrived, the shy children invariably made themselves scarce.

Dressed in her new navy pinafore, the idea of school appealed to Helena until Monday morning arrived. As the week progressed, so grew her enthusiasm for school and by Friday, were it not for the weekend break she would have happily continued onto school regardless. But, by the following Monday, getting her there was again an uphill battle. To make their daughter a part of the 1959 school break-up and fancy-dress ball, Anna created a costume from the children's rhyme book character of 'Mary-Mary Quite Contrary' and dressed her daughter in a blue frock with a matching bonnet and added a miniature watering can for her to carry. Children's school concerts and dances were a great social event for all the locals, and these functions were held at the Julatten community hall in what is today known as Geraghty Park. It was an opportunity to socialize with one another and make new acquaintances in the community which often was the making of lifelong comradery. On such occasions, someone always played the piano, and with the floor adequately dusted with sawdust, the men took their partners and waltzed around the dance floor. Later on, these dances were even hyped up with local bands coming from Mossman adding a more modern flavour of music for the younger attendees. One such Mossman group were 'The Stars' with Johnny Sciacca and his band players.

Between dances, men generally grouped outside talking while the women busily prepared supper, to be served halfway through the evening. While the dance floor remained unused the children took the opportunity to utilise it and at great pace slid up and down on the floor from one end of the hall to the other.

Anna was an attractive woman and did not go unnoticed. Once an out-of-town chap indiscreetly approached her at a community dance and asked if she would step outside with him! Anna was horrified when she realized it was a proposition and reminded him, in no uncertain terms, that she was a married woman with children.

When it was time for the family to finally move from Euluma Creek to Julatten, they already had numerous friends and acquaintances and Anna was welcomed by the Parents and Citizens Association to help support the local school at Julatten.

Jan's 13 Mareeba Bacon Factory share certificates. Circa 1958

Jan's 27 Mareeba Bacon factory share certificates. Circa 1959.

CHAPTER 26

Julatten: 1960

Jan and Anna moved from Euluma Creek in early 1960. They rented a small house from Mrs. Adele Koll, who lived next to Bushy Creek. The property had recently been bought from the Mildren Family by her son Endel, but Adele was taking charge of all rental business.

Julatten had a long history of mining, timber cutting, and dairy farming. It was once a prosperous township with its own butter factory, which had opened in 1924, a bakery, a shop, a billiard room for entertainment, and above all, it was on the rail link to Mareeba. However, being situated on the Bushy and Rocky Creek floodplain, it must have proved inconvenient and challenging during the wet season as water would rise and surround the buildings.

Slowly over the years the township went into decline. After the dairy farmer's cooperative disputes and community upheavals, the butter factory was forced to close in the 1940s amidst concerns of nepotism and unfair payment for their butter fat. Eventually, all locally produced milk and cream went onto Malanda and Millaa-Millaa on the Atherton Tablelands. All that remained on the current site near the running creek were two small cottages now owned by the Koll family and the ruins of the dilapidated butter factory on the block next door. However, the railway station remained in Kevin Gadd's paddock across the road.

The new township hub of Julatten was re-established a short distance uphill, away from future flood threats. When Jan and Anna arrived, the hub consisted of a new school master's residence for newly appointed teacher Wally Crear and across the road a high set Primary School which had been built some decades earlier. A small community library next to the school and further on the Post Office and its residence then owned and run by the Major family. Next door was a free-standing dwelling which bounded onto the grocery store then owned and operated by Charlie and Vera Knight. Beyond the schoolyard and still standing at the time, were the dilapidated ruins of what was once the previous residence of past school headmasters; Michael Pedrazzini and numerous others including Wally Crear's predecessor Charlie Todd. This old timber building was eventually pulled down, and much of its usable timber was deployed to build Bill and Noreen Mildren's new home next door to where Jan and Anna were about to move to. In the 1950s, before Jan and Anna arrived to Julatten from Euluma Creek, the schoolmaster's residence had been temporarily housed in their dwelling until the new teacher's accommodation was finally erected opposite the school.

Bushy Creek State School began in 1922, and although its original location, albeit temporary, commenced elsewhere and remained for longer than the anticipated three months; it initially consisted of a room in a dwelling provided by William Mildren, where the students were housed and taught by the school's first primary teacher, Miss Dorothy Andersen. However, William Mildren was keen for a permanent new school to be built within the community precinct closer to where the new Post Office had been built.

Although James Mildren had granted land for the new school in early 1923, the structure needed to be built by February 1924[1]. When finally constructed in 1924 on the higher acquired land, the school retained the name of Bushy Creek until it was changed much later in 1975, to Julatten State School.

During the initial establishment of Bushy Creek township which later became Julatten, the railway extension from Mt. Molloy was already being considered, together with further construction of various bridges to facilitate road transportation within the area. One bridge that would create intrigue in later years would be the Rifle Creek bridge near Mt. Molloy. It was constructed as a high narrow bridge allowing the movement of vehicles over it only in the one direction at a time and so it remains at the time of writing this book.

Shortly before Anna and Jan moved into the district, a story had been circulating that two women, Mrs. Leila Alston from Julatten and Mrs. Williams from Rumula, had actually achieved the impossible and passed one other in their vehicles midway across the bridge. Whether myth or fact, it certainly made talk of the district. Their vehicles would have been much smaller by today's standards, and whether each refused to give way to the other on approaching the bridge remains conjecture. Or maybe they just had a point to prove! Mrs. Williams who lived almost opposite the railway siding in Rumula, was a talented piano player, and many locals received music lessons from her until she left the district.

Some say that Anna and Jan's Julatten residence started its humble beginnings at Mt. Carbine as one of two miner's cottages relocated to Bushy Creek, but this was only conjecture, as no real evidence had ever come to light. However, Alfred Inglis a descendant of the Inglis family who once lived in Julatten, said he was sure the two cottages had been built by the Mildren family in about 1910.

In the late 1950s, following the upgrade and maintenance of the road, including the Bushy Creek bridge and the Rocky Creek causeway, a substantial main road's camp had been established on the neighbouring block behind the butter factory. Upon completion of road works, slabs of concrete flooring and a disused and rusting old truck remained. The vehicle once belonged to either Jack Crothers (local timber cutter from Mt. Molloy) or Snowy Baker (Main Road's foreman), or perhaps both at some stage. The truck rested in the paddock behind the family dwelling when Jan and Anna first arrived and it remained there for some time, overgrown with grass. It was yet another source of temptation for the children in its rusted and derelict condition. However, the old butter factory ruins, a crumbling relic beside their house, posed the most danger.

The children, especially young Johnny, were keen adventurers and found the old butter factory intriguing, if not dangerous. It was a ruination of rusted refrigeration coils of cooling pipes still standing precariously gathered on high cement blocks amongst the concrete rubble. These soon collapsed when the incorrigible youngster climbed on top. The cooling pipes concertinaed down, somehow leaving a gap for Johnny to fall through and survive unscathed, escaping the cascading rubble like a cat with nine lives. Their arrival to their new home was also marred by the sight of a huge python nearby that had just feasted on a wallaby. These incidents did not seem to have the haul markings of an encouraging beginning at Julatten. The close by well was another source of intrigue for young Johnny. On numerous occasions he managed to clamber down the deep shaft and back up again along a fitted steel pipe onto the well cavity. Much later while mowing the grass he even threw the burning lawn down the well mower after it caught fire. It had of course been tinkered with and once again Johnny had to retrieve it by rather ingenious methodology before being caught out.

With time to spare, Jan gave Anna driving lessons in their green Zephyr. With the children watching from the back seat and Jan directing her, Anna became nervous at the prospect of it all. Although the road was a narrow dirt track with enough room to manoeuvre and well away from major traffic, Anna would oversteer the car whenever passing trees near the edge and almost veer off the road into the opposite ditch. After a few nerve-wracking lessons, Jan lost patience, and Anna lost confidence and the will to drive.

During this time, while waiting for future work prospects to eventuate, Jan decided to explore the nearby densely forested mountains just beyond where they were living. The closest, Mount Kooyong, had already been partially cleared for cattle grazing. Its steep grassy slope made easy access for about two-thirds of the way up before reaching into the thick mountainous rain forest near its summit.

The family had just finished lunch, and Jan told Anna he was going for a walk and would return later that afternoon. With evening approaching and no sign of her husband, Anna put the children to bed, went next door to Bill and Noreen Mildren's place, and shared her concerns about Jan. After some discussion with further neighbours, it was already too dark for any search party to be sent out. So, instead, it was decided to mount a search for Jan; first thing in the morning. Anna had a sleepless night of worry when just on breakfast early the next morning, Jan casually walked into the kitchen.

As overjoyed as Anna was, she now had to give him the news that a large-scale search party was gathering that very moment to look for him. Jan was not impressed. Feeling foolish but relieved, Anna hastily rushed next door to Bill and Noreen's place to cancel the search. Jan reprimanded her that she should never have doubted his ability as a bushman and that he always knew where he was. However, on that occasion, he penetrated the dense forest much further than expected. With light fast fading, he preferred to camp amongst the trees rather than fight his way out with lawyer vines constantly gripping and scratching him. He had climbed one of the trees and told Anna he could see the lights of nearby farmhouses below, so he knew exactly where he was; he was not lost!

Quite early in the New Year, the family received a visit from a stranger. Jan had been recommended to him by Ned Cobb from the Daintree. Jan was between work at the time, and all his equipment was sitting idle at Julatten. He had been bothering Anna with notions of migrating to New Guinea or Rhodesia which did not please her.

Rob Whelan introduced himself as a grazier from Laura Station and offered Jan contract work to supply timber for cattle yards, sheds, and fences. Jan with his ample machinery was more than adequately prepared for such a task, so it was easy for him to accept the offer. But, before Jan could speak up, Anna was quick off the mark, and much relieved with the offer of work, she immediately recommended her husband wholeheartedly to Rob. Rob fondly remembered this introduction many years later and laughed, "How could I refuse to employ this man after such a glowing endorsement from his wife?"

This chance encounter would begin an enduring friendship that would last for the remainder of their lives.

Helena had just started school and, living only a short distance away, shared the walk with the other schoolchildren. However, shortly afterward, Helena developed a mysterious illness that was problematic to diagnose. After lapsing into numerous sudden fevers, she was eventually admitted to Mossman Hospital and transferred onto the Cairns Base Hospital to the Children's Infectious Ward. It was her first experience with aboriginal children, and as a shy country child, she found solace amongst them as the white kids were often spiteful.

Luckily, Jean Ingles, daughter of Walter Ingles, a long-time resident of Julatten whom Anna and Jan had been acquainted with, was now living in Cairns and regularly visited Helena in the hospital. Jean kept Helena in stock with sweets, which she readily shared with her new aboriginal friends. Eventually, Helena was diagnosed with probable QFever and made a full recovery.

Finally, the wet season receded and Jan packed his truck with all his machinery and headed for Laura with only his dog Kiki for company. Anna was relieved that Rob Whelan's offer had come at that precise moment when their inopportune lives had been in limbo. Anna was happy to remain in Julatten, settling herself and the children into some orderly domestic routine while Jan organized a place for them to live on Laura Station.

Adele Koll, Anna's landlady and immediate neighbour, was an elderly Estonian woman who was generous, kind-hearted, and always meant well with her advice. Adele keenly observed what was going on in Anna's back yard especially with the children but more so young Johnny who was prone to mischief. Anna found her interference intolerable at times and vowed many times that if Jan did not buy the house from her, they would all have to move.

In 1927 Adele had migrated to Australia from Palamuse in Estonia with her husband, Osvald Koll and son Endel. They eventually bought and settled on a farm at Tamaree, a short distance from Gympie, until her husband passed away in early 1930.

After their Tamaree property was devastated by fire, they moved north to the Atherton Tablelands, where Adele and her son Endel lived for some time.

During the outbreak of WWII, Endel joined the army, and Adele worked various jobs, mainly as a cook. She was also a hairdresser-beautician in her spare time, but after the war, she continued working predominantly as a cook at various Main Road's camps. She eventually drifted toward Tobacco work around Mareeba and Dimbulah until she and her son finally settled in the Julatten district.

Mrs. Koll's companion, Paddy Groves, was of part-Aboriginal descent. He was some years younger and a jolly and affable fellow. Paddy, being of mixed race, was born to Rosie, an aboriginal woman at what was in his youth known as Weatherboards. The Groves family of Scottish descent then owned the property, and Rosie was employed in the capacity of domestic duties. In those days, it was customary for many children born to Indigenous families on cattle properties to take on the name of the owners. Paddy always claimed that his father was of German heritage. Weatherboards was only a short distance from Mt. Molloy, and at one time, it was a Cobb and Co. staging stopover to replenish the coach with fresh horses on route over the Old Bump Road down to Port Douglas. Today this property is known as Wetherby Station, and at the time when Anna and Jan arrived to Julatten, it was owned by Maurice and Elizabeth de Tournouer.

Paddy had two older brothers; Archie, who barely out of his teens, died tragically in a logging accident, while Shelley worked as a labourer and lived transiently at the Mossman Mill barracks. He later moved and settled alone in a shack along Euluma Creek-Black Mountain Road until he passed away in 1962.

During WWII, Paddy joined the 17BN Volunteer Defence Corps and, during this time, helped to man the Radar Station on the eastern ridge of Black Mountain. Paddy frequently visited Anna's place as he enjoyed the children's company. A keen fisherman, he often took the children fishing and introduced them to some of his little-known about fishing haunts. His visits were for no other reason than to plan their next fishing expedition or chat with Anna's children about what kids generally love to chat about. Mrs. Koll began to sense an adversary in Anna. Anna was horrified when she learned Mrs. Koll had reported to Jan that he should watch his wife carefully as she had her eyes set on her Paddy. Angered by these unfounded allegations, Anna did not receive much sympathy from her husband, who only laughed and suggested that she sort out her romantic entanglements. However, Paddy remained unperturbed by the gossip and oblivious that he was at the centre of a romantic duel and remained a great mate with the children,

Mrs. Koll worked in the tobacco industry, grading and stringing leaf, but mainly in the Mareeba-Dimbulah-Paddy's Green area and occasionally at Mary Farms. When the tobacco season was over, for the remainder of the year, she and Paddy would cultivate a large market garden and sell their vegetables in Mossman or wherever there was a market for their produce.

By then Anna was well acquainted with Addy Jenkins, recently widowed and with children Johnny and Kenny of similar ages to Anna's three. For extra income both she and Addy decided to go tobacco stringing at Mary Farms. While Jan was at Laura, Anna did a season there stringing on various farms belonging to Italian families, De Iacovo, Lombardi, and Sato in the Mary Farms district.

While Helena was at school, Addy and Anna, with their children; Johnny and Kenny, and Anna's two, Johnny and Diana, would spend the day stringing tobacco before returning home later in the afternoon. Anna found this work both educational and of financial benefit. She reasoned that her knowledge would become useful to Jan when later they established their own tobacco farm.

In May of 1960, Anna received a letter from the Minister of Immigration approving for her to be Naturalized. It was an auspicious occasion as, at long last, she would become an Australian Citizen and become eligible to vote. Even though of Czech origin, Jan had become a British Subject. Hence at the time, there was no need for him to become an Australian Citizen, but for Anna, it was an opportunity to be welcomed in from the cold and become one of the same within society. So, on the 11th of May 1960, Anna was naturalized at a ceremony in Mareeba presided over by the then Chairman of Mareeba Shire Council, Cedric Davies.

Photograph 290: Julatten Railway station circa the late 1950s
(Courtesy Adele Koll's photo collection).

Photograph 291: Margaret Lewis' family L-R Christine, Gaye, Michael and Julie. Absent eldest son Rodger.

Photograph 292: Jan and Anna & children Johnny, Helena, and Diana, day of Anna's naturalization in Mareeba 1960.

CHAPTER 27

Laura Station: 1960-1961

At the end of the May school holiday, Jan took Anna and their two younger children to live at Laura Station, where Jan established his work and living quarters. They arranged to maintain the Julatten house and left it fully furnished for whenever they returned. Helena was placed to board with the Knight family to continue her schooling while the rest of the family prepared to leave for Laura. They moved with only bare domestic basics but shifted all their chickens with them. Jan had already sourced fold-up wire beds with horse-hair mattresses and made provisions for some rudimentary furniture to fit out their new camp. Loaded with fresh supplies and household essentials, they set out for the Cape in their red International truck.

The trip to Laura Station became Anna's introduction to bush camping, an experience just short of disaster. It was the tail end of the wet season, so flooded road crossings were still problematic. On their first night after numerous holdups, it was late when they finally pulled up by the side of the road and set up camp on Spring Creek. Preparing dinner for her tired and disgruntled family, Anna made a broth with some chicken meat and placed the pot wedged in between some rocks to simmer over a fire. One of the stones split apart and capsized the pot, spilling out the contents. Only chicken pieces were spared and retrieved, barely satisfying the hungry family. Anna was almost in tears and at the end of her tether. It had been a long and frustrating day, set back by flash flooding from an unexpected late rain event. By the time they arrived at their destination in Laura, Anna was desperate for a bath to rid herself of all the embedded dust and mud.

Late in the evening when they passed through Laura Homestead, Rob and Margaret Whelan met them, and Anna later complained to her husband that Margaret did not even offer them a cup of tea. Jan ignored the complaint, as he knew too well and appreciated that folk in the bush did not hold up people when hurrying to reach home.

That night the only place to bathe was in the close-by water hole, so Anna and Jan braved the water in the dark and had their wash. The following morning when Margaret Whelan arrived at their camp bearing fresh meat, Anna was embarrassed for pre-judging her so unfairly and was at a loss how to thank her for such generosity. Margaret was horrified to learn from Anna that on the previous night, she and Jan had actually swum in the waterhole.

"You know this place has crocodiles, and a huge one lives in that waterhole where you swam last night. Don't ever do that again!" She sternly warned Anna.

Jan had constructed a medium-sized two-roomed timber shack with timbered floors. The shack was divided by a wall, the kitchen with its wood stove and pantry shelves on one side, and across at the other end an area for the kerosene fridge and family kitchen table. The sleeping quarters were through the kitchen door into the back half of the shack. This room was again divided into two sections by a stockpile of wooden boxes used to store clothes and surplus supplies. Jan and Anna's bed space was on one side, and the other half accommodated the children. One large window with a wooden shutter opened the sleeping quarters to the outside. This allowed airflow to circulate from the front kitchen door and window through to the rear bedrooms. However, one major downfall with timbered dwellings in these parts was that most softwood buildings were prone to wood borers; small beetles that dwelled in the wood and burrowed through the timber; if left untreated or unmanaged, buildings would soon hollow out and collapse. Anna had her line of defence. Each morning the children would be given a screwdriver to prod the vermin in their holes, killing them. Anna also encouraged her army of lizards and geckos to help with these menacing beetles. This, however, introduced another dilemma, as Diana would catch reptiles and bring them in for Anna. One day she brought in a snake wrapped around her wrist, as she held tightly onto the hapless reptile's head and presented it to Anna as a lizard!

The hut stood a short distance from Jan's timber mill and some distance from the nearest water hole, probably with good reason so that the children would not wander off for a swim where saltwater crocodiles were known to frequent.

With so many kangaroos about, Anna wanted to make Kangaroo Tail Stew and, for some time, pestered her husband to shoot a kangaroo for her. He did so dutifully, even if reluctantly. It would be the first and only time he would do such a thing, as for one; they did not enjoy the taste of the stew, and secondly, as retribution, Anna was left to raise a hairless Joey. He would become known as Laurie and thrived with her love and attention. Later as he grew, he would leave the safety of his pillowcase hanging by the door and join the family for breakfast. His fetish was milky tea which he lapped from a tin can placed on the floor by the kitchen table. After any misdemeanour for which Diana was found culpable, she would sit on the floor in a corner and sulk, sucking her two middle fingers and covering them with the corner of her shirt. Laurie would follow and sit next to her, sucking one of his feet! Ultimately, Anna had to make green cloth booties for the Joey; otherwise, he would have sucked his feet raw.

On one of Margaret Whelan's visits during cattle mustering to deliver tucker to the stockman's camp, she took along Sylvia, a young Aboriginal girl from their station, and Diana. It would be Diana's first encounter with native children of her own age. Anna recalled afterward when Margaret told her the story; how for a short while, the two shy little girls eyed one another off in the back seat of the car until, after obvious curiosity, Diana made the first move and leaned toward Sylvia, gently touching her, and innocently enquiring, "Didn't you have a bath this morning?"

Sylvia nodded shyly, and replied "Yes!"

The logic of skin colour at a young age for many European children, like Diana, who had their first encounter with aboriginals in the bush, was simple; if you did not appear white; it must be that you are covered in dirt like her brother Johnny often was, and in need of a bath.

Rob Whelan laughed about a similar incident that occurred at the time when he once teased Johnny, who was covered in dirt and sawdust, and told him he wasn't Johnny Kanak but a black boy.

Young Johnny was indignant and burst forth, "No! I am Johnny Kanak!"

The children only received pocket money whenever they went into Laura township. Johnny, by now, was preoccupied building billy-carts from offcuts of timber and nails he managed to scrounge from his father. He was also working out how batteries operated so he could have working lights on his mobile contraptions. When they arrived in the Laura town, Johnny immediately bought a packet of nails and then eagerly joined the circle of eager young aboriginal children surrounding Diana as she shared her lollies amongst them all. Diana being so fair-haired, was nicked-named Snowy as she stood out in her crowd of friends. Long after all the lollies were gone, Johnny still had his bag of nails.

The arrangement with Helena's schooling plans worked well until Charlie and Vera Knight sold their shop and moved from Julatten. To complete her first year at Bushy Creek State School, Helena stayed with Marion and Robbie Jenkins for a few weeks. Their two oldest children, Marion and Billy, had already left home, and at the time, they only had Bobby and Lesley with them. This all went well for the final weeks of the year, and before the holidays started, Jan and Anna returned to Julatten to collect Helena.

The wet season had set in early by December of that year, so it was imperative to collect Helena and hastily return with fresh supplies so Christmas could be spent on Laura Station. The truck was the only way to travel during the wet season. Although slow, it was sturdy and reliable, and while Anna and Jan sat in the front discussing future prospects, the children slept under cover in the back.

The unsealed road from Mt. Molloy through to Mt. Carbine, and over the Desailly and Byerstown Ranges and onto Laura, took a slightly different course in those days. It was merely a rocky and gravel track fording a series of creeks, gullies, and rivers where flood water would quickly rise after rainfall and block traffic for hours, if not days. Speer Creek and the series of Kelly St. George and Reedy St. George crossings were notorious for hold-ups. The roads were unpredictably slippery and boggy during these times, so it was often a slow and arduous trip.

If, during the wet season, the upper reach of the Laura River stream at the base of the Byerstown Range was already in full flow but still not necessarily blocking the road, then it was reasonable to assume that further downstream, the Laura River would be in flood. Numerous smaller water courses feeding into this system, namely Ruth's Creek, Red Bank Creek, Quartz Creek, and Hell's Gate Creek, would also be rising. With its low wooden bridge over the first approach of the Laura River, Carroll's Crossing, it was still occasionally passable, if lucky. However, further on, road access near the confluence of Kennedy Creek and the Laura River would certainly be flooded and, in most cases, impassable. At this confluence of the Laura River, the deluge of rising water would flood the river bed and spread rapidly creating a backlog completely inundating the low wooden girded bridge under metres of swirling current.

Overland trips into Laura town remained quite problematic during the wet season as the Laura River to the south would block vehicles, and likewise, the northern Laura crossing just outside of Laura town. Both crossings had to be negotiated in order Jan reach their Laura camp.

During the many trips culminating in a great deal of night travel, Jan rarely drove his truck with headlights on. He had remarkable night vision and enjoyed the ambiance of the twilight as his eyesight adjusted to approaching darkness. Under a full moon, it was even better, as there was more than sufficient light to guide him. Traffic was sparse, and the road familiar after so many slow and regular trips.

On one of these trips near the Byerstown Range, while the children slept in the back tucked in amongst boxes beneath a tarpaulin, Anna experienced an eerie feeling of being followed and whispered to Jan that a light had been following them for some time. It seemed to come no closer nor drift further away but only followed at a constant distance. Jan refused to be drawn into any fear speculation and remarked that it was only a light, perhaps from a bright star. Unconvinced and needing to be distracted, Anna prayed it would simply vanish and leave her alone, so she began to sing. The longer the glowing bright ball continued to follow them, the louder she sang. Although Anna had a good singing voice, no doubt by now, her husband would have wished he had a convincing explanation to silence her.

Anna later learned about the Min-Min light phenomenon, an inexplicable ball of light that manifests in certain outback areas of Australia and can never be reached or touched but always maintains a uniform distance. Anna believed she saw one of the same on that night along the Byerstown Range.

During summer, before the onset of the monsoonal season, temperatures around their Laura camp would become almost insufferable and stiflingly hot and humid; and night insects would flourish in abundance around any sort of light. Jan had a generator attached to the front of his tractor, and while the tractor engine ran, it generated power for lights which came by way of an extension lead. At the time, their refrigerator was kerosene, not electric, but the downside of generated power was not only the noise, but the hordes of unusual insects that these bright lights always attracted. If any free-standing kerosene lamps were lit for only short durations and placed over a pan of water, these dimmer lights were a more effective way of minimizing insects crawling all over you as most drowned in the water. However, lights or no lights, insect invasions were unavoidable as windows were unscreened and had to remain open to allow the breeze in to cool the hut.

During such times, to achieve a more comfortable sleep, it was preferable to be outside rather than toss and turn in bed inside the hut warding off sticky and smelly bugs that crawled over everyone in their bedding. Watching fireflies flittering above in the dark rafters might have been soothing for the children but during these weather conditions, it was regular practice to move all the beds outside at night and hang mosquito nets from nearby saplings and trees. Ultimately, the family grew accustomed to cattle wandering about and grazing beside them during these restless nights under the stars.

During the early 1960s, crocodile shooting around Lakefield and Laura was very much the 'big hunters' recreational game, and very little control was exercised over numbers shot. Although hunters were cautioned to skin and salt the hides rather than leave them to rot and contaminate water holes, many amateurs lacked the knowledge how to properly preserve these hides for sale. For a while, Jan employed two young Romanian chaps who were passing through on an Australian adventure.

Roman and Andre were keen to shoot a crocodile, but their inexperience in skinning and preserving the beast's skin resulted in ruination.

Ron Pocock, the local Laura policeman, had a great passion for crocodile shooting. Ron was a keen shot, and although Jan himself was handy with a gun and well acquainted with Ron, Jan left crocodile hunting well alone.

As mentioned in Bryan Peach's book 'Crocodile Men' published in 2000 [1], Anna related in the book her story when she and Jan lived on Laura Station. They had been camped at a waterhole by Rocky Creek, further up on the Kennedy and she observed a crocodile near where they bathed and wash their clothes. Diana and Johnny were with them while Helena remained at school in Julatten. In the end, Ron Pocock took care of the beast and, with Jan's tractor, hauled his monstrous trophy out of the river.

As dangerous as the saltwater crocodiles were, they feared man and his gun during these times, and while their numbers had dwindled drastically, these reptiles often would rather hide than confront their foe. It did not mean it was safe to swim amongst them. Quite on the contrary, as they still had to eat, but they were more shy and only prone to taking habitual visitors at waterholes such as cattle and kangaroo and human beings if they persistently visited the same spot in their habitat. Although Crocodiles are at the top of the food chain, in those days whenever fishing for barramundi, they rarely attempted to steal the fish from the anglers.

Luckily, Jan and Anna lived some distance from any large waterhole, but it was never far enough where children were concerned, as they would often wander off with their dog Kiki while Jan and Anna were busy milling timber.

One day the children returned home anxious and stressed, piggybacking Diana with her leg in a tourniquet. They reported to their father that she had been bitten in the water by a snake or crocodile, which they had not seen. Although impressed with their first aid attempt, Jan's praise soon turned into a good scolding after learning they had been paddling in the crocodile-infested waterhole. Jan and Anna were horrified. Snake or crocodile bite; this soon became secondary as the children were reprimanded and warned about the dangers and the stupidity of swimming with crocodiles. In that particular waterhole at the time, a large salty was known to inhabit the place and had been observed numerous times by passing stockmen droving cattle.

While Anna lived in Laura, there were many more alarming instances to contend with but there were equally as many enjoyable moments to distract her from the mundane chores of baking, caring for the children, and helping Jan with milling timber.

One particular family pleasure was barramundi fishing. While Jan worked, Margaret Whelan, with her children, often collected Anna and her three and went on a day's fishing trip to the Normanby River. Here, in season, the big fish would bite at certain times of the day, and everyone would have the exhilaration of trying to land one of these highly prized fish. In the end, Anna's kerosene refrigerator would be so full of barramundi, with little room for anything else. In time, her family would start complaining about constantly eating fish.

After the wet season, when the Laura River finally receded into a small sandy watercourse, Margaret would take Anna and the children on picnics behind Laura Station homestead. Here, all the children would play and swim in the safety of these clear and sandy shallows while this much-diminished river flow would now trickle its way in narrow streamlets through the vast sandy bed. Still one of the native women would remain on watch just in case of unexpected menace.

On another occasion, Rob and Margaret's daughter Lydia, together with Helena, and Johnny were mounted on saddled ponies and joined the tail end of a muster as cattle were being herded into the homestead yards. This was Lydia's time to shine as she led and instructed the other two on what to do. Anna enjoyed watching her children grow and play in the bush until she invariably had to referee skirmishes that would break out amongst them.

Generally, the children played alone but close enough to be within Anna's sight while they created their fantasy world, made mudpies sprinkled with different coloured sawdust, and played out make-believe games that often included, Kiki and Laurie.

Living so far from amenities and the luxury of freshly baked bread, Anna learned to bake her own, although many of her first attempts were deemed unsuccessful. But as always, with perseverance, she soon mastered the art and became well-versed in yeast baking. Her bread became as acclaimed as her plum jam buns and apricot dumplings. During these baking sessions, Anna would invariably reward the children, each with a baked doll made of platted bun dough and decorated with raisins. 'Panenka' was the female doll for the girls, and 'Panák' was the male version for Johnny.

In late January of 1961, the countryside was once again amid monsoonal rain when Helena was about to resume her second year at school. At the time, there was no school at Laura, and Anna could not teach her by correspondence as her English was not to an acceptable standard. So, once again, their daughter was placed with a local family in Julatten. As always it was a race against inclement weather forecasts to get her back to school on time.

Flooded creeks and rivers between Laura and Julatten always created obstacles for vehicles along the road. While crossing Red Bank Creek some distance south of Laura, Jan almost stalled his truck midstream in the deeper than expected red swirling current. Some watercourses had low-level bridges, some had culverts, but most were rocky or sandy creek bed crossings. During monsoonal downpours, it was always imperative to be familiar with water levels and have an abundance of patience while sitting-out delays until swollen streams receded.

During that year, Helena boarded with Bunny and Cairen Sides. Cairen was of European descent, while her husband Bunny, himself a WWII veteran like Jan, was the son of Jack Sides, a WWI Gallipoli return soldier. Jack and his wife, Florence were both school teachers who once taught at Euluma Creek, but now retired and living close by on the family farm at Julatten.

Bunny and Cairen were acquaintances from when Anna and Jan first started farming at Euluma Creek. Many years later Cairen would jovially remind Anna, how on one occasion, Jan visited their farm and on raising his hat in greeting, astonished everyone with a head full of tiny bows plated into his hair. Never to be too embarrassed for long, Jan apologized for his unusual hairstyle, explaining his daughter had been practicing her hairstyling skills while he dozed. Unfortunately, he had forgotten about his hair do when donning his hat, but luckily only the Sides' witnessed his coiffure and not everyone else in town! During this time, Bunny and Cairen only had their son Peter, who was a year or so younger than Helena. The two children got on well, but according to Cairen, Helena always kept Peter in his place.

Each night before bedtime, Cairen taught them both to pray in German. For whatever reason, Helena informed Peter she had relatives in New Zealand, so at prayer time, Peter insisted on praying for them as well; "Lieber Gott schau mein Familie, und Freunde im New Zealand!" Dear God, look after my family and friends in New Zealand!

At one stage Bunny Sides worked for Jan in Laura for a short time. He, like Les Webb, had his experience with wild bores and once found his sleeping quarters invaded by wild pigs. Bunny quickly evacuated his lodgings during the night, and in the morning, Jan found him perched high on the timber stack. But unlike Les, Bunny remained working for a bit longer.

Having deposited their daughter in the care of the Sides family, Jan and Anna and the two younger children returned back to Laura. The usual hold-ups along the Desaily Range kept them waylaid, but flooding became more problematic after Red Bank Creek. Jan hoped the southern bridge approach to Laura at the confluence of Laura River and Kennedy Creek would still be open to traffic. They were desperate to reach their Laura camp by evening and in the pouring rain Jan took his chances with the bridge crossing and proceeded slowly forward. The water was already running over the bridge and swirling around the edges as debris rushed by with the rapidly rising water. He soon realized the water was becoming too high to cross when the truck suddenly stalled midway, with rising water flow beginning to heave against the heavy and sturdy vehicle. Anna prayed for help; otherwise, there would have been very little chance of saving the truck with its load and, more importantly, themselves and the children. Like a God-sent saviour, an apparition appeared and approached them through the rain. Anna could not believe that her prayer had been answered so quickly and just in time! A road worker who had just returned on foot from Laura town with his camp supplies had caught sight of the distraught family in their partially submerged truck. Fortunately, his grader was nearby, so he towed the stricken family's vehicle over the flooded bridge to safety.

In April of 1961, Diana became ill while at Laura Station and had to be medevacked to Cairns with Bush Pilots. While she screamed, not wanting to be taken on board, Johnny screamed, wanting to get on the plane. Ultimately, Johnny had to settle for an apple from the Pilot, Bill Forwell. Because of unforeseen emergency evacuations by aerial ambulance, everyone living in the Cape at the time contributed to its fund, and Diana's emergency retrieval cost in the vicinity of £28.

Even though he had only flown briefly in Australia, Bill Forwell was a competent Ex. RAF pilot who became well known and respected throughout the Cape and would remain flying until July 1967.

When Diana was ready for discharge from the hospital, it was early May, so Jan drove to Cairns to collect her and arranged to collect additional supplies from Burns Philip Merchants. On his way, he collected Helena from Sides' place, and together they travelled onto Cairns. Jan later told Anna how sad and lonely and lost their little Diana appeared as she stood in the hospital ward in oversized hospital pyjamas. And how her little sad face lit up when she saw him beckoning her to the door where he and Helena waited to collect her.

The trip back to Laura was memorable for only one reason, they came across an unusual road kill by the roadside. It happened near Butchers Hill Station, along the Laura Road, which today traverses the property's grazing land that is now a part of the agricultural community of Lakeland Downs. Jan was intrigued by the carcass and believed it to be an animal similar to the Tasmanian Tiger[2], as none had been recorded on the mainland, it puzzled him how it got there as he had not seen anything like it before. It had a relatively small head with a strong jawline, a thick tapered tail with heavy hind legs, and partially circumferential stripes around the lower torso. It would always remain a family enigma.

On arrival at their Laura camp, Johnny ran to greet his father. He had far more pressing news to share with his dad rather than greeting his sisters; and showed Jan a fistful of spent cartridges. He explained to his father how his mother had wasted all these bullets trying to shoot a crocodile in a tree and missed each time. For Anna, it was embarrassing enough having missed so many shots after firing at a snake swallowing a frog; but then to have it repeated that she thought it was a crocodile up there, as she must have originally told her son, was even more humiliating.

Jan shared with his wife that he felt sorry for Helena being placed so far from the family and decided she had suffered enough and should be located elsewhere closer to them to do her schooling. So, after the May holiday, when her school term was about to resume, it was decided to look for an alternate solution. Jan had recently built some sheds and yards on King's Plain Station for the owners, the Christenson family. Fred told Jan that their son Spencer boarded in Cooktown to attend school. Jim and Betty Waters owned and ran Hill Crest Guest House at the base of Grassy Hill. They also took in paid school borders from outlying stations and were most willing to accommodate Helena for £81.5.9 until the end of the year. At the beginning of each of these last two school terms in 1961, Jan, Anna, and the children drove into Cooktown, and placed Helena with the Waters family. After a brief top up with supplies and any available spare part machinery items, they all returned to Laura.

The road between Laura and Cooktown was rough, dusty, and slow going, so it was always a long and tiring trip there and back in the one day. However, it was much closer and more convenient than travelling back and forth from Julatten each time.

On one of their return trips from Cooktown after having delivered Helena to Hill Crest, their Zephyr broke down, breaking an axel near Trevethen Creek. Jan hitched back into Cooktown some 10 miles away to try and obtain a replacement part, but failing to do so, he could only order one to be shipped to him. He hitched back to the car with some provisions and once again set out, leaving Anna and the two children with the car while he hitched toward Laura some 100 miles further on to retrieve his truck and recover his family and the broken-down car. Anna and the children remained overnight by the roadside. She made a makeshift camp and surrounded herself with large sticks and rocks should someone came along and threatened them. While her two children slept in the car, Anna settled outside and kept guard. It was a long night without incident, as road traffic was sparse in those days. Only the lowing of noisy cattle in the distance disturbed the peace.

By morning a huge mob of cattle moved past them, herded by stockmen on horses, but no one even barely noticed the family shrouded in a cloud of thick dust as they huddled in the car and watched the noisy stock pass by.

During the day, while Anna waited for Jan, her two children played close by the road until a car pulled up, sending the children scuttling for cover in the bush. An older lady exited the car, approached Anna, and asked if she was OK. The woman introduced herself as Mrs. Doreen Wallace and said she was concerned when she saw two children playing by the roadside. After introducing herself, Anna spoke about her predicament but reassured Mrs. Wallace that her husband should be along soon.

Anna later learned that Doreen Wallace and her husband Charlie owned Butcher's Hill, the large cattle property at the road junction of the Cooktown and Laura turnoff, which Anna and Jan often passed on their numerous trips between Julatten and Laura. This casual off-the-road introduction was seemingly how many people met on the Cape. It would remain a family connection that would carry on long after the Wallaces sold Butchers Hill and themselves moved into the Julatten district. They would eventually buy a property along Hunters Creek that Archie and Grace Betchel once owned and establish their cattle stud of 'Cambrae' and jointly with Bill Edmonds also set up the Droughtmaster cattle stud of 'Wallace Vale'.

By late afternoon Jan returned in his truck, collected his family and loaded the car. While the children sat in the front with him, Anna chose to sit inside the car loaded on the back of the truck as they trundled down the dusty and bumpy road.

Once in Laura town, one of the locals from George Watkins' Pub teasingly yelled at Anna, "I wouldn't sit up there for all the rice in China!"

At the time and for some time afterward, Anna wondered what all the rice in China had to do with her sitting in the car. Such a turn of phrase had not been in her vocabulary before!

At the end of each school term, Betty Waters would send Helena home on the Cooktown-Laura Rail Motor[3] and place her in the care of the conductor with explicit instructions to deliver the child to her waiting parents in Laura. It was a slow trip over 67 miles of hilly, mostly savannah countryside. The journey took some hours as the rail motor invariably pulled into numerous rail sidings on its journey to Laura. Outside of Cooktown it first stopped near the race course and airdrome and further afield Marton, Jansen, Flaggy, and Wilton, dropping off random passengers and goods until it approached the sidings of Alderbury, Normanby, Welcome, and Deighton where mail and goods were dropped off for these isolated cattle stations. The rail motor would finally reach Laura by about mid-day before returning to Cooktown. Although this rail road was originally destined for Maytown in the Palmer Gold Fields, its construction never got past the Laura-Maytown bridge over the Laura River.

Helena probably would have enjoyed her holiday in Laura were it not for the compulsory hour of spelling lessons that Anna insisted on to improve her daughter's vocabulary. Before being allowed to listen to The Children's Half Hour on Radio ABC, Helena would endure a spelling lesson every afternoon as Anna lined up tins and packets of Spaghetti, Sugar, Tea, Marmalade, Flour, Milk, Coffee, Plum Jam, and anything else in the larder that she deemed her daughter needed to know how to spell. What the child lacked in comprehensive basic spelling for her class age, she far exceeded and made up in words beyond class expectation, except she was never tested on these.

Situated next to their Laura shack, Jan built the children a timber play house, and inside, it was fitted with a wooden table with attached seating. It was roomy enough for the three of them to play inside, but like with all timber structures, it too was subject to wood borers. The task was set for the children; to look out for these critters and bring the pests to their demise. Their little play house later accompanied them onto Kennedy Camp, but luckily the table with its seating was left behind at their main hut.

Upon returning from Kennedy, Jan tried to retrieve the children's playhouse with his tractor, but the wet season had already set in, and the black soiled flats dotted with water-logged ant beds already warned that this swampy land was too boggy and impassable.

Unfortunately, Kennedy Camp had become isolated for the duration of the wet season, and sadly, their playhouse would never be seen again. Only the table and seating would remain as a reminder of their little cubby house.

In early November of 1961, Jan made two purchases. One was the acquisition of the Julatten house at Anna's insistence, which, up till then, they had been renting. The other was a block of land on the McIvor River north of Cooktown. Jan had won the McIvor block by ballot, costing him the princely sum of £425. He had also wanted to secure the block next to it, but Bill Hood beat him to it. Now that he had land, Jan could begin to plan what to do with it.

The McIvor property was on fertile river flats, next to neighbours Bill and Sylvia Hood. The Hoods had already experimented with growing tobacco, peanuts, and beetroot crops, and everything seemed to thrive in this fertile and well-watered soil. However, the most significant hindrances were poor roads and distance from any supporting market and industry infrastructure. The expense of cartage was a further consideration as it far outweighed any profitability.

On purchasing the land, Jan visited the district and accepted an invitation from Bill Hood to go fishing and crabbing on the Morgan River. Most of the region was impassable with vehicles, so quite some distance was done on foot. When the foot-weary expedition returned with little to show for their fishing, while bathing Jan fell into a deep sleep in the bathtub. Sylvia Hood later recalled, telling Anna that at first, she and Bill feared he had died in the tub.

Jan wanted to grow tobacco but soon realized it would become problematic transporting tobacco leaf for sale in Mareeba. His McIvor property was isolated and quite some distance north of Cooktown. The soil might have been rich, but the two roads servicing the McIvor district were the Upper Road and the Lower Road, both rough and generally impassable during the wet. Both roads terminated at McIvor River and crossed the river a short distance apart before branching off to service several landholders on the northern side of the river.

The Upper Road, the wet weather road, crossed the higher and hillier countryside to the west and forded the McIvor River over a concrete causeway that would still be rendered impassable during the wet.

The Lower Road, the dry weather road further east, crossed over low-lying sandy country. Although a wooden bridge over the McIvor

River was at the end of this road, it was further downstream from the causeway and this road was always impassable during the wet season. Another major obstacle was the need for a school. Although Bill and Sylvia had children and had lobbied for a school, it failed to eventuate. A school of short duration later ended up on the Starkey River further north, but it, too, eventually folded.

Jan made numerous trips between Laura and Julatten, mostly without breakdowns or mishaps. On one occasion however, nearing the Palmer River crossing, on his way to Laura, his truck capsized near the appropriately-named Capsize Creek. Jan realized he had very little leeway from an approaching truck as it hurtled toward him down the gravel slope. Charlie Barrett from Mareeba was behind the wheel and headed toward Jan in a dust cloud. To avoid a head-on collision, Jan swerved off the road toward the edge and capsized his loaded truck into the water table. Anna did not get to hear about this incident for some time after as otherwise, no doubt, Charlie Barrett would have received a visit from her!

Capsize Creek achieved its notorious name a decade before when an incident occurred involving main road engineer Rollo Gallop [4]. Travelling uphill, his vehicle failed to negotiate the steep slope and stalled, running backward. His brakes failed, and he ended capsized in the gully.

Jan had recently applied for and bought an agricultural leasehold block on the Laura River, a short distance from Laura town and opposite Olive Vale Station. He bought Lot 112 as it was one of the larger blocks suitably sized for agricultural purposes. It was on the banks of the Laura River and had riparian water rights. The land was about one or two miles out of town, with road access along the old railway line, before turning off onto a side track toward his property.

In December of 1961, shortly after Helena's final trip home on the train from school in Cooktown, the Cooktown to Laura railway closed, with all rail lines pulled up. The portion of the track near Jan's block formed a readymade road for the landholders within the vicinity. Jan's block and a few other neighbouring parcels of land were once a part of reserved land for soldier's settlement that failed to fulfil its purpose.

Lot 112 had previously been a tobacco farm owned by Hugh Cowper, who virtually walked off it due to hardship. Some remnants of tumble-down infrastructure remained, most of which had been burnt during the intervening years, but it still had a habitable shack. Next door was Jack Howell's property, and it too once had been a tobacco farm, now sitting idle with crumbled remnants of old curing barns.

At the time, Jan also applied for Fairview, a small block north of Laura on the old overland telegraph track (OTT). It was initially an integral part of the overland telegraph line through to the Cape, and Fairview housed a section of the communication exchange system that was still operational.

After Jan and his family bid goodbye to their hut on Laura Station, he moved his machinery and timber milling operation onto the newly acquired block in Laura. With the remaining house contents, he made the shack habitable for when next Anna and the children arrived.

Although the shack needed attention, notably the leaking roof, its internal walls were plastered with old newspapers to keep out the chill in winter. Numerous buckets were placed strategically on the floor during the wet to catch the falling drips. It was very primitive but initially sufficed Jan as his base camp.

The family would eventually spend Christmas together in this new abode. Even though it was only the beginning of the Monsoonal season, their make-shift home was well above the high-water mark.

The wet season in the Cape has a special feel, culminating in the highly anticipated event which would break the otherwise dry and unbearable heat of the parched countryside. As monsoonal clouds gathered, the humidity increased, making days hot and sticky with muggy nights and little or no breeze to offer relief. Clothes would stick to sweaty bodies, and during the evenings, the mosquitos would swarm and descend along with a multitude of other insects. The monotony of cicadas buzzing incessantly and the arrival of harmless millipedes covering the ground in thousands; was a sure sign that rain was eminent. The first cloud burst offered immediate relief to the stifling heat, but it was only a brief reprieve until the rains really settled in.

During the day, the children would run about scantily dressed in shorts and play in newly formed puddles, returning home covered in mud. Beyond the hut, along a track down to the river flats and onto the river, Jan would take the children to swim in the sandy shallows while the river still barely flowed. For most, The Laura River was a dry sandy river bed interspersed with permanent water holes often flush with barramundi and occupied by saltwater crocodiles. Only when rain fell over the river's headwaters would it come to life, creating small waterways through its dry sandy bed until the stream grew in volume and flowed eastward toward the Normanby River and its tributaries and into Princess Charlotte Bay.

A short distance from Jan's hut, the water course passed over a slate bar where small rapids would form whenever the river flowed. Anna would hear the water burbling over these rapids from their hut whenever the river rose to sufficient heights. But when the 'big wet' finally arrived, a peaceful, albeit eerie silence would permeate and mask the river's presence during the night, and Anna always knew what to expect the following morning. Looking out through the window at dawn, Anna would be met with a vast spread of swirling and murky water below when overnight the Laura River, having broken its banks and flooded the lower flats, was now lapping up against the track coming down from the nearby steep embarkment upon which their shack stood. It was an amazing sight, but the flooded river rarely encroached further. It would only be during one of those exceptional weather events, one in fifty or one-hundred-year floods, that the river would rise further and pose the threat of unrivalled inundation.

Photograph 293: Anna, Diana, & Johnny on Laura Station 1961.
Photo courtesy Whelan Family collection.

Photograph 294: Some of Cooktown school children 1961.
Photo courtesy Palmer Family collection.

CHAPTER 28

Return to Julatten: 1962

By the beginning of 1962, Anna and Jan's two younger children, Diana and Johnny, were due to start school.

The family's return to Julatten pleased Adele Koll to finally have permanent neighbours. Despite their earlier neighbourly misunderstanding, matters of the heart were now long forgotten, and Adele was looking forward to having someone to chat with across the garden fence.

Their rented house and land purchased from Endel Koll (Adele's son) in November of 1961 was now jointly owned by Jan and Anna. It was intended to be used as a base during their children's education until Jan built a new home on their Laura property. For the time being, it was a place Anna could call her own, but with it still came the annual deluge of flood water from Bushy Creek, which Anna grew to live with over the years.

Although the house was relatively low-lying, flood waters, whenever the creek broke its banks and peaked, never entered inside but only surrounded the dwelling, after which the waters would rapidly recede. This remained the case for several years until an engineer in the public work's department deemed the culvert across the road near the bridge potentially responsible for much of the flooding and so had it removed. As Anna always maintained, this culvert initially served its purpose for a good reason; to free the excess flood water built up in the natural watercourse parallel with the creek. This culvert aided the flow of the water via the small anabranch and headed it back downstream into Bushy Creek just beyond the bridge. Although the gully could be deep and swift-flowing when flooded, it prevented this water from spreading out sideways onto her property and further down the causeway. By removing the culvert and partially filling in the hole beside the roadside, the flood water began to spread more freely across the bridge and down the causeway toward Rocky Creek, creating a backlog of flood water that rose between the two flooded streams and spread back, delaying runoff. Instead of being a rapid flow of water knee-high, the causeway became a body of water, chest high in the middle, which ultimately blocked traffic for hours. Anna had many years of observing this wet season phenomenon, during which time her rationale fell upon deaf ears. Instead, the flood water rose around her house and remained there for lengthier periods. Ultimately, she would have her house raised to avoid water entering.

Once settled in, Anna began planning how best to utilize her land and where to plant her fruit trees and vegetables. The house yard was large, with numerous dilapidated old buildings. Their green Zephyr was now housed beneath one of them, a rather wonky old garage under a large mango tree. Several nearby large mango trees and an old box tree grew creating a retreat for the children, and a challenge to climb, especially for Johnny.

Anna had a well for water only a short distance from the house, which now had a pump, but with a rather small and inadequate tank on an even more inadequate and wonky stand, it still nevertheless gravity-fed water to the house. Many improvements were needed, but Jan had his heart set on Laura rather than becoming too embroiled in Anna's plans.

When school commenced, and Anna settled into her family routine, Jan returned to Laura while the monsoonal season still held off. He was by now working on his block in Laura, so he had plenty of work awaiting him and was always anxious to get back before weather setbacks hindered progress. For him, it was a case of starting from scratch, as curing barns and bulk sheds had to be rebuilt before his first tobacco crop could be planted.

Once the wet season subsided, he would return home at regular intervals to have family time and stock up on provisions for his camp.

Although alone and missing his family, Jan was never lonely in the bush and his biggest plight at his camp were the nocturnal visitations from quolls or then colloquially better known as Spotted Native Cats. These inquisitive creatures would raid his camp at intervals and create havoc in the kitchen larder. Arriving during the night under Kiki's radar, they would run along the open rafters before encamping amongst food stores for a night of frivolity in search of bread and meat or anything edible, even delving into opened canisters containing flour, sugar, coffee or tea. They would create a ruckus as tins, plates and saucepans were toppled, leaving behind an unruly mess with trails of flour or whatever other food stuffs the culprits pilfered, as they escaped the scene.

The children adapted well to school life, made friends, and slowly adjusted to speaking English. It was a one-teacher school, taking grade one students every alternate year, so Johnny and Diana started off in grade one together. Wally Crear, their headmaster, had one problem though, he had to separate the two in class as both would only speak Czech to each other when Johnny needed to explain the lessons to Diana.

Next-door neighbour, Paddy Groves, once more befriended the children, and again weekend fishing expeditions were planned with often excellent results, arriving home with full bags of sleepy cod.

Paddy also had regular work as a labourer, on what is today the Mulligan Highway. He worked with Main Road's gangs, building bridges and doing maintenance work between Mt. Carbine and the Byerstown Range. However, no sooner home, Mrs. Koll would corner Jan and plead him to go to Mossman and find Paddy, who, with his recent pay cheque, would have escaped Mrs. Koll's clutches and headed for Mossman to enjoy some quality time with his kindred folk.

Paddy drove a black Dodge DB. It had a soft top cover covering both the front and its opened rear back wooden platform seating, a vintage vehicle if not an antique by today's standards. Smartly dressed, he would often drive Mrs. Koll to the local shop or where ever else she needed to go. They were an odd couple, if not in total harmony, as Paddy, dressed in his white shirt and Sunday best trousers and wearing a hat, escorted Mrs. Koll, equally smartly dressed, sporting one of her numerous floral hats. She was of petite stature as she sat next to him, and it was often only her hat that was generally visible as they drove down the road.

Once, just prior to school holidays, the Nankervis family left their three newly acquired goats in Anna's care while they continued onto Cairns on business.

George Nankervis was the local mechanic in Laura, so Jan and Anna knew them well. On occasions during the wet season, the two families would travel to Laura in convoy and so make river crossings less hazardous with each looking out for the other.

During this goat-sitting saga, Anna's children were initially delighted, enthusiastically taking the goats on lengthy walks. But it was not long before the novelty wore off. The goats soon became bored after so much attention, and in return were soon chewing on everything left lying about; clothes on the line, blankets, soft toys and books and any surplus food or grain in their wake. As a result, friendships soon became strained, and none too soon for Anna, when finally, the troublesome trio were whisked off by their owners.

For Anna, goats had been very much a part of her childhood but here these animals seemed to have greater freedom to roam and it was not uncommon for the neighbouring farmer's goat to frequent Mrs. Koll's vegetable garden. On one such occasion the poor old lady had not only the goat to contend with, but also his wandering companions. While the goat and duck wreaked havoc with her indoor plants on the front veranda, the partially blind horse stood waiting for them like a sentinel beside the opened door.

The annual Mossman Show was always a family affair, and Jan did his best to be home to enjoy the day out with the children. One of the highlights for the Julatten folk was the wood-chopping event. The Julatten district had its own worthy representatives; Billy McKean, Wally Crear, and Paddy Groves. They were of champion status and, between them, won many titles and trophies.

Anna always had religious woes to sort out in her family. It was not that she enforced her ideas onto her children; it was more that she wanted to keep them within the fold of some faith. In those days, the state schools had weekly visits from clergy of different denominations, and each child attended Christian lessons in their parent's chosen faith.

Anna's children struggled with the rigid routine of Catholicism and were even given homework. One of the lessons was to learn and recite the catechism by heart; failing to do so, they would be punished and warned that "they would be kicked down the stairs!" Well, that was what Anna was told by her three children.

Anna became aware that she was not alone in her concerns, as others had jumped denominations as well, so she wasted no time in addressing the issue with the headmaster and withdrew her children from the catholic fold, and had them transferred to the Anglican padre, Father Ernest Gribble, an elderly gentleman with a missionary background. The children found Father Gribble interesting and entertaining and even looked forward to his scripture lessons, especially those involving pictures and slides from his missionary work in Papua New Guinea. Their eyes had been opened to another world, making them aware that not everyone lived as they did. Anna would often be greeted with fascinating tales of black women breast-feeding piglets (highly prized in New Guinea society then) and stories of how wigs of hair could walk! She eventually realized it was a metaphor; as head lice were so prevalent and endemic in those communities, the thought of so many nits would make your hair crawl!

For the children, the fascinating feature of living by Bushy Creek was not only the creek but that they were close to the rail tracks along which a train arrived twice weekly at nearby Julatten rail siding. The steam engine on Wednesdays would deliver goods and mail, and the rail motor on Fridays would transport passengers onto Mareeba and return back on the same day passing through Mount Molloy, Julatten, and Rumula. During holidays or late Friday afternoons after school, the children would stand by the roadside, and the rail motor would stop and collect them for a round trip onto Rumula and back. It was only a few miles down the track but it was the highlight of their week.

Mount Kooyong Chalet, once owned and operated by Miss Keitha Salisbury and Miss Barbara Parkman, was situated upstream on Bushy Creek in the Rumula-Julatten district. It had been constructed before the war by local Estonian immigrant and builder, Peter Pink. It was an impressive building for its time, erected from locally logged timber. The residence comprised of numerous guest rooms, a large stone fireplace within the entertaining area, and surrounded by verandas. By all accounts, it had been a swanky place in the heydays before the war, with guests well provided for with plenty of music, dancing, and clinking of champagne glasses.

With the onset of WWII, Mt. Kooyong's and numerous other arable properties were petitioned by the Australian Government and farmed with assigned workers from the Women's Land Army replacing men who had been otherwise drafted into Military Forces. This farm produce was in part to help feed the Army and AirForce bases on the Atherton Tablelands. Mrs. Ivy Booth was one of the Land Army girls seconded to Mt. Kooyong and became well acquainted with Keitha and Barbara.

After the war, Mt. Kooyong eventually returned to some of its former gaiety for a while, offering local residents and those from further afield, chalet accommodation and meals. However, by the latter part of 1950, Keitha and her friend Barbara departed, and for a short time the business came into new hands.

The Roe family, food caterers from Cairns, took it on and retained it as Chalet accommodation with restaurant meals; a sort of honeymooner's retreat.

During the early months of 1962, Mt. Kooyong Chalet was once again returned to one of its original owners, Keitha Salisbury, who now had returned as Mrs. Alcorn with her husband, David, a minister of the Presbyterian church from Brisbane. David Alcorn was a friendly and kindly chap who recently had his leg amputated.

Before the war, Keitha had trained as a nurse and was a worldly and well-educated woman. She had travelled extensively worldwide, and her passion for learning took her to places like India and Kashmir, where she familiarized herself with the benefits of alternative medicine and meditation. With Keitha's vast nursing experience, she managed David through his illness, taking on a more homeopathic approach, that was favoured by both of them. Barbara Parkman did not return on this occasion, instead, it was Keitha's long-time friend, Jean McMillan, a South African by birth, who remained long enough to help clean and sort out the Chalet before its next lease of life, and then finally parting company for good with Keitha.

The Chalet, with its previously indulging clientele emersed in restaurant-gaiety over music and cocktail parties, soon became a thing of the past as David Alcorn forbade any alcohol or dancing on the premises. Instead, Mt. Kooyong was transformed into a Convalescent Chalet and thus, entered its new era.

While Mt. Kooyong was being revamped, Anna was introduced by Ivy Booth a mutual friend, to Keitha and David Alcorn, and Jean McMillan.

Anna was initially employed to help launder, mend, and iron the huge bundles of curtains and table linen ware from the Chalet's more exuberant days, a paid task she was happy to take on and so began Anna's association with Keitha and Mt. Kooyong.

Next to Anna's house, an adjoining piece of land with the old butter factory, soon became a consideration too good to miss when it was advertised for sale by Public Auction a few months after the family bought their house.

Anna quickly pointed out to Jan that this additional land would benefit them because, as a stand-alone one-acre plot without water, it probably had little value to anyone else in this rural setting. But oddly enough, many in the neighbourhood seemed eager to bid for it. Anna had a friendly rival in Darby Edwards, albeit an understanding one, who was interested in purchasing the land for himself. However, Anna finally convinced him that it would serve him little purpose as the block had no water and would be more beneficial to her, so, in the end, she was the only bidder and acquired the add-on land in October 1962.

During the May and August school holiday break of that year, the family packed up again and returned to Laura. The children enjoyed the bush and the freedom it offered, and besides, they missed their father who for extended periods was only too often absent from their lives.

Photograph 295: Anna with Diana, dog Kiki and cat Paddy at Julatten, Circa 1964.

Photograph 296: L-R Jaryn, Shaun & Vladimir Kurovec; Anna's nephews.

CHAPTER 29

A Year of Unbearable Sorrow: 1963

Anna readily made friends within the Julatten community and had numerous supportive neighbours while Jan remained away for lengthy periods in Laura working on his tobacco farm. During this time Anna became concerned with their son Johnny, as his speech development seemed to lag behind that of his sisters. His Czech language was good, but he needed help grasping the spoken English language. He understood well, but his spoken words were less fluent and coherent. Phyllis McClure, a local farmer's wife with experience in speech elocution, came to the rescue and offered to give Johnny lessons.

The McClure children, Elise and Narelle, were similar in age to Anna's three, and for a while, they all attended school together in Julatten. Phyllis and Anna's friendship grew due to Johnny's regular elocution lessons, and Phyllis was always on hand to offer Anna support and reassurance with his progress. Later when the McClure family sold their farm to Bill and Kitty Edmonds and moved to farm sugarcane in Mossman, Anna missed Phyllis and her friendly and bubbly personality, albeit along with her chain-smoking habit. Shortly afterward, the McClures moved yet again, and after only one brief visit, the two families eventually lost touch.

At the commencement of school, Jan once again returned to Laura. As always, the monsoonal season brought heavy rain and flooding. Bushy Creek broke its banks, and flood water rose around the house. Unfortunately for the children, school continued as usual, but on weekends if the floods persisted, the children had plenty to do; sailing Johnny's corrugated iron canoes down the flooded causeway between Bushy and Rocky Creeks. Although these canoes leaked like sieves, the rather swift stream, barely knee-deep midway down the causeway and with grassy paddocks on either side, the water course was deemed relatively safe for the children to play in.

Years later, when engineers from the public main road's department reconfigured some of the drainage systems, diverting the flood flow to spread, this causeway became a formidable stream, too deep and dangerous for any canoeing ventures.

Jan returned home once more, just a few weeks before the May school holidays were scheduled to start, and the family all attended Tom Brown's movie theatre in Mt. Molloy. It was a memorable occasion, watching 'Hatari,' an African wildlife movie which had only been released some months earlier. It was filmed on the Serengeti in Tanzania Africa amongst its flourishing wildlife and in its adventure narrative John Wayne starred the major role.

Before Jan left for Laura, he had a pleasant evening with his children, laying under the stars on a blanket, looking skyward to see who could first spot a satellite. Kiki, his dog, remained with them while Anna cooked dinner. Jan's plan was to return just before the commencement of the school holidays in May and then for them all to spend two weeks with him in Laura. The next day, Jan departed and with Kiki returned to Laura. By now, Anna had full employment nursing at Mt. Kooyong.

On Wednesday evening at about 8 pm on the 1st of May 1963, an unexpected knock on the door suddenly startled Anna. The children had barely gone to bed, and she was about to settle for the night. Opening the door, Anna saw Keitha Alcorn facing her, and before words were even spoken, she reached out and braced Anna while Constable Beckworth the local Mt. Molloy policeman stood behind them. The news was devasting. In recent times Jan had complained to Anna about transient pain and numbness in his left arm, and she also recounted his frequent dreams about walking through a beautiful garden, like the Garden of Eden.

Anna screamed with grief and collapsed to her knees, while the children jolted from their slumber, began to cry. It was a night of confusion, despair, and hopelessness, with Anna and her children floundering in an awful nightmare scenario, unable to escape its gripping wake.

Jan had passed away earlier that afternoon in Laura town. He had driven in from his property to buy some aspirin as he had been suffering from a terrible headache. According to George Watkins, the local publican and shop proprietor, Jan had told him; that he was going to lie down for a while on the bench beneath the community shed a short distance away until his headache subsided. Jan would never wake up again and was found shortly afterward, with Kiki sitting faithfully beside him.

That evening, Keitha packed up Anna and her family and took them to stay with her at Mt. Kooyong.

Over the next few days Anna remained numbed with grief, while Keitha arranged Jan's funeral and put into process Anna's legal affairs. Jan had died without a will, so the public curator's office in Cairns immediately took control, executing probate of Jan's estate, and arranging to distribute his assets as they saw fit. This would only be the beginning of Anna's nightmare.

An Anglican funeral with Father Ernest Gribble presiding was arranged at St. David's Church in Mossman. There was an outpouring of grief, and Anna received many condolence cards from people she barely knew. Back then, it was not encouraged for young children to attend funerals, so Anna agreed that her children were too young and would not understand the meaning of the service. However, whoever appropriated this, gave no thought to the closure it would have given the children to see their father buried rather than believing he had deserted them.

News always travels fast in a small community and by the time the children returned to school, after the May holiday break, they were already subjects of curiosity. Sudden death in a family was not an expressed grief shared, but rather a shy distancing of silent respect. Only Elise McClure, with tears pouring down her cheeks, approached Helena and hugged her.

Anna lived at Mt. Kooyong with her children for several weeks and was eventually joined by Kiki brought down from Laura by a family acquaintance. Even Paddy, the family's grey kitten, joined them at Kooyong and created an amusing distraction for one of the lonely inmates.

Sadly, only a few weeks later, David, Keitha's husband, suddenly passed away from a heart attack, so this time, it was Anna who offered Keitha solace in return.

When Anna finally came to terms with her fate, but still grieving the loss of her husband, the family returned home and resumed life as best as they could. From there on, every penny counted, as now Anna's earnings alone, would have to sustain her and the children.

Photograph 297 & 298: (L-R) David Alcorn & Johnny 1963. Johnny & Kiki at Kooyong 1963.

Photograph 299: Keitha Alcorn with Anna & children May 1963.

Photograph 300: At Jan Kanak's Funeral; Rev. Father Ernest Gribble and Anna with Keitha Alcorn, Mossman Cemetery, May 1963.

CHAPTER 30

Julatten: A Tree Without Branches

Alone in her grief as a single parent, Anna became her children's mother and father figure and began to carve out a life for them all. Without Jan's support, she now had to make all the hard decisions herself. Time for her would be of the essence, as she would have to work and be there for her children. She felt an overwhelming black cloud hovering overhead and rapidly bearing down on her, bringing uncertainty and the threat that she may even lose her home.

With her children at school and Kiki at her feet, she surveyed her backyard and wondered what life would be like for them from now on. If only she could secure her home, she knew she could become self-sufficient with all this land, even if much of it would need to be cleared and placed under a fruit orchard and vegetable garden to feed them. If Anna's elderly neighbour, Mrs. Koll, could do it, so could she!

Anna's house may have been old but it still extended a warm welcome. A huge vine may have weighed down the front porch, but this glorious fire-orange honey-suckle canopy made the place look inviting, and Anna loved flowers. In Anna's mind, several mango trees, which bore large crops of fruit in season, could remain, as the fruit was edible and could also be used for chutneys. However, some of the other large trees offering little except shade, and numerous old and dilapidated outbuildings; all would need knocking down to make way for progress. There was little room for sentimentality but instead practicality.

Anna's proposed new garden, which extended beyond the house yard, was a mass of blad

y grass and trees with undergrowth that was useless in its present state and only harboured vermin and snakes; it was this area that would need clearing. Her house yard had plenty of potential. The granadilla vine, which grew behind the outside toilet, almost covering it, seemed to cling onto anything within reach. However, it was still laden with violet flowers and pendulous ripening fruit. The passion fruit vine, also laden with fruit, strung itself along a dilapidated trellis made of fencing wire which ran parallel with the clothesline. Both these frameworks extended toward the tall but dead tree around which the wired espaliers entwined its girth. Attached to this dead snag was also a radio antenna. Long before Anna's arrival, someone used a very long ladder or courageously climbed over 20 feet up to the tip and tied the aerial wire which extended from the house. Nevertheless, it still provided a safe perch for kookaburras, chicken hawks, and other wildlife overlooking the yard observing the goings-on below.

This landmark tree also formed the corner post of the chicken run. More often than not, Kiki did her penance there, tied to the tree for raiding the chook house for eggs. Anna stared at the lifeless tree, its life, long spent, but it still supported life as it took centre stage in her backyard. It was a tree without branches.

Putting aside her rather fragile and futile dreams for the future, Anna faced more immediate and looming issues that needed her undivided attention. Jan's estate was being addressed and needed to be wound up, and she had to make some decisions. If it had not been for Rob and Margaret Whelan's assistance and advice, Anna would have long succumbed to the pressures of the Public Curator's Office to sell everything. Having died intestate, in their eyes, it was a case that Jan had owned everything and she nothing. Even with the recent purchase of additional land with only her name on it and the shared interest in her present home, it was not enough to satisfy them, as they demanded to know where her money had come from to buy this land. With Rob Whelan's intervention and representing her interests, it soon became evident that the Curator's office would be dealing with a man rather than a grieving widow easily beguiled to give into them.

The process evolved into a rather nasty situation from which Anna soon learned who her genuine friends were. As Jan's everyday debts were being accounted for and cleared, it was soon evident that some people with unscrupulous intent were creating invoices that never existed. With Rob's meticulous information gathering, these people were soon filtered out, and Jan's estate proceeded ahead. After agreeing to sell all of her husband's machinery, Anna used her own share of the estate to help finance the purchase of all Jan's properties. Anna received genuine offers of financial help, for which she was most appreciative, but ultimately, she chose to do all her financing through banks.

For all that transpired throughout that difficult period of settling Jan's estate, Anna remained forever grateful to Rob and Margaret Whelan for their unwavering support and assistance and their genuine concern that she was justly treated with a fair outcome. For Anna, it was the beginning of yet another journey that she had to undertake once again alone, but this time with the added responsibility of three young children.

Photograph 301: Helena, Johnny with dog, Anna & Diana, Julatten 1964.

Photograph 302: Jaroslav & Lois Kurovec with Vladimir, Shaun and Jaroslav circa 1956.

Book Two: Life in Australia

CHAPTER 31

Life Without Jan: 1964-1968

Anna's priority in life would always be her children. She decided she would never remarry and instead live life uncomplicated without the imposition of someone else's rules and ideas governing her family. Ultimately Anna would become her own woman and stand her ground. Her path was never meant to be easy from the onset, as she realized but she was determined to forge ahead as a single parent, a widow no less, and prove to herself she could do it. People in the community were generally supportive, but like in many instances, once a husband dies, quite often, shared main-stay friends go with him. However, Anna had a presence and personality that attracted people, and she soon began accumulating new friends from all walks of life and who were often much younger than herself. In later years, when her children had grown up and left home to carve out their own lives, Anna became a mother figure to many.

In the beginning, with three young children at school, Anna had to maintain work through a series of different jobs to support herself and her family. Her earlier psychiatric nursing career in New Zealand now paid dividends, as she was able to work as a nurse's aide at Mt. Kooyong, dealing with the elderly and their often-demented states of mind. However, she quickly applied herself to earning extra money during seasonal tobacco work. She would string and later grade tobacco leaf before it was bundled, baled, and sent to Mareeba for sale. Whichever job Anna had, she had to remain close to home for her children.

She was never deterred by hard work and could put her hand to any task offered, no matter how demanding. Tobacco work was often easier to accommodate, as on weekends, the children could join her stringing tobacco leaf and themselves earning pocket money. Once, while helping to sucker tobacco (removing the lesser quality leaves, flowers and suckers from the tobacco bush before maturation), Anna worked alongside an aboriginal chap, Sid Green. On that particular day, he suddenly stopped and became quiet and distant.

He then whispered to her, "Hear them curlews, Misses? Someone in my family has just died!"

He seemed so convinced what he foresaw was real. When Anna next saw him, he had just returned from his mother's funeral. Anna was not superstitious but believed many aboriginal people had a strong association with their totems and these native callings which seemed deeply embedded into their cultural folklore and psyche, enabled them to preempt and prepare for such premonitions.

Life resumed and took on a different normality while Anna continued to work and attend to her children's schooling needs. The children mostly enjoyed school; the girls were bright and energetic while Johnny lagged scholastically, his mind often wandering and taking him beyond the bounds of the schoolyard.

During mid-July of 1963, after one of their much-anticipated scripture lessons with Father Gribble, the children excitedly disclosed to Anna that an 'atomic bomb' had exploded on Iron Range in Cape York. Anna was mortified, as in recent years, much had been said and protested about the French doing atomic testing on Bikini Atoll in the Pacific. The story that unfolded was intriguing, nevertheless. It seemed only the children's word in this case, implying that Father Gribble told his little flock of believers that something of an explosive nature had been detonated near Iron Range in Cape York. Wally Crear, their school teacher, was unaware of any such event occurring or having been discussed in Anglican scriptures. The children insisted that during this scripture lesson, Father Gribble revealed he had been asked to administer to a local aboriginal community in the area and assist with their relocation before this test was carried out. He had shown the children photo slides of the event, during which time he indicated he had been privileged to observe it with a gathering of witnesses as the payload of TNT exploded. Many decades later, it became publicly exposed and known as 'Operation Blowdown' [1].

The photo slides captured the devastation this explosive TNT experiment had caused, flattening a considerably huge circular area of trees and vegetation within the rainforest. It had remained unmentioned and kept from the general public until about 2001, when declassified government material became assessable. Back then, nobody would have paid too much attention to the children's wild tales of bomb explosions in the Cape, but Father Gribble's troubled conscience perhaps prompted him to share this event with them. After all, he had to help relocate the local aboriginal tribes from their community and then witness the devastation on their land caused by some 45 tons of TNT.

Although Anna's children eventually settled at school following their father's passing in 1963, a few months later, an unexpected event shook the Nation on Friday, the 22nd of November of that same year. USA president (JFK) John Fitzgerald Kennedy had been assassinated. Anna and the children heard about it on the wireless on Saturday, as it was broadcast on the early news. Anna was shaken and saddened as the tragic news unraveled. On that day, reeling from such unbelievable tragedy, the family was gathered by the roadside discussing the situation with Arthur Duck, the baker from Mount Molloy, as he was doing his Saturday morning bread delivery.

America was a long way from the centre of every Australian's life. Still, it struck a chord when this cowardly slaughter was carried out of a very popular and charismatic President. The day remained etched into the memories of so many who bore witness to the news on that day. Later when the Australian Women's Weekly Magazine published an article about the funeral, the first thing the children noticed was the presence of JFK's children at the funeral. It opened up old wounds and questions for Anna's children;

"Why were they allowed to attend their dad's funeral, and we weren't allowed to attend our daddy's funeral?"

The children were still silently grieving the loss of their father, but they had to bury this grief and remain strong for their Mum.

In 1963 shortly after Jan's death, Jaroslav Kurovec, Anna's brother, arrived from South Australia to offer his condolences and help. After all, he had been one of Jan's closest friends. Anna sensed that it may have been more advice he was offering as he arrived with two of his friends, Ken Pope and Rudy Schnrier. It may have been in all innocence, but Anna soon took offense to the presence of the additional male company and was quick to point out that she was not on the market for a new husband and accused her brother of trying to play matchmaker.

Jaroslav soon realized that his sister could more than stand on her own two feet. Although she had been pleased to see her brother, she wished he had come alone and not with an entourage of men. Sadly, it would be the last time she would see him, as he, too, suddenly passed away five years later in July of 1968.

In the latter part of 1963, a transport entity from the bygone days was being re-enacted and celebrated. It was the Cobb & Co stagecoach service [2] incorporating a Royal Flying Doctor Service fundraiser. The horse-drawn coach, along with its backup of horses at regular staging intervals, aimed to cover the distance between Port Douglas and Melbourne, heralding its past transportation of mail and passengers and promoting the RFDS. It was hoped to visit as many places as possible as it made its way along more conventional roads. Besides, many of the original coach routes were either too remote or no longer accessible.

The commemoration created excitement amongst the locals as the procession passed through Julatten along the gravel and dusty road onto Mt. Molloy before heading south on its epic journey. At the time, some old folk still remembered this service, either having been passengers on it or in some rarer cases employed to drive it [3].

The Julatten-Mount Molloy district was well versed with Cobb & Co history as it was once the Bump Road near Euluma Creek that afforded the coach service link from the Hodgkinson Goldfields in the hinterland to the coastal town of Port Douglas. Once up and over the Bump Road summit, two better locally known staging posts for this service were Weatherboards near Mt. Molloy and another further south along the Little Mitchell River near Yalkula. It was a historic moment, and although many paid to partake in travelling on the coach for short distances, Anna's finances were such that it wasn't affordable for all her children to take a ride, so instead, covered in dust and with wide-eyed enthusiasm, they observed the procession from the roadside.

Throughout the 1960s, Anna remained employed in a permanent part-time capacity at Mt. Kooyong, and it was during this time that many changes at the establishment were beginning to surface.

Mt. Kooyong had become an aged care facility and had to be regulated according to the health standards deemed appropriate by the government regulatory body that dictated funding for its purpose. Although Matron, as Keitha became affectionately known by all, abided by most rules, there were always grey areas that she skirted around to suit herself for the betterment of her inmates. She had a set bed capacity, but that did not deter her from taking in others in need. These extras were not accommodated on the premises but rather in close-by disused and converted buses and caravans parked permanently amongst the trees in her extended garden. She gave these people a home and a sense of purpose and made them feel a part of her bustling household. Keitha even gave up her own room and slept in a curtained-off corner on the verandah with all her possessions stacked about her.

Matron also had a fondness for animals, but the children added to her menagerie with additional woes when tamed bandicoots fed by them at night became regular guests in the kitchen and had to be rounded up and evacuated off the premises. Keitha owned a border collie named Tiger, who mellowed with age and fitted in well with her inmates; a spoilt Siamese cat called Cleopatra and an Angora goat called Marc-Anthony. For most, all these animals had free range of the premises.

Marc-Anthony was no exception in making his presence evident when one day he was caught out on Keitha's bed, helping himself to various note-worthy records and documents.

During Anna's time there, Matron employed Olive Keys in the office with Eunice Davidson, Kitty Speer, and Lorna Days as principal Registered Nurses. Zara Wildenhauer, a nursing friend of Keitha's from former days returned for a short while and she and Anna became well acquainted. Mary Brown was chief cook for some time, and numerous other nursing, domestic and auxiliary staff passed through the establishment at varying times. In a nutshell, Keitha gave most Julatten folk employment, whether she needed them or not.

A few elderly chaps, albethey colourful characters, notably Tommy, Pat, and Johnny, lived from time to time near the premises in refurbished caravans and old decommissioned buses. They were all noteworthy kitchen hands with a designated task, and each occupied a specific spot in the kitchen, thus assisting the wheels of culinary production to keep turning. With his white cane, Pat sat in one corner beside the door and peeled the potatoes while Johnny assisted him in delivering the peeled vegetables to the cook. Tommy was in charge of the scrap bucket, but Tommy and Pat did not see eye to eye, so at all times, Tommy avoided confrontation with near-blind Pat. Such was their unhappy disposition. Although Pat was legally blind and confessed to seeing nothing, he never missed an opportunity to whack Tommy with his cane whenever the poor chap with his bucket of scraps crept past him. Pat always insisted it was an accident as he never saw Tommy coming.

Tommy had another arch enemy: Marc-Anthony, Matron's Angora goat. One day while Anna was on duty, Keitha came rushing by with all her bedding under her arms, announcing that the health inspectors were on the way up from Cairns. Orders were shouted in all directions. Firstly, all unregistered inmates had to be removed from the premises and ushered back into their garden quarters or, where ever convenient, seated on the verandah as visitors.

As per health regulations, the freshwater tank which generally only held fresh river water had to be chlorinated for the visit and ultimately was overdosed with an undisclosed number of chlorine bags emptied into it. All the animals had to be rounded up and locked well away from the premises. Tommy was in charge of Tiger and in this case locked the dog in the bird aviary, while someone else took charge of Marc-Anthony.

While doing a last-minute check of the kitchen, Keitha caught sight of her cat Cleopatra and unbeknown to the cook, rather unceremoniously shoved the indignant creature into the flour cupboard beneath the kitchen bench.

While Keitha entertained the health inspectors with cups of tea over the general discussion about her establishment, numerous inmates began knocking on her office door, complaining about sore eyes from the tap water. She reassured them sweetly that someone would shortly give them their eye drops as she gently but persuasively escorted her visitors out of the office and away from the centre of crises; in a direction that she deemed would be of more interest and less distraction.

The kitchen, mandatory for the inspection, was last on the list, and the facility had to be thoroughly checked. The cook, fully preoccupied with lunch, opened the bench cupboard for some flour when a white streak shot out, startling her and leaving behind a trail of flour on the floor. Keitha caught sight of the flour-covered escapee, and before her visitors did so, she calmly turned them around and headed them off in another direction. When the inspection was done and dusted and the gentlemen once more on their way back to Cairns, the water tank was immediately emptied and replenished with fresh water.

Tommy's sudden appearance with Marc-Anthony in hot pursuit came right on queue as otherwise, it may have caused an embarrassing moment for Matron and her inspectors. Someone had locked Marc-Anthony inside Tommy's caravan, and when he opened the door, the two met face-to-face, both suddenly with an urge to escape in the same direction! Tommy, eager to run for refuge, was terrified, while the goat, agitated and hot to trot, pursued him in great haste.

Whenever Anna was on night duty, she had numerous startling encounters while doing security checks at Mt. Kooyong. Snoring noises from behind cushions on the lounge would create alarm, and when prodded, an even more alarmed Tommy would jump out in the dark. He always managed to sneak in before lockdown and hide somewhere, as he hated sleeping alone in his caravan.

At the time, a rather glamorous, if not exotic and outspoken lady by the name of Phyllis had been promised a public relations job by Keitha. Keitha had so many ideas milling about in her head that one project often melted into another, and for a while, Phyllis was left in limbo. After being given mundane tasks that were completely out of her scope of practice and witnessing the often-chaotic routine of the place, Phyllis realized she could serve little purpose and resigned from her yet-to-be-appointed position; "I can't possibly work on this funny farm!" She was heard to say. Luckily at the time of visiting Health Inspectors, Keitha was saved from embarrassment when one of her mobile gentleman residents absconded. Dressed in his pyjamas and slippers, he made his was to the highway and flagged a car to Mossman. He convinced the driver he needed to be in Mossman to buy the Mossman Sugar Mill! His absence became evident when Mt. Kooyong received a call enquiring if one of their residents were missing. There was never a dull moment at Mt. Kooyong!

But, funny farm or not, Mt. Kooyong had a pulse of its own, and the elderly inmates were always well looked after by caring staff overseen by Keitha, who dedicated her life to caring for others. Keitha was fond of children and even had her brother Frank and his four children stay there for a few years.

In the early 1960s, when Mt. Kooyong was more of a convalescent Chalet, children often lived in with their convalescing parents. They even attended the local school for a while. Children seemed a constant, either as visitors or belonging to staff, and on occasions, even Ivy Booth brought along her grandchildren Raymond and Margaret. Of course, Anna's children were never far away.

Keitha put all these youngsters to good use, encouraging them to play cards with the elderly residents. Over Christmas the children were responsible for creating a Christmas Pantomime and entertaining the elderly with scenes from the holy scriptures. This would often be overshadowed by rowdy skits, followed by singing and dancing with residents in swaying hula-hula skirts taking to the stage, after which the ever so-graceful and petite Christine Evans trying to perform her fairy ballet rendition from The Nut Cracker Suite, while the record player crackled out Tchaikovsky's theme. Even Santa Clause was acted out by one of the children, and Helena took on the role on one occasion. It was always jolly as gifts were handed out and the elderly mingled with the children dancing and swaying to Hawaiian melodies.

But as free as the children were, Sundays were always days of worship, and they formed the pivot of the choir; and there was no getting out of it. Keitha was never seen to discriminate one religion over another, and clergies of all principal denominations took their turn to preside over Sunday service. Even Keitha's dog Tiger would sneak in until she had to haul him off a rather embarrassed Anglican priest when the dog became too familiar with the poor chap during his sermon. The children would snicker in amusement, but one frown from Matron's direction would silence their glee.

Mt. Kooyong was where the old met the young on even turf, giving everyone a sense of appreciation of one another. Anna was a gifted masseuse and many of the residents and even staff benefitted from her deep massages. Keitha in particular with her chronic back problem had numerous sessions with Anna. Through Keitha, Anna came to the notice of Schellberg, a prominent chiropractor and masseuse in Cairns, who offered her an assistant job but Anna had to decline due to family and work commitments. Anna along with many other staff had a sense of belonging to Mt. Kooyong while Keitha fussed about them. But Keitha could also be a hard task master.

From 1963 through to 1964, while trains still ran from Mareeba to Julatten, Anna would order cases of green Grannie Smith apples in season from Stanthorpe to ensure her children always had fruit to eat. Apples were always a treat for the children, as were pineapples sourced in caseloads from Mossman. Pineapples were not only eaten for their fruit alone but the prickly skins with juicy flesh still attached were boiled down to make juice.

The regular train service also fulfilled another purpose; the annual visit from the school dentist. For a while, it saved Anna regular trips to Mareeba to have her children's teeth checked. Still, Anna's concern with their teeth would become her constant preoccupation, as afterward, at the end of each school term, the children would have ready-made appointments awaiting them.

Anna's other idée fixe was her children's need for fresh milk. As once before, while at Euluma Creek, she again aspired to have her own milking cows, but in the interim, Anna arranged to milk a cow on Kevin Gadd's nearby farm. Her children grew up familiar with milking cows and often helped. On one occasion, while doing the milking, Diana and John went off horseback riding, with Diana falling off and breaking her arm. Johnny recollected the incident well; it happened on the day Martin Luther King was assassinated. But Diana undoubtedly had a more vivid and less historical memory of it, as she ended up with her arm in a cast.

Always trying to be self-sufficient, Anna often reared pigs for pork. Although the children would become attached to the animals, to Anna's way of thinking, they served only one purpose. Animals always majored in Anna's life, and her children grew up with horses, two of whom became loved pets. Trigger was a frisky, black part-Shetland pony. He was as cunning as he was adorable. But adoration came on his terms, and he always knew how to snatch bread from the children's hands before the bridle came near his neck. Trigger never jumped fences, he crawled beneath them, rider and all!

The children enjoyed many delightful years with him, but he was never accommodating with male riders, so Johnny rarely scored a mount that did not result in him being bucked off. However, Trigger was partial to bananas and chicken mash. Once, Anna heard noises coming from the shed where she stored her grain; fearing being burgled, she armed herself with a large stick and stealthily approached the door. About to strike out and tackle her intruder, a black head and muzzle covered in white mash sheepishly peered around the corner, confronting one other in a startled stupor.

Soon afterward, another orphan foal named Comet was gifted to the children, so Trigger, at long last, had a partner in crime.

During the tobacco season, Anna and the children would earn extra money doing lengthy weekend nights stringing tobacco leaf either for Kevin Gadd or Eric and Agnes Anderson, and later after 1968 for Olive and Harvey Keys. After meeting Dawn and Bernie Voerman from Red Rock's Nursery in Mareeba, Anna's tobacco work extended onto their farm as well, during which time a close family friendship grew, mostly founded on mutual interest in plants and gardening.

In early 1964, Anna's sister-in-law Lois Kurovec arrived for a visit from South Australia with mutual friend Jean Blann. It was a follow-up trip to Anna's brother's previous visit. Anna was pleased to see them both, as Jean and her husband Bob Blann had been Jan's closest friends, and Jean being jovial and easygoing, soon became a favourite with Anna's children. Lois would visit on further occasions with her then three grown-up boys, two of whom: Jaryn and Shaun, would already be married to Tanya and Annette, respectively.

Again in 1964, but toward Christmas, Anna had yet another surprise visit. Margaret Lewis, her fondest friend from New Zealand, arrived with her two younger children, Gaye (now known as Allison) and Michael, who were similar in age to Anna's three children. It was a memorable stay and one that the children enjoyed immensely. To them, Margaret was their real 'Auntie' even if by default. They all visited Green Island for the first time and then spent a week at Newell Beach. 'Mary Poppins' with Julie Andrews had recently been released, and Anna's children, having not heard about the film, were fascinated and equally delighted as Gaye taught and sang the ditties from the movie.

Gaye was a great narrator and read 'Brer Rabbit' every evening to them, whereas Mike was the financial whiz. When the children sold the watermelons, they had planted earlier for Christmas, Anna's children shared their proceeds with their New Zealand guests under Mike's expertise accounting. For Anna, it was the first time she had someone to talk to who really understood her and could share all her ups and downs since losing Jan. Margaret knew them from when they shared together much happier times during their New Zealand and South Australian days. With their children content to play together, the two women had plenty of time to reflect on their lives.

In later years, Margaret would return on several more occasions to visit Anna. It was always a special time of reminiscing and contemplation for them both, made easier by then with all their children grown up. Anna and Margaret were like chalk and cheese in character; Margaret was more sensitive to other people's plights and misfortunes, whereas Anna was straightforward and practical, but above all, what bonded them was that each shared a great sense of humor and an unwritten agreement to differ in opinion without offending each other.

Alice and Ray Richards were a farming couple living in Julatten at the time. They had arrived from Koah (near Kuranda) and bought a farm that once boasted the most stylish home ever built in the Rumula district during the early 1900s. It was built by brothers Frank and Henry Evans and was made solely of locally harvested timber. Its grand style consisted of numerous guest rooms and even indulged in a large ballroom. However, by the time the Richards' arrived and bought it from Frank Evans in the 1960s, on the agreement, Frank remained with them; the home was already in need of major repairs.

Over the years, Alice would become a testament to its decline, as on numerous visits, Anna would greet Alice covered in bruises from where she had fallen through the floorboards.

Ray was never one to be confined to farming, or carpentry; he was of the social kind and enjoyed cricket, tennis, and dances. He had a flirtatious nature and quite often was MC at the dances and, for a while, drove the school bus while entertaining those around him with often outlandish and humorous tales. Alice was more reserved, quite the opposite of her husband, and had been an accomplished pianist but shied away from playing at too many social functions. She much preferred to write a weekly column for the Cairns Post Newspaper on 'Julatten affairs,' and often much to Anna's annoyance featured her mundane life as the topic of introduction.

At the time, Alice operated as a local door-to-door saleswoman upon the demise of 'The Watkins Salesman' franchise, a door-to-door salesman who once regularly drove through country areas selling everything from potions and lotions to kitchen utensils, cloth, and other merchandise.

Alice operated her much smaller enterprise between Julatten and Mareeba and only sold Avon, Nutrametics, and fabrics while at the same time gleaning news for her column, most of it gossip doing the neighbourhood rounds. During these regular visits over prolonged cups of tea, Anna would listen patiently to Alice's woes as she related tales of misadventure and snake home invasions; generally, pythons which Ray, her husband, always had the propensity in failing to capture the offender and allowing this hapless creature to escape and reappear yet again on another day somewhere else in the house. In most cases, it was a triumphant escape for the wretched reptiles. One night a python fell from the ceiling onto their bed and slithered into the wardrobe through which Ray immediately shot a huge hole, missing the terrified albeit very fortunate reptile. Next time they had a snake visitation, he barreled a hole through Alice's new stove as the bullet missed its intended victim and penetrated their water tank behind the kitchen wall. Again, the reptile escaped with its life intact while another emergency began to emerge. These stories would have been far more worthy of entertainment in the Cairns Post than Anna's dull domestic life! However, Alice and Ray were good friends despite all their shortcomings, they were decent people who always helped Anna. On numerous occasions, they would drive Anna and the children to Cairns to attend the annual Children's Christmas party, sponsored by Cairns Legacy; a charity organization supporting children and families of return war veterans.

Many happy memories remained from these events, with one Christmas party at the Cairns airport hangar with the Webb Trio, Marilyn,

Laurence, and Carmel singing. The Webb family were acquaintances from Anna's earlier Euluma Creek-Julatten days. Other parties were held in Kuranda and even at Aloomba, where everyone was transported in a rather rickety boat owned and operated by a well-known local Cairns entity, Tom. It was always an adventure for the children.

When the film 'The Sound of Music' first came to Cairns in 1965, it was again Ray and Alice Richards who took Anna and her children to see it. Later the children were treated to a swim in a popular spot on the Barron River. Swimming in this same spot on the river today would be a treacherous folly as it is now abundant with protected estuarine crocodiles!

When the train ceased running to Julatten in 1964, Ray and Alice took on a taxi/bus/mail delivery service between the Julatten district and Mareeba.

By now, graziers Charlie and Doreen Wallace were well ensconced into the Julatten community after selling their station 'Butchers Hill,' on which today most of this grazing country supports the community of Lakeland. Doreen was an accomplished pianist and always willing to play at many Julatten dances and concerts. She became fondly known as Granny Wallace, as many of her relatives from the Cape attended these occasions.

Both Doreen and Charlie were enthusiastic racegoers, owning racehorses. For a brief moment, many local keen punters and followers hoped Charlie's latest acquisition, 'Zarook,' would make it to the Melbourne Cup and win. Julatten was never to be honored with this accolade, but nevertheless, this majestic creature happily saw out his days at 'Cambrae' along Hunters Creek.

Charlie's cattle associate, Bill Edmonds at the time owned and operated a bulldozer. While residing at Julatten, he cleared large swathes of land for cattle grazing, and offered to clear Anna's overgrown acreage at the rear of her house yard. Old tree stumps were pulled, over-growth was uprooted, and all the concrete foundations from the previous Main Road's Camp were dug up and removed, the last standing testament to foreman, Snowy Baker, who years before, based himself at the camp and oversaw works on the local roads and bridges.

This newly cleared acreage finally made Anna's land usable, and she wasted no time planting a large citrus orchard with various exotic fruits. It also created a regular job for Johnny, and with the new Victor mower, he mowed grass between rows of planted trees, keeping him occupied for hours on end and out of mischief.

Anna always found camaraderie in her local community, and as a widow with three young children there were numerous people who always helped her.

One such family were the Bruntons. Bill and his wife Ethel Mary owned and ran the local Julatten store which they had earlier purchased from Charlie and Vera Knight.

Bill was English and had immigrated to Australia, met and married local Mossman girl Ethel Hingley and in semi-retirement eventually made their way to Julatten. Bill or Brother Bill as he was affectionately known, was a busy man and his poor long-suffering wife was often left with running the store while he attended numerous committee meetings including those of the Mossman Hospital Board. He became involved in the Julatten community; a regular participant at the school PNC meetings and many grateful locals at the time attributed and recognized his efforts in Bushy Creek State School remaining opened. At one stage pupil numbers had dwindled to about 13 with mounting government pressure to close the school and transfer the pupils onto Mt. Molloy School which at the time had a larger enrollment of children. W.J. Brunton made it his mission that this did not happen and he succeeded.

On occasional Saturdays, Bill would give Anna a lift to Mossman so she and the children could visit Jan's grave at the Mossman Cemetery. The trip down the winding and unsealed Rex Range often left Anna feeling car sick as Bill whizzed down the track beeping his car horn at every bend.

Anna gifted Bill and Ethel a pup named Nipper, an off-spring from her dog Kiki. This pup was much loved and thoroughly spoilt by the Bruntons and one which gave Bill no end of trouble, always chewing either all his left or all his right slippers.

New orders for slippers had to be placed to Mossman over the telephone exchange, often accompanied by colourful language directed at his dog and which would come to the attention of the local Post Mistress Mrs. Major listening in on the conversation. Without thinking, she would intercept by reminding such language was unacceptable. Needless to say, verbal sparks were added to the dialogue whenever Brother Bill caught her out!

Anna's English was quite accomplished by now, although she always spoke with a thick European accent. Despite frequent misinterpretations coupled with her unique turn of phrase and sense of humour, Anna often found herself at the brunt of her own misreading.

Once when fish fingers were fast becoming popular and deemed a treat for children regardless of the taste, or rather lack of it, Anna was unpacking her grocery shopping when one of her children piped up in excitement,

"Oh! Woh! You have bought us Bird's Eyes!"

Anna's heart dropped as she grabbed the packet and apologized, "Bird's eyes! They were supposed to be fish fingers!"

Anna always admired pretty things, especially decorative cards, regardless of the verses included. Once, her daughter received a beautiful card with Anna's usual personal message written inside; except the card read, "Happy Birthday Grandfather!"

Many years later, Anna would laugh at these indiscretions whenever mentioned.

For Anna, 1966 was a year of significant changes. Firstly, the nation converted from Pounds, Shillings, and Pence into Dollars and Cents, followed by Bob Menzies resigning from office as Australia's Prime Minister and replaced by Harold Holt.

All the while the Vietnam War continued to rage with the conflict supported by Australian conscripts. It was an era when mothers feared for their sons and hoped that a peaceful solution would soon eventuate before their sons came of age and were called on to join the war.

By early to mid-1966, the school's headmaster, Wally Crear and his family were transferred from Julatten; soon to be replaced by new-comers Greg and Shirley Hobbs.

Anna always believed that school teachers laid the foundations for their pupil's future. Wally Crear, who was there for most of her children's schooling, was one such headmaster who introduced his classes to interesting facts outside everyday community living. Wally was a great teacher and instrumental in teaching the children respect for their country.

Each morning at the start of class, the Australian flag was hoisted and flying high, the children stood to attention with their right hand over their heart and sang the national anthem, 'God save the Queen.' Back then, 'Advance Australia Fair,' today's anthem, was just a song with national sentiment and which Wally had the foresight to teach his pupils to sing all its verses.

He also pointed out to them where during WWII, a trench had been dug at the front of the school near the flag pole, and used as an air-raid shelter for pupils and staff whenever Japanese enemy planes flew over. This trench now long covered over, remained as a long and narrow rectangular dip in the ground signaling its passing testament to the war.

Under Wally Crear's stewardship, the children were taught to square dance and waltz, becoming accomplished in the progressive barn dancing and waltzes such as the Pride of Erin and the Prince of Wales Schottische. So, by the time the children finished school, each could hold their own when going to dances.

However, it was not only his musical accomplishments that stood out, teaching them to sing and play on small plastic flutes, but making time in class to listen to the wireless as Sonny Listen and Cassius Clay (before becoming Mohamed Ali) battled it out in the boxing ring for the world heavyweight titles. He also introduced the children to the virtuosity of Melbourne Cup sweeps as everyone bought a horse for a penny and listened eagerly for their horse to fly past the winning post.

One thing that Anna was grateful to Wally for, was that he taught his students the value of money. With every child having their own Commonwealth Bank passbook, each would bring their pennies and thruppence bits on Wednesdays and have the money banked into their accounts at the post office. None of the children at the time knew what the other had to bank, and it was always kept discrete, but by the time the children left primary school, each had a bank account with some money in it.

Wally Crear's lasting legacy was his timber work, and there would not have been too many in the community who did not own something that Wally made. He helped Anna with many carpentry house renovations and even built linen cupboards for one of the rooms.

From making puppets for school plays, to playing marbles, or darbs as they were called, to learning the art of sporting games, Anna was always kept busy with her children's interests. There was no end of marble bags sown as her children came home with bags swollen with marbles won, only to return home the next day with their coffers empty after losing most of them in a game. It at least taught them good sportsmanship and how to win and lose humbly.

For the short duration that the Hobbs family remained in the district, they greatly impacted the small community of Julatten. Greg was a great motivator with children, and during sports, he encouraged training rather than just competing at lib. Although the school inter-house (Leichardt versus Kennedy) sports day was low-key and fun, for their events on the inter-school programme Greg took a more serious approach for the first time in training the children for their school sports day in Mossman. From track and field events to ball games; tunnel ball, leader ball and overhead ball, Bushy Creek State School could not afford to discriminate the best from least abled athletes and everyone had a go as they prepared for competition against the large schools of Mossman State Primary and St. Augustine's Catholic School, and the smaller neighbouring schools of Miallo, Rocky Point, Daintree and Cassowary. It was a huge surprise when the small school of Bushy Creek won the Inter-school Aggregate Athletics Shield in Mossman. The school, totaling only seventeen pupils were all smiles that year when for the first time the children all wearing their red and royal blue school colours proudly embraced the Aggregate Shield.

Some years earlier, through the P&C (Parents and citizens), Anna helped to instigated the sport's uniform design. The girl's tunic was a short white pleated dress with a bold blue and red band near the hemline. The boy's white trousers also had a similar blue and red band along both sides of the shorts. For once, the little bush school had an identity rather than competing in mufti clothes.

Helena even came away with the senior athletics champion trophy. A few weeks later, she and Graham Brown competed in The Far North

Queensland Junior Athletic Championships in Cairns, winning minor accolades.

One noteworthy occasion for Bushy Creek School, apart from the mandatory arbor day, the annual planting of a tree, was when the School Inspector arrived on his annual visit. It was the only time Anna sent her children to school wearing shoes. Generally, all the school children were barefooted at the time, and on occasions such as this, they would be shoed and neatly dressed in their sports tunics.

For the school children, these school visitors were an integral part of the ongoing education system ensuring it was being upheld to state wide standards. The annual mini agricultural day, during which time the children displayed their prowess in gardening; mainly growing watermelon and pumpkin, bee-keeping and honey-extracting skills, and how to conduct an actual general meeting with elected committee members carrying out the roles of Chairman, Secretary, and Treasurer were enthusiastically carried out to the benefit of the official visitor and families alike. Above all, the highlight of the day was the calf parade, where entries were judged on training and interactional behaviour between calf and child rather than alone on the pedigree and breeding of the animal. This privilege rested solely with the visiting Inspector to be judge and jury in this competitive arena of animal husbandry.

Though a little lively, Linda Edmonds presented with a stately pure-bred Droughtmaster calf, a progeny from her father's Wallace Vale Stud. On the other hand, Helena, John, and Diana each trained one of Bill Mildren's dairy herd calves. The exercise all came down to handling and the relationship that developed over the past few weeks between child and calf. Helena's calf was named 'Star'. Even though it was a beautiful-looking heifer, its pedigree did not match Linda's well-bred calf. When the prizes were awarded, and Linda took out the red ribbon for second place, Bill Edmonds, her father, was ropeable. His reprisal was loud and clear for those who cared to listen for days, if not weeks, afterward;

"What would a bloody School Inspector know about cattle, giving Billy Mildren's mongrel calf first prize?"

Although Mt. Molloy and Julatten schools were only some nine kilometres apart, the two schools never interacted as Mt. Molloy was aligned with Mareeba and Julatten with Mossman. However, it would be newly arrived headmaster Greg Hobbs who would instigate a concert between the two schools for the first time. As all the children prepared with recitals and plays, Anna's three and local lad Gregory Rebetzke made papier-mâché puppets. Anna busily helped to create and sew puppet costumes for the King, Queen, Royal Princess, and Royal Doctor. 'The Royal Belly Ache' may have not rivaled 'The Tin Tookie Puppets,' which toured the country then, but it was certainly a class act of its own.

The end of year break-up day was always a time of fun for everyone as children competed in sack bag races, egg and spoon races and three-legged races and then indulged in water melon and ice cream. In those days refrigeration of ice cream was on dry ice stored in a green oval cylindrically shaped canvas container. The dry ice was an ever-ending source of curiosity with consequences whenever some of the boys got their fingers or worse still, their tongues' stuck to it.

The annual fancy dress ball and Christmas party was an event anticipated by all even if Santa at times arrived late. He was often suffering jet lag; from an over indulgence of pre-Christmas celebratory drinks and excuses such as his sleigh and rein deer becoming tangled up in lantana soon wore thin even with the youngest of believers!

1966 was Helena's final year at Bushy Creek State School and initially unknowingly for her, she was being prepared to leave home once more to attend boarding school in Charters Towers.

Greg and Shirley Hobbs became Anna's most staunch allies and friends and whenever Anna needed help to care for Diana and Johnny, such as when Anna had to take Helena to enroll at school at Charters Towers, Greg and Shirley were there to help.

In late January, Anna and Helena boarded the train in Mareeba and journeyed onto Cairns and Townsville. Whether Anna fully explained to Helena the nature of the trip, remains questionable.

In Townsville, the connection to Charters Towers on the regular Inlander Passenger Service did not correspond, so Anna had no choice but to take the evening goods train. Feeling already exhausted with her rather contrary and tiresome daughter, it was a long and tedious trip with regular stops and shunting of wagons along the way.

Arriving into Charters Towers in the early hours of the morning, Anna called a taxi, a rather obliging Mr. McDonald, who informed her during their conversation, that he had two daughters, Pam and Judith attending Blackheath College as day girls and highly recommended the school as the best for girls in The Towers.

Off-loaded at the prearranged address, a house belonging to Mrs. Carrington, Anna found the key, let herself in, and braced for the next task ahead in preparing her daughter for admission to her pre-enrolled Anglican boarding school of St. Gabriel's.

Later while downtown doing pre-school shopping, Anna spoke with numerous mothers with daughters being fitted out for school uniforms, and all who again recommended Blackheath College as the preferred option for young girls.

Although co-educational with Thornburgh Boys College, Blackheath however maintained separate accommodation facilities for the girls. Blackheath was once named 'Yelvatoft,' a grand old lady of notable architecture from by-gone days, was now overseen by a rather formidable and strict headmistress, Miss Jessie Landsberg. Anna needed no further convincing and instead, enrolled Helena at the Presbyterian and Methodist College, graciously embracing its motto, Sine Domino Frusta,' and departed for home.

On St. Patrick's Day in 1967, Paddy Groves, Mrs. Koll's companion of many years, suddenly passed away. It was a sad occasion for many who knew him and remembered him as a jolly and affable plump chap. Paddy was known for his wood-chopping prowess, and he, along with Bill McKean and school teacher Wally Crear had won numerous wood-chopping accolades at the local district shows.

Paddy had been a friend to many and a great fishing mate to even more, especially the children. He was the son of Rosie, who at his birth lived on Weatherboards Station (now Weatherby) near Mt. Molloy, where he and brothers Archie and Shelly grew up as part aboriginal lads. Paddy was laid to rest in the Mossman Cemetery and was greatly missed by all within the Julatten community.

As a neighbour, he had been a great fishing mate to Anna's children.

In July of 1967, Julatten was making headlines in the aviation industry when a Cessna 172, piloted by Bill Forwell[4], came down on the 18th of July somewhere in the mountain range near Mt. Lewis.

Anna was saddened as eight years earlier, Bill Forwell flew a very ill Diana from Laura Station onto Cairns Base Hospital.

Many held out that he and his passengers would be found alive as a massive search was conducted. Many locals, such as Bill Edmonds and Anna, believed that they heard the plane in a particular direction which pointed toward a location behind Julatten within the rainforest ranges, close to Mt. Lewis.

Initially, the countryside was scoured far and wide locally, but the search eventually spread further afield, due to so much confusion and confliction of stories from various local folk.

Just over a year later, by the end of July 1968, the Cessna plane wreckage with three human remains was discovered by a ranger, a comparatively short distance from a road on Mt. Lewis. It was found in the direction and vicinity where some locals had originally postulated it had gone down. It was a sad farewell for Bill Forwell and his passengers, but at least it gave closure to the families of the loved ones lost on that fateful day.

Between 1967 to 1968, Anna juggled her finances, keeping one child at boarding school and preparing for her other two to follow.

Once again, Greg Hobbs stepped in and paved the way to have Johnny enrolled in Abergowrie Agricultural College, an all-boys Catholic boarding school near Ingham.

By now, Johnny was answering to John, and by the time he began his secondary schooling at Abergowrie, Greg and Shirley had returned to Ingham after Greg resigned from teaching.

When Anna relocated to Charters Towers with Diana and Helena to school them as day borders at the Presbyterian and Methodist College of Blackheath, the Hobbs family once more offered support by inviting John from boarding school to stay with them over long weekends. Since his father's passing, John always had to contend with an all-female household.

For some time, until his untimely passing, Greg Hobbs continued to mentor John and provided him with a "father-figure" in his life.

Photograph 303: Bushy Creek State School Julatten students with school teacher Wally Crear circa early 1966. (L-R) back row; Marilyn Clayton, Helena Kanak, Fay Brown, Graham Brown; next row; Elizabeth Pashen, John Kanak, Linda Edmonds (following row) Diana Kanak. David Smith, Gregory Rebetzke, (next row) Verony Whyte, Judith Crear, Mavis Pashen, (next row) Russell Crear, Danny Dayes, Gregory Jenkins, and front row (L-R) Lesley Jenkins, Cheryl Clayton, Warren Brown, and Johnny Pashen.

Photograph 304 & 305: (L-R) Anna with brother Jaroslav Kurovec, Johnny, Diana & Helena in their sport uniforms,1963. Lois Kurovec & Anna with Helena, Diana & Johnny at Newell Beach 1964.

Photograph 306 & 307: (L-R) Anna with children at Helena's Anglican communion 1965. Johnny and Diana at the calf parade Bushy Creek School 1967.

Photograph 308, 309 & 310: (L-R) Diana, John, & Helena, Anna's children at Bushy Creek State School fancy dress ball 1963. (Anna made the girl's costumes).

Photograph 311: Anna's Family portrait, 1966.

CHAPTER 32

Charters Towers: 1969-1972

Following Jan's death, Anna reestablished regular communication with his family in Hošťálková while keeping a steady flow of letters between her own family at Krhová and Lhotka. Although it had been an overwhelming time for her emotionally and financially, she did not burden her family with what was trivial compared to their lives. However, despite her financial hardships, she always put aside some money for them in Czechoslovakia.

Anna regularly received parcels of crocheted tablecloths and doilies lovingly handmade by her mother. As much as Anna appreciated these heart-rendering gestures, she repeatedly urged her mother to save them for her family at home. Anna was acutely aware of how her people struggled with so few commodities available, as most everything they lacked; Anna had a ready supply in Australia. For her Czech family, if any quality luxury goods were available, these were exorbitantly expensive and, for most, could only be purchased with foreign currency.

TUZEX[1] was a chain of state-owned stores in Czechoslovakia that functioned until 1992. Here were sold selected commodities and luxury items only in exchange for foreign currency. With Tuzex or Darex vouchers, it was possible to obtain certain goods, but these vouchers only had a limited use-by-date and could not be re-exchange for foreign currency. So, between sending money and parcels of fabric and anything else Anna deemed unavailable, she tried to lessen their want for some niceties in life.

By now, Anna's grandparents, Jan and Františka Stolař, had passed away, and her younger sisters had all married except Bo. Eliška married Jan Voda and had two children; Dušan and Eliška. Helena married Robert Pavlik, whom Anna knew well from her childhood days and they had a daughter, Růženka. Anna's youngest sister Jarmila married Josef Švec, and they had a son Svatopluk. It was only Bohuslava (Bo) who would remain single.

Anna's oldest sister Zdeňka having married Miloslav Hurtík many years earlier, had four mostly grown-up children, Milosh, Zdeněk, Jarek, and Pavla. All were either married or attending university.

Because of the Political circumstances of the day and her earlier outlawed departure, Anna was regarded as a persona non grata in her home country. For them, she ceased to exist. However, this changed once government bureaucrats needed her signature to sign over the Kurovec property still in her name. Anna was never going to return to her homeland and was relieved when the opportunity presented to pass on the family home to her older sister Zdeňka, albeit now a much-reduced landholding. Sadly, this formal property transfer came at considerable cost to Zdeňka. Regardless, Anna encouraged Zdeňka to plant trees in the old orchard and again sent money to help with this proposed project.

During this period, the question of František Kurovec's buried handgun resurfaced. Anna tried to be helpful, but she pointed out to them, her memory was dulled by the passing of time, and all efforts to locate it proved futile. Perhaps Anna did not want it found and unearthed after all this time, only to regurgitate unpleasant memories which probably were best left buried. In all probability, one day, it will be unearthed and recovered with a metal detector if it has not already rusted away.

While Anna's family continued to exist under stringent constraints in Czechoslovakia, for a while, hope came with Alexander Dubček [2]. Attempting to reform the communist government, President Dubcek presented 'socialism with a human face' by lifting censorship on media and paving the way for what would become known as the Prague Spring. His political career soon ended when the Warsaw Pact invaded the streets of Prague in August 1968. Once again, the rule of communism tightened, and all over again, Anna feared for her family's welfare.

At the beginning of 1969 Anna had already embarked onto another phase in her life when she moved temporarily to Charters

Towers, renting various houses over the next three years while her girls attended Blackheath College and John boarded at St. Theresa's College in Abergowrie near Ingham. Out of necessity, once again, the family became divided so that Anna's children could all have an equal opportunity for a better education. During term semester breaks, they would all return home to Julatten, and for a short time, their lives would resume as normal. But Anna's children were already growing up fast.

For a while, Anna had Ivy and Alec Booth care-take her house in Julatten while they were in limbo about where next to build their new home. This arrangement only lasted for a short time; afterward, Anna preferred to leave her home vacant so she and her family could come and go ad-lib. There was always plenty of work awaiting them whenever they returned home.

In the late 1960s, Charters Towers was transitioning into a modern metropolis. It was a town still dusting off its post-goldrush era with a lingering air of bygone days. Graced with stunning architectural buildings, beautiful Queenslander homes although many in need of repair, and quaint miner's cottages and dwellings, the township, to the casual visitor, appeared like a rustic settlement nestled in a dry, inhospitable bowl of Chonky apple trees surrounded by bare rocky hills.

Most old dwellings still had outside toilets, 'dunnies,' and many of the houses Anna rented at the time were no different with the night-cart man running his weekly service in the early hours of the given day.

Anna still had her husband's dog Kiki, a faithful companion, and where ever Anna went, old Kiki followed close behind. The children had grown up with her, so she was more than just a family pet. Although now an elderly dog, Kiki still attracted various suitors!

Whenever Kiki was 'in season,' Anna would lock her in the toilet for the night, but that did not stop other dogs from hanging about. At one particular rental property the outside toilet had to be entered and attended to through the front door rather than through a rear hatch door. It must have come as an awful shock for the night cart man, if not a horrifying experience, when one night he opened the 'dunny' door, and a dog desperate to get out flew out at him. Anna heard the commotion outside and shuddered but dared not venture out with the ruckus of dogs barking and the poor night cart man cursing. Luckily, he had yet to carry out his task, so his empty hand bucket was probably a handy deterrent to ward off the dogs. Fortunately for Anna, no complaint was lodged, just a note, as at the time, there were no work, place, health, and safety measures in place, nor was it mandatory to have dogs desexed.

By this time, Kiki had matured well into old age. With Anna now living next door to Mr. Knapp, a retired animal veterinarian, he willingly assisted Kiki as she finally transitioned into the next world and joined her master. After a long and adventurous life, Kiki was sadly laid to rest in Charters Towers.

Charters Towers had its own fair share of interesting characters, if not eccentric ones. One old woman, who today would be regarded a national treasure, would be seen in her horse-drawn cart, collecting selective pieces of rubbish as she made the rounds of the streets. She was like a specter who had materialized from another age, generally oblivious of others while she scrounged the streets for any discarded and interesting items. Many kept their distance, and children feared her as she often cursed them while mumbling to herself and her grey horse. She seemed to dwell in a time of past hardship; to many, she was simply known either as the 'Bag or Rag Lady'. While Mrs. Gerty Patterson trolled the streets of Charters Towers, on the other side of the globe in the USA, on the 20th of July 1969, a man was about to put foot on the moon. This irony would best be summed up in Reg Lindsey's song, 'Armstrong,' a soliloquy when the world awakened from its ephemeral existence and was propelled into a new age of rapid technological advancement and achievement.

During April of 1970, when the British Royals toured and partook in Australia's Bi-centenary Celebrations, they arrived in Townsville as a part of their itinerary. Anna was proud when John and a few other local recipients received their 'Duke of Edinburgh Award' from the duke himself. Anna owed a deep gratitude to Greg and Shirley Hobbs for mentoring him while at Abergowrie and opening his eyes to the possibility of such personal achievement.

Anna's stay in Charters Towers was enriching, making new friends and acquaintances through Mrs. Ivy Carrington's introductions. Ivy Carrington was Rob Whelan's mother, a lasting family connection from Anna's Laura days. Anna appreciated this connection as it introduced her to local grazing families with whom she found employment cleaning their homes on a rotational basis. Anna was always a willing worker, and although humbled by their apparent cattle grazing status, she was extended friendship as she struck a chord with these country folk.

Anna was well-read and had a great interest in pioneering history. These people were a part of that history, and by the time she left Charters Towers, Anna was well-versed in many of their ancestral backgrounds. During her domestic work in Charters Towers, Anna worked for Dr. Jock Allingham and his wife, Lorna, from Fletcher Vale Station. Anna was always in awe of his family's pioneering history and WWII service, one which she could relate to as a subsequence of her own war experiences. She also worked for Shirley Symes from Merricourt Station and Betty Webb from Victoria Downs Station. All these women offered affectionate comradery, and Anna was never left feeling lesser of a person in their presence.

At the time, Thea Shadforth, for whom Anna also worked, became one of her special confidants and friends. Thea was one of three sisters, the other two being Norma and Verna, daughters of the late Walter Lawrence, who once owned Wrotham Park near Chillagoe and, together with other eminent graziers of his time, helped to pioneer the Braham cattle industry in North Queensland. Thea and her husband, George Shadforth, owned Slogan Downs Station, and here once a week, Anna helped Thea with her housework.

Once while polishing Thea's silver on the eve of the 1971 Melbourne Cup, Anna had a premonition that the horse Silver Knight would win the prestigious race. But unfortunately, no bets were placed as Anna did not gamble. Anna did have one passion, and that was attending auctions and bidding for affordable antiques and bric-a-brac. Whenever she had spare money to spend on herself, she would browse through old second-hand shops or attend one of Dungavell's auctions in Charters Towers to see if she could buy a bargain. She once returned home with an old adjustable wooden armchair that had been auctioned, and she the winning bidder. This particular armchair allegedly once graced a boardroom somewhere within or near the old Stock Exchange and was supposed to be of some significance, being perhaps even the chairman's chair. This was all supposition, of course, but shortly after acquiring it, some interested parties approached her, but Anna refused to part with her newly acquired treasure. During this time in Charters Towers, many old period buildings were not all heritage listed. This would happen later when the town's rich history grew to become a recognized and valuable state asset.

Through Helena's school friend Dallas, both attending Blackheath, Anna met Frances and Hillman Isaacs. Dallas' father, Hilly, worked for the railways, and his irregular hours while driving trains often created absences from home, so it often left Frae, as Frances was known, at the helm. Anna was most grateful when during holiday breaks and on certain weekends, Frances invited Helena to join Dallas on a short vacation to Magnetic Island and on other occasions, excursions to Ravenswood. The township was some 40km over a dusty and gravel road inland from Mingella, a small settlement on the main highway in an eastly direction from Charters Towers.

While in Ravenswood, Frae visited her sister Grace and family, and the girls explored the township. Later in the evening they attended the local dance with friends. These trips often coincided with dances that were prevalent in isolated bush towns enabling young locals to gather and be entertained with others living scattered throughout the district.

Ravenswood, nestled in the arid savannah landscape, was surrounded by disused mine shafts, interspersed with Chonky apple bushes, and languished in its past glory as a mining town. Although, at the time, self-proclaimed mayor Percy Keen tried to keep its golden dream alive, its heady days as a gold mining town were well and truly over. However, the town's turn of the 19th century architectural facades still graced the dusty streets, while numerous miner's cottages scattered within the township were practically obscured by the prickly overgrowth of abundant Chonky apple shrubs.

When the Burdekin Dam to the south of Ravenswood was completed in 1987, the township received a boost, followed by the resurgence of gold mining which injected a new flow of hope into the area. Today Ravenswood is linked by a sealed road to the outside world.

Apart from occasional classroom pranks that tended to overshadow Anna's daughters' scholastic achievements, Anna had an overall satisfactory relationship with the boarding school and had admirable respect for head mistress Jessie Landsberg.

After the school's speech night in 1971, a number of the graduating students were invited to have their final hurrah, a get-together at the Dallas' home. Frae, Dallas's mother oversaw the occasion, and all was above board while the boys and girls enjoyed themselves. The next day Anna was reproached by someone who actually did not have all the facts, and claimed that her daughter and others were responsible for inviting certain students to the get together without parental permission thus, defying school rules. Anna was disheartened by such trivial nonsense that was totally baseless and untrue. Anna held her silence about it throughout the years and it was only much later that Helena learnt about her alleged misdemeanor that night.

When Helena finished at Blackheath College, Diana became unsettled at the school. Eventually, by the end of 1972, Anna enrolled Diana to board at the Anglican school of St. Ann's, now known as The Cathedral School in Townsville. Thus, Anna's time in Charters Towers ended, and she returned home to Julatten. However, Anna remained in touch with Frae and Hilly Isaacs, and on several occasions, they visited her in Julatten.

Photograph 312 Anna's sisters post-war; Eliška & Jan Voda.

Photograph 313: Helena & Robert Pavlik.

Photograph 314 & 315: (L-R) Anna's sister Bohuslava Kurovcová. Diana & Anna at Charters Towers show 1968.

Photograph 316: Adele Koll, Anna, Louie Nohl & sister Sophie, & Diana 1968.

Photograph 317: Anna with Ivy Booth at Julatten 1969.

Photograph 318: Anna's sister Jarmila & Josef Švec with their son Svätopluk.

Photograph 319: Anna's grandparents Frantiska & Jan Stolař 15th August 1953.

Photograph 320: Hillman, Dallas & Frances Isaacs in Auckland NZ 1975.

CHAPTER 33

Anna Returns Home to Julatten

During 1973, Anna returned to work at Mt. Kooyong in Julatten. Many things had changed at her old work place, but it was still forging along as an aged-care home. As some of the previous staff still remained, Anna fitted in once more, as if she had never left the place.

With her two younger children still at boarding school and Helena now finding independence with work in the bank, Anna still had to earn and save scrupulously to pay for her children's education. She had more time to herself, her garden, and her growing menagerie of animals, but also still had to contend with annual floods and unwanted nightly visits from pythons raiding her hen house. Somehow, she managed to ward off all these obstacles and persevere on.

During one particular wet season, Anna was working a series of night shifts at Mt. Kooyong. Whenever Bushy Creek flooded, it spread water over a considerable flood plain that cut off farms and homes, and without exception, Mt. Kooyong. One evening just as the floods were subsiding, Anna was abruptly awoken at home by Keitha Alcorn coming to recover 'the body' so it could be immediately dispatched to the mortuary in Mareeba. Anna stared back blankly in shock, if not horror, as she was certainly not harbouring any dead bodies in her home! Not being put off, Keitha's growing irritation and impatience persisted as she pressed for answers.

"Well, Dearie! The body is supposed to be here with you! Where is it, then?" Anna had no idea.

Keitha grew flustered as behind her, the impatient undertakers were breathing down her neck, needing to retrieve the missing body as soon as possible. Finally, Nevil was located and called upon as he was the last person known to have been with the wrapped corpse when he was instructed to load it on board the tractor and cross the rising creek near Mt. Kooyong. Nevil later admitted he wasn't game to deliver the body to Anna's house as instructed, knowing full well Anna would not entertain such a notion and he 'sure as hell' was not spending the night with the corpse in his house. In his wisdom, without time to inform anyone; he placed it safely in the Community Hall just a short distance from Mt. Kooyong, reasoning it was at least partly on its way to Mareeba even if not quite making it as far as Anna's place.

In December of 1974, Anna received a letter sent by Josef Hikel from Krhová, who was known to Anna's sister Eliška. At the time, Josef was visiting his son in California and promised to relay a message to Anna from her family. Surprisingly none of Anna's family had received any letters from her in the past six years! Josef suspected her mail had been intercepted, and all her family in Krhová and Lhotka were anxious about her.

It was distressing news for Anna as, unbeknown to both sides, they were caught up in some sort of bureaucratic censorship, that left neither party knowing what was going on. Anna had always been meticulous with her letters, not to be political, or overly critical of anyone as she suspected any suspicious innuendos could become problematic for her family at home. After receiving the letter from Josef Hikel Anna wrote again to her family and hoped she would reconnect with them.

In 1975, while Diana was preparing for a career in nursing, she needed to apply for a copy of her birth certificate. Her original certificate lay lost amongst Anna's letters and documents and could not be located in time for Diana's nursing application. A copy ultimately arrived but revealed what Anna had probably been dreading all along; a record of step-sister Milada Violet Kanak, whose existence, so far, had been concealed from Anna's children. Oddly, Violet's name had not appeared on Helena's nor John's South Australian birth certificates; it was only recorded on Diana's Queensland birth document. It had not been a deliberate act on Anna's part to conceal this evidence, in as much she was only honouring a pact she had made with her late husband, who many years before agreed to tell his children about Violet when they were old enough to understand. After his death, Anna believed the matter would never arise again.

While she tried to explain the situation to Diana, in NZ, Margaret Lewis was equally surprised that Helena was ignorant of her step-sister and was busy pacifying Helena giving her reasonable excuses for this grave omission. It would be many years later, in 1983, when John and Helena visited Hošťálková, that their aunt, Jan's sister Anna Syptáková, more than happily furnished them with her ex-sister-in-law Elsie Carter's address details. She encouraged them at the time to contact Elsie in Great Britain. This intrusion, as Anna perceived it to be, would ultimately create much consternation between the two sisters-in-law!

In July of 1975, Adele Koll, Anna's long-time neighbour, and friend who had been ill for some time, passed away. Anna had divided much of her time between caring for Adele and working at Mt. Kooyong. As sad as it was, Adele had already suffered considerable discomfort before finally agreeing to be transferred to Mareeba hospital where she passed away.

Endel, Mrs. Koll's only son, was an eccentric old chap who lived a hermit-like existence in the rainforest. He was a dedicated miner, scratching for wolfram in the hills near Mt. Perseverance, and despite his isolation, he was still very well-read and well-versed with prices of metals and ores on the commodity's market.

Endel wrote regular letters to Anna and John, often lengthy and difficult to decipher, describing the current market and how money was to be made in mining and that perhaps John should be encouraged to take an interest. Some months after Adele's death, Endel Koll was ready to finalize his mother's estate and sell her house. He had no desire to maintain a home in the community for his own purpose, so Anna made him an offer. He declined her offer because she already owned a house! He did, however, agree to sell it to Helena and John. With Anna's assistance, the purchase was made, and from there on, Anna took charge of renting the house and, subsequently, its own share of equally eccentric, if not unconventional, tenants.

Julatten had become a hub of diverse lifestyle dwellers, all blending into the community in one way or another. The region seemed to attract an eclectic array of identities; from artistic, alternate, neurotic, and indifferent, to actresses and folk from aristocratic backgrounds like one Lady Selina... and even years later; additional Lords and Ladies, mostly all genuine people seeking more peaceful, if not a self-sufficient and productive existence. Amongst them also were drop-outs of society who sought refuge from conventional responsibility. Living in this pure mountain air and often concealed in the rain forest from neighbours, some of these folk sought to live out their alternative lifestyle in a manner that often bought them to the attention of vigilant police. And some of Anna's tenants were no different!

Anna had one endearing young couple who rented next door, and although they led a rather questionable, if not unconventional lifestyle, they were friendly and respectful to Anna.

One day they came to ask permission to host a party for their friends and extended an invitation to Anna out of politeness. They no doubt expected Anna to decline politely, but instead, out of curtsey, Anna accepted. Anna later recalled that, at the time, she felt genuinely sorry for the couple's impoverished circumstances. On her arrival they were all seated on the floor in a circle, sharing one cigarette. She said she could not have partaken as there was so very little of the 'cigarette' left to go around, and at the time, wished she had a packet of cigarettes to give them.

One of Anna's more eminent tenants were Hungarians Jozsef and Anna Balogh. Anna Balogh also worked at Mt. Kooyong as an assistant nurse, while Jozsef whiled away time dedicated to his life of art. Jozsef Balogh [1] was a Hungarian portrait artist of some accomplishment. Although he had been commissioned to paint high-profile figures such as Queen Julianna of the Netherlands, horse trainer Bart Cummings, and cricketer Greg Chappel, to name a few, he and his wife Anna were always short of money. His acclaim as an artist never soared to grand heights, and for most of the time that Anna knew them, they seemed down on their luck and struggling financially.

Although some of Jozsef's art had been acquired by the then-visiting Shah of Iran and his entourage, he and Anna Balogh only ever managed to save enough money for boat trips abroad of short duration, taking along their Combi Van to explore some exotic country that would inspire Jozsef to paint.

Occasionally, they would contact Anna for a loan to assist their passage back to Australia. But whenever finances became too tight for them, Jozsef would trade Anna some of his art as repayment for his debt. Anna enjoyed art and was always willing to oblige as she regarded his works of reputable standard and hoped one day he would be recognized as a great Australian artist. Jozsef had often asked Anna to sit for him, but she never desired a portrait of herself… Shame she did not ask her children's opinion.

After many years of financial mismanagement, failed ventures lacking funds to sustain outlandish fads, and Keitha Alcorn's failure to heed the advice of her board directors, Mt. Kooyong's fate was finally sealed, and it was all over. It was heartbreaking for Keitha and her fellow staff after so many years of well-intentioned hard work and sacrifice. On the 29th of August 1975, Mt. Kooyong, with its 'Koorawatha Foundation' now insolvent, went to auction and was sold. It was a heavy blow to a community of local workers who needed to go elsewhere for employment. But Mt. Kooyong would rise again from the ashes of Keitha's failed dreams and become yet again a Nursing Home for the Aged.

Keitha Alcorn finally returned to New Zealand, where she received recognition for accomplishments in services to her community and receive the 1990 Commemoration Medal from then minister for Health Helen Clark [2].

In the latter part of 1975, John bought a Mini Moke and taught his mother to drive. Anna's life was about to be set in motion on wheels as she grasped the art of driving and finally, with confident independence, broadened her navigational horizons.

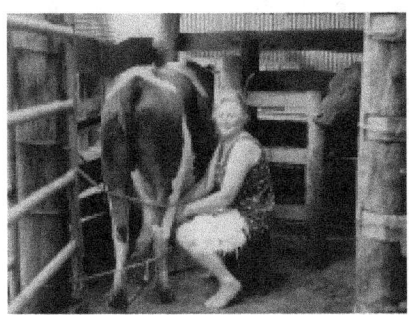 

Photograph 321 & 322: (L-R) Anna milking her cows at Julatten. Anna with her growing cattle herd at Julatten.

Photograph 323 & 324: (L-R) Anna having time out with her geese and chickens at Julatten. Bushy Creek in flood with water around Anna's house.

Photograph 325 & 326: (L-R) Anna's home at Julatten. Anna with her crop of Lychees in her backyard.

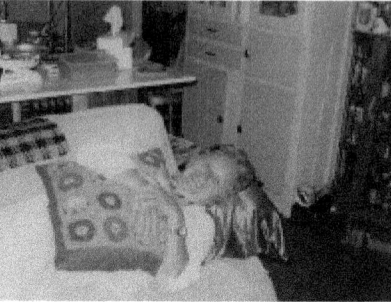

Photograph 327 & 328: (L-R) Anna with her Mini Minor at Julatten. Rest time for Anna at home.

Photograph 329: Anna holding kitten Mish-Mish, with Korky the cockatoo at home in Julatten.

Photograph 330: Anna with John and Helena at Cairns airport 1983, the year her children visited CSSR.

CHAPTER 34

Anna's Life After Mt. Kooyong: 1976-1997

From nursing, Anna turned her hand to cooking and worked in hotels owned by Olive and Harvey Keys in Millaa-Millaa and Judy and Jeff Baldry in Mt. Molloy. By now, Anna was mobile, and her driving opened up new opportunities outside of Julatten.

Anna became quite proficient at driving and, in 1976, bought a Mini-Minor car and finally began to drive further afield from Mareeba. She was always a cautious and courteous driver and would help anyone side-lined by the roadside. Her courtesy even extended to the local policeman trying to conceal himself from roadside traffic to set up his radar speeding trap. He was none too pleased when she pulled up next to him, offering her assistance!

One of Anna's more memorable trips from Millaa-Millaa while working for Olive and Harvey Keys at their hotel was when she called into Kairi and purchased some laying hens. These poor creatures had been housed in cages, so initially they were not very mobile. She placed her half dozen hens into hessian bags, gently tying them together in pairs to each other's leg, and left the hens sitting loosely in their bags in the rear seat of her car. During her trip, Anna stopped briefly in Mareeba at Tobacco Growers to buy a few things. She parked her car at the rear of the store near the railway line and left the windows partially opened for ventilation. While paying at the cash register, Anna noticed a crowd gathering in the car park, all amused by something happening outside. The cause of the commotion soon became apparent when Anna caught sight of six dazed hens toddling off on their newly found legs and heading along the rail tracks. Unfazed by all the fuss, Anna herded them back together and returned her feathered crew into the car. Anna could always laugh at her shortcomings and was never one to dwell on embarrassment for too long.

With Anna's girls living away from home, working and independent, John was still completing his degree in civil engineering at Rockhampton Institute of Technology. By now, Anna had more time to dwell on her own interests and pursue with her hobby farm, adding beef cows to her little dairy herd. Initially, Anna started with two dairy cows she bought from Bill Jorgenson to provide herself and her friends with fresh milk.

Having become well acquainted with Doreen and Charlie Wallace since their earlier arrival in the mid-1960s, Anna also became friends with their daughter Joyce Ahlers from Maitland Downs. Before long, Anna purchased the occasional Droughtmaster heifer to add to her herd. It was an interest and a hobby for Anna, never destined to make money.

During the early 1980s, while John was still living at home after graduating in engineering and working at Mt. Carbine, Anna received a call from Erland and Marjory Erlandson from the Darling Downs. They had been her late husband's friends, with whom Anna had maintained contact since Jan's passing, if only annual Christmas cards. In all that time, Anna had never met them, and now she could finally speak with them face to face. The Erlandsons had been on a brief holiday to Cairns and invited Anna and John to dinner. Anna was in a quandary... It was already the wet season and raining, and her Mini Minor was being repaired. They only had the open-air Mini-Moke as their means of travel, and there was no hint that John might even suggest taking her down to Cairns on his motorbike. In the end, she and John devised an ingenious plan. Early in the afternoon, they drove to Cairns in the open-air Mini Moke, and soaked to the bone, they changed into dry evening clothes at the airport, where they left the vehicle before catching a taxi into the city. They all met and had an enjoyable dinner with the Erlandsons, and afterward that evening, Anna and John returned by taxi to the airport and drove back home to Julatten in the Mini-Moke. Anna always found a way to overcome obstacles.

At the time, Anna had an engaging and sincere family living briefly next door: Norm and Paddy Howsan and their four children, Robin, Wayne, Tanya and Cherry. Norm was mining tin near Mt. Lewis then, and Paddy kept herself busy with handy crafts, needlework, and general sewing. One day Paddy rushed to Anna's place in a terrified state, reporting she had a snake inside her house. Anna was never one to be perturbed by these reptiles and immediately came to her rescue, but in doing so, she was bitten by it. After disposing of the snake, and with Paddy in total apoplexy on account of Anna being bitten, Anna tried to coax Paddy to drive them both to Mareeba hospital for medical attention. Paddy, pale and shaken by the ordeal, could not trust herself at the wheel, so Anna drove them both into town.

In the Hospital, Anna was examined by the doctor, and it was recommended that she stay under observation and overnight in the ward. With Paddy still trembling and distressed by the snake saga and no staff around, Anna quietly discharged herself and drove Paddy back home to Julatten. In the end, it was pointless returning to the hospital.

Anna and her late husband had been both politically savvy. They both supported the conservative political party and throughout Jan's life in Australia he had only known Bob Menzies as Australia's Prime Minister. Sir Robert G. Menzies served his second time as PM of Australia from 1949 to 1966 after which he resigned and was succeeded by Harold Holt. Although Anna always voted Liberal National, any Politician regardless of persuasion was not beyond her scrutiny, especially those with extreme left and socialist views. These she would label racketeers and add, "Gather them all together in a sack bag and drop them in the middle of Moscow… and then they will know what communism is all about!"

Unashamedly Anna supported the National Party, becoming a member and throughout her voting life, always presented on election day to hand out for her local member and enjoy some light hearted argy-bargy with locals of opposing views.

During one political campaign in Julatten, Anna met with Premier Sir Joh Bjelke-Petersen and his wife Florence who later became Senator Flo. Anna's most memorable moment during this function was chatting with Flo, exchanging pumpkin scone recipes, which, no doubt at the time, Anna would have had her own scones provided with coffee and tea for the occasion.

Anna was always willing to help, and nothing ever seemed to inconvenience her. She once received a visit from a blond woman bespectacled in large dark sunglasses who came looking for cement to finish a job on her property along Black Mountain Road. As they rummaged together through Anna's shed, Anna was sure she knew this woman from somewhere.

Finally, she asked, "I am sure I know you from somewhere?"

Diane Cilento lifted her sunglasses and introduced herself.

Some years later, when Diane Cilento's Karnak Playhouse was established in Whyanbeel near Mossman, Anna used to get numerous phone calls enquiring about bookings for Karnak. In the days before the internet and web pages, your fingers walked through the telephone directory. Kanak came before Karnak, and in the end, Anna kept the appropriate phone number handy and politely passed it on to the enquirer. Anna never needed to be annoyed. She often had lengthy chats with the people on the other end of the line before they continued their inquiry on the correct number.

Anna had many offbeat occurrences, no more unorthodox when riding in a rocking chair on the back of an open utility truck. During the early 1990s, Anna's daughters returned to live and work closer to home. The girls shared a house recently built at Pebbly Beach; at which time it was sparsely furnished. Anna was always keen to help out with furniture she had accumulated over the years from auctions, and after restoring the pieces, these often cluttered her house. One such item was an old rocking chair with reupholstered cushions, which she considered would make a useful piece of furniture for her girls. She arranged with her good friend and helper Cherry Pashen to deliver it from Julatten to Pebbly Beach, a distance of some 40 km via the Rex Range. Anna was always pedantic with her furniture and, in this instance, horrified Cherry when she insisted on sitting in the rocker to ensure it did not fall off, even though securely tied down in the Toyota tray-back! It went without saying the trip to Pebbly Beach was slow, if not overwhelming for Cherry, with an elderly lady perched on a rocking chair out in the open. A rather tense and near embarrassing moment occurred when a police car passed them. The poor chap was probably so dumbfounded and caught unaware to act decisively. No doubt he would have imagined he had just seen old granny from 'The Clampetts' (An American Hill Billy show) in her rocking chair cruising by. Thankfully, Anna and Cherry arrived at their destination unhindered or apprehended.

In 1988 Endel Koll passed away, and some years later, in 1997, a letter arrived addressed to Anna from the Estonian Baptist Mission Church. These people were trying to contact Endel, Adele's son. It was an intriguing letter informing Anna that a 'pot of treasure' consisting of sixteenth-seventeenth and eighteenth-century gold and silver artifacts had been unearthed on the Koll family farm in Estonia. The befuddled enquirers had received confusing information from another local source in Julatten suggesting Mrs. Koll had come from Ethiopia. Anna duly notified them of Endel's passing and suggested that the treasure trove remained in Estonia as she was sure Adele and Endel would have wished for that.

Many decades later, and after Anna's passing, interest in Adele's life would re-emerge. This time, historians from Palamuse Museum in Estonia arrived in Julatten to research Adele's life in Australia. Adele Koll née Pärtelpoeg was none other than the muse for Estonia's acclaimed novelist Oskar Luts, whose character Raja Teele in his novel 'Kevade,' which translated means 'Spring', was based on Adele.

In 1977 John and Helena visited the family property in Laura for the first time since their father passed away. From there onward, whenever Anna's children returned home on holiday, camping trips to Laura together became a special time for her. Anna was an outdoor person who loved to head for the bush, camp outdoors, and relive memories. From 1986 through to 1994, Anna made numerous trips back to Laura with her children, visiting places that, while she lived there, she never had the opportunity to see.

Much had remained the same in Laura during her first trip back in 1986. The pub and shop still fronted onto a dusty road, but now it had a school and medical clinic, and many of the natives once living in a camp down on the Laura River were now housed in town. The old railway station was long gone, but the old goods shed was still standing at the time. It, too, would later be abandoned and removed. During this visit, Anna met up with an old local identity, Scotty, and together they sat under the mango tree in front of the pub and over a beer and some pies reminisced about the good old times. Another curious resident, a tame but rather plucky emu, snooped about circling the table, trying to snatch a pie from anybody who was not being overly vigilant.

In 1989, Anna returned again, but this time joined her children on their first trip to Maytown, travelling from Laura down the Laura-Maytown Coach Road track. At the top of the ridge, a smaller side track detoured from the main one and descended sharpy down a notoriously narrow and stair-like passage which was a rough and steep cut-out once used by teamsters and their drays headed for Maytown in the Palmer Goldfields. Now this rough piece of terrain is only used by 4x4 enthusiasts. Anna and her family challenged this bumpy and steep track that took hours to traverse a relatively short distance down to Maytown on the Palmer River. By late afternoon after a hot and gruelling journey travelled at a snail's pace, they finally set up camp on the Palmer River and, all alone in the wilderness, spent a memorable night camping under the stars.

Anna loved entertainment, and anything classical was always a great favourite. Her favourite singing artist was Jim Reeves, and his many songs always reminded her of days spent with Jan. She also enjoyed ballet. Still, in earlier times, such cultural entertainment was rarely seen in Australia's far north. However, when ballet dancer Eileen Fifield appeared in Innisfail, Anna made sure she attended.

Anna and Olive Keys once received complimentary tickets to attend Des O'Connor's concert in Cairns. Through Anna's family, Des arranged tickets for her and a friend to attend his performance, but unbeknown to Anna at the time, he had anticipated meeting her. Unfortunately, this meeting did not eventuate, as once the concert was over, Anna and Olive did not remain behind to meet with the entertainer as many others would have. He was very popular with the older 'blue rinse set.'

Anna's then son-in-law Robert, was a keen music buff but not the type of music Anna viewed to her liking. However, he had a heart of gold where animals were concerned as his wife could vouch for the destitute strays he collected and brought home. He was a city lad but Anna's animal menagerie amused him.

Anna had a healthy and happy brood of chickens, regular layers maintaining her in a steady supply of eggs. In his wisdom Robert decided to rearrange all the nesting boxes until all the hens became anxious and flustered and refused to lay. He pointed out to Anna the reason her hens refused to lay was because they were unhappy, they should each have a rooster of their own to make them happy.

Anna looked at him in disbelief... She had heard many suggestions in the past but this one left her astonished.

Anna attended World Expo in Brisbane in August 1988 and invited her old New Zealand nursing colleague Jarmila Bílek to join her. Together they caught the train to Brisbane, and at the invitation of Mr. and Mrs. Ross, Judy Baldry's parents, they spent their stay with them; a gesture that Anna very much appreciated. Anna had been excited and anticipated Expo well in advance, and for the week while she was in Brisbane, she spent every day attending as many venues as possible. For Anna, it was pure fascination, but Jarmila soon tired of it after a day, complaining of sore feet. Anna would not be deterred, and made the most of her cultural enlightenment with or without Jarmila.

By now, vast changes were happening on the other side of the globe.

Soviet leader Mikhail Gorbachev[1] introduced 'Glasnost' (openness) and 'Perestroika (restructuring and modernizing), and with the fallout of the 1986 Chornobyl nuclear plant disaster, the regime of the old United Soviet Socialist Republic (USSR) finally began to crumble. With the Berlin Wall and the 'Iron Curtain' collapsing, all eastern bloc countries under USSR constraint were finally experiencing freedom and with their release, the USSR ceased to be, eventually becoming Russia. In November of 1989, the Velvet Revolution[2] of the then Czechoslovak Socialist Republic (CSSR) became a nonviolent transitioning of power to the newly elected government of Czechoslovakia, under President Václav Havel[3].

With the age-old disharmony between the Czech and Slovak nations, a dissolution of Czechoslovakia[4] occurred in December of 1992, dubbed as the 'Velvet Divorce' giving the now Czech Republic and Slovakia, each an autonomous independence of government but still remaining unified. At long last, Anna could telephone her family and talk. This became a regular occurrence, often emotionally charged with lengthy chatter with her sisters. They were now free to say whatever they wanted. Still, due to these lengthy personal calls overloaded with emotional chatter, important family matters were often overlooked, so Anna continued to follow up with lengthy letters. For the Czech people, it might have been a quantum leap into the 21st Century with the younger generations embracing democracy, but for the older generation, it was a huge adjustment from being cared for, no matter how frugally in the past, to adjust to financial independence. The older generations themselves could not any longer achieve the aspirations of youth they had been denied so long ago, instead it was now for the young people to embrace. Many older folk admitted their vulnerability, admitting they preferred the security of communism.

In 1993, Anna returned to Laura yet again, assisting her children with fencing the eastern boundary of her property after National Parks and Olive Vale Station fenced off the northern and western portions along her border. Anna was in her element during these trips, and while she travelled in the front of the old Toyota tray-back with John, the girls braved the elements in the back. During this period, Anna received a letter and subsequent visits from Bronwyn Gilham, whose father, Hugh Cowper, once owned the Laura block. It was interesting to shed light on its past history, even if it spelled hardship and sadness for the Cowper family, who had settled on the property in 1946. Hugh Cowper attempted growing tobacco, but it brought no sustainable income for the family as distance over rough roads to transport tobacco to markets was a contributing factor. Consequently, the family did not remain long as hard work for such little gain, and family pressures became detrimental to their existence. In the end, the family walked off the property. They left behind infrastructure that had long disappeared when Jan bought the place in 1961.

On the 3rd of June 1992, The Mabo judgment was brought down in Australia, a significant decision giving Eddie Mabo[5] and his people native title over the Murray Islands in the Torres Strait. For those observing from a distance, it was almost fait accompli as these people had a continuous, if not uninterrupted, association with their islands both culturally and traditionally. In early 1993 Anna received notice of a pending native land claim on Lakefield National Park, including the Cliff

Islands in Princess Charlotte Bay. Along with the Native claimants, all owners of neighbouring properties were invited to partake in the process. At the time, except for Marina Plains at the mouth of the Annie River, all previous grazing leases, including Bizant, Breeza Plains, Lakefield, and Laura Stations, were now all part of Lakefield National Park. Shortly afterward, Louie Komsic from Marina Plains would have his own battle to contend with, an outcome that seemed predetermined even before the process began and one which did not go in his favour. Bordering the eastern boundary of Lakefield National Park at the time were grazing leases of Birthday Plains, Kalpowar, Jack Lakes, Mount Jack, Battle Camp, and Escort Creek, and on the western boundary, other grazing leases of Olive Vale Station, Koolburra, Morehead, Mary Valley, Artemis, Violet Vale, and Lily Vale, including Anna's northern property boundary which touched onto the park, thus making them all common neighbours with Lakefield National Park.

A historical stock route once used by northern graziers ran from the now-declared National Park through Anna's property and beyond to the Laura River. Anna was a small fish in terms of land size, but she had one consolation, her land was freehold, but the stock route of no determined title other than crown land was her major concern at the time. Everyone bordering on the national park had concerns regarding how this native title determination would ultimately impact them. Major concerns with any national park were the containment of feral pigs, invasive weeds, fires, and general straying cattle secreted within these parklands. If unchecked, these roaming animals could contract and spread tuberculous, creating a costly pandemic for nearby grazing properties. With the native title, it was feared it would just add another layer of bureaucracy in controlling outbreaks of disease, pests and weeds.

When the proceedings began in Cooktown, about twelve entities, including Anna, were party to the process apart from the scores of claimants from family and tribal groups, all claiming their right to the land. Most were familiar local family names, but numerous others came from places where their ancestors had moved to in more recent times. The tribunal disallowed any legal representation at the table during hearings for those party to the claim except for the native claimants themselves. The native claimants were well represented by knowledgeable anthropologists, those savvy with the legal system, and bureaucrats. The Tribunal hearing began in Cooktown on 11th January 1994 and would move from place to place within the national park over the course of time, finalizing in Brisbane. Initially, the claim was based on traditional affiliation and historical association rather than economic or cultural viability. However, without the other two considerations, it would have left little or no option to show how the native people would manage this land. Their Proposed Management Plan was to be presented at the tribunal hearing before their claim.

It took over twenty-nine days to accomplish, no doubt an expensive burden for the taxpayers; an exercise to determine something that soon became apparent to those present; was a foregone conclusion with or without their input. It was time-consuming for all others, apart from the claimants and their paid representatives, as most invited participants could only leave their work for a short while to attend and sit about listening to witnesses, giving evidence of proof of their entitlement.

For Anna and Helena, it was sufficiently expensive just flying back and forth from Cairns to Cooktown on the occasions required of them. The road into Cooktown and beyond was unsealed, and it took several hours to get there. When the Tribunal hearing moved onto Bizant and Breeza outstations, it became ludicrous for Anna to contemplate attending. It would have been a long overland journey and even more expensive to charter a plane for the exercise. Besides Anna's immediate concern, the stock route, was no longer the topic of consideration, and whatever else transpired in discussions further afield was well out of Anna's domain. However, there still remained an expectation that once signed to the process as an interested party, it was up to Anna to follow it through and remain involved throughout the process regardless of no benefit while the claimants pursued with their claims further afield.

Some tribunal members even advocated that Anna be removed from the list of interested parties due to her perceived lack of interest!

Traditional affiliation and historical association with this land may have been significantly addressed. Still, when it came to economic or cultural viability, no rational plans were put forward at the time so there was no avenue for grazier's input to contribute to the outcome. For those party to the process, bigger issues were carefully circumvented in the proceedings such as the long-term recreational use of the national parks under native title. Until then, National Parks were less restrictive, with free camping and fishing accessibility.

Although some who were party to the process wanted to be included in the future management of Lakefield National Park, no offers at the time seemed forthcoming. As it transpired, at the outcome of the Tribunal, the unfulfilled promises that nothing would change for white men accessing Lakefield National Park were, in the end, either diluted or eventually forgotten. Moreover, it was only the beginning of things to come, as gradually, other native title claims began to roll out over the Cape.

Any cohesion between the claimants and those invested in the economic development of the Cape (be it tourism, mining, or grazing) would become fractured, with many eventually realizing their worst nightmare; rigid negotiations between tribes becoming a lengthy and convoluted process, albeit costly and laced with a minefield of bureaucratic red tape.

With Cook Shire's rate base significantly eroded by newly created national parks throughout the Cape, now mostly under native title, little consideration had been given at the time to who would become financially responsible for road maintenance, upkeep, and accessibility. Would it be the taxpayer?

Ultimately much would rest with National Parks and Wild Life to maintain upkeep, which depended on taxpayer funding. Throughout this process, recreational freedom of movement that was once taken for granted; had become eroded for mainstream campers and fishermen, except for those entitled under legislation and many significant areas became accessible only by the claimants themselves. It was a sad time for many, as native claimants were pitted against white folk, many of whom had been on friendly terms for years and, in some cases, even related. One poignant moment was when a well-known elder and friend to many, the now late Jack Harrigan, approached Anna and Helena, extended his hand in apology for the animosity this land tribunal hearing had created, and even divided so many who once had been friends of long standing.

"I am so sorry it has come to this, but I hope we can still be friends."

His plea was a genuine apology on behalf of his people. He also hinted that the whole process was not of their instigation but rather by those who were employed to act on their behalf. Anna and others received an 'avalanche of material,' as Pamela Dickenson, Anna's solicitor at the time, so eloquently put it. Their requests for submissions, a mere formality, in the end, came to nothing.

For many who were party to this Native Land Tribunal, it was no more than a charade, a one-sided hearing which whitewashed concerns and diluted promises. During scheduled sittings in Brisbane between the 21st to the 24th of November 1994, and with all submissions presented and considered, an inconsequential verdict was returned to those party to the process (other than the claimants);

"Will not suffer any detriment as a result of the land grant, as Aboriginal land"[6].

Nobody in the first instance ever begrudged these people acknowledgment of lands that their ancestors once roamed and their need to be custodians to protect certain cultural heritage sites. It was an acceptable proposal. But, to claim large swathes of land much of which seemed abandoned by the claimants when so many tribes had migrated toward established centres for whatever purpose, did not constitute in the views of many, a continual and uninterrupted association with this country. Instead, it left the non-claimants nervous and apprehensive of what might be in store for them in the future.

Without full disclosure of their proposed intent for all these claims, and the way the tribunal hurriedly conducted itself without transparency in favour of one group and blindsiding the other, it began to create a wedge of suspicion between the parties. At the time, there had been no official preparatory consultation between tribunal representatives and participating minor parties to prepare for the process ahead. For those, except the native claimants, it was an undertaking at the table without legal representation for the minor parties.

All Tribunal proposals could only be heard and addressed with expert assistance and instructions from supporting sources present, but it failed to accommodate the invited non-indigenous participants with the same rights and assistance at the table during these hearings.

Had the approach to handing down this legislation been more conciliatory, bipartisan, and transparent; for those later seeking to negotiate deals with various tribes, it may have averted many future delays and costly pitfalls.

In the end, Anna's stock route remained unaffected. Although she had applied to have it closed, it was refused, and so the stock route remained.

Today this inessential stock route originating somewhere within the National Park and still traversing her land is of little or no purpose to anyone else, except to Anna, although not hers to claim.

Eventually, it had to be fenced off to prevent livestock from entering the National Park.

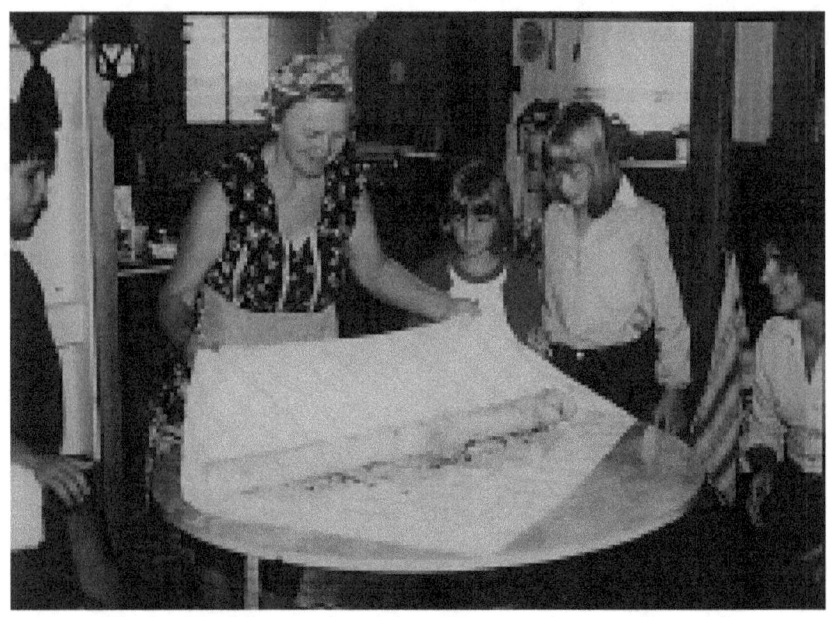

Photograph 331: Anna demonstrates how to make an apple strudel.

Photograph 332: Anna preparing noodles.

Photograph 333 & 334: (L-R) Anna at home for Christmas 1988. Anna at home with Leo.

Photograph 335 & 336: (L-R) Anna with family & her Kurovec nephews & family. Anna with Josepf and Anna Balogh and their cat Marchart.

Photograph 337 & 338: (L-R) Aerial view of Anna's Julatten property at the centre of the picture. Anna at home in Julatten.

Photograph 339 & 340: (L-R) Anna with her friend Margaret Lewis from NZ in 1988. Anna & NZ friend Jarmila Bílek 1988.

Photograph 341, 342 & 343: (L-R)Anna with Judy Novak 1992. Anna enjoying a night out at "Going Bananas" Mossman, 1988. Diana and Anna in Laura 1986.

Photograph 344: Anna in Laura with Diana and Helena 1986.

Photograph 345 & 346: (L-R) Anna in Laura 1986.
Anna, Helena & John with Scotty at Laura Pub 1983.

Photograph 347 & 348: (L-R) Fencing on Anna's Laura Property 1994.
Laura railway goods shed still standing in 1988.

Photograph 349 & 350: (L-R) Old timber house on Anna's property on McIvor River.
Anna, John & Diana on Grassy Hill Cooktown.

Photograph 351 & 352: (L-R) Anna with Judy Baldry in the 1970s.
A few drinks at the Mt. Carbine Pub post-March 1990 Federal election; Anna and Helena with Marie (Handley) Reynolds.

Photograph 353 & 354: (L-R) Anna at home, deep in conversation, 1992.
John's graduation in Rockhampton with Anna & Diana 1978.

Photograph 355: Anna in her garden in Julatten 1992.

Photograph 356: John, Diana, Anna & Helena at Pier 319 Port Douglas 1985.

Photograph 357: (L-R) Anna, Diana & John seeing Helena off at the Cairns International airport 1985.

Photograph 358: Robyn, Paddy Howsan, Tanya, Anna Kanak, Cherie & Wayne Howsan in Julatten early 1980s.

Photograph 359: Anna with her daughter Helena 2003.

Photograph 360: Anna's children Diana, Helena & John in Laura 1986.

Photograph 361: Kurovec Family Port Lincoln; Shaun, Vladimir, Lois (their mother) & Jaryn.

CHAPTER 35

Anna's Life Full-circle: 1998-2008

Anna had remained self-sufficient throughout her life and no more so than when her children grew up, and she, once again, took up gardening with great gusto and passion. She always maintained a garden growing vegetables and herbs, always fresh from the earth to her table. She was passionate about flowers that she propagated and grew in abundance, and she always proudly displayed her magnificent blooms for visitors. She had green fingers and could bring a plant back from near extinction.

She created her nursery where she nurtured many plants, ferns, and orchids, some exotic, unusual, and even rare.

For a while, she propagated from seed, native Black Bean, and Karri Pine plants and grew them abundantly for the local council to plant. She had these trees growing on her property and felt it was a shame that after each year, so many seeds were wasted in nature and rarely produced seedlings. At heart, Anna was a conservationist and did her bit to green her little piece of earth.

Along with her flora came fauna, and she was especially fond of sulpha-crested cockatoos, not so much those in the wild but more so those rescued and domesticated.

She had inherited one such bird from a situation where his presence in suburbia was no longer acceptable due to his disorderly behaviour! She later reared another featherless fledgling, becoming its mother and mentor as the tiny creature imprinted on her. Cocky, as he was simply named, learned to talk albeit with an accent and grew into quite a character. He was a great watchdog, sharing his place with a gaggle of geese that kept vigilant surveillance of the yard.

A visitor once called out to Anna from the front gate and was answered with a simple "Hello!"

The chap called out again, only to be greeted with the same "Hello".

Eventually, the voice added, "Want a cupa tea?"

Believing it must be Anna somewhere in the garden, he was startled when asked, "You like Cocky?"

He soon discovered he was conversing with a bird before Anna finally emerged from beyond her garden.

Anna was a foodie, even before the actual term gained popularity, and she loved to cook and eat what she made. Cooking may have begun out of necessity, but it soon became a lifelong passion in which she excelled. Everyone who visited was often met with delightful aromas from her kitchen, and she never failed to reward her guests with culinary delights over a cup of tea. Her cuisine read like a menu from a Michelin-star restaurant.

Anna's taste in food was Eurocentric as she enjoyed cooking Czech recipes and other eastern European dishes, including Italian. Beside her jar of pickled gherkins always stood bottles of olives to complement her pasta dishes, homemade pizzas, and lasagnes. Anna's signature dishes probably stemmed from her preferred taste for Czech food as she became known for her Apple strudel, sweet steamed apricot dumplings, apricot or plum jam buns, Moravian potato salad, apple pie, and a variety of goulashes and soups accompanied by homemade noodles and savory dumplings. She also made excellent brawn (a cold-cut terrine) and mastered the art of pumpkin scones.

Despite her exotic tastes, Anna embraced bacon, eggs, and steak, often treating her children with crumbed veal and fried crumbed cauliflower. But, above all, Anna loved to entertain, and whenever her children were home, she would put on a BBQ, supply all the meat and salads, and invite the neighbourhood for a night out. Although she provided some beverages, the guests were always recommended to bring their own. Anna did not drink, but socially on such occasions, she would dabble in a shandy. Only on rarer occasions did she take a tipple of Slivovice; in this case, a homemade plum brandy, with which her Czech family kept her in stock.

Christmas lunch was never celebrated without additional guests, some of whom had nowhere else to dine, and graciously accepted Anna's invitation. Anna's cooking rarely saw disaster or embarrassment. However, on one occasion, when the children were still young, she anticipated a visit from Bernie Voerman from Red Rocks Nursery in Mareeba. He was passing through and delivering some plants for her, so for afternoon tea, Anna proceeded to bake buns. Young Johnny, fancying doing some cooking of his own, mixed up a concoction of laying mash, shell grit, secretly an egg or two, and with added water, made a stodgy mixture which he asked his mum to bake as a treat for Kiki the dog. When Bernie arrived, Anna's kitchen was filled with the wafting aroma of freshly baked buns sitting on the window sill, cooling. Over a cup of tea and a plate of unusual biscuits sitting in the middle of the table, Bernie picked up a hard cracker. He bit into it, politely commenting on its unusual texture and taste. Horrified and embarrassed, Anna could not apologize enough for her oversight and her son's least appetizing biscuits!

One culinary delight Anna relished in and rarely shared with her family, was pickled herrings; definitely an acquired taste.

Toward the end of March, just before Easter in 1998, Anna became nostalgic about her past and announced to her family that on Sunday, the 29th of March, she would be celebrating fifty years since leaving her home country during Easter Monday the 29th of March, 1948.

Previously, Anna had been restrained about her past and rarely spoke to her children of the war years as those days seemed no longer relevant. She had been more motivated by the present and future. However, on this day, she finally unburdened her shackles of the past. She allowed her nostalgia to flow freely as she began to bring up her past and reminisce about her last years at home before finally escaping with Jan (later her husband) and Domin Červenec. Their sudden and hurried departure late on Easter Monday evening of 1948 had become the axis of her unfolding saga.

After some cajoling, Anna agreed to an interview by the Cairns Post, and a short narrative with photographs appeared in the paper on the 4th of April 1998. Shortly afterward, Anna received a phone call from Colleen Ingold, who lived at Wongaling near Mission Beach. She had seen the photograph and Anna's story in the Cairns Post and had forwarded it to her Czech friends in Wollongong, who she thought might be interested, as they, too, had escaped Czechoslovakia after the war.

When Walter and Alena Herrmann saw her picture, Alena, after a thoughtful pause, said, "I know this lady!"

Walter agreed, and both remembered where they knew her from. Some fifty years onward, Anna's face still remained etched into their memories that to that day, they still recognized her. The Herrmanns used to see her several times a day in the children's kitchen at Ludwigsburg refugee camp Germany in 1948. At the time, Walter and Alena had a babe in arms; their daughter Christine and Anna would give Alena extra sustenance for the baby. Although they did not know one another by name then, images remained firmly imprinted and so began a new chapter in Anna's life.

After finally reunited, Alena and Anna agreed to an interview with Fiona Sharpe Wright from the Cairns Post newspaper. Their story was printed with their photograph on the 26th of August 1998, but the occasion was to have an even stranger twist to it. Alena Herrmann and Colleen Ingold and their house model Angela had a long association from their younger days working together in a boutique in Wollongong. They had lost contact with Angela over the years, but throughout the interview, Fiona was bothered by the familiarity of the Herrmann name. Further questioning revealed that Fiona was Angela's daughter, and serendipitously, Anna's daughters knew Angela from working with her at Cairns Hospital. From there onward, every year until 2008, Alena and Walter would visit Anna and relive their lives through these precious passages of past times.

In 2000, Anna had yet another surprise visit. This time it was her youngest sister Jarmila and great-niece Kaťka, granddaughter to their brother Vladimír who in 1945 died tragically in Mauthausen, just before the end of WWII. Once again, the Cairns Post featured Anna, but this time with her sister Jarmila as they were reunited at the Cairns airport after fifty-two years. Although Anna and Jarmila had much catching-up to do, it was a very young Jarmila that Anna remembered and left behind, as much of Anna's growing-up years had been shared with her older sisters.

In 2002, Jarmila returned to Australia yet again but did not visit Anna this time. Instead, Jarmila sent their sister Helena to Cairns alone, who was about to accompany Jarmila on a tour to New Zealand. Sisters Anna and Helena were both distraught with Jarmila's insensitive arrangement; a reunion anticipated all their lives to be reduced to only one overnight stay. Sensibly, Jarmila remained in Brisbane, awaiting Helena's return the following day.

Although it was to be a memorable, if not heart-wrenching, reunion for the now elderly sisters, it nevertheless caused great consternation that their youngest sister Jarmila could plan the trip to only suit herself and be indifferent to the other two. For Anna, this was an unforgivable folly.

Helena assured Anna she would have preferred to remain with her rather than trapesing around New Zealand with Jarmila, in a country she neither had a connection with nor needed to visit.

Despite their short reunion, Helena and Anna stayed up all night reminiscing, weeping, hugging, and holding onto what precious little time together they had been granted. Both realized it would be their only and last opportunity to ever see one another during their life time. It was a fleeting encounter that neither would have traded for anything else in the world; a once-in-a-lifetime reunion that they both had waited so long for after so many years apart, but sadly cut short.

Anna had always been well-read and had a life subscription to 'National Geographic,' a monthly magazine where she gleaned interesting facts about places in the world and enjoyed discussing these with visitors. She read many classic novels, none more pleasing than 'Seven Little Australians' by Ethel Turner, identifying well with a large family living through happiness, tragedy, and sadness.

She also enjoyed Iain Douglas-Hamilton's books on African wildlife. However, one of her favourite authors was Frank G Slaughter, once a practicing American surgeon who turned into a novelist, writing about medical science intrigue. Anna would read anything that came her way, albeit even controversial material such as 'The Little Red Schoolbook' that had been banned in Queensland in 1972 and which she managed to obtain a copy of. Its material may have been risqué, but tame compared to what school children are exposed to today.

Although Anna's spoken English always carried a heavy accent, her comprehension, and reading were exceptional. Anna had studied Latin at school, so words with Latin roots were often easily deciphered. After all, all catholic services had once been performed in Latin.

Years before, when Indonesia had gained a bloodless post-war independence from the Dutch and its subsequent invasion in 1962 with the Dutch's expulsion from West Papua; (now known as Iran Jaya), this conflict was a little too close to Australian shores for comfort. With Indonesia's strenuous opposition to the Federation of Malaysia in 1963 and President Sukarno's support of the Communist Party of Indonesia, it became an unnerving prospect to many Australians having communism so close to their doorstep[1]. Anna was no exception. After all, she had escaped one Communist regime only to be within cooee of another. Her primary consideration was always her family, and she even contemplated applying to migrate to Canada! However, in the interim, she decided to learn Indonesian and took a correspondence course.

After Papua New Guinea gained independence from Australia in 1975, calm prevailed, and no further invasion seemed imminent. Thus, Anna's enthusiasm for Indonesian eventually waned, her tutorials folded, and she redirected her energy elsewhere. She was becoming a woman prepared for all seasons.

Her children were never angelic, and Anna had her share of anxious and disciplinary moments, as all parents do with their children. The three often waged backyard scuffles in varying combinations of two against one, but their life was generally free of any rigid constraints, and with so much outdoor space they were active and spent much of their time fishing and exploring the nearby creek. Their scrapes and falls from trees, bikes, and horses and later motor bikes; sometimes they learnt the hard way with the odd broken arm or leg requiring hospital treatment. It nevertheless taught them resilience and pay heed to the dangers outside the parameters of their home and their mother's constant bothering about them.

The children had plenty of imagination and were curious, drawn to the outdoors rather than indoor activities and played well together without too much need for added interaction from visiting neighbourhood children.

The night sky always held a fascination for them, trying to spot the rare satellite or falling star. While briefly in Mareeba hospital during 1965, John told his mother how a thoughtful young nurse piggy-backed him outside so he could see the comet that was visible at the time. It was probably Comet Ikeya-Seki, but in those days, all comets sighted were generally mistaken for the fabled Halley's Comet.

Anna readily had premonitions, like when Helena and Diana attended a Blackheath and Thornburgh Reunion in Charters Towers in about 1973. As Anna was to be in Mareeba on the day in question, she specifically asked Mary Blain at the Julatten Post Office exchange to redirect any phone calls to her friend's place in town.

When the phone call arrived at Frantz and Lina Latenza's place that her daughters had been in a minor vehicle prang, Anna was prepared for the phone call and news. Frantz and Lina remember it being very uncanny.

Anna quietly prided herself on her children as they grew into responsible adults, and each individually carving out a niche in their lives. They had not always remained geographically close, but she always knew where they were, and she never had cause to fear that they would bring shame, although, on numerous occasions, she did not necessarily always agree with their ideas and plans.

Anna only had one regret: she was never given grandchildren. On numerous occasions she certainly babysat many of their much-loved 'fur babies', but it was never quite the same looking after animals as one's own grandchildren. Maybe, it was her fault for instilling into them the resolute idea that there was so much more to life with the world at their feet rather than settling down too early. Anna had seen her world even if blazoned by war and afterward not in the most appealing of circumstances, but she was grateful her children had been spared this anguish of war, never needing to suffer her experiences. Still, she always desired her children to broaden their horizons and encouraged them to travel and experience life and see for themselves what a lucky country Australia was and never forget their fortunate upbringing.

Anna maintained contact with her sisters, nephews and nieces, and in-laws in the Czech Republic but more so with her brother Jaroslav's family in Australia. With her Australian relatives, Anna had more immediate social contact. Her nephews, Vladimir (Vladge), Jaroslav (Jaryn), and Shaun, visited her at different times with their families.

When Jaryn and Tanya had daughters Heidi, Zoe, and Whitney, Anna took a keen interest and had special affection for her great nieces and similarly great nephews Isaac, Aaron, and Liam; Shaun and Annette's children. After all, they were her closest and strongest blood link to her Kurovec family. Anna had contributed to her ancestral tree, yet her offspring failed to generate new buds for future generations so the Kanak ancestral branch slowly withered. However, the Kurovec name continues to thrive in Australia, and at the time of writing this, Anna would have been proud to add great-great nephews and nieces to her ancestral line.

For most of her life, Anna remained healthy, and apart from minor health hiccups during her later years, Anna experienced only one major health alert. Still, once diagnosed and treated, she successfully overcame it. During this period, she had a wonderful haematologist she held in high esteem. Whenever she had her follow-up visits, he would become a regular recipient of her home-grown albeit frozen ducks, a gesture of gratitude for his caring bedside manner. All her life, Anna had been happier to give rather than receive.

In 2006, Anna declared she would hang up her work boots and retire. She had already accumulated ninety years of living, and from there on, she relied more than ever on close friends; Cherrie, Betty, and mainly Kate, and her own family to help her. On the 23rd of October in 2008, Anna passed away, and her ashes, as she wished, were interred with her husband Jan in the Mossman cemetery. She did not want any part of them to be returned to her homeland. Father Mia McSweeney, who had been a close friend to Diana and Helena during their nursing days, presided over Anna's funeral.

At last, Anna's journey had come full circle.

Photograph 362 & 363: (L-R) Diana & Helena.
Anna with Helena Diana & John, Cairns Family Xmas 1999.

Photograph 364: Diana, Helena, Anna, Jarmila, and Kaťka
ready to visit Green Island in 2000.

Photograph 365: Helena, Anna, and her sister Jarmila Švecová at Archer Point
near Cooktown 2000.

Photograph 366 & 367: (L-R) Helena's 50th Birthday 2003. Margaret Lewis' son Michael with Anna & Diana 2007.

Photograph 368: Anna with Alena & Walter Herrmann, Colleen Ingold (centre) & Helena 2003.

Photograph 369: Anna's great nieces Heidi, Zoe & Whitney Kurovec.

Photograph 370: Anna's great nephews Aaron, Liam & Isaac Kurovec. Courtesy Kurovec Family.

Photograph 371: Anna in John's shed with John & Max and watchdog Gearbox the turkey 2004.

Photograph 372: John Kanak, Anna's son in Charters Towers 2014.

Photograph 373: Jan and Anna's final resting place in Mossman Cemetery. RIP.

Photograph 374: Adel Koll's headstone in Mareeba Cemetery. RIP.

Jan Kaňák's Citation 2005.

A Tree Without Branches: Anna's Journey

Epilogue

While living abroad I desired to write but I did not pursue this notion too seriously. I dabbled in poetry, wrote a few essays; all unpublished, except for a small article for a UK Travel magazine, coincidentally about my first visit to Czechoslovakia.

Once I returned home to Australia, I finally found my writing mojo and rather ambitiously, my writing journey was to be initiated with the rather dubious task of attempting to pen a memoir; none other, than my mother's story!

Throughout writing my mother's memoir, I was for most, overwhelmed with the scope of it all, but also too easily side tracked by my lack of total trust in my ability to commit to such an undertaking. Hence, I found time to write several shorter fictious stories that better suited my preferred genre.

Often on these totally unrelated and misguided writing trajectories in midst of more fanciful ideas, my conscience would draw me time and time again, back to my mother and I realized it was my procrastination that failed to advance me over this inevitable chasm I had created between her story and my ability to complete it.

Excuses, such as waiting for an impetus from some higher power to outdo my many frivolous distractions was not something that miraculously happens but inadvertently the COVID-19 pandemic did help. It reminded me just how fragile life really was here on earth, and here, there was no room for procrastination, but instead, seriously get on with projects before it became too late. Besides I had already done so much work and research on my mother's life that it would have been a shame to shelve it all.

Having returned to my much-overdue project, over 12 years had passed since my mother's death. My initial excuse to myself, that I must first get over the grief of losing a mother and allow things to rest for a while, was beginning to spell apathy on my part. With such passing of time, enthusiasm can often wane and to pick up from where I had left off prior to her death, I would now need to become more objective as I only had what I earlier had amassed from our many conversations. However, this latent approach to completing my mother's memoir did have some compensations; namely it allowed me time to access and read through some of her private papers and letters which I had not done before.

When I finally resumed writing the memoir, it brought new meanings to each chapter I had compiled from past conversations with my mother, and where previous revelations had exposed new aspects of her life which she occasionally dismissed or even failed to acknowledge as significant, these often brushed-aside bits of information, together with more recently unearthed material began to marry together and create a fresh start to her life's narrative.

As growing children, the life we shared with our mother was far removed from the never spoken tragedies left behind in Czechoslovakia. There was never any comprehension on our part what our mother went through after the war just to be here in Australia.

For Anna, the price of freedom bore many unpleasant memories which had been stifled and not spoken about, as initially, there was never a need or an opportunity to share them with anyone close to her.

In the early 1960's living and rearing a family in an unfamiliar country where small communities although welcoming, some still could harbour indifferent attitudes toward foreigners.

Having survived WWII barely two decades before, memories were still raw for many and foreign names immediately singled out families as being different and coming from Europe, whether they be refugees or past enemies.

This was further highlighted by Anna's thick foreign accent whenever communicating in broken English and which could often be difficult to understand.

It would always be challenging for Anna especially now that she was a widow with only her children to comfort her.

However, Anna herself was not about to surrender to such trivial adversity and instead strived to push aside obstacles until she was accepted as an equal amongst her peers.

At home, our lives were rich in family values; though not always appreciated at the time, all we ever wanted to be, were ordinary Australian kids, eating Australian food, speaking Australian, and being accepted as one of them despite our differing backgrounds.

We often felt that our mother was far too un-Australian, strict, and unyielding with us. Whenever she publicly redressed us in Czech, people would stop, stare, and whisper, which was the ultimate humiliation and embarrassment that set us apart.

Although financially poor, we were never starved of food, clothing, or shelter, nor were we deprived of our mother's constant surveillance and protection. On the contrary, our mother protectively over saw all our needs and constantly reminded us the importance of a good education and instilled values that taught us; that personal achievement can only come through personal endeavour, hard work, and not granted as a free meal ticket on a silver platter.

However, nobody outside our family encouraged us to speak Czech or even hinted that being bilingual was an asset or indeed a privilege.

It was discouraged at school, as our teacher felt inadequate whenever my brother and sister conversed.

In the school ground there were the usual intermittent scuffles as we tried to assert acceptance and recognition within our peer groups. Still, the cruel impact of ill-spoken words far outweighed any physical pain, mainly when it was directed at our family. Playing in the schoolyard, we were often at the brunt of discriminatory teasing inflicted by innocent children, ignorant of the unintentional hurt it may have caused.

Intentional or unintentional verbal discourse generally originated within families, and what children repeated in the schoolyard was only what had been heard at home.

Once during John's very early schooling days, he awoke during the night sobbing in floods of tears. Anna, thinking her son was ill, consoled him as he spilled out his misery and told her that one of the children told him' "Mumma Kanak is a silly old cow!" Anna was upset that such school yard nonsense could be so detrimental to the psyche of a small child.

This acute isolation separating us from an already established network of school yard comradery would often contribute to self-deprecation and shame that can only be identified by those in similar circumstances where Australian society is punctuated with migrant families trying to assimilate against negative attitudes.

We all just wanted to be ordinary Australian kids, but burdened with these perceived obstacles, we still managed to have a happy and productive childhood and integrated unscathed into the community during our growing years.

As I muddled through her recollections and collections of conversations in the forms of numerous taped recordings, scribbled notes on scraps of paper, and later her Czech letters, I tried to refine Anna's story to the best possible outcome.... the truth.

Ultimately in the end, I had to accept that no memoir can never accurately or completely portray a life without the input from the subject. To rely totally on someone else's memory for an account of another's life often loses credibility and authenticity, but sadly, all too often, that is the only option.

Regrettably, many of us leave the recording of family history until far too late. To consciously allow for family time and listen to our elders is all too often delayed or forgotten, with the notion that they will be there tomorrow. Sadly, for many of us, such opportunities never return.

I made several visits to my mother's ancestral homeland; twice at the height of communist occupation, during which time foreign visitors were few and often monitored with interest; and subsequently additional visits upon the fall of the 'Iron Curtain' in 1989-90, heralding the collapse of the communist USSR and its hold over the Eastern Bloc countries. From there on visits to the Czech Republic were no longer intimidating but embraced all visitors as in any global democracy.

Regardless of this reformation, my mother still maintained a deep seeded mistrust and always feared for our safety whenever we visited her homeland.

Epilogue

My mother's family were religious Catholics, so questions regarding our beliefs and practices were often on the table for discussion during which time, I always had to tread diplomatically and with impartial tact, depending on which branch of the family I was with. At home in Australia, we were a mixture of non-practicing Catholics and Anglicans, and our upbringing was not necessarily shaped by any one particular religious doctrine.

During earlier family discussions in Czechoslovakia, we were often overwhelmed with the many questions directed at us, and due to our lack of full comprehension of the spoken Czech language, their responses to our quizzing, were often lost in translation and not always fully understood or remembered by us with any certain clarity.

We were always regarded as the lucky relatives from Australia, so whenever I began to delve into my mother's past, I was often met with chagrin comments from my generation;

"Why do you want to dig about in the past? We care nothing of it. We only look to the future!"

Even though I had sufficient conversation Czech to get by while questioning family about my mother's life, I still needed a better language understanding in order to gain their trust and cooperation, so as to reassure them that I was only searching for answers to my mother's past and ancestry and not seeking out any long-lost inheritance.

My mother's past, for most, had remained closely guarded for many years, and much of it was never spoken about. Therefore, there was always reluctance from her family to discuss war-time activities but instead focus on their happier childhood memories. All else remained buried.

However, Uncle Robert Pavlik was an exception. He was more open, and in English readily imparted a wealth of knowledge about the war years and his personal experiences.

During these visits to Czechoslovakia and later the Czech Republic, I began to sense a touch of snobbery, subtle jealousy, and underlying suspicion amongst some of the family as I received varying accounts of family life. Even though my mother never spoke ill of anyone, subtle hints of sibling rivalry, suspicion, and jealousy, and occasionally divisions within the family, albeit unacceptance of new members, and circumstances at the cost of fortunes gained or lost, all played into the theatre of their lives. I may have unintentionally rattled a few skeletons in the closet, bearing secrets close to their hearts. Still, I soon realized my mother's family was no different from any other.

My mother's siblings were a mixed bunch of personalities. Her elder sister Zdeňka had married early and acceptably, to a school teacher. She, in many ways, was like my mother, kind, considerate, and jovial, with a great sense of humour.

Their brother Vladimir, having died young, was deemed to have married outside family expectations, and hence there grew a divide that had to be subtly negotiated to avoid needless discourse.

The other brother Jaroslav, chose an Australian wife, albeit of German ancestry. However, this was deemed an acceptable marriage and as a result, Lois remained an enigma, as nobody had ever met her until well after her husband's death.

Sister Bohuslava, or 'Bo' as she preferred to be called, never married. Nobody seemed ever good enough for her, and she was probably the most judgmental of all the siblings. Nevertheless, she always made it her business to monitor all family matters closely and kept my mother constantly updated. Whether there was bias in her family reports or just clever manipulation, I think my mother knew her well enough to be able to read between the lines.

Eliška was also distanced from most of the family soon after she married, and excuses were always made why we should not visit her family.

The youngest of the family, Jarmila, had probably made the right choice, married a man of questionable business connections according to some family sources, and lived sufficiently distanced not to become too embroiled in most family issues.

Helena, the second youngest sister, remained close to the heart of family life and married a WWII veteran, Robert Pavlik who was quite a few years older than herself and one who had been well acquainted with the Kurovec family. Their only daughter, my cousin Růženka was mainly raised by her grandmother, her father's mother, as both her parents had to work. She always maintained her grandmother as her real family, even though she was extremely close to her father. Her mother, Helena, and my mother were probably the most intimate of all sisters and, in many ways, similar. What land they owned they would never sell regardless how desperate the circumstances may have been. In later years, after Helena's husband passed away, she became even more reluctant to sell her home for a more practical existence.

Helena was incredibly proud of her daughter and her many achievements, but their relationship was often complex, as it can be between mothers and daughters. For example, Helena would invariably overrule her daughter's medical advice and instead seek and follow the 'medical opinion' from her Catholic Priest, a stubborn trait of independence that seems to run deeply in the Kurovec family. However, these 'blessed opinions' were probably not the best medical remedies for her numerous aliments.

Although Helena's ancestral farmhouse once belonged to great-grandfather Stolař, it had now been extensively renovated by Růženka and her husband, Lumír. Despite vastly improved renovations, Růženka always feared for their safety. Her mother lit the downstairs corridors with burning candles to shine a path for her deceased husband and ancestors. In addition, Helena's rigid and unwaning Catholic Faith often created more division than cohesion.

Of all of my mother's sisters, Helena was probably the aunt I mostly gravitated toward. Despite her constant anxiety and worrying about things she had no control over, Helena could never relax long enough and smell the roses, no matter how calm the waters were. However, whenever I visited, her constant fussing and preoccupation with me kept her mind from other things. I appreciated that her life must have been one emotional rollercoaster ride.

Their cousin Marta lived well away from the Kurovec epicentre of disquiet. She was a refined woman who took no sides but kept in contact with her cousins, and rarely contributed to the palaver of family intrigue. Moreover, she was the daughter of a Kurovec who succeeded in life, whereas her cousins were the product of lost fortunes who had to make their own way in life. Marta and her cousin Jarmila became close in later years, so no doubt Marta would have been updated with all the latest hurly-burly of events within the Kurovec circle. If there was smoke, Jarmila, much like her sister Bo, was all too happy to stoke the fire!

Even though I met all of my mother's sisters and all of my father's sisters I regret never having met any of my grandparents.

My father's mother, grandmother Anna Kaňákova passed away in 1965, two years after my father. They had been close, as mother and only son quite often became.

Upon my father's passing, she had told her family that she had a dream during which Jan visited her to say goodbye. By the time the news of his death filtered from Australia and reached them in Hošťálková, they almost anticipated it.

Initially, the family thought it would have been better not to tell their aged mother about her son's death, but in the end, the elderly mother realized her premonition had been correct.

My mother's mother, Grandmother Rosalie Kurovcová, experienced a similar dream in 1968 when her son Jaroslav passed away in Australia. The family had arrived to deliver the news of his death but did not have the heart to tell her when instead, she informed them she had dreamt her son had visited her. In her dream, she had awoken to see Jarda (as she called him) sitting at the end of her bed. He told her he had come to say goodbye. Sadly, my grandmother passed away in December of 1982, and only eight months before my brother John and I were due on our first visit in 1983. She had so desperately wanted to meet her Australian grandchildren, but her ailing health failed her, and instead, she left several bottles of red wine 'Bull's Blood' to celebrate our arrival.

I learned later that my grandmother had led a sorrowful and lonely existence ever since my grandfather (her husband) died in 1947 and especially after my mother's departure in 1948. Contrary to all assurances my mother had received over the years from her family that Rosalie had been well cared for, it was Zdeňka and her husband Milos who regularly called by to help her. On these occasions, Grandmother would bring out the 'Borůvka Brandy (blueberry brandy), and she and Milos Hurtík would partake in a few drinks, much to his Zdeňka's disdain. During that period, it had been alleged that my grandmother had become quite partial to her brandy. For how long this habit persisted, I do not know, but in reality, it was a tragic way to numb the sorrows of a lifetime, trying to forget the pain and disappointments that must have plagued her as she silently grieved for the life she no longer had. Her loneliness, losses, and heartache must have been overwhelming during her declining years while she silently suffered this cruel twist in fate, a burden she alone had to carry. In some ways, I am relieved that my mother never knew how unhappy and lonely her mother Rosalie had been.

When Rosalie passed away in 1982, she wished to be buried in her Stolař family's crypt in Krhová, not with the Kurovec family. But her daughter Helena had other ideas and, against her mother's wishes, created family division by insisting otherwise. It seemed that even after death, Rosalie's soul could not rest in peace.

In 2000 I met Jarmila, my mother's youngest sibling, when she and Katka, (their great niece and granddaughter to their brother Vladimir), visited my mother in Australia.

By then, Jarmila had severe scoliosis, but this did not deter her from enjoying life, and with her gregarious nature and uninhibited ways, she was always on the go. She surprised my mother, who was quite the opposite; conservative and softly spoken.

In 2004 Jarmila returned yet again to Australia, but this time with her sister Helena. Jarmila chose not to visit Anna but instead dispatched their sister Helena alone to visit her. By then, Helena's husband Robert had passed away two years earlier in 2002, so Jarmila probably managed to coax Helena into travelling with her on the promise of a meeting with their sister Anna.

In late 1974 I went on a working holiday to New Zealand. Before returning to Australia the following year, I spent a month in Auckland with my mother's dear friend Margaret Lewis. While staying with her during February of that year, I received a letter from my sister Diana, who had recently completed secondary school and was preparing to commence nursing in Brisbane. At the time, I, too, had applied to do nursing, but rather in New Zealand than in Australia, and I had been waiting for a response from the New Zealand Nursing Board while I remained in Auckland. Diana explained that she had recently obtained a copy of her birth certificate. To her surprise, it had some additional, information that neither John nor I had on our South Australian birth certificates.

Diana wrote, "Did you know we have a half-sister Milada Violet Kanak?"

Suddenly, my family was not as perfect as I had always believed. My father had passed away eleven years prior, and nothing to arouse such a notion had ever been mentioned or even suspected.

I became upset with the news while Margaret tried to console me;

"Didn't your mother ever tell you?"

In August of 1974, before my New Zealand trip, I received money from my dad's estate and noticed that one of the beneficiaries was a Milada Violet Kanak. I was puzzled at the time by this person and asked my mother who she was. I remembered that my mother acted strangely and was hesitant, so I added, "Is this dad's mother?" although no longer alive, I naively thought she had been a beneficiary.

My mother looked almost relieved and answered, "Yes."

So, in 1974, this opened a can of worms for me. I decided there and then that I would find my half-sister one day. However, it would be almost forty years before achieving this, primarily because my mother discouraged us from delving into my father's past marriage.

I first visited Czechoslovakia with my brother John in the autumn of 1983 while the country was behind the 'Iron Curtain' and under Communist rule. For many years, our mother wanted us to visit her homeland and especially meet her mother, Rosalie Kurovcová. Unfortunately, Grandmother passed away the previous year in December of 1982, only a short time before our arrival. Despite this sad setback, my mother still encouraged us to go, well, at least in the beginning, so hopefully at least we could meet remaining relatives and be introduced to my father's family as well. Our pending arrival became an eagerly anticipated event as news travelled amongst all our Czech relatives, and the fact that we were now living and working in London made our visit all the more eminent. It would be a landmark moment in the lives of my mother's family, as at last, those who remembered her would finally meet two of her Australian children.

Planning our trip from London into any close-by Eastern Bloc country was expected to be easy and manageable. After all, it was only a short distance across the Channel to the continent compared with the travel we had already accomplished. We soon discovered for any Western European traveller, a journey into Eastern Europe was not without its web of unusual requirements and prerequisites. Our preparations involved some unorthodox, time-consuming, and costly outlays compared to most democratic countries we had already visited. For any visa to be granted, we each had to exchange the equivalent of £8 per day, a condition placed on every foreign tourist visiting Czechoslovakia. This was an additional prerequisite to visa costs or any other costs incurred with our rite of passage. Through a Czech firm in London known as Čedok, we negotiated this currency exchange at the low government official rate and, each received money vouchers in Czech Koruna equivalent for our specified length of proposed visit. This transaction would validate our visa on date of entry and be strictly adhered to on our departure date to ensure we did not overstay in Czechoslovakia.

In Great Britain in the early 1980s, the money we handed to Čedok was a costly amount for any young traveller on a shoestring budget. But, in the end, we had little to show for it except the privilege of being allowed to visit and stay in our mother's country. Czech Koruna could not buy much for young travellers except food from local stores.

As the time neared for departure, I began having scary dreams and reservations, not made any easier by concerned and cautioning letters from Mum, who was starting to have latent regrets about encouraging us to go. As an extra consideration, we had been advised by the Australian Embassy in London not to travel alone but rather in a tour group. We were cautioned that group travel would be safer. Still, if we insisted on travelling there independently, we were reminded that there was no Australian Embassy or Consulate in Prague, only a British Embassy but with no guarantee of assistance to Australians in the event of unexpected difficulties. The closest Australian Embassy was in Vienna, which wasn't encouraging as Austria was on the other side of the 'Iron Curtain.' However, if worse came to worst, our only alternative would be to liaise with the British Embassy in Prague and perhaps they could provide some Consular help or a safety net in the case of any unforeseen trouble.

My father, Jan Kaňák, became a British Subject after WWII when he returned to the UK. He eventually migrated to Australia on a British passport. In 1983 we did not capitalize on our eligibility for dual citizenship as, at the time, we were not contemplating permanent work in the UK. For our proposed travel to Czechoslovakia at that time, any organized tours were out of the question. In contrast, the possibility of applying for special leave from a tour group to attend family reunions would have been untenable due to restricted tour group movements which had to be adhered to. Besides, we already had family arrangements in place, and at the time Czechoslovakia was not exactly on the list of highly desirable tourist destinations.

Unfortunately, during this time many newspapers were flush with reports about attempted escapes out of Czechoslovakia. Those ending in recapture and subjected to retributions made headlines in the both east and the western media outlets. But those who successfully did make it to freedom, their escape generally went unreported in the east with only their families gaining all the attention by the authorities. At the time, I read about a young man I believed to be an engineer who attempted to hot-air balloon across the Czech border, only to be captured. This story made headlines and added to my mother's already anxious predisposition. The fact that this fellow was an engineer touched a raw nerve with my mother, which propelled her into fear overdrive for John.

Once again, she pleaded with us to forget the crazy notion of visiting a country she long ago escaped and suspected had remained unchanged from those days. She feared the worst for us, and nothing could sway her beliefs. She blamed herself wholly for generating our keen interest to follow through with our visit.

I kept a travel diary at the time and left it deliberately in London with my other belongings; money, airline tickets, and personal effects.

Epilogue

On the last page of my journal, I placed an entry, "Should we not return and this comes into your hands, Mother… DO NOT ATTEMPT TO COME TO CSSR YOURSELF; promise me that." Not that she would have heeded such instructions anyway, but looking back, I certainly must have had the jitters about our pending trip.

Rather naively, if not recklessly, I reasoned, "What would anyone want with a nurse who barely speaks Czech and knows nothing of their internal politics? But, on the other hand, maybe John might have been useful as a civil engineer even if he didn't speak the language!" Initially, most of my anxiety was probably due to guilt from disobeying my mother's wishes. It rested on my conscience; "What if she is right?" Our trip to pending doom caused my mother great anguish as her letters and telephone calls continued to show. In hindsight, it was probably an overreaction from all concerned parties because we were headed into a country that was then secreted from most western intelligence. Nobody possessed factual evidence of torture and inhumane treatment of visiting foreign tourists. Finally, it was our selfish and reckless youth with a unanimous resolve to proceed, that played down any notion of harm. After all, there were more dangers in East London, let alone in East Europe.

When I learned much later about my parents' lives and their partisan collaborations during the war, I began to appreciate my mother's fear. She probably had every reason to suspect someone in a dark trench coat lurking in the shadows of Prague's streets, waiting to settle an old score with us on her behalf. Except that Russians were not interested in settling scores on behalf of the Nazis but settling scores regarding her and dad's escape under Russian stewardship, were always going to be the unknown consideration. Some years later before the fall of the Iron Curtain, our cousins, Jaryn and Shaun Kurovec were refused Czech visas on the bases they were both in the Australian Police Force at the time!

Having overcome most foreseeable hurdles, our unanimous decision was to go ahead, so we finally departed London by train for Dover on Saturday, the 1st of October, in the coolness of autumn, leaving behind the bleak and cloudy weather of the London skyline.

Otherwise, 1983 seemed like a good year; Australia had just won the America's Cup for the first time in some 126 years of sailing and 24 challenges, Peter Vizzard won the World Hot Air Balloon Championship at Nantes, France, and Vicki Cardwell took out the Women's World Open Squash Title. But then, we were off to Czechoslovakia for the first time, and would this be a win for us also?

On board the ferry, 'Maria Esmeralda,' the weather remained brisk and windy as we sailed across the Channel toward Oostende in Belgium. Slumped down on the deck with our heavy backpacks stuffed with gifts and covered in Australian paraphernalia resembling a mobile advertisement billboard for 'Oz,' there was no mistaking from where we hailed.

The Channel crossing to Oostende was unremarkable, and we arrived in time to connect with the night train for Munich. Everything was going to plan as all tickets had been pre-booked and paid for with allocated seating. We had planned to travel directly to Nuremberg, but the October Fest seemed too good an opportunity to miss. So, we altered our route and remained on the train heading toward Munich. Our Belgium train conductor happily agreed to our sudden destination changes and said he didn't care where we went as long as we had a ticket for his section of the train journey. He jokingly added that it would be the German conductor's problem to sort out when train staff changed at the border. Belgium seemed accommodating and laid back, but the Germans were another thing, as they were sticklers for routine and order and intolerant of sudden changes. We soon discovered that our friendly Belgium conductor probably had relished the mayhem we were about to cause at the German border, upsetting their strict routine. It did cost us dearly, but to Munich we did go.

Once there, I telephoned Mum and told her that all was well in 'East Germany' and that we would soon be going to Czechoslovakia. Before I realized my error, she gasped in horror, "What are you doing in East Germany?"

I quickly corrected myself, and after a rather lengthy and expensive telephone exchange, I finally convinced her we were both safe in Munich, West Germany.

Failing to locate the Australian contingent at the October Fest, we finally gave up and instead joined the beer-swilling Germans in their great hall. The locals embraced us wholeheartedly, and without understanding German except for "Brust!" we soon swilled and spilled our beer with them. The friendly and jubilant mob continually replenished our beer steins, so we had no choice but to remain joined in camaraderie as we sat, stood, and swayed to robust singing and emptying of mugs on cue. At the same time, an ever-ending encore of celebratory toasts was called. By the end, barely maintaining horizontal posture, we topped our day with a gravity-defying whizz on a roller coaster, leaving us in a state of inebriated exuberance along with tens of thousands who celebrated Oktoberfest on that day. Then, finally, our bodies began to resist all equilibrium and slowly defy gravity.

It had been a cold and dark night if not a disruptive one, from all the post-Octoberfest celebrations, when I finally resurrected my body from one of the most uncomfortable sleeps, I had ever endured at a railway station. The rugged platform in Munich, which served as my bed for the night, was a far cry from the romantic tales of nostalgic train travel. It was an experience I cared never to repeat, as in the small hours of that cold morning, we finally bordered a train heading toward Nuremberg. Even worse, this night train was old and dilapidated, with no seat reservations necessary and with very uncomfortable and hard seating. 'Backpackers' was not a fashionably coined term back then, so to most, we were no better than travelling vagabonds on the road to somewhere.

The night train was full of USA Army personnel on their way to the Augsburg military camp. They seemed a happy group of polite young men, sharing our carriage and filling it with a haze as they sat about smoking and talking. But, unfortunately, some of our fellow German passengers were not as polite. A young army chap protected me from a drunken marauding German who was no doubt headed home but could not refrain from moving in on a defenceless femme fatale.

At Augsburg, we once more waited in the cold before finally embarking on the final leg of our journey to Nuremberg, a trip that had been planned to take place some days before. After this minor diversion and a few days behind schedule, we finally arrived at Nuremberg railway station at 5:00 am on the 3rd of October.

In my unpractised and broken Czech, I telephoned Aunt Helena and explained that today we would depart on the 11:12 am train from Nuremberg to Prague. After some apparent confusion and an uncomfortable pause, followed by a flurry of dialogue beyond my comprehension, I prayed that my message somehow had scraped through. But, how much of my garbled Czech Aunt Helena actually understood remained to be seen, as it left me feeling embarrassed about how deficient I had become in my native tongue. More importantly, would anybody be meeting us in Prague?

Having arrived in Nuremberg early on a Monday morning, we had plenty of time to kill as there was hardly any human activity near the railway station. Instead, we walked via the covered wooden bridge pathway to the close-by park and nibbled on roasted nuts while we sat on a park bench beneath a large oak tree. It was well into Autumn as leaves of red and gold were falling about us. The air had a chill as the misty rain drizzled and dampened us. An older man was walking his dog at a distance, and a few people wearing their all-weather coats walked purposefully across the park. While we sat there in silence, each contemplating one's thoughts, a squirrel appeared from nowhere, ran up my jean-clad leg, and began to help itself to our packet of nuts. We were amazed and fascinated by this beautiful creature as we had never seen a live squirrel before. Its precocious antics kept us amused as the hours dwindled by. We had no idea then that these delightful furry little creatures could carry rabies. Nor did I not for one moment imagine that life in the neighbouring country of Czechoslovakia, yet some distance down the rail track, could be any different from what we had so far experience in mainland Europe.

As we stepped off platform 13 into our carriage, the cold silence and sparsely occupied seats added a sense of foreboding as this trip to Czechoslovakia was fast becoming a reality. I would have been highly relieved if our journey at that point had been unexpectedly cancelled. However, the train finally pulled away from the platform and all uncertainty evaporated out of the window. We were now on our way to Prague, like it or not!

It was not a joyous trip by any means. Our carriage was only sparingly filled with two Belgium students, a Czech couple, ourselves, and a rather sullen old woman who glared at us. No one spoke; we sat uncomfortably in our seats, reluctant to move. It was, indeed, a very silent journey through the beautiful countryside, which finally, after some hours, brought us to the border town of Cheb.

Epilogue

At the border, the train screeched to a stop, and there we remained as if deserted and forgotten, waiting anxiously for what might happen next. There were no announcements, and all the German train crew except the passengers disembarked the train and hurriedly disappeared. We sat like the spectres of long-lost souls staring out the windows of a ghost train destined for trial rather than a holiday.

After some time, a lurch forward jolted us from our idle state, and the train moved slowly forward once more, this time crawling steadily onward as it creaked and screeched over rail tracks hemmed in either side by two high wired fences. At Cheb these two opposing structures were about five metres high and spaced apart by several hundred metres of no man's land. On both sides, this wired barrier was dotted with well-lit looming watch towers, spaced apart at regular intervals. The towers followed the barrier contour as far as the eye could see, eventually shrinking in size as the border fences on both sides disappeared into the distance. At different locations along the border, the height of this electrified double-fenced fortification varied as did the distance of the no-go zone between them; to anywhere from a few hundred metres to several kilometres apart. The no-go zone strip of land was further shielded with concealed land mines, but always overseen by armed guards in the observation towers, well-spaced to cover the entire distance of the country's barrier. Escape through this blockade looked impossible.

I wondered briefly if anyone was actually driving the train as it slipped through no man's land, policed only by those in the high security towers on either side. This seemed to be the only hint of human presence besides us on the train.

Although still mid-afternoon, it felt like darkness had come early, and beyond invisible to the naked eye was the east; for the most part, concealed and only imagined to be a distant and sombre country rarely heard about. Over the lonely stretch of earth that no one seemed to occupy but only observe from tower tops, we slowly proceeded like in a bubble where uncertainty was the only definable emotion—time seemed to have stood still for what felt like eons. While we transited through this hologram of non-existence, we suddenly screeched to a halt. We had pulled up alongside a dimmed and shabby railway station swarming with uniformed personnel, pushing, shoving, and lining up to board the train. The Cheb railway station on the Czech border guarded and monitored all rail entry into Czechoslovakia from the west and vice versa. Once stationary, the train doors swung open, and customs officers, security, and armed soldiers swarmed into the carriages. Their presence terrified and stifled us with their loud and gruff execution of duties. No greetings or introductions; the whole shouting exercise was so surreal that it portrayed a glimpse of life from another era, 50 years in the past, as if we had uninvitingly invaded their space through a time warp and were propelled back into the war years.

Firstly, passports with visas and relevant documents were demanded as immigration officials seized them, leafed through them, casting a cursory glance at the appropriate owners before stamping the page and shoving the documents back at them. Customs officials followed on as passengers were stripped of anything deemed illegal, and promptly confiscating from these hapless travellers, their western magazines, newspapers, and books, while soldiers poked and prodded compartments, cases, and bags, probing beneath seats and making everyone duck and squirm to avoid the brunt of this frenzied rummage. We could only stare in silence, bracing ourselves for what was next to come. There were no pleasantries or apologies, only the deafening commotion of people being interrogated, shouted at, and generally intimidated by this rigorous routine. The old woman who sat opposite us was quite severely reprimanded by one of the immigration officials as she had overstayed her visa in the West. Even though I had disliked her intimidating and sneering presence, I felt sorry that anybody should be treated like a criminal and penalized for what was possibly an unintentional and unavoidable oversight in travel plans.

This confrontation disturbed me, and I shuddered, "Welcome to Czechoslovakia!" While we sat quietly, not appearing to be overly interested but taking in all that was happening in our carriage, we could only dread our turn when the official had finished with the old lady opposite us. The uniformed official finally glared at us and grunted, "Passports!"

He indicated something about our stay, to which I replied in English and to which he gruffly mumbled back in Czech, "Stupid English!"

We were relieved that at least our passports and visas were in order, and the documentation did not hint in any way that we had Czechoslovakian connections or relatives. There had been no need to include our mother's maiden name on our visa application, and with a name like Kanak, it could originate from any part of the world, and we only spoke English. Our passports reaffirmed that we were Australian citizens. I had been reading 'Schindler's Ark' by Thomas Keneally, and on a last-minute impulse, decided to leave the book behind in London and instead brought along a Cleo magazine. When the customs officer approached us, as a cooperative gesture of obedience, I offered him my magazine after having witnessed newspapers and magazines being confiscated from others. He roughly leafed through the pages quickly, and without opening the sealed pages that concealed more provocative images, he found nothing too sexually explicit or politically corruptive and shoved the magazine back at me. Still looking dissatisfied but finding everything in order, he thrust our documents back at us, reiterating audibly in Czech for anybody listening, "Bloody stupid English tourists!"

I smiled politely and thanked him in English. Then, not wanting to draw unwanted attention, I gratefully settled for being a stupid tourist rather than alerting him that I fully understood his derogatory remark.

It seemed like hours detained at the Cheb border while the bureaucratic, time-consuming sabotage went on feverously up and down the train. Then, finally, all went quiet, and every official disembarked. The armed soldiers, two to three a-breast, blocked every passenger exit while the train remained stationary. I could hardly imagine where we would want to escape except make a mad dash back up the rail tracks into Germany.

The remainder of the journey onto Prague took on a lighter mood, including our sullen old lady, whom other Czech passengers had joined. Nevertheless, she glared at us and whispered to the person beside her that the English were dirty and untidy. I almost had a helpless desire to apologize for our state of presentation, but in the end, I bit my tongue, withholding any attempt to communicate with her. Instead, I nudged John and handed him a comb suggesting he go and tidy himself in the toilet closet before we arrived in Prague. My brother always seemed to have a personal aversion to combs, and his hair, although short, often looked spiky and dishevelled.

Moreover, we were both tired and desperately needed sleep. We had already been on the road for over four days since leaving London. When John returned, the old lady looked uncomfortable and embarrassed and offered us apples as an apparent apology. I politely declined, looked away, and left her to swallow the humiliation of underestimating fellow travellers' comprehension of other languages.

Nearing Prague, the evening landscape in the weakening late sun was quite stunning. The heavily forested valleys and mountains of green firs, interspersed with beech and oak trees were already turning on a spectacular hue of Autumn colour. In the distance, amidst swirls of evening mist and smog, more smoke rose from coal-fired indoor burners as the facades of blackened but beautiful old medieval buildings began to seep through the haze.

It was 6:40 pm when we finally came to rest at Prague's central railway station. As we disembarked our diesel train, the smell of coal-fired steam filled the air bringing with it the acrid but sweet nostalgic sense of a bygone era.

For a moment, we froze in awe of a massive green locomotive belching smoke up into the blackened overhead rafters as it propelled forward, drawing power with each laborious effort from its slow and deliberate mighty thud of steam-driven pistons. It was slowly pulling out of the station, spewing steam all over the platform and covering passengers as they eventually re-emerged from its blanket of fog. Enraptured by its presence, we stood mesmerized by the sheer grandeur of this magnificent and enormous locomotive. This was a sight long gone from our industrialized western society. In contrast, here, steam harnessed power still resonated throughout the railway station filling the air with smoke that poured out of this vast mythical coal-driven monster. A sense of excitement mixed with nostalgia lingered. The smell was so intoxicating with its mixture of steam and soot as the smog floated upward, adding yet another layer of black. Again, it was so fitting for an era we thought was long gone. Its lingering smell flooded us with our childhood memories of the 1960s when locomotives, diminutive in comparison, would pass our home in Julatten, delivering goods from Mareeba every Wednesday.

As reality kicked in, we were already swept up in a sea of grey melancholia, with sombre faces milling about us. People in grey clothes were jostling and propelling us forward amongst the evening flow of homeward-bound commuters. Suddenly we felt conspicuous and exposed; clad in jeans and brightly coloured backpacks, we tried to mingle into a sepia image of the past. Eva with her photographs spotted us first and quickly directed her husband, Zdeněk, in our direction. Our cousin Zdeněk was my mother's nephew. He was the son of Mum's elder sister, Zdeňka. Even though Zdeněk was only a young lad when my mother left, he vividly remembered her on her last visit before she departed. She had given him a small alarm clock as a token of fondness and one which he treasured and played with during his childhood.

Zdeněk spoke reasonable English, but as Eva didn't, she left it to him to greet us. Later Eva told us she had first spotted the backpacks with all the colourful Australian emblems, namely the kangaroo and Australian flag. Only then was she drawn to the faces that resembled those in the photographs she was carrying.

In 1983, there were so very few tourists around Prague that any visiting foreigners stood out in crowds. In hindsight, fear of remaining stranded somewhere would have been the least of our concerns as our family would have soon found us even if having to meet every train from Cheb.

As Zdeněk was keen to converse in English, for the time being, I was reprieved from further embarrassing myself with my limited childhood Czech. But, on the other hand, John showed no inkling in speaking Czech, although as a youngster, he was fluent, and to this day, I often wonder just how much he understands without admitting it. Zdeněk and Eva's son Milan at the time was a young teenager and keen on music, so our vinyl album featuring western pop groups was well received. At the time, any imaginative notion of the Internet was only a figment of science fiction make-believe, so the latest Western World Atlas was also appreciated.

The following day, we made our mandatory presence known to the 'VB' or security police and subsequently, from then on, reported to them at any new district we travelled to and remained at for any duration. For visitors like ourselves, we had to observe specific protocols and comply to avoid drawing unwanted attention and flow-on consequences to our host families. However, at no time did we ever experience threatening behaviour or any untoward curiosity from the police. They only showed interest in us as Australians and were always courteous and welcoming.

Contrary to popular myth and much to my relief, albeit perhaps disappointment as unlike in spy books and movies, no KGB agents ever skulked about on street corners or shadowed us! If they existed, they were invisible to the inexperienced eye, and had no need to bother themselves with two Australian tourists when there may have been bigger fish to fry. However, the presence of black marketeers shadowing side streets and ally ways was always challenging to avoid. Hard currency was most desirable and could be cashed at a far better rate than officially, but this transaction was illegal and had consequences if caught. In Prague in 1983, we each exchanged our mandatory £112 vouchers at the official rate in Čedok, receiving a paltry sum of Krc 1,910, but this was still much money by Czech earning standards of the time. This sum could have been quadrupled on the black market at considerable risk. We were not even tempted to do business with these side-street shysters, as my cousin Zdeněk referred to them.

There was so little to buy in government shops with local currency besides food, household items, and odd essentials when available. Our mandatory money vouchers served no practical purpose other than a compulsory acquisition of foreign currency, exchanged at a minimally low rate into Czech Koruna, thus giving us no access to quality or duty-free goods. Our fistful of Czech Koruna may have at the time equated to more than a monthly earning for the average Czech citizen, but for us, it had a limited purpose. Of the little, we managed to spend, the remaining money we gave to our host families to contribute toward some of our daily upkeep.

Tuzek, a state-run organization similar to duty-free shops, accepted only foreign currency or bank vouchers and travellers' cheques, enabling you to buy luxury goods such as Bohemian crystal, jewellery, perfumes, and merchandise we take for granted in western society. These quality goods were far too expensive for regular shoppers and, in many cases, not always value for money. But the Bohemian crystal that Tuzek sold was of the finest quality and not found in any state government shops. Even in most western retailers, inferior quality crystal was less expensive and readily available, whereas the highly prized intricately designed Bohemian crystal was generally only found in top-end retail market outlets such as Harrods in London and specialty and jewellery shops where they attracted a hefty price tag.

All hotels, meals, and tours, including luxury souvenirs, had to be paid for in hard currency. The option of credit cards at the time did not exist in Czechoslovakia, with only the next best choice being Traveller's Cheques in US Dollars or British Sterling currency. These again attracted a hefty government commission and were exchanged at the low official rate. We learned later that border officials would demand any left-over Koruna upon our departure on the undertaking that if we ever returned, it would be refunded. I often wondered how many returning visitors ever succeeded.

In Prague, we were free to roam alone or accompanied by Zdeněk. We walked for hours along the many wide streets of Nové Město (the new city) or Stare Město (the old town), where narrow-cobbled lanes such as Zlatá Ulice (Golden Street) secreted antiques and antiquarian bookshops and pokey nooks crammed with dusty historical artworks. Discreet bars serving cheap beer could be found amongst these shops, while close-by Church steeples towered high above the city. Numerous baroque bridges gracefully spanned the Vltava River, while beneath the supporting arches, majestic swans floated by. We did feel vulnerable and very visible at times, as it was only us amongst a smattering of other foreigners that weaved through the local populous. But simultaneously, we felt safe as nobody unduly bothered us.

I remember the first time we stood in anticipation, waiting to observe the medieval charade and listen to the chimes of the town clock striking the hour in the Old City Square. The square, once empty, momentarily filled with a few people, probably only to synchronize their watches, and after the hour struck, the square emptied just as quickly, and all became quiet again. There was no need to rush out and secure standing space to observe this ancient timepiece. There were no 'Macdonald's, fast-food chains, or heady bars, only discreet minimalistic restaurants and bars snuggled into the narrow-cobbled side streets and shouldering on to other small curio shop fronts.

In Prague during this visit, we met a young English couple who, like ourselves, were touring alone and had just arrived from Poland. They were amazed at the number of goods in shop windows within the old city square precinct. In Poland, they could not even buy toothpaste at the time, and when it did become available, long queues posed even more frustration. During this time, shop windows within Prague square were not abundantly laced with frivolous items but instead had spartan displays of practical things, like boots and saucepans. Today this same area in the old city square is lined with luxury Parisian fashion shops, jewellery shops selling exquisite Swarovski crystals and expensive gems, high-end antique shops, alfresco dining and bars. It is crowded, especially during the summer when standing space needs to be secured well in advance before the hour strikes again carrying out its hourly charade in the old cobbled square. You are no longer the solitary spectator but a participator in a tidal tsunami of sightseers, all clambering to glimpse Prague's past grandeur as the city succumbs once more to changing moods. However, we were also privy to visit many neighbouring castles as Zdeněk drove us into the country side so we could appreciate some of Bohemia's stunning and historic medieval architectures, once home to by-gone kings and Nobility, and ruling despots.

In the early 1980s, we were undoubtedly spoilt and had this magnificent city virtually to ourselves, shared only with random foreigners and tourists who stood out in crowds and were easy to pick out while wandering the streets of Prague. However, most visitors did not venture too far beyond Prague, and the foreigners seen were mostly from other communist countries, either working or studying here. During this inaugural visit, I prided myself on being one of them; a Czech with similar features, language, and ancestral bloodline connecting me to this place. But regardless of this perception, we remained virtual strangers standing apart from those about us for no other reason than being conspicuous by our foreign appearance that did not blend so readily into this culture. We deliberately dressed simply in jeans and t-shirts. Still, it did not disguise the fact that our faded jeans bore desirable Levi or similar labels that only western society could afford to wear. This alone spurred the curiosity of many young onlookers which I found quite disconcerting, especially when silently scrutinized while cornered on a crowded commuting metro train. But, once undressed of my western cloak, I felt embarrassed and inadequate to share in their emotions. Their sad eyes seemed to come from lonely souls, piercing through me as I stood being examined for no other reason than being a foreigner. Did they know they were being held to ransom by their own country? And what did they think when they stared at our clothing and faces? Their eyes saddened me as I braced myself, wishing I could melt into the walls and become invisible to these deeply woeful and glazed expressions while staring into my inner soul and making me the centre of a daunting charade. However, they did not seem to exude envy but perhaps a curious desire to be able to dress and appear as free and unconventional as we were. If they pitied themselves for what they had missed out on in their youth, this guise they kept well concealed and perhaps only too aware that they were powerless to shake off the shackles of political deprivation.

Observing people while they travelled on the metro, like during the mundane act of commuting home from work, it was perhaps this inequitable moment that one chanced to capture people at their most vulnerable, as they dropped their guard during that fleeting space of time and their national pride drifted into a state of indifference, exposing the actual human being. I shall always remain moved by these encounters.

At the time, a metro ticket cost only Krc1, and the train fare from Prague to Valašské Meziříčí cost only Krc 64. To finally meet with our country relatives, we travelled alone on the train, hoping not to disembark at the wrong station. It was a slow journey, taking some five hours through breathtaking, lush scenery. On arrival, we were introduced to our family and their incredible country hospitality generated from what little they possessed in their simplistic life.

The table was always laid out with home-baked sweets and buns, strong coffee, and even stronger Slivovice. Most main meals generally consisted of pork, potatoes, cabbage, various soups, salami, and cheeses with bread. In addition, there was roast rabbit for lunch after Sunday church for special family occasions. Luckily, this was not extended to us then, as I was not accustomed to eating our fluffy bunny friends. But, much to my surprise, I remembered Aunt Helena presenting us with a sealed jar of vegemite so we could feel more at home. Our mother had posted it; otherwise, our relatives would never have heard of such a condiment or ever had the desire to use this Australian taste-acquired spread.

We spent many hours listening to Uncle Robert Pavlik telling us about the war, stories which he only related in English so his wife Helena did not become embroiled in them. He never spoke to anybody else about the war except to John and myself at the time. He had perfect mastery of the English language with a quaint British accent. He acquired English while in the UK during the war and maintained it by listening to BBC radio and thus keeping abreast of western world affairs. He recalled his war days, negotiating dangerous feats alone or alongside other soldiers, who were probably known to my father or uncle and were comrades at arms while training at Cholmondeley. Many of his war compatriots had already gone to early graves by then.

Later, I tried to recollect these precious stories and piece them together, but by then, time had already short circuited my inattentive brain and short attention span for such things that, today, I have only myself to blame for this folly.

Much later, upon the fall of communism and Czechoslovakia's separation from Russia's eastern bloc neighbours, Uncle Robert Pavlik would be posthumously decorated and honoured as a WWII Czech General. But, of course, he never aspired for it. Still, it was a solemn but proud moment for his remaining family to receive this recognition on his behalf, an accolade in Czech history that he deserved and which had been denied him by the previous Soviet regime.

Money earned in Czechoslovakia was minimal compared to western standards. With what little could be saved, some could be contributed toward holidays, especially during Winter when families could go skiing into some of Czechoslovakia's world's best ski fields.

Everyone prided in having a job and was paid equally no matter how menial or inessential the task was. It was pointed out to us that only those in government and authority with dubious connections within the system seemed to prosper. The regime was so entrenched in corrupt activities that it made these select few officials, financial beneficiaries of this highly unproductive system. There were always whispers of corruption when somebody had more than someone else, but whether it was authentic or simple jealousy, it rarely went beyond discussion at the family table. So, at the humble end of the food chain, there was no incentive to better oneself, especially if the pay did not equate to the diligent effort made resulting in the quality of work proudly achieved.

A good education did not necessarily equate to better pay and privileges. On the contrary, it only opened the eyes to all the system's injustices. In short, life was primarily same-same for everyone who was not privileged. Moreover, within this society came secrecy and often limited socialization, so neighbours or acquaintances outside of family circles were often discreetly avoided so as not to engage in potentially harmful gossip that could create outside suspicion or intriguing innuendos concerning private family affairs. For John and I it was only a fleeting visit and more of a curiosity to finally meet family without regard for our ancestral roots or history. My travel journals, at the time, paint a vastly different life in Czechoslovakia compared to the 21st century since its breakaway from Soviet influence. Never the less, it was a life unparallel to our childhood upbringing in Australia.

Even though this journey was our first into Czechoslovakia as visiting tourists, it nevertheless fell under the umbrella of national security as any visiting foreigner had to be satisfactorily identified. My cousin's husband was legally obligated to report to his workplace of our presence. Having failed to do so would have only raised questions, suspicion, and trouble for his family if it was later revealed that foreign visitors had been staying. Many would have thought it shallow of character and improper to do so, but it was a requirement by their law, and the expectation to comply was the norm. Therefore, we accepted it without reservation as it was the premise of their societal law in a country where we were merely guests.

Once bustling with activity in pre-war years, local towns and villages were now silenced from frivolous gaiety and functioned purely as conduits to a harsh industrial economy that the communists controlled. Most of the urban landscape was scarred by bleak socialist modernization of bland and cramped high rise accommodation blocks, now grotesquely out-measuring once beautiful medieval buildings and villas. Many old structures lay in ruins, dilapidated and crumbling at the mercy of this Spartan modernization. Most suffered from the lack of available funding to creatively preserve a heritage that neither held value nor was a priority for the government's bureaucrats. However, efforts were still made to protect the more viable and valuable medieval castles, forts, and ancient monastic relics by using the skills of various artisans and craftsmen at low pay to resurrect these significant landmarks now in the ownership of the state. So, it was not all doom and gloom for the country's crumbling heritage.

The countryside was mostly peaceful, perhaps concealing a darker side from which we were constantly screened. Family members always escorted us and rarely ventured into villages unless we were driven there for some meaningful purpose. Nevertheless, we could still see numerous stunning castles, churches, and ancient medieval buildings from the car window.

For whatever reason, along with everyone else, Aunt Helena insisted on using the communal laundry, where she did her weekly and major family washing. I remember seeing white electrical goods stored in her attic and wondering why she did not use these machines. A washing machine would have made all the difference rather than sharing the downtown communal laundry. Owning these goods was one consideration, but fitting, maintaining, and replacing worn parts possibly far outweighed the use of these appliances at a time when private contractors were unheard of and only worked for the government. I once accompanied Aunt Helena to this local communal laundry to do our washing, which she insisted on doing anyway. I was amazed at the organized chaos around us while waiting patiently to secure an allocated position in the laundering area. The laundry mechanism was archaic, resembling a noisy ramshackle factory of bubbling, steaming, and gurgling waterworks. All the washing, rinsing, and wringing of clothes was done manually, but water and sudds seemed plentiful while clothes were scrubbed and beaten clean. Whatever the downfall of this open-air laundromat, it nevertheless fulfilled the daily needs of everyone in an efficient sort of way.

In 1983 we were introduced to a beautiful country with an ever-changing landscape that could challenge any other in the world for its sheer beauty and uniqueness. For now, this considerable tourist potential lay dormant like a sleeping giant. So, we alone enjoyed the autumn landscape, basking in the glorious colours of burnt amber, gold, and russet red trees that extended as far as the eye could see.

Epilogue

We visited the Tatra Mountains, the beautiful snow-capped peaks in what is now Slovakia. During winter, skiing and numerous winter sports were available here for ski enthusiasts and anyone else fortunate enough to be visiting.

There was no definitive border between Slovakia and the Czech side as it was then all one country. The roads were not great highways but adequate thoroughfares to accommodate holiday traffic from neighbouring communist countries. Although not always perfect, these sporadically used roads took us to many beautiful and fascinating places under the watchful eye of our chaperons.

We witnessed no traffic jams nor encountered crowds or queues, as our hosts continually shielded us with a commitment to our safety and continually diverted us from any potential hazards. Throughout this visit, we had the opportunity to meet many elderly family members who would later figure in my mother's story. We did not discuss the past or the future, only the now. Many were already in their twilight years, and today I regret not reaching out to every one of them and listening to their stories. At the time, everyone was more interested in our lives in Australia, as they had a deep fascination with our lifestyle, and besides, we were some of their first relatives to visit from the West.

During this time, we met all of my mother's sisters except Jarmila. We also met all of my father's sisters, but sadly, all our grandparents had passed on by then. In addition, there were great uncles and great aunts whose place in the family tree I did not fully appreciate at the time, but in hindsight, many of whom I would have dearly wished to meet with again and share in their stories. Today my greatest regret is that most of the family history that was available then is now mostly lost due to my ignorance.

In Hošťálková, we learned more about my father's first marriage, and I was even offered Elsie Pidgeon-Carter's address in England by my father's second elder sister, Aunt Anna Syptáková. At the time, I wanted to contact Elsie, learn about my half-sister Violet, and glean further information about my father. Unfortunately, my mother was reluctant to entertain such a relationship, and after only one letter to Elsie, I let matters drop mainly to appease my mother. Anna Syptáková and my mother were never on best of terms, even more so after my father passed away. In hindsight, during our visit my aunt had exercised the upper hand, which she probably knew would annoy my mother.

During our initial visit to Hošťálková, we were given my father's Cholmondeley photograph album, a memento consisting of a small collection of photographs while training at this camp in England during WWII. We were also presented with our father's family bible, which had part of their family tree outlined on the blank forwarding pages. The Kaňák family were of Evangelist/Lutheran following; although not an outwardly religious family, they kept their beliefs very much to themselves. Another family treasure my father's family bestowed upon me was the classic children's storybook about fireflies. It was called 'Broučci,' written by Jan Karafiát, a famous Czech writer. Many years earlier, when we were only small, our mother recited these tales at bedtime and filled our weary little heads with adventures of happy little creatures carrying their lanterns and flitting throughout the night as we drifted into sleep. While I was a child, these stories ignited my imagination beyond anything else I would later encounter in children story books. However, this brief visit with my father's family was fortuitous in another way. We were warned against visiting Aunt Jarmila and her family near Ostrava due to joint Russian-Czech military manoeuvres in the vicinity. The warning came from our army cousin, who informed us that any presence of foreigners would not be taken lightly in view of these exercises. The inevitable consequence for those caught violating or perceivably trespassing too close to military training was one I did not need to be reminded of. It had been a close call had we not visited my father's family, as the following day, we were scheduled to go to Ostrava and visit Jarmila. For the first time since arriving, I realized there were actual perils if ignorant or uninformed about sensitive activities. On this occasion, I would have been much happier to leave immediately had I had the chance. I didn't translate the situation to my brother until well after we had left the country. Besides, on that day, he was otherwise too occupied being initiated by the Kaňák male members into the art of drinking Slivovice, very much to my Aunt Helena's annoyance. Sadly, our visit to Hošťálková was of short duration as we were in the custody of the Kurovec clan, and our movement outside of our mother's family was very much under the jurisdiction of Aunt Helena.

Epilogue

The trip into Czechoslovakia had been an adventure for John and I, and anything that happened from the ordinary made it all the more tantalizing. On Sunday, the 16th of October, day 14 of our visa, we boarded the 8:10 pm train from Prague to return to Cheb on the German Czech border. Nearing midnight, we finally arrived at Cheb, and again we were greeted by 'the Czech welcoming committee' as military personnel swarmed over the train like bees. Exiting Czechoslovakia proved even more intriguing than our arrival some two weeks earlier. During this occasion, I estimated somewhere between eighty and ninety personnel. Outside was dark and chilly; the only visible light came from small lantern-like bulbs swaying in the breeze as they hung sparsely above the deserted platform. It was the eeriest feeling I had ever experienced at any border check.

For some time, there seemed a deathly silence outside beyond the chaos inside our carriages where it was business as usual with heavily coated military guards shouting and trampling up and down corridors, poking gun buts into every inconceivable crevice. I half expected Shultz or Col. Klink (from the American comedy show, Hogan's Heroes) to appear at any moment! The whole scene could have been mistaken for an old black-and-white war film setting, and we the actors, waiting on cue to break into action. To this day, this memory remains indelibly imprinted in my mind as if it only happened yesterday. John and I felt safe and assured that we had nothing to hide and that our visas were in order, provided immigration stamped and checked us out before midnight. However, the customs officers were particularly overzealous, searching and cross-examining every passenger, and it sent shivers down my spine. It was as if they were searching for something or someone and would only relent once whatever it was, was unearthed.

Passengers were ordered to stand up as guns were poked underneath their seats and into their bags. Hand luggage was searched, and loud, harsh dialogue echoed down the corridors. We happily handed over what little Czech currency we had, some Krc150 from me and Krc 260 from John, and as they did their meticulous paperwork, we were informed we had three years to return and reclaim the money. At that very moment, returning was the last thing on my mind, and all I wanted was to get away; the sooner and the further away, all the better.

If we did return and dare request our meagre refund, I could not even begin to imagine what this negotiation would create; the chaos of bureaucratic red tape, hurdles, and paper trails, and the efforts for this restitution far exceeding its monetary worth. In this case, the cash and receipts probably ended up in someone's back pocket, as we did not receive formal paperwork. One official customs chap indicated he would like to inspect our backpacks further. Fortunately, he was suddenly called away by a fellow officer interrogating a nearby passenger, so we were overlooked and spared any further inquisition and forgotten about.

This time the exterior of the train and beneath the carriage compartments was being thoroughly checked as soldiers clambered beneath and banged away with the butts of their rifles, probably searching for dissidents trying to escape. The deafening commotion ceased as suddenly as it had begun. We sat inside the brightly lit carriages alongside the shadowy and dimly lit railway station for the next two hours.

The Czech officials had disappeared, and once again, only the doubled-up guards remained to block all exits of the carriages. To the untrained eye, we may have appeared like criminals during the war about to be transported to a detention camp. It may have triggered a fear not unsimilar that ran through the hearts of all those refugees, but 40 years on, in 1983, at least the war was over, and there was some self-assurance that this was only a minor hold-up and we would soon be delivered over the border. For the time being, no one dared to get up or move, and we all sat silently staring out into the darkness, facing our own somewhat despondent reflections staring back at us through the closed windows. It was to be one of my most prolonged two hours of waiting, and we were still on Czech soil, yet only a stone's throw from West Germany and democracy.

For most of the time, I sat with my face pressed against the window peering into the darkness, trying to focus on the steel and wire structures that separated two worlds; on one side of the fence for close to half a century since the war, a closed society suppressed and still languishing in the past with most of its people ignorant of western progress. While on the other side, a free-thinking democracy that respected and advocated human rights but was powerless to help those on the other side of the fence. To be on the cusp of such an inhumane division was genuinely heart-wrenching. And for all this inequality, only a fence separated the two ideologies. But, back then, I did struggle to make sense of this man-made barricade that divided with such unyielding provocation.

"Oh! For God's sake! Why not just knock it down? After all, it's only just a high fence!"

But, for now, our transition into Germany remained blocked and taunted by these high, intimidating doubled partitions of barbed wire. It was lit like a soccer field but instead dotted with concealed explosive devices, and high above, lookout towers guarded this hallowed ground in between, not with friendly commentary of rivalry but guns! During our wait, I pondered who maintained no man's land between these two heavily patrolled parallel fences and on the free side; who cared enough to pay for the upkeep of this structure. I was sure the Germans had better things to do than trouble themselves with this grotesque barricade.

Finally, we were moving, ever so slowly, as screeching wheels turned on the icy cold steel rails. Our mood lightened as we progressed into no man's land, each carriage door still doubly guarded. Just short of the border exit beneath brightly lit searchlights, the train stopped yet again, and all train staff, including our military guards, disembarked and left us, while once more, the train began to move forward. With all army presence dispersed, I again wondered who was left in charge of our moving train. We crept toward the West German border and halted at last; but this time under bright lights greeting us and bustling activity along the railway station platform as personal and additional passengers began gathering to embark. At last, we reverted to the present world as we knew it, leaving behind the past.

The mood and atmosphere immediately lightened while the new German crew and everyone else began boarding the carriages. Passengers became mobile, standing to stretch their cramped bodies as they talked and joked with fellow travellers. The noise was almost deafening but embracing after such protracted stillness and silence. At no time did we have to change trains on this journey into Nuremberg while the train pitched and swayed with renewed energy, whistling and clattering rapidly into the oncoming dawn.

It was a cold and miserable day in Nuremberg when we arrived at 9:00 am. Even though we had another 16 hours before we boarded our train for London, no bleak weather could dampen our spirits after a triumphant and safe return from Czechoslovakia. Like the cheeky little squirrel in the nearby park, we like it were free spirits sharing our lives in western society. From London, John returned to Australia after being recruited as an engineer with Balfour Beatty while still in England, and I went onto Egypt to live and work in Cairo for the next five years. Reflecting on our first visit to Czechoslovakia, it was like a privately guided tour, protected from the local populace, steered discreetly through the countryside, and unnoticed by anybody except those escorting and receiving us.

In 1985 my sister Diana arrived to Cairo on a visit from Australia with her then-husband Robert. Once more Czechoslovakia was on the travel itinerary. The country as before, was still a communist state beyond the 'Iron Curtain.' It was Diana's first visit there which she was looking forward to and at my mother's insistence, I was to chaperone them. As I still had sufficient leave accrued, I was once more on my way to Czechoslovakia.

After spending some weeks with me in Cairo, Diana, and Robert returned ahead of me to the continent on pre-booked flights while I flew onto London to organize my visa, train travel, and Čedok money vouchers. Being a seasoned traveller, I made all my seating reservations well in advance as we were now in the height of the European Summer, and tourists would be everywhere. The final hurdle was to meet my co-travellers in Nuremberg, from where we would continue onto Cheb by train and finally into Prague. As arranged, we met, but due to their oversight for not pre-booking all train seats, it made for some interesting train travel later on in Europe. In the first instance, for my co-travellers, it was a case of getting early to Platform 6 at Nuremberg Station and being the first to board the train, and pray not everyone had made their reservations. Somehow it all worked out, with Diana and Robert managing to secure seats adjoining me in the carriage.

For me, it was an unexpectedly early return to Czechoslovakia, and my anxiety jitters from my earlier trip were well and truly buried by now. This time I felt prepared for anything the communist bureaucracy might throw at us. My biggest concern at the time was Robert, who, over the past weeks in Cairo, could create chaos and confusion without too much effort. Moreover, he possessed the knack of walking away from the mayhem he created without any heed of consequence. He could be funny and entertaining but never audacious, only down right annoying when he found your weakness and got the desired reaction by pressing all the right buttons.

After contacting cousin Zdeněk and his wife Eva in Prague, who were expecting us, and informing them of our train schedule, my newly acquired Arabic language was very much in its infancy. It became a blend of 'Czech-Arabic.' Unfortunately, the Arabic word for the pronoun I was similar in sound to my mother's name Anna so our poor relatives became confused and unsure if our mother would be arriving as well. Late afternoon on the 1st of August 1985, I once more set out from Nuremberg, this time accompanied by Diana and Robert, onto yet another journey beyond the 'Iron Curtain.' Germany had been celebrating 150 years of rail that year, and the countryside was beautiful as we headed onto Cheb. It was hard to believe that almost half a century before, all this countryside had been a war zone.

We each exchanged our compulsory £80 for Krc 1,200 at the border town of Cheb, validating our visa for Czechoslovakia, and I mentally noted that the foreign currency requirement had not changed but the rate of exchange since my last visit had dropped from Krc17 to 15Krc for each pound sterling, but on this occasion, we were staying for ten days rather than two weeks.

The border crossing seemed less intimidating than on my first visit, but true to their bureaucratic form, we again sat in our carriage for two hours waiting to proceed. It was an anxious wait for Diana, but not before wide-eyed Robert started to fidget and complain, saying he wanted to exercise his democratic right to know what was happening. I looked at him and warned him that if he brought unnecessary attention to himself and was hauled off the train, I was not coming to his aid. He had a choice; Put up and shut up! Or else, at his peril, see how communists dealt with dissatisfied and demanding foreign customers.

We arrived in Prague at about 8:00 am, and much to our relief Zdeněk and Eva were there to meet us. Unused to travelling light, Robert and Diana came loaded with two large and heavy suitcases, as opposed to my backpack. As we could not fit into Zdeněk's little Škoda, we all caught a taxi for Krc 35 and followed the Škoda toward the district of Braník in Prague.

During the early morning traffic, travelling through the undulating spread of Prague, it was a symphony of traffic humming in rhythm to the bleak monotony of its everyday routine. Around us, wafting smog shrouded the tops of old building facades that clung to the streets as we veered away from the city centre toward the solemn and stark, but neatly spread suburbia. Finally, after a brief wash and tidy up and a much-appreciated hot and robust coffee with Zdenek and Eva, we were ushered off to the Police station (VB), where we registered our presence with our respective hosts. This was done again with minimal fuss, much to our hosts' relief.

Surprisingly, the streets of Prague were occupied with noticeable numbers of young Vietnamese, Korean, and Cuban people. We were informed they were students on an exchange program from friendly communist countries. Still, I soon learnt that this same open friendliness was not offered to the Arab nations, especially those from Lebanon, and nor did the government of the time encourage students from other Western democracies.

During our many long walks through Prague packed with historical marvels, Zdeněk once again proudly showed off his beautiful city. All this seemed lost on Robert as his enthusiasm was devoted elsewhere. Robert focused on the social landscape rather than its history, as he remained intrigued with its intimate functionality, which mostly gravitated toward food and what the locals were doing. As we hiked through the parklands, Robert was fascinated with the trees that grew in these areas, and collected pears and apples in their pre-ripened state, continually offering them to Diana to taste whether she wanted to or not.

Prague has always been a fascinating gothic city raised from medieval times with an ever-ending source of delightful architecture, landscaped parks, and historical monuments, which even I happily revisited, retracing my steps from my previous visit as there was always something new to glean. Unfortunately, the shops were still bare of exciting curios, for tourism as we know it, had yet to catch on, and foreign tourists were not especially catered for. Only government businesses and department shops continued catering to local needs as there was no place for private enterprise within the Communist system. State-owned eateries served simple food, stodgy but hearty meals, and likewise, government shop windows spared any frivolity and only displayed and sold spartan commodities for every day-use.

I retraced my walk over St. Charles' Bridge (Karlův Most), still a peaceful experience, especially in the evenings when swans glided gracefully beneath the bridge on the Vltava River. There was never more than a handful of people sharing my space as I strolled and absorbed the stunning architecture and the historical statues, albeit with grotesque human faces maligning the bridge. Their history had a more sinister birth when past religious conflicts were widespread. The Presidential Palace, 'Hradčany,' on the opposite side of the Vltava River was the seat of many ancient noble rulers and modern-day presidents. Over shadowed by the high steeples of St. Vitus Cathedral, a catacomb of narrow-cobbled side streets still revealed exciting nooks where old antiquarian books and antique shops lay hidden in obscurity. In musky corners, treasures of old books, maps, coins, postcards, stamps, antique figurines, and paintings clustered together, some long forgotten but still collecting dust. Chances of acquiring a genuine historical piece was always possible. But chances of getting it out of the country without confiscation by customs at the border was unfortunately less likely. Visiting this area one can only marvel at the beauty of Prague's bridges that brought together the old and the new city.

Zdeněk explained that things were slowly improving, and even now, some people were beginning to work for themselves in a sort of way. These repair works that government factories no longer wanted to do, offered an opportunity for budding entrepreneurs to rent premises, create a business, and dabble in potential capitalism, which was still a dirty word to most, describing it as the double standard of systemic corruption.

We visited numerous neighbouring medieval castles shrouded in ancient history standing majestically some surrounded by moats, gardens and dense forests. We stopped by popular markets where locals could buy souvenirs, postcards, wood carvings, and pottery. However, the constant and open barrage of black marketeers plaguing these potential tourist spots always remained a constant and annoying cause of frustration as they hounded foreigners for hard currency.

On the 8th of August, we departed Prague by train and headed toward Valašské Meziříčí in Moravia. It was a cold and bleak day with rain for most of the trip. For me it was Deja vu, a return train journey that John and I had undertaken nearly two years earlier. I felt I was on familiar territory while vaguely familiar names of passing villages and rail sidings whizzed past. At Hranice, we were met by the Pavlik family and driven onto Krhová, where again, we were welcomed and stayed with Uncle Robert and Aunt Helena at what was once our great-grandparent's Stolař family home.

In contrast, our mother's sister Aunt Zdeňka had to pay Krc 30,000 to the government to transfer the Kurovec Lhotka property from my mother's ownership. Although my mother was regarded as a 'persona non grata' here in Czechoslovakia, she was still acknowledged as someone who could be contacted through solicitors to sign over her property. It was never a question of my mother wanting to retain the family home, but it hurt her that her sister had to pay for something she rightfully should have inherited in the first place. Such was the government system.

One evening during our visit, amid a storm with echoing thunder and flashes of lightning surrounding us, Uncle Robert embarked yet again in English on WWII history. Aunt Helena, not understanding what was being spoken, became impatient and interrupted the conversation on numerous occasions but, in the end, managed to remind us all that on the 25th of August, it would soon be our mother's 69th birthday, and so, began an exciting debate that left us all in limbo about our mother's age.

Our presence in Valašské Meziříčí was low-key, and our local outings were generally kept to visiting the cemetery to pay respect to the dearly departed and light candles for them. So, when we were to see Helena's sister, our Aunt Bo, who was in the hospital then, it created another dilemma for our host. The hospital visit would have been a fascinating experience for Diana and I as we were both nurses. Still, it was a disappointment as we were briskly and silently ushered in, made our brief acquaintances with Aunt Bo, and just as quickly ushered out and taken elsewhere. Embarrassingly, we felt that everywhere we went, it always developed into a significant operation for the family, which we would have preferred to avoid. However, we did have some wonderful and memorable moments with them. We were always taken to stunning places such as the ski region of Bumbalka, where at least my sister Diana could have the satisfaction of stepping onto what is now Slovakia. We also visited our dad's family in Hošťálková, meeting all his sisters; our aunts, and later returning to catch up with the remainder of our Mum's family at their ancestral home in Lhotka, where she grew up, and where in the garden, we shared fond times with our Mum's sisters Zdeňka and Helena.

This trip to Czechoslovakia was not always smooth sailing. My patience was tested numerous times while travelling with Robert, my brother-in-law. Uncle Robert and Robert had a guarded relationship and mostly avoided one another. Uncle Robert was never judgemental but at times his own patience was being tested as well.

Robert was good natured and always keen to understand everything, but offering to help Uncle Robert was not exactly welcoming, especially when it concerned the coal heating system. After all the dwelling was cold otherwise, so heating was essential and it was only Uncle Robert who was totally in charge of operating the household heating.

One evening after one such episode of well-intentioned advice, Uncle Robert pulled me aside and, not pointing the finger directly at anyone, confessed, " We aren't particularly keen on Arabs in this country!"

Suspecting friction was about to develop, for the first time I came to my brother-in-law's defence and diplomatically pointed out that he was a third to fourth generation Lebanese-Australian who came from a well-respected family and who were all practising Christians. I fully sympathized with Uncle Robert, but somebody had to keep the peace.

Not understanding a word of Czech, Robert was always keen to participate in all conversations. With the assistance of his dictionary, by the time he discovered the correct word and blurted it out, the conversation had progressed well beyond where he was still at, but Aunt Helena was always very accommodating and patiently listened to him regardless.

Robert had an annoying habit of fiddling and adjusting things even if these things were in perfect working order. Many times, I wanted to believe it all happened quite unintentionally, but after at least three bathrooms that I knew of in Cairo during his brief visit there, two in my apartment, and one at the Meridian Hotel, had all met with some disaster with Robert's tinkering, it came as no surprise when Zdeněk's downstairs toilet met with the same fate. How the chain from the overhead water chamber miraculously fell off into Robert's hands beggars' belief, and I soon realized that it was more than just a simple coincidence when all these water closets met with their waterloo. At least for now, we were still spared any such incident at our aunt's and uncle's place.

Our departure from Czechoslovakia seemed swift. Aunt Helena had us up at 4:00 am, and all the family was organized to meet at the railway station for our grand farewell. After much confusion and seating deliberation, which was probably sorted out by Aunt Eliška, then employed by the railway, we were finally all seated in the same carriage and sent off on our way. Back in Prague, laden with all the heavy and bulging baggage, we were alone and had to find our own way to the Main Prague Railway Station and to the platform where we would catch the train from Berlin bound for Vienna. Luckily it was late, so we had time to be there ready and waiting well before its arrival.

This time the border crossing at Grund seemed an anticlimax after all the earlier drama at Cheb, and even the border guards on the Czech side seemed more amenable while doing their inside, outside, and underneath checks of the train. This intriguing formality almost faded into oblivion as we proceeded out of the country. However, it was interesting to note that this border crossing between Austria and Czechoslovakia at the time had a triple-structured fence, and once again, my heart went out to those we had left behind. Finally, we crossed over at Grund into Austria, while the train blew its whistle loud and long, letting us know we were once again in the West.

After living away from home for over the past decade and a half, of which I spent over five years abroad, I finally returned to be closer to my family. In early 1998 on one of my regular home visits from Pebbly Beach, my mother unexpectedly announced that it would soon be 50 years since she had left her homeland. This sparked my waning interest, followed by intense dialogue about her past. Finally, she was ready to talk and share with me some of her life's adventures to the extent that I decided without reservation to document the details of these conversations.

My mother was initially sceptical about my proposal to write her story.

"My life was so ordinary and boring. Why not instead write about the animals from your childhood? They were far more interesting!" She insisted, and so began a temporary diversion about her grandmother Stolařová who had created for her grandchildren, bedtime stories about animals from their family farm. Without waiting for my objection, she began, "One day, an old half-blind horse was taking his friends for a ride in his cart when he drove off the road and capsized them all into the mud. The clever hare jumped off far and wide, and so did the cunning fox. The cranky goose flew over them, but the lazy fat pig fell flat into the mud on top of the fastidious young goat! 'Help, my leg is broken!' Bleated the goat beneath the weight of the pig …."

I tried to avoid becoming too side-tracked. But ultimately, I succumbed to her suggestion and eventually wrote my own animal fantasy, 'Scallywags of Bushy Creek,' and delayed her inevitable memoir.

During these chats, we broached the subject of our early lives in South Australia. I was barely three years old when we departed for North Queensland, but I had vivid snippets of my life there and several recounts needed to confirm how accurate my memory was.

One particular memory at the time was my obsession with a newly surveyed road near Mareeba, which I always pointed out to my parents, telling them in Czech (the only language I spoke), "See that road? It goes to Port Lincoln!"

My parents were always puzzled by my repetitive and emphatic assertion of its destination whenever we passed this surveyed road. However, in due time all was forgotten, and we moved on. I raised this subject with my mother and asked her if she ever wondered why I was so emphatically bloody-minded about where it went.

"We did wonder at the time what bought on such thinking!"

I explained, "When leaving Wangary in South Australia, a similar-looking unsealed road leading onto Port Lincoln was being surveyed for new roadworks. As a child, I had no notion of distance, and although we had travelled for some six weeks over thousands of miles from Wangary onto Mareeba, I believed that both roads were the same."

If my parents had asked me then, I am sure I would have pointed out the wooden crossed pegs down the centre, just like both surveyed roads shared at the time, and this clue might have solved their conundrum. Children are very logical. If two things look alike, then in their naïve logic, they must be one of the same things, or at least that is how I figured it out as a child. My father went to his grave, never knowing the truth about my so-called irrational thinking, but my mother was quite intrigued and almost relieved that this age-old enigma had finally been put to rest.

It would be another twenty years before I returned to Czechoslovakia, and this time it would be a country divided into the Czech Republic and Slovakia. When the Berlin Wall fell in 1989, Czechoslovakia was still in the grips of Communism. However, with the Velvet Revolution of the 19th of November 1989, the hold by oppressors began to slip away slowly, and renewed tensions between Slovakia and Prague re-emerged. Once the 'Iron Curtain' was pulled down, so with it on the 1st of January 1993 came the rebirth of democracy and the Socialist Republic of Czechoslovakia ceased to exist. In its place, the newly independent states of Slovakia and the Czech Republic emerged.

On the 10th of July 2005, I yet again returned to Prague. It would be at Václav Havel International Airport, or 'Ruzyňe Letiště,' as it was then called, and arrived to a surprisingly low-key security reception. From where I had just arrived in the United Kingdom, Heathrow was hardly comparable, having just undergone recent bomb threats.

The Czech nation's hopes of self-determination had finally come to fruition after being held back from humanitarian ontogenesis for so long. On that overcast day, it had been an emotional moment for me, setting foot on Czech soil and wishing my mother had been with me to witness the change; a change that would finally transition her country into a democracy of free-thinking people; something she had wished, for so long.

Epilogue

I was met by my cousin Růženka and her husband Lumír, along with their pampered dog Danoušek, or Dani for short. Armed with dictionaries and an electronic translator, they greeted me, and I, in return, only arrived with the hope that they could understand my somewhat impoverished Czech. By now, Uncle Robert, Růženka's father, had passed away, leaving the younger generations to sort out their communication skills, even if with rather inarticulately-spoken visiting relatives.

On that bleak, rainy afternoon, we flew down a modern dual-lane carriageway heading toward south Moravia. Their car was a new Audi, and to my horror, from the back seat, I could see the speedo climbing and hovering on what I believed to be 160km per hour. I prayed it was not in miles while I politely asked what the legal speed limit was in the Czech Republic. This did not deter Lumír, and he continued to speed along like everyone else. "Welcome again to the modern Czech Republic," I thought, and I was more than relieved when they suggested a stop at MacDonald's. Yes, MacDonalds had also made its way to the Czech Republic! As it turned out, this pit stop was not for my benefit but for Dani, who was partial to Macca's chicken nuggets.

Unexpectedly, my accommodation arrangements had been changed since departing for the Czech Republic as my host Aunt Helena had recently suffered a minor stroke and was in hospital undergoing tests and preparing for rehabilitation. My first two weeks were to be spent with Aunt Jarmila at Paskov near Ostrava, after which I would stay with my cousin Růženka and her husband, Lumír. Jarmila, my mum's youngest sister, had already visited Australia on two previous occasions, and during her first visit, I finally became acquainted with her. Jarmila's home was initially a large two-story dwelling, but much of it is now occupied by her son Svatá. At the rear was Jarmila's abode, an attached two-storied apartment that may have once served as an office and a small warehouse. I came to this conclusion because she had enough stuff there to open up a hardware shop.

Upstairs was pokey, especially for the two of us, but it satisfied Jarmila's needs. Even though she was minimalistic with her furnishings, she had plenty of old appliances, which she must have inherited from her business days with her late husband. I was especially keen to provide for myself and even buy a functional coffee plunger, but Jarmila had other ideas. From an electric oven converted into a cupboard, she fetched something outdated resembling a percolator. Jarmila controlled the roost and as her guest, I had to abide by her master plan. Despite her scoliosis, she still drove a car which she told me were her legs, giving her total independence from everyone, including her son. I wanted to know all about my mother's family history, but invariably the topic of conversation turned to what Jarmila wanted to discuss.

I heard everything barring what I had come to research. Jarmila had been barely sixteen when my mother left, so perhaps it was a big ask to expect any significant revelations from her. Her recollection of the war years and family history was vague at best but primarily self-centred; she wasn't easy to deviate from her pet topics of self-interest, and conversations rarely led down avenues of what I wanted to know. Ultimately, I think she made things up just to appease me. My stay with Jarmila made for some exciting moments, as I soon discovered, with her often erratic and buoyant temperament. She had a heart of gold, but with it came her idiosyncrasies.

Her daily routine consisted of visiting the cemetery each morning and attending to her late husband Josef's grave, bringing fresh flowers, changing the water from the previous day, and lighting a few candles. He had already been dead for several years, but she maintained this ritual for personal gratification.

Once we left the cemetery, her piety evaporated. I soon learned that Jarmila was prone to some very colourful language and equally colourful gossip, most of which I did not care to know about. We travelled far and wide within the area, and I was most grateful for these sightseeing trips, but they did come at the expense of some erratic driving. I soon found a Tesco Store and bought several bottles of wine to calm my shaken nerves each evening. However, through Jarmila, I would meet my Mum's cousin Marta Berková who then lived with her husband Vladimír in Havlíčkův Brod.

While still with Jarmila, rather unexpectedly, I was invited to call in on my father's side of the family for an impromptu but brief, ceremonial formality. I knew nothing of it beforehand, but it had been especially prearranged to coincide with my visit. The whole affair certainly put a spoke in the wheel of Jarmila's daily routine, and she let it be known. I apologized for the unexpected inconvenience over which I had no control but was assured it would only be a brief ceremony at Hošťálková, the village of my father's birth. I had planned to visit them all independently afterward, so why it could not have been delayed till then, I dared not ask.

Jarmila's established order of the day was always adhered to, and I accepted her daily cemetery drill. In the end, I would eventually choose to remain in her car and wait, saving her the complicated task of locking and unlocking her vehicle. The distance to Hošťálková was not far, but Jarmila decided to take me via Svaté Hostýn, which my Mum and her sisters often visited as young girls. This made the trip somewhat longer but, for me, an exciting diversion. Unfortunately, our visit to Svaté Hostýn coincided with bad weather, and where the chapel was situated at the summit of the mountain, it was extremely cold and windy. I was compelled to remain seated in the chapel with Jarmila and listen to the Latin service. I understood nothing, a service that Jarmila no doubt had planned to attend. However, even to her surprise but perhaps a bonus, a rather elaborate Requiem Mass followed for one of the late cardinals.

Svaté Hostýn was a beautiful white and ornate chapel perched at the summit commanding fantastic views on a fine day. I imagined that things would not have been much different when Mum and her sisters visited as young girls so many years ago. As my mother had described to me, this long, well-worn concreted stairway up to the chapel was still lined with souvenir huts.

Arriving finally, at Hošťálková, I was hurriedly escorted by my father's family and ushered into the town hall, and presented to the local mayor. It was a private affair that had to coincide with my visit as the initial public commemorative service had been conducted some time before. This ceremony was a part of the town's 500th Anniversary celebrations that had occurred earlier that year. Unbeknown to my family in Australia, an earlier posthumous citation for my father's war service and efforts during WWII had been included as an official recognition on behalf of the village. This later private ceremony had been hastily put together for my benefit so I could receive his accolade from the local municipality mayor in person. It was an emotional but proud moment, one best received by my brother, had he been there, being the only son of this accorded WWII soldier. Although this visit was quickly organized, we remained for the afternoon, and I had a brief opportunity to enquire about some family matters. I had planned to return later with my husband Max when he finally joined me. Everyone was eager to talk about their recent events and ask about family happenings in Australia, so no one was too keen to enter discussions about the war years. Besides, my older relatives with possible answers were far too preoccupied with their recent losses of loved ones.

I was taken to the cemetery to search and photograph some old headstones bearing the 'Kaňák' name. However, I was constantly redirected to other names and graves of recently deceased people who were not necessarily linked directly to me. I also learned that Grandmother Anna Kaňáková was buried together with her daughter in a grave bearing only her late daughter's family name. Maybe one day, this will be rectified, and her name will also be added to the headstone. I was intrigued with one particular 'Kaňák' headstone, but my enthusiasm was promptly doused when my cousin's husband told me it was not my relative but one of his. I was astonished, as the Kaňák name seemed no longer common in the district, and I was acutely aware that my family in Australia was at the terminus of our Kaňák line; my brother being the last surviving male bearing the name. It was already impossible to find another living 'Kaňák' in Hošťálková who was a direct bloodline relative.

Cemeteries may appear lonely and morbid, but for many, they hold a wealth of fascinating histories, like an encyclopedia of ancestral roots. If only these cemetery records of our early ancestors were upheld and readily available, then it would have assisted me better in tracing my father's ancestral tree. However, it did occur to me that in the past, old established families with minimal migration out of their villages probably were more likely to intermarry with cousins, as Hošťálková had once been an isolated village in the valley. Today, this population has become mobile and younger ones leave home searching for work and education, finding partners who come well outside of their own villages.

A day later, after our early morning cemetery ritual, Jarmila unexpectedly announced that we would be visiting her cousin Marta Berkova in Havlíčkův Brod, a distance of some 370km westward in the direction of Prague. At such short notice, we were both ill-prepared for such a journey as Jarmila's impulsive decision did not allow consideration for the distance and time it would take to drive to Havlíčkův Brod; but then I did not take into account how fast my aunt could drive. Once in the car, Jarmila presented me with an old Czech road map and told me to navigate. That morning, it seemed time consuming just negotiating our way out of her garage and reversing down the driveway, so I half expected a tedious trip ahead. Having not factored Jarmila's driving impatience into this journey, I had little idea that this was just the calm before the storm. Once behind the wheel, Jarmila became another woman, impetuous, aggressive, and disagreeable with all other drivers, believing they were at her mercy as she sped down the highway. Unequipped for any heart-stopping road experience, my nerves and sense of direction were like a defective compass, jumpy and unidirectional, taking me some time to settle down and gauge which road and where we were headed. As a result, I felt overwhelmed with my responsibility as I am not at the best of times noted for my navigational skills, albeit from an old Czech map.

Even though I finally mastered the map with some confidence, Jarmila insisted on directions at each intersection, too slow to respond to her command she would ignore me, so my navigational assistance fell upon deaf ears. It was not long before we became hopelessly lost. Ultimately, she had to pull over and ask a stranger for directions. He pointed her in one direction, so invariably she shot down the road on an opposite course, cursing his ignorance and lack of knowledge. Finally, I gave up navigating, letting the map slip onto the floor. I had no choice but to place all blind faith in my driver and hoped my concentration and prayers, with some divine intervention, would prevent a head-on collision with oncoming traffic.

Jarmila had little tolerance for road courtesy, so whenever a slower vehicle ahead finally offered an opportunity to pass, she accelerated past, giving the poor driver rude hand gesticulations for being too slow. I hung onto my door as we weaved in and out of traffic, half expecting the latch to release at any moment and leave me hanging over the road beneath. Instead, as Jarmila speedily navigated the route, so did her incessant talking match the pace of speed. She talked non-stop about anything and everything and instructed me to look out the window and enjoy the scenery. How could I? With both eyes glued to the road and anticipating at any moment the need to evacuate my seat and leap to safety, I was fast becoming a nervous wreck.

In the Czech Republic, it is common to have religious shrines or icons every few kilometres apart by the roadside. Jarmila would release her hand from the steering and cross herself at each one, followed by a short inaudible prayer. I was speechless as only minutes before; she had been sacrilegiously cursing some poor driver.

There, all traffic is to the right with left-hand drive, so whenever we overtook anybody, I always felt I was about to connect with road side trees as she swerved the vehicles. Jarmila believed in using entirely her side of the road, so the proximity felt like a whisker apart between all passing cars. On one occasion, Jarmila decided to overtake two lorries in tandem. After some improper gesturing at the first lorry driver, Jarmila shot in between the two, so much that I screamed, believing we were about to hitch onto the lorry ahead of us. Unfazed, she cursed them both and crossed herself at the next shrine before passing the truck ahead of us. During each overtaking lap, I reapplied my grip on the door and, at the same time, leaned instinctively toward Jarmila like a rally driver. Negotiating many sharp bends, I could have just as irrepressibly ended up in the driver's seat with her. Her turbulent driving and intermittent praying certainly had a detrimental effect on my psyche and left me feeling shattered, with white knuckles numbed from my steel grip on the door while both feet were about to melt through the floor. I am sure this trip could have been likened to Le Mans!

When Jarmila finally decided on a brief road stop, I could barely fumble my way out of the car, stand upright on jelly legs, and run for the nearest large tree. Then, for the first and only time on that trip, I finally noticed how beautiful the surrounding countryside was. Beside me, a crystal-clear stream bubbled over mossy-covered rocks as it disappeared into the dark woods. I feared less what might lurk in amongst those trees than on the road with Aunt Jarmila.

On our approach into Havlíčkův Brod, Jarmila knew only one speed: with her foot down, and at the entrance into the town we raced through the roundabout in the wrong direction, entering it on the left rather than on the right. I screamed as on coming cars screeched to a halt allowing Jarmila to squeeze through.

I muttered something about going the wrong way on the roundabout, to which she sharply replied, "This roundabout wasn't here the last time I visited."

Epilogue

It was already late afternoon when we arrived, so I was relieved we were invited to spend the night with the Berk family in Havlíčkův Brod. I would spend the evening with Helena Strusova, Marta's daughter, while Jarmila, Marta, and her husband Vladimír would spend the evening together. Marta Berková was the daughter of Alois Kurovec, my mother's uncle and brother to her father. Marta was warm, calm, and softly spoken, poles apart from Jarmila's loud and bombastic presence. On that visit, Marta told me a little about her life. Later, when I revisited Marta without Jarmila, she was informative about life in Krhová and gave me her version of events on how the partisans attempted to derail the German train during the war. Marta's daughter Helena, who was about my age, managed time away from her busy schedule at the local hospital. After my ordeal with Jarmila, Helena was a breath of fresh air and serenity while we talked well into the early hours.

Helena is a cardiologist, so the following day she invited me to the hospital where she worked. I had an informative tour of their maternity ward and the baby cardio-thoracic unit, where Helena consulted.

Our return journey had traits of the previous, but it seemed to take less time. Jarmila was like a homing pigeon; once on the way, little stopped her. She continually crossed herself at every Religious 'signpost.' For some reason, I felt I should have as well, but my eyes could not leave the road nor unwrap my hands from my knuckle-white grip on the door handle. This unofficial endurance rally that I had been subjected to with Jarmila was an experience I wished never to repeat, as I am sure only the grace of God saved us.

When we finally returned, I learned Cousin Růženka had been trying to contact me since the previous day. When I told her we had just returned from Havlíčkův Brod, there was a prolonged silence at the other end of the phone before she finally asked if I was, OK? I was informed that my stay with Jarmila had been shortened and that she and Lumír would pick me up early the following day.

This trip, from the start, was to be a journey of utmost endeavour to unearth as much as I could about family history. I had resolved to speak my best Czech and be understood, but more to the point, I also had to understand them. I realized over time that no amount of learnt written phrases ever bridged language barriers, it was always conversation Czech; no matter how inarticulate or broken it was, that always paved the way to better communication and understanding.

The remaining elderly generation often had a very black-and-white view of war years, reflecting which side of politics they leaned toward. But my carefully laid out plans soon became obfuscated when I realized how onerous it was to delve into a past that so many young Czechs preferred forgotten. None were eager to converse about war history but instead about their future.

By now, my great grandparent's home at Krhová had been fully renovated by Růženka and Lumír, who had their quarters upstairs, while Aunt Helena, who had inherited the place, lived downstairs. Růženka was a doctor and had a busy schedule as a radiologist at one of the larger hospitals in the vicinity. Her husband Lumír acted as my guide and chauffeur as we drove about chasing after family history, visiting cemeteries and historical sites, and delving into archives in Vsetin, where many documents of interest were uncovered. He was of considerable help, and although not too bothered with Kurovec's history, he went out of his way to try and unearth and bring to light as many of my ancestors as he could find, for which I am eternally grateful. In the evenings, I chatted with Růženka about family matters.

As Aunt Helena was still away, I stayed with them in their apartment, which was once a spacious attic. One evening quite unexpectedly, Růženka raised the subject of our great-uncle Bohuslav Stolař. He was generally never spoken of by the Kurovec family due to disquiet surrounding the circumstances of his death. Růženka, like myself, was more spiritual than religious, but our great uncle's death remained a bit of an enigma to us both. I had been staying with them for some days when this discussion unfolded. I generally slept well in any environment, but earlier during my stay, I had a bizarre dream about a young male stranger, totally unknown to me. It was a disturbing dream, but on waking, I thought my subject must have been sad, if not angry, and a frustrated chap. It was not a nightmare but a rather sad dream, so I thought nothing more of it.

Epilogue

I felt relaxed in their homely environment until Růženka hinted if anything had bothered me while staying here. It was an open-ended question I took it as a polite way of asking if everything was OK. I had hardly reason to complain even when Dani, their big dog insisted on sleeping at the foot of my bed. It was then that Růženka disclosed that our great-uncle Bohuslav was thought to have hung himself in their attic, probably in the rafters above their bedroom. I was quite taken aback, as I had heard various versions of his death, but this one took me by surprise. It was only then, when Růženka further asked me if I had sensed anything untoward in their house, that I recalled my recent dream. As it was a one-off dream without any disturbed sleep afterward, I let it be, and so as not to add further fuel to this intrigue, I said no more.

Some weeks afterward, I returned to Prague by train and met up with my husband, Max, recently arrived. Having done 'my family thing,' the rest of the time was spent touring together by car throughout the countryside and only visiting briefly those I had not been able to catch up with. Earlier, when I had visited Hošťálková, I had been promised assistance from my older cousin Jarek Palá, to research my father's war records. In his youth, he remembered my father, and when a few days later, we returned there; I finally received some breakthrough news about solving a dilemma that had eluded me for some time.

I finally had the name of the prison in Hungry where my father and many other Czech partisans had been imprisoned during the war. My mother often referred to it as Tolonhazy, and at the time, no amount of research on the internet shed a clue. It was called Toloncz Haź, a notorious prison in Hungry. Cousin Jarek also shed light on other war stories about my father, all of which were a revelation to me. However, even then, to google Toloncz Haź on the internet led me to a dead end, and it was not until I accidentally came across a book 'Narrow Escapes!' by Miloslav Bitton that I learned he too had been at Toloncz Haź. This at least confirmed that such a prison existed, but for the time being, it still did not solve where this prison was situated. Some years later, when we visited Budapest, I began to wonder if the Citadel and this prison were one of the same.

Today as I continue to research history on the internet, which is being continually replenished, I now know that this notorious state prison of Toloncz Haź was situated on Mosonyi Street in Budapest.

On that day, as a last-minute idea, Max and I drove my cousin Draha and her husband Ruda Fila to Bulhary. We left Hošťálková at about lunchtime as I wanted to see where my father had last lived before escaping from Czechoslovakia. In 1948, my father's niece Draha had only been in her early teens, but she still remembered the place. It was already late afternoon when we finally arrived at Bulhary, so we had little time to locate the house. We were eventually directed to No. 75 and were met at the door by a rather suspicious and unfriendly old woman. It turned out after my father left; she was of the very same family who was awarded his property by the Communist Government. She did not sit comfortably with us, especially when she learned I was the daughter of 'that soldier.' In the end, my cousin convinced her we were visiting for no other reason but as curious tourists, so she reluctantly allowed us into the backyard. I was thrilled to finally see where my Mum and Dad had spent their last days in Czechoslovakia. I found the well near the house where my father had concealed his weapons before escaping. It was a short but very satisfying visit, and I vowed to return one day. As a parting gesture, the old woman offered to sell me the property. She said she had three sons, and none of them were interested in living in Bulhary.

My father's family gave me photocopies of old photographs and my father's pocket-sized New Testament, which he carried with him during the war. His family leaned toward Evangelical/Lutheran teachings, whereas my mother came from a Catholic background. But never once during my visit did my father's family ever broach the subject of religion, a stark contrast to my maternal side.

Later, leafing through my father's New Testament, I found specific passages underlined, which left me wondering if, deep down, he was a religious man or perhaps these verses just gave him solace while suffering the horrors of war and later his divorce. One can probably unfold many interpretations of these verses, even suggesting these passages contained codes to decipher war messages, but I prefer to think they were meaningful verses for my father at a time when he needed to believe in his faith. However, on the back page remains a reference in Arabic numeracy which he may have jotted down to remember a certain number while in Lebanon.

Epilogue

Although I do not recall my father being religious, he preferred to leave these matters with my mother and allowed her to raise us as she deemed appropriate. In truth, I did not really know the man behind the mask of my dad as he passed away all too soon when I was barely ten years old.

Upon my return to Havlíčkův Brod, Helena, Marta's daughter (my second cousin), showed us many places of interest in the neighbouring district. At the time without the hindsight of more concise WWII knowledge, I did not realize how central Havlíčkův Brod had been to the planning of Operation Anthropoid when Czech parachutists from the UK made preparations that culminated in the final and fatal assault on Reinhardt Heydrich in Prague during WWII. Later when I read 'Seven Men at Daybreak' by Alan Burgess, I realized only then, how close I had been to the place where these patriotic and heroic measures had been planned by these Czech resistance fighters who would ultimately sacrifice their lives for their country.

Being Max's first visit to the Czech Republic, we explored Prague. We attended the famous Black Theatre (Černé Divadlo) and saw 'Prague Cats' in its small but rather old and cramped auditorium. The Black Theatre often travels worldwide, so we were lucky, if not privileged, to catch one of their shows.

We drove about widely, sightseeing, and added churches, castles, and palaces to our historical repertoire of exciting places. But none could compare with Český Krumlov, further south of Prague along the Vltava River, which was once the summer palace of the ousted Royal Hapsburg family.

Travelling east to west within the European Union and passing between once divided countries, border checks were now relaxed, barely hindering motorists as the Czech Republic and Slovakia were now absorbed into the mix of this European democracy. But as history shows, unexpected or unacceptable events can suddenly change the dynamics of any political theatre.

In 2010, two years after my mother passed away, we had an unexpected visit from Louie Nohl and his son Steven. Louie lifted the lid on a decades-old secret shared by him and my father that they had kept from my mother. Louie, who by now was living once more in the Czech Republic, returned on holiday and, during his visit, revealed to my brother something that he could never disclose while our mother had been alive; otherwise, as he put it, "She would have killed me!"

Louie had been an old acquaintance of my fathers from their South Australian days and who, under very different circumstances, had also immigrated to Australia from Czechoslovakia. Louie had visited us at least twice while my father was still alive, and then once more in the 1970s with his sister Sophie after my father's passing. He was a colourful character and at least twelve to fourteen years younger than my father. My mother was always wary of him as he was too free-spirited for her liking, and she always felt he would lead her husband astray; but little did she know how close to the truth she had been.

During one of his earlier visits, while we were still dairy farming at Euluma Creek, Louie was employed by my father to help cut railway sleepers for the Mossman Sugar Mill. In 2010 Louie confessed to a series of events, when at his instigation he induced my father into a lucrative deal for a princely share in £800. During this period, the Forestry Inspector led an intense Forestry Department investigation to track down those responsible for the disappearance of a huge hickory tree. Somebody unknown had allegedly cut it down, milled it, and removed it without leaving any trace. Many were questioned, some suspected, but in the end, nobody was charged as there was insufficient evidence to arrest anyone. However, it was always believed by those investigating the case at the time that it must have been sawn by one of the larger timber mills within the district.

At the time, a well-known Hotel in Cairns would become the beneficiary of some quality timber. When I heard the story from my brother some years after Louie passed away, I was glad my mother had been spared the details, as no doubt she would have vented her anger at Louie for this nefarious act.

On one particular visit to New Zealand in 2013, I requested the release of my mother's archival documents from a Wellington repository. To my surprise, amongst these documents and immigration papers, new information helped to shed light on a few remaining questions. My mother could be spare with detail sometimes, and I always believed her voyage to Australia on board the 'Wanganella' was only for a short holiday, with her return passage from Sydney booked through Thomas Cook. She allegedly had planned to visit her brother in South Australia for a few weeks, but, at the time, she had been presented with a crystal dressing table set and a silver cigarette lighter by her nursing colleagues. This always intrigued me why such an extravagant going-away gift, when she was going only on a short holiday, even though accompanied by an excessive number of trunks destined for some remote community near Port Lincoln. These archival records put to rest one quandary in particular as it highlighted that on the day of embarking 'The Wanganella' on the 28th of August 1952, it was her birthday, an earlier omission she made when we discussed her journey. She also added that she intended to return to New Zealand, but circumstances after arriving at Port Lincoln took her down a very different road. It would only be years later while reading her Czech letters when researching her story that I learnt of another important omission, her engagement to my dad, which she failed to acknowledge while she was still alive. At least this explained why she travelled with so many trunks. She probably only intended to return if things did not work out with my father, so hence the paid return passage to New Zealand.

While in New Zealand, I managed to retrace some of her recreational jaunts, but one that I found most poignant was Mount Manganui on the mid-eastern coast of North Island. Here on the beach, perhaps not in as glamorous style, I sat on the very rocks, a prominent rocky outcrop where in an old black and white photograph, she and friends posed so many years ago. Sitting there, I tried to sense that moment in her life where and when she and her Czech girlfriends probably had their first swim in the open sea.

In 2016 my husband and I once more passed through the Czech Republic. This time I came with renewed hope of filling in the gaps that stared back at me from my old notes. I had been hoping for that grand final hurrah to give me all the answers.

A lot happened in the intervening years between 2005 and 2016. My mother and her sister Bo both passed away in 2008, and later Aunt

Helena in 2014. By then, their youngest sister Jarmila was in aged care. Some years before, Vladimir Burk, Marta's husband, had also passed away along with many other elderly relatives on both sides of my family. Sadly, with time comes change, opportunities are lost, as many treasured family stories no longer echo in conversations with the emerging youth. The past is no longer significant to them, as this new generation is only interested in their future.

During these intervening years, I remained busy piecing together ancestral members of both Kurovec and Kaňák families with the aid of Ancestory.com.

One day an email message reached me; "I think my half-sister might be your half-sister!"

After many years of searching and procrastinating, I finally found Milada Violet Kanak. Violet was nine years older than I, married with a family and grandchildren, and still living in England. Unfortunately, our pending trip to Europe was on a tight schedule, and this time we had not included Great Britain. Instead, we arranged to meet in Yprés in Belgium as we were scheduled to visit there. Although no thought had been given to this choice of town at the time, it was rather serendipitous as during WWII, our father at some stage would have fought in battle close by.

Violet had arrived with her husband, Ralph, their elder daughter Geraldine, and her husband, Paul. It was almost bittersweet to learn that I was already an aunt by the age of thirteen but knew nothing of it. Our meeting was an emotional one, but as we were now older and set in our ways, sibling similarities that may have existed were often masked, leaving behind strangers. Violet was a warm and sensitive sister, but her daughter Geraldine and I struck up an immediate entente cordiale.

I expressed my sadness and profound disappointment that our dad had left a daughter behind on the other side of the world, without as much as speaking about her. Violet seemed very pragmatic and accepting of our father's actions and reiterated that he should not be solely blamed as it was not all his doing. Alice, her grandmother who brought up Violet, was a strong-willed woman who intervened, disallowing Elsie and her small daughter to follow him back to Czechoslovakia after the war.

Three years after Violet's birth in 1944, her parent's marriage was finally over by 1947. Violet recalls seeing our father for the last time when she was three or five. One witness at her parent's wedding was our father's cousin Karel Kutěj another Czech who also turned up at Cholmondeley during the war and who remained in the UK for a while after Jan had left. He occasionally visited Violet and her mother until Elsie's divorce became final.

Upon divorcing our father, Elsie later remarried and began a new family. When meeting Violet, her mother still lived at home but had already developed marginal dementia. Nevertheless, she still recalled our father and many events of the day and how together they would go to a place in London where Czech army uniforms were fitted to size and tailored for the soldiers. She allegedly always kept a photo of him. Although I remain no wiser about how they met, Elsie Carter finally passed away in early March 2023.

During our 2016 trip to the Czech Republic, we were independent and free to return to Bulhary alone, and once more explore my father's village. By now, the township of Bulhary had smartened up as parts of the place were being used as film props for a popular Czech TV series. Again, we visited No. 75, where previously my father had lived, and unbelievably, the same old woman still occupied the house. Thirteen years since our previous visit, we again introduced ourselves to her, yet again, she received us coldly. There was no warm welcome but rather the feeling of intrusion while she eyed us off suspiciously as if not wanting to remember who we were. After all, thirteen years ago, when trying to locate my father's dwelling, an old village man referred to my father as 'that soldier' and did not want to enter any further discussion. No doubt, for those then still alive and recalling the 1948 Easter fiasco, it must have been a dark memory for them, whether they were; informers, victims, or simply bystanders.

We found where, in 1948, my parents took their chances and escaped crossing the stream beneath the rail bridge. Today, this swampy terrain of creeks and waterways is primarily overgrown with natural vegetation. In contrast, back then, it would have been covered in winter snow, and much of the vegetation cleared, so all rail tracks, for security reasons, would have been fully exposed. The railway remains in use, but parallel to it is a commemorative pathway reminding all those who walk along it, how many lives were lost while trying to escape through the

'Iron Curtain'. Although my parents fled in 1948, just before it had been erected, I still feel my parents should be included as the success story of those dark times and be remembered. 'Escaped here on the evening of Easter Monday, the 29th of March 1948, Jan Kaňák, Domin Červenec, and Anna Kurovcová'. But then, no locals knew their story.

We returned to Hošťálková, and once more, my family's hospitality was warm and welcoming. It was now the younger generation at the forefront of family representation who was embracing our visit and extending the welcome on behalf of their aging relatives. Unfortunately, my most valuable source of information, cousin Jarek Palá had by now passed away, taking with him the answers to questions I was still wanting to ask.

My cousin Lenka had inherited the Kaňák family home at No. 125 Hošťálková. She was the younger daughter of my father's sister Anna Syptáková. My mother and Lenka had always maintained a cordial relationship with regular communication, and my mother was particularly fond of Michal, their adopted son and only child. Sadly, Michal passed away in 2003, aged only twenty-five leaving Lenka and her husband with no other children.

Sometime before our arrival, Lenka had passed away, and as she and her husband had no natural children of their own, the Kaňák ancestral home ended up with Lenka's husband. This created angst and family division when he passed on the property to his side of the family, and then moved elsewhere with a new partner. Lenka's elder sister, my cousin Drahomíra or Draha as she was generally known, had also lost her husband Ruda by this time. Much of the conversation centred on immediate family bereavements, concerns and the injustices of Lenka's family home.

I strolled past the Kaňák ancestral home, but it was now shut to me and in the hands of strangers, so I realized a part of my father's history was fast disappearing along with it. It no longer seemed the same when on by gone visits, I could share my time between Lenka's Kaňák family dwelling and Draha's home. During this visit, nobody really wanted to speak about the past or divulge additional information about my father's cousin Karel Kutěj and his family.

We continued onto Valašské Mezirici and Novy Jičín and reunited once more with my mother's remaining family. Aunt Jarmila was now in aged care, and with Aunt Helena gone and the Stolar ancestral home sold, it left me with a sense that my family roots were also shrivelling up. Nevertheless, out of it still came renewed hope of breaking ties with the past, focusing on families in the present, and looking to their futures. The younger generations left behind were now able to resurrect their lives from the crumbling mortar of these old institutions where the past no longer mattered and was all but gone. In their eyes, it was time to unshackle the past and move on.

Back in Prague, we planned to visit the Orthodox Church of St. Cyril and Methodius on Resslova Street, where in 1942, Czech resistance fighters responsible for Reinhard Heydrich's assassination were eventually captured and executed by the Nazis. Heydrich's death was followed by the horrendous annihilation of entire villages like that of Lidice, which, when we visited, left us emotionally devasted by this catastrophic retaliation.

My interest in the church was not only of historical value but of curiosity arising from my mother's account that my father had volunteered for Special Operations (SOE) while in the CIABG. Suitable recruits were sent to Arisaig in Scotland and trained for selection to prepare for 'Operation Anthropoid,' an exercise which ultimately succeeded in ending Heydrich's life and his cruel infliction upon so many Czechoslovak people. During this period, my father allegedly fractured his collarbone during an awkward parachute jump while training, which precluded him from selection and further training for these classified missions.

On the Monday of our visit in late August of 2016, it was raining, and the church, unbeknown to us, was closed on Mondays, but through Max and his fortunate encounter at the church door with John Marten from Manchester, our luck had changed. John Marten was leading a group of privately prebooked English journalists on a church tour, and we were allowed to tag along. The then soon-to-be-released film 'Anthropoid' was being previewed for the UK audience. Through research and data available to date, I have failed to correctly identify any records attributed to my father's intended part in this patriotic role. Therefore, I can only assume he had failed to be selected due to injury and never made it as far as Arisaig.

Later, before departing Europe in 2016, we drove to Mauthausen in Austria to seek out my Uncle Vladimír's resting place, my mother's brother who had spent his final hours there. The previous evening, we spent a pleasant stay at Melk on the Danube River within easy reach of Mauthausen. Our comfortable accommodation was beyond comparison to the stark and chilly reality, a spectre of the human travesty that today is the Museum of Mauthausen. Within the now silenced barrack walls remains a history of shame and deprivation where wretched souls were executed, gassed or otherwise, for no other reason than being Jewish or believing in freedom. The concentration camp of Mauthausen is a relic of these WWII Nazi atrocities.

During this journey to unravel family history, I learned beyond doubt that Vladimír was arrested by ZbV KDO 31 (German commando) on the 7th of March 1945 and imprisoned at Brno. On about the 6th or 7th of April, he was moved from Brno and placed on Transport KL3 to KT Mauthausen (Concentration Camp), comprising over two hundred prisoners of the 'most dangerous kind' who were to be executed! On the 9th of April, they all arrived in cattle wagons and, from the railway station, walked to Mauthausen Concentration Camp, where they were held all day without food or water. As there was no room for these prisoners, they were later herded into the bathrooms for the night, and the next day, April 10th, they were all gassed.

I finally left Mauthausen feeling angry and despondent without any closure or resolution for what had happened in 1945. My uncle Vladimír had been executed there just weeks before the war ended and although his records were documented on their electronic database, his name failed to appear on the large granite tablet where every soul having died there was named. This oversight added to my grief, but I was assured it was up to his immediate family to correctly identify his records before being added. Again, I felt helpless and sorrowed that he had been overlooked, but I agree it is up to his immediate remaining family to rectify.

In 2018 we travelled to the Ayre Peninsula in South Australia, where my parents first started married life together, giving me a sense of homecoming. I had not returned to South Australia since leaving at the age of three, and it was here that my brother and I were born and took our first steps, and, without doubt, my sister was conceived, after which time we moved north to Queensland. It was here that my earliest memories began as a smattering of images that, to this day, still remain vivid.

I walked through Wanilla Forest, my first home now protected indigenous land, and later, at Wangary, where I reflected on moments in the company of Helen Sheppard. Being close in age, we had once shared times as children on what was then her family's sheep and wheat property. Things change, but glimpses of the past still linger. The most poignant moment, however, was when Peter, Helen's brother, took us to neighbouring Puckridge's property, and I wandered through the forest amongst the gnarled trees and sawn-off tree stumps, a legacy remaining from when my father fell these trees so many years ago. His haunting presence remains as heaps of hard and bleached wooden off-cuts remain from the early 1950's scattered in piles and preserved over decades by the heat and dry climate but, thankfully, not reduced to ashes by the ravage of fires that from time to time have scurred the South Australian landscape. I also learnt that the Puckeridge family have an archival film of my father cutting timber which one day I hope to see.

We visited the popular seasides featured frequently in my family album; old black and white photographs of Coffin Bay, Farmer's Beach, Tumby Bay, and Port Lincoln Pier on Tasman Terrace, all of which held special memories for my parents. During our stay in Port Lincoln and while lunching at a small café, I serendipitously came across a friendly and elderly lady Judith Parker who just so happened to know friends and acquaintances of my parents. I had been keen to search out Mary O'Hara's family and hoped by some sheer stroke of luck that she or her family were still alive. Sister O'Hara had been my Godmother, and I just wanted to acknowledge her obligation and thank her for volunteering to protect a child in the advent of adversity. But I also wanted to tell her I had survived without calling upon her obligation. Mary O'Hara had been a nursing sister at the Port Lincoln Hospital where I was born. Our reunion was not to be, as I was informed, she was long gone, and there appeared no one remaining from her immediate family in Port Lincoln.

Sadly, before completing this memoir, my cousin Zdeněk Hurtik who had always been there for us whenever we visited the Czech Republic, passed away in 2018 and Marta Berková, my mother's cousin, followed in 2020. In 2022 my mother's sister-in-law, Jaroslav's wife, Lois Kurovec, passed away.

Since visiting the Czech Republic in 2016, I maintained regular telephone contact with Aunt Jarmila my mother's last surviving sister. Although residing in aged care Jarmila kept her own mobile phone so every year near Christmas, I would call her. On New Year's day having missed my Christmas call to her, I rang and as usual Jarmila did the talking while I patiently listened. She was bright and cheery, content in her place of abode, and maintained she was well cared for. She spoke of family who had visited her and gave glowing reports about her great-grandchildren. Little did I realize that this would be our last conversation as later in April 2023, aged 88 Jarmila passed away and with it, closing another family chapter.

In my mother's memoir, I felt obliged to use as many of her photographs as possible, which frames a glimpse into her personal life through these pictorial windows. Only she knew what bearings these snapshots had at those precise moments. But, like with many photographs, these will one day pass onto strangers who will have no relationship with them or a need to keep them, and like so many pictures of the past, they will end up in the dustbin, gone forever.

As I reflect upon my mother's life, I recall our numerous conversations over the years and her ability to prioritize over what she deemed trivial.

Once during late February 1986 at a time when social media was unheard of and only Reuters Reporters placed strategically around the globe reported on world events, the Philippines were the focal point of interest as dictators Ferdinand and Imelda Marcos were being ousted out of their country.

At that precise moment I was also having a crisis of sorts of my own. I had been skiing in Austria and on my return to Cairo became standard at Vienna airport. Cairo was under siege after rioting by police and with curfews in place, flights in and out of Cairo were being restricted.

Epilogue

Finally arriving I was met and collected at the airport by our driver from the A.O.I. (Arab Organization for Industrialization) my employer whilst in Egypt, and nervously dispatched home through the deserted and eerily quiet streets. Above in the evening sky, military choppers dotted the sky enforcing the curfew.

Arriving at my apartment I immediately placed a call to my mother in Australia to report I was safe and well.

Her response, "I am so pleased you have returned to Cairo as I was so worried you might break a leg while skiing." She was always so practical!

Although I learnt that our company vehicles were brazenly marked with large visible A.O.I. letters over the bonnet to avoid being shot at, it seemed our Egyptian crisis went mostly unnoticed elsewhere in the world.

I had many precious moments with my mother during her later years and whenever I visited her and especially on my birthdays, she always insisted, I come home and visit. She always made these occasions special and celebrated them with her freshly made apple strudel and then sent me home with a bowl of apricot dumplings; meruňkové knedlíky, my favourite. These memorable instances will always remain with me, not only because of her exceptional culinary skills but because it was her way of expressing love and enabling us to have precious mother-daughter moments. Therefore, whenever I think of my mother, my thoughts always stray homeward to the warmth she exuded while at the same time wonder how she would have meshed into her own society at home, now in the 21st century. Would she, like me, fear for the Czech culture and identity and its language? After all, it was once almost lost and may yet again face extinction with the advent of rapid Anglicization through entry into the European Union and shared markets.

Her own reflection on life was never of regret except where she wished she had been granted more time with my father and which no doubt would have taken her and us down a very different path, a destiny that was never to be. She missed him very much throughout her life. Never one to waste money, she on rare occasions reminisced about her return passage to New Zealand one which was never used or redeemed and one which so long ago closed a chapter on her previous station in life. Besides, she never had a need to return to New Zealand again. Anna always looked forward and not back on missed opportunities as she made her journey through one door, leaving behind a chapter of that life while navigating through the next revolving door. In the end she achieved what she set out to do and was content with her lot in life.

Over the years, while I travelled and visited my mother's haunts and crisscrossed her old tracks, I always discovered something new to slot into this narrative. I must acknowledge without reservation, that much of what I have written could not have been procured without those who contributed anecdotal tales, jolted my memory with reminders of past events, and occasionally even corrected my narrative. As with the completion of any lengthy memoir, it often comes at the expense of time, which many of my mother's dear and remaining friends may not have an abundance of, but for those who still remember her and do read this book, I hope it does not disappoint.

It has been a long and convoluted journey from beginning to end, seeking a past that finally brought me to where I am today. But for me also, it is time to leave what remains unknown about my parents' lives and move forward instead of looking back for time-old answers. Like any memoir, no doubt somewhere in the future, additional pieces of my mother's life will unexpectedly surface and fit snugly into place, but in the end, not change the outcome of her life.

Helena E Kanak 2024.

Acknowledgements

Without the contribution of so many and the encouragement of friends, this book may not have seen the light of day.

My unwavering gratitude goes to everyone who helped me fill these pages with memories and family recollections, including so many of my mother's dear friends, many of whom sadly are no longer with us, but each who contributed a story.

Special thanks to everyone I spoke with, emailed and wrote to and those who over the years generously contributed information, enabling this story to be told.

To my relatives in the Czech Republic who over the years provided me with documents, photos and their personal family stories which they willingly shared.

My cousin Růženka's husband Lumir, who obligingly and with good humour accompanied me to way out places, gleaning information and exploring cemeteries with me to gain further insight into my Kurovec ancestors.

My late cousin Zdeněk who generously introduced us to the city of Prague and its history and together with his wife Iva always made us feel welcome, and his brother Milosh who always found time to take us out in Prague and whenever we visited my ancestral town in Moravia, introduce us to their country hospitality along with his siblings Pavla and Jarek.

My Kanak family descendants in Hošťálková who gave of their time to show my father's heritage and always welcomed me with open arms.

Here in Australia, the Kurovec family, namely my cousins; Shaun who made time to take me to places around Port Lincoln which otherwise I would not have found, Jaryn who sadly passed away earlier this year (2024) much, much too soon, and who always lent a willing ear as we discussed my mother's story; sadly, never to read the final draft, and Vladge who kept me updated with our forever expanding ancestral tree.

To my newly-found sister Violet Langworthy and her family from the United Kingdom, who enlightened me with family history while our father was still married to his first wife, their mother Elsie, and who, at the time of writing this, had entered her 100th year but passed away in 2023..

The Shepperd family from South Australia, especially Helen and Peter, for sharing their memories and kindly showing me where my father over 67 years ago cut timber on Puckeridge's property, a firsthand walk through the forest, and be able to stand amongst trees in a virtually untouched landscape since my father last milled his log before leaving for Queensland.

To Judith Parker, a total stranger I accidently met in a café in Port Lincoln and who just happened to know everyone! And Bronwyn Gilham highlighted how difficult life had been for them in Laura on the very block my father would acquire many years later.

Special acknowledgment and thanks to Mr. Jeff Callaghan, now retired from the Bureau of Meteorology, who responded to my email and headed me in the right direction while in my mind I was attempting to navigate the route from my mother's rudimentary sketch of towns and places we passed through, on my family's journey from South Australia to Queensland. A time I barely remembered my family driving north during some of the most severe weather conditions in history that culminated from the 1955 to 1956 floods.

Sincere gratitude to the late John Stevenson, and his wife Jan, especially John, who volunteered time and information, helping to piece together my family life when we newly arrived from South Australia to Mareeba and settled temporarily in a hut on his family farm by Atherton Creek.

Special thanks to Colleen Ingold, who reunited Alena and Walter Herrmann with Anna and prioritized yearly reunions.

Betty Lawford for her knowledge of historical facts about Julatten, and Olive and Harvey Keys, who graciously wrote the foreword for this book.

Many thanks to my brother John who remembered with clarity certain events I had long forgotten and always put me straight on those I needed to get accurate.

And Diana, my sister who occasionally read transcripts but remained impartial throughout, preferring to maintain privacy rather than sharing all with the world! I respect her decision.

I principally must acknowledge my late mother Anna, who left behind not only her life's legacy but letters albethey Czech, which I unearthed and patiently read to complete her memoir.

And finally, thank you to my dear husband Max, who not only suffered my protracted absences from our domestic life but steadfastly accepted my determination to complete this saga. At a time while I madly typed away at the computer, zoning out in the office and often wondering to where all this was leading me. I very much appreciated his efforts and dedication digging up information and researching WWII battles, which directly linked to my father's participation. He often corrected my numerous assumptions as we pieced together my father's narrative. Knowledge of my father's war years was scant at the best of times, but through research and endeavour, inroads were made, giving some light to questions and answers I wasn't old enough to ask before my father's untimely passing. Thank you, Max!

A Brief History of Czech Lands and the Birth of a Nation

I have added a brief history to better understand the Nation of Czechoslovakia which today forms the countries of the Czech Republic and Slovakia. This brief history is by no means complete and at the very least a complex one; an undertaking more worthy of a learned historian, rather than myself. Instead, with Czech history available on the internet, Wikipedia, and what my mother passed on, I have very briefly outlined, in some chronological order, the better-known rulers, national heroes, despots, and historical events that helped define the nation.

In about 300 BC, a Celtic tribe called the Boii[1] roamed within the Czech lands, which gave this region the name Bohemia. These Boii were pagan tribesmen who, from time to time, were invaded and ruled by other dominant tribes. They were eventually forced out by Germanic Marcomanni and Quadi tribes, which soon afterward, in about 450AD, were themselves wiped out by Attila the Hun[2]. By the sixth century, early Slavs, with their pagan cultures[3] and various language dialects, arrived and occupied this region. These people were descendants of Polesia[4] from the farthest edges of central Europe.

During the seventh century, the Slavic tribes inhabiting these areas were consequently ruled over by the Avars, whose harsh rule provoked Slavic rebellions and brought about the short-lived Slavic Kingdom. As the legend goes; during the eighth century, a tribal leader named Krok had three daughters; Kazi, a healer with knowledge of herbs; Teta, the religious one and Libuše, who was beautiful and wise. Upon Krok's death, his daughter Libuše was chosen, and although unheard of that a woman could rule over a tribe, she first had to find a husband.

One popular myth was that a white horse followed by tribal elders had been sent over the hills. In a reverie, Libuše forecast that this horse would come upon two spotted oxen and a ploughman named Přemysl, and so began the Přemyslid Dynasty[5]. Independence and empire building followed, and from Vyšehrad, Libuše envisioned a great city that would become Prague. The Přemyslid Dynasty would rule Bohemia for the next

600 years until eventually succumbing in 1306.

During the ninth century, when a Slavic state was created in Moravia under the rule of Prince Mojmír[6], more tangible history was recorded. Mojmír's successor, Rastislav[7], beseeched the Pope to send Christian Apostles with knowledge of the Slavic language to end sun god worshipping and fertility rites practiced by the Slavs[8]. Two Greek brothers, Cyril and Methodius were dispatched by the Byzantine Emperor and created a Cyrillic script from the Slavic language. However, with pressure from Frankish and German priests, the Slavic language was soon prohibited.

From earlier invasions, this region had become a mixing pot of ethnic nationalities, later including the nomadic Romany tribes with their own language, who arrived during the tenth century. These 'Gypsy' people migrated from the east through Hungry and spread across Europe, with many remaining in Slovakia, Moravia, and Bohemia. When religion finally arrived, the kingdoms were ruled by religious monarchs, and this new culture engulfed most of the tribes and converted them to Christianity, namely Catholicism.

With the continual reign of Přemyslid Kings throughout coming centuries; Prince Václav, also known as Good King Wenceslas, who reigned until 929, managed to maintain humanity and peace, but he neglected Slavic interests and sold out to the Germans.

Over the centuries, the Slavs had endured the rule of the Byzantine Empire, the Holy Roman Empire, the Austro-Hungarian Empire, and the Germans. They almost lost their Slav identity and language while always remaining at the epicentre of mercenary invasions and bloody battles.

By 1278 King Přemysl Ottokar II aspired for the crown of the Holly Empire, forcing Rudolf of Habsburg into the Battle of Marchfeld, during which Ottokar II was killed. Ottokar II's successor Václav II (Wenceslaus), continued to conquer much of Romania, Poland, Croatia, and Hungry. By 1306, the Czech Přemyslid Dynasty ended with alleged Habsburg agents assassinating Václav III, Heir to the throne, thus, leaving no successors.

In 1310 the Holy Roman Emperor, John of Luxembourg, aged only fourteen, ascended to the throne as King of Bohemia. He later married Elisabeth of Bohemia, the daughter of Václav II, thus giving him an authentic Přemyslid link.

At the battle of Crecy, John of Luxembourg died, and his son Charles IV would rise to become Holy Emperor, King of Bohemia; and so, began the golden age of Prague.

Having escaped the 'Black Death' of 1348 which ravaged much of Europe, Prague became an opulent city under Charles IV. Charles IV was a devout Christian, but his reign was plagued with church corruption making many clergy wealthy land owners, thus creating anti-clerical uprisings. Following Charles IV, his son Wenceslas IV created unrest with the Catholics by refusing the destruction of Protestant writings by English theologian, reformer, and translator of the Bible; John Wycliffe [9].

John Wycliffe was the medieval forerunner of the Protestant Reformation and was an influential dissident within the Roman Catholic priesthood. In 1403 Jan Hus [10], Rector of Prague University and influenced by John Wycliffe's doctrines, began his own campaign against the corruption of the Catholic Church and against Wenceslas; who, although being a champion of the common people, lacked moral and intellectual integrity. These actions declared Jan Hus a heretic, and in 1412 Wenceslas IV advised Jan Hus to leave Prague in order to quell escalating attitudes against the monarchy. Wenceslas' brother, Sigmund, King of Hungry, summoned Hus to appear before the General Council at Constance. Hus attended the hearing in good faith but was imprisoned after refusing to recant his beliefs. On his 46th birthday, the 6th of July 1415, Jan Hus was burnt at the stake.

His tenets of Hussitism, contained in the Four Articles of Prague, demanded the unrestricted preaching word of God, communion in both kinds, removal of estates and possessions from monks and clergy, and strict punishment of sins committed by members of the church. Jan Hus became a martyr to his fellow Czech Utraquist followers who embodied hope with the symbolic chalice and his motto 'Truth Wins.' Upon Wenceslas IV death, his brother Sigmund took over the Bohemian throne without encountering too much rage from the Utraquist nobles.

In 1432 General Jan Žižka [11], a follower of Jan Huss, and a radical Hussite, led the Táborité (a faction within the Hussite movement) against medieval Catholic practices. Apart from the Taborites, the Hussites were splintered into various sects; Adamites, Orebites, Sirotci, Ultraquists, and Praguers.

Fighting the crusaders, Jan Žižka and his 'Warriors of God' won numerous battles all the way to the Baltic. Žižka used unorthodox and innovative tactics, exploiting geographic features and maintaining strict discipline with his fighters.

He became a National hero, and upon his death, it was said, "The one whom no mortal hand could destroy was extinguished by the finger of God."

For most, the Hussites remained united during times of attack. However, their class beliefs strained relationships between the moderate middle-class intellectual Praguers and the extreme Taborites who band all class divisions and held their services only in Czech.

The Pope reluctantly invited the Czechs into peace negotiations, but the Taborites remained suspicious of such propositions. However, the Praguers happily united with Rome and made way for dialogue with the Papal city while decimating over 13,000 Taborites at the Battle of Lipany in 1434.

Shortly afterward, in 1436, the 'Basle Compacts' were signed, making all Czechs 'Faithful Sons of the Church' and accepting Utraquist demands of communion in both kinds. However, the 'Basle Compacts' made no mention of church corruption. Prague was soon admonished by a Papal envoy questioning their un-Roman practices. The envoy denied any knowledge of the signed agreement between the Utraquist and the Roman church. Still, seeing the document, the mediators made a hasty withdraw with the stolen papers, which were later recovered upon capture.

During this national religious class anarchy, the rather weak and readily swayed King Ladislaus of Habsburg relied on advice from his native-born Utraquist, George of Poděbrady [12]. Persuaded to take poisoned wine, King Ladislaus posthumously made way for Poděbrady to rise to the throne in March of 1458. Poděbrady stamped out fanatical Taborites, suppressed schismatic pacifist Christians, and kept diehard

Catholics aside without alienating Rome.

Upon George Poděbrady's death in 1471, Kings from the Jagiellonian Dynasty[13] ascended to the throne and reigned in absentia from Hungry. During that period, it altered the Hussite balance of influence and created a vacuum again filled by ruthless nobles who ruled mercilessly over the peasants. The spread of Lutheran ideas aligned with Hussitism flared tensions with the Utraquist, who feared admonishment from Rome.

In 1526 Jagellon King Louis II drowned during the battle of Mohács, and the Estates of Bohemia finally elected Austrian Duke Ferdinand I of the Habsburg Dynasty as King of Bohemia. A dynasty that would rule until 1918.

Ferdinand systemically suppressed all Protestant dissidents, appointed German Catholics to key official positions, and declared German the official language, thus violating the King's constitution and oath. By 1556 the Jesuit Order took control of higher education throughout the kingdom and tutored the sons of leading nobles.

In 1562 Maximilian II hoped to divide Bohemia by suppressing the unity of the Czech Brethren and supporting the Utraquist movement rather than the middle-class Catholics. Through allowances, the King's verbal 'Confessio Bohemica' set out sections of Hussite and Lutheran learnings and freed Bohemia from the Roman Church. But in his wake, Maximilian left Christianity divided, which did not help him achieve his other political goal; that being the eviction of all Turks out of Hungry.

Maximilian's successor Rudolf II[14] moved his court from Vienna to Prague, and for the first time in two hundred years, Prague became central to the Empire. The emperor removed himself from political activity and fostered artistic, scientific, and mystical research. While Europe entered the thirty-year war, Rudolfine Prague was so distanced that it became a nirvana of religion, medieval chemistry, and astrology.

During this war period, Prague was invaded by Saxon Protestants and reclaimed by Wallenstein [15], a Bohemian-born Protestant General. In 1606 Wallenstein converted to Catholicism and rose through the ranks to become a leader in the Imperial Catholic Army, a great asset to the

Habsburg Empire. However, the Emperor's Jesuits despised him despite his numerous military accolades and conspired to do away with him.

Even though the emperor attempted to outlaw all non-Catholic worship in 1599, the threat of Islam from the Turks made the Habsburgs quickly realize that Protestants were far preferable to Islam. The Empire relied heavily on military and financial support from the Protestant Estates.

Eventually, Matthias [16], brother of Rudolf II, took over from the shrinking King and shaped a peace treaty with the Hungarians and Turks, thus forcing Rudolf II out of Hungry, Austria, and Moravia and leaving him only to rule in Bohemia. After signing the 'Letter of Majesty' and reinstating some Protestant integrity, Rudolf II suspected his brother Mathias was also about to oust him out of Bohemia, so he summonsed his cousin Leopold to invade. Rudolf II was finally deposed in 1611.

Mathias and his successor Ferdinand II were ardent Counter-Reformation Catholics who vexed the Bohemian Estates.

The towns of Hrob and Broumov became the epicentre of unrest when the Bishop of Prague ordered the destruction of a Protestant Chapel and the closure of another. Both Chapels had been built following the guarantee of the 'Letter of Majesty.' The emperor further banned the Estates from meeting, so on the 23rd of May 1618, Count Thurn[17] marched onto the Royal Castle and met with the Emperor's Roman Catholic deputies Slavata and Martinic, both of whom had been accused responsible for the ban. Together with their secretary, they were catapulted out of the window, landing in a pile of swilling trash but lived on to relate their elaborated valour. Prague's defenestration (to be thrown out of the window) grew into a symbolic and contentious act throughout Europe, and so began the term 'defenestration.'

During the seventeenth-century cold war, one pivotal event was the election of Frederick of the Palatinate to the Bohemian throne. He was the son of James I of England and Ireland and the head of the Protestant Union of German Princes. For the first time, it upset the balance of power four to three in favour of the Protestants against Catholic electors within the Holy Roman Empire.

Ferdinand II was ready to retaliate and defend his sovereignty, but Bohemia's Frederick of the Palatinate was ill-prepared for battle.

Nevertheless, the Czechs maintained faith in Frederick and hoped the all-powerful Protestant Princes of Europe would unite behind him and defend Bohemia. By November 1620, Ferdinand II had assembled the support of the merged Roman Catholic League of Spain, Italy, Poland, and Bavaria. Frederick had only managed to round up the support of the Protestants of Transylvania.

The Battle of Bilá Hora on the 8th of November 1620 saw the demise of Frederick's army, and only after his escape had he learned that English troops were standing by some twelve miles away waiting to be summonsed to battle.

Upon the first anniversary of Prague's earlier defenestration, twenty-seven Protestant nobles and scholars were decapitated in Prague's Old Town Square. Many of the less privileged had their tongues wrenched out, hands chopped off, and heads impaled onto the columns of Charles Bridge spanning the Vltava River. Ferdinand II had annihilated one-third of Bohemia's population to rid it of dissidents and confiscated over three-quarters of the land to pay for war tariffs. Over thirty thousand wealthy Protestant families were dispossessed of their possessions and sent into exile, while German immigrants filled the depopulated towns and villages.

Estates belonging to the Protestant nobles were confiscated and handed to loyal Catholics and those from abroad. The Czechs were subsequently heavily taxed, the proceeds used to beautify Vienna and pay off war debts. The peasants were forced into slavery, and the ruthless Jesuits came to re-educate them, while the royal court once more returned to Vienna and Ferdinand II ruled by Royal Decree. The Habsburg's hereditary claim was yet again settled. Bohemia would remain isolated, with the Habsburgs having the casting vote on any future Holy Emperor.

Although Protestant General Wallenstein had earlier switched sides in 1606, the Czech people's hope of any victory still lay with him when in 1634, he entered Bohemia. However, the same year, he was assassinated by Irish mercenaries in Cheb.

In 1650 a Czech named Jan Comenius[18] inspired his people to keep the faith and helped to maintain their hope with these desperate words, "I believe that after the tempest of God's wrath shall have passed, the rule of thy country will again return unto thee, O Czech Nation."

However, toward the end of that century, much of the population had already reverted to Catholicism, and many notable changes quickly followed. German replaced the spoken Czech language, and nobility was educated in German schools. Charles University became Charles-Ferdinand University, and the Jesuits taught there in Latin. A lifetime of Czech heritage now lay with the illiterate peasants. It was a period of oppression but ironically produced some of Prague's most stunning works of Baroque architecture of today.

During the mid-eighteenth century, following Charles VI her father, Empress Maria Theresa[19] was the only woman to become a sovereign ruler within the Holy Roman Empire. Even though she lost Silesia to the Prussians; she founded the Viennese Medicine school, promoted education, restructured the Judiciary system, and reformed land leases and ownership; thus, changing the serf system and allowing peasants to make a living. Her successor Joseph II [20] instrumental in 'The Edict of Tolerance' (a declaration of religious reform), granted worship freedom to other religious sects. He had little tolerance for the Church and rid the system of Jesuits, closing down monasteries and freeing the Jews from ghettos. Although he was condemned for the Germanization of the central bureaucracy and the decline in Czech culture, he was still credited with educational reform, religious tolerance, and social reforms, which meant the peasants could marry without their master's permission. Still, the grave oversight of this good news was that it all occurred in German.

Under Emperor Leopold II [21] (brother to Joseph II), his short reign toward the late eighteenth century came amidst growing unrest within the empire. However, he still uplifted the revival of the arts. This revival continued with historians, linguists, artists, and composers contributing to a previously infertile cultural landscape. Leopold even established a chair in the Czech language at Prague University. With peasants who had never abandoned their Czech roots and language, they were, for the first time having their literature published in Czech. However, one of his harshest legacies was to force the serfs freed by his brother back into servitude.

During the Napoleonic wars, Leopold's successor Emperor Francis II[22], suffered numerous defeats, and by 1806, he would become the last

Holy Emperor. Instead, as Francis 1, he became the founder and first Emperor of the Austrian Empire.

At the beginning of 1848 and through to 1849, the Empire underwent rolling disruptions; it was the beginning of the Industrial Revolution[23]. In 1848, Prince Alfred Windisch-Gratz[24], head of the Bohemian army, fired upon a peaceful demonstration after a stray bullet had killed his wife. This provoked a riot in Prague's Wenceslas Square, followed by a declaration of martial law. In the same year, when Emperor Frantz-Joseph I[25] ascended to the throne amid this terror, he issued the March Constitution declaring all Habsburg territories one entity. He ruled from the Imperial Parliament in Vienna. He was troubled by nationalism throughout his reign, but his patriarchal authority held the Empire together. Although he was generally respected, the Czechs waited impatiently for political changes within the monarchy and were frustrated with no sign of Czech and Slovak independence from Austria or Hungary.

During this revolutionary period, many Czechs from poorer classes who only spoke Czech began moving from villages throughout Bohemia and Moravia and elsewhere, leaving behind their homeland and ancestral roots, which dated back to centuries of civilization. Also, during this Nationalistic strive, many Czechs began to demand equal rights and for their language to be used in schools and government. The arts, music, and literature prospered, but only the assertion of political ideology remained thwarted. While Hungarians gained independence during this reform, the Czech's claim for independence was largely disregarded.

Born in 1876 in the small village of Hodslavice, František Palacký[26] politician and historian; belonged to the Czech National Revival Movement, which often clashed with Imperialists. Palacký, known as one of the three 'Fathers of the Nation;' (the other two being Charles IV and Tomáš Garrigue Masaryk), was of the old guard of Czech deputies and accepted as a part of their concessions, an electoral system favouring the Germans in Bohemia. But the young Czechs, following the teachings of Jan Hus and with the support of the Realist Party Leader, Professor Tomáš Masaryk, focused on moral issues that highlighted the Czech history of the Hussites and National Revival.

During the elections to the Diet in 1891, the young Czechs had a landslide victory as numerous established families embraced their newly revived national identity and, with renewed enthusiasm, resuscitated their intellectual and traditional culture. This change finally gave rise to a working-class political movement and Catholic parties. It would become the beginning of political, social, and economic reform and rapid industrialization.

In 1914 a Bosnian-Serb assassinated Archduke Franz Ferdinand, nephew of Emperor Franz Joseph and heir presumptive, which ignited the Austro-Hungarians to war against the Kingdom of Serbia. This would become the catalyst of WWI.

Tomáš Masaryk,[27] philosopher, and politician, was born in Hodonín Moravia in 1850. He was the son of a Blacksmith and a German-educated mother and received his education in Brno and Vienna. In 1878 he married Charlotte Garrigue, an American Protestant with French Huguenot ancestry, and took on her maiden name and became known as Tomáš Garrigue Masaryk. Throughout WWI, Tomáš Masaryk had become instrumental in organizing the Czechoslovak Movement of Independence and, with it, became the head of the Czechoslovak National Council. WWI had helped with the downfall of the Austro-Hungarian Empire and thus effectively ending the empirical rule of the Hapsburgs that lasted just over 390 years from 1526 to 1918.

The Czech people had sided with the Allies by supporting their war efforts, and with this, a gamble had paid off for Masaryk and Edvard Benes, who received support for an Independent State in return. With the Habsburg Dynasty now ended and with the assistance of the USA, President Woodrow Wilson witnessed this peaceful transition of power, creating a provisional government for the newly liberated nation under Tomáš Masaryk.[28] So, finally, on the 28th of October 1918, with the recently founded Republic of Czechoslovakia proclaimed, Tomáš Garrigue Masaryk became the first President. The New Republic included the former Imperial provinces of Bohemia, Moravia, Slovakia, Sub-Carpathian Ruthenia, and part of Silesia.

The past had been an age of disquiet and persecution, interspersed with religious wars, revolutions, and denial of a heritage that took centuries to regain. Under this egalitarian and democratic rule, Tomáš Masaryk reformed social structure, including the practice of all free religious beliefs. He devoted himself to the political education of the Czech nation and introduced a free and compulsory education system for all Czech people.

The government equally capitalized on opportunities created and left behind at the demise of the Habsburgs and their Austro-Hungarian Empire. The new government now had control of Bohemia, the breadbasket and the Empire's food supply, and the wealth of mineral resources; coal and iron ore with established industrial infrastructure inherited from the now defunct Austro-Hungarian Empire. With a stable currency and a stable and equitable government preparing to redistribute land, it created an optimistic feeling of economic recovery with social and justice reforms. But it was still a country of many nationalities!

The Slovaks were predominantly agricultural people ruled by the Magyars and not the Habsburgs, whereas the Czechs looked upon the Church as their symbol of freedom. The Slovaks resented being patronized by Prague. Bubbling ethnic rivalry and tensions also added to the problem of Czechs resenting the well-educated German-speaking Jews who were concentrated principally around Prague.

On the other hand, the Germans had formed 23% of the population throughout the country and were, for most, well-educated and wealthy. They ran their own schools and universities and had their own political parties, which presented a huge obstacle in unifying the nation.

Finally, in 1920 the Constitution declared it to be a state of 'Czechoslovakian people' who spoke the 'Czechoslovakian language' and who at last would be recognized in their own right as a nation of Czech people; a free democratic society independent from past ties, while being directed down a path of recovery, peace, and stability. And so, the Republic of Czechoslovakia began to rise from the ashes of past tyrannical rule and imperial injustices.

After Tomáš Garrigue Masaryk's inauguration as president in the inaugural election of 1918, he would be re-elected three consecutive times before finally resigning from office in 1935 and handing over to the then-newly elected Edvard Beneš[29].

Tomáš and his wife Charlotte had six children Alice, Herbert, Jan, Anna, Elenora, and Olga, with only their son Jan following his father into politics. Both Tomáš Masaryk and Edvard Beneš had earned international respect as their nation flourished into a liberal democracy. On September 14th, 1937, Tomáš Garrigue Masaryk died at Lany Castle. By then, Edvard Beneš, who had already succeeded him in 1935, would reign as president until 1938. His post would be relinquished after failed political safeguards exposed his government to Nazi invasion[30].

During this interim period in 1938, the leadership would fall into the hands of short-lived President Emil Hácha until March 1939, when Hitler invaded and established a Czechoslovakian Protectorate under Nazi German rule. Soon afterward, in September 1939, the rest of Europe entered WWII, putting the country back into turmoil and Czechoslovakia's promising future once more into doubt.

References

Part 1, Chapter 1, Moravia: Rural Life in Lhotka nad Bečvou
[1] Article: 'Radegast (mythology).' (2023, January, 28). In Wikipedia. https://en.wikipedia.org/wiki/Radogost_(mythology)

Part 1, Chapter 3, Kurovec Family Life in Lhotka
[1] Article: '1st Czechoslovak Independent Armoured Brigade.' (2023, January, 5). In Wikipedia. https://en.wikipedia.org/wiki/1st_Czechoslovak_Independent_Armoured_Brigade
[2] 'Historical Development of Land Ownership in the Czech Republic Since the Foundation of Czechoslovakia until Present' (2018). From Czech University of Life Sciences, Prague; Authors Ludek Homolac and Karel Tomsik. https://www.czu.cz/en

Part 1, Chapter 4, A Prelude to War
[1] Article: 'Konrad Henlein.' (2023, April, 2). In Wikipedia. https://en.wikipedia.org/wiki/Konrad_Henlein
[2] Article: 'The Maginot Line - 11 Fascinating Facts about France's Ill-fated Fortifications.' (2023) In Military History Now. https://militaryhistorynow.com/
[3] Article: 'Munich Agreement.' (2023, February, 23). In Encyclopedia Britannica, Inc. https://www.britannica.com/event/Munich-Agreement
Article: 'First Vienna Award.' (2023, March, 24). In Wikipedia. https://en.wikipedia.org/wiki/First_Vienna_Award
[4] Article: 'How 802 Square Kilometres of Land Caused a World War.' (2023). In History of Yesterday; Author Dhruv Shevgaonkar. https://historyofyesterday.com/
Article: 'Zaolzie.' (2023, April, 9). In Wikipedia. https://pl.wikipedia.org/wiki/Zaolzie
[5] Article: 'Occupation of Czechoslovakia (1938-1945).' (2023, April, 5). In Wikipedia. https://en.wikipedia.org/wiki/Occupation_of_Czechoslovakia_(1938%E2%80%931945)
Article: 'Protectorate of Bohemia and Moravia.' (2023, April, 1). In Wikipedia. https://en.wikipedia.org/wiki/Protectorate_of_Bohemia_and_Moravia
[6] Article: 'Józef Tiso.' (2023, April, 4). In Wikipedia. https://en.wikipedia.org/wiki/Jozef_Tiso
[7] Article: 'Invasion of Poland.' (2023, March, 30). In Wikipedia. https://en.wikipedia.org/wiki/Invasion_of_Poland
'Chronicle of the 20th Century.' (1990). Author John Ross, Contributor Jacques Legrand. https://catalogue.nla.gov.au/Record/1765803

Part 1, Chapter 5, Krhová and Lhotka: Anna's War Under Nazi Occupation
[1] Article: 'František Moravec.' (2022, October, 13). In Wikipedia. https://en.wikipedia.org/wiki/Franti%C5%A1ek_Moravec
[2] Article: 'History of 17th November-International Student's Day.' (2023) In OBESSU Online. https://www.obessu.org/resources/news/17th-of-november-and-its-historical-meaning/
[3] Article: 'Heinz's Memoirs, Chapter 1 Ostrava, Czechoslovakia: A Brief History.' (2023) In vogl.org.uk. https://www.vogel.org.uk/memoirs/index.html
Article: 'Heinz's Memoirs, Chapter 8 Alfred Goes to War May-July 1940.' (2023) In vogl.org.uk. https://www.vogel.org.uk/memoirs/chap08.html
[4] Article: 'Assassination Operation Anthropoid 1941- 1942.' (2002, September, 17). In Internet Archive; Authors Michal Burian, Aleš Knížek, Jiří Rajlich, Eduard Stehlik. https://archive.org/details/assassination-en1
Article: 'Assassination of Reinhard Heydrich.' (2023, April, 9). In Wikipedia. https://en.wikipedia.org/wiki/Assassination_of_Reinhard_Heydrich
[5] 'Massacres and Atrocities of World War II; The Lidice Massacre.' (1942, June 10). In George Duncan's Massacres and Atrocities of World War II.
Lesser-Known Facts of World War II; George Duncan's Historical Facts of World War.

References

[6]Article: 'Jan Žižka Partisan Brigade.' (2022, July, 28). In Wikipedia. https://en.wikipedia.org/wiki/Jan_%C5%BDi%C5%BEka_partisan_brigade

[7]'Nešli Stejnou Cestou: Osudy Parašutistu a Konfidentu Gestapa.' (1994, January, 10). Authors Čestmír Šikola and Jaroslav Pospíšil. https://www.goodreads.com/book/show/25405790-ne-li-stejnou-cestou

[8]'ČR-Moravský zemský archiv v Brné.' (2001, January). Authors Miloslav Hurtík, Žofie Kurovcová, Čestmír Smolká.

'A Member of the Resistance, Čestmír Smolká, Died.' (2018). Author Ivan Pytela. https://www.memoryofnations.eu/en/smolka-cestmir-1924

[9]"Transport KL3 do Mauthausena.' (2023). In Holocaust Encyclopedia. https://encyclopedia.ushmm.org/content/en/article/mauthausen

Part 1, Chapter 6, End of World War II: V-E Day 8th May 1945

[1]Article: 'CAST Czech and Slovak Things.' (2000-2011). http://www.geocities.ws/czechandslovakthings/index.htm

[2]Article: 'Alois Liška.' (2022, July, 12). In Wikipedia. https://en.wikipedia.org/wiki/Alois_Li%C5%A1ka

[3]Article: 'United Nations Relief and Rehabilitation Administration.' (2022, October, 17). In Wikipedia. https://en.wikipedia.org/wiki/United_Nations_Relief_and_Rehabilitation_Administration

[4]"Naše Noviny.' (2023, April, 10). http://www.nasenoviny.net/

[5]Article: 'Iron Curtain.' (2023, April, 7). In Encyclopedia Britannica. https://www.britannica.com/event/Iron-Curtain

[6]Article: 'Košice Government.' (1998, July, 20). In Encyclopedia Britannica. https://www.britannica.com/topic/Kosice-government

Part 1, Chapter 7, Anna's Escape Plans

[1]Article: 'Investigation on the Death of Ex Foreign Minister Jan Masaryk Closed.' (2021, March, 11). In Prague Morning. Author Marielle F. https://www.praguemorning.cz/?s=Investigation+on+the+Death+of+Ex+Foreign++++Minister+Jan+Masaryk+closed

[2]Article: 'Klement Gottwald.' (2023, March, 10). In Encyclopedia Britannica. https://www.britannica.com/biography/Klement-Gottwald

Part 1, Chapter 8, Pulgary (Bulhary)

[1]Article: 'Sten.' (2023, April, 10). In Wikipedia: https://en.wikipedia.org/wiki/Sten

Part 1, Chapter 9, The Escape: From Pulgary to Poysdorf

[1]Article: 'Vienna Offensive.' (2023, March, 31). In Wikipedia. https://en.wikipedia.org/wiki/Vienna_offensive

[2]Article: 'Allied-Occupied Austria.' (2023, April, 10). In Wikipedia. https://en.wikipedia.org/wiki/Allied-occupied_Austria

Part 1, Chapter 10, Vienna (Vídeň): Czechs on the Run

[1]Article: 'Potsdam Conference.' (2023, April, 7). In Wikipedia. https://en.wikipedia.org/wiki/Potsdam_Conference

[2]Article: 'Allied-Occupied Austria.' (2023, April, 10). In Wikipedia. https://en.wikipedia.org/wiki/Allied-occupied_Austria

[3]Article: 'Lipizzan.' (2023, April, 10). In Wikipedia. https://en.wikipedia.org/wiki/Lipizzan#:~:text=The%20breed%20has%20been%20endangered%20numerous%20times%20by,the%20Disney%20movie%20Miracle%20of%20the%20White%20Stallions.

Article: 'Operation Cowboy/How American GIs and German Soldiers Saved the Legendary Lipizzaner Horses in the Final Hours of WW2.' (2018, November, 25). In Military History Now. https://militaryhistorynow.com/2018/11/25/operation-cowboy-how-american-gis-german-soldiers-joined-forces-to-save-the-legendary-lipizzaner-horses-in-the-final-hours-of-ww2/

[4]Article: 'Steyr DP Camps in Austria.' (Unknown). http://www.dpcamps.org/steyr.html

Part 1, Chapter 12, West Germany: Regensburg – Burg: 1948

[1]Article: 'Allied Occupation of Germany, 1945-1952.' (2009, January, 20). In US Department of State

Archives. https://2001-2009.state.gov/r/pa/ho/time/cwr/107189.htm
[2]Article: 'LN: Most Czechs fleeing homeland after 1948 coup were men.' (2016, January, 14). In Prague Daily Monitor. Authorly Martina Čermákova. https://praguemonitor.com/news/national/14/01/2016/2016-01-14-ln-most-czechs-fleeing-homeland-after-1948-coup-were-men/
[3]Article: 'Šumava National Park.' (2023, March, 10). In Wikipedia. https://en.wikipedia.org/wiki/%C5%A0umava_National_Park
[4]Article: 'Abandoned and Forgotten & Little Known About Airfields in Europe.' (2011, April, 15). https://www.forgottenairfields.com/airfield-burg-378.html
[5]Article: 'Czech Refugees in the Papers of the National Archives of Hungry.' (2022, October, 26). Author Daniel Miklos. https://www.researchgate.net/publication/328504378_Czech_Refugees_in_the_Papers_of_the_National_Archives_of_Hungary
[6]Article: 'Alois Liška.' (2022, July, 12). In Wikipedia. https://en.wikipedia.org/wiki/Alois_Li%C5%A1ka
[7]Article: 'Baa Corporation.' (2023, March, 27). In Wikipedia. https://en.wikipedia.org/wiki/Bata_Corporation
[8]Article: 'Occupation and the Emergence of Two States (1945-1961).' (Unknown). In GHDI. https://ghdi.ghi-dc.org/chapter.cfm?subsection_id=110
[9]Article: 'International Refugee Organization.' (2022, June, 17). In Wikipedia. https://en.wikipedia.org/wiki/International_Refugee_Organization

Part 1, Chapter 13, Ludwigsburg:1948-1949
[1]Article: 'Displaced Persons Camps in post WW2 Europe.' (2023, March, 9). In Wikipedia. https://en.wikipedia.org/wiki/Displaced_persons_camps_in_post%E2%80%93World_War_II_Europe
[2]Article: 'Rudolf Slánský.' (2023, April, 23). In Wikipedia. https://en.wikipedia.org/wiki/Rudolf_Sl%C3%A1nsk%C3%BD
'Rudolf Slánský: His Trials and Trial.' (Unknown). In Wilson International Centre for Scholars. Author Igor Lukes Woodrow. https://www.wilsoncenter.org/program/cold-war-international-history-project
[3]Article: 'Brenner Pass.' (2022, October, 26). In Wikipedia. https://en.wikipedia.org/wiki/Brenner_Pass
Article: 'Western Railway (Austria).' (2023, March, 29). In Wikipedia. https://en.wikipedia.org/wiki/Template:Western_Railway_(Austria)
Article: 'Turin.' (2023, April, 8). In Wikipedia. https://en.wikipedia.org/wiki/Turin
[4]'Australian Migrant Ships 1946-1977.' (2006). Author Peter Plowman. Published by Rosenberg Publishing. https://books.google.com.au/books/about/Australian_Migrant_Ships_1946_1977.html?id=P_vfFx5npJUC&redir_esc=y
'ISTG: Immigrant Ships Transcribers Guild: SS Dundalk Bay.' (2022). https://www.immigrantships.net/v5/shipsv5/dundalkbayv5.html

Part 1, Chapter 14, Part 1, Family Life
[1]Article: 'Hošťálková.' (2022, June, 1). In Wikipedia. https://en.wikipedia.org/wiki/Ho%C5%A1%C5%A5%C3%A1lkov%C3%A1

Part 1, Chapter 14, Part 2, Jan's Brief Czech Military Career
[1]'Military Archives.' (2015). In My Czech Roots. https://www.myczechroots.com/archives/military-archives
[2]Article: 'Battle of Czajánek's Barracks.' (2022, October, 20). In Wikipedia. https://en.wikipedia.org/wiki/Battle_of_Czaj%C3%A1nek%27s_barracks
[3]Article: 'Resistance in the Protectorate of Bohemia and Moravia.' (2023, January, 4). In Wikipedia. https://en.wikipedia.org/wiki/Resistance_in_the_Protectorate_of_Bohemia_and_Moravia
[4]Article: 'The Czech Embassy Tells its Story.' (2018, July, 19). In Embassy of the Czech Republic Budapest. https://www.mzv.cz/budapest/en/about_the_embassy/index_2.html
[5]'Narrow Escapes!' (2013, December, 20). Author Miloslav Bitton. Published by Bass drum Books. https://www.ebay.com.au/p/195245231
Article: 'Miloslav Kratochvil Bitton: Military officer who fought as one of "The Rats of Tobruk" and went on to fly Spitfires protecting Lancaster Bombers.' (2014, April, 28). Author Phil Davi-

References

son. https://www.independent.co.uk/news/obituaries/miloslav-kratochvil-bitton-military-officer-who-fought-as-one-of-the-rats-of-tobruk-and-went-on-to-fly-spitfires-protecting-lancaster-bombers-9299064.html

Article: 'Colonel Miloslav Bitton – Obituary.' (2014, April, 27). In The Telegraph. https://www.telegraph.co.uk/news/obituaries/10791093/Colonel-Miloslav-Bitton-obituary.html

[6]Article: 'French Foreign Legion.' (2023, March, 27). In Wikipedia. https://en.wikipedia.org/wiki/French_Foreign_Legion

[7]Article: 'Invasion of Yugoslavia.' (2023, April, 10). In Wikipedia. https://en.wikipedia.org/wiki/Invasion_of_Yugoslavia

[8]Article: 'Mandate for Syria and the Lebanon.' (2023, February, 24). In Wikipedia. https://en.wikipedia.org/wiki/Mandate_for_Syria_and_the_Lebanon

Part 1, Chapter 14, Part 3, France: A Short but Bitter Fight

[1]Article: 'Marseille – First Capital of the Resistance.' (2022). In Alliance Française de Londres. https://www.alliancefrancaise.london/Marseille-First-Capital-of-the-Resistance.php

[2]Article: Phoney War: (2023, May 23) In Wikipedia. https://en.wikipedia.org>wiki>Phoney_War

[3]'On all Fronts: Czechoslovaks in World War II.' (2000). Editor Lewis M. White. Published by East European Monographs. https://books.google.com.au/books/about/On_All_Fronts.html?id=x-7E0wgEACAAJ&redir_esc=y

Article: 'Second Lieutenant Alexander Burger (1922).' (2008-2023). In Memory of Nations. https://www.memoryofnations.eu/en/burger-alexander-1922

Article: 'Czechoslovak Exile Units of WWII.' (2014, June, 7). In Military History Online. Author Kai Isaksen. https://www.militaryhistoryonline.com/WWII/CzechExilesOfWWII

Article: '12th (Eastern) Division.' (2023, February, 20). In Wikipedia. https://en.wikipedia.org/wiki/12th_(Eastern)_Division

[4]Article: 'Panzer Division.' (2021, April, 20). In Military Wiki. https://military-history.fandom.com/wiki/Panzer_division

[5]Article: 'Battle of Sedan: (1940).' (2023, April, 9). In Wikipedia. https://en.wikipedia.org/wiki/Battle_of_Sedan_(1940)

Article: 'The Battle of Arras.' (2023, April, 9). In Britannica. https://www.britannica.com/topic/Battle-of-Arras

Article: 'Battle of Arras (1940).' (2023, January, 29). In Wikipedia. https://en.wikipedia.org/wiki/Battle_of_Arras_%281940%29

[6]Article: 'Dunkirk Evacuation.' (2023, February, 15). In Wikipedia. https://en.wikipedia.org/wiki/Dunkirk_evacuation

[7]Article: 'Paris in World War II' (2022, April, 1). In Wikipedia. https://en.wikipedia.org/wiki/Paris_in_World_War_II

[8]Article: 'Battle of France.' (2023, April, 11). In Wikipedia. https://en.wikipedia.org/wiki/Battle_of_France

[9]Article: 'Fieseler Fi 156 Storch.' (2023, March, 3). In Wikipedia. https://en.wikipedia.org/wiki/Fieseler_Fi_156_Storch

[10]Article: 'Junkers Ju 87.' (2023, April, 11). In Wikipedia. https://en.wikipedia.org/wiki/Junkers_Ju_87

[11]Article: 'German Air Force.' (2023, April, 9). In Wikipedia. https://en.wikipedia.org/wiki/German_Air_Force#:~:text=The%20German%20Air%20Force%20%28German%3A%20Luftwaffe%2C%20lit.%20%27air,of%20the%20Bundeswehr%2C%20the%20armed%20forces%20of%20Germany.

[12]Article: 'Schlieffen Plan.' (2023, March, 23). In Wikipedia. https://en.wikipedia.org/wiki/Schlieffen_Plan

Article: 'Schlieffen Plan, German Military History.' (2023, March, 31). In Britannica. https://www.britannica.com/event/Schlieffen-Plan

[13]Article: 'CAST Czech and Slovak Things.' (2000 – 2021). Author Richard Gaskell. http://www.geocities.ws/czechandslovakthings/index.htm

[14]'A History of the Second World War.' (1969, January, 1). Author B.H. Liddell Hart. https://www.goodreads.com/book/show/26220176-a-history-of-the-second-world-war

Article: 'Battle of France.' (2023, April, 11). In Wikipedia. https://en.wikipedia.org/wiki/Battle_of_France

'The Fall of France in the Second World War.' (2019). Author Dr. Gary Sheffield. https://link.springer.com/book/10.1007/978-3-030-03955-4

Part 1, Chapter 14, Part 4, 1940-1944: Cholmondeley Cheshire and Formation of CIABG
[1] Article: 'The History of Cholmondeley Castle.' (2022, April, 13). In Castrum to Castle. https://castrumtocastle.com/english-castles/cheshire-cholmondeley-castle/
[2] 'CAST World War 2 'Mutiny' at Cholmondeley Castle.' (2000 – 2004). Author Richard Gaskall. http://www.geocities.ws/czechandslovakthings/WW2_mutiny.htm
[3] 'CAST World War 2 The Czechoslovak Brigade.' (2000 – 2011). Author Richard Gaskell. http://www.geocities.ws/czechandslovakthings/WW2_CzSkB.htm
[4] 'CAST World War 2 Czechoslovaks in the Pioneer Corps.' (2000 – 2004). Author Richard Gaskell. http://www.geocities.ws/czechandslovakthings/WW2_pioneers.htm
[5] 'CAST World War 2 The Czechoslovak Brigade.' (2000 – 2011). Author Richard Gaskell. http://www.geocities.ws/czechandslovakthings/WW2_CzSkB.htm
[6] 'CAST World War 2 The Czechoslovak Brigade.' (2000 – 2011). Author Richard Gaskell. http://www.geocities.ws/czechandslovakthings/WW2_CzSkB.htm
[7] 'Biography of Army General Alois Liška.' (2000). Published by Steen Ammentorp. https://generals.dk/general/Li%C5%A1ka/Alois/Czechoslovakia.html
[8] 'Seven Men at Daybreak.' (1960, January, 1). Author Alan Burgess. https://www.goodreads.com/book/show/1824529.Seven_Men_At_Daybreak
[9] 'Tripartite Pact World War II.' (1940, September, 27). In Britannica. https://www.britannica.com/topic/Tripartite-Pact
[10] 'CAST World War 2 The Czechoslovak Brigade.' (2000 – 2011). Author Richard Gaskell. http://www.geocities.ws/czechandslovakthings/WW2_CzSkB.htm
[11] 'CAST World War 2 The Czechoslovak Brigade.' (2000 – 2011). Author Richard Gaskell. http://www.geocities.ws/czechandslovakthings/WW2_CzSkB.htm
[12] Article: 'WO 171/3467 War Diary of 22 Liaison HQ.' (Unknown). In The National Archives. https://discovery.nationalarchives.gov.uk/details/r/C14378
[13] 'CAST World War 2 The Czechoslovak Brigade.' (2000 – 2011). Author Richard Gaskell. http://www.geocities.ws/czechandslovakthings/WW2_CzSkB.htm
[14] 'Biography of Major General Jan Mikuláš Kratochvíl.' (2000). Published by Steen Ammentorp. https://www.generals.dk/general/%C4%8Cihak/Jaroslav/Czechoslovakia.html
[15] Article: 'Siege of Tobruk.' (2023, March, 10). In Wikipedia. https://en.wikipedia.org/wiki/Siege_of_Tobruk
Article: 'Syria-Lebanon Campaign.' (2023, April, 9). In Wikipedia. https://en.wikipedia.org/wiki/Syria%E2%80%93Lebanon_campaign
[16] 'CAST World War 2 The Czechoslovak Brigade.' (2000 – 2011). Author Richard Gaskell. http://www.geocities.ws/czechandslovakthings/WW2_CzSkB.htm
[17] 'Flames of War: The 1st Czechoslovak Independent Armoured Brigade Group.' (Unknown). Author Jonathan Forsey, Published by CIABG).
Article: '1st Czechoslovak Independent Armoured Brigade.' (2023, January, 5). In Wikipedia. https://en.wikipedia.org/wiki/1st_Czechoslovak_Independent_Armoured_Brigade
[18] Article: 'Karel Klapálek.' (2005). In Military Wiki. https://military-history.fandom.com/wiki/Karel_Klap%C3%A1lek
'Klapalkova-Kosutova, Olga: Voják Vypravuje.' (1948). Published by Družstvo Moravského kala spisovatelů in Brno Czechoslovakia.
[19] 'CAST World War 2 The Czechoslovak Brigade.' (2000 – 2011). Author Richard Gaskell. http://www.geocities.ws/czechandslovakthings/WW2_CzSkB.htm
[20] 'CAST World War 2 The Czechoslovak Brigade.' (2000 – 2011). Author Richard Gaskell. http://www.geocities.ws/czechandslovakthings/WW2_CzSkB.htm
[21] 'CAST World War 2 The Czechoslovak Brigade.' (2000 – 2011). Author Richard Gaskell. http://www.geocities.ws/czechandslovakthings/WW2_CzSkB.htm

Part 1, Chapter 14, Part 5, 1944-1945: Siege of Dunkirk and Finally Home
[1] Article: 'Battle of Caen.' (2023, April, 10). In Wikipedia. https://en.wikipedia.org/wiki/Battle_for_Caen

References

[2] Article: 'Falaise Pocket.' (2023, March, 31). In Wikipedia. https://en.wikipedia.org/wiki/Falaise_pocket
[3] Article: 'Wormhoudt.' (2022, December, 10). In Wikipedia. https://en.wikipedia.org/wiki/Wormhout
[4] Article: 'Waffen-SS.' (2023, April, 5). In Wikipedia. https://en.wikipedia.org/wiki/Waffen-SS
[5] Article: 'Hawker Typhoon.' (2023, March, 23). In Wikipedia. https://en.wikipedia.org/wiki/Hawker_Typhoon
[6] Article: '1st Czechoslovak Armoured Brigade.' (2023, January, 5). https://en.wikipedia.org/wiki/1st_Czechoslovak_Independent_Armoured_Brigade
[7] 'CAST World War 2 Token Force or Kominovaný odil (combined detachment).' (2000 – 2011). Author Richard Gaskell. http://www.geocities.ws/czechandslovakthings/WW2_tokenforce.htm
[8] 'CAST World War 2 Token Force or Kominovaný odil (combined detachment).' (2000 – 2011). Author Richard Gaskell. http://www.geocities.ws/czechandslovakthings/WW2_tokenforce.htm
[9] Article: 'Prague Offensive.' (Unknown). In Military Wiki. https://military-history.fandom.com/wiki/Prague_Offensive
[10] Article: 'Ferdinand Schörner.' (2023, March, 13). In Wikipedia. https://en.wikipedia.org/wiki/Ferdinand_Sch%C3%B6rner
[11] 'CAST World War 2 Token Force or Kominovaný odil (combined detachment).' (2000 – 2011). Author Richard Gaskell. http://www.geocities.ws/czechandslovakthings/WW2_tokenforce.htm
Article: German Instrument of Surrender (2023, July 1) from Wikipedia. http://wikipedia.org>wiki>German_intrument of surrender
[12] 'CAST World War 2 Token Force or Kominovaný odil (combined detachment).' (2000 – 2011). Author Richard Gaskell. http://www.geocities.ws/czechandslovakthings/WW2_tokenforce.htm
[13] 'Unconditional Surrender and the Aftermath' (by Gustav Svoboda). (2000, July, 15). In 'On All Fronts: Czechoslovaks in World War 2.' Author Lewis M. White. https://www.amazon.com.au/All-Fronts-Czechoslovaks-World-War/dp/0880334568
[14] 'CAST World War 2 The Czechoslovak Brigade.' (2000 – 2011). Author Richard Gaskell. http://www.geocities.ws/czechandslovakthings/WW2_CzSkB.htm

Part 1, Chapter 14, Part 6, Jan's WWII Aftermath
[1] 'My Home Coming' (by Alois Šeda). (2000, July, 15). In 'On All Fronts: Czechoslovaks in World War 2.' Author Lewis M. White. https://www.amazon.com.au/All-Fronts-Czechoslovaks-World-War/dp/0880334568
[2] 'Partia Ingrata' (by Gustav Svoboda). (2000, July, 15). In 'On All Fronts: Czechoslovaks in World War 2.' Author Lewis M. White. https://www.amazon.com.au/All-Fronts-Czechoslovaks-World-War/dp/0880334568
[3] 'Vařák's Clearing.' (2023). In Forgotten Fates – Ratibor. Authors Ondřej Haša, Roman Babica and Stanislav Haša. https://dev.obecni.net/en/obec/stezka/zapomenute-osudy
[4] Article: 'Ludvík Svoboda.' (2023, March, 30). In Wikipedia. https://cs.wikipedia.org/wiki/Ludv%C3%ADk_Svoboda
[5] Article: 'Jan Masaryk.' (2023, April, 1). In Wikipedia. https://en.wikipedia.org/wiki/Jan_Masaryk

Part 1, Chapter 15, New Zealand: Annas Dream
[1] Article: 'Port of Aden.' (2022, November, 9). In Wikipedia. https://en.wikipedia.org/wiki/Port_of_Aden
[2] 'Checklist of the Birds of New Zealand, Norfolk and Macquarie Islands, and the Ross Dependency, Antarctica.' (2010). Published in association with the Ornithological Society of New Zealand Inc. https://www.birdsnz.org.nz/wp-content/uploads/2021/03/NZ-Checklist-of-Birds-2010.pdf

Part 1, Chapter 16, Wellington, New Zealand
[1] Archives New Zealand: Internal Affairs (Te Tara Taiwhenua): Anna Kurovcova: AAAC 504 (Box 191) AL 30260 (R23658897) ABKF 6794 W5585 (Box 1631893 (1631893)) "Dundalk Bay" 1949: ACGO 8376 1A 52 (Box 120 No.15 (R20964 584)).

Part 1, Chapter 17, Anna: Tokanui Psychiatric Hospital
[1] Article: 'Women and Girls for that Nursing Career Train as a Psychiatric Nurse.' (1949, December, 10). Published on Page 2 of The Gisborne Herald.

[2] Wikipedia: Tokanui Psychiatric Hospital.
Patient Journeys: Stories of Mental Health Care from Tokanui to Mental Health Services, 1930's to the 1980's; Chapter 7 by Catharine Coleborne.

Part 1, Chapter 19, Winter Engagement in Takapuna
[1] Wikipedia: Tasman Empire Airways Limited; TEAL - 1940-1965...
New Zealand History – TEAL becomes Air New Zealand 1 April 1965.
[2] Wikipedia: RMS Strathmore; launched 4th April 1935. She served as a troop carrier during WW2 but was refitted after 1948 and resumed service with P&O until 1963.

Part 1, Chapter 20, Sunnyside Asylum Christchurch
[1] Article: 'Sunnyside Hospital.' (2023, February, 3). In Wikipedia. https://en.wikipedia.org/wiki/Sunnyside_Hospital
Article: 'Sunnyside Hospital.' (2023). Christchurch City Council Libraries. https://my.christchurchcitylibraries.com/sunnyside-hospital/
[2] Article: 'Auckland Star.' (2022, July, 6). In Wikipedia. https://en.wikipedia.org/wiki/Auckland_Star
[3] Article: 'The New Zealand Herald.' (2023, April, 1). In Wikipedia. https://en.wikipedia.org/wiki/The_New_Zealand_Herald
[4] Article: One dose of Architecture, taken daily: Building for Mental Health in New Zealand.' (2014). Author Rebecca McLaughlan. Victoria University of Wellington. https://researcharchive.vuw.ac.nz/handle/10063/3424
Article: 'Maudsley, Sir Henry Carr (1859-1944).' (2006). Author K.F. Russell. https://adb.anu.edu.au/biography/maudsley-sir-henry-carr-7528
[5] Article: 'Hornby Lodge/ Stoneycroft.' (2023). Christchurch City Libraries (Ngā-Kete Wānanga-o-Ōtautahi). https://my.christchurchcitylibraries.com/hornby/
[6] Article: 'George Ross (Farmer).' (2022, November, 29). In Wikipedia. https://en.wikipedia.org/wiki/George_Ross_(farmer)
[7] 'Historia Nunc Vivat. Medical Practitioners in New Zealand 1840-1930.' (2003). Author Rex Earl Wright-St Clair. Published by Rex Earl Wright-St Clair and Cotter Medical History Trust. http://wmhs.org.nz/medpractinnz.pdf
Article: 'Heavenly Creatures, 7.1 List of people.' (1991). http://www.adamabrams.com/hc/faq2/Section_7/7.1.html
Article: 'Parker-Hulme Murder case.' (2023, March, 18). In Wikipedia. https://en.wikipedia.org/wiki/Parker%E2%80%93Hulme_murder_case
[8] Article: H.M.A.H.S. Wanganella.' (2023). In Monument Australia. https://www.monumentaustralia.org.au/themes/conflict/multiple/display/32334-h.m.a.h.s.-wanganella/
Article: 'MS Wanganella.' (2023, March, 11). In Wikipedia. https://en.wikipedia.org/wiki/MS_Wanganella
[9] 'The Porirua Hospital Museum.' (2016). https://poriruahospitalmuseum.flh.nz/History
[10] 'Swiss Cradle Song.' Māori Farewell Song. (2001, September, 19). Authors Dr. Angela Annabell, Gordon Spittle, Roger Flury, & Peter Downes. https://folksong.org.nz/poatarau/index.html

Book Two, Chapter 21, Life in Australia
[1] Article: 'Category: Minnipa (ship, 1927).' (2018, September, 19). In Wikimedia. https://commons.wikimedia.org/wiki/Category:Minnipa_(ship,_1927)

Chapter 22, Wangary SA: 1955-1956
[1] Article: 'Yallunda Flat, South Australia.' (2022, October, 10). In Wikipedia. https://en.wikipedia.org/wiki/Yallunda_Flat%2C_South_Australia#:~:text=Yallunda%20Flat%20is%20a%20locality%20in%20the%20Australian,from%20the%20local%20landform%20of%20the%20same%20name.

Chapter 23, On the Road to Queensland: 1956
[1] 'A Comparison of Weather Systems in 1870 and 1956 Leading to Extreme Floods in the Murray-Darling Basin.' (2018, June, 11). CSIRO Publishing Journal of Southern Hemisphere Earth Systems. Author Jeff Callaghan. Bureau of Meteorology, Brisbane.

References

Chapter 24, Mareeba: 1956-1957
[1] Article: 'Vodyanoy.' (2023, February, 23). In Encyclopedia Britannica. https://www.britannica.com/topic/vodyanoy

Chapter 25, Euluma Creek: 1957-1959
[1] 'The Bump Track.' (2023). Douglas Shire Historical Society (NQ) Inc. https://www.douglashistory.org.au/local-stories/bump-track?rq=BUMP
[2] Review article: Taylor and Francis online/ https://doi.org./10.1080/08120099.2020.1821773 Historical Journal of Earth Sciences. An internal Geoscience journal of the Geological Society of Australia. ISSN: (Print) (Online) journal homepage: https://www.tandfonline.com/loi/taje20. A review of historical earthquakes in Queensland utilising the Trove Newspaper Archive as a primary source: Vo l68, Issue 4: D. Rubenach, J. Daniell, P. Dirks, & J. Wegner. Published on line 11 October 2020. Page 10 Table 4 earthquake details/ Cairns 1958 Date 1/12/1958 Time AEST 8.35pm Original epicentre location 16°30'S, 145°30'E Original Magnitude 5......Page 14 Cairns 1958...a magnitude 5 earthquake occurred off Cairns......

Chapter 26, Julatten:1960
[1] Public State Records: Letter from Premier's Department, dated 5th February 1924. https://www.qld.gov.au/law/court/court-services/access-court-records-files-and-services

Chapter 27, Laura Station: 1960-1961
[1] 'Crocodile Men: History and Adventures of Crocodile Hunters in Australia' (2000) Author Brian Peach. https://www.goodreads.com/book/show/5834319-crocodile-men
[2] 'Thylacine (Tasmanian Tiger) Sighting Reports Database.' (2023, April). https://recentlyextinctspecies.com/thylacine-archive/thylacine-sighting-reports 'Shadow of the Thylacine; One Man's Epic Search for the Tasmanian Tiger.' (2013, April, 29). Author Col Bailey. https://www.goodreads.com/book/show/17879654-shadow-of-the-thylacine
[3] 'The Cooktown Railway'. (1980). Author K.W. Knowles. https://catalogue.nla.gov.au/Record/1511329
[4] 'Roads in the Wilderness.' (2009). Author Lyall For. Published by the Queensland Department of Main Roads. https://www.cambridge.org/core/journals/queensland-review/article/abs/lyall-ford-roads-in-the-wilderness-development-of-the-main-road-network-in-far-north-queensland-the-first-100-years-brisbane-queensland-government-department-of-transport-and-main-roads-2009-isbn-9-7819-2071-9081-405-pp-4000/C623B7614CE4608FC5ECC8BA5CD354E4

Chapter 31, Life in Julatten Without Jan: 1964-1968
[1] Article: 'Operation Blowdown.' (2022, October, 4). In Wikipedia. https://en.wikipedia.org/wiki/Operation_Blowdown
[2] 'Cobb and Co Heritage Trail.' (2023). https://www.bathurstregion.com.au/cobb-co-heritage/
[3] 'Marsha Mildren Julatten Local.' (2012). http://mbahistsoc.org.au/locations/location-julatten.html
[4] 'Bushies: The Fascinating Story of Bush Pilots Airways.' (2023). https://bushpilotsairways.com.au/our-history/

Chapter 32, Charters Towers: 1969-1972
[1] Article: 'Tuzex.' (2022, July, 15). In Wikipedia. https://en.wikipedia.org/wiki/Tuzex
[2] Article: 'Alexander Dubček.' (2023, April, 2). In Wikipedia. https://en.wikipedia.org/wiki/Alexander_Dub%C4%8Dek

Chapter 33, Anna Returns Home to Julatten
[1] 'Landscapes of Change.' (2016). Artist Jozsef Balogh. Kingaroy Regional Art Gallery 2016. southburnett.com.au/Exhibition
[2] 'A Great New Zealand Nurse.' (2009). Author Keitha Alcorn. Publisher Neville and Ashley Salisbury. https://natlib.govt.nz/records/21533596?search%5Bi%5D%5Bsubject%5D=Nurses+--+New+Zealand+--+Biography&search%5Bi%5D%5Busage%5D=All+rights+reserved&search%5Bpath%5D=items

Chapter 34, Anna's Life after Mt. Kooyong: 1976-1997
[1] Article: 'Mikhail Gorbachev Championed 'Glasnost' and 'Perestroika'. Here's How They Changed the World.' (2022, August, 30). Author Olivia B Waxman. https://time.com/5512665/mikhail-gorbachev-glasnost-perestroika/
[2] Article: 'Velvet Revolution.' (2023, March, 29). In Wikipedia. https://en.wikipedia.org/wiki/Velvet_Revolution
[3] Article: 'Václav Havel.' (2023, April, 9). In Wikipedia. https://en.wikipedia.org/wiki/V%C3%A1clav_Havel
[4] Article: 'Dissolution of Czechoslovakia.' (2023, March, 13). In Wikipedia. https://en.wikipedia.org/wiki/Dissolution_of_Czechoslovakia
[5] 'Overturning the Doctrine of Tera Nullius: The Mabo Case' (1992). https://aiatsis.gov.au/sites/default/files/research_pub/overturning-the-doctrine-of-terra-nullius_0_3.pdf#:~:text=The%20Mabo%20decision%20altered%20the%20foundation%20of%20land,could%20seek%20recognition%20of%20their%20native%20title%20rights.
[6] 'Report of the Land Tribunal on the Aboriginal Land Claim to Lakefield National Park North Queensland.' (1996, April). https://catalogue.nla.gov.au/Record/1057747

Chapter 35, Anna's Life Full-Circle: 1998-2008
[1] 'Australian Diplomacy Toward Indonesia 1965-72 (2004). A study of Fear in Australian Foreign Policy. Author Karim Najjarine. https://www.jstor.org/stable/20638302

A Brief History of Czech Lands and the Birth of a Nation
[1] Article: 'Discover Czechoslovakia.,' (2018, May, 17). In encyclopedia.com. https://www.encyclopedia.com/history/modern-europe/czech-and-slovak-history/czechoslovakia
Article: 'Boii.' (2023, April, 7). In Wikipedia. https://en.wikipedia.org/wiki/Boii.
[2] Article: 'Atilla.' (2023, April, 6). In Wikipedia. https://en.wikipedia.org/wiki/Attila#:~:text=Attila%20%28%2F%20C9%99%CB%88t%C9%AAl%C9%99%20%2F%2C%20%2F%20%CB%88%C3%A6t%C9%99l%C9%99%20%2F%3B%20fl.,Bulgars%2C%20among%20others%2C%20in%20Central%20and%20Eastern%20Europe.edia
[3] Article: 'Slavic Paganism.' (2023, March, 30). In Wikipedia. https://en.wikipedia.org/wiki/Slavic_paganism c paganism - Wikipedia
[4] Article: 'Polesia.' (2023, February, 12). In Wikipedia. https://en.wikipedia.org/wiki/Polesia
[5] Article: 'Přemyslid Dynasty.' (2023, January, 19). In Wikipedia. https://en.wikipedia.org/wiki/P%C5%99emyslid_dynasty
[6] Article: 'Mojmir I of Moravia.' (2023, April, 2). In Wikipedia. https://en.wikipedia.org/wiki/Mojmir_I_of_Moravia
[7] Article: 'Rastislav of Moravia.' (2023, April, 2). In Wikipedia. https://en.wikipedia.org/wiki/Rastislav_of_Moravia
[8] Article: 'List of Slavic Deities.' (2023, March, 31). In Wikipedia. https://en.wikipedia.org/wiki/List_of_Slavic_deities
[9] Article: 'John Wycliffe.' (2023, March, 28). In Wikipedia. https://en.wikipedia.org/wiki/John_Wycliffe
[10] Article: 'Jan Hus.' (2023, April, 6). In Wikipedia. https://en.wikipedia.org/wiki/Jan_Hus#:~:text=Jan%20Hus%20%28%2F%20h%CA%8As%20%2F%3B%20Czech%3A%20%5B%CB%88jan%20%CB%88%C9%A6us%5D,and%20a%20seminal%20figure%20in%20the%20Bohemian%20Reformation.
[11] Article: 'Jan Zizka.' (2023, March, 15). In Wikipedia. https://en.wikipedia.org/wiki/Jan_%C5%BDi%C5%BEka
[12] Article: 'George of Poděbrady.' (2023, April, 2). In Wikipedia. https://en.wikipedia.org/wiki/George_of_Pod%C4%9Bbrady
[13] Article: 'Jagiellonian Dynasty.' (2023, April, 5). In Wikipedia. https://en.wikipedia.org/wiki/Jagiellonian_dynasty
[14] Broadcast: 'The Habsburgs and Rudolf II' (1995). On Radio Prague.
Exhibit 1997. https://archiv.radio.cz/en/static/history-of-radio-prague
Article: 'Rudolf II, Holy Roman Emperor.' (2023, April, 1). In Wikipedia. https://en.wikipedia.org/wiki/Rudolf_II,_Holy_Roman_Emperor

References

[15] Article: 'Albrecht von Wallenstein.' (2023, March, 31). In Wikipedia. https://en.wikipedia.org/wiki/Albrecht_von_Wallenstein

[16] 'Matthias Corvinus of Hungry,1443-1490; 'The Raven King' also King of Bohemia.' (2023, April, 11). In New World Encyclopedia.

[17] Article: 'Jindřich Matyáš Thurn.' (2023, March, 20). In Wikipedia. https://en.wikipedia.org/wiki/Jind%C5%99ich_Maty%C3%A1%C5%A1_Thurn

[18] Article: 'John Amos Comenius.' (2023, April, 5). In Wikipedia. https://en.wikipedia.org/wiki/John_Amos_Comenius

[19] Article: 'Maria Theresa.' (2023, April, 7). In Wikipedia. https://en.wikipedia.org/wiki/Maria_Theresa

Article: 'Silesian Wars.' (2023, March, 22). In Wikipedia. https://en.wikipedia.org/wiki/Silesian_Wars

[20] Article: 'Joseph II. Holy Roman Emperor.' (2023, April, 1). In Wikipedia. https://en.wikipedia.org/wiki/Joseph_II,_Holy_Roman_Emperor

[21] Article: 'Leopold II, Holy Roman Emperor.' (2023, April, 4). In Wikipedia. https://en.wikipedia.org/wiki/Leopold_II,_Holy_Roman_Emperor

[22] Article: 'Francis II, Holy Roman Emperor.' (2023, April, 3). In Wikipedia. https://en.wikipedia.org/wiki/Francis_II,_Holy_Roman_Emperor#:~:text=Francis%20II%20or%20I%20%28German%3A%20Franz%20II.%3B%2012,coronation%20of%20Napoleon%20as%20Emperor%20of%20the%20French.

[23] Article: 'History of Europe, Napoleonic Wars.' (2023). In Encyclopedia Britannica, Inc. https://www.britannica.com/topic/history-of-Europe/The-Napoleonic-era

Article: 'Formation and Collapse of Austria-Hungary.' (2023). In Encyclopedia Britannica, Inc. https://www.britannica.com/summary/Austria-Hungary#:~:text=Austria-Hungary%2C%20or%20Austro-hungarian%20Empire%2C%20Former%20monarchy%2C%20central%20Europe.,Transylvania%2C%20Carniola%2C%20K%C3%BCstenland%2C%20Dalmatia%2C%20Croatia%2C%20Fiume%2C%20and%20Galicia.

Article: 'Revolutions of 1848 in the Austrian Empire.' (2023, April, 3). In Wikipedia. https://en.wikipedia.org/wiki/Revolutions_of_1848_in_the_Austrian_Empire

Article: 'Otto von Bismarck.' (2023, April, 6). In Wikipedia. https://en.wikipedia.org/wiki/Otto_von_Bismarck

[24] Article: 'Alfred I, Prince of Windisch-Grätz.' (2023, March, 13). In Wikipedia. https://en.wikipedia.org/wiki/Alfred_I,_Prince_of_Windisch-Gr%C3%A4tz

[25] Article: 'Franz Joseph I of Austria.' (2023, April, 5). In Wikipedia. https://en.wikipedia.org/wiki/Franz_Joseph_I_of_Austria#:~:text=Franz%20Joseph%20I%20or%20Francis%20Joseph%20I%20%28German%3A,until%20his%20death%20on%2021%20November%201916.%20

[26] Article: 'František Palacký.' (2022, November, 9). In Wikipedia. https://en.wikipedia.org/wiki/Franti%C5%A1ek_Palack%C3%BD

[27] Article: 'List of Presidents of Czechoslovakia.' (2023, March, 7). In Wikipedia. https://en.wikipedia.org/wiki/List_of_presidents_of_Czechoslovakia

[28] Article: 'Czech Republic.' (2023, April, 8). In Wikipedia. https://en.wikipedia.org/wiki/Czech_Republic

[29] Article: 'Edvard Benes.' (2023, April, 8). In Wikipedia. https://en.wikipedia.org/wiki/Edvard_Bene%C5%A1

[30] Article: 'Emil Hácha.' (2023, April, 2). In Wikipedia. https://en.wikipedia.org/wiki/Emil_H%C3%A1cha

From the Publisher

Explore the extreme highs and lows of one incredibly courageous woman's life story, penned by her eldest daughter, Helena Kanak. Working with Helena on 'A Tree Without Branches, Anna's Journey' has been an incredible honour. Helena has created a detailed and intriguing memoir to capture her mother's journey from war-torn Czechoslovakia to the green hills of Julatten.

Her story touched me personally as a descendant of strong European men and women. I commend Helena's tenacity and dedication to ultimately honouring her mother in the most loving way; by sharing her story.

I wish Helena Kanak all the success and happiness in her new endeavour as a published author. Undoubtedly, 'A Tree Without Branches, Anna's Journey' will touch the hearts of many and bring Czechoslovakian (and other European) Australians together.

Crystal Leonardi
Bowerbird Publishing
www.crystalleonardi.com